Also by David Faber

SPEAKING FOR ENGLAND

MUNICH, 1938

Appeasement and World War II

DAVID FABER

SIMON & SCHUSTER
New York London Toronto Sydney

Simon & Schuster
1230 Avenue of the Americas
New York, NY 10020

Originally published in Great Britain as *Munich* in 2008
by Simon & Schuster UK Ltd.

First Simon & Schuster hardcover edition September 2009

SIMON & SCHUSTER and colophon are registered trademarks
of Simon & Schuster, Inc.

For information about special discounts for bulk purchases,
please contact Simon & Schuster Special Sales at 1-866-506-1949
or business@simonandschuster.com.

The Simon & Schuster Speakers Bureau can bring authors to your live event. For
more information or to book an event contact the Simon & Schuster Speakers
Bureau at 1-866-248-3049 or visit our website at www.simonspeakers.com.

Manufactured in the United States of America

1 3 5 7 9 10 8 6 4 2

Library of Congress Cataloging-in-Publication Data
Faber, David.
Munich, 1938 : appeasement and World War II / David Faber.
p. cm.
Includes bibliographical references and index.
1. Munich Four-Power Agreement (1938) 2. World War, 1939–1945—Causes.
3. World War, 1939–1945—Diplomatic history.
4. Europe—Politics and government—1918–1945. I. Title.
D727.F34 2009
940.53'112—dc22
2008044896

ISBN 978-1-4391-3233-3
ISBN 978-1-4391-4992-8 (ebook)

PHOTO CREDITS
1, 4, 5, 6, 8, 9, 10, 12, 13, 15, 16, 17, 18, 20, 21, 22, 23, 24,
25, 27, 28, 31, 32, 33, 34, 35, 36 © Getty Images
2 © Solo Syndication/ Associated Newspapers Ltd.
3, 7, 26, 29, 30 © AKG Images
11© Bayerische Staatsbibliothek München Hoffmann
14 © Corbis
19 © NI Syndication

For my mother
who remembers the Czech refugees
at Birch Grove

Contents

Prologue

■

Heston

COUNSEL: Mr. Chamberlain. You are charged that on the night of September 30th, 1938, you did indecently expose yourself at the windows of your home, No. 10 Downing Street, clad only in a scrap of paper and shouting "Peace With Honour," "Peace With Honour." How say you, guilty or not guilty?
CHAMBERLAIN: I'm not sure.

Alan Bennett, *Forty Years On*, 1968

Friday, September 30, 1938, was a clear, sunny, late summer's day. Throughout the afternoon, huge crowds had been gathering at Heston Aerodrome, west of London, many of them lured there by the blanket coverage in the morning newspapers. The Prime Minister, Neville Chamberlain, would be making a triumphant return from his meeting with the German Chancellor and Führer, Adolf Hitler, at Munich. "PEACE!" screamed the headline in the Beaverbrook-owned *Daily Express*, the three-inch-high letters set in the largest typescript ever seen on the front of a British newspaper.[1] "No conqueror returning from a victory on the battlefield," gushed *The Times*, "has come adorned with nobler laurels."[2] In a special report, entitled "LONDON GOES TO HESTON," the *Evening News* published details of the best means of getting to the airport, whether by car, bus or train. Additional buses had been provided on all the major routes from central London to nearby Cranford, while extra staff had been summoned for duty at Hounslow West Underground station to meet the crowds arriving on the District and Piccadilly lines.[3]

The airport at Heston was nine miles west of London, and had opened for business in 1929 as a private air club. Until June 1936 it had been the principal terminal for British Airways' daytime passenger operations, when services had been transferred to the newly modernized Gatwick Airport. However, flooding problems which led to a persistently waterlogged runway at Gatwick, and the prevalence of fog at Croydon, where British Airways took temporary refuge, had led to the airline returning to Heston in May 1938. Yet air travel was still a comparatively rare luxury for the privileged few, and Heston was situated in a quiet rural setting, well outside London's ever-expanding suburbia.[4] As the afternoon wore on, the traffic on the Great West Road became increasingly congested, to the extent that, as more and more cars converged on the area, the narrow approach roads to the airport ground to a halt in both directions. Many onlookers, desperate not to miss witnessing the moment of Chamberlain's return, simply abandoned their cars beside the road, and decided to walk the last mile or so instead.

By 5 P.M. there were several thousand onlookers cramming the approach roads, and pressed up against the perimeter fence of the airport. The police had eventually been forced to close the roads in the immediate vicinity of the airport, and to prevent anyone further from gaining access who was not in possession of an official police pass. Many, however, were already safely inside, and had been waiting for several hours. Just inside the airport gates were schoolboys from nearby Eton College, who, "on their own initiative had sought and obtained permission to be there," and had formed an impromptu guard of honor along the tree-lined avenue that led to the main terminal.[5] Others had climbed onto the roofs of the airport buildings, or had gathered behind the rope and timber barriers that marked out the landing enclosure. On the tarmac itself, an impressive array of VIPs had assembled, headed by the Lord Chamberlain, the Earl of Clarendon, who had been sent to represent the King and had arrived in good time. Alongside him was the Lord Mayor of London, Sir Harry Twyford, assorted Cabinet ministers, the High Commissioners of all the Dominions, and the ambassadors of France and Italy, together with the German chargé d'affaires.

Only the Foreign Secretary, the Earl of Halifax, had been less well organized. He and his wife had been collected from his home in Eaton Square by the Permanent Under-Secretary at the Foreign Office, Sir Alexander

Cadogan, and they made painfully slow progress through the heavy traffic. As they approached Heston the sunshine gave way to a sudden, heavy downpour of rain, and at one stage Cadogan was forced to drive his car down the wrong side of the road, almost unable to see through the windshield. A quarter of a mile from Heston, on hearing the distant sound of an aircraft, Cadogan accelerated, and crashed his way through the crowds at the gates, the Foreign Secretary brandishing his police pass at the hapless constables on duty. At 5:38 P.M. the waiting crowds, by now drenched by the sudden cloudburst, also heard the roar of aircraft engines, and a few moments later the outline of the silver airplane could be made out against the thick, gray cloud.

The aircraft in question was the very latest addition to the British Airways fleet, a Lockheed 14 Super Electra, call sign AFG-N, which had been delivered from the United States at the beginning of September. Just a fortnight earlier it had set a new aviation distance record during its maiden flight, traveling nonstop to Stockholm and back in just over ten hours. A few days previously it had also carried Chamberlain on his second visit to Germany, indeed only the second time he had ever flown—to Bad Godesberg on the Rhine, by way of Cologne. On that occasion, Chamberlain had later described his return to the Cabinet.

> That morning he had flown up the river over London. He had imagined a German bomber flying the same course. He had asked himself what degree of protection we could afford to the thousands of homes which he had seen stretched out below him and he had felt that we were in no position to justify waging a war to-day in order to prevent a war thereafter.[6]

Just as Cadogan pulled up alongside the other waiting cars on the tarmac, the Prime Minister's plane landed, followed by a second identical aircraft carrying his supporting officials. Both aircraft taxied toward the waiting crowd of dignitaries, press correspondents and the general public. Possibly because of the heavy rain, the pilot appeared to overrun the main airport terminal, and he eventually came to a halt outside a nearby hangar, forcing the reception committee to half-walk, half-run to ensure that they kept up. As the door swung open, the crowd surged forward as Chamberlain appeared. It had been a long and tiring journey, but he looked animated enough, and waved his hat at the assembled, cheering throng.[7] "I've got it!" he shouted at Halifax. "I've got it!"[8] At the foot of the aircraft steps the Prime Minister was met first by Lord Clarendon, who handed him a letter. "From the King, From the King." An excited murmur went round the crowd. Next to greet him was Lord Halifax, who doffed his bowler hat, and shook hands with the Prime Minister.[9]

As the waiting journalists closed in around him, cameras and microphones were hastily erected to record his words. The BBC, their coverage anchored by the television reporter Richard Dimbleby, broke into their output to cover Chamberlain's speech live on the radio, while both television and newsreel cameras recorded the proceedings for broadcast that evening. Chamberlain paused for a moment, before addressing the crowd. "There are only two things I want to say," he began.

> First of all I received an immense number of letters during all these anxious days—and so has my wife—letters of support and approval and gratitude; and I cannot tell you what an encouragement that has been to me. I want to thank the British people for what they have done. Next I want to say that the settlement of the Czechoslovak problem which has now been achieved is, in my view, only a prelude to a larger settlement in which all Europe may find peace.

At this point he paused again. He slowly removed a single sheet of paper from his breast pocket, carefully unfolded it, and held it aloft for the crowd to see. "This morning I had another talk with the German Chancellor, Herr Hitler," he continued, "and here is a paper which bears his name upon it as well as mine. Some of you perhaps have already heard what it contains, but I would just like to read it to you."[10]

> We, the German Führer and Chancellor and the British Prime Minister, have had a further meeting today and are agreed in recognising that the question of Anglo-German relations is of the first importance for the two countries and for Europe.
>
> We regard the agreement signed last night and the Anglo-German Naval Agreement as symbolic of the desire of our two peoples never to go to war with one another again.

At these words, the remainder of his carefully prepared statement was drowned out by the ovation of the crowd, and the noisy renditions of "For he's a jolly good fellow" and "Rule Britannia" which followed.[11]

The King's handwritten letter invited Chamberlain to visit him immediately.

My Dear Prime Minister,

I am sending this letter by my Lord Chamberlain to ask you if you will come straight to Buckingham Palace so that I can express to you personally my most heartfelt congratulations on the success of your visit to Munich. In the meantime this letter brings the warmest of welcomes to one who by his patience and determination has ensured the lasting gratitude of his fellow countrymen throughout the Empire.

Yours sincerely and gratefully, George RI[12]

As his car left the airport, with Halifax sitting at his side in the back seat, Chamberlain was mobbed by the waiting crowds; mounted police were forced to clear a path. The Etonians cheered, hundreds of young children waved miniature Union Jacks, and women threw flowers through the open car window. The nine-mile drive to London took an hour and a half and, as Chamberlain himself later recalled, the roads "were lined from one end to the other with people of every class, shouting themselves hoarse, leaping on the running board, banging on the windows and thrusting their hands into the car to be shaken."[13]

As at Heston, so it was too at Buckingham Palace, where crowds had been gathering for much of the afternoon. "Indifferent to the heavy rain," reported *The Times*, "they stood, densely packed, a happy throng, their hearts full of relief and a deep sense of thankfulness towards the man who had lifted a great weight from their minds." As dusk fell, the air of anticipation grew. At 6:15 P.M. Mrs. Annie Chamberlain arrived from Downing Street. When she had taken her daily walk in the park that morning she had been cheered by a large crowd, among which a number of women had been so overcome with emotion that they had fainted. Now, as the rain stopped, a rainbow, "hailed by some as an omen," appeared above Buckingham Palace. Half an hour later Chamberlain's car finally came into view. Motorists sounded their horns, and the crowd rushed to fill the space outside the palace gates, leaving only a narrow passage for the car to get through. As the Prime Minister disappeared into the bowels of the palace, the crowd began to chant: "We want Chamberlain! We want Neville."[14]

Just before 7 P.M. the huge double doors on the balcony of Buckingham Palace opened to a huge roar from the rain-drenched crowd. The King and Queen stepped out first, followed by the Prime Minister and Mrs. Chamberlain. For a few minutes the four of them stood there, waving to the crowd and smiling broadly; all the while illuminated by the violet beam of an enormous searchlight, mounted on a fire engine outside the palace. The crowd soon found its voice, singing a medley of tunes including "For they are jolly good fellows," "Rule Britannia" and the National Anthem. The King motioned Chamberlain to step forward, and for two minutes the Prime Minister basked alone in the glow of the searchlight and the crowd's adulation.[15] It had been, wrote the King to his mother, Queen Mary, "a great day. The Prime Minister was delighted with the result of his mission, as we all are, and he had a great ovation when he came here."[16]

When Chamberlain left the palace, the throng again surged around his car, before he was driven slowly down the Mall, and into Whitehall, where the crowds had also been gathering for several hours. In spite of the rain, there was a carnival atmosphere. Flag and souvenir sellers were doing a brisk trade on the street corners, as were the evening newspaper vendors: "Public Hero Number One!" they cried. The crowd of thousands was restive but good-natured, having passed the time singing such old favorites as "O God our help in ages past" and "Pack up your troubles." Each new arrival at the famous black door had been mobbed, including three large van loads of flowers that had been delivered. At last, Chamberlain's car pulled into Downing Street. By now the crowds were so tightly packed in, and the road so impassable, that mounted police with megaphones were compelled to clear the narrowest of paths for the Prime Minister's car, with two policemen riding on its running boards. At the entrance to No. 10, the Chamberlains could hardly open the car door to get out. Women in tears were crying "Thank you, thank you." Members of the Cabinet, who were themselves trying to get to the door of Downing Street, mingled with the general public. Eventually the Chamberlains managed to squeeze through the crowds, and to reach the comparative haven of 10 Downing Street.[17]

Yet even the front hall was scarcely any less crowded. As Chamberlain made his way upstairs to a first-floor window, his Parliamentary Private Secretary, Lord Dunglass, heard someone shout out to him. "Neville, go up to the window and say 'Peace in our time.' " Chamberlain swung round and replied angrily: "No, I don't do that sort of thing." Somewhere on the stairs, however, which were packed tightly with people, he changed his mind.[18] He was mindful of Disraeli's celebrated remarks when he too had returned to Downing Street in July 1878, having concluded the Peace of Berlin. At 7:27 P.M. Chamberlain waved to the crowd from an open window on the first floor of Downing Street. "Speech! Speech!" the crowd shouted. Chamberlain held up his hand, and motioned to the crowd to fall silent.

My good friends, this is the second time in our history that there has come back from Germany to Downing Street peace with honour. I believe it is peace for our time. We thank you from the bottom of our hearts.

At this the crowd again roared their approval. Chamberlain paused, and turned to the crowd one last time. "Now I recommend you go home," he concluded, "and sleep quietly in your beds."[19]

1

■

Hitler Sees His Chance

The question for Germany ran: where could she achieve the greatest gain at the lowest cost. . . . Germany's problem could only be solved by means of force and this was never without attendant risk. . . . It was [his] unalterable resolve to solve Germany's problem of space at the latest by 1943–45. . . . The descent upon the Czechs would have to be made with "lightning speed" . . . even as early as 1938.

Adolf Hitler, Reich Chancellery, November 5, 1937

In England, for instance, far too many people have an entirely erroneous conception of what the National Socialist régime really stands for. Otherwise they would lay less stress on Nazi dictatorship and much more emphasis on the great social experiment which was being tried out in Germany.

Sir Nevile Henderson at a dinner of the Deutsch-Englische Gesellschaft,
June 1, 1937

There was some talk about the Führer; of his qualities, artistic, romantic, sensitive. It was all very cheery and light-hearted.

Lord Halifax, Berlin, November 17, 1937

In Berlin, Friday, November 5, 1937, was a characteristically cold, dull, early-winter's day. Unusually, however, Adolf Hitler was in town. As André François-Poncet, the French ambassador and senior overseas diplomat, had complained to his own Foreign Minister that summer, Hitler was increasingly "devoting less and less time to public affairs." He preferred instead "to spend more of his time at his house at Obersalzberg and much less in the capital city." By and large he was happy to leave the principal areas of domestic policy to those "who had seized them for themselves," while he "concerns himself, insofar as he does, with foreign policy [and] primarily occupies himself in new and grandiose construction projects, especially for the beautification of Berlin, which haunts his imagination."[1] There seemed that day to be nothing to break the calm that hung over the district of the city known locally as the *Diplomatstrasse*.

At midday the Propaganda Minister, Dr. Joseph Goebbels, as he did frequently, made the short trip across the Wilhelmstrasse from the Propaganda Ministry to the Reich Chancellery for lunch with Hitler, and returned to work that afternoon, reflecting on the wide range of topics they had discussed. In recent weeks Goebbels had noticed that Hitler had begun increasingly to turn his eyes toward Czechoslovakia, but at lunch that day they had agreed that Germany was not yet in a position to take action, although the Czechs were now facing pressure from all sides. They had also agreed on the position of Hjalmar Schacht, the Economics Minister, whose long-running opposition to Hitler was now to lead to his enforced resignation. Finally, noted Goebbels, the Führer was to have "General Staff talks" later that afternoon.[2]

Accordingly, as dusk fell, the chiefs of the army, the navy and the Luftwaffe, together with the War Minister, made their way to the Reich Chancellery for what they too thought was to be a routine meeting. Over recent weeks the commander-in-chief of the navy, Admiral Erich Raeder, had expressed growing concern at what he believed to be the inequitable allocation of raw steel supplies to the armed forces, to the advantage of the Luftwaffe, and the detriment of the navy. Raeder had strongly pressed his case with the War Minister, Field Marshal Werner von Blomberg, arguing that much needed naval expansion was being seriously hampered by the lack of supplies. Blomberg had in turn urged Hitler to call a meeting to arbitrate on the dispute, and when Hitler reluctantly agreed, it was Blomberg who had issued the invitations to the three service chiefs. When Raeder arrived, a suspiciously friendly Hermann Göring, the commander of the Luftwaffe, took him to one side, and reassured him that he had already discussed the matter with Hitler that afternoon. The primary purpose of the meeting was to speed up armament development, and in particular "to put pressure on [the commander-in-chief of the army] General Werner Freiherr von Fritsch, since [Hitler] was dissatisfied with the rearmament of the Army."

Nobody, however, could understand why the Foreign Minister, Constantin Freiherr von Neurath, had also been invited, including, so it would seem, Neurath himself. Göring later claimed that Hitler had explained to him that it was because he "did not want the thing to look too military," and hoped that Neurath's presence would emphasize, to Fritsch in particular, the importance of rearmament to the "foreign political situation."[3] It is more likely that Hitler knew of the Foreign Ministry's general opposition to what he was going to say, and that the meeting afforded him an ideal opportunity to deliver an explicit warning to his Foreign Minister. The meeting began at 4:15 P.M. The only other participant was Colonel Friedrich Hossbach, the senior armed forces' adjutant on Hitler's staff, who took his place opposite his chief at the table in Hitler's study. It soon became clear to the select gathering that this was to be no ordinary get-together. The subject to be discussed, began the Führer, was of such importance that in any other country it would necessitate a full Cabinet meeting, but he had rejected that idea precisely because of the gravity of the matter and the necessary secrecy. What he was to tell them, he intoned solemnly, "was the fruit of thorough deliberation and the experiences of his 4½ years of power." In the event of his death, his words should be treated as his last will and testament, his "*testamentarische Hinterlassenschaft*."[4]

Around the table there was a sharp intake of breath, as all eyes were fixed on Hitler—"even Göring was tense." Hossbach, realizing that what was to follow was clearly of importance, hurriedly got out his diary and began to take down notes.[5] The young adjutant was a close confidant and admirer of General Ludwig Beck, the Chief of the General Staff, who had not been invited to the meeting. However, Beck's critical view of the broad thrust of Hitler's foreign policy, and in particular his anxiety that German military action in central Europe would set off a general war which Germany was bound to lose, was a theme with which Hossbach was already familiar. A written record of such a portentous statement would clearly be of great interest to him.

It quickly became clear that Hitler was to pursue a topic that was already familiar to his inner circle. On June 24, Blomberg had issued a "Top Secret" directive to the three commanders-in-chief. Only four copies had been circulated, and it had been immediately obvious to the recipients that it had been inspired by Hitler himself. Blomberg had begun by emphasizing that in theory Germany had no need to fear immediate attack from any quarter.

> Nevertheless, the politically fluid world situation, which does not preclude surprising incidents, demands constant preparedness for war on the part of the German armed forces . . . to make possible the military exploitation of politically favourable opportunities should they occur. Preparations of the armed forces for a possible war in the mobilization period 1937–38 must be made with this in mind.

Furthermore, there were two distinct eventualities for war, for both of which plans were already well advanced. First, war on two fronts, with the main theater in the west, probably as a result of a sudden attack by France: to be code-named *Fall Rot*, or "Case Red." The second possibility might also involve war on two fronts, but the principal struggle would be to the southeast, code-named *Fall Grün*, or "Case Green." This option was considerably more aggressive in nature.

> The war in the East can begin with a surprise German operation against Czechoslovakia in order to parry the imminent attack of a superior enemy coalition. The necessary conditions to justify such an action politically and in the eyes of international law must be created *beforehand*.

Czechoslovakia was to be "eliminated from the very beginning," and occupied. In addition, a number of "special case" scenarios were to be catered for, including "Case Otto," which would initiate armed intervention in Austria in the event of any attempt to restore to the throne there the young exiled pretender, Otto of Habsburg.

> Making use of the domestic political dissension of the Austrian people, there will be a march to this end in the general direction of Vienna, and any resistance will be broken.[6]

Thus in the Reich Chancellery on November 5, Hitler began, unusually for him, to read from a prepared text and to expand on his theme.

> The aim of German policy was to make secure and to preserve the racial community [*Volksmasse*] and to enlarge it. It was therefore a question of space [*Lebensraum*].
>
> The German racial community comprised over 85 million people and, because of their number and the narrow limits of habitable space in Europe, constituted a tightly packed racial core such as was not to be met in any other country and such as implied the right to a greater living space than in the case of other peoples. Germany's future was therefore wholly conditional upon the solving of the need for space.

The political climate in Europe posed the greatest threat yet to the German race, both in terms of arresting its decline in Austria and Czechoslovakia, and indeed of maintaining its very existence within Germany itself. In the absence of any expansion of living space, "sterility was setting in, and in its train disorders of a social character." Hitler went on to raise, and subsequently to dismiss, a number of possible alternatives. Autarchy, or self-sufficiency, would only be achievable in a limited form in respect of raw materials, and would be quite impossible in terms of food supplies. Similarly, it was hopeless to anticipate German economic growth by relying solely on an increased share in the world economy, even if there were to be a boom on the back of worldwide rearmament. Nor could sufficient living space, raw materials or food be found in some far-flung colonies, not even those to which Germany had a valid claim. The sea routes which served them were controlled by Britain, and he rejected in principle the "*liberalistisch-kapitalistischen*" view that space could be found not in Europe, but in the exploitation of Germany's pre–First World War colonies.

Having discarded such alternatives, Hitler turned to the core of his argument.

> The history of all ages—the Roman Empire and the British Empire—had proved that expansion could only be carried out by breaking down resistance and taking risks; setbacks were inevitable. There had never in former times been spaces without a master, and there were none today; the attacker always comes up against a possessor. The question for Germany ran: where could she achieve the greatest gain at the lowest cost?

It was clear where he believed that the opposition would lie. Germany "had to reckon with two hate-inspired antagonists, Britain and France, to whom a German colossus in the centre of Europe was a thorn in the flesh." But Britain was in a state of decadent decline and could only defend her colonial empire with the help of others. And France, although in a stronger position in terms of her empire and the military strength that it brought her, had internal political difficulties that greatly weakened her. In conclusion:

> Germany's problem could be solved only by means of force and this was never without attendant risk. . . . If one accepts as the basis of the following exposition the resort to force with its attendant risks, then there remained still to be answered the questions "when" and "how."[7]

At this point Hitler, who never felt at ease speaking from behind a desk, stood up, paced about the room, and finally came to a standstill, his legs astride. He now began to outline three possible scenarios in which new territory could be acquired by force. His opening argument was typical of his style, that "time was not on Germany's side, that it would be imperative to act by 1943–5 at the latest." Thereafter, it would be too late to benefit from Germany's massive rearmament program and the relative superiority it had brought about. Certain weapons would no longer be secret, reservists called up by draft would be older, and a food crisis might well become a reality as

a result of a lack of foreign exchange. At the same time, the Nazi movement's leaders were aging, the birth rate was falling, and the standard of
living might decline—all in all, there was a very real prospect of a potential
"weakening-point of the regime." If he were still alive, "it was his unalterable
resolve to solve the German problem of space by 1943–5 at the latest."[8]

There were two further possible scenarios which might oblige him to
take action even sooner. If France was to become so severely wracked by
internal strife, or so embroiled in a war with another power that the French
army was rendered useless for war against Germany, then "the time for
action against the Czechs had come."

> Our first objective, in the event of our being embroiled in war, must be to
> overthrow Czechoslovakia and Austria simultaneously in order to remove
> the threat to our flank in any possible operation against the West. . . .
> Britain, and probably France as well, had already tacitly written off the
> Czechs and were reconciled to the fact that this question would be
> cleared up in due course by Germany.

He made this assumption on the basis of likely difficulties for Britain within
the empire, principally in Ireland and India, and a reluctance again to
become involved in a lengthy European war. In the meantime, French
involvement in a foreign war, possibly allied to Britain and almost certainly
against Italy, was "coming definitely nearer" given the continuing tension in
the Mediterranean over the civil war in Spain. He was therefore "resolved
to take advantage of it whenever it happened, even as early as 1938," while
"the time for our attack on the Czechs and Austria must be made dependent on the course of the Anglo-French-Italian war." In conclusion, he
warned his audience, an attack against Czechoslovakia would "have to be
carried out with 'lightning speed' [*blitzartig schnell*]."[9]

In recent months, Hitler had grown increasingly disillusioned with
Britain, his attitude that of a spurned lover. His dream that the two countries might enter into an alliance to carve up the world between them,
inspired by a war between Britain and Italy over Abyssinia, had by now all
but evaporated. It was all too clear that Britain had little or no intention of
standing up to the Italian dictator, Benito Mussolini, as Hitler had hoped.
He had therefore reached the conclusion "both that Britain's ostensible

willingness to appease Germany with concessions was a sham intended only to separate Germany from Italy and also that despite its deep-rooted hostility to Germany, Britain was too weak to fight."[10] By contrast he had come increasingly to admire Italian strength in successfully defying both Britain and the League of Nations over the invasion of Abyssinia.

After two hours on his feet Hitler brought his speech to an end. He was under no illusion as to the shock his remarks would cause, and he was not to be disappointed. His audience was stunned. As Hossbach noted, "there was a heavy silence in the Führer's gilt and marble office," as everyone did their best to avoid eye contact with each other.[11] And although Hossbach devoted considerably less space in his written minute of the meeting to the discussion that followed, it is clear that it too lasted some two hours, and that the "sharpness of the opposition . . . did not fail to make its impression on Hitler, as I could see from his changing expressions."[12] For once, Hitler's powers of persuasion had failed him. Blomberg, Fritsch and Neurath all expressed concern, although not, it must be said, because they were struck down by any violent moral disagreement with the Führer. Hitler's plans for *Lebensraum* were well known to them, and talk of annexing Austria and invading Czechoslovakia was nothing new. What was new, and what caused such shock, was Hitler's suggestion that Germany should use early force to achieve her aims. For the first time he had presented his generals with a tangible timetable for aggression against two neighboring countries, an action for which they felt Germany was militarily woefully underprepared, and which would lead inevitably to a general war which they would lose.

Blomberg and Fritsch spoke first. It was essential, they urged, whatever the circumstances, to avoid provoking a war with France and Britain. Fritsch drew attention to the strength of the French army, and warned that France enjoyed sufficient military superiority both to engage in war with Italy on her Alpine frontier, while simultaneously holding back sufficient force to launch an offensive against Germany in the Rhineland. Blomberg expressed grave reservations about the weakness of German fortifications in the west, while stressing the comparative strength of the Czech fortifications to the southeast, "which would gravely hamper our attack." Even Neurath eventually found his tongue, venturing the opinion that Hitler's optimism as to the likelihood of an imminent war between Britain, France and Italy might be misplaced. But Hitler remained adamant that "the summer of 1938 was the date which seemed to him possible for this." To the suggestion that Britain and France might show a greater interest than he anticipated in the politics of central Europe, he merely reiterated his earlier assertion that "he was convinced of Britain's nonparticipation."[13]

After a few minutes of desultory discussion on the issue for which the meeting had been called in the first place, the participants filed out into the cold of a Berlin evening at 8:30. Raeder, who appears to have contributed little to the actual discussion in the Reich Chancellery, later claimed at Nuremberg, presumably in an effort to avoid the noose, that "it was definitely my opinion that this speech was intended purely as Göring had suggested [to speed up armament development] . . . and that things were not quite so serious as they had been painted. I certainly did not feel that I had heard an announcement that our foreign policy was to be fundamentally changed."[14] But the evidence of the other participants suggests otherwise. Fritsch was so concerned at the immediacy of Hitler's proposals that he offered to abandon his planned holiday in Egypt, which he was due to take a few days later on health grounds. But Hitler reassured him that there was no imminent prospect of war. And Neurath later testified at Nuremberg that it had been "quite obvious to me that the whole tendency of [Hitler's] plans was of an aggressive nature. I was extremely upset at Hitler's speech, because it knocked the bottom out of the foreign policy which I had consistently pursued."

In fact, Neurath was so shaken by the tone and content of Hitler's speech that in the days that followed he apparently "suffered several heart attacks."[15] Yet on the very next day, November 6, he was still well enough to visit Fritsch and the Chief of the General Staff, General Beck, who had already been briefed on the meeting by Hossbach, and on whom the impression was said to have been "shattering."[16] The wholly optimistic intention was "to get Hitler to change his ideas," and it was once again delegated to Fritsch to tackle the Führer on the military considerations of invading Austria or Czechoslovakia, at a meeting he was to have at Obersalzberg before leaving for Egypt. Neurath was to seek a similar interview to dispute the political and diplomatic ramifications of Hitler's proposals.[17]

Fritsch did indeed see Hitler on November 9, and although no record survives of the meeting, we may assume that the army commander-in-chief repeated the military arguments he had made a few days earlier at the Reich Chancellery. But the Führer was growing increasingly antagonized by the emerging opposition to his plans, and he dismissed Fritsch's concerns out of hand. When the following day Hossbach finally got around to writing up the minutes of the meeting, Hitler steadfastly refused even to look at them, in spite of several requests from his adjutant to do so. And Neurath's appeals to secure a similar interview as that granted to Fritsch repeatedly fell on deaf ears. Hitler refused absolutely to entertain his Foreign Minister, and instead locked himself away for a lengthy rest at his mountain retreat at Berchtesgaden. Neurath was not to see him for a private appointment until the middle of January.

One person who had not been invited to the meeting at the Reich Chancellery was Admiral Wilhelm Canaris, the chief of German military intelligence, the Abwehr. He knew that the meeting had taken place, and that it had been important, and he believed that he should have been informed of what had been discussed. But six days later he had still heard nothing, and he did not feel that he knew the other participants well enough to confront them. Then, on November 11, he found himself in the office of Beck, an officer he greatly admired, and with whom he had recently become increasingly friendly. Both men shared a deep concern that Germany was being dragged into a war for which she was ill-prepared, but Canaris, ever the intelligence officer, at first said nothing, until Beck suddenly blurted out to him: "Hitler is leading Germany into the grave and he must be stopped before it is too late." Beck had only just finished reading Hossbach's report of the previous week's meeting, and now showed it to Canaris, who immediately understood its significance. His "face became more and more serious . . . and his expression showed Beck plainly that Hitler's plans appeared to him sheer madness."

"Hitler will bring about a war in the worst possible conditions because his whole argument is based on erroneous assessments," began Canaris.

Beck agreed. "It will be necessary to break the spell that Hitler has cast on the German people."

"That is easier said than done," replied Canaris. "I do not believe that an armed insurrection or a popular revolt has the least chance of happening.

The police are in the hands of the SS and the Party controls the means of information and propaganda. The majority opinion is favourable to the Führer. How can we bring home to the German people, which wants peace, that Hitler's plans are leading them to the slaughter-house?"[18]

On November 12 Beck committed his thoughts to paper, and presented them to Blomberg. Challenging the pessimistic outlook that only force could solve Germany's problems, he supported the policy espoused by Schacht and Neurath, that increased participation in world trade was vastly preferable to military expansion.

> The enormity of French and British opposition to any extension of German living space or German power is beyond question. But it is out of place to label this opposition as irrevocable or insurmountable. . . . Politics is the art of the possible. It would therefore be far better first to exhaust all possibilities in trying to arrange some settlement, especially in view of the mutual power relationships. Moreover, such a policy would be more intelligent, even should it come to some future confrontation.[19]

Brave words indeed, had they reached the Führer's ears. However, the ever-pliable Blomberg had in any case already modified his own position, his earlier doubts having proved short-lived. He was now subtly making known Hitler's views to the upper echelons of the Wehrmacht, so that by Christmas a new directive had been issued, detailing the army's revised mobilization plans for an offensive, rather than defensive, war against Czechoslovakia. Blomberg had little interest in Beck's concerns.

▪ ▪ ▪

On October 13, 1937, a glossy invitation landed on the Whitehall desk of the Lord President of the Council, Lord Halifax, from Eric Parker, the editor of the *Field* magazine. An accompanying letter informed Halifax that the invitation had been dispatched "at the wish of Prince Loewenstein . . . from the German Hunting Association to the International Sporting Exhibition" which was shortly to take place in Berlin. The exhibition was to be held under the patronage of the Reichsjägermeister himself, the Chief Game Warden of the Reich, Hermann Göring.[20] Halifax's love of hunting, and his position as Master of his local pack of his hounds, the Middleton in Yorkshire, was well known, and a supplementary program of events promised "big game and small game shoots in East Prussia, Pomerania, Mecklenburg, Kumark, Schlesien, Saxony and Brunswick." A multiple-choice system of box ticking indicated the likely scale of the slaughter, including "red deer, fallow deer, wild boar, hares, pheasants and rabbits." Halifax's initial choice suggested that he wished to shoot foxes in Saxony on November 10 and 11.[21]

The following evening Halifax attended a dinner at the Foreign Office in honor of the Yugoslav Prime Minister, Milan Stoyadinovitch. After dinner he found himself engaged in casual conversation with Winston Churchill, at the time still a Conservative backbench Member of Parliament, and the Foreign Secretary, Anthony Eden. Churchill later recalled that Halifax "said in a genial way that Göring had invited him to Germany on a sports visit, and the hope was held out that he would certainly be able to see Hitler. He said that he had spoken about it to the Prime Minister, who thought it would be a very good thing, and therefore he had accepted." Churchill formed the distinct impression that "Eden was surprised and did not like it,"[22] and Eden himself later confirmed that initially he "was not eager, but saw no sufficient reason to oppose it."[23] Halifax, however, interpreted the conversation altogether differently, claiming that "after some chaff about my shooting foxes," and even after he had "pooh-poohed the idea," Eden had continued to support the proposed visit and promised to speak to Chamberlain about it. He subsequently only accepted the invitation after "their joint exhortations to me to take the opportunity."[24] Chamberlain too thought that "Anthony . . . would be quite happy" about the visit.[25]

Once the invitation had been issued, the idea of a Halifax visit was enthusiastically taken up by Britain's recently appointed ambassador to Germany, Sir Nevile Henderson. A highly experienced diplomat, Henderson had served in a wide variety of often difficult posts around the world. He had particularly impressed during his time as minister in Belgrade between 1929 and 1935, where he had been considered "a good man and a good shot," qualities on the back of which he had built a constructive relationship with the dictatorial King Alexander, and the Regent Prince Paul. "You have done splendidly in Belgrade and made a great name for yourself," wrote Sir Robert Vansittart, the Permanent Under-Secretary at the Foreign

Office. "Now it is time to have some of your life in the sun and in the First Eleven." To Henderson's disappointment, the "sun" initially meant a posting to the diplomatic backwater of Buenos Aires, away from "what was considered the charmed European Inner Circle."[26] He was not, however, to have to wait long to join the "First Eleven."

The outgoing ambassador in Berlin, Sir Eric Phipps, had never made any secret of his distaste at having to deal with Hitler. Indeed, the then Prime Minister, Stanley Baldwin, had long since been advised that "if it is our policy to get alongside Germany then the sooner Phipps is transferred the better."[27] Henderson, on the other hand, was perceived as having precisely the qualities needed to get close to a dictator. One former ambassador, under whom Henderson had served in Constantinople, praised his "jujitsu methods in diplomacy"[28] and, ironically, it was largely due to the influence of the staunchly anti-appeasing Vansittart that Henderson was ultimately preferred to two other candidates and plucked from the relative obscurity of Buenos Aires to move to Berlin in April 1937. "Sir Nevile has done his stint in South America," said Vansittart. "He shall have his reward."[29]

Henderson embarked upon his career in Berlin with some trepidation, plagued initially by a sense of his "own inadequacy for what was obviously the most difficult and most important post in the whole of the diplomatic service." However, a strong fatalistic streak quickly led him to the somewhat grandiose assumption that he had been "specially selected by Providence for the definite mission of . . . helping to preserve the peace of the world."[30] His first meeting with Chamberlain only served to reinforce his conviction "that he was the personal representative of the prime minister's, rather than the Foreign Office's, policy in Berlin."[31] His Private Secretary at the embassy later confirmed that Henderson had indeed "received very precise instructions from the Prime Minister to improve relations with Germany and to establish good relations with the Nazi leadership. Although his German was not very fluent, he was extremely assiduous in cultivating the German leadership and in putting across Chamberlain's policy. He never questioned the instructions he received from Chamberlain. He believed they were correct and he carried out that policy loyally right to the end."[32]

An immaculately dressed bachelor with a "fey streak," Henderson's appointment was greeted with a mixture of surprise and concern, both in London and in Berlin. His reputation among those who worked for him was for aloofness, a problem accentuated by the old-fashioned design of the embassy itself, an "imposing yellow and white Palladian building at the Unter den Linden end of the Wilhelmstrasse."[33] Essentially a private residence for the ambassador, complete with servants' hall and wine cellar, embassy staff were forced to work in cramped conditions in the basement. Henderson's head of chancery, Ivone Kirkpatrick, found him to be a "human chief with whom it was a pleasure to work." Equally, however, Kirkpatrick soon recognized that there was to be "a new regime," and that Henderson was "determined to tame Hitler by kindness."[34] The military attaché described him as a "celibate and caustic chief,"[35] while his Private Secretary thought him "an old style diplomat, with a good presence and courteous manner. He was not an intellectual man, he was not a subtle man, but he was very persistent and had the courage of his convictions. He did not suffer fools gladly."[36]

It did not take long for Henderson to cause a stir. One of his first public duties on arrival was to speak at a dinner held in his honor by the Deutsch-Englische Gesellschaft. His host was the Duke of Saxe-Coburg and Gotha, with whom he felt comfortable, as they had been at Eton together.[37] However, the audience also included Heinrich Himmler, the SS Reichsführer; Viktor Lutze, the chief of staff of the SA, the Nazi brownshirt storm troopers; General Erhard Milch, Göring's Secretary of State at the Reich Air Ministry; and Alfred Rosenberg, the Nazi Party's key ideological theorist. "In England," Henderson told his audience, "far too many people have an entirely erroneous conception of what the National Socialist régime really stands for. Otherwise they would lay less stress on Nazi dictatorship and much more emphasis on the great social experiment which was being tried out in Germany."[38] The speech earned Henderson the sobriquet in certain British newspapers of "our Nazi British ambassador at Berlin,"[39] while the American ambassador there, William Dodd, complained that Henderson had effectively "informed the German Government that England would make no objections if Hitler seized Austria and Czechoslovakia."[40]

Whether or not Henderson's prowess with a shotgun and rifle had indeed been a contributory factor to his appointment, he soon became a close friend and regular guest of the equally hunting-obsessed Göring. For some reason, however, nobody seems to have pointed out that it was common knowledge that Hitler, on the other hand, loathed any form of field sports. Henderson was appalled to discover that Britain, alone of all the European countries, was not to be represented at the forthcoming hunting exhibition and, with direct help from the Foreign Office, he quickly set about acquiring a "highly satisfactory" collection of trophies from around the world, including some which had been shot by the King and Queen.[41] He urged Halifax to accept the invitation and, after initially dragging his feet, on October 21 Halifax finally did so. He hoped, he wrote, that he would "see something in the way of German sport," but tactfully pleaded that on doctor's advice he would "rather not actually shoot myself, having strained my shoulder a week or two ago." He would be coming as a spectator only.[42]

At the end of October Henderson visited London, headquartering himself at Brown's Hotel off Piccadilly. One senior politician with whom he sought an interview was the Shadow Foreign Secretary, Hugh Dalton. "He did not make a very good impression on me," recorded Dalton, "either in respect of political intelligence or character." In anticipation of the meeting Dalton had sought a briefing from François-Poncet, who had complained that "Henderson leaned too much towards the Nazis." Henderson's response was to launch into a lengthy diatribe denigrating the work of his predecessor, Phipps, "a most unsuitable appointment." On arrival in Berlin he had "found an impossible state of things . . . it was common talk that there was no British embassy there at all. It was only a branch of the Quai d'Orsay." Dalton was furious. "It was not really either very gentlemanly or very clever to jeer at his predecessor in Berlin to a complete stranger," he wrote. Undeterred, Henderson then suggested that Göring should be invited to London—"a little flattery, a new Order, another uniform, and a little country-house life, might work wonders with him."

That evening Dalton saw Eden in the House of Commons, and warned the Foreign Secretary that his ambassador in Berlin had "been explaining in detail all the concessions which he thought we should offer to Germany." Eden, sounding "a little vexed," replied quietly: "I wish he would not go on like this to everybody he meets."[43] In fact, it had not taken Eden long to realize that Henderson's appointment had been a grave mistake, "an international misfortune" as he later described it, although at the time "no one foresaw the opinions he was to hold." Henderson, he complained, "far from warning the Nazis, was constantly making excuses for them, often in their company."[44] In the words of another Foreign Office official at the time, Henderson "had almost become Hitler's ambassador to us, rather than our ambassador to Hitler."[45]

During Henderson's visit to London, the differences of opinion as to the merits of Halifax's proposed visit, between the Foreign Office on the one hand and Downing Street on the other, soon became apparent. Chamberlain had by now seized on the trip, and the hoped-for meeting between Halifax and Hitler, as a crucial component of "the far-reaching plans which I have in mind for the appeasement of Europe."[46] After seeing the Prime Minister at Downing Street, Henderson enthused to Halifax that "the way the P.M. put it to me yesterday, your visit takes on quite a different aspect." Hopefully it would "open a door on to a road along which progress is really possible."[47] A further meeting at the Foreign Office, between Henderson, Halifax and Eden, came to an altogether different conclusion. Eden cautioned Halifax that while in Berlin he was to do no more "than listen and confine himself to warning comment on Austria and Czechoslovakia." At the same time he had "impressed on Sir N. Henderson the need for doing all we can to *discourage* German intervention in these two states." At all costs, Germany must be kept "guessing as to our attitude."[48]

When Henderson returned to Berlin he found that preparations for the visit were not running as smoothly as he had hoped. Eden had already made a point of warning the embassy that "it would clearly be undesirable that Lord Halifax should accept this invitation unless we could be reasonably sure that he would see some persons in authority."[49] However, Hitler himself had no desire to play ball. Even before Hitler's speech at the Reich Chancellery on November 5, his Foreign Minister, Neurath, had complained to Henderson that the Führer "had made so many advances to Great Britain without a result that he might now see no reason to jump at a hand so reluctantly held out to him." The reaction at the Foreign Office to this attempt at blackmail was decidedly cool. "It will appear to the Germans that we are pressing that [Lord Halifax] should be received by the Chancellor," minuted William Strang, the head of the Central Department, while Sir Orme Sargent, an Assistant Under-Secretary, complained that he did not "at all like this cadging for an invitation from Hitler."[50]

In fact, as Neurath had already discovered to his own cost, after the meeting at the Reich Chancellery, Hitler had locked himself away at his home at Berchtesgaden, sulking at the negative attitude of his generals and his Foreign Minister. He had no intention whatsoever of returning to Berlin for a meeting in which he had no interest, let alone for anything even vaguely connected to a hunting exhibition. A further flurry of telegrams between an increasingly anxious Henderson and his superiors in London made it clear that if Halifax was indeed to see the Führer, he would have to make the pilgrimage to his mountaintop aerie himself. The problem was how to make it look as though he had been invited there, and was not imposing himself on a reluctant Hitler. Henderson did at least find a willing ally in Foreign Minister Neurath, who, having listened with apparent horror to Hitler's anti-British diatribe on November 5, was now desperate both to find an opportunity to tackle the Führer personally, and to talk up the more general prospects of peace talks with Britain.

Neurath first suggested to Henderson that Hitler, who "was anxious to rest for a few days at Upper Salzburg," would be prepared to receive Halifax in Berlin, but only once the hunting exhibition was finished in late November. Otherwise a long journey to Berchtesgaden would be necessary.[51] Henderson endorsed this advice in a telegram to the Foreign Secretary on November 7, pleading that he could "not express too strongly my hope that it will be found possible to agree to date proposed by Chancellor for meeting with Lord Halifax. I am altogether convinced that present opportunity is one which we should not allow to pass." Only the previous day, he enthused, Göring had assured him that "he had seldom heard Herr Hitler speak more enthusiastically in favour of an understanding with Great Britain"—a shamelessly brazen remark for Göring to have made, given that just a few hours earlier he had been listening to Hitler's diatribe at the Reich Chancellery. Henderson went on to make the extraordinary suggestion that the hunting exhibition might be kept open after its planned closing date, "if it is really considered indispensable to provide ostensible pretext for visit." This was too much for Vansittart, who minuted on the telegram that Henderson was being "very naïf," quite correctly gauging the prevailing frame of mind toward Britain in Berlin as at best "extreme mutability," but more likely "adverse, both as regards Hitler's mood & the inspired press."[52]

Eden arrived back in London on the evening of November 6, after five days in Brussels on League of Nations business. He was not best pleased to discover that both Henderson and Downing Street had been pressing ahead with plans for Halifax's trip, in spite of the goalposts having moved. He had only agreed to the visit reluctantly in the first place, and on the understanding that it would be to Berlin, ostensibly to visit the exhibition. "Here was the precise sequence of events," he later recorded, "I had wished to avoid."[53] He sent a terse message to Henderson warning that it was of "the greatest importance at the present time that no encouragement whatsoever should be given the German Government for believing that His Majesty's Government would contemplate any settlement at the expense of the political independence of the nations of Eastern and Central Europe."[54] Two days later he returned to the fray, acidly observing to Henderson that the suggestion that Hitler should receive Halifax after the exhibition had finished "would lend the visit a very different aspect and would, in fact, deprive it of its main advantage to us." For Halifax to visit with the main aim of meeting Hitler "would arouse such publicity and speculation as would almost certainly defeat its purpose of an informal entry into contact."[55]

During the evening of November 7 a "cabal," representing "almost the entire decision-making elite of the Foreign Office," met privately after hours at Eden's London home. Among those present were Lord Cranborne, the Minister of State; Oliver Harvey, Eden's Private Secretary; Sir Alec Cadogan, at the time the senior Deputy Under-Secretary; Sir Orme Sargent, an Assistant Under-Secretary; William Strang, the head of the Central Department; and Rex Leeper, the head of the Press Department.[56] While the discussion covered a broad range of current Foreign Office policy issues, including Italy (possible recognition of the Italian conquest of Abyssinia) and Spain, as well as Germany, the overriding view of the meeting was that, while they all "favoured [an] approach to Hitler and offer of a bilateral declaration of our policy . . . none of us liked the idea of the Halifax visit," not least because of the danger of it "producing [a] plausible and vague account of Hitler which would have a soporific effect on the Cabinet."[57] Time was to prove their fears entirely justified.

By now Chamberlain was becoming increasingly frustrated with the painfully slow progress in organizing Halifax's trip to Germany. He had no doubt where the blame lay. "All my plans seem to be going agley at the moment,"[58] he complained to one of his sisters. When he first heard of

Foreign Office opposition to the visit, he had been "really horrified . . . another opportunity to be thrown away. But really, that F.O.! I am only waiting for my opportunity to stir it up with a long pole."[59] On November 8 Chamberlain summoned Eden to Downing Street, a meeting which, according to Harvey, "went very badly." The Prime Minister's principal complaint was that the "F.O. never made a genuine effort to get together with dictators," a criticism which Eden no doubt took as a compliment.[60] On his return to Brussels the following day, Eden telegraphed back to London that "from point of view of our position in Europe and public opinion at home it is essential to avoid giving the impression of our being in pursuit of German Chancellor."[61] Cranborne was dispatched to emphasize this position to Chamberlain in person, but reported back only that the "P.M. and Halifax are absolutely determined that visit shall take place regardless of fact that H. is forcing himself on Hitler, and of the impression it will produce on the Germans of our anxiety to run after them."[62]

On the evening of November 9 Chamberlain addressed the Lord Mayor's Banquet at the City of London Guildhall and, in the course of a long passage on foreign affairs, dropped a broad hint. He promised that relations with Germany and Italy were to be built "upon a basis of mutual friendship and understanding," but that, since any future agreement would be "more hopefully pursued by informal discussion than by public declamation," he intended to "abstain from further words upon the subject."[63] The following afternoon it therefore came as no surprise when the late editions of the London *Evening Standard* carried the bold headline "LORD HALIFAX FOR GERMANY." Although the story took second place on the front page to the news that the former Prime Minister, Ramsay MacDonald, had died at sea on board a liner bound for South America, the impact of the story was still considerable.

> The "Evening Standard" understands that plans are being made for Lord Halifax, the Lord President of the Council, to visit Germany in the near future. He will have an interview with Herr Hitler. It is proposed that Anglo-German relations should be discussed.[64]

That evening Chamberlain addressed the annual dinner at the Savoy for the Conservative backbench 1922 Committee. He promised that he was about to make a "gesture of friendship" to Germany, and announced that he was "sending Lord Halifax" to see Hitler. The Conservative backbench MP and diarist, Chips Channon, recorded that the "P.M. had a rapturous reception and was cheered long and loudly when he sat down."[65]

That news of the visit was now in the public domain played into Chamberlain's hands. "I have had a very difficult time with the F.O. over the Halifax visit," he grumbled to his sister. "In fact I have had to fight every inch of the way. . . . However the fortunate misfortune that the news somehow leaked out finally made it impossible to go back and since then the battle has raged around Halifax's instructions."[66] This was a reference to the argument which now ensued as to the precise wording of any formal Anglo-German declaration. The Germans were insistent that it should be emphasized that there had been no invitation from Hitler, precisely the scenario Eden had feared. Meanwhile the Foreign Secretary's supporters, realizing that the visit was now inevitable, resorted to complaining bitterly at "the precipitancy with which the P.M. and Halifax have pressed on with this visit in A.E.'s absence, knowing that A.E. did not favour it." This, they claimed, showed a "shocking lack of solidarity and even of common decent behaviour." Even Harvey, Eden's loyal Private Secretary, repeatedly pressed his chief to threaten resignation.[67] The rumors of Eden's concerns conveniently found their way into the *Daily Express*, which reported that the decision to send Halifax had been "made without consulting the Foreign Secretary, who knew nothing of the proposal or the decision until he saw it in the newspapers." He was, by all accounts, "furious."[68]

It was therefore fortuitous in the extreme for the Foreign Office "cabal" when on Saturday, November 13, the *Evening Standard* (a stablemate of Lord Beaverbrook's *Daily Express*) followed up its earlier scoop with a yet more sensational story, below the banner headline "HITLER READY FOR TRUCE—NO COLONIES DEMAND FOR TEN YEARS":

> The British Government have information from Berlin that Herr Hitler is ready, if he receives the slightest encouragement, to offer to Great Britain a ten-years "truce" on the Colonial issue. During the "truce" the question of Colonies for Germany would not be raised. In return for this agreement Herr Hitler would expect the British Government to leave him a free hand in Central Europe.[69]

The article unleashed a torrent of vitriol in the German press, which Henderson, in a state of near-panic, reported to London in a series of telegrams. In a lengthy statement, the official Nazi news agency, National-sozialistische Parteikorrespondenz, described the article as a collection of "impudent statements . . . an invention from beginning to end and deliberate falsehoods." It was "the height of sensation mongering and of tendentious poisoning of the atmosphere."

> If Lord Halifax's visit is to take place in such an atmosphere the question must seriously arise whether it would not be more useful in the interests of political appeasement to postpone it for the moment and to allow it perhaps to take place if the Press, in Great Britain particularly, evinces that calm which is usually called decency and truthfulness in other countries.[70]

Henderson claimed to have it on good authority that both *Evening Standard* articles had been written anonymously by one Vladimir Poliakoff, a former diplomatic correspondent of *The Times* and well-known commentator on European affairs under the pseudonym "Augur." Poliakoff had allegedly received the information from "persons in Foreign Office who were against the visit," and was "continuing to receive inspiration from the same persons for the same purpose."[71] For good measure Henderson added his own opinion that the rebuttal had almost certainly been drafted by Hitler himself, who "was furious with *Evening Standard* not only for giving impression that Lord President would bring concrete proposals but also for giving publicity to [the] visit, the arrangements for which he wished to keep as secret as possible."[72]

The following day Vansittart composed an indignant reply for Eden to send to Henderson. "Poliakoff has been barred at the Foreign Office for some time past," he asserted, and the suggestion that the leak had emanated from that quarter was, therefore, "wholly unfounded." Eden strongly rebuked his ambassador for failing "to counter these stories" more strongly, and sharply criticized the Germans, and implicitly Henderson also, for making the assumption in the first place that the Foreign Office was opposed to Halifax's visit. "There are 'no persons in Foreign Office who were against visit,' nor, as you are well aware, are these *our* methods."[73] Eden may or may not have realized it, given that the telegram had been drafted by Vansittart, but both assertions were bare-faced lies. The influence of Vansittart, the senior official at the Foreign Office, was crucial in all this, as were his close ties to the Secret Intelligence Service, MI6.

Historically SIS officers serving overseas had assumed the cover of passport control officer in the British embassy. The PCOs were supposed to spend the majority of their time collecting information for their masters in London, while the routine office work of issuing visas was left to junior staff. However, after Hitler's rise to power, "limited resources, shortage of outstanding talent, the refugee problem, scandals at The Hague and Warsaw, its increasingly transparent cover and the growing demand within Whitehall for intelligence from Nazi Germany"[74] had brought the system to the point of collapse. As the demand for exit visas grew proportionately with the Nazi persecution of Jewish communities, the actual work of gathering intelligence became permanently disrupted. The head of SIS, Admiral Sir Hugh "Quex" Sinclair, therefore decided, in collusion with Vansittart, to try to find an alternative method of channeling intelligence back to London. Their solution was the creation of a top secret network of business contacts throughout Europe, known as the "Z Organisation," which would cover the PCO network, and could carry on working independently should SIS itself become compromised during wartime. The new organization was kept secret even from other SIS staff, and was based out of alternative headquarters, at Bush House in Aldwych, rather than at SIS's traditional nerve center at Broadway Buildings in Victoria.

A key member of the Z Organisation was Frederick Voigt of the *Manchester Guardian*, the doyen of central European correspondents and a confidant of Vansittart. Formerly based in Berlin, where the Gestapo had once tried to assassinate him, Voigt was well versed in the way in which Vansittart did business. The leak to Poliakoff, he confirmed privately to his editor, was only one part "of the fight against Halifax's trip [which had] become desperate." Admittedly the Foreign Office had "rarely resorted to a scheme so desperate as to counteract a dangerous political move by making a disclosure to a stunt newspaper." But this was precisely what had happened. Poliakoff had been told about the planned visit "so that it would receive stunt publicity and be denied by the Germans."[75] It now appeared entirely possible that Vansittart's tactics might pay off, and that the visit would be canceled.

However, in a clear sign of the increasing bitterness that characterized the conflict between Chamberlain at Downing Street, and Eden across the road at the Foreign Office, the Prime Minister now resorted to his own aggressive spin tactics. His Chief Press Secretary, George Steward, was put to work to brief certain newspapers about the importance of Halifax's visit, and the foolishness of the *Evening Standard* article. The *Daily Telegraph* obediently described the article as an "inexcusable indiscretion." Its claims were "as unauthentic as they were ill-timed and mischievous. Nothing could have been better calculated to dissipate the spirit in which alone such conversations can fruitfully be conducted."[76] *The Times* concurred, criticizing the "mischief" caused by the story, which it dismissed as "quite unfounded speculation."[77] Eden was appalled. "This morning's newspapers (especially *Times* and *Daily Telegraph*) contained the most exaggerated account of scope of Halifax's visit," complained Harvey. Meanwhile the briefing note that Eden insisted Rex Leeper should distribute on behalf of the Foreign Office, "emphasizing [the visit's] informal and limited character and the fact that it implied no change in the present policy of H.M.G.," was not even published.

It was obvious to Eden that the inspiration for these stories emanated from the very top. Indeed, so angry was he that he dragged himself out of his sickbed where he was recovering from flu, and came into the Foreign Office to see Halifax, who he discovered to be equally concerned at the likely difficulties he might now face. After later seeing Chamberlain also, Eden confessed to Harvey that the interview "couldn't have gone worse." In a now celebrated exchange, the Prime Minister accused his Foreign Secretary of being "feverish," and advised him "to go back to bed and take an aspirin!" Showing further insensitivity given that Eden had only just returned to work, Chamberlain also suggested that he should take a holiday for a further rest. Most incredible of all, Chamberlain assured Eden with a straight face that he "also deplored exaggerated press accounts and undertook to see the Press himself and correct them."[78] It had, of course, been Chamberlain who had been responsible for briefing the press in the first place.

If they had any remaining doubts as to the British government's good intentions, the Germans were further reassured by an extraordinary meeting that took place on the day of Halifax's departure. Steward invited the press attaché at the German embassy, Dr. Fritz Hesse, "a rather close friend," to visit him at Downing Street. There he promised Hesse privately that "Chamberlain had been extremely angry about the article" in the *Evening Standard,* and had made "exhaustive investigations" into its origins. Steward agreed that it had probably been written by Poliakoff, but identified the source as the Italian embassy in London. He further wished Hesse to assure the Führer that "the *Evening Standard* was a paper to whose utterances no particular importance was to be attached."[79] Over the coming months Steward was to brief Hesse regularly, leading one historian to describe his behavior as being "strictly against his code of conduct as a civil servant . . . if he was acting on his own initiative, then his activities were frankly treasonable."[80] If he was not, then his orders can only have come from the Prime Minister.

▪ ▪ ▪

Halifax arrived in Berlin on the morning of Wednesday, November 17, and was briefed by Henderson over breakfast at the embassy. Göring, he was told, "was *very* keen indeed on the establishment of complete understanding between us; as was Hitler." His first official appointment was at a family lunch with Neurath, who was still smarting at Hitler's refusal to see him since the meeting at the Reich Chancellery two weeks earlier. Neurath was regarded by the British embassy as a "diplomat of the old school, a gentleman among gutter-snipes,"[81] and Halifax clearly felt at ease. The Neuraths were "nice people and most friendly," he recorded unquestioningly, "with two little brown dachshunds just like Jemma, over which we made much common ground." There was also "some talk about the Führer; of his qualities, artistic, romantic, sensitive. It was all very cheery and light-hearted."[82]

After lunch he paid his first visit to the hunting exhibition, admirably described by his biographer as a "gruesomely Teutonic affair,"[83] the huge crowds overseen by battalions of uniformed Nazi officials. The most notable exhibit was a giant stuffed panda, while Poland won the first prize for a European country and Britain, much to Henderson's delight, came top in the overseas category. The French sent an entire pack of hounds, complete with huntsmen in red coats, brandishing horns. As background accompaniment, a gramophone reproduced the roar of a wild stag, while a huge, judiciously placed world map reminded visitors of the overseas colonies lost by Germany at Versailles. However, much to Halifax's pleasure, it soon became obvious that he was himself the prize exhibit. The German for "Tally Ho!" is "Halali!," and he soon acquired the nickname "Lord Halalifax," much to the delight of his German hosts. He made an almost regal progress through the throng, which reminded him of the "crowds of one's supporters at an election," acknowledging the cheers and Nazi salutes by doffing his hat. He later expressed mild concern at the manner in which his bodyguard of uniformed Nazis roughly brushed aside the curious onlookers from the path of the tall, languid English celebrity.

At the end of his visit, he faced the world's press, and their request that he should "broadcast a few words of appreciation in English, which it appeared discourteous to refuse!" But he could "think of nothing to say except how wonderful it was."[84] Back in London, reaction to his first day in Berlin was mixed, even at times within the same publication. The *Evening Standard* printed a scathing cartoon by its celebrated cartoonist Low, quoting Halifax's praise for the organizers—"Great Britain and every country owe a debt of gratitude . . . for the encouragement given to sport by this exhibition." Hitler, meanwhile, proudly showed off a collection of sporting trophies on the wall, with two empty plaques reserved for Austria and Czechoslovakia. Elsewhere in the paper, alongside a photograph of Halifax and Henderson posing nervously beside a giant set of genuine antlers, the paper's editorial writer disagreed with Low's conclusion.

> Low is a great cartoonist to whom the "Evening Standard" allows independence of expression. And, as our readers know, the political opinions of Low often differ drastically from those of the "Evening Standard," as expressed in its leading articles.
>
> The idea that Britain will play a merely passive and defensive part in discussions with the German government is a preposterous misunderstanding of the position. The foreign policy of Mr. Chamberlain . . . is based not upon fear or upon weakness, but upon realism.[85]

The following evening Halifax left for Berchtesgaden, accompanied by Neurath, Paul Schmidt, Hitler's ubiquitous interpreter, and Ivone Kirkpatrick, the head of chancery at the British embassy. Kirkpatrick, a "small, dapper and decisive man . . . possessed of an incisive mind,"[86] was the sole member of staff at the embassy with whom Henderson apparently felt comfortable, even though his views often conflicted with those of the ambassador. In the words of one junior diplomat serving in Berlin at the time, Kirkpatrick was "a sort of spare wheel to the coach . . . very bright— too bright in a way—and he was very loyal."[87] As a fluent German speaker, he was to play an important role in the various meetings with Hitler over the coming months. The Führer had thoughtfully provided his special train for the journey, and Halifax and Kirkpatrick enjoyed a carriage to themselves, complete with sitting room, bathroom and two sleeping compartments. The white-coated attendants seemed naturally to assume that, like all Englishmen, Lord Halifax would require a fresh whisky and soda every half-hour.

At 9:45 A.M. the train pulled into the station at Berchtesgaden, situated beside the River Ache, and halted at the private platform, with its own vast triple-arched exit, which had been built exclusively for Hitler's use. They were met by storm troopers in five-ton armored and tracked Mercedes cars, and were driven out through the security post by the river, and on up the mountain to Hitler's home, the Berghof. The first fresh snow of the winter lay on the ground, and the views were spectacular in the clear morning light. As Halifax prepared to alight from the car, just where a path had been swept clean of snow at the foot of the steps leading up to the house, he looked out of the window and at eye level could see only "a pair of black trousered legs, finishing up in silk socks and pumps." Assuming this diminutive creature to be a footman, come to open the door for him, he was poised to hand his coat to this helpful servant when a rapidly paling Neurath hissed at him in a hoarse whisper, "*Der Führer, der Führer.*" A closer inspection above waist height did indeed reveal a khaki tunic complete with swastika armband, and a diplomatic crisis was narrowly averted before the visit had even begun.[88]

The Berghof was Hitler's spiritual home. His life in the Bavarian mountains above Berchtesgaden had closely mirrored his own political fortunes. He had first hidden in a small wooden hut on the mountain when a warrant was issued for his arrest after the so-called Beer Hall Putsch in Munich in 1923. He later rented a summer cottage in which to put the finishing touches to *Mein Kampf,* and in 1933 acquired the Haus Wachenfeld, which became the Berghof, and which he then had almost completely redesigned in 1936. When he was at home the swastika flew proudly above the house. Although Hitler liked to portray it as a snug, country home, in truth the Berghof was the hub of a huge complex, a Nazi settlement created by Martin Bormann, who had ruthlessly evicted the former villagers from their homes, either by burning them down or simply removing their roofs. In their place had sprung up a secure *Führergebiet*, a fenced-in community where the chalets and farmhouses had been turned into military installations, barracks and luxurious homes for senior Nazi officials. Göring, Goebbels, Rudolf Hess and Albert Speer all had their holiday homes there.

In March 1936, *Country Life* offered its readers a glimpse into Hitler's lifestyle at the Berghof in a gushing feature article, entitled "HITLER AS A COUNTRYMAN—THE 'SQUIRE' OF WACHENFELD." Hitler, the magazine assured its readers, had "keenly artistic tastes," and was a "passionate lover of music—especially that of joyous Mozart, whose birthplace was a bare ten miles away." Over the years the "rude frame shack" that had been the Berghof had "blossomed into a villa . . . a cosy but modest *chalet* perched at 2000 ft. above Berchtesgaden." It was here that the Führer now spent "his happiest hours," keeping "a generous table for his statesmen guests," while always "the lifelong vegetarian himself." He "looked out upon a panorama of incomparable beauty," while the house itself was decorated in a tasteful "light green." On one important point, however, *Country Life*'s correspondent was badly misled. "The only ladies ever invited to the *chalet*," he claimed, "are Frauen Göring and Goebbels. It is well known that Herr Hitler shrinks from feminine society."[89]

In fact, ever-present at the Berghof, especially when Hitler was there for any period of time, was his mistress Eva Braun. Rarely seen, and never heard by his official guests, Braun was allowed to cheer herself up by inviting her lady friends to stay. They were good-time girls, Hitler's valet later recalled, with "the manners of their Bohemian Munich world . . . frivolous women, occasionally offensive." They talked "openly of the most intimate things" at the dinner table, would "walk around half-naked" in front of the SS servants, and used to "talk loudly about the actors' physiques" when one of Hitler's favorite films was shown in the evening. "They quite openly worked their way through the unusually tall soldiers in Hitler's bodyguard."[90] The austere, high Anglican Halifax would doubtless have been appalled by Braun's biographer's assertion that "the atmosphere at the

Berghof, below its ordered surface, was intensely erotic," and that "Hitler's stout henchmen had virtual *droit de seigneur* and made full use of it."[91]

Throughout the 1930s a succession of well-meaning British politicians had beaten a path to Obersalzberg, few of whom had subsequently returned home with an entirely critical view of the Führer. Now it was to be the turn of Halifax, the latest in a long line of politicians who thought that they could do business with the dictator. Hitler greeted Halifax warmly at the foot of the steps and led him up into the house, and then on upstairs into his study. The room was overheated and the atmosphere stifling, and when Halifax removed the heavy coat and two woollen pullovers in which he had traveled, his thin frame appeared to his hosts even more gaunt than usual. Hitler wanted the surroundings to be deliberately low-key, and the two principals, together with Neurath and Schmidt, sat in armchairs around an inconveniently low coffee table. Kirkpatrick noticed that from the outset Hitler was in a "peevish mood," and having invited Halifax to begin the discussion, the opening exchanges were "distinctly sticky."[92] Halifax thanked Hitler for agreeing to a meeting "upon which the whole future of civilisation might well depend," but warned that he had "brought no new proposals from London," at which an angry frown darkened the Führer's face.[93] The ensuing three-hour conversation, according to Halifax's biographer, was to "constitute the high-water mark of Halifax's appeasement."[94]

Shrewdly, Hitler invited Halifax to identify the subjects he wished to discuss, whereupon the Lord President tailed off into a lengthy eulogy on the merits of Nazi Germany.

> Although there was much in the Nazi system that offended British opinion (treatment of the Church; to perhaps a less extent, the treatment of Jews; treatment of Trade Unions), I was not blind to what he had done for Germany and to the achievement from his point of view of keeping Communism out of his country and, as he would feel, of blocking its passage West. And taking England as a whole, there was a much greater degree of understanding of all his work on that side than there had been some time ago.[95]

These were, considered Halifax, "great services . . . and if the public opinion of England took up an attitude of criticism from time to time, it might no doubt be in part because people in England were not fully informed of the motives and attendant circumstances of certain measures taken in Germany."[96]

Halifax ended his opening statement by assuring Hitler that Britain had no desire to drive a wedge between Berlin and Rome, and put forward the tentative suggestion that some form of four-power agreement, also involving Italy and France, might perhaps provide the best chance for peace. Hitler waved the idea away on the grounds that it would be impossible to achieve, and instead launched into a lengthy, rather tedious monologue of his own. It was time, he insisted, for the world to recognize Germany's status as a "Great Power," and to "get away from the Versailles mentality." Halifax assured him, somewhat obsequiously, that "nobody wished to treat Germany as anything but a Great Power," but that "nobody in their senses supposed the world could stay as it was for ever." To this Hitler replied that there were only two alternatives, "the free play of forces that meant war, and settlement by reason." This gobbledygook was followed up by a more comprehensible and familiar tirade about the difficulty of doing business with democratic countries, and that "all his offers, disarmament and political, had been wrecked on this rock."

At last Halifax showed his political teeth and bluntly told the Führer that if there was to be no progress between them until such a time as "Great Britain ceased to maintain a democratic system," then clearly "I had wasted my time coming to Berchtesgaden and he had wasted his time receiving me."[97] Hitler was taken aback by this outburst from the mild-mannered Halifax, but soon recovered his composure and again offered his guest the floor, asking what further issues he would like to discuss. Halifax briefly raised the topics of the League of Nations and disarmament, both of which Hitler batted away with further platitudes about America's continued absence from the League and his own rejected proposals to abolish bombing. Still he pressed Halifax. Was there anything else?

It was at this point that all Halifax's good intentions foundered. He should have had ringing in his ears Eden's warning that he was to "confine himself to warning comments on Austria and Czechoslovakia," but for some reason he chose completely to ignore the Foreign Secretary's counsel.

I said that there were no doubt other questions arising out of the Versailles settlement which seemed to us capable of causing trouble if they were mishandled, e.g. Danzig, Austria, Czechoslovakia. On all these matters we were not necessarily concerned to stand for the status quo as today, but we were concerned to avoid such treatment of them as would be likely to cause trouble. If reasonable settlements could be reached with the free assent and goodwill of those primarily concerned we certainly had no desire to block.[98]

There were, he concluded, "possible alterations in the European order which might be destined to come about with the passage of time." This was precisely the message that Chamberlain had encouraged Halifax to deliver, but equally the one offer that Eden had feared. "I wish that Halifax had warned Hitler more strongly against intervention in Central Europe," he later complained.[99]

Having heard all he needed to know, Hitler immediately lost interest in the conversation. He disingenuously expressed support for Germany's existing agreements with Austria, and hoped that a similar agreement could be reached with Czechoslovakia. He emphasized his wish to "get away from the atmosphere of 'imminent catastrophe,' " promising his visitor that "the situation at present was not dangerous." Halifax, however, seemed unsure as to how he should treat Hitler's rather lame joke that "if you believed the press, you could of course expect to wake up one day to see German armed forces in Vienna or Prague."[100] After a further lengthy but ultimately aimless discussion about colonial issues, Hitler somehow managed to keep a straight face when wrapping up the three-hour morning session with an assurance that "Germany herself set great store by good relations with all her neighbours."[101] It had been, of course, only a fortnight since he had warned his generals (and Neurath, now sitting alongside him) that they should prepare for the invasion of both Austria and Czechoslovakia.

The meeting duly broke up for lunch, taken in a "hideous dining room" on the first floor, furnished with a large satinwood table and pink upholstered chairs. Hitler ate a vegetarian meal of soup, mixed vegetables and walnuts, while his guests were invited to partake of "a rather indifferent meat lunch," served by three SS waiters in white mess jackets. The wineglasses, however, were kept filled, although Hitler stuck to his own "hot concoction out of a glass in a silver holder." From a "social point of view," reported Kirkpatrick, "the lunch was a frost." Hitler was in a furious temper throughout, Neurath clearly felt uncomfortable, and Halifax found it difficult to get involved when everything had to be interpreted for him. Kirkpatrick manfully made several attempts to initiate a conversation, "but they all collapsed pitifully under Hitler's determination not to play." Talk of the weather provoked the riposte that "the weather prophets are idiots; when they say it is going to be fine it always rains and when they foretell bad weather, it's fine." A brief discussion on flying was brought to an early end by the assertion that "only a fool would fly if he can go by train or road."

A similar attempt to review the Berlin hunting exhibition reduced the Führer to near-apoplexy.

> I can't see what there is in shooting; you go out armed with a highly perfected modern weapon and without risk to yourself kill a defenceless animal. Of course Göring tells me that the pleasure lies not in the killing, but in the comradely expedition in the open air. Very well. I merely reply: "If that's the case, let's spare ourselves all bother and make a comradely expedition to a slaughter-house where in the greatest comradeship we can together kill a cow in the open air."

Satisfied that he had had the last word, he sat back with an angry gesture of defiance. He joined in the conversation only once again, when talk of Hess's newborn baby son gave him an opening to lecture his guests on the iniquities of the falling Austrian birth rate, caused by the miserable economic conditions that were the result of Austria's continuing separation from Germany. Kirkpatrick noted tartly that the Führer "behaved throughout like a spoilt, sulky child."

After the "painful ordeal" of lunch, Hitler took his guests downstairs to the main drawing room, famous for its enormous leaded picture window, a single sheet of glass which could be lowered in its entirety into the ground. Two SS officers were summoned to insert car starting handles into two sockets, and then duly wound the window noiselessly down into the floor, giving the room the feel of a covered terrace, with spectacular views out over the mountains and on to Austria. So impressed had former Prime Minister David Lloyd George been when he visited Hitler in 1936 that he had installed a similar mechanism at his home at Churt in Surrey. The party took their coffee in wicker upholstered chairs, set out around low round tables. At each end of the room was a grand piano, the walls were covered with pictures from museums, and two large tapestries could be rolled back to reveal a cinema screen.

Hitler's mood had not improved. He liked to watch two films a night, preferably featuring his favorite actress, Greta Garbo, and he now took great delight in telling Halifax that one of his favorite films was *The Lives of a Bengal Lancer*, depicting "a handful of Britons holding a continent in thrall. That was how a superior race must behave and the film was compulsory viewing for the S.S." Talk of India encouraged him to berate the former Viceroy over the failings of British policy there. There was no need to tolerate disorder or to waste time in negotiating—"Shoot Gandhi" was his simple remedy, "and if that does not suffice to reduce them to submission, shoot a dozen leading members of Congress; and if that does not suffice, shoot 200 and so on until order is restored." Throughout this tirade, Halifax "gazed at Hitler with a mixture of astonishment, repugnance and compassion. He indicated dissent, but it would have been a waste of time to argue."[102] Schmidt was struck by the extraordinary contrast between the two men, the "deeply religious Yorkshire nobleman, the enthusiastic protagonist of peace, and Hitler, wilful and uncompromising by nature, and now rendered even more so by his recent successes and the now manifest weakness of his opponents."[103]

On the train back to Munich, Neurath, clearly embarrassed, apologized for Hitler's poor demeanor. Halifax, meanwhile, committed to paper his reminiscences of the day's events.

> Hitler was on the whole very quiet and restrained, except now and again when he got excited: over Russia or the press. Very much alive, in speech—eyes moving about all the time, and points being reinforced by sharp gestures of the hands. I can quite see why he is a popular speaker. The play of emotion—sardonic humour, scorn, something almost wistful—is very rapid. But he struck me as very sincere, and as believing everything he said. As to the political value of the talk, I am not disposed to rate this very high.
>
> Although perfectly friendly and courteous, he showed a certain reserve, which may have been due partly to tiredness, but was, I think, mainly attributable to a feeling that we had a different sense of values and were speaking a different language.[104]

They may well have been speaking a different language, but Hitler had understood Halifax perfectly and was in a considerably less contemplative mood. Although he had had little enthusiasm for the meeting in the first place, he had in fact got all he wanted and more from "the English Parson."[105] His valet noticed that he was now "in the best of moods and . . . rubbed his hands and slapped his thighs as if he had already concluded a good deal." That evening he joined Eva Braun and her friends for dinner, listening as they "poked fun at Halifax's garb and his long, wizened physique." But Hitler came to Halifax's defense, "praising him as a clever politician who fully supported Germany's aims." Most important, he told them, "Halifax had assured him that Britain would not stand in Germany's way in respect of its Austrian policy."[106] Eden would have been appalled.

Halifax and Kirkpatrick, with Schmidt as their guide, spent the evening in Munich, visiting the newly built Führerbau, the two Temples of Honor to the dead of the 1923 putsch, and the block of flats that was Hitler's Munich home. After dinner they returned to their train, and arrived back in Berlin the next morning in time for breakfast. At lunchtime Halifax was driven an hour or so out of Berlin to Göring's vast 100,000-acre estate at Karinhall. His host met him in the courtyard, wearing brown breeches and boots all in one, a green leather jerkin covered by a fur-collared coat, a green leather belt from which was hung a dagger in a red leather sheath and, to complete the effect, a green hat with a large chamois tuft—"altogether a very picturesque and arresting figure," recalled Halifax.[107] During a tour of the heavily wooded estate in a horse-drawn shooting break, Göring proudly showed off the enclosures where he kept his elk and bison, as well as his extensive forestry operation.

The vast stone and thatched house was "like nothing I have ever seen," recorded Halifax. The never-ending series of immense rooms, and the huge central hall, were all crammed "with art treasures of different sorts, pictures, tapestries, sculptures, carvings," all looted from various museums.[108] A month earlier, the Duke and Duchess of Windsor had also been Göring's guests at Karinhall, and the Duchess has left a vivid description of their own tour of the house.

It contained a private gymnasium in the basement, equipped with weight-lifting apparatus, an electronic exercising horse, horizontal bars, and a massage apparatus bearing the Elizabeth Arden trade-mark.

The entire attic was given over to a playroom for the children of Göring's relations. It was stocked with enough children's toys to equip a shop. Spread around the room was the most elaborate toy railway I have ever seen—yards and yards of intricately connected track, dozens of switches, coal tipples, charming little stations, and any number of locomotives and cars of different types. The Field-Marshal, kneeling down in his white uniform showed us how it worked. The deftness with which he directed the trains up and down the tracks, opening and closing switches, blowing whistles, and averting collisions, suggested that he must have spent a good deal of his time in the attic.[109]

The Duchess failed to mention Göring's final touch—an intricate system of wires which allowed model airplanes to "fly" across the room, dropping miniature bombs on the railway below.

Halifax's lunch, which included raw beef and was "uneatable," was served by "parlour maids in some country-peasant costume, and by footmen dressed in eighteenth century liveries, green and white plush, breeches, gaiter-spats, reversed cuffs and caught up tails of the coats."[110] Afterward Göring and Halifax, with Schmidt interpreting, retired to talk. Schmidt had driven out to Karinhall early that morning to brief Göring on the previous day's proceedings, and did not "conceal how badly things had gone." Göring, however, who had also spoken to Hitler by telephone, was an altogether more genial host. The subjects of conversation were largely the same as they had been at Berchtesgaden, but Göring dealt with them "with infinitely more diplomacy," and remained quiet and calm throughout the meeting. As far as he was concerned any problems could be settled by negotiation; "under no circumstances shall we use force," he assured Halifax.[111] The good cop/bad cop technique had worked to perfection.

In a much quoted passage, which Halifax's reputation has never wholly lived down, he later reminisced about meeting the man who had set up the concentration camps, and presided over the Night of the Long Knives.

I was immensely entertained at meeting the man himself. One remembered all the time that he had been concerned with the "clean-up" in Berlin on June 30th, 1934, and wondered how many people he had been, for good cause or bad, responsible for having killed. But his personality, with this reserve, was frankly attractive. Like a great schoolboy, full of life and pride in all he was doing, showing off his forest and animals, and then talking high politics out of the setting of green jerkin and red dagger . . . a composite personality—film star, great landowner interested in his estate, Prime Minister, party-manager, head gamekeeper at Chatsworth.[112]

In the view of Halifax's biographer, Göring's "innate depravity seemed to escape him," while nothing in his "upbringing had equipped him with the instinct to fathom the true wickedness of these men."[113]

The following day Henderson invited Joseph and Magda Goebbels to tea at the embassy on the Wilhelmstrasse. "I had expected to dislike him intensely," recalled Halifax, "but am ashamed to say that I did not."[114] Goebbels had gone one better than Göring, and had actually traveled to Berchtesgaden in person the previous day to receive his orders from Hitler. Now he too was charm personified. His principal concern was the British press, and he complained bitterly at the hostility of the Berlin correspondents to Nazi Germany in general, and Hitler in particular, who he felt deserved greater respect as head of state and the national symbol of Germany. Halifax gently pointed out that many of them had served in Berlin for many years. Had they suddenly become dishonest? Goebbels replied "with a shameless and charming smile: 'We did not complain in the past because Germany was not rearmed. We complain now because we are strong enough to do so.' "[115] Nevertheless, Halifax promised to speak to the Prime Minister and Foreign Secretary about the matter, and "had no doubt that His Majesty's Government would do everything in their power to influence the Press to avoid unnecessary offence."[116]

Halifax returned to London to be met by muted press reaction. This was partly because he had urged restraint on the local correspondents before he left Berlin, and partly because his return coincided with the news that the Duke of Windsor had settled out of court an action he had brought for libel against the publishers William Heinemann. The supposedly libelous allegations, contained in a book, *Coronation Commentary* by Geoffrey Cox, included the suggestions that the Duke had been forced to abdicate only because ministers had been desperate to get rid of him, that he had prolonged the crisis to hold out for more money, and "had at times had recourse to other sources of courage." Most brazen, his King's Counsel had assured the court that the allegation that the Duchess had "occupied, before his marriage to her, the position of his mistress . . . was entirely untrue. No suggestion could be more damaging or more insulting." Perhaps fortuitously for the Duke, the case had been settled before he was called to the stand to give evidence on this particular matter, much to the regret of the Lord Chief Justice, Lord Hewart, who was presiding. He told the court that he would much rather that the allegations had not been withdrawn and that he had been allowed to dispense justice; indeed, so "foul and cruel" were they that they "almost invited a horse-whipping."[117]

On November 24 Halifax reported on his visit to the Cabinet. He prefaced his remarks by warning that "his impressions were subject to the considerations that his visit was very brief, that he might have been deceived, or his judgement might have been at fault." But he had everywhere "encountered friendliness and a desire for peace," especially among the public at the hunting exhibition, where "he had been warmly received by the general crowds." Göring had assured him, apparently with Hitler's approval, that "he could see no circumstances in which the two countries would fight," and that "not one drop of German blood would be spilt in Europe unless it was forced on them."

> Lord Halifax's general conclusion, therefore, was that the Germans had no policy of immediate adventure. They were too busy building up their country, which was still in a state of revolution. Nevertheless he would expect a beaver-like persistence in pressing their claims in Central Europe, but not in a form to give others cause—or probably occasion—to interfere.

Amazingly, Eden seemed satisfied with this conclusion to a visit which he had originally so strongly opposed, and "expressed great satisfaction with the way the Lord President had dealt with each point in his conversations with the Chancellor."[118] Chamberlain was more delighted still, boasting to his sister that:

> The German visit was from my point of view a great success because it achieved its object, that of creating an atmosphere in which it was

possible to discuss with Germany the practical questions involved in a European settlement.

It was no part of my plan that we should make or receive any offer. What I wanted H[alifax] to do was to convince Hitler of our sincerity & to ascertain what objectives he had in mind and I think both of these objects have been achieved. But Hitler and Goering said repeatedly & emphatically that they had no desire or intention of making war and I think we may take this as correct at any rate for the present.[119]

Halifax had indeed shown Hitler sincerity, but the Führer "had instead deduced weakness." He now knew that Britain would happily entertain the prospect of possible changes to the existing, post-Versailles order and would almost certainly not go to war to prevent the expansion of the Reich for which he longed. "Halifax," wrote his biographer, "let Hitler see his chance."[120]

2

Scandal in Berlin

What influence a woman, even without realising it, can exert on the history of a country and thereby on the world.

Colonel Alfred Jodl, January 26, 1938

The outcome of the Blomberg-Fritsch affair amounted to the third stepping-stone—after the Reichstag Fire and the "Röhm-Putsch"—cementing Hitler's absolute power and, quite especially, his dominance over the army. With the military emasculated. . . . Hitler's personal drive for the most rapid expansion possible was unshackled from the forces which could have counselled caution. The danger-zone was being entered.

Sir Ian Kershaw, *Hitler 1936–45: Nemesis*

Field Marshal Werner Freiherr von Blomberg, Hitler's Minister of War and commander-in-chief of the armed forces, was a far from popular figure in the higher echelons of the army. It was widely felt that he failed to present the army's view sufficiently forcefully to Hitler, and that his fawning admiration for the Führer clouded his professional judgment. Behind his back he was sneeringly referred to as "Hitlerjunge Quex," after the Hitler Youth hero of a propaganda film who was prepared to sacrifice his life for Hitler. He was considered impulsive, easily influenced and too friendly with the Nazi Party hierarchy for the liking of the aristocratic old guard among the German officer corps.[1] The British embassy in Berlin too recognized that he was "completely dominated by Herr Hitler whose words he quotes on each and every occasion." Blomberg, on the other hand, believed that he was much more "a man of the world" than his army contemporaries, having studied and traveled in Russia, the United States and throughout Europe.[2] He was pointedly pro-British, and had relished acting as Hitler's representative at the coronation of King George VI in May 1937, where Chamberlain had found him to be "a very pleasant agreeable man of the world who talks extremely good English."[3]

Although he had registered a passing unease as Hitler unveiled his expansionist plans at the Reich Chancellery on November 5, Blomberg's doubts were short-lived. As he left the meeting he told Admiral Raeder that Hitler's speech "had not been meant so earnestly and was not to be judged so seriously. He believed that the Führer would settle these questions peacefully."[4] Yet he refused to discuss Fritsch's concerns with him, or even to acknowledge Beck's written memorandum, which was submitted to him on November 12. Instead, he set to work updating the one aspect of the Führer's orders over which he had personal control, the coordination of military planning. By December 21 he was ready to issue a new military directive, amending the provisions for Case Green, the existing plans for a lightning invasion of Czechoslovakia.

> When Germany has achieved complete preparedness for war in all fields, then the military conditions will have been created for carrying out an offensive war [*Angriffskrieg*] against Czechoslovakia, so that the solution of the German problem of living space can be carried to a victorious end even if one or other of the Great Powers intervene against us.[5]

Blomberg, meanwhile, had other, more personal, matters on his mind. He had married his first wife, the daughter of a retired army officer, in 1904, but she had died in 1929 after a long illness, leaving him with five grown-up children. Now fifty-nine, and growing increasingly tired of a lengthy and lonely widowhood, at some moment during September 1937 he met, and soon become infatuated with, a considerably younger woman. Legend varies as to whether he first met her on a park bench in the Tiergarten while out for his daily morning walk, or at the local hostelry where she worked. But the fact remained that Fräulein Margarethe Gruhn, known to her friends as Erna or Eva, was thirty-five years younger than the War

Minister and came from a vastly contrasting social background. She had been born in 1913, the daughter of a cleaner and a gardener at the Royal Palace in Berlin, but after her father died in the First World War, her mother, Luise, lost her job and took up work instead as a masseuse. After working for her mother for a while, the two apparently fell out with each other, and a few years before her meeting with Blomberg, the young Erna had set out on her own in the world.[6]

At some stage Erna secured a job as a stenographer at the Reich Egg Board, possibly with Blomberg's help, but, as he became increasingly besotted with his newfound lover, he became aware also that he was competing for her affections with another, younger man. The obvious course of action was for him to marry Erna, although he was well aware that the snobbery and prejudice that were prevalent among the army's aristocratic officer corps would lead to dismay among his colleagues at the proposed union. Incredibly, given that Göring had long coveted Blomberg's job for himself, it was to the Luftwaffe chief that Blomberg chose to turn. He confided in him that he was having an affair with a "girl of the people," and inquired confidentially whether it would be in order for him to marry her, given that she was also "a lady with a past." Göring, who had himself married an actress after the death of his first wife, assured him that the Third Reich was actively struggling to overcome just such social prejudices, and that the field marshal's high standing would not be compromised one iota. Indeed, such a marriage would help to bridge the social divide that unfortunately all too often still existed, and he would personally intervene with Hitler to secure the necessary support to fend off any criticism from within the officer corps.[7]

A few days later an agitated Blomberg felt emboldened to return to see Göring again, with a further request for assistance. His younger rival for Erna's affection was refusing to bow out quietly—could Göring possibly come up with a way of discreetly removing him from the fray? Göring shamelessly continued to play the role of well-wisher and promised that he would do what he could. The president of the Reich Grain Office was summoned, and agreed to find a suitable, well-paid position for Blomberg's rival in Argentina. The startled young man was duly sent for and informed by Göring that his passage was booked, and "that his health demanded a drastic change of climate." It would be in his best interests to leave immediately.

Doubtless grateful that he had avoided being shipped instead to a concentration camp, the rival suitor "accepted his fate philosophically," but before setting out on his voyage called on Göring one last time. He felt it only right, he informed his unlikely benefactor, to warn him that Fräulein Gruhn was a woman of highly questionable character, and "had a rather more lurid personal history than she had probably told the field marshal."[8] He strongly advised Göring that Blomberg should give careful consideration as to whether or not he should marry her.

His own impending nuptials were not Blomberg's only cause for celebration. His daughter Dorothea was engaged to be married to Lieutenant Karl-Heinz Keitel, the son of General Wilhelm Keitel, the chief of the Wehrmachtsamt, the Armed Forces Department within the Ministry of War, and thus effectively Blomberg's chief of staff. The elder Keitel had recently noticed that Blomberg's behavior had become increasingly bizarre, and that the field marshal had taken to driving out on his own, in civilian clothes, to a hotel in Oberhof, in the Thuringian forest. On December 15 Keitel's assistant, Colonel Alfred Jodl, noted in his diary that "The General Field Marshal is in a high state of excitement. Reason not known. Apparently a personal matter. He retired for eight days to an unknown place."[9] Blomberg's adjutant refused to confide in Keitel, claiming that his chief was visiting a lady in Oberhof who had broken her ankle skiing.

In mid-December 1937 the First World War veteran General Erich Ludendorff died, and Hitler decreed that he should have a state funeral in the Feldernhalle in Munich. It fell to Blomberg to give the funeral oration. Keitel commandeered a special train, complete with Blomberg's new personal carriage which he had recently been given by Hitler, to take the field marshal's entourage to Munich. However, Blomberg failed to board with the others in Berlin, and the train was forced to take a detour to collect its principal passenger at Oberhof, where he was once again enjoying a few quiet days with Erna. After the funeral Blomberg persuaded Hossbach to let him have a few minutes alone with Hitler, and he repeated the bare facts of his earlier conversation with Göring, again conceding that his fiancée was a girl of humble origins. Hitler, like Göring before him, warmly endorsed the idea of Germany's senior military officer bridging the class divide in this way. Indeed, so enthusiastic was he to emphasize his complete rejection of any suggestion of snobbery that he insisted that he and Göring act as witnesses. As a result Blomberg felt suitably confident to spend Christmas with Erna at Oberhof, away from his own family, and on his return to confirm his plans to Keitel. "It was no disgrace," he insisted defensively, "in our modern National Socialist Germany to marry a 'child of the people' and he did not care a hoot for the gossip in so-called society." He had confided in his children, who had happily given him their blessing.[10]

The wedding was to take place quietly on Wednesday, January 12, in one of the state rooms at the War Ministry in the Bendlerstrasse. The wedding party was kept deliberately small in accordance with the low-key occasion, and included just Erna's mother, Blomberg's former naval adjutant, an old friend and his three current adjutants. Blomberg arrived in ordinary uniform, proudly wearing his Iron Cross, while his bride was dressed in a gray dress and silk blouse, with no jewelry, and carried a bunch of red roses. They waited nervously in silence, until Hitler and Göring arrived together at noon. Hitler was wearing a plain brown storm trooper's uniform tunic, but with no swastika armband, while Göring, never one to miss an opportunity to dress up, was in full-dress uniform of the air force, complete with all decorations. Blomberg presented his bride to the Führer, who in turn handed her a bouquet of yellow roses, before he and Göring took their places either side of the couple for the civil ceremony. At its conclusion all four signed the register, and, as was the custom, the registrar handed the newly married couple a copy of *Mein Kampf*, as Hitler looked on impassively. One of Blomberg's adjutants later noticed that it had been left on the table when the guests departed.[11]

News of the marriage and Hitler's participation appeared prominently, albeit with no accompanying comment, in that evening's Berlin newspapers. The announcement caused a considerable stir, and was greeted with incredulity by the majority of senior Nazis, many of them friends of Blomberg, who had had no idea that the field marshal was planning to remarry. The lack of detail and photographs in the reports, however, immediately caused suspicion and rumors soon began to circulate. The publication a few days later of a photograph of Blomberg and his new wife on their honeymoon, apparently taken in front of the monkey enclosure at Leipzig zoo, did little to still the gossip. The *Daily Mail* took it upon itself to fill the gap and investigated the story with alacrity. "Field Marshal von

Blomberg," it announced, "has astonished his friends and colleagues by getting married." Reports suggested that the bride was variously from Hamburg or Geneva, and that the ceremony had taken place "in a hospital, where, it is said, the bride is being treated for an injury received while skiing."[12] Blomberg's original cover story had by now gained credibility.

Showing considerable ingenuity, the paper's Berlin correspondent managed to track down Frau Gruhn to a "small workman's shack in Neukölln, a working class district of Berlin." "We have probably been more surprised than anyone else," mused Frau Gruhn, describing herself as a "State-registered masseuse." Her daughter, she assured the reporter, had gone to work as a typist in the War Ministry after leaving school. "We knew she had been getting on well, but we did not dream that she had become friendly with the Field Marshal." Meanwhile the page opposite this scoop ran a trailer for the paper's forthcoming serialization of Agatha Christie's latest thriller, *A Date with Death* (later entitled *Appointment with Death*)—"a gripping first-rate story in which the excitement and interest never flag."[13] As the *Daily Mail* briefly became the most widely read newspaper in Berlin, the city's residents were enjoying a first-rate story of their own.

The happy couple's honeymoon was cut short by the sudden death of Blomberg's mother, and he returned for the funeral, at Eberswalde near Berlin, on January 20. The sense of mystery surrounding his new wife was only heightened by her appearance at the graveside, so heavily veiled that it was impossible to see her face, and her hurried departure before anyone could talk to her afterward. By now the trickle of malicious rumors was becoming a torrent. The following day Fritsch's adjutant took a telephone call in his office, and when he refused to put the anonymous caller through to the commander-in-chief in person, the voice at the other end of the line shouted back: "Then tell the general that Field Marshal von Blomberg has married a whore." With that he hung up, leaving the adjutant staring incredulously at the telephone receiver. He reported the call to Fritsch, who in turn discussed it with Beck and Hossbach, but in spite of much shaking of heads the army hierarchy failed to accept the proffered bait and move against Blomberg.[14]

On the same day, however, Erna Gruhn's true background was finally revealed. There are a number of explanations as to how her police file may have found its way onto the desk of the chief of the Berlin police,

Count Wolf Heinrich von Helldorf. One has the wife of a Berlin police inspector discussing the latest gossip surrounding Blomberg with her husband, who, on checking his files in the Residence Registry Office the next morning, was astonished to discover that Erna was indeed known to the Berlin police. Another has a police official overhearing a little girl on the street, boasting to her friend that "Mother Gruhn has gotten herself a fine new son-in-law, a field marshal." A further account describes how a drunken prostitute is arrested one night and boasts that she is not so bad if girls like her can aspire to rise to the highest places. And the most detailed has an officer in the Bureau of Moral Offences recognizing Erna's name on a number of pornographic photographs which had recently come into the office.[15]

By whatever tortuous means it may have arrived there, the fact remains that by late morning on January 21 a bulging dossier detailing all of Erna Gruhn's past misdemeanors lay open on Helldorf's desk. The dry legal language could not conceal the clear implication that the wife of Field Marshal von Blomberg, the Minister of War and commander-in-chief of the armed forces, was a prostitute. It had apparently been common knowledge that her mother was running a brothel under the camouflage of her massage parlor, and had two convictions against her name for procuring and prostitution. Eva too had come to the attention of the Berlin police at an early age, and was also registered in the file as a prostitute, having "used her domicile for naked orgies." As well as a more mundane conviction for stealing, she had also acquired a lengthy record for having "posed for pornographic photographs with partners of both sexes; further she had made commercial transactions in the said photographs," five of which were included in the dossier. Incredibly, she had at the time taken out an action against the photographer, complaining that he had only paid her sixty marks for her trouble.[16] The images had apparently "been obscene enough to sell tremendously."[17]

Helldorf was well known to British diplomats as an ardent Nazi, "a bully . . . notorious for rowdy attacks on Jews" who had gambled away a substantial fortune.[18] However, nothing in his training had prepared him for this eventuality. As he looked at the face of the nude girl in the incriminating photographs, he was "thunderstruck" at the possibility that it might be Frau von Blomberg.[19] He quickly realized that if he acted as properly as he should, and took the file to his ultimate superior, Heinrich Himmler, he would be providing the SS with an invaluable weapon with which to black-mail the head of the armed forces. Only recently he had dared to step outside official channels by taking evidence that the Under-Secretary in the Propaganda Ministry, Walther Funk, was homosexual, direct to Goebbels. He had been severely reprimanded for doing so, and it was therefore a considerable risk for him to consider doing the same again.

Bravely, however, Helldorf decided to bypass the SS and take the evidence instead to Blomberg's nearest associate, General Keitel. The conversation began cautiously, with Helldorf delicately inquiring whether Keitel could identify the new Frau Blomberg from a passport-style photograph on her registration card. Keitel had to admit that he had only seen the young lady on one occasion, when she had been heavily veiled at Blomberg's mother's funeral. Helldorf was incredulous, pointing out that Blomberg and Keitel were soon to be related by marriage, and insisted that Keitel call Blomberg there and then to ascertain the truth. Unfortunately for Blomberg, he was out of Berlin attending to his late mother's affairs and could not be reached. Finally Helldorf came out with the unvarnished truth, and showed Keitel the full dossier. As the future father-in-law of Blomberg's daughter, Keitel could not conceal his embarrassment, and his first thought was that Helldorf should leave the evidence with him, and he would show it to Blomberg on his return to Berlin. But Helldorf refused; it was too late for a cover-up, too many people were already in on the story. Lamely, Keitel, who wanted nothing more to do with the whole sorry saga, referred Helldorf to Göring, "who as a witness at their wedding had, of course, met and seen the young lady."[20]

Having seen Keitel, Helldorf telephoned Arthur Nebe, the chief of the Reich Criminal Police, and asked him to come round to his office. Although Nebe was a general in the SS, Helldorf trusted him, and knew that he preferred to keep Himmler, and his Gestapo chief, Reinhard Heydrich, at arm's length. As Nebe cast a cold eye over the file's contents, Helldorf impatiently asked him what he made of it. "It is evidently an attempt to destroy Marshal von Blomberg," replied the police chief. "It is a *coup*, well prepared and well executed, probably by the Gestapo." When Helldorf interjected that the Gestapo as yet knew nothing of the affair, Nebe scoffed. "Do you really believe that Heydrich, who keeps files on everybody from Hitler and Göring downwards, including yourself and myself, did not know that Erna Gruhn was a prostitute? You may be sure that when the most important man in the German army marries, Heydrich knows all about this lady." The only question in his mind was who had "pushed this prostitute at the Field-Marshal."[21]

Not only had he failed to warn Blomberg of the dark clouds that were circling, but the spineless Keitel, so desperate was he to wash his hands of any further involvement, had rung Göring's office personally to make the appointment. In the words of one observer at the time, Helldorf was now "being asked to carry the bomb with its lighted fuse to the very place where the most spectacular explosion would be welcomed." The following morning, a Saturday, Helldorf drove out to see Göring at Karinhall. Göring did not like having his weekends disturbed, and greeted his uninvited guest brusquely: "Well, what's it about?" As Helldorf began slowly to recount his story, Göring paced impatiently back and forth around the room, listening with increasing interest as Helldorf reached his inevitable climax. Göring went over to a window, threw it open, took a deep breath and exclaimed: "This is the last straw."[22] How far he was acting out a role, and how far he was genuinely shocked, Helldorf was unable to judge.

Two days later, during the early evening of Monday, January 24, the staff at the Reich Chancellery were nervously awaiting the Führer's return from a stay at Obersalzberg. Hossbach was hanging about in the entrance hall, anxious to inform him of a request he had received from Blomberg for an urgent audience. At that moment an unusually apprehensive Göring arrived with his adjutant, Colonel Karl Bodenschatz, clutching a brown file in his hand. To Hossbach, Göring immediately launched into a lengthy tirade about the unfortunate affair of Field Marshal Blomberg, and how "it always fell to his lot to bring particularly unpleasant matters to the Führer's attention." He then continued into Hitler's outer office, where he encountered Captain Fritz Wiedemann, Hitler's personal adjutant, who found the Air Minister to be in a state of considerable agitation, pacing around the room "like an angry lion." To his casual request as to whether all was well, Bodenschatz whispered conspiratorially: "I am telling you, Blomberg will have to get out; he has married a whore!"

When Hitler finally arrived, he and Göring were closeted together for a considerable time, and all contemporary reports suggest that the Führer was genuinely stunned at what Göring had to tell him, letting out a despairing cry: "Nothing is spared to me." Wiedemann later found him "crushed," walking around his office in a trancelike state, head bowed, and hands clasped behind his back.[23] For Hitler, there were a number of factors that made the situation even worse that it might initially have appeared. It transpired that the indecent photographs of Frau Blomberg and her erstwhile lover had been taken by a Czechoslovak Jew. Scurrilous rumors that later did the rounds of Berlin suggested that Hitler "took a bath seven times the next day to rid himself of the taint of having kissed the hand of Frau Blomberg." Worse still, the potential blow to his international prestige, having stood as witness at the wedding, was too horrific to contemplate. That night he lay awake worrying at how to avoid a loss of face. "If a German Field Marshal marries a whore," he lamented to Wiedemann, "anything in the world is possible."[24] Göring was told to see Blomberg the following day and insist that he get an immediate divorce, or better still a full annulment of the marriage on the grounds of gross deception. In the meantime, he was to be barred from the Chancellery and forbidden to wear uniform.

Rumors of Blomberg's impending demise were soon rife throughout the political and diplomatic circles of Berlin. Colonel Jodl recorded in his diary that "telephone calls from [Erna Gruhn's] friends are supposed to have reached the generals from public houses in which they celebrated the social rise of their 'colleague.' "[25] At Abwehr headquarters on Tirpitzufer, Admiral Canaris was warned that rumors were circulating by his chief of staff, Colonel Hans Oster, a close friend of Wiedemann. Like a number of others, Canaris was perplexed as to why Keitel had not warned Blomberg of the existence of the dossier, and was perturbed at Göring's close involvement in what should have been a purely army affair. "Blomberg can't be saved," Goebbels recorded in his diary. "Only the pistol remains for a man of honour. . . . The Führer as a marriage witness. It's unthinkable."[26] But Göring, with his eye now firmly on stepping into Blomberg's shoes, was playing for altogether higher stakes. If Hitler meant to allow Blomberg to keep his job on the sole understanding that he brought his marriage to a speedy end, then it was vital for Göring's plans that Blomberg was not informed of this fact, and that he remained defiantly married.

When Göring called on Blomberg at the War Ministry on the morning of January 25, his demeanor was businesslike, even brutal. Eschewing any opening niceties, he informed the horrified field marshal that "certain matters in the distant past" of his wife had come to light, and that he was to be relieved of his post and discharged from the army. He falsely told Blomberg that the army high command was demanding his resignation, and failed utterly to pass on Hitler's message that an annulment of the marriage might lead to his keeping his job. Göring may even have failed to make clear the full details of the charges against his wife that were contained in the dossier. Blomberg, believing that he had nothing to gain by divorcing his new bride, refused absolutely to contemplate such a move, insisting that he was deeply in love, and complaining bitterly at "such unspeakably unfair treatment." Why should he not enjoy the freedom customary to anyone in his choice of wife? Göring replied tersely that he could "please himself about the marriage, but the dismissal was absolutely final."[27] The conversation lasted just five minutes, and after Göring had left his office, Blomberg's nervous adjutants opened the door a crack to reveal "the hale and hearty field marshal staggering, a broken man, to his private rooms behind the office."[28]

Blomberg, however, was not the only senior officer in the armed forces whose world was about to collapse. While Göring was reading him the riot act at the War Ministry, back at the Reich Chancellery Hitler was holed up with the trusty Hossbach. They were discussing the question of Blomberg's succession. Hitler was furious that he had been betrayed by Blomberg, who had told him nothing of his wife's past, and yet had happily allowed him to act as a witness at the wedding. Although Hossbach already had an inkling of what had happened, he was appalled at the grim detail and furious that the good name of the officer corps had been dragged into such a quagmire of immorality. He was still coming to terms with the implications of what he had learned when suddenly, completely out of the blue, Hitler shifted the conversation away from Blomberg and on to Fritsch. The commander-in-chief of the army, he declared solemnly, was homosexual, and would have to go as well. The evidence had been in his hands for some time. Hossbach was stunned.

Göring was well aware that Fritsch would be the obvious candidate to fill the vacant post of War Minister. He had therefore taken the opportunity quietly to remind Hitler of the existence of an SS file, created by Himmler in 1936. It contained the accusation that Fritsch had been subjected to persistent blackmail by a Berlin rent-boy on account of alleged homosexual activity in 1933. When originally shown the accusations, Hitler had refused to believe them, had forbidden an investigation, and had ordered the file to be burned. Now he asked Himmler to "reconstruct" the file, a simple task for the SS chief as it had in fact been sitting for the past two years in a safe in Heydrich's office. By the morning of January 25 it was back on the Führer's desk, delivered in person by Himmler—not only in pristine condition, but in a remarkably expanded form. Hossbach read it with horror, clearly understanding the appalling implications of a second scandal so soon after the first. Throughout the day, and late into the night, he tried to convince Hitler that the charges against Fritsch were absolutely without foundation and clearly a clumsy manipulation. By the time he left the office to return home that night he had decided on his course of action. Although Hitler had expressly forbidden him to warn Fritsch of the accusations against him, Hossbach drove straight to the Bendlerstrasse, where Fritsch had his private apartment in the War Ministry, and confronted him. Fritsch was horrified and, in uncharacteristically colorful language, vehemently rejected them as a tissue of "stinking lies."[29]

The following morning, January 26, Hossbach returned to work and immediately sought an interview with Hitler. He admitted that he had been to see Fritsch, recounted their conversation, and again tried to reassure his chief that the allegations were completely without foundation. Hitler listened calmly and made a convincing show of appearing relieved. All would be well, and Fritsch could, after all, become Minister of War. Later that morning, unknown to Hossbach, Blomberg arrived at the Chancellery at Hitler's request for a final meeting. The Führer was calm, but firm. The scandal of the field marshal's marriage was too much for the Reich to bear and, with great sadness, he had decided that it was time for them to part company. Blomberg again protested his innocence and, to Hitler's annoyance, played down the serious nature of the accusations against his wife, insisting that she was but "a simple girl of the people." But by now Hitler had heard enough and, as quickly as he could, shifted the conversation on to the issue of the succession. Having told Hossbach just a short time earlier that Fritsch was back in the running, he began by informing Blomberg that the commander-in-chief of the army was a homosexual and therefore not in contention.[30]

Blomberg tried to hide his surprise, and probably his pleasure too, that he was not alone in his misfortune. He even concurred that he thought such a prospect entirely conceivable. Fritsch, he agreed, was not a "woman's man," and the general, a lifelong bachelor, might well "have succumbed to weakness."[31]

"In that case," Blomberg said, "the choice must fall on Göring." Now it was Hitler's turn to look surprised.

"Not possible," he replied. "He has neither the patience nor the application to work."

"In that case," continued Blomberg, "the Ministry of War must revert to the Führer himself."[32]

Such a radical idea clearly held an immediate appeal for Hitler, who promised to consider it, but pointed out that he would need someone to do the intensive staff work that would be required.

"What's the name of that general who's been in your office up to now?" Hitler asked.

"Oh, Keitel," replied Blomberg. "There's no question of him; he's nothing but the man who runs my office."

Hitler seized on this at once. "That's exactly the man I am looking for."[33]

Having been told, untruthfully, by Göring that it was the army hierarchy that had been at the forefront of demands for his dismissal, it is hardly surprising that Blomberg decided to get his own back before his own departure. Having delivered the army into Hitler's hands, he then proceeded to identify a list of generals who were not in his opinion sufficiently supportive of the aspirations and machinery of National Socialism. Beck was later to brand the former War Minister a "scoundrel [*Schuft*]" for this final act of treachery against his erstwhile colleagues.[34] Hitler, however, seemed pleased with the information and, according to Jodl, "by his superhuman kindness, succeeded in comforting the *Feldmarschall*. He told him: As soon as Germany's hour comes, you will be at my side, and everything which happened in the past will be forgotten." Blomberg too later claimed that Hitler promised him "with the greatest emphasis that I would take over the supreme command in wartime."[35] In the meantime, he would continue to draw his full salary, and would be provided with the sum of 50,000 marks to enable him and his new wife to travel abroad for what Blomberg believed was to be a year's holiday.

Blomberg returned to the War Ministry to clear his desk, and told Keitel that he was to report to the Führer in civilian clothes that afternoon. Blomberg recounted the details of his earlier interview, in particular Hitler's promise that he would be recalled to active duty in time of war. However, it was transparently plain to Keitel that his old friend "was clutching very strongly at these words," and that Hitler had no such intention whatsoever. Keitel reproached Blomberg for not having confided in him sooner, indeed before he had taken such a momentous step as marriage, and tried one last time to persuade his chief to initiate divorce proceedings, and thus possibly to hang on to his job. But Blomberg indignantly rejected the idea, even for the sake of their respective children, soon to be married themselves. It had been a "love-match on both sides," and he would "rather put a bullet in his head than do that." With that he rushed from the room, the tears streaming down his face.[36]

The following day Blomberg set off on his belated honeymoon, effectively to spend a year in exile, with Hitler's golden handshake in his pocket. He told his friends that he was embarking on a voyage to the Indian Ocean, but went first to Rome and then on to Capri for a holiday, from where news filtered back that the newlyweds were thoroughly enjoying themselves in the warm Italian sunshine. An enterprising reporter from the *Daily Express* tracked the happy couple down to their island hideaway, from where he filed a feature on Frau Blomberg that could hardly have been further removed from the scandalous reputation she had left behind in Berlin.

> She is a tall woman, large-boned, well rounded. In a flowing white robe and crown she might play Brunnhilde. In modern dress, she is that large comforting type of woman whom you know would make you a good cup of tea, and would always have a newspaper laid out for you on the breakfast table. Her eyes are blue-grey, and she looks at you in a quietly fearless way. Her profile is cleanly chiselled. Her broad forehead slopes to a smallish nose. Her lips are full and mobile. Like most Germans she has a hearty, healthy appetite.[37]

Lord Beaverbrook's scoop-seeking correspondent was not the only unwanted guest to track down the Blombergs in Capri. In a bizarre, tragicomic final twist to the story, they were pursued there by a young naval officer, Baron Hubertus von Wangenheim, who had acted as Blomberg's adjutant at the Wehrmachtsamt. Wangenheim had been despatched by Admiral Raeder in a final effort, as Keitel had made before his departure, to persuade Blomberg to divorce his wife and thus save the honor of the officer corps. However, the arrogant and overzealous young officer far exceeded his instructions. On finding Blomberg in his hotel, he first described in gruesome detail the full litany of Erna's previous indiscretions, and then thrust his revolver into the field marshal's face with the suggestion that he should do the honorable thing. Blomberg, who was by now enjoying married life far too much even to consider such nonsense, waved the young fanatic away and wrote angrily to Keitel, complaining that Wangenheim "apparently held entirely different opinions and a different standard of life." Keitel was furious that Wangenheim had gone to Capri without his permission, and that the clumsy attempt to offer Blomberg the honorable way out had shown "an extraordinary arrogance on the part of this young officer who believes it is his duty to be the guardian of the honour of the officer corps." Göring, meanwhile, was so angry that he threatened to have the young officer shot. A dead field marshal was the very last thing that either he or Hitler needed at that precise moment.[38]

Keitel kept his appointment with Hitler at the Reich Chancellery later that afternoon, having first been summoned to see Göring, who was now busily canvassing for support as Blomberg's successor. He had already persuaded Wiedemann to put his name forward, but Hitler had dismissed the idea out of hand.

"Out of the question. He does not even understand anything about the Luftwaffe."

Keitel received much the same reply when he repeated the suggestion a few hours later.

"Never," exclaimed Hitler, "he is much too easygoing and lazy. I am going to take direct command of the Wehrmacht myself."

When Keitel then recommended Fritsch as next in line for the post, he too was shown the incriminating dossier alleging homosexuality. Hitler made it clear that he was now seeking a successor for both Blomberg and Fritsch, and flattered Keitel, inviting him to become his chief of staff, with the prospect of further self-improvement in due course. Keitel's first task was a distasteful one, a "thankless duty," he complained. Hitler was furious with Hossbach for having disobeyed orders, and going behind his back to warn Fritsch of the accusations against him. Hossbach "had broken his confidence and he never wanted to see him again." Keitel was to dismiss him forthwith and find the Führer a new adjutant.[39]

▪ ▪ ▪

Colonel General Werner Freiherr von Fritsch, the commander-in-chief of the army, was a gifted officer of the old school. A typical General Staff character, he sported a monocle, was stiff and reserved, but determined. His professional ability and his fierce loyalty to the army ensured that he was widely admired and respected. The army in turn demonstrated its allegiance to him, and his authority as commander-in-chief was unquestioned. Unlike Blomberg, he did not rely for his prestige on Hitler's personal favor, and the Führer felt uneasy in his presence. He tended to keep out of politics, except when it impinged on army matters, for instance when he spoke out in opposition to Hitler's plans at the Reich Chancellery on November 5. Bravely, he had never made any attempt to conceal his long-standing hostility to the Nazi Party, nor the contempt he felt for Himmler and the SS in particular. As a result, Himmler had been plotting his overthrow for some time. Similarly, it is unlikely that Hitler had either forgiven or forgotten Fritsch's display of defiance, and once Blomberg had been safely removed, it was to Fritsch, and the earlier allegations against him, that Hitler now turned his attention.

The dossier had its genesis over five years earlier, in November 1933. One cold winter evening that month, an unremarkable member of the city's underworld was loitering in the dimly lit lobby of the Potsdamer Platz railway station, on the Wannsee suburban line in downtown Berlin. Otto Schmidt was an occasional male prostitute, thief, blackmailer and extortionist. When necessary, he was also a police informer. That night, as was often his custom, he was keeping a careful eye on the comings and goings outside the station's public washroom, a venue he knew to be a lucrative source of easy blackmail. His patience was soon rewarded. A group of army and navy officers approached, accompanied by a man of advanced middle age, with a monocle, wearing a dark coat with fur collar, and carrying a cane with a silver handle. After talking for a short time, they split up to go their separate ways, and the man excused himself and went into the washroom.

Not long after he came out with a young man whose face was immediately familiar to Schmidt—Josef Weingärtner, a well-known local rent-boy, who went by the sobriquet of "Bavarian Joe."

Schmidt surreptitiously followed the two men along a dark alleyway beside the perimeter fence of the station, until they reached the cover of some scaffolding against a local building. Keeping his distance, he waited until they emerged from the shadows sometime later and then quickly separated. Assuming the anonymous man had paid Bavarian Joe for homosexual sex, Schmidt approached the rent-boy and asked point-blank what had taken place. Weingärtner, though shocked, confirmed his suspicions, whereupon Schmidt quickly tracked back to the station platform where his intended mark was boarding a train. Having caught up with him in his carriage, to the old man's horror, Schmidt gravely informed him that he was "Criminal Commissar Kröger" of the morals police, and confronted him with the shameful scene he claimed to have just witnessed. He was prepared, however, to turn a blind eye for a suitable sum in return. After some debate as to what might constitute a suitable payoff, the terrified gentleman identified himself as Cavalry Captain Achim von Frisch, and offered 200 marks, all that he had in his wallet at the time. The similarity of his name to that of the commander-in-chief of the army was to prove the latter's undoing.

Schmidt dismissed the amount as insufficient, but agreed to accompany Frisch to his home in Ferdinandstrasse, in the suburb of East Lichterfelde. There, Frisch went into his apartment, leaving Schmidt outside, and emerged soon after with a further sum, still only a down payment toward a newly agreed figure of 500 marks. The following morning Frisch went to his local bank, withdrew more money, and later met Schmidt in the waiting room of the station at East Lichterfelde, where the full 500 marks was finally paid over, accompanied by brandy and cigars. Frisch believed that he had done enough and was now in the clear, but in the time-honored manner of all blackmailers, Schmidt returned just a few days later and confronted Frisch with another man, supposedly his police superior, who demanded his own cut. This time a sum of 2,000 marks was agreed, half to be paid immediately and half in a few weeks' time. When the further rendezvous took place, again in the station waiting room, Schmidt turned up with yet another "detective." The three of them proceeded to drink vast amounts of beer and whisky (so much so that the bar owner still remembered them four years later), and finally Frisch handed over the final payment of 1,000 marks.

Sadly for Frisch, but inevitably, even this supposedly final disbursement failed to satisfy the bloodsucking Schmidt, who turned up from time to time to demand further payments, always accompanied by a heavy drinking session. The old cavalry officer's health declined rapidly, apparently worn out by the stress of being so persistently blackmailed, and he was forced to employ a nurse, which he could scarcely afford anyway. Having bled him dry, one day Schmidt passed his house with a friend and boasted that there lived a man he once "laid on the cross," his most successful sting ever.[40] But Otto Schmidt was soon to fall victim himself to the changing political climate in Germany.

In the aftermath of the Röhm affair of June 1934, and in an effort to divert attention from the savagery of his actions, Hitler chose in part to justify his liquidating the leadership of the SA by emphasizing the homosexual depravity of Ernst Röhm and his followers. Although Hitler had never appeared to have taken much interest in this issue previously (and was shortly to promote a notorious homosexual, Walther Funk, to be Minister of Economics), this was enough to give the green light to a relatively underemployed Gestapo that the full power of the Nazi state's repressive machinery should be used to purge those committing this most heinous of crimes. It was an ideal opportunity for the Gestapo greatly to expand its sphere of influence. A "Reich Centre for Combating Homosexuality" was established as Gestapo Department II-H, and a homosexual witch-hunt was instituted, resulting in hundreds of men being rounded up, brought before special courts on an assembly-line basis, and hauled off to concentration camps.

It was not long before the Gestapo hit upon an ingenious idea for quickening the pace of the process of investigation and conviction. Instead of searching for homosexuals themselves, it proved infinitely easier to trawl through the prisons of Germany and find the low-life degenerates who had made a living out of spying on, and then blackmailing, homosexuals in the past. Clearly they would be only too happy to spill the beans in return for a reduction in their own sentence. Otto Schmidt had been in and out of custody since his teenage years, and by 1936 he was back in prison, serving a seven-year sentence. When first approached for interview by the local police, he cheerfully recounted in full the details of quite literally hundreds of homosexuals whom he had blackmailed in the past. Among them, he claimed, was a senior army officer by the name of Frisch. When the file reached Department II-H at Gestapo headquarters, the name that called to mind the commander-in-chief of the army inevitably attracted the immediate attention of the department's chief, Joseph Meisinger, "a corrupt, repulsive, sordid figure, addicted to the cruder methods of conducting investigations and detested by more fastidious associates."[41]

Schmidt was delivered into the custody of the Gestapo, and at his first interrogation was shown a photograph of Fritsch in full regimental uniform, above a caption giving his name and military rank. Schmidt, who was by now enjoying his moment in the limelight and was only too happy to please his interrogators, duly identified him as the man he had seen at the Potsdamer Platz station, and whom he had subsequently blackmailed. Meisinger could not believe his good luck. The news that the SS now had a weapon with which to attack Fritsch soon found its way to Heydrich, then to Himmler, and finally to Hitler himself. It was at that stage, in 1936, that Hitler was supposed to have expressed his revulsion at the very idea of Fritsch being homosexual, and ordered the file to be burned, an order which Himmler had notably disobeyed. Thus it was that two years later the dossier reappeared, in pristine condition, on the Führer's desk in the early hours of the morning of January 25, 1938.

Fritsch had already been on his guard, even before Hossbach defied Hitler's orders by visiting him to warn him of the accusations contained in the dossier. Just two days previously he had been visited by an old friend, who had received an anonymous telephone call warning him that: "You are a friend of General von Fritsch. He is in the greatest danger."[42] Further disturbed by his conversation with Hossbach, Fritsch had subsequently spent a sleepless night mulling over the issues in his mind, and trying to explain the source of the allegations against him. He recalled the few occasions during the winter of 1933–34 when he had lunched alone with fatherless boys of the Hitler Youth, in a charitable, and wholly innocent, effort to support the Reich Winter Aid Campaign. He could only conclude that the predicament with which he was now faced must have originated from some accompanying malicious, but inaccurate, gossip. The following morning he called Hossbach and invited him to a meeting in the riding ring of the War Ministry, but his story of the Hitler Youth boys served only to unnerve his most ardent supporter.

Hossbach returned to the Chancellery and again confronted Hitler, demanding to know why the charges, which he had refused to believe in 1936, had now suddenly acquired such prominence. If the material was so damning, why had Hitler continued to work with Fritsch for those two years? Hitler mumbled that Fritsch had been indispensable during the period of military rearmament, and implied that he might once again be back in the running for the post of War Minister. Hossbach replied that Fritsch wished only to remain in his existing post. However, Hitler later told both Blomberg and Keitel that even that was out of the question, due to the charges of homosexuality that had been brought against him. And any generous feelings he may indeed have harbored toward Fritsch were all but obliterated by the constant comings and goings of Göring, Himmler and Heydrich throughout the day. By late afternoon Hitler was again warning Hossbach that the charges against Fritsch were all but proven. "Homosexuals," he gravely informed his adjutant, "the highest and lowest alike, are all liars."[43] Fritsch was to be suspended from duty with immediate effect. Hossbach then proposed that Fritsch should face a tribunal of honor, composed of army generals, but Hitler brushed that suggestion aside also.

He did, however, agree to consult the Minister of Justice, Franz Gürtner, who was summoned to the Chancellery. Gürtner was a representative of the ministerial old guard, from the days of pre–Third Reich government. He had kept his head down and, largely by telling Hitler what he wanted to hear in a cool and calm manner, had managed to survive in his job. He was known to be weak-willed, and when Hitler called him to the Chancellery that afternoon he almost certainly knew that Gürtner would be happy to do his bidding. Hitler thrust the Fritsch dossier into his hand and demanded that Gürtner provide a written opinion there and then. He emphasized, as he was to do over the following days, that Schmidt's evidence had always proved reliable in cases in which he had testified (this was, in fact, the exact opposite of the truth, since Schmidt's police file made it clear that he was a professional liar who had never been taken seriously in the past). Gürtner hurriedly scribbled out an opinion, declaring that the documents showed Fritsch to have been accused under Article 175 of the penal code, that he had not as yet cleared himself of the charge, and that "in the form in which the documents lie before me they can provide the basis for a charge by the public prosecutor."[44]

Hitler finally agreed to Hossbach's insistent suggestion that Fritsch should be given the opportunity of being confronted with the evidence against him in person. "It is not for von Fritsch to exonerate himself," he added, "as he will only tell lies. Our purpose is to confront him with a witness named Schmidt who is detained by the Gestapo." In fact Schmidt had been released from prison after giving his original testimony in 1936, but had conveniently been recently taken back into custody by the Gestapo. Now, on Himmler's instructions, a senior Gestapo officer, Franz Josef Huber, was despatched to fetch him from the internment camp where he was being held.[45] That evening Hossbach summoned Fritsch to the Chancellery by telephone and went down to meet him in the entrance hall, primarily to warn him about the intended confrontation with Schmidt, before leading him upstairs to Hitler's library. In the words of one historian, it was to be an experience for Fritsch for which "his long training as an aristocrat, an officer and a gentleman had scarcely prepared him."[46]

The interview began with Hitler, Göring and Fritsch in the room. Hitler came straight to the point, demanding to know if the allegations were true, and offering to have the whole affair hushed up, and Fritsch sent far away from Germany. Fritsch listened carefully to the charges, and then vehemently protested his innocence. Schmidt had meanwhile arrived at the Chancellery with Huber and an accompanying guard of Gestapo officers. One of Hitler's personal adjutants was so appalled at the disgusting state Schmidt was in, that he insisted that he be shaved and generally cleaned up before being taken into the Führer's presence. Huber and Schmidt then took up their positions at the foot of the Chancellery staircase, and at an agreed signal Hitler and Göring led Fritsch out onto the landing above. Huber and Schmidt slowly climbed to the top of the stairs, whereupon Hitler gazed at the seedy-looking ruffian before him and asked if he recognised Fritsch. Schmidt paused, pointed dramatically at Fritsch and, far from being overawed by the occasion or the company he was in, replied confidently, "That's the man."[47] Fritsch, his high-minded sensibility outraged by the very presence of such a creature in the inner sanctums of German government, appeared too dumbfounded to speak.

Back in the library Fritsch repeatedly and calmly protested his innocence. He had never laid eyes on Schmidt before, and again gave the
Führer his word of honor, as an officer and a gentleman, that he had nothing to do with the whole sordid affair. Only then did he make a mistake.
When Hitler asked if he could think of any reason why he might have
aroused any suspicion of homosexuality, Fritsch foolishly referred to the
incident with the Hitler Youth boys. Hossbach, who had been deliberately
excluded from the interview, had failed to warn him to keep off the subject
in spite of his own reservations, and the admission had precisely the opposite effect on Hitler to that which Fritsch had hoped for. His composed
demeanor also counted against him. He had steeled himself to stay calm
and in control, but his lack of histrionics made Hitler more suspicious still.
"Just imagine, Wiedemann," Hitler confided to his adjutant later that
evening. "Now it is suddenly not two but four fellows with whom he has had
to do. Now this matter can no longer be kept secret. All I wanted was to
hear from his own mouth the proof."[48]

Hitler decided that Fritsch's guilt was established beyond doubt. "Here is
word against word," recorded Goebbels in his diary. "That of a homosexual
blackmailer against that of the head of the army. And the Führer does not
trust Fritsch any longer."[49] Hitler again suggested that his senior general
should disappear quietly on the grounds of ill-health, but Fritsch understood only too well that such a course of action would represent a public
admission of guilt. He refused, and demanded instead that he be tried by
a court of honor of his fellow officers. Hitler bluntly informed him that he
was now on indefinite leave and showed him the door. Still shell-shocked by
what had happened, the humiliated and exhausted Fritsch was shown to his
car by Hossbach, still indignantly protesting his innocence. When Hossbach
returned, Göring rushed out of the Chancellery library, threw himself on a
sofa with his hands covering his face and, howling melodramatically, proclaimed Fritsch's guilt: "It was he, it was he, it was he!" he repeated, over and
over again.[50]

Although it was now midnight, Hossbach asked Hitler's permission to
call General Beck, now the senior army officer on duty, at home. A car was
sent to collect the chief of staff, who hurriedly made his way to the
Chancellery in civilian clothes and went straight into conference with Hitler
and Göring. He found them both in a state of extreme excitement, Göring

pacing the room like a wild animal, and Hitler rocking about nervously on his sofa, dripping with perspiration. Hitler's opening gambit shocked Beck: when and where had he last lent money to Fritsch? It seemed that the Gestapo had been unable to locate a bank account in Fritsch's name anywhere in the East Lichterfelde area—hardly surprising as it had not, of course, been Fritsch who had paid off Schmidt. As Beck lived in that part of Berlin, it had been assumed that he had made funds available to Fritsch instead. Beck angrily denied ever having lent money to the head of the army, and was then horrified to be told the precise nature of the charges against both Blomberg and Fritsch. Although he already had an inkling of the former, the latter came as a complete bombshell to him, and he immediately supported Fritsch's own request that the matter should be dealt with by a military court.

Much to the annoyance of both Hitler and Göring, whose purposes were well suited by bundling the two scandals together, Beck chose to make a clear distinction between them. In Blomberg's case, he took a surprisingly hard line, insisting that the depravity of his lapse was so serious that he had automatically excluded himself from the army. As he was later to lecture Keitel: "One cannot permit the highest-ranking officer soldier to marry a whore; he should be forced to divorce the woman or else be taken off the list of officers; he could no longer be the commander of even a regiment."[51] In the case of Fritsch, however, there were still numerous questions to be answered and the dignity of the army demanded a thorough investigation by the army itself. Although it was by now the middle of the night, Beck drove to see Fritsch in his apartment in the Bendlerstrasse, finding him in a despairing state. After a lengthy conversation he returned to the Chancellery convinced of Fritsch's innocence. When he reported that Fritsch was standing steadfastly by his story, and now enjoyed his, Beck's, support, Hitler reluctantly agreed that Göring, Beck and Fritsch should meet the following morning to hammer out the details of a judicial review of the case.

Beck woke up on the morning of January 27, reluctantly convinced that Fritsch lacked the necessary stomach for a fight to deal with the allegations against him. Taking matters into his own hands, he drove out to see Göring at Karinhall, only to find that the meeting with Fritsch had been canceled, and that Göring was loudly proclaiming Fritsch's guilt to anyone who would listen. At that very moment, the browbeaten Fritsch was submitting to the ultimate humiliation, interrogation by the Gestapo at their infamous head-quarters in Prinz Albrechtstrasse, just around the corner from his own apartment and military headquarters. Given that the Gestapo had no juris-diction over the military, and thus no way of forcing Fritsch to appear before them, it seems incredible that he agreed to enter the lion's den at all, but he clearly believed that it was the only way in which he could con-vince Hitler of his innocence.

Even the Gestapo themselves were unsure whether he would appear. When he arrived in civilian clothes at 10 A.M., he was greeted at the entrance by a nervous Franz Huber, the officer who had brought Schmidt to the Chancellery the day before, and who now conducted Fritsch to the interview room on the third floor. As they made their way down the long corridors of the old building, Fritsch was vaguely aware of a number of shadowy figures loitering in doorways and window alcoves. The Gestapo had picked up some of Berlin's better-known young homosexuals, includ-ing Bavarian Joe, who were being given the opportunity to catch a glimpse of Fritsch so that they could later positively identify him as a client. Fritsch's performance during the interview was again spiritless and lackluster, even when confronted with Schmidt for a second time. His interrogators pro-voked him repeatedly. "But Colonel General, a man with such a squeaky voice must be a homosexual."[52]

The legal process now slowed to a snail's pace. Hitler was reluctantly forced to concede that Fritsch should face a military court over the allega-tions, and the defendant retained the services of Count Rüdiger von der Göltz as his counsel. Keitel summoned the head of legal affairs at the Wehrmacht, Dr. Heinrich Rosenberger, and instructed him to draw up a memorandum on the affair for submission to Gürtner, the Minister of Justice. Rosenberger was another officer of the old school, and was imme-diately skeptical. On receiving his report, Gürtner strongly advised Hitler "not to take proceedings against General von Fritsch on the basis of this sort of documentation." Indeed, Gürtner realized that he had not been shown all the relevant documents, and made it clear that his advice would have been stronger still had he known the full truth. "The evidence is very flimsy," he warned the Führer, "and the case should be seriously reviewed before any further step is taken."[53] Hitler ignored this advice, but agreed to a pre-hearing investigation by two military judges. Ominously, a parallel investigation was to be carried out by the Gestapo.

The case against Fritsch soon unraveled, as Schmidt's story came under increasing scrutiny. Even within the Gestapo there were doubters. After Fritsch's interrogation at Prinz Albrechtstrasse, Huber had become so suspicious that he and two fellow officers had Schmidt picked up, and taken to the house in Ferdinandstrasse, where they subjected him to intense questioning. Schmidt then showed them the nearby bank, from which he claimed Fritsch had withdrawn the money, but Huber remained unconvinced. That evening, after his colleagues had left for home, he decided to have a quiet look around some of the other offices at Gestapo headquarters, in particular those of Meisinger's Department II-H. There, lying openly on a desk, was a file of bank statements in the name of Captain von Frisch, dating back to 1933. The comprehensive list of withdrawals tallied precisely with the payments listed in the dossier on Fritsch. Huber felt "as if he had been stung by a tarantula."[54]

The military judges too quickly realized that this was a case of mistaken identity, albeit a deliberate one. In spite of the Gestapo's best efforts, Bavarian Joe was located, and denied absolutely that his client at the Potsdamer Platz railway station in 1933 had been Fritsch. This should have been the end of it, but Hitler intervened personally to insist that their investigation continued. Schmidt's story too was riddled with inaccuracies. He told them Fritsch was a smoker, which he was not in 1933; he claimed he had been wearing a fur-lined coat, such as Fritsch did not possess; he was mistaken as to his rank at the time; and Fritsch had never lived anywhere near Ferdinandstrasse in Lichterfelde. When the judges finally got around to visiting Lichterfelde for themselves, they found both the house where Frisch lived, and the bank where he kept his account. Although his nurse told them that he was too ill to be moved, he did agree to be interviewed in bed. The ailing captain, a sick and broken man, confirmed under oath that it had indeed been he who had for so long been the object of Schmidt's blackmail.

As the nurse showed the two judges to the door, they were startled to be told by her that the Gestapo too had recently visited Frisch—clear evidence that they knew it to be a case of mistaken identity, but had continued the investigation anyway. The same officers had also visited the bank in

Lichterfelde. But the Gestapo was not yet ready to throw in the towel. That evening the elderly and frail Frisch was taken into "protective" custody, and subjected to a terrible beating in the cells at Prinz Albrechtstrasse. Bravely, however, he refused to change his story. Schmidt, meanwhile, was hurriedly forced to change his. Terrified by Gestapo threats, he now made the wholly implausible claim that there had been two completely distinct events, and that he had been blackmailing both a Fritsch and a Frisch. The Gestapo stuck steadfastly to this newly agreed version of events, and when the investigating judges visited Hitler to suggest that the case should be dropped, they were again ordered to continue their inquiries. "As long as the witness has not withdrawn his charge," said Hitler, a beaming Himmler at his side, "the case for me remains unsettled."[55]

■ ■ ■

Throughout the last week of January, a state of extreme tension gripped Berlin. Rumors circulated unchecked. At first it was reported that Blomberg and Fritsch had been sacked. The French ambassador heard that Fritsch had been forced to cancel a dinner engagement because he had been arrested. The generals, it was said, were in open revolt and planning a military coup, a rumor which gathered momentum when it was announced that Hitler had canceled his planned fifth-anniversary speech at the Reichstag on January 30. This, it was alleged, was because of the discovery of an army plot to surround the Reichstag and arrest the entire Nazi government. Within the Chancellery, the mood was no less feverish, as Hitler realized that he was facing an international public relations disaster, a potentially devastating blow to his prestige both at home and abroad. "The wildest rumours are circulating," moaned Goebbels. "The Führer is at the end of his tether. None of us has slept since Monday."[56]

It was obvious to Hitler that a bold stroke was required to halt the wagging tongues, and restore his reputation. He was still faced with the problem of finding a successor for both Blomberg and Fritsch. Although he knew perfectly well how fervently Göring coveted Blomberg's job, as he had already made clear to Blomberg himself, to Keitel, and to Wiedemann, he had no intention of satisfying this particular yearning. He was scathing on the subject of Göring's military competence, and had no intention of concentrating so much power in the hands of his second-in-command. Hitler now recalled his farewell interview with Blomberg. "The Ministry of War must revert to the Führer himself," had been his parting words. Goebbels too had come up with a similar idea. "In order to put a smoke-screen round the whole business," he confided to his diary, "a big reshuffle will take place."[57] Keitel too recognized that Hitler "was making use of the current bad odour left especially abroad by the departure of Blomberg and Fritsch to carry out a major Cabinet reshuffle."[58]

Within a few days, the reshuffle was complete. In all fourteen generals were removed, and fifty-one other posts were reallocated, many within the Luftwaffe. The naval command was left intact, a reward for Raeder's abject submissiveness during the crisis. Fritsch was replaced by infantry General Walther von Brauchitsch, who had been strongly endorsed by Keitel, and supported by Blomberg, in an effort to keep out the unpopular General Walther von Reichenau. Far from being a staunch Nazi, Brauchitsch was regarded within army circles as a distinguished example of the Prussian aristocratic tradition and as "an efficient and ruthless commander" by the British embassy.[59] By coincidence, he was himself going through a particularly messy divorce of his own, and had recently even been considering retirement. After several days of negotiation, during which Brauchitsch was holed up in a Berlin hotel waiting for news, Hitler offered personally to provide the 80,000 marks he needed to pay a final, one-off settlement to his wife. This, coupled with the previously adulterous nature of his second marriage, ensured that the servile and dependent Brauchitsch would remain forever in Hitler's debt.

As compensation for missing out on Blomberg's job, Göring was promoted to field marshal, while among the casualties was the long-suffering Foreign Minister, Neurath. Having in vain requested an audience with the Führer following the Chancellery meeting on November 5, he eventually wrote to Hitler in early December indicating his desire to resign. Hitler ignored the letter. On January 14 Neurath was present when Hitler met the Polish Foreign Minister and ambassador, Józef Beck and Józef Lipski, and was upset to discover that the mood and language of the Hossbach meeting continued to prevail. Hitler again revealed his preoccupation with Austria and Czechoslovakia, declaring "with absolute firmness that he would not hesitate to march immediately . . . as quickly as lightning."[60] Immediately after the meeting Neurath again plucked up the courage to confront the Führer. His policy, he protested, "would lead to a world war," and he "would have no part in it." But Hitler stuck to his guns, and eventually Neurath, according to his testimony at Nuremberg, told him that if he was determined to pursue his expansionist plans, then "he would have to find another Foreign Minister, and that I would not be an accessory to such a policy."[61]

In fact, Hitler had already decided to sack him. "The Foreign Office are not cooperating," recorded Hans Lammers, the chief of the Reich Chancellery. Hitler "had for some time now decided to replace Neurath with Ribbentrop."[62] Joachim von Ribbentrop was at the time still ambassador in London, and Göring argued strongly against his appointment as Foreign Minister. But Hitler was determined "above all to change the Foreign Office because only such a change would make a strong impression abroad and would be likely to divert attention from the military affairs."[63] Even then, Neurath's sacking was executed in a typically cowardly manner. On February 2 Hitler attended a party to celebrate Neurath's sixty-fifth birthday and fortieth anniversary in the foreign service. When Neurath quietly reminded him of his resignation request, Hitler countered that he could "never let you leave my side. You must make this sacrifice for me." To Neurath's daughter he boasted: "You know, this man is like a father to me. I can't let him go."

Two days later, having just returned to his office from a perfectly amicable meeting with Hitler, Neurath was summoned back to the Chancellery. Leading him out of his crowded office into the Wintergarten, Hitler's opening words were blunt. "Look, I have appointed Ribbentrop as my new foreign minister."[64] At Göring's suggestion, Neurath was compensated with a new post, as chairman of the Secret Cabinet Council. When Hitler naively pointed out that no such council existed, Göring replied that "the expression would sound quite nice, and everyone would imagine that it meant something." A few names were jotted down on a piece of paper, but most were never even told of the council's existence, and for Neurath it was a wholly meaningless appointment. According to Göring the council never met once, "not even for a minute."[65] The diplomatic reshuffle was completed by new appointments to the key ambassadorial posts in London, Rome, Tokyo and Vienna. The ambassador to Rome, Ulrich von Hassell, regarded as an advocate of restraint, was visiting Berlin at the time, and read of his sacking in the morning newspaper over breakfast at his hotel.

On February 4 the Cabinet met for what was to prove to be the last occasion during the lifetime of the Third Reich. Blomberg and Fritsch, announced Hitler, had resigned on health grounds. "From now on I take over personally the command of the whole armed forces," he told them.[66] The War Ministry was abolished. In its place Hitler created the Supreme Command of the Armed Forces, the Oberkommando der Wehrmacht, or OKW. Hitler appointed himself Supreme Commander, with the pliant Keitel as his chief of staff. Shortly before midnight on February 4, a communiqué announcing the changes was broadcast on radio, leading to blanket coverage and frenzied rumor in the following day's newspapers. "STRONGEST CONCENTRATION OF ALL POWERS IN THE FÜHRER'S HANDS," screamed the Nazi Party's newspaper, the *Völkischer Beobachter.*[67] In London, the *Daily Express* reported that Blomberg was the victim of a "Potsdam clique of senior officers of the army, who typify today the stiff-backed Prussianism of the Kaiser régime." On February 5 the same paper blazed the headline "KAISER HITLER . . . Makes himself Supreme War Lord."[68]

Later that afternoon Hitler addressed his shell-shocked generals. They stood around him in a semicircle, in a large hall in the Chancellery, as he described what had happened to Blomberg and Fritsch. Quite deliberately, he read aloud the most gruesome details that he had been able to glean from police reports, and Gürtner's dossier on Fritsch. The generals were "flabbergasted," and "cut to the quick" by the allegations against colleagues they had believed to be "men of spotless honour."[69] For the proud officer corps, this was an unbearable indignity for their honor to suffer, but they were forced to bear it without complaint. The army had suffered a devastating blow. There were no objections; no one said a word. They had been "outwitted, demoralised and bribed."[70] Hitler knew perfectly well that he had never been entirely accepted by those two upper-class bastions, the army and the Foreign Ministry, and as a result had always distrusted them. Now, at precisely the moment his expansionist policies were beginning to cause alarm, "the army had demonstrated its weakness and without a murmur of protest swallowed his outright dominance even in the immediate domain of the Wehrmacht."[71]

▪ ▪ ▪

The military court of honor set up to try General Werner von Fritsch on charges of homosexuality under Article 175 of the penal code finally convened on March 10 in the Preussenhaus, once the home of the Royal Prussian House of Peers. It was chaired by Göring, flanked by Raeder for the navy and Brauchitsch for the army. The public and the press were, naturally, excluded. Fritsch, in full regimental uniform, was unimpressed by Göring's latest toy, a blue field marshal's baton, and in a direct challenge refused to stand when the hearing opened. Schmidt spent the first morning repeating his accusations until, shortly before noon, an adjutant of the Wehrmacht rushed into the courtroom and conferred with Göring. The field marshal immediately suspended proceedings, citing "reasons touching on the interests of the Reich."[72] In fact, Hitler had just given the order to invade Austria, the Anschluss was underway, and the commanders-in-chief were needed at their posts. Whether by intent or good fortune, the invasion of Austria gave Hitler the pretext he needed to divert attention from Fritsch's imminent acquittal, and to prevent any resulting uprising within the army.

The trial resumed on March 17 and concluded the following day. Schmidt did his best to stick to his story, but eventually broke down under sustained questioning from Göring, who, realizing that there was no way back for Fritsch, understood that an acquittal would be irrelevant anyway. Perversely, he began to play the role of the fair-minded judge. Under further pressure, Schmidt admitted he had been intimidated, but refused at first to say by whom. When pressed by Fritsch's defense counsel, he replied that Commissioner Meisinger of the Gestapo had told him only that morning that "if I retract my evidence, I will go to heaven."[73] Fritsch was duly acquitted and the trial brought to a close, but incredibly without any reference to the role of Himmler or the Gestapo in the whole affair. There was to be no public rehabilitation of Fritsch, nor was he reinstated to a senior post in the army. He accepted his fate with the same calmness and silence with which he had met the allegations throughout. On the outbreak of war he returned to his former regiment, and was killed—very possibly deliberately seeking his own death—during the invasion of Poland in September 1939. No proceedings were ever taken against the Gestapo, but neither did they forgive Otto Schmidt for failing them. In April 1938, he disappeared without trace.

∎

3

The Last Frail Chance

The trouble with Anthony Eden is that he was trained to win the Derby in 1938; unfortunately he was not let out of the starting stalls until 1955.
                                                                Harold Macmillan, April 23, 1975

I fear the difference between Anthony and me is more fundamental than he realises. At bottom he is really dead against making terms with the dictators.
                                                        Neville Chamberlain, October 15, 1938

I fear that fundamentally the difficulty is that Neville believes that he is a man with a mission to come to terms with the dictators.
                                                                Anthony Eden, January 17, 1938

It is always best and safest to count on nothing *from the Americans except* words.
                                                        Neville Chamberlain, December 17, 1937

Immediately after Christmas 1937 the Edens took a holiday at the Parc Palace Hotel in Grasse, on the French Riviera. The Foreign Secretary hoped to have some time to himself to indulge his two favorite pastimes, swimming and tennis, but the world of politics was never far away, and on January 5 he lunched with Churchill and Lloyd George, who were also on holiday nearby. Both, he recorded, were "strongly opposed to any recognition of the Italian conquest of Abyssinia."[1] The Prime Minister, meanwhile, had enjoyed a more homely Christmas and New Year, entertaining his family at Chequers, and reveling in his shooting prowess. The only major diversion with which he had to contend was a spectacularly self-indulgent letter from the former King, the Duke of Windsor, now wintering, like Eden, in the south of France. Over seven handwritten pages the Duke spelled out a long litany of grievances which he insisted could only be tackled by Chamberlain himself. "I cannot refrain from saying," he concluded, "with the frankness you would expect of me, that the treatment which has been meted out to my wife and myself since last December, both by the Royal Family and by the Government, has caused us acute pain."[2]

Once he had sent a suitably tactful reply, Chamberlain returned to the more pressing matter of European affairs. He remained wholly unconvinced by Eden's opposition to de jure recognition of the Italian conquest of Abyssinia, and indeed to entering into discussions with Mussolini at all. A protracted, and at times acrimonious, correspondence ensued between Whitehall and Grasse. On January 9 Eden warned that "Mussolini is, I fear, the complete gangster and his pledged word means nothing. It would be most unfortunate to take any action at this moment which gave Mussolini the appearance of a diplomatic triumph." Chamberlain disagreed entirely. "The one way in which we can maintain our moral position," he countered, "is to make recognition part of a general scheme for appeasement in the Mediterranean & the Red Sea."[3]

In fact, Eden's holiday was to be brought to a premature end, not by further developments in Europe, but by an initiative originating on the opposite side of the Atlantic. On the evening of January 11, the American Under-Secretary of State, Sumner Welles, called on the British ambassador in Washington, Sir Ronald Lindsay. He brought with him a secret message from President Franklin Roosevelt, to be transmitted to the Prime Minister in person. The President had become increasingly concerned at the progressive deterioration of the international situation. While recognizing British efforts to reach agreement with Germany and Italy, he wished to undertake an equivalent initiative of his own in support of British diplomacy. Lindsay appreciated immediately the importance of the President's proposals, observing to Welles that they represented "the first hope I have had in more than a year that a new world war can be prevented."[4]

Throughout the night of January 11 Lindsay transmitted a series of telegrams to the Foreign Office, all of which, "at personal request of President," he insisted should "be treated with more than ordinary secrecy. They are to be regarded as message direct from him to Prime Minister and any divulgation [sic] of their purport or even existence would defeat President's object."[5] The ambassador went on to describe the essence of the President's plan. Subject to the British approval he was now seeking, he proposed to call together the entire Washington diplomatic corps on January 22, and to make his announcement in person. He would speak of the decline in diplomatic standards between countries, the disconcerting pace of international rearmament, and the appalling effect that scientific advances had produced on contemporary weaponry. In particular, he feared the terrible consequences that modern warfare might have on civilian populations.

Roosevelt hoped to secure unanimous agreement between all nations on a new set of "essential and fundamental principles which should be observed in international relations." These would include the "most effective methods for achieving limitation and reduction of armaments"; equality of access for all to "raw materials and other elements necessary for their economic life"; and, "in the unhappy event of war, rights and obligations of Governments . . . and laws and customs of warfare whose observance neutrals may be entitled to require." In a coded reference to the Treaty of Versailles, he spoke also of the need to implement "international adjustments of various kinds . . . in order to remove such inequities as may exist by reason of nature of certain settlements reached at termination of the Great War." The United States, meanwhile, would continue to maintain its well-known "traditional policy of freedom from political involvement," in other words its military neutrality.[6] In conclusion, Lindsay emphasized that for the time being the President was communicating his thoughts to the British government alone. "He will only proceed with his scheme if *not later than January 17th* he receives an assurance from you that it will meet with cordial approval and whole-hearted support of H.M. Government."[7]

By now there was a new Permanent Under-Secretary at the Foreign Office. After serving as British ambassador in China, Sir Alexander Cadogan had been recalled to London by Eden in 1936. On January 1, 1938, a lengthy and somewhat tortuous announcement from the Foreign Office stated that the long-serving Permanent Under-Secretary, Sir Robert Vansittart, was to be "promoted" to become the government's Chief Diplomatic Adviser, and was to be replaced by Cadogan. The announcement gave rise to widespread comment. Vansittart's position was a new one and, although high-sounding, it was in fact little more than a sinecure. Chamberlain's delight was obvious.

> After all the months that S.B. wasted in futile attempts to push Van out of the F.O. it is amusing to record that I have done it in 3 days. . . . Van has accepted my proposal. Indeed I did not give him any alternative! When Anthony can work out his ideas with a sane slow man like Alick Cadogan he will be much steadier. Van had the effect of multiplying the extent of Anthony's natural vibrations and I am afraid his instincts were all against my policy.[8]

Cadogan was considered a safe pair of hands, "not only intelligent, efficient, imperturbable, loyal, economical in language, and thoroughly conventional, he was also 'sound' in judgement, and reserved but not without charm."[9]

By mid-afternoon on January 12 Lindsay's telegrams had been deciphered, and dispatched to Chequers for the Prime Minister's attention, accompanied by an explanatory minute from Cadogan. "The President certainly has courage," he acknowledged, "and we must not discourage him, although the prospects of the success of his scheme are problematical and the risks, maybe, great."[10] Privately, however, Cadogan thought that "this is not the way to do business."[11] The following morning a further telegram arrived from Washington. Lindsay, himself a former Permanent Under-Secretary and ambassador in Berlin, was a well-respected and widely admired diplomat. Known to be "little given to effusion or to any display of emotion,"[12] he now urged the government to support Roosevelt's "genuine effort to relax the tension of the world."

> Destructive criticisms, reservations or attempts to define the issues more clearly can only accomplish very little in favour of anything you may wish to put forward while they will create a disproportionate bad impression in thoughts of Administration. I therefore urge respectfully but very earnestly that His Majesty's Government reply to this valuable initiative with a very quick and very cordial acceptance.[13]

But the Prime Minister proposed to do no such thing. "The plan," he confided to his diary, "appeared to me fantastic and likely to excite the derision of Germany and Italy."[14] To his sister he complained that the President's approach had come as a "bombshell," and had caused him "the most strenuous and anxious endeavours."[15] He was concerned that both countries would use it as an excuse to postpone discussions, and interpret it as an attempt to divide the dictators. At the Foreign Office, Cadogan recognized that Chamberlain "hated" the President's idea, but was understandably reluctant to "snub him."[16] Cadogan therefore prepared a conciliatory draft reply to Lindsay, which he proposed should first be sent to Eden in the south of France for approval. However, Chamberlain vetoed even this suggestion (on the supposed grounds that the telephone line to Grasse would not be secure). He ignored both Lindsay's telegram of support and Cadogan's draft reply, and instead agreed a telegram to Washington which, by his own admission, "in very guarded terms indicated a possibly hostile reception."[17] In effect, wrote one of Eden's biographers, it was a rejection "written in terms of complacency and superiority . . . there are few more calamitous documents in modern international politics."[18]

Cadogan did manage to persuade a reluctant Chamberlain to recall Eden from holiday. Still blissfully ignorant of the impending transatlantic diplomatic crisis, on the morning of January 14 the Foreign Secretary was finally called to the telephone to speak to Cadogan, who, while he could give no details down the line, insisted that Eden return home immediately. It was arranged that he should leave Cannes by train that night, and then fly home from Paris. A diplomatic bag, containing all the relevant papers, was dispatched from London to meet the train at Marseilles at 10 P.M. In the event, all Cadogan's plans went awry. The bag missed the train at Marseilles, and all flights from Paris were canceled due to high winds. Eden took the train on to the Channel, made a turbulent sea crossing, and finally arrived at Folkestone late the following afternoon. Even then, the sea was so rough that the boat collided with the harbor pier, causing considerable damage. He was met there by Cadogan and Harvey, with "troubled faces and a large file of papers,"[19] but they were at last able to brief him on the events of the previous few days in the train on the way back to London.

Eden was "outraged, and uneasy at the way in which this opportunity had been handled."[20] He knew that he could perfectly well have been reached in

Grasse through the British embassy in Paris, and while not necessarily convinced by every detail of the President's proposal, he was concerned at the wider implications of snubbing the Americans at such a crucial moment. That evening he dined with Cadogan, and soon after dinner a message arrived from Lindsay indicating that Roosevelt was willing to postpone his initiative for a short time, but expressing disappointment at Chamberlain's reply, which Welles described as "in the nature of a douche of cold water."[21] Eden wasted no further time. Without consulting Chamberlain, he composed a telegram there and then to Lindsay, contradicting the Prime Minister's earlier message. He expressed concern that "the President may be registering disappointment at finding what he considers to be a negative attitude on our part. That, I am convinced, was not the impression which it was intended to convey." Matters had been exacerbated by his own absence abroad, which had precluded consultation with Chamberlain on such "far-reaching proposals." He would speak to the Prime Minister in the morning in an effort to break the impasse.[22] The telegram was dispatched from the Foreign Office at 2:30 A.M. and, for good measure, Eden telephoned Lindsay to emphasize its contents.

On the morning of Sunday, January 16, Eden motored down to Chequers. Although outwardly friendly and apparently in good spirits, Chamberlain was clearly riled by his Foreign Secretary's actions of the previous night. In the course of a frosty lunch, and a long country walk that afternoon, the two men remained as far apart as ever in their views. Eden strongly supported Anglo-American cooperation and acceptance of Roosevelt's initiative, but Chamberlain stubbornly continued to insist that it would "confuse our own efforts." They then argued over Mussolini and the de jure, or formal, diplomatic recognition of his conquest of Abyssinia. "The less strong Mussolini was," insisted Eden, "the less he appealed to Hitler." Recognition of his newly conquered empire would, he believed, only serve to "increase his authority, and, therefore, make him more attractive to Hitler."[23] But Chamberlain remained unimpressed, and was anyway, unknown to Eden, already planning a further secret diplomatic initiative of his own with his sister-in-law, Lady Ivy Chamberlain, who was at the time in Rome, and the Italian ambassador in London, Count Dino Grandi.

Roosevelt's written reply arrived in London on the morning of January 18. Reluctantly, he agreed to postpone making public his proposal, but Lindsay warned privately that the President's "disappointment had been distinctly felt." To Eden's delight, Roosevelt expressed his grave concern at the possible de jure recognition of Abyssinia, which he believed would have a harmful effect on public opinion in America. Lindsay emphasized the point in his covering letter.

> It would rouse a feeling of disgust; would revive and multiply all fear of pulling the chestnuts out of the fire; and it would be represented as a corrupt bargain completed in Europe at the expense of interests in the Far East in which the United States were intimately concerned.[24]

That evening Eden endured a stormy two-hour meeting with Chamberlain, who insisted that he would continue to request that Roosevelt delay his initiative, if necessary indefinitely, while he himself pursued a settlement with Mussolini. According to Harvey he also "admitted that there was a fundamental difference between him and A.E. and left the impression that one or the other must go."[25] He did, however, agree that the matter should be brought before the Foreign Policy Committee of the Cabinet the following day. "I fear that fundamentally the difficulty is that Neville believes that he is a man with a mission to come to terms with the dictators," complained Eden. His principal objection to the Roosevelt plan was that "it would greatly irritate the Dictator Powers."[26]

The Foreign Policy Committee met a number of times over the coming days to consider the President's letter. At the meeting on January 19, Eden found himself sitting next to Sir Thomas Inskip and, peering over his colleague's shoulder, saw that the Minister for Coordination of Defence had scribbled on his notes: "Eden's policy to line up the U.S.A, Great Britain, France—result war."[27] The Prime Minister, meanwhile, much to Eden's disgust, resorted to reading out a lengthy extract of a letter from his sister-in-law in Rome as justification for his refusal to deal with Roosevelt. The meeting was informed that Grandi had now returned from leave in Italy, and had confirmed in a meeting at the Foreign Office that de jure recognition of Abyssinia remained the price for any further conversations with Italy. Eden found himself isolated, and was forced to endure a rough ride from his Cabinet colleagues. After a lengthy debate, Cadogan was deputed to redraft Chamberlain's reply to Roosevelt. That evening Eden invited Cadogan,

Cranborne, Harvey, and his Parliamentary Private Secretary and close confidant, Jim Thomas, to dinner. It was pointed out to him that however much he wanted to resign, it was all but impossible for him to do so on this particular issue, one which would have to be kept secret from the general public.

Overnight Chamberlain partially changed his position, and when Eden saw him at lunchtime the next day he seemed less sure of himself. He now suggested a compromise solution involving a parallel approach: the Roosevelt initiative *and* talks with Mussolini would be pursued simultaneously. Given the President's firm stand on Abyssinia, Eden thought this unrealistic, but at the Foreign Policy Committee that afternoon he found some of his ministerial colleagues were now less entrenched in their opposition. Harvey assumed that "the P.M. had clearly been shaken up by feeling that A.E. would resign." It was agreed that Eden should draft three new telegrams, keeping British options open. That evening there was a further meeting of Eden's supporters at his home, after which Harvey summed up the feeling that "A.E. would be better outside the government as the 'old gang' will watch to trip him again. Anyway, he can afford to be as firm as he likes as now they realise he would resign on it they are afraid of him. We know now that the P.M. hates American co-operation and wants to make peace with the dictators."[28]

The Foreign Policy Committee met twice on January 21. Chamberlain had been to Birmingham overnight, and had returned in a bad mood in time for the first meeting at 11:30 A.M. Eden presented his draft telegrams, but no agreement was reached. A further meeting convened at 3 P.M., Eden's fourth attempt to argue his case. But his colleagues continued to back the Prime Minister, and eventually a compromise was reached whereby four telegrams were dispatched to Washington. The first was a short personal message from Chamberlain to Roosevelt, expressing gratitude for the deferral of any announcement, recognizing Roosevelt's disappointment, and concluding that the Prime Minister "warmly welcomes the President's initiative," and would do his "best to contribute to the success of his scheme whenever he decides to launch it."[29] A second message set out at length British thinking behind the recognition of Abyssinia, and for seeking appeasement in the Mediterranean. The other two telegrams were to Lindsay, bluntly warning him that he was walking a diplomatic tightrope. He should at all costs avoid shared responsibility with America for the proposals, in case they received a bad press when made public. If that were to happen, it was equally vital that Roosevelt could not make the claim that he had been encouraged by London. ·

There was some relief in Washington both at Chamberlain's halfhearted welcome for the initiative, and at the understanding that de jure recognition would only come about as part of a general settlement with Italy. The President, reported Welles, "regarded recognition as an unpleasant pill which we should both have to swallow and he wished that we should both swallow it together."[30] But Roosevelt's initiative was now, to all intents and purposes, dead and buried. On January 25 Eden returned to the League of Nations in Geneva, and was therefore again absent when the President quietly announced that he was postponing his initiative, using as a pretext Hitler's increased grasp on the reins of power after the reshuffle in Berlin on February 4. When Winston Churchill got around to writing history, as he promised that he would, he wrote that "no event could have been more likely to stave off, or even prevent, war than the arrival of the United States in the circle of European hates and fears." Chamberlain's rejection of Roosevelt's overtures represented "the loss of the last frail chance to save the world from tyranny otherwise than by war."[31]

▪ ▪ ▪

While he spent much of January skirmishing with his Foreign Secretary over Roosevelt's offer, the Prime Minister was also quietly making plans of his own to open talks with Mussolini, by initiating parallel secret negotiations in London and Rome. He had identified two possible opportunities: first, while Eden was on holiday in the south of France, and then again when he was away on League of Nations business in Geneva. His plan was to reach agreement with Grandi before Eden returned to London. On January 9, with Eden still safely abroad, he decided that the moment had come for him to reject his Foreign Secretary's advice "in favour of a method of my own."[32] That method was to involve his sister-in-law, Lady Ivy Chamberlain, the widow of his late half-brother, Austen. She had first met Mussolini while accompanying her husband to the Locarno conference in October 1925, since when, according to Halifax, she had become "a warm but naïve admirer of the Italian cause."[33] In December 1937, some months after

Austen Chamberlain's death, Ivy returned to Rome, where she took up residence in the Grand Hotel.

It was not long before she felt fully assimilated into Roman political and diplomatic society, writing breathlessly to Chamberlain that she was being wined and dined by "the people who count." She had even received a "spontaneous" invitation from the Duce, who "shook both my hands and kissed them," while reminiscing about happy days in Locarno. "If nothing else," she boasted, "I have put the British embassy on the map here." But there was a downside to all this frenetic socializing. "Every day at every meal," she complained, "I have to combat the feeling against Anthony."[34] On New Year's Eve she secured a personal audience at the Palazzo Chigi, the Italian Foreign Ministry, with Count Galeazzo Ciano, Mussolini's son-in-law and Foreign Minister. She took with her a letter from Chamberlain reaffirming his determination to open talks with Italy. Ciano appeared to be delighted. "You were right! This is *most* useful," he assured her. "I will tell the Duce of this letter."[35] Privately he was less enthusiastic. The letter, he complained, contained "nothing new, simply the old complaints about the anti-British propaganda of Radio Bari and the Italian press, and a reaffirmation of general goodwill for negotiations with us. We shall see . . ."[36]

Chamberlain's London go-between was of an altogether different character. Sir Joseph Ball was a former long-serving MI5 officer who, in 1927, had been recruited by the then chairman of the Conservative Party, J. C. C. Davidson, to run the party's publicity machine. Davidson later recalled that Ball was "tough and looked after his own interests," and he was particularly impressed that the former intelligence officer was "steeped in Service tradition, and has had as much experience as anyone I know in the seamy side of life and the handling of crooks." In 1929 Ball became the first director of the newly created Conservative Research Department, where he became a staunch ally and angling companion of the department's chairman, Neville Chamberlain. Ball's skills were soon put to good use, he and Davidson running "a little intelligence service of our own, quite separate from the Party organization." In particular he managed a network of agents that successfully infiltrated Labour Party headquarters and the printing press where all Labour's pamphlets and policy documents were produced.[37]

Among Ball's contacts was one Adrian Dingli, a barrister of Maltese-Italian-English extraction. Dingli had been raised in Malta, the son of the country's Chief Justice, had served with the Royal Marine Artillery during the First World War, and subsequently settled in London. From his chambers in the Middle Temple he acted as legal counsel to the Italian embassy, becoming a confidant of the ambassador, Count Grandi, while as a member of the high Tory Carlton Club he became acquainted with Ball. At some stage during 1937 he offered to supply Ball with "secret information about Italian diplomatic moves."[38] The two men were to meet regularly to exchange information throughout the remainder of 1937, but all the evidence suggests that the opening of a secret channel between them was to be to the benefit of Italy rather than Britain.

On January 10 Ball told Dingli that the Prime Minister "wished to know whether Grandi would obtain permission from Rome to start 'talks' in London with the PM." Dingli was suspicious, but Ball assured him that, with Eden abroad, Chamberlain was acting Foreign Secretary and that "the suggestion represented the view of the PM."[39] Grandi was in Rome at the time, and Ball knew that any message sent en clair by telegram would be deciphered by British intelligence and passed to the Foreign Office, and thus to Eden. Incredibly, it necessitated a series of guarded telephone calls between London and Rome to convey the gist of Chamberlain's message without the information reaching the ears of his own Foreign Secretary. It was agreed that Chamberlain and Grandi would meet in London on January 17.

To the Prime Minister's annoyance, this first attempt to conduct covert international diplomacy behind the back of his Foreign Secretary was thwarted by Cadogan's insistence that Eden be recalled from his holiday to deal with the Roosevelt offer. With Eden arriving back in London on January 16, the planned meeting was quietly canceled. Not to be outdone, Chamberlain's next step was a quite extraordinary one. With Ball's assistance, he drafted a letter from Grandi to Eden requesting a joint meeting with the Prime Minister and Foreign Secretary. Although uneasy that this gave the false impression that it was the Italians pursuing Chamberlain, rather than the other way around, Grandi could hardly turn down a draft letter in Ball's handwriting on Chamberlain's Downing Street letterhead. The letter was typed out, taken to Grandi for signature, and duly dispatched to Eden. Meanwhile Ball, Grandi and Dingli met at the Italian embassy to decide how best to assist Chamberlain and "neutralise any obstruction by Eden."[40]

On January 21, during its evening news broadcast, the BBC announced that "no efforts to improve Anglo-Italian relations were at all contemplated." The announcement caused consternation both at the Italian embassy and at Downing Street, and Ball was directly authorized by Chamberlain to refute the story. Under pressure from Ball, the following evening the BBC declared that the story had been inaccurate, but it had already been taken up by some of the Saturday newspapers, and the following day by the *Sunday Times*. Fearing that the Italians would use the negative publicity to shelve the coming talks, Ball assured them that Chamberlain was "much incensed" by the coverage, and had personally ordered him to issue a rebuttal to all the major news outlets. Ball further emphasized that Chamberlain had spoken firmly to Eden, told him to toe the line, and instructed him to unearth the original source of the story. Although Ball reported that Eden had now become "sulky," Chamberlain still hoped that the talks could commence once the Foreign Secretary returned from his forthcoming trip to the League of Nations.[41]

While in Geneva, Eden was given access to French intelligence material by the Foreign Minister, Yvon Delbos, suggesting that Italy was shortly planning to increase, rather than to scale back, military involvement in the Spanish Civil War. On his return to London, Eden drafted a Foreign Office minute making his position clear.

In any event it is surely true that so long as the Spanish situation continues with recurrent bombing of the civilian population by Italian aeroplanes and other manifestations of Italian intervention in one form or another, there cannot be an improvement in relations between this country and Italy.[42]

His concerns appeared to have been justified in early February, with the news that a British merchant ship, the SS *Endymion*, had been sunk by an unidentified submarine, presumed to be Italian, in the Mediterranean. A few days later a further British ship was sunk, this time from the air. The government retaliated by resuming the so-called Nyon patrols to protect neutral shipping in the area, while Eden summoned Grandi to warn him that the navy would sink any submerged submarine it encountered in the British zone. This hardening of the British approach paid off, and on February 4

Grandi told the Foreign Office that the Italian government too would resume its part in the Nyon patrols.

Although Eden believed that he had regained the upper hand, he was unaware that Chamberlain had recently stepped up his own unofficial diplomacy in Rome. Lady Chamberlain spent February 1 sightseeing, and was almost breathless with excitement when she returned to her hotel to find that "Rome was being combed for me . . . the Duce wished to see me at 7 P.M.!" Ciano sent a car to collect her, and accompanied her to the Palazzo Venezia, where Mussolini informed her that he understood she had received an important letter from her brother-in-law. He wondered if she might consent to let him know what it said. Lady Chamberlain agreed only too readily to read it to him, while Ciano made a great show of translating the passages that Mussolini claimed not to understand. "He is not too sure of his English," reported Ivy, "though he likes to talk it!"[43] That Mussolini knew of the letter's existence, indeed of its contents, was no surprise. For one thing, Ivy had already boasted to half of Rome that she had received the letter, and had told the British ambassador, Lord Perth, that "the Prime Minister had stated in it that he expected to have Anglo-Italian conversations well started before the end of February."[44]

Furthermore, security at the British embassy in Rome had long been woefully inadequate. Documents had been stolen on a small scale for many years until, in 1935, the thefts were organized in a more formal manner by the "P. Squad" of Italian Intelligence ("P" stood for *prelevamento*, or withdrawal), which specialized in the removal of secrets from foreign embassies. The British had not put up much of a fight. A trusted and well-liked Chancery servant, who had worked at the embassy since 1914 and was considered by diplomats to be "a sort of friend of the family,"[45] was later discovered to have been in the pay of the P. Squad for many years. Over a long period of time he removed secret documents and ciphers from the embassy at will, passing them to his handler in the street outside. The documents would be taken away, photographed, and replaced within an hour and a half. A number of security reviews, including one following the theft in 1937 of a diamond necklace belonging to the ambassador's wife, consistently failed to reveal this appalling breach in security.[46]

Although she had no authority to do so, Lady Chamberlain assured the Duce that under her brother-in-law's influence the Cabinet was coming round to the idea of recognizing his conquest of Abyssinia, and that it was hoped conversations could begin at the end of the month. Mussolini replied that he "entirely agreed with the P.M.'s point of view," that he was himself "working in a very realistic spirit," and that once the conversations began it was his "earnest wish to re-establish the good relations between our countries."[47] This message was conveyed by Ciano to Perth, who forwarded it on to London with an accompanying private telegram informing the Foreign Secretary of Lady Chamberlain's actions. Unsurprising, Eden was furious, both at the secrecy surrounding the meeting, and the resulting undermining of his position. It was now clear that the Prime Minister had been communicating with her behind his back.

"I have just seen in full the various messages which have come through from Lady Chamberlain in the last few days," he wrote to Chamberlain. "I confess that what I read there causes me considerable apprehension which is not allayed by this morning's news that Lady Chamberlain is to stay for another month in Rome."

> Without wishing to be unduly punctilious, I am sure you will understand that this kind of unofficial diplomacy does place me in a most difficult position. It recreates in Mussolini's mind the impression that he can divide us and he will be the less ready to pay attention to what I have to say to Grandi. Mussolini has clearly and, as he would, very skilfully, taken advantage of the opening which Lady Chamberlain has afforded him.[48]

Chamberlain, who had of course written to his sister-in-law precisely in the hope that she would pass on his message to Mussolini, feigned surprise.

> I am sorry that my sister-in-law's unorthodox procedure has caused you apprehension. I don't really think however that she has done any harm although . . . I will tell her very definitely that my letters are to be shown to no one.[49]

While Ivy Chamberlain had been flirting with the Duce, in London Sir Joseph Ball had stepped up his own efforts to promote Anglo-Italian relations. His publicity campaign was running at "full blast," and Grandi was delighted to hear that "every possible persuasion was being placed on the

Press to conform to the desired object of reversing public opinion about Italy."[50] Typical was the *Daily Mail* of February 9: "BRITAIN TO HASTEN NEW TALKS WITH ITALY—ALL ISSUES TO BE DISCUSSED. COUNT CIANO FOR LONDON?" The paper's diplomatic correspondent solemnly provided further details for his readers.

> I am able to state authoritatively that the British Government is eager to press forward new negotiations with Italy with least possible delay. Count Grandi, the Italian Ambassador, is to see Mr. Eden at the Foreign Office to-day. It is felt in political quarters that already there has been far too much delay in seeking a solution of the differences between Britain and Italy.

Full legal recognition of Abyssinia would be conceded "as part of a general settlement," while the problems of anti-British Italian propaganda were only "of secondary importance."[51]

Eden, for whom recognition was out of the question and propaganda was crucial, was understandably irritated. He knew the suggestion that Ciano should be invited to London had come from Lady Chamberlain, and correctly guessed that the press campaign bore "all the hallmarks of authoritative inspiration."[52] Harvey too noted that "according to the [Foreign Office] News Department, this campaign can only have come from No. 10."[53] But when Eden confronted Chamberlain about the article in the *Daily Mail*, the Prime Minister flatly denied any responsibility—a barefaced lie. For once, however, Ball had been forced to break his cover. He sought an assurance from his Italian informant that his "name would never be mentioned by G[randi],"[54] but a few days later Harvey recorded that "a curious story reaches me that press campaign about Italy was given out by Sir Joseph Ball at Conservative Head Office, NOT from No. 10. By whose authority I wonder?"[55] Eden accurately surmised that such exaggerated coverage would be interpreted in Rome as a sign of increasing British eagerness, even desperation, a concern confirmed by Ciano's diary. The Italian Foreign Minister was suspicious, both of British motives and even of his own ambassador in London, who he thought had become overzealous. "Grandi has started off in top gear," he noted disapprovingly, "and wants authorization to begin the conversations. I have drafted a telegram, recommending calm and prudence in face of this British zeal for reconciliation, which might after all be a manoeuvre of Eden's."[56]

The Saturday morning newspapers were full of stories about an alleged Chamberlain-Eden divide. Chamberlain complained bitterly to his sister that they were "as mendacious & vicious as any of the Continental rags. . . . It is all untrue in every respect. I saw Anthony on Friday morning and we were in complete agreement, more complete perhaps than we have sometimes been in the past."[57] It was an assertion that would have surprised Eden. The following morning the *Sunday Times*, edited by W. W. Hadley, one of Chamberlain's most ardent supporters in the press, issued what it described as a formal "*démenti*," under the headline "A POLITICAL CANARD."

> There is no truth in the stories published yesterday of acute differences between the Prime Minister and the Foreign Secretary and of a consequent Ministerial crisis. Though the reports vary in scope and detail, they agree in representing Mr. Chamberlain as the adventurous spirit in foreign policy and Mr. Eden as the advocate of more cautious and slower action. I have the highest authority for saying that there is not a word of truth in all this. The Prime Minister and Mr. Eden are in complete agreement.[58]

Two events now combined to quicken the pace, both in London and Rome, toward an early opening of formal talks between Britain and Italy. First, news began to filter through from Germany that on February 12 Hitler had summoned the Austrian Chancellor, Kurt von Schuschnigg, to Berchtesgaden, and had subjected him to a furious browbeating, resulting in an "agreement" which marked the beginning of the end for an independent Austria. Intelligence reports reaching the Foreign Office strongly suggested that Mussolini had given tacit support to Hitler, who it was feared would now pursue his policy to its logical conclusion, and seize Austria by force. In return, it was assumed that Hitler had given Italy a free hand in Spain. It was certainly the case that Mussolini had recently told his Foreign Minister that he was "in favour of the nazification of Austria," and after Schuschnigg's visit to Berchtesgaden he again expressed his pleasure. "The Duce has seen the Austro-German agreement," reported Ciano. "He says he regards it as a logical and inevitable development in the relations between two German countries."[59]

On February 16 Ciano wrote to Grandi, ordering him to speed up his efforts in London in light of increased German aggression toward Austria.

> To use a phrase of the Duce's—which is as usual most effective—we find ourselves in the interval between the fourth and fifth acts of the Austrian affair. When will the fifth act begin? It is impossible to foresee. But it is not beyond the bounds of possibility that this tempo may increase. This interval, and this interval alone, can be used for the negotiations between us and London.[60]

From the British ambassador in Rome came an urgent message from Ciano for Eden, "that an early start should be made with Anglo-Italian conversations in view of certain future happenings." Although Ciano had been "studiously vague," Perth assumed "that recent events in Austria have given Italian Government a nasty jolt and that they are anxious about future."[61] Lady Chamberlain was more emphatic still. After lunching with Ciano she contacted Perth begging him to forward a personal letter to Eden, in which she warned ominously that "time is everything. Today an agreement will be easy but things are happening in Europe which will make it impossible tomorrow."[62]

Chamberlain was impressed by the urgency of these appeals, but was more convinced still by the disconcerting news given him by Ball, to the effect that Grandi was under growing pressure from Rome, and becoming increasingly nervous about his own position. He was threatening that if his letter to Eden of January 19 were made public, he would have no choice but to reveal that the Prime Minister himself had been its author, if only "to protect Italy's honour." Worse still, if no meeting took place within the next few days, he would leave London, probably for good.[63] Faced by these twin threats of blackmail, one personal, one political, Chamberlain recognized that his Italian policy was in danger of collapse. Eden had long made it clear that he believed any preliminary talks with Grandi should not include the Prime Minister, but Chamberlain was now in a hurry. To Eden's astonishment, and without revealing his source, he indicated that he knew that Grandi had already asked for a meeting, and that he intended to grant his wish.

Twice Eden tried to summon Grandi to the Foreign Office but, in a deliberate snub, Grandi simply refused to attend. He appreciated only too clearly that while Eden would insist on discussing uncomfortable topics such as Spain and Austria, the Prime Minister, in his anxiety to avoid being implicated by Grandi's letter, would be considerably more accommodating. Initially, Grandi claimed that he was awaiting a letter containing instructions from Ciano, while the following day he gave the quite extraordinary excuse that he was too busy playing golf. He was indeed a member of the exclusive Wentworth Golf Club outside London, and boasted to Ciano that he had "put [Eden] off again, bringing up as a pure excuse that I had a golfing engagement (I hate golf but pretend to play it when necessary)."[64] Ball, meanwhile, was tipped off by the SIS that Grandi was deliberately staying at Wentworth to avoid meeting Eden; he was warned to accept the next invitation he received, as it would be for a meeting with the Prime Minister himself.

On the morning of February 18 Eden made the short walk across Downing Street to No. 10. He had tried in vain to persuade Chamberlain that he should not entertain Grandi, but once it became clear that the meeting would take place, he instead sent a letter of warning to the Prime Minister. Grandi, he warned, would be coming with the sole purpose of making "an earnest appeal for the immediate opening of conversations in Rome."

> It does not appear that he will bring us much in the way of a contribution about Spain. My own strong feeling is that we must be very careful not to commit ourselves either way in response to Grandi's prayer—if a prayer it be. Such information as we have here tends to strengthen the view that there is some kind of agreement between Rome and Berlin and that Mussolini has, or thinks he has some kind of *quid pro quo* from Berlin in return for his acquiescence in Austrian events.[65]

Eden's standing had been strengthened by the enthusiastic endorsement of his views by a well-attended meeting of the Conservative backbench Foreign Affairs Committee in the House of Commons the previous evening. Churchill, in particular, had urged his colleagues to rally behind the Foreign Secretary. At 11:30 A.M. Grandi was ushered into the Cabinet Room for a meeting which must rank as one of the most extraordinary in British diplomatic history.

Eden was not to know that the Prime Minister had already "determined to stand firm even though it meant losing my Foreign Secretary."[66] Chamberlain opened the meeting by expressing his concern at recent events in Austria. What, he asked, was the attitude of the Italian government? Grandi expressed regret at Hitler's actions, which he admitted had not been entirely unexpected, but when challenged by Chamberlain over the existence of a secret understanding between Italy and Germany, he denied absolutely that any such agreement existed. His concern was that "Germany was now at the Brenner and it was impossible for Italy to be left alone in the world with two great potential enemies—Germany and Great Britain."[67] This led in turn to the rehearsal of a litany of anti-British grievances, to which Eden listened quietly. Grandi, he later wrote, was:

> a very skilful diplomat, and did his stuff admirably. Whenever he paused, N.C. encouraged him. He sat there nodding his head approvingly, while Grandi detailed one grievance after another. The more N.C. nodded the more outrageous became Grandi's account until in the end it would almost seem that we had invaded Abyssinia. If N.C. had kept his head still we should have been spared two-thirds of this.

Chamberlain then invited Grandi to throw light on the warnings from Ciano and Ivy Chamberlain that talks should commence as soon as possible in view of "the possibility of certain future happenings." Although Eden assumed that this was no more than "characteristic Fascist blackmail,"[68] Grandi skillfully sidestepped the question by reiterating that "if it was impossible to improve relations with Great Britain, then it would be necessary for Italy to draw still closer to Germany."[69] Chamberlain seemed pleased by this reply, conforming as it did to his own interpretation of events. Until now Eden had listened quietly, maintaining, in Grandi's words, a "hostile silence," but when the ambassador insisted that any talks must take place in Rome, he "intervened in a sharp tone," and returned to the subject of Austria. Chamberlain "gave visible signs of disappointment and irritation."[70] Grandi merely replied that "he had no instructions at all to mention Austria," which failed to satisfy Eden. But when he looked across at the Prime Minister, "to see if he had seized the point," Chamberlain "only looked impatient to get on."[71]

The meeting concluded with a discussion on Spain, and in particular the possibility of the withdrawal of Italian troops. Grandi was again non-committal, apologizing that he might have been over-optimistic as to the likelihood of this during previous discussions with Eden. It was agreed that Chamberlain and Eden would talk matters over, and Grandi was asked to return at 3 P.M. A furious row then ensued. Chamberlain bluntly told Eden that when Grandi returned he intended to inform him that conversations would open immediately, that Perth should be recalled from Rome to receive instructions, and that he would personally make the announcement that very afternoon. Eden objected strongly, pointing out that no progress had been made over Spain, and that he refused to be blackmailed by the "now or never" telegrams from Rome. Chamberlain became "very violent,"[72] and began to shout at the Foreign Secretary, pacing up and down the Cabinet Room as he did so.

"Anthony, you have missed chance after chance. You simply cannot go on like this."

"Your methods are right," replied Eden calmly, "if you have faith in the man you are negotiating with."

"I have," said Chamberlain.[73]

Reluctantly, the Prime Minister agreed that the Cabinet should be consulted before any decision was taken, and Eden returned to the Foreign Office for lunch, to find that the mood there had turned angry. Much of the fury was directed at "that jackass Ivy," as Cadogan described her,[74] or in Cranborne's words, the "rather stupid lady who had been spoon fed by two very clever and unscrupulous men."[75] It was agreed that Eden should stand firm, and that if the Cabinet disagreed with him then he would resign. After lunch he again argued with Chamberlain, but he held to his line, and when Grandi kept his appointment at 3 P.M., he was told that there would be a special Cabinet meeting the following day, and that he would get his answer on Monday. Later that afternoon Sir John Simon, the Chancellor of the Exchequer, called on Eden at the Foreign Office. "Take care of yourself, Anthony," he concluded. "You look rather tired. Are you certain that you're all right?" Although Simon claimed to be "as fond of Anthony as if he had been his own son," he told Jim Thomas, Eden's Parliamentary Private Secretary, that he was becoming increasingly concerned that the Foreign Secretary "was both physically and mentally ill." He suggested six months holiday, a suggestion Thomas angrily rejected, pointing out that Eden had only just returned from a relaxing holiday in the south of France.[76] The whispering campaign had begun.

In what was perhaps one of the most bizarre diplomatic dispatches ever written, Grandi briefed Ciano on the meeting at Downing Street.

> They were—and revealed themselves as such to me in defiance of all established convention—two enemies confronting each other, like two cocks in true fighting posture. The questions and queries addressed to me by Chamberlain were all, without exception, intentionally put with the aim of producing replies which would have the effect of contradicting and overthrowing the bases of argument on which Eden had previously constructed, or by which he had attempted to justify, his miserable anti-Italian and anti-Fascist policy in opposition to Chamberlain.[77]

It had always been his intention, he boasted, "to drive a wedge into the incipient split between Eden and Chamberlain and to enlarge it more if possible,"[78] and in this he appeared to have succeeded. Eden left that afternoon for his Leamington constituency, "very bitter at the way his colleagues treat him and feeling he cannot go on like this,"[79] while even Chamberlain now recognized that he was "on the eve of a Cabinet crisis."[80]

The front pages of the Saturday morning newspapers were all dominated by the news that four members of the notorious so-called Mayfair Gang of aristocratic jewel thieves, who had left a Cartier jeweler for dead at the Hyde Park Hotel, had been sentenced to hard labor and the "cat." Inside, however, most papers also contained the first indications that all was not well in Whitehall, and by the time the Cabinet assembled at 3 P.M. a large crowd had gathered in Downing Street. Eden had prepared himself over lunch with his inner circle of Foreign Office advisers, all of whom had urged him to take an uncompromising line, and he was loudly cheered by the crowds as he made the short walk across Downing Street. He was not to reemerge for more than three hours.

Chamberlain opened the meeting by apologizing for dragging ministers away from their homes on a Saturday, before embarking on a tedious, hour-long discourse on the history of negotiations with Italy. Most of the Cabinet had absolutely no idea why they were even there. Halifax passed a note to

Sam Hoare, the Home Secretary, who was sitting beside him, "to ask what was the purpose of this rather boring lecture on history."[81] With consummate skill, Chamberlain set out from the first to trivialize his differences with Eden. The main issue, he insisted, "was not one of principle, as to the desirability of an agreement with Italy, but rather of method, timing and whether the present moment was opportune or not." This was "one of those opportunities that came at rare intervals and did not recur . . . an opportunity to show Signor Mussolini that he might have other friends than Herr Hitler." Not "to embrace the opportunity would be not only unwise," he concluded, "but criminal."[82] Eden replied, "rather ineffectively,"[83] repeating his reasons for his opposition to opening talks with Italy: his belief that Mussolini was untrustworthy; his suspicion that Grandi had lied about a German-Italian deal over Austria; the need for Italian troops to be first withdrawn from Spain as an act of good faith; and the danger to British international prestige of appearing to surrender to blackmail by dictators, giving the "impression of scuttle in London," and causing "panic among our friends."[84] He felt unable to refer to Roosevelt's approach.

Chamberlain then threw the discussion open to the rest of the Cabinet, the majority of whom supported him unequivocally. Even Eden's natural allies appeared confused. "He did not, or so it seemed to me, state his case very well," recorded Duff Cooper, the First Lord of the Admiralty, "and I felt that anyone who had not already made up his mind must have been convinced by the Prime Minister."[85] Eden accepted defeat, but warned that he "could not recommend to the House of Commons and argue in favour of a course in which he did not agree. If his colleagues decided against his view, he hoped they would find someone else to help them to carry through this decision."[86] His words triggered "a gasp of horror"[87] around the table, but Chamberlain was unmoved, and "remarked drily that this was a distressing situation, the more so because he held the opposite view so strongly that he could not accept any other decision."[88] He did, however, agree that in view of the seriousness of the situation they should reconvene the following day, a Sunday.

Toward the end of the meeting Halifax had suggested a compromise, to the effect that an official announcement might be made at once that talks would begin, but only, it would be stressed, when affairs in Spain had been satisfactorily resolved. That evening he called at the Foreign Office, along with Oliver Stanley, the President of the Board of Trade, to try to broker the compromise.

> I felt at once that the atmosphere, emanating mainly from Bobbety [Cranborne], was very much pro-resignation. It produced on me some-what of the effect I should have expected from the corner of a boxing ring when the 2nds received back the pugilist & restored his vitality by con-gratulations & encouragement. I could almost hear them saying, I thought, "You have done very well. You have won the 1st round. Hold firm & all will be well!" We talked for some time in a rather restless atmosphere of whiskies & sodas, & cigarettes, but without, I felt, making any impres-sion, & when we came away Oliver Stanley said to me, "He has been through Hell to make up his mind, & he's d——d well not going to unmake it."[89]

Sir Joseph Ball too had been far from idle. That Saturday evening he warned Grandi that, if Eden resigned, Chamberlain would need a coup de théâtre to impress his critics, "to demonstrate the superiority of the views he has taken and of his resulting action." Ideally, suggested Ball, this should be in the form of an announcement that Italian troops were to be withdrawn from Spain. Grandi telephoned Rome for instructions, and Dingli later called Ball in the country to say that the ambassador expected a favorable reply, and that Chamberlain should be made aware of this immediately. On Sunday morning, Dingli called the Italian embassy, on Ball's instructions, to emphasize that Chamberlain was desperate for a positive reply as soon as possible, in order to strengthen his hand in the Cabinet meeting. He also passed on a further request from Ball, to the effect that Chamberlain would be grateful if the Italian press could be persuaded to refrain from acclaim-ing the likely events of that day as "a triumph of the dictators over democracies."[90]

Sunday, February 20, was a cold, wet, windy day, but widespread newspa-per coverage ensured that the crowds had begun to gather in Downing Street from early morning. Shortly after noon Chamberlain sent for Eden, and asked if his views had altered. It was no more than a formality, since Chamberlain had already made up his mind that Eden should be forced to resign, and was now actively colluding with the Italian government behind his Foreign Secretary's back. Eden, in any case, agreed that "the difference between us was vital and unbridgeable and that the only way out was resignation."[91] To Eden's astonishment, however, Chamberlain then told him that the Italian government had accepted his formula for the withdrawal of troops from Spain. "Have they Neville?" asked Eden incredulously. "I have heard nothing of it. No word has reached the Foreign Office and I am still Foreign Secretary." Chamberlain appeared embarrassed, but pressed on. "I cannot tell you how I heard it, but you can take it from me that it is true."[92] In fact, an hour before the Cabinet was due to meet, Dingli met Ball off a train at Waterloo station, and the two men shared a taxi back to Westminster. Ball was given Grandi's "complete assurances" that Chamberlain's request that all Italian volunteers should leave Spain "had been agreed to by Rome."[93]

By the time Cabinet ministers began to arrive, Downing Street was packed, and extra police had been called in to control the throng. Eden was greeted with loud cheers and cries of "Stick to your guns."[94] Chamberlain began by passing on the good news from Italy. Eden, however, had nothing to add to what he had already said: he could not recommend a policy to Parliament with which he disagreed. "He could not disguise," he continued, "that there was a difference of outlook on foreign affairs generally between himself and . . . the Prime Minister." For the first time he alluded to the Roosevelt offer. He then thanked his colleagues, and reaffirmed his intention to resign. Chamberlain too now conceded that there were "differences of deeper outlook," and agreed that resignation was "inevitable."[95] The Cabinet was stunned. It had been widely assumed until then that the sole point of disagreement was the narrow policy issue of talks with Italy. Most of those present had never even heard of Roosevelt's offer, or had any idea of the level of antipathy between Prime Minister and Foreign Secretary. The meeting, "strenuous and ineffectual,"[96] according to Eden, dragged on for over three hours, as numerous compromises were put forward. William Ormsby-Gore even offered his own place in the Cabinet to Eden.

At 4:45 P.M. the meeting adjourned, and Chamberlain reluctantly agreed that a subcommittee be convened under Halifax's chairmanship in a last-ditch attempt to reach a compromise. During the adjournment a number of ministers tried to persuade Eden to stay and, when the main meeting reassembled, Halifax again put forward his compromise solution, inviting

Eden to accept the formal opening of conversations, provided that Italy accept the British formula for the withdrawal of volunteers from Spain. At 6:20 P.M. an exhausted Eden left Downing Street to return to the Foreign Office, where his supporters were growing increasingly alarmed "lest he should be giving way under the third degree methods of the Cabinet."[97] The *Daily Mail* recorded the scene.

> The door opened and the light of a lamp revealed Mr. Eden alone, his face pale, and one hand nervously fidgeting with the lapel of his greatcoat. He had the look of a weary, worried man—his forehead puckered, his lips tight below the Eden moustache.

The cheering crowds struggled to break through the police cordon.

> "Good old Eden. We want Eden. No pact with Italy. Arms for Spain." Head bent, shoulders sunk under his coat, hair ruffling in the wind, he walked swiftly across the street to his room in the Foreign Office, pursued by the cheers.[98]

Ball had one last, crucial role to play in support of Chamberlain. At 7 P.M. he telephoned Dingli to say that the Prime Minister now "desired a preciseness" in Grandi's assurances, a formal confirmation that Italy would indeed withdraw its troops from Spain. The significance of such an assurance was that it would help to ensure that any other ministers who were considering resignation would most likely refrain, and that "therefore the crisis would be limited to the resignation of only Eden."[99] In Rome the excitement was intense. "The crisis is perhaps one of the most important that has ever taken place," recorded Ciano. "I have authorized Grandi to take any step which may add an arrow to Chamberlain's quiver."[100] An hour later, Eden returned to Downing Street. He could not accept Halifax's compromise, and therefore had no option but to resign. Oliver Stanley said that he too must consider his position. One final, last-minute attempt to find a middle way was brushed aside by Chamberlain, who instead asked for Eden's letter of resignation. At 10 P.M. this was read to a further meeting of the Cabinet, the last of a long day. Thanks to Ball, Chamberlain was also able to pass on Grandi's further assurances, as authorized by Ciano, in respect of Italian intentions in Spain. It had the desired effect. Stanley agreed that he had now "had an opportunity to think the matter over and he could see no benefit to the country from further differences. Consequently he was prepared to take his part with his colleagues in facing the difficulties to come."[101]

The following morning large crowds gathered outside Eden's home to cheer him as he left for the Commons, where "the excitement was immense, and the lobbies buzzing."[102] He took his seat on the government backbench below the gangway, the traditional place for a former minister to make a statement of resignation. Cranborne, who had also resigned, sat beside him. From Churchill, Eden received an enthusiastic letter of support. "It seems to me vital," he wrote, "that you should not allow your personal feelings of friendship to your late colleagues to hamper you in doing full justice to your cause."[103] There was similar advice from Lloyd George, but still Eden refused to do serious damage to the government. While Cranborne launched a withering attack—"for His Majesty's Government to enter on official conversations would be regarded not as a contribution to peace but as a surrender to blackmail"[104]—Eden's speech was strong and competent, but cautious. Above all, he failed to explain coherently exactly why he had resigned. The senior Tory backbencher Leo Amery, for example, who should have been a natural ally, recorded that Eden "left the impression that there was really no issue to resign upon."[105]

Chamberlain's job was made easier by the reluctance of other ministers to follow Eden's lead. Harry Crookshank, a junior minister at the Board of Trade, sought guidance from his Secretary of State, but found Stanley diplomatically "uncommunicative." Crookshank then warned the Chief Whip that he "was very wobbly," but he could find no other junior ministers who shared his anxiety, and finally he wrote to Chamberlain "calling attention to apparent discrepancies" in the Prime Minister's recent statements. He was quickly won over by a combination of flattery, and an assurance "that there was no change of policy."[106] Of all his colleagues, Eden was most disappointed by Stanley's refusal to resign with him. "The Stanleys have been trimmers ever since Bosworth field," remarked Lady Cranborne bitterly when she heard the news.[107] Ball's publicity machine too went into overdrive. "I heard what a magnificent speech you made," he wrote to Chamberlain following the debate, "and how completely you destroyed the cases made by Eden and Cranborne." He had, he boasted, "taken certain steps privately" to disparage Eden and Cranborne in the Conservative-inclined press.[108]

The majority of newspapers did indeed support the Prime Minister, the *Daily Mail* among those that dutifully played their part.

> The country will be relieved to learn that Mr. Eden resigned from the Government last night. Mr. Eden's policy during his two years as Foreign Secretary has produced uncertainty at home and bewilderment abroad. The Daily Mail has never seen eye to eye with him. It is to be hoped that in his future political career he will profit by his experiences and mistakes. Above all, the country is fortunate in having a Prime Minister to whom it can give its fullest confidence—a statesman who handles the nation's affairs, both domestic and foreign, with realism and sound common sense.

The paper's diplomatic correspondent echoed the briefing that was widely circulated by ministers and, of course, Sir Joseph Ball.

> Health reasons have played their part. One of Mr. Eden's colleagues said to me last night: "Mr. Eden was overwrought this week-end, and there is no doubt that his condition was the culmination of months of strain and hard work. But I must say that the differences between us were very slight. I regret his decision."[109]

The anonymously quoted minister was almost certainly Simon, who later felt compelled to deny to Eden that he had been spreading gossip. "I heard that you were attaching some credence," he wrote, "to a rumour that I had told the National Liberals in connection with your resignation that this was influenced by health reasons, or that your decision was to be explained because you weren't fit. I had said nothing of the kind."[110] But supporters of Eden knew the truth. "The story was spread by the Whips that A.E. was ill," complained Harvey. "This is, of course, Simon's effort."[111] Chamberlain told his sister that "first the Cabinet, then the House of Commons and now the country have rallied to my side." In fact, during a debate on a vote of censure called by the Opposition on February 22, he indulged in an acrimonious exchange with Lloyd George, "in which that unscrupulous little blackguard tried to make out that I had done something dishonourable."[112] Lloyd George was quite correct. When challenged as to why he, rather than Eden, had been the first to be told of the Italian decision to withdraw troops from Spain, Chamberlain had indeed seriously misled the House. In an effort to conceal Ball's activities, he initially claimed that he had received the news in a written message from Grandi on the Monday morning, after Eden had resigned. When challenged by Lloyd George, he contradicted himself, telling the House that "Count Grandi communicated the contents of the telegram early on Sunday morning." Then later during the same exchange, he claimed that on Sunday morning he "received through a friend who knew Count Grandi an intimation that he had received a favourable reply, and I told the Cabinet so."[113] They were three entirely different explanations.

From Rome, Ivy Chamberlain cooed with ill-disguised pleasure. "The whole of Rome is rejoicing," she reported, "as if a load had been lifted." Even Ciano had made a point of congratulating her at his own party. "It is *wonderful*," he had told her, "*now* we can have peace with England, we told you Mr. Eden hated Italy."[114] From Berlin, Henderson reported that "of course everybody here is at heart profoundly relieved at Eden's departure."[115] It was left to Churchill to describe his contrary emotions in an oft-quoted passage in his memoirs.

Late on the night of February 20 a telephone message reached me as I sat in my old room at Chartwell (as I often sit now) that Eden had resigned. I must confess that my heart sank, and for a while the dark waters of despair overwhelmed me. In a long life I have had many ups and downs [but] . . . in its darkest times I have never had any trouble sleeping. But now, on the night of February 20, 1938, and on this occasion only, sleep deserted me. From midnight till dawn I lay in my bed consumed by emotions of sorrow and fear. There seemed one strong young figure standing up against long, dismal, drawling tides of drift and surrender, of wrong measurements and feeble impulses. Now he was gone. I watched the daylight slowly creep in through the window, and saw before me in mental gaze the vision of Death.[116]

4

■

The Loaded Pause

German Austria must be restored to the great German Motherland.

Adolf Hitler, *Mein Kampf*

Austria is the little world in which the big world holds rehearsal.

Guido Zernatto, Secretary General, Fatherland Front

In the early hours of Saturday, February 12, 1938, a train carrying the Chancellor of Austria, Dr. Kurt von Schuschnigg, pulled into a quiet railway siding outside Salzburg, close to the border with Germany. Schuschnigg had left Vienna the previous evening in great secrecy, disguised as though bound for a weekend's skiing in the Tyrol, in a sleeping carriage which had then been uncoupled from the train at Salzburg. He was accompanied by the State Secretary at the Foreign Ministry, Dr. Guido Schmidt, his adjutant Colonel Bartl, and a detective. He was under no illusion as to the potential danger of his mission. Before leaving Vienna he had sent for Dr. Richard Schmitz, the Mayor of Vienna, and told him that if he did not return from Germany Schmitz was to assume the chancellorship. Before leaving the train in Salzburg he also summoned the local Austrian Security Director and warned him, in strict confidence, where he was going and that if he were not back by nine o'clock that night, the frontier with Germany was to be closed and the country put on a state of alert.

■ ■ ■

Schuschnigg had become Chancellor in 1934 when, at the age of just thirty-six, he succeeded Engelbert Dollfuss, who had been assassinated by Austrian Nazis. A lawyer by training, he had served in Dollfuss's Cabinet as Minister of Education and, although anti-Nazi, he shared many of his mentor's pan-German beliefs. Well born, well educated and dignified, he was perceived as a "man of impeccable Old World Austrian manners." But he was also reserved, and his natural shyness could make him appear cold and disdainful. His critics viewed him as a "narrow-minded man but, within his limits, an intelligent one."[1] Dollfuss had once remarked that what was "good and healthy" in National Socialism was already part of his own political program. Schuschnigg attempted to emphasize those "good and healthy" points by imitating many aspects of German Nazism in the expectation of "taking the wind out of the Nazi sails." He hoped that an Austrian Nazi "would no longer envy Germany if he could find the best features of Nazism in his native country."[2] It was to prove a hopelessly optimistic ambition.

On July 11, 1936, Austria and Germany signed the Austro-German agreement, which "recognised the full sovereignty of the Federal State of Austria in accordance with the statements made by the Führer and Chancellor on 21 May 1935." It also stipulated that both governments would regard "the internal political structure of the other country, including the question of Austrian National-Socialism, as an internal affair of the other country, which it will influence neither directly nor indirectly."[3] But while Schuschnigg was full of good intentions, the agreement served only to heighten German pressure on Austrian independence, what one historian has described as a "policy of peaceful penetration."[4] At the same time Austria was becoming increasingly unable to rely on the level of Italian support that had been enjoyed in the early 1930s, while the expectation that robust intervention would be forthcoming from France and Britain was also fading fast.

Throughout 1937 the Austrian Nazis, encouraged both financially and morally by Berlin, stepped up their terror campaign. Bombings became an everyday occurrence, while Nazi demonstrations, often violent, became commonplace, especially in the outlying provinces. Increasingly, Hitler turned his eye to fulfilling his Austrian dream.

Since his childhood days in Linz he had believed that the future of Austria's German-speaking population lay within the Reich. The first point of the Nazi Party Program of 1920 demanded "the merger of all

Germans . . . in a Greater Germany," and on the very first page of *Mein Kampf* Hitler wrote that "German-Austria must return to the great German mother-country, and not because of any economic considerations. No, and again no: even if such a union were unimportant from an economic point of view; yes, even if it were harmful, it must nevertheless take place. One blood demands one Reich."[5]

By the end of 1937, however, economic factors had achieved equality of importance with ideological beliefs. Not only did Austria command an important strategic position in central Europe, she could also provide much needed material resources to a German economy suffering under the pressure of rapid and forced rearmament; both factors had been stressed by Hitler at the Reich Chancellery meeting on November 5. The appointment earlier that summer of his economic adviser, Wilhelm Keppler, to run party affairs in Austria had further strengthened his hold over an increasingly fractious Nazi leadership in Vienna, at the expense of Foreign Ministry influence. And in mid-November, the visit of Lord Halifax to Berchtesgaden had merely confirmed in Hitler's mind that neither the British government, nor indeed the French, would do anything to save Austria from German aggression.

In Vienna, gallows humor told of an impatient Führer, locked away at Obersalzberg, poring over hundreds of picture postcards of Vienna, and other Austrian towns and cities, in an effort to identify sites for local Nazi headquarters. Pinned up on the wall, it was said, was a huge street plan of Vienna, beside which Hitler sat "for hours at a draughtsman's table, designing architectural monstrosities by which he is going to replace some of Vienna's soft and dreamy baroque facades after his triumphal entry as conqueror." In January 1938 François-Poncet reported to the Quai d'Orsay that Hitler was openly boasting, "I shall soon have Schuschnigg's head."[6] And while the Austrian Nazis stepped up their campaign of insurrection, Hitler's ambassador in Vienna, Franz von Papen, suggested that the time had come for the Führer to meet personally with Schuschnigg to apply the threat of force. "Only by subjecting the Federal Chancellor to the strongest possible pressure," he wrote, "can further progress be made."[7]

Having agreed to meet Hitler, Schuschnigg tried first to strengthen his own position. On January 25 the Viennese *Reichspost* published an interview with the Nazi deputy leader and Gauleiter of Vienna, Dr. Leopold Tavs, in which he openly challenged the government, asserting that the police would never dare to prosecute Austrian Nazis for fear of German retaliation. This gave Schuschnigg the pretext he needed, and that evening police raided the headquarters of the so-called Committee of Seven in the Teinfaltstrasse. The committee, a panel of prominent Austrian Nazis, had been formed in early 1937 in an attempt to build bridges between the ruling party, the Fatherland Front, and supposedly moderate Nazis. But it soon became clear that the Seven "were more interested in dynamiting bridges than building them,"[8] and it was well known that their offices in the Teinfaltstrasse were the headquarters of the Nazi underground in Vienna. Tavs was arrested, and the police discovered a cache of secret documents, many of them orders signed by Hitler's deputy, Rudolf Hess. The so-called Tavs Plan provided for a sustained series of the most provocative illegal acts of defiance, including bombings and assassinations, to be carried out in March and April 1938. It was hoped that these outrages would lead to a heavy-handed government crackdown, which would in turn justify armed intervention by the full military might of the Reich, by then to be massed on the Austrian border.

The most extraordinary aspect of the plan was the proposition that a surprise attack should be mounted on the German embassy by Nazis disguised in the uniform of storm troopers of the ruling Fatherland Front. The embassy was to be burned to the ground and, incredibly, the German ambassador murdered. Quite how Papen felt when he discovered that his fellow Nazis were planning his assassination, neither history nor Papen himself has related. An aristocratic diplomat and politician of the old school, and himself a former Chancellor of Germany, Papen had helped bring Hitler to power in 1933, for which he had been rewarded with the Vice-Chancellorship. He subsequently served as ambassador in Vienna from 1934, and believed that he had become indispensable to Hitler in helping prepare for the absorption of Austria into the Reich. Papen was therefore left "speechless with astonishment," when on February 4 in the wake of the Blomberg and Fritsch affairs, he was informed by telephone from Berlin that he was one of those ambassadors to be sacked in Hitler's reshuffle.[9]

Schuschnigg was concerned at the loss of a diplomat who was widely believed to exercise a restraining influence on Hitler, a character assessment in which he was badly mistaken. "Papen unfolds a plan to bring down Schuschnigg," recorded Goebbels shortly before Christmas. "The cat doesn't leave the mouse alone. But that's good. Schuschnigg is getting too strong and cheeky [*frech*]."[10] In reality, Papen was Hitler's principal agent in the plot to overthrow Schuschnigg. The Austrian Chancellor demonstrated similar naïveté in his dealings with the apparently moderate Nazi leader, the Viennese lawyer, Arthur Seyss-Inquart. Believing that he could win the sympathy of Seyss, and conclude an agreement before meeting Hitler, Schuschnigg foolishly entered into a series of secret negotiations. But, in the words of one historian, "his belief that Seyss was loyal was a pathetic delusion."[11] The so-called Ten Points (*Punktationen*) agreed between Schuschnigg and Seyss included a number of major Austrian concessions. But Seyss was in constant contact with his German masters, and ensured that Hitler was fully briefed as to Schuschnigg's likely negotiating position long before he got to Berchtesgaden.

Just a few days after sacking Papen, Hitler suddenly changed his mind and summoned him to Berchtesgaden. Papen found the Führer "exhausted and distrait." But when he resurrected the idea of a Schuschnigg meeting, which had previously been postponed because of the Blomberg and Fritsch crises, Hitler welcomed the idea with alacrity. Papen was ordered back to Vienna, and told to arrange it "within the next few days." His protestations that it was only forty-eight hours since he had been sacked were brushed aside. "I beg you, Herr von Papen," implored Hitler, "to take over the affairs of the Legation again, until the meeting with Schuschnigg has been arranged."[12] Schuschnigg was, understandably, suspicious. But Papen assured him that the 1936 agreement would be honored, and that "the suggested discussion will deal with such misunderstandings and points of friction as have persisted after the agreement of 1936." A communiqué would be published to this effect after the meeting, Austria's independence would be preserved, and there would be no "aggravation of Austro-German relations." Schuschnigg also insisted on a formal invitation, that the meeting would be conducted to an agreed agenda, and that absolute secrecy be maintained. "The worst that can happen," promised Papen, "is that after the meeting we are exactly where we are to-day. The Führer told me so himself."[13]

▪ ▪ ▪

When day broke on February 12 it was a frosty, bitterly cold winter's morning. Schuschnigg and his colleagues exchanged their carriage for a waiting car, and drove the few miles along an empty road to the border at the River Salzach, where he was met by Papen. Schuschnigg found the former ambassador in high spirits, but was immediately put on his guard by his casual announcement that the Berghof was crawling with military top brass. General Wilhelm Keitel, the chief of the newly created OKW; Walter von Reichenau, the military district commander for the Munich region, and "one of the most thoroughly nazified generals";[14] and Hugo Sperrle, the Luftwaffe commander in Bavaria and veteran of the Condor Legion, "who had been demonstrating his capacity for levelling cities in Spain."[15] All had been summoned by Hitler, and Schuschnigg was right to be concerned. Hitler had warned Keitel that there would not be much to do, but he wanted his commanders there "only so that Schuschnigg would see a few uniforms around."[16] During the journey to Berchtesgaden, the Austrian Chancellor witnessed ample evidence of the German military might concentrated near his border. And as they made the final ascent up the icy mountain road to the Berghof, passing through checkpoints and close to military barracks, Schuschnigg was aware of the soldiers' faces pressed inquisitively against the frosty windows. Many of them, he knew, were so-called Austrian Legionnaires, Austrian Nazis who had fled across the border, and were now being trained as a paramilitary strike force for use against Austria.

At eleven o'clock, a "pale, bleary-eyed and unshaven" Schuschnigg arrived at the Berghof.[17] He was greeted in an ostentatiously polite manner by a tense Hitler, wearing a brown storm trooper tunic with swastika armband and black trousers, surrounded, noted Schuschnigg, by his "military chorus." As they made their way to Hitler's upstairs study, where the meeting with Halifax had taken place, Schuschnigg quietly took in his surroundings. The furnishings were "tastefully, not ostentatiously arranged; there were many flowers; on the walls were heads by Lenbach and a particularly beautiful Madonna by Dürer."[18] He began the conversation with typical Austrian courtesy, flattering his host. "This room with its wonderful view has doubtless been the scene of many a decisive conference, Herr Reichskanzler." But Hitler cut him short. "Herr Schuschnigg, we did not gather here to speak of the fine view or of the weather."

Schuschnigg tried a more formal approach, expressing the optimistic hope that the meeting would remove all outstanding differences between the two countries, and assuring Hitler that his sole intention was to "follow a policy friendly towards Germany in accordance with our mutual agreement."[19] At this, Hitler exploded:

> So you call this a friendly policy, Herr Schuschnigg? You have done everything to avoid a friendly policy. Besides, Austria has never done anything that would be of help to Germany. The whole history of Austria is just one uninterrupted act of high treason. I can tell you right now, Herr Schuschnigg, that I am absolutely determined to make an end of all this.[20]

Schuschnigg stood his ground. "For us Austrians," he replied calmly, "our entire history is an essential and inseparable part of German history. Austria's contribution in this respect is considerable."

"Absolutely zero—I am telling you—absolutely zero," screamed back Hitler. "Every national idea was sabotaged by Austria throughout history; and indeed all this sabotage was the chief activity of the Hapsburgs and the Catholic Church."

"All the same, Herr Reichskanzler," countered Schuschnigg, "many an Austrian contribution cannot possibly be separated from the general picture of German culture. Take for instance a man like Beethoven . . ."

"Oh—Beethoven? Let me tell you that Beethoven came from the Lower Rhineland."

"Yet Austria was the country of his choice, as it was for so many others. Nobody would, for instance, refer to Metternich as a German from the Rhineland."

"I am telling you once more," ranted Hitler, "that things cannot go on in this way."

> I have a historic mission, and this mission I will fulfil because Providence has destined me to do so. It is my life. Who is not with me will be crushed. I was predestined to accomplish this task; I have chosen the most difficult road that any German ever took; I have made the greatest achievement in the history of Germany. . . . And not by force, mind you. I am carried along by the love of my people.

After an hour of listening to this, Schuschnigg asked that Hitler enumerate precisely his complaints. "We will do everything," he promised, "to remove obstacles to a better understanding, as far as it is possible."

"That is what you say, Herr Schuschnigg. But I am telling you that I am going to solve the so-called Austrian problem one way or the other. Do you imagine that I don't know that you are fortifying your border against the Reich?" Schuschnigg denied this, but Hitler's threats were becoming more menacing.

> Oh, no? You have made rather ridiculous efforts to mine the bridges and roads leading to the Reich. Listen, you don't really think you can move a single stone in Austria without my hearing the most accurate details about it the next day, do you? I have only to give an order, and in one single night all your ridiculous defence mechanisms will be blown to bits. Who knows? Perhaps you will wake up one morning in Vienna to find us there—just like a spring storm. And then you'll see something. I would very much like to save Austria from such a fate, because such an action would mean blood. After the Army, my S.A. and the Austrian Legion would move in, and nobody can stop their just revenge.

"I am fully aware that you can invade Austria," admitted Schuschnigg. "But Herr Reichskanzler, whether we like it or not, that would mean bloodshed. We are not alone in this world, and such a step would probably mean war."
Hitler remained unimpressed:

> It is easy enough to talk of war while we are sitting here in our comfortable easy-chairs. But war means endless misery for millions. Don't think for one moment that anybody on earth is going to thwart my decisions. Italy? I see eye to eye with Mussolini, the closest ties of friendship bind me to Italy. And England? England will not lift one finger for Austria. Not long ago an English diplomat sat in the very chair you are now sitting in. No, you can't expect any help from England.[21]

They had been alone together for two hours, and Hitler had done most of the talking. He had bullied and shouted, shaken his fist, and pounded the table. He had threatened to "give the order to march into Austria immediately," before bursting into tears as he spoke of "My people—my dear, dear, tortured German people." But Schuschnigg's calm exterior only served to enrage him still further. "Listen to me, I tell you, listen to me! I am the greatest of all Germans—the greatest German who has ever lived, do you hear? I am going to march in—my people call me." At one point Schuschnigg coolly took out his cigarette case, prompting Hitler to scream at him. "I allow no one to smoke in my presence."[22]

Eventually Hitler rang a bell, the doors opened from the outside, and they were led downstairs, past a bust of Bismarck, to the dining room. When Schuschnigg commented on the Madonna by Dürer, Hitler retorted that it was his "favourite picture because it is so thoroughly German." Lunch was taken in the company of Hitler's henchmen, "served by tall, handsome SS men in snow-white steward uniforms."[23] During the meal Schuschnigg could think of little except Hitler's earlier threats, ringing in his ears. He spoke little, and appeared "worried and preoccupied." Hitler, on the other hand, suddenly became "polite and calm." He talked animatedly of his love of cars, and of the autobahns he was building for them; of the skyscrapers he was having designed, which would be the tallest in the world, taller even than those in the United States; and of a massive bridge which was to be built across the mouth of the Elbe to impress visiting Americans. Sperrle recounted some of his experiences of the war in Spain, but conceded privately that he had "no idea why he had been invited."[24] Schuschnigg, all the while, remained "silent, reflective and as a pale as a ghost."[25]

After lunch the Austrians were shown into the great hall, with its huge picture window. They were offered coffee and liqueurs, and were then left to kick their heels for a further two hours. The chain-smoking Schuschnigg, having asked again, was at last allowed to smoke and enjoy a stiff drink. The three generals, together with Hitler's press chief, Otto Dietrich, loitered nervously at the other end of the room. Throughout the morning, while Schuschnigg was being subjected to Hitler's browbeating, Papen and Ribbentrop had been locked away, busily compiling a documentary list of German demands. Papen thought Ribbentrop insufferably pompous, and it was obvious that he understood nothing of Austrian politics. But a list of demands, a typed, two-page draft "agreement," was at last prepared, and Schuschnigg and Schmidt, his Foreign Affairs Adviser, were summarily presented with it. Schuschnigg felt relieved that there was at last something tangible to consider.

His sense of relief quickly evaporated. Hitler's demands represented, to all intents and purposes, an ultimatum that the full machinery of Austrian government should be made over to the local Nazis within a week. The principal demand was that Seyss-Inquart should be appointed Minister of the Interior, responsible for public security, with "full and unlimited control of the police forces in Austria."[26] Another Nazi, Dr. Fischboeck, was also to be appointed to the Cabinet as Minister of Finance, to prepare for "the assimilation of the Austrian into the German economic system." The ban on the Austrian Nazi Party was to be lifted, all Nazi officials who had been relieved of their duties were to be reinstated, and all Nazis in prison were to be granted an amnesty and freed within three days. The German and Austrian armies were to establish closer links, while another Nazi sympathizer, Edmund Glaise-Horstenau, was to become Minister of the Armed Forces.[27] Most dangerous of all, in Schuschnigg's view, was the assertion that "everyone is free to profess the National Socialist creed," and that "National Socialist groups will be permitted to develop legal activities in accordance with Austrian laws."

Ribbentrop explained each paragraph in pedestrian fashion, but insisted that the document had to be accepted as a whole. Schuschnigg, however, recognized clearly that the document as drafted would presage the end of Austrian independence, and he refused to agree to it. He referred to the now worthless agreement he had made with Papen before coming to Berchtesgaden. But it was not long before he began to weaken. Naively, he inquired whether he "could count on the good will of Germany, whether the Reich Government had at least the intention to keep its side of the bargain," and then seemed satisfied with Ribbentrop's reply.[28] Papen disingenuously expressed surprise at the severity of the terms, but assured Schuschnigg that if he signed, "from that time on Germany would remain loyal to this agreement and that there would be no further difficulties for Austria." After securing two minor and obscure changes to the document, Schuschnigg was summoned back into Hitler's presence. The Führer, as always when agitated, was pacing furiously up and down his study. "Herr Schuschnigg," he began. "Here is the draft of the document. There is nothing to be discussed. I will not change one single iota. You will either sign it as it is and fulfil my demands within three days, or I will order the march into Austria."[29]

Schuschnigg capitulated, but although he agreed to sign the document, he warned that his signature was effectively of no value. Under the Austrian constitution only the President had the legal power to ratify such an agreement, and while he would endeavor to persuade the President to accept it, he could give no guarantee.

"You have to guarantee that," raged Hitler.

"I could not possibly, Herr Reichskanzler," replied Schuschnigg calmly.[30]

At this Hitler lost all semblance of self-control, and flew into a furious rage. At last Keitel, who had been waiting around, bored stiff, all day, was given his role to play. "General Keitel! Where is Keitel? Tell him to come here at once!" screamed Hitler.[31] Keitel ran down the corridor "with much clattering of weapons," and rushed into the room just as Schuschnigg was leaving—"fully armed and wearing boots and spurs, he looked like the god of war, Mars in person." Hitler was "snorting with rage, with flashing eyes." Once Schuschnigg was safely out of earshot, Hitler roared with laughter.[32] "There are no orders," he told Keitel. "I just wanted to have you here."[33]

The ploy worked. Terrified, Schmidt noticed an immediate change of mood, and feared imminent arrest. Half an hour later they were ushered back into Hitler's presence. "I have decided to change my mind," he told them, "for the first time in my life. But I warn you this is your very last chance. I have given you three additional days to carry out the agreement."[34] With that a dazed Schuschnigg signed the protocol, engaged in some further small talk with a now calmer Hitler, and declined his host's invitation to stay for dinner. When he requested that the final communiqué make mention of the July 1936 agreement, as promised by Papen, Hitler flatly refused. Austria must first implement the terms of the agreement in full. By now it was 11 P.M., and an exhausted Schuschnigg was driven down the mountain, in almost total silence, accompanied by the duplicitous Papen. It was a gray, foggy winter's night. As they drove toward the border and, beyond it, to Salzburg, Papen tried to break the oppressive silence and to cheer up his Austrian friends. "Well now," he exclaimed. "You have seen what the Führer can be like at times. But the next time I am sure it will be different. You know, the Führer can be absolutely charming."[35]

A stunned Schuschnigg arrived back in Vienna at 3 A.M. "I cannot believe that it really happened," he kept repeating to his friends. "I cannot believe that anyone could have treated me like this."[36] Well aware that he had only three days to confirm Austria's acceptance of Hitler's terms, he set to work that same day to try to convince President Wilhelm Miklas that there was no alternative to the Nazi ultimatum. Miklas was a "plodding, mediocre man of whom the Viennese said that his chief accomplishment in life had been to father a large brood of children." However, he also exhibited "a certain peasant solidity," and after fifty-two years in the service of the state, he was not to be rushed.[37] He was willing to grant an amnesty to those Nazis who were still in prison, but would not agree to the appointment of Seyss-Inquart as Interior Minister. Nevertheless, on February 14 Papen reported to Hitler that Schuschnigg hoped "to overcome the resistance of the President" by the following day.[38]

Hitler, meanwhile, was leaving nothing to chance. Keitel, on his return to Berlin from Berchtesgaden on February 13, immediately summoned Admiral Canaris and Colonel Jodl to see him at the Bendlerstrasse. Goebbels was also present at the meeting. It was the Führer's wish, Keitel told them, that "military pressure by shamming military action should be kept up until the 15th."[39] The plan was to simulate sufficient military activity on Austria's frontier to oblige Miklas to ratify the agreement. While there was to be no actual movement of troops, an elaborate hoax was to be perpetrated on the Austrian government. This was to be achieved by utilizing the Abwehr's network of agents in Austria to "spread false information, appearing perfectly probable, which will cause it to be supposed that military measures have been taken against Austria." Likely rumors would include the cancellation of leave in the 7th Army Corps, the stockpiling of military equipment at vital sites in Augsburg and Munich, and the reinforcement of frontier police on the Austrian border. Major General Wolfgang Muff, the German military attaché in Vienna, was recalled to Berlin; alpine units were said to be undertaking maneuvers in mountainous regions; and there was to be "increased military radio activity in the Bavarian frontier sector, to make it appear that troop concentrations are being built up."[40]

The plan was telephoned through to Hitler for approval, and was endorsed by him at 2:40 A.M. At dawn, Canaris and two of his most senior lieutenants left for Munich to implement the Führer's instructions. "The effect is quick and strong," reported Jodl the following day. "In Austria the impression is created that Germany is undertaking serious military preparations."[41] Jodl was correct. So effective was the simulation that Canaris's senior local officer was concerned that the British might believe that a real invasion was imminent. Miklas duly ratified the agreement on February 15, the last possible day of grace. The following day the amnesty was announced (it caused considerable problems as many of those released were former police officers who now had to be reinstated), and the Cabinet reorganized. Seyss-Inquart disingenuously feigned surprise when informed of his appointment, but was soon on a plane to Berlin to receive his instructions, and to consolidate his position among Austrian Nazis.

Arthur Seyss-Inquart, "the first of the quislings," offered the ideal facade of respectability to the Nazi leadership in Austria. Papen thought him a "conscientious, tolerant and intelligent man whom no one believed capable of precipitating any wild adventure." A Sudeten German by birth, he came from a solid middle- to upper-class background, and had been raised in an atmosphere of only moderate German nationalism. A pleasant-mannered, intelligent young Viennese lawyer, he ran a successful legal practice and had always avoided the worst excesses of his "bomb-throwing" fellow Austrian Nazis. Since 1918 he had been an avowed theoretical supporter of union with Germany, but he appeared modest and reasonable, refused to join the Nazi Party, and spoke consistently of the moral necessity of achieving his aims by peaceful means. His more hard-line Nazi colleagues were suspicious of him, in particular of his successful academic career, his flourishing law practice, and his tolerance of Jews. He was, they thought, "more a Catholic than real Nazi."[42]

In 1936 Seyss had become a State Councilor, since when he had "concentrated his efforts, aided by Papen and other German officials, in burrowing from within."[43] As his political masters in Berlin had predicted, he easily succeeded in winning Schuschnigg's confidence, largely due to the similarities between the two men. Both came from wealthy families, both were intellectuals and lawyers, and both were devout and practicing Catholics. They had both served their country in similar regiments during the First World War, Seyss-Inquart returning with a serious wound which caused him to limp for the rest of his life. Both were moderate pan-Germans, and neither supported the use of violence. As one historian has written of Seyss, he "was not, in fact, a conscious traitor; treachery grew out of his actions but did not inspire them." He believed himself to be an Austrian patriot, "seeking to lead his countrymen, peacefully and voluntarily, into the *Zusammenschluss*, or fusion with Germany."[44] But Schuschnigg's trust in him was still to prove sorely misplaced.

The news that the Austrian Chancellor had been to visit Hitler in his mountaintop lair caused considerable excitement in Vienna. The trip had been planned in such secrecy that neither Nazis nor Nationalists were entirely sure what to make of it. The diplomatic community too was taken by surprise. Although Schuschnigg had warned the French and British ambassadors in advance of his plans (the latter had strongly counseled him against going), there was widespread incredulity as news filtered out of the exact circumstances and conclusions of the meeting. Schuschnigg ordered his official news agency to play down its significance, but it soon became clear that he had suffered a major diplomatic disaster. The British ambassador in Vienna, Michael Palairet, telegraphed to London that Schuschnigg's position had been "seriously weakened,"[45] and that the agreement marked the "first step to complete Nazification." He had been assured by Guido Schmidt, newly appointed as Foreign Minister and in the throes of altering his allegiance, that "Seyss-Inquart was honest in his attachment to Austrian independence and was also a practising Catholic."[46]

In London the political focus remained on the ongoing issue of conversations with Italy, and the buildup to Eden's resignation. There was little enthusiasm for speaking up for Austria. On February 15 Cadogan recorded that there was "a flap about Austria" at the Foreign Office, and then summed up what was the majority view. "Personally, I almost wish Germany would swallow Austria and get it over. She is probably going to do so anyhow. What's all this fuss about?" When Vansittart demanded a formal protest, Cadogan complained: "*What* is the good of brandishing Austria under Hitler's nose when we can't do *anything* about it? As I say, I shouldn't mind if Austria *were* gleichgeschaltet."[47] Harvey reported that even Eden was "determined not to get into the false position of giving the Austrians advice and then being saddled with the responsibility if they accept advice and the situation gets worse." His own conclusion was that "we cannot fight for Austria and we must be careful not to raise false hopes in Vienna." Austria's incorporation into the Reich was now "probably inevitable, and to stop it from outside is impossible and indefensible."[48]

While that may have been the view in political and diplomatic circles, Goebbels recognized that the press were not so forgiving. "The world's press rages," he recorded. "Speaks of rape. Not entirely without justification."[49] The British government was therefore understandably sensitive lest it be accused of having contributed in any way to Austria's predicament, reacting angrily to a report from Palairet suggesting that Hitler had informed Schuschnigg "that Lord Halifax had completely approved of Germany's attitude towards Austria." Palairet had vehemently denied that this was the case, but Schuschnigg complained sorrowfully that "of course England and France would do nothing to save Austria and that Italy could do no more than show displeasure at any German move."[50] The problem was exacerbated by Schuschnigg's misguided attempts to reassure the British and French that all was well, publicly refusing all expressions of concern, and doing his best to dampen down any sense of alarm. Privately, however, he admitted to local diplomats that the Führer had treated him appallingly. "Never," he told the French Minister, Gabriel Puaux, "has a head of government been treated by a foreign leader as I was treated by Hitler. Is this a madman who thinks he is a God?"[51]

Mussolini, meanwhile, had already advised Schuschnigg to yield to Hitler's demands, describing the protocol signed at Berchtesgaden "as a logical and inevitable development in the relations between two German countries."[52] The French government, on the other hand, invited Britain to join with them in issuing a strongly worded joint démarche in Berlin, but Eden poured cold water on the idea, even when an appeal was received from Schuschnigg that "it would be of the greatest help to him if you could speak firmly in Berlin of His Majesty's Government's interest in seeing Austria's independence preserved."[53] For Henderson, it was bad enough that he was asked to raise the subject at all. "I deprecate too definite a line here as regards Austria," he wrote privately to Halifax. "With the best will in the world, we cannot help Austria and even the pretension to do so is far from being 100% justifiable."[54]

▪ ▪ ▪

The province of Styria, in southeast Austria, was the most overtly pro-Nazi region in the country. Resentment at the loss of territory to the new state of Yugoslavia after the First World War had fueled local radicalism, and had "turned the region into a hotbed of Austrian Nazism."[55] It was estimated that 80 percent of the population of the provincial capital, Graz, was sympathetic to National Socialism, while the majority of local officials, civil servants and both lecturers and students at the university were thoroughly Nazified. By early 1938 the local Nazis were well organized and brimming with confidence, and news of the Berchtesgaden agreement served only to reinforce their growing sense of power. Life-size pictures of Hitler appeared in shop windows, the police increasingly ignored the growing number of Nazi parades, and the ban on wearing the swastika in public was openly flouted. On the evening of February 19, huge pro-Nazi demonstrations in Graz forced the temporary closure of the university.

The following evening Hitler made his long-awaited speech to the Reichstag. It had already been postponed once as a result of the Blomberg and Fritsch affairs, and now he made up for lost time, speaking for over three hours. It was the first occasion on which one of his speeches had been broadcast in its entirety over Austrian radio, and his favorite British journalist, George Ward Price of the *Daily Mail,* was present to ensure that his readers back home would be able to sample the atmosphere.

> Informal and intimate was the setting inside the Kroll Theatre for the German Chancellor's speech. The dominant feature of the crimson-carpeted and walled building, the great golden reproduction of the Eagle and Swastika that make up the symbol of Nazi sovereignty was mounted on an illuminated background. It was a test of Herr Hitler's oratorical powers that for a whole hour he continued to reel off tables of figures of German production without losing the attention of his audience. There was an infectious enthusiasm in the triumphant tone. He had the air of being in excellent health, and his face looked fresh and clear.[56]

While the Führer may well have been in the rudest of health, the content of his speech was far from friendly.

> Over ten million Germans live in two of the States adjoining our frontiers. This in itself is sufficiently distressing. It is intolerable for a self-respecting World Power to know that across the frontier are kinsmen who have to suffer severe persecution simply because of their sympathy, their feeling of union with Germany. To the interests of the German Reich belongs also the protection of those fellow-Germans who live beyond our frontiers and

are unable to ensure for themselves the right to a general freedom, personal, political, and ideological.[57]

The sole concession he had made to Schuschnigg at Berchtesgaden, a promise that he would include a passage respecting the independence of Austria, was ignored.

The effect was immediate, his thinly veiled threat only serving to encourage further the already confident Austrian Nazis. Four days later, on the evening of February 24, Schuschnigg replied with a defiant speech of his own to the Austrian Bundestag. Demanding an end to further concessions to Germany—"we must call a halt and say: Thus far and no further"—he made an emotional appeal to Austrian patriotism in support of independence.[58]

> Austria can live and will live. It will never voluntarily give up its national existence. Our watchword remains "True German and red-white-red until we're dead."[59]

In the main square in Graz 20,000 Nazis gathered to listen to Schuschnigg over a public address system, and reacted by tearing down the loudspeakers and demanding that the pro-Nazi mayor hoist the swastika over the city hall. The following day every student at the university was wearing a swastika armband, the illegal "Heil Hitler" greeting was being widely used, and old Nazi marching songs were being sung in the streets. While Schuschnigg's defiance had briefly raised the morale of his supporters, it had also exacerbated the existing tensions within Austria, and inevitably served only to irritate Hitler still further.

On March 3 Henderson visited the Reich Chancellery for a long-awaited interview with Hitler. At the end of January, as the crisis over Eden's impending resignation was reaching its climax, he had been recalled to London for discussions that were intended to follow up Halifax's visit to Berchtesgaden. On January 24 Chamberlain announced his plans to make colonial concessions to Germany to the Cabinet's Foreign Policy Committee, describing them as "the opening of an entirely new chapter in the history of African colonial development."[60] It did not seem to worry either Chamberlain or Henderson that the majority of the territories with which he proposed to appease Hitler did not even belong to Britain. Henderson was instructed to emphasize that all outstanding differences between the two countries would be open for discussion. The Blomberg and Fritsch affairs, and Schuschnigg's visit to Berchtesgaden, had delayed the meeting for some weeks, and by the time Henderson was finally summoned to see Hitler, Eden had resigned as Foreign Secretary, and been replaced by Lord Halifax, to Henderson's obvious delight. "Since I regard an understanding with Germany as indispensable if we are not slowly or even rapidly to drift into war again," he wrote to Halifax, "I cannot regard either Eden's resignation or your own appointment with anything but the utmost relief."[61]

However, when the meeting did finally take place, the moment was, by Henderson's own admission, "an ill-chosen one," and the Führer "was consequently in a vile temper, and made no effort to conceal it." Henderson began by refuting accusations in the German press that he had come to propose a bargain—a "*Kuh-handel,*" or cow-deal as it was described. Hitler "remained crouching in his armchair with the most ferocious scowl on his face," and when Henderson had finished he "let himself go." For an hour Hitler harangued the hapless ambassador on a whole range of his favorite gripes: his unsympathetic portrayal by the British press, unwarranted interference in central Europe, the meddling of British bishops in German church affairs, and Members of Parliament in Germany's political affairs, and the iniquities of Bolshevism. He appeared utterly disinterested in the issue of colonies, but made clear his views on Austria, and the "sad fate of Nazi-loving Germans there." Only 15 percent of the population supported Schuschnigg, he claimed, and if Britain opposed a just settlement, Germany would have to fight. He would, he promised, "intervene like lightning [*blitzschnell*]."[62]

According to the German transcript of the meeting, which was forwarded on to Henderson the following day, the ambassador was reported as having disowned the protests of his counterpart in Vienna following Schuschnigg's browbeating in Berchtesgaden, and had "declared that he, Sir Nevile Henderson, had himself often advocated the *Anschluss.*"[63] Although Henderson replied by return, stressing that he had said no such thing, he did admit to having "sometimes expressed personal views which may not have been entirely in accordance with those of my Government."[64] But the damage had been done. The combination of Halifax's remarks the previous year, the replacement of Eden by Halifax as Foreign Secretary, and now Henderson's lukewarm condemnation of German policy in Austria, all led Hitler to believe that he would face no significant opposition from London. His avowed aim remained, however, that "the just interests of the German Austrians should be secured and an end made to oppression by a process of peaceful evolution."[65]

Schuschnigg's dramatic announcement on the evening of March 9 changed everything. Sensing that the pro-Nazi mood in Graz was increasingly infecting the rest of the country, he decided that "the moment for a clear decision had come."[66] Addressing a large crowd in Innsbruck he declared that in just four days' time, on Sunday, March 13, he would hold a national plebiscite on the future of Austrian independence. The Nazis had long advocated such a referendum themselves, confident that a straightforward question on union with Germany would prove successful. Indeed, Hitler had most recently advocated a plebiscite during his meeting with Henderson, albeit one in which he would decide on the question to be asked. But Schuschnigg had foreseen such a move, and announced that he would ask the Austrian people to support "a free and German, independent and social, Christian and united Austria; for freedom and work, and for the equality of all who declare for race and fatherland." Rejection of such a proposal would be the equivalent, as one (American) historian later wrote, of asking an American to reject "the Stars and Stripes, apple pie, and motherhood."[67]

In an effort to leave nothing to chance, Schuschnigg also took a leaf out of the Nazis' own electoral handbook. The brief interval before the plebiscite was due to take place would ensure that the startled Nazis had little time to prepare, especially in the mountainous provinces where they would be electorally strong. The electoral register was not up-to-date, the most recent elections having been held in 1930; the minimum voting age was set at twenty-four, thus excluding large numbers of young Nazis; and only "yes" ballot papers, with the Austrian red-white-red stripes on both sides, were to be issued—if you wanted to vote "no," you had to bring your own ballot paper. Although Seyss-Inquart was able to persuade Schuschnigg to modify some of these regulations, the Austrian Nazis still believed that the plebiscite would be rigged. Schuschnigg also asked Mussolini to support the plebiscite, but received the curt reply "*C'è un errore!* [It's a mistake!]."[68] Mussolini warned the Austrian military attaché in Rome that Schuschnigg "should have played for time and not precipitated things. Tell the Chancellor," he continued, "that he is handling a bomb which may explode in his hands." Schuschnigg replied that it was too late to abandon his plans. "Then tell him," replied the Duce, that "Austria is no longer any concern of mine."[69]

In Berlin the news was greeted initially by a stunned silence. Hitler's first reaction was incredulity, one that soon gave way to fury. In the words of one distinguished historian, he "responded as though someone had trodden on a painful corn. He had received no warning, and had made no preparations. It was clear to him that the 'evolutionary solution' was dead. He must either act or be humiliated."[70] His immediate actions were largely improvised, and made at breakneck speed. That evening he summoned Göring and Goebbels to the Chancellery, and vented his rage at Schuschnigg's "extremely dirty trick . . . to dupe [the Reich through] a stupid and idiotic plebiscite." But they could not agree on a suitable response, and discussed a range of alternative options, including Nazi abstention from the plebiscite, and a nationwide leaflet drop over Austria. Later that night, Goebbels was called back for a further meeting, and found the leading Austrian Nazi, Glaise-Horstenau, also present. "The Führer drastically outlines for him his plans," recorded Goebbels, who stayed with Hitler until 5 A.M. Hitler was now "in full swing," and showing "a wonderful fighting mood. He believes the hour has arrived."[71]

The following morning, March 10, the Reich Chancellery was a hive of activity. Jodl noted that the "Führer is determined not to tolerate it." General von Reichenau was summoned back from Cairo where he was representing Germany at a meeting of the International Olympic Committee, while General Milch of the Luftwaffe was hurriedly recalled from a holiday in Switzerland. Göring, meanwhile, was due to preside over the opening day of the military tribunal hearing the Fritsch case, which, as we have seen, he immediately adjourned, before making his way to the Chancellery. The Wehrmacht too was taken by surprise. When Keitel was summoned to see Hitler at 10 A.M., as he correctly guessed to be told to prepare for the immediate invasion of Austria, he took the precaution of first conferring with Jodl and General Max von Viebahn, the Chief of the Military Operations Staff at the OKW. Fortunately for Keitel, the resourceful Jodl remembered Case Otto, originally intended as no more than a backup plan in the event of an attempt to restore Otto of Habsburg to the Austrian throne, but now the only available strategy for military action against Austria. "Prepare Case Otto" ordered Hitler.[72]

Of all those caught unaware by the rapid pace of events, Hitler's new Foreign Minister, Joachim von Ribbentrop, was perhaps the most unfortunate. He had chosen that week to return to London to say his formal farewells as ambassador, and now found himself stranded there while the greatest event of his diplomatic career so far was unfolding in Berlin. As news filtered through to him, he rang his Private Secretary at the Wilhelmstrasse, Reinhard Spitzy, and ordered him to find out what was going on at the Chancellery. Spitzy was at first told "to mind his own business and that Ribbentrop's views were of no interest," but no sooner had he returned to his office than he was summoned back to see Hitler in person. "I want you to fly to London immediately and deliver this letter to Herr von Ribbentrop," began Hitler. "He is to answer it at once in writing. You are to return immediately with his reply. There is no time to lose. An aeroplane is standing by. It's Fritsch's old machine." When Spitzy inquired politely what the message was about, Hitler exploded. "This fellow Schuschnigg is trying to deceive me . . . we have just heard that he intends to spring on us a plebiscite on the question of Austrian independence. What is more, he is employing all manner of dirty tricks to make sure the result goes his way. Such behaviour is unheard of, and I refuse to tolerate it."[73]

Spitzy arrived in London early the following morning to be met by a pack of journalists at the airport. Ribbentrop, meanwhile, was due to hold his final meeting with Halifax at 11 A.M. The new Foreign Secretary had already assured the Cabinet that he would demonstrate "a mixture of disappointment, reproach and warning," during the conversation. "Once war should start in Central Europe, it was impossible to say where it might not end or who might not get involved."[74] Ribbentrop was greeted at the Foreign Office by a noisy, hostile crowd chanting "Ribbentrop get out," and he asked Halifax to do what he could to get the Austrian plebiscite canceled. Privately, Halifax thought Schuschnigg's behavior "foolish and provocative,"[75] but Palairet had telegraphed from Vienna that he thought the plebiscite a "risk worth taking,"[76] and Halifax therefore insisted to Ribbentrop that it should be allowed to proceed, "free and undisturbed."[77] Ribbentrop, thought Cadogan, was "quite hopeless and wooden and useless.

H[alifax] read him a lecture—or sermon—not too frightfully well, I didn't think."[78] It is possible that Halifax was already in possession of SIS intelligence material warning that an invasion of Austria was likely. The previous night, before returning to Berlin from Cairo, Reichenau had first telephoned the local German minister to inform him that the Anschluss was imminent. The call had been intercepted, and the details sent through to the Foreign Office.[79]

Back at OKW headquarters in the Bendlerstrasse, Brauchitsch was away on official business, but Keitel contrived to apportion responsibility for the military preparations more evenly by sharing his concerns with Beck.

"The Führer requires you to report to him immediately on the dispositions made for the Wehrmacht to enter Austria," he ordered Beck.

"But we have prepared nothing," replied Beck despairingly. "Nothing has been done, nothing at all."

"What about Plan Otto of June 1937?"

"That was a contingency plan for preventing a Habsburg restoration. It's not the same thing." Beck nevertheless took what plans they had over to the Chancellery.

In spite of Beck's concerns at the battle-readiness of a number of armored divisions, Hitler was adamant that his orders be carried out. "Am I or am I not the Supreme Commander of the Wehrmacht?" he shouted. "At a time when I need to act like lightning you tell me that nothing is ready, and that all must be improvised at the last moment. Do what you like but our troops must be in Vienna on 12 March!"[80]

For the next five hours, the senior generals at the Bendlerstrasse drafted the necessary orders. There was little time available. It was already Thursday, and the troops needed to be ready to march by Saturday at the latest. The 7th Army Corps—based at Munich—and the 13th Army Corps—at Nuremberg— were both mobilized immediately on the Austrian border, together with the 2nd Panzer Division. All invading troops were placed under the command of General Fedor von Bock of the 8th Army, stationed at Dresden. At 4 P.M. Beck summoned General Heinz Guderian, the newly appointed commander of the motorized 16th Army Corps, and told him that "if the Anschluss is to be carried out, this is probably the best moment to do it." Guderian was to mobilize the 16th Army Corps, and to alert and assemble the 2nd Panzer Division, in readiness for the push into Austria.[81] The Luftwaffe too was placed on full alert at airfields throughout Bavaria under Sperrle's command. Their role would be "to show and drop propaganda material [and] occupy Austrian airfields," and later to "support the ground forces if required and hold other bomber units ready for special tasks."[82] At midnight Goebbels went again to see Hitler. "The die is cast," he recorded. "On Saturday march in. Push straight to Vienna. Big aeroplane action. The Führer is going himself to Austria." Goebbels then returned to his own ministry, where he worked on propaganda arrangements through the night. "Again a great time," he noted. "With a great historical task. It's wonderful."[83]

At 2 A.M. on the morning of March 11, Hitler issued "Directive Number One" for Case Otto. In his rush to occupy Austria, however, he forgot to sign it until almost twelve hours later.

TOP SECRET

1. If other measures prove unsuccessful, I intend to invade Austria with armed forces to establish constitutional conditions and to prevent further outrages against the pro-German population.
2. The whole operation will be directed by myself.
3. The forces of the Army and Air Force detailed for this operation must be ready for invasion on March 12, 1938, at the latest by 12:00 hours.
4. The behaviour of the troops must give the impression that we do not want to wage war against our Austrian brothers. Therefore any provocation is to be avoided. If, however, resistance is offered it must be broken ruthlessly by force of arms.[84]

In Vienna, Schuschnigg had gone to bed that night still confident that his gamble in calling a plebiscite had paid off. But at 5:30 A.M. he was brusquely shaken from his sleep by the loud ringing of the telephone beside his bed. It was his Chief of Police, Dr. Skubl, one of the few senior police officials who had kept their jobs after Seyss-Inquart's appointment as Minister of Security. The news was bad. The German border at Salzburg had been closed an hour earlier, all German customs officials had been withdrawn, and rail traffic between Germany and Austria had been halted. It was a gray, drizzling morning, and by 6:15 A.M. Schuschnigg was on his way to his office, only stopping briefly en route at St. Stephen's Cathedral. There, as dawn broke and early mass was read, the Chancellor of Austria sat restlessly in a pew, contemplating the meaning of Skubl's message, before furtively making the sign of the cross. At the Chancellery in the Ballhausplatz everything was still quiet. He rang police headquarters and issued orders that a precautionary police cordon be placed around the inner city and government buildings. His consul-general in Munich telephoned to warn that the German divisions stationed in the city had been mobilized. When Schuschnigg summoned his Cabinet colleagues to an emergency meeting, only Seyss-Inquart could not be found.

The previous evening Papen had received an urgent summons to return to Berlin, and had left Vienna in a private plane at six that morning. Seyss-Inquart had accompanied him to the airport, where he then waited for a further flight to arrive from Berlin carrying his fellow minister, Glaise-Horstenau, who brought with him instructions from the Führer. At 9:30 A.M. the two of them arrived at the Chancellery.

After a perfunctory apology for being late, Seyss-Inquart bluntly informed Schuschnigg of Hitler's anger. "The Reich is in great excitement about the plebiscite," he warned. "Hitler is said to be beside himself. Everybody is furious."

Schuschnigg defended himself, pointing out that it was entirely in accordance with the agreement reached at Berchtesgaden.

"No, no you cannot say that," interrupted Glaise-Horstenau. "This plebiscite is really the limit. It was bound to annoy the Führer. One should never have started it."

Seyss, meanwhile, had orders from Göring himself. "The plebiscite has to be postponed within the hour," he commanded.[85]

Hitler had one further demand: Schuschnigg was to resign in favor of Seyss-Inquart.

When Papen arrived at the Reich Chancellery at 9 A.M. he found chaotic scenes and a palpable tension in the air. It was extremely rare for Hitler to make a public appearance before 10 A.M., yet the main reception room outside his study was already heaving with a curious assortment of ministers and hangers-on, "everyone who by reason of duty, curiosity, employment or intrigue, had any connection with the subject discussed." In Ribbentrop's absence in London, Hitler had recalled Neurath to act in an advisory capacity, principally to calm the foreign diplomatic corps when news of the invasion became known. Goebbels, after a sleepless night, was much in evidence "with his cohorts from the Propaganda Ministry," Himmler was strutting around "surrounded by a dozen giant S.S. officers," while Brauchitsch and Keitel were decked out in full military uniform. Hitler himself "was in a state bordering on hysteria." He had clearly still not made up his mind as to what he should do next.[86]

At about the same time Spitzy returned from London. Having left Croydon late the previous night, he arrived at Tempelhof Aerodrome at 8 A.M., and was rushed to the Chancellery in a motorcade, clutching Ribbentrop's lengthy letter of reply. Hitler, though angry at the delay, was delighted with his Foreign Minister's answer.

> What now will England do if the Austrian question cannot be settled peacefully? Basically, I am convinced that England of her own accord will do nothing in regard to it at present, but that she would exert a moderating influence upon the other powers.[87]

"It's exactly as I thought," exclaimed Hitler. "We needn't fear any complications from over there. Tomorrow we shall deal with Austria!" He "rubbed his hands together, slapped himself on the thigh and dismissed [Spitzy] in the best of spirits."[88] A few hundred yards away, at the British embassy, Henderson too was absorbing the contents of a message, one he had received early that morning from his consul-general in Munich: a large concentration of troops and police was moving eastward through the city toward the Austrian border.

Henderson immediately ordered the embassy's military attaché, Colonel Frank Mason-MacFarlane, to call on the Director of Military Intelligence at the OKW, General von Tippelskirch, and to confront him with this news. The general was apparently unavailable, but a senior staff officer assured Mason-MacFarlane that the information was quite incorrect, and that no unusual troop movements were scheduled to take place that day. The military attaché, however, refused to believe such an unconvincing assurance, and instead set out to make his own reconnaissance of the Austrian border. Hardly had he left the outskirts of Berlin than his car became embroiled in a column of over 3,000 armed police and SS troops "moving towards Austria in buses, bakers' vans, pantechnicons and a mass of other miscellaneous vehicles."[89] In the meantime his assistant military attaché was called to OKW headquarters, where a visibly embarrassed junior officer admitted that Mason-MacFarlane had been misled earlier in the day. He offered profuse apologies, and disclosed that "the political situation had made it necessary to stage a strong demonstration on the Austrian frontier." The purpose was twofold: to prevent "disorders of Marxist origin from spreading to Germany [and] to protect the genuine Germans against the above Marxist elements."[90] In conveying this information to the Foreign Office, Henderson could not resist the opportunity for a jibe of his own. Although he could not "judge the motives which have inspired him," Schuschnigg's decision to call the plebiscite seemed "precipitous and unwise."[91]

Ribbentrop, meanwhile, was still kicking his heels in London. Having sent Spitzy back to Berlin with his letter for the Führer, he held a huge farewell reception, inviting everyone he had ever met in London, at the newly redecorated German embassy in Carlton House Gardens, overlooking the Mall.[92] The following morning, as preparations for the invasion of Austria were reaching a climax in Berlin, he hosted a small breakfast party for a number of his most intimate British friends, including the MP Nancy Astor, and the Minister for Coordination of Defence, Sir Thomas Inskip, "whom Ribbentrop regarded as the most pro-German of the British ministers."[93] According to Ribbentrop, Inskip assured him "that if Germany would be patient, the Austrian question could certainly be solved sooner or later in the German sense. He could definitely state that the British Cabinet would not decide in favor of military intervention by England, if the Austrian question was solved in the German sense. However, it would be a different matter if Germany settled this question by force, or—to put it more clearly—if she solved it by military means. A large-scale conflict might result, in which England could become involved."[94]

It was customary for senior departing ambassadors to present their letter of recall to the King, and afterward to be entertained to lunch at Buckingham Palace. In Ribbentrop's case, however, the King discreetly requested that he might be excused such an ordeal, on the grounds that the ambassador had "been conspicuously unhelpful" during his time in London.[95] Instead Ribbentrop paid a brief visit to the palace, during which he denied all knowledge of the unfolding events in Austria. "I replied," the King later recounted, "that I understood he was Foreign Minister of Germany. I thought after that it was wise not to press the matter further."[96]

Ribbentrop and his wife then made their way to Downing Street for lunch with the Chamberlains; the other guests included Churchill, Cadogan, Inskip, Halifax and Simon, all with their wives. Lunch was "a grim affair"[97] and, as it drew to a close, a messenger arrived from the Foreign Office with two telegrams for Cadogan. After first reading them himself, Cadogan passed them to Halifax, and in turn to Chamberlain. Churchill noticed the Prime Minister's "evident preoccupation," and, at a signal from her husband, Mrs. Chamberlain invited her guests through to the drawing room for coffee. It was obvious to everyone that it was time to leave, but the Ribbentrops "did not seem at all conscious of this atmosphere," and, as a result, "a general kind of restlessness pervaded the company, and everyone stood about ready to say good-bye."[98]

Eventually Frau Ribbentrop was persuaded to leave for home on her own, while Chamberlain, accompanied by Halifax and Cadogan, took her husband down to the Prime Minister's study. The telegrams were read out loud: one from Henderson, containing news of German troop movements on the Austrian border; the other from Palairet in Vienna, giving details of the ultimatum handed to Schuschnigg, who now asked for advice from the British government. Halifax then "talked to Ribbentrop most gravely and seriously begging him before it was too late to ask his chief to hold his hand."[99] But Ribbentrop claimed to know nothing of troop movements or an ultimatum, and expressed strong doubts about the accuracy of the reports, merely repeating now familiar complaints about Schuschnigg's "breach of faith" in calling the "fraudulent" plebiscite. The discussion, reported Ribbentrop, "took place in a tense atmosphere and the usually calm Lord Halifax was more excited than Chamberlain, who outwardly at least appeared calm and cool-headed."[100] Later that afternoon Halifax visited the German embassy for a prearranged farewell meeting over afternoon tea, and gave Ribbentrop an even "more serious talking to," again with little effect.[101]

In his memoirs, written while on trial for his life at Nuremberg, Ribbentrop attempted to apportion blame on Halifax for failing to prevent the Anschluss. Halifax had assured him that "the British people would never consent to go to war because two German countries wanted to merge," and he claimed that at their meeting on March 10 Halifax had "accepted the situation calmly and with composure."[102] In fact the Foreign Office record of the meeting states that while Ribbentrop stubbornly disclaimed all knowledge of the events taking place in Vienna, Halifax objected strongly to the "exhibition of naked force."[103] Halifax's biographer maintains that "meaningful negotiations with Germany were hampered by the terminal denseness of Ribbentrop,"[104] a view echoed by Chamberlain. "In talking to Ribbentrop I am always overcome by a feeling of helplessness," he complained to his sister, of the lunch at Downing Street. "He is so stupid, so shallow, so self-centred and self-satisfied, so totally devoid of intellectual capacity that he never seems to take in what is said to him."[105] In truth, once he was back in London, Ribbentrop was never in a position to influence events in Berlin—indeed he was deliberately excluded from the decision-making process. Spitzy refused to pass on any information, on the pretext that the telephone line was almost certainly being tapped, while Göring insisted that he stay in London, supposedly to "monitor British reactions." Hitler too was perfectly happy to have the calmer Neurath temporarily back in charge at the Foreign Ministry. However loudly Ribbentrop screamed at Spitzy down the telephone, as events unfolded in Berlin and Vienna, the German Foreign Minister was forced to follow proceedings on the BBC.

Göring's long-held ambition to incorporate Austria into the Reich was widely known. When the Duke and Duchess of Windsor had visited Karinhall the previous year, the Duke observed that above the fireplace in the library was a map of Germany colored green, showing Austria fully incorporated into the Reich. Göring was delighted when the Duke raised the subject. "I've just had it made—a fine example of new German cartography," he chuckled. When the Duke commented further that German cartographers seemed to have "novel, and I might add, expansive ideas," Göring could scarcely control himself. "Ho, ho," he cried, "you refer, Sir, to the incorporation of Austria into Germany. Well, I needed a new map, and since Austria will soon join Germany—voluntarily, of course—it seemed more economical to anticipate the event."[106] Guido Schmidt had been shown the same map when he visited Karinhall during the Hunting Exhibition—"good huntsmen knew no frontiers, Göring told him with a grin."[107] And when Mussolini had studied it, and shown no adverse reaction, Göring had taken it as sign that Italy would not oppose an Anschluss.

Now, on the afternoon of March 11 in the Reich Chancellery, it was indeed Göring who seized the initiative, and "grasped with both hands the lead vacated by the vacillating Hitler."[108] Schuschnigg had been assured by his chief of police that the streets of Vienna were still under government control, but had also been warned that the police, now infiltrated by Nazis released under the amnesty agreed at Berchtesgaden, could no longer be relied upon. In the meantime news filtered in from Graz that Nazi loud-speaker vans were already touring the streets announcing the cancellation of the plebiscite and Schuschnigg's resignation. Desperate to avoid loss of life, Schuschnigg decided to postpone the plebiscite, and summoned Seyss-Inquart and Glaise-Horstenau to tell them so. At 2:45 P.M. Göring placed the first of a series of telephone calls to Vienna, and was informed by Seyss that Schuschnigg had agreed to call off the plebiscite, but was refusing to resign as Chancellor.

Göring now realized, as he later testified at Nuremberg, that "finally, that possibility which we had long and ardently awaited was there—the possibility of bringing about a complete solution." From that moment on, he claimed, "I must take 100 percent responsibility for all further happenings because it was not the Führer so much as I, myself, who set the pace and, even overruling the Führer's misgivings, brought everything to its final development."[109] He replied to Seyss that the cancellation of the plebiscite would not be enough and, having conferred with Hitler, he called back twenty minutes later to emphasize the point. Schuschnigg must resign, and Seyss must be appointed as Chancellor. If he did not hear back within the hour, he would assume that Seyss had been prevented from telephoning. "If these conditions are not fulfilled," Schuschnigg was to be told, "the German armies will move on Austria."[110] Seyss went quiet, and was so shocked that he "turned pale."[111]

Seyss-Inquart and his fellow Austrian Nazis feared a German invasion almost as much as Schuschnigg, and were still hoping for *Gleichschaltung*— the "coordination" of Austria, rather than full Anschluss—to forestall the arrival of German troops. Hitler's special agent for Austria, Wilhelm Keppler, had by now arrived from Berlin, bringing with him the draft of a telegram which Seyss was ordered to send to Hitler. It requested the prompt dispatch of German troops to Austria to put down widespread disorder. Seyss, how-ever, refused to send it, pointing out that there were no such problems. Indeed, the only signs of disorder were among the Nazis themselves. Since early morning Austrian SA and SS units had been gathering in towns throughout the country. In Graz there were violent clashes, and by late afternoon the SA and SS were marching in Graz, Salzburg and Innsbruck, and they soon began to occupy municipal and provincial government buildings. At 3:30 P.M. Schuschnigg finally resigned. He had first put in a call to Mussolini, but later canceled it, knowing that it would be a "waste of time." Sure enough, a message arrived from Rome that the "Italian Government declares that it could give no advice under these circumstances in case such advice were asked for."

The Austrian Nazi leadership, including Keppler, Seyss and Glaise-Horstenau, now established themselves in a makeshift office in the Chancellery, the very heart of the Austrian government. Schuschnigg was powerless to stop them, remarking only that the Chancellery "looked like a disturbed bee-hive," with Seyss-Inquart and Glaise-Horstenau holding "court in one corner," surrounded by a group of "strange-looking men, with close-cropped hair, some of them completely shorn, and most of them with heavy sabre-scars across their faces."[112] Everyone, however, had failed to take into account the brave stubbornness of the Austrian President Miklas. He accepted Schuschnigg's resignation, but adamantly refused to appoint Seyss in his place. In Berlin the tension initially eased when it was wrongly announced that Seyss had been made Chancellor. "Tell Brauchitsch immediately that the orders for the troops to march have been cancelled," Hitler told Keitel. Brauchitsch breathed a sigh of relief at the news. "Thank God we have been spared that," he told Papen.[113]

Göring, however, was clearly enjoying himself. Hitler's Luftwaffe adjutant, the aristocratic Captain Nicolaus von Below, described him as being "in his element," the complete "master of the situation."[114] But at 5:26 P.M. Seyss himself came on the line again to contradict the earlier rumor. He had not been made Chancellor, and there was no sign of Miklas agreeing to the appointment. Göring again exploded. "Go immediately to the President," he ordered Seyss, "and inform him that if he does not accept our demands then and there, then the troops which are already stationed all along the borders will march, and Austria will have ceased to exist. Tell him also that we are not joking."[115] But still the resolute Miklas held out. At 6 P.M. Vienna radio announced that the plebiscite had been postponed, and that the entire Cabinet had resigned, but there was no mention of new appointments. At 6:28 P.M. Göring was back on the phone to Keppler and Seyss-Inquart. When they told him that Miklas still refused to concede, he ordered them to give the President a second ultimatum, warning that he would "give marching orders to the troops within five minutes."[116] "I informed the two gentlemen," Miklas later testified, "that I refused the ultimatum . . . and that Austria alone determines who is to be the head of government."[117]

Dusk was falling, and Schuschnigg made one last tour of the Chancellery. The corridors were crowded with young Nazis, a look of contempt in their eyes, while outside he could hear the demonstrations, the Nazi songs, and the tramp of marching feet. He made one last effort to persuade Miklas to appoint Seyss, but the old President remained adamant. "He would not appoint a Nazi as Austrian Chancellor" and complained bitterly: "You all desert me now, all of you."[118] A radio microphone was hastily set up in the room where, four years earlier, the former Chancellor Dollfuss had been assassinated. At 7:47 P.M. Schuschnigg made his farewell address to the nation. He revealed that he had been compelled to resign by the German ultimatum, and refuted as false the reports emanating from Germany of "disorders by the workers, the shedding of streams of blood and the creation of a situation beyond the control of the Austrian Government."[119] Such reports, he declared, "were invented from A to Z."[120] "We yield to force," he told the Austrian people. "As we have no desire, even at this grave hour, to shed German blood, we have ordered our army to withdraw without resistance. . . . I thus take leave of the Austrian people, saying from the depths of my heart—God protect Austria!"[121]

It was now the turn of the German military attaché in Vienna, General Wolfgang Muff, to be the bearer of bad news. Miklas still refused to yield. "It was very dramatic," Muff told Göring. "I spoke to him for almost fifteen minutes. He declared that under no circumstances will he yield to force."

"So? He will not give in to force?" inquired Göring incredulously.

"He does not yield to force," confirmed Muff.

"So he just wants to be kicked out?"

"Yes," said Muff. "He is staying put."

For the first time all evening Göring laughed. "Well, with fourteen children a man has to stay put. Anyway, tell Seyss to take over."[122]

When Keppler called Berlin again an hour later, he confirmed not only that Miklas was remaining steadfast in his refusal to resign, but that Seyss-Inquart was now refusing to send the telegram requesting German military assistance. Göring replied that the telegram did not need to be actually sent, but that Seyss needed only to say that he agreed with its contents. In fact, Keppler sent it himself half an hour later, but by then it was immaterial anyway. A mere *Gleichschaltung* was no longer going to be enough to satisfy Göring, and at 8:45 P.M., after a considerable amount of cajoling, he finally persuaded Hitler to give the order to march.

> Secret—High Command of the Wehrmacht.
>
> Subject: Operation Otto.
>
> 1. The demands made on the Austrian government in the German ultimatum have not been met.
>
> 2. The Austrian armed forces have been ordered to withdraw before the advance of German troops and to avoid fighting. The Austrian government has ceased to operate.
>
> 3. To avoid further bloodshed in Austrian cities the German Wehrmacht will commence movement into Austria at first light on 12 March in accordance with Directive No. 1. I expect every effort to be made to reach the assigned objectives as quickly as possible.
>
> Adolf Hitler.[123]

Later that evening Hitler received the call for which he had been nervously waiting all day. From the moment he had decided on invasion, he had been worried about the reaction of Austria's former protector, Mussolini. On March 10 he sent his personal envoy, Prince Philip of Hesse, the son-in-law of the Italian king, by private plane to Rome with a personal message for the Duce, explaining the action he was poised to take, and asking for the understanding and sympathy of his fellow dictator.

> In my responsibility as Führer and Chancellor of the German Reich and likewise a son of this soil, I can no longer remain passive in the face of these developments. I am now determined to restore law and order in my homeland.

He assured Mussolini that the "definite boundary" between Germany and Italy would continue to be "the Brenner."[124] At 10:25 P.M. came the long-awaited reply, in a telephone call from Prince Philip in Rome. Throughout the afternoon and evening, the power supply in the Reich Chancellery had struggled to maintain the telephone connection between Berlin and Vienna.

Now Hitler and the "corpulent" Göring, in a thoroughly undignified manner, were forced to squeeze their way into the switchboard operator's booth to take the call.

Hitler grabbed the receiver. He was "standing with one foot on the sofa, and excitedly twisting the curtain cord, [and] pulled it so hard that the entire curtain came away and fell onto the sofa."[125] He heaved a sigh of relief at Prince Philip's news.

> I have just come back from the Palazzo Venezia. The Duce accepted the whole thing in a very friendly manner. He sends you his regards. . . . Schuschnigg gave him the news. . . . Mussolini said that Austria would be immaterial to him.
>
> Then please tell Mussolini I will never forget him for this!
> Yes, Sir.
> Never, never, never, no matter what happens! I shall be ready to go with him through thick and thin—through anything!
> Yes, my Führer.
> You may tell him that I do thank him from the bottom of my heart. I shall never forget him for this, no matter what happens. If he should ever need any help or be in any danger, he can be convinced that I shall stick to him whatever may happen, even if the whole world gangs up on him.[126]

The hapless Miklas finally surrendered at midnight, and Seyss-Inquart was appointed Federal Chancellor. At last Göring could relax, and he left the Chancellery to make his way the few blocks to the former Prussian parliament building, the magnificent Haus der Flieger, on the Prinz Albrechtstrasse. He was to act as host for the evening at a glittering ball for over a thousand guests, including government officials, foreign diplomats and the Nazi Party hierarchy. The entertainment was to be provided by the orchestra, singers and ballet of the State Opera. From the outset, the atmosphere in the great hall was one of "electric tension and impending tragedy," and the overseas guests in particular felt that there was "an unseemliness in music and dancing" while Austria was being dismembered.[127] Throughout the day the diplomatic community had heard the rumors of the German troop concentrations on the Austrian border, and before the party began they had listened to the broadcast from Vienna of Schuschnigg's emotional resignation speech. In the Haus der Flieger, the absence of army and Luftwaffe officers was obvious, and those who were present slowly melted away during the course of the evening.

Henderson, who had already lodged one formal protest during the day with Neurath at the Foreign Ministry, attended reluctantly. The Polish ambassador and Czechoslovak Minister had dined together beforehand, where "an atmosphere of utter tension and depression prevailed."[128] In Göring's absence, a surreal atmosphere of false normality pervaded the proceedings—bands played, couples waltzed, and diplomats from around the world sat clustered at round tables, engaged in animated discussions about the day's events. At one point Kirkpatrick arrived from the British embassy, bearing further instructions for Henderson from London. As he pushed his way through the throng of guests to the top table, the huge room fell silent. Kirkpatrick removed two crumpled pieces of paper from his pocket, which Henderson read slowly, before nodding. "You could have heard a pin drop in the great hall," recalled Henderson, as "2,000 pairs of eyes watched" for his reaction.[129]

At last Göring arrived, "plastered with orders and decorations."[130] He immediately sought out the Czechoslovak Minister, Dr. Voytech Mastný, and escorted him to a private room. Austria, he assured him, was a "German family affair," and the night's events had no significance for Czechoslovakia, so long as the Czechs did not mobilize. "I give you my word of honour," he continued, "that Czechoslovakia has nothing to fear from the Reich."[131] As everyone waited for the performance to begin, Göring then tore a strip of paper off his program, and scribbled a note on it, which he passed to Henderson, stretching across the wife of the American ambassador. "I will explain everything to you," he promised.[132] Mastný, meanwhile, hurried back to his delegation to telephone Prague for instructions. He returned to the Haus der Flieger in a state of high excitement, and in turn assured Göring that there would be no Czech mobilization. Göring was delighted. He was not only speaking for himself, he told the gullible minister, but for the Führer also, who had vested all power in him as he traveled to Austria. "Your Excellency, listen carefully," he concluded with a flourish. "I give you my personal word of honour—*Ich gebe Ihnen mein Ehrenwort*—that this is a question of the Anschluss of Austria only, and that not a single German soldier will come anywhere near the Czech border."[133]

Back in the Ballhausplatz in Vienna, the rooms at the front of the Chancellery were no longer safe from the throng below. A group of young boys scaled the building's facade to hoist a swastika, and Seyss went out on to the balcony to try to calm the crowd, but was forced back inside. He offered to take Schuschnigg back home in his car, or to arrange sanctuary for him in the Hungarian embassy across the street. Schuschnigg's supporters had even organized a plane to be kept ready and waiting at Aspern Aerodrome, to fly the deposed Chancellor into exile. But Schuschnigg declined all such offers, and left with Seyss-Inquart, first shaking the hands of his former sentries, by now themselves reduced to tears. The whole building had been occupied, and the grand staircase was lined by civilians wearing swastika armbands. Schuschnigg was bundled into the car with Seyss, with Nazi guards on the running boards for their protection, and slowly, through the huge crowds, he was driven home from the Chancellery for the last time. He was to spend the next ten weeks under house arrest, before being moved to a cell at Gestapo headquarters in Vienna. He spent the war in a concentration camp, first at Dachau, and then at Sachsenhausen.

Seyss-Inquart made one last attempt to halt the invasion. Acting on his instructions, at 2:10 A.M. Muff telephoned the Austrian desk officer at the Foreign Ministry in Berlin to request that "the alerted troops should remain but not cross the border." If they had already done so they should be withdrawn. Keppler also came on the line and supported the request. Hitler had retired to bed at midnight, satisfied with a good day's work, and was far from happy to be roused from his sleep. His adjutant telephoned back to Vienna: the Führer was absolutely insistent that "the entry could no longer be stopped." Muff's only reaction, a courageous one in the circumstances, was that "he regretted this message."[134] Throughout the night Keitel too received a number of calls from fellow Wehrmacht officers begging that the invasion be called off. At 4 A.M. he heard from Brauchitsch and Viebahn, the Chief of the Military Operations Staff at the OKW, both urging him to intervene with Hitler and have the operation canceled. But he lacked the courage even to pass the message on.[135] In Vienna, President Miklas too made his way home for the last time. "I was completely abandoned," he reflected, "both at home and abroad."[136]

5

■

A Spring Storm

Who knows? Perhaps you will wake up one morning in Vienna to find us there—just like a spring storm.
>   Adolf Hitler to Kurt von Schuschnigg, Berchtesgaden,
>   February 21, 1938

Dear Czecho-Slovakia,
I don't think they'll attack yer
But I'm not going to back yer.
>   Attributed to Neville Chamberlain by Hilaire Belloc,
>   March 24, 1938

Europe, like an artichoke, was ready to be eaten leaf by leaf.
>   Joseph Paul-Boncour, Foreign Minister of France, March 1938

Early on the morning of Saturday, March 12, hundreds of Sperrle's Luftwaffe planes took off from Bavarian airfields. Some flew direct to Austrian airports, where they delivered high-ranking German officials, while most circled lazily over Vienna, Linz and other cities dropping thousands of propaganda leaflets. At 5:30 A.M. German troops began crossing the border at Bregenz, Innsbruck, Kufstein, Braunau and Salzburg. During the night, General Guderian's 16th Army Corps had assembled from all over Germany, and was now massed just across the border from Austria at

Passau. At the head of the column was Guderian's former command, the 2nd Panzer Division, behind which came the motorized Waffen SS formation, the SS-Leibstandarte Adolf Hitler, under the command of SS-Obergruppenführer Sepp Dietrich. The SS-Leibstandarte was Hitler's private bodyguard, the command of which made Dietrich ultimately responsible for Hitler's personal safety, and a trusted confidant. At Guderian's suggestion, the tanks that rolled into Austria were decked out with greenery and flags of both countries, "as a sign of friendly feelings."

The initial stages of the invasion, however, ran far from smoothly. The SS-Leibstandarte had come from its barracks in Berlin, while the 2nd Panzer Division had made a 200-mile journey through the night. The commanding officer, General Rudolf Veiel, had with him neither maps of Austria, nor sufficient fuel to make further progress. In place of the maps, Guderian provided him with a tourist's Baedeker guide of Austria, while supporting fuel columns were improvised, making use of borrowed trucks and petrol stations along the route. The jump-off had been scheduled for 8 A.M., but it was not until an hour later that the first tanks crossed the border, the frontier barriers already raised in welcome. There was no resistance. Everywhere the invading forces were "joyfully received." First World War veterans, proudly wearing their medals, waved as the tanks passed by. At every stop women came out of houses decorated with swastika flags, bearing flowers and food for the soldiers. "Their hands were shaken, they were kissed, and there were tears of joy."[1]

But progress was painfully slow, due largely to the lack of fuel, the icy roads made more treacherous still by a heavy snowfall, and the poor mechanical performance of the older tanks. Many of the young drivers had been recruited directly from the early stages of their training. Observers who followed the armored column from Salzburg to Vienna found that dozens of disabled tanks and armored vehicles had been ditched, often leaving the road blocked. Churchill later claimed that the "German war machine had lumbered falteringly over the frontier and come to a standstill."[2] By Guderian's own admission some 30 percent of his panzers had to be abandoned, while Jodl put the figure between Passau and Vienna as high as 70 percent. By noon, however, Guderian had arrived in Linz, where he immediately set about securing the roads around the town in expectation of Hitler's arrival. From Vienna, the British ambassador reported that 2,000 fully armed German troops had been landed at Aspern Aerodrome in 200 transport planes, at the rate of almost a plane every minute. "German and Austrian troops are fraternising," he added ominously.[3]

At 6 A.M. that morning several military airplanes, filled to overflowing with Nazi Party and Wehrmacht top brass, and escorted by a fleet of fighters, had left Tempelhof Aerodrome in Berlin. Hitler traveled with Keitel, and at Oberwiesenfeld Aerodrome in Munich they were met by a fleet of gray, six-wheeled Mercedes cars, all open-topped in spite of the cold weather. Hitler drove first to the German side of the Austrian border at Mühldorf am Inn, where the commander-in-chief of the invading 8th Army, General von Bock, had set up his forward command post. Satisfied with what he heard from Bock concerning the advancing troop formations, Hitler continued on into Austria, crossing the small bridge that represented the border shortly before 4 P.M. at his birthplace, Braunau am Inn. There he was greeted by pealing church bells, and "acclaimed with an unending roar of welcome" by the thousands of ecstatic supporters lining the streets. After an emotionally charged speech of welcome from the new Mayor of Braunau, who had only been released from prison the previous day, Hitler stopped briefly outside the Pommer Inn where he had been born almost forty-nine years earlier. He was, apparently, "visibly moved by it all."[4]

From Braunau the cavalcade set off for Linz, the Upper Austrian capital. At Lambach, where Hitler had lived as a child, he ordered his driver to stop outside the cloister where he had once taken singing lessons. Progress was slow, due principally to the jubilant crowds that thronged the sides of the road, cheering and crying as the Führer passed. Women rushed forward at the car, throwing flowers onto the hood; children were held above their parents' heads to get a better view; and in the villages local bands struck up in welcome. For hours on end, Hitler stood bolt upright in his open-topped car, arm outstretched in salute. When he finally reached Linz, long after dark, he was greeted by Seyss-Inquart and other leading Nazis, as well as by a hysterical crowd of 100,000 people—"The streets, the rooftops, the balconies, the windows and even the trees and street lamps were full of screaming, shouting people."[5] From the balcony of the town hall he addressed the huge crowd below, pausing frequently as the cries rang round the old market square—*"Sieg Heil! Ein Volk! Ein Reich! Ein Führer!"* Guderian, standing beside him, noticed that Hitler was "deeply moved . . . the tears were running down his cheeks."[6]

> If Providence once called me forth from this town to be the leader of the Reich, it must in so doing have charged me with a mission, and that mission could only be to restore my dear homeland to the German Reich. I have believed in this mission, I have lived and fought for it, and I believe I have now fulfilled it.[7]

Their late arrival in Linz, and the sheer scale of the crowds in the town, forced Hitler and his entourage to abandon plans to drive on directly to Vienna. Instead, they checked into the already overcrowded Hotel Weinzinger on the banks of the Danube, the proprietor proudly surrendering his own suite for Hitler's use. The hotel's main lounge, however, which was lavishly decorated with stuffed animals' heads, provoked a stern retort from the anti-hunting Führer. The food soon ran out, and the single telephone in the hotel had to be reserved initially for Hitler's personal use. It took nine hours even to get a line to Berlin, and it was finally decided that priority be given to the Nazi-admiring George Ward Price of the *Daily Mail*, who had secured a scoop by conducting a short interview with Hitler himself. "His need," recorded Spitzy without a trace of irony, "was greater than ours, as it was of the utmost importance that at least one of the world's newspapers should report an accurate and unbiased view of events."[8]

A further reason for the delay was a request by Himmler to be allowed an additional day in Vienna to "perfect security arrangements," principally by rounding up "thousands of undesirables."[9] He had beaten both the Wehrmacht and Hitler into Austria by some hours, having left Tempelhof in a military transport plane at 1 A.M. He was accompanied by his most senior officers, including Walther Schellenberg, Chief of his Foreign Intelligence Service, and Adolf Eichmann, an officer of the anti-Jewish section of the SS Protection was provided by a gang of Reinhard Heydrich's thugs from the SD. They landed in Vienna at 4 A.M., to be met by the sinister Ernst Kaltenbrunner, head of the Austrian SS, and went immediately to the Chancellery in the Ballhausplatz, where they found a scene of bustling activity. Himmler's aim was to take immediate precautions against any possible resistance, and his primary target was the files of the Austrian Intelligence Service on political opponents and the Jewish community. To his horror, Himmler discovered that Admiral Canaris of the Abwehr, a man he trusted not one iota, had gotten there even earlier, along with a special detachment of Abwehr officers. They had already removed all the relevant dossiers, and in particular five files held by the Austrians on Hitler, Göring, Himmler, Heydrich and, most important for Canaris, on himself.

Hitler's coup had been timed to perfection, and if the reactions of the other major powers had not already influenced his actions, they assuredly did so now. In Moscow Nikolai Bukharin, Genrikh Yagoda and Alexei Rykov, along with eighteen other members of Lenin's former Politburo, were awaiting the death penalty, having been convicted of treason at the last of Stalin's great show trials. In Washington the German ambassador called on the Secretary of State, Cordell Hull, who had already studied the content of Hitler's speech in Linz, and was "obviously still thoroughly impressed by the proclamation." From the gist of the few, tame questions that Hull then asked, the surprised German envoy concluded that "it was apparent that he thoroughly understands our action."[10] In France there was no government at all, the administration of Camille Chautemps and Yvon Delbos having fallen on March 10. Léon Blum was to assume a caretaker role as Prime Minister, but would not take permanent charge for another four days. "France, as usual, has been caught bathing," scoffed Chamberlain to his sister, "and the world looks to us."[11]

▪ ▪ ▪

At 10:30 A.M. on Saturday, March 12, the British Cabinet met in emergency session. Chamberlain began by casually apologizing that "although there was probably not very much that could be done, he had thought it right that the cabinet should meet." He and Halifax then described the events of the previous forty-eight hours, including the meetings with Ribbentrop, the lunch at Downing Street, and the flow of telegrams from Berlin and Vienna. In reply to Schuschnigg's appeal for help, Halifax had stated that he "could not take any responsibility of advising the Chancellor to take any course of action which might expose his country to dangers against which His Majesty's Government are unable to guarantee protection." At this, Chamberlain could not resist sardonically reminding his colleagues that

"Doctor Schuschnigg had not asked advice before announcing the plebiscite which had caused so much trouble." It was obvious that "Herr Hitler had been meaning to take this action for some time and Doctor Schuschnigg's blunder had given him the chance." The Italians had refused all dialogue on the matter, Henderson's protests had been batted away, and, all in all, there was not much more that could be done.[12]

Throughout the day in Berlin, it fell to Göring and Neurath, much to Ribbentrop's fury, to field protests from the world's diplomatic representatives. For Neurath, it meant being required to "tell some flat lies," but he stuck resolutely to the line that Schuschnigg's provocative action had forced Austrian nationalists to demand a new government, which in turn had freely requested the assistance of German troops to avoid bloodshed. For the "respectable bureaucrat and diplomat of the old order," it was, recorded his biographer, "a sorry performance."[13] Henderson first spoke to Neurath on March 11, and then communicated the formal written démarche that he and Kirkpatrick had composed at the Haus der Flieger. The British government, it stated, felt "bound to register a protest in the strongest possible terms against such use of coercion backed by force against an independent State."[14] Unfortunately, Henderson managed substantially to undermine the force of the protest by admitting to Göring at the party that he "reluctantly agreed that Dr. Schuschnigg had acted with precipitate folly" in calling the plebiscite.[15] It was a view which drew a sharp retort from Halifax, who was "disturbed" to read the ambassador's comments. "It may well be your personal view," he chided Henderson. "But I cannot help feeling that by the admission to General Göring you cannot but have diminished the force of the protest."[16] Hitler was anyway unrepentant. "England has sent me a protest," he boasted. "I would have understood a declaration of war; to a protest I shall not even reply."[17]

Hitler remained holed up in the Weinzinger Hotel for most of Sunday, March 13, the day on which Schuschnigg's plebiscite was to have been held. That morning, however, he did venture out briefly to the nearby village of Leonding, accompanied by his faithful valet Heinz Linge, to lay a wreath on his parents' grave, just across the churchyard from the old family home. For a few minutes he stood in silence, alone at the graveside, before visiting his former primary school, where he was greeted by a number of old school friends. Everywhere he went he was forcefully struck by the warmth of the reception, and gradually his views on the future governance of Austria began to change. Until now, he had on balance preferred the concept of Zusammenschluss, a merger of the two countries, with himself as titular head of both, but with Vienna retaining a measure of domestic autonomy. Certainly Seyss-Inquart refused to accept that the invasion necessarily entailed the end of Austrian independence, and still "fancied he was stage-managing the creation of a Catholic Nazi Austria."[18] In Berlin, the Minister of the Interior, Dr. Wilhelm Frick, was busy preparing a draft law that would place Austria "under Germany's protection," but would not lead to full Anschluss.

However, it was rapidly becoming clear that neither Britain nor France proposed to take any concrete steps to halt Hitler's march. "It is fate, Linge," he told his valet. "I am destined to be the Führer who will bring all Germans into the Greater German Reich."[19] He was told that foreign newspapers were already accepting full Anschluss "as a *fait accompli*," and during his interview with Ward Price he hinted that Austria would become a German province, "like Bavaria or Saxony."[20] At some moment that Sunday Hitler finally heard formally from Mussolini. "I congratulate you on the way you have solved the Austrian problem," ran the Duce's telegram. "I had already warned Schuschnigg." Hitler was delighted, thanking him effusively for his support. "Mussolini," he replied, "I shall never forget you for this [*Ich werde Ihnen dieses nie vergessen*]."[21] When Göring heard the "joyous welcome" in Linz over the radio, he sent off a message: "If the enthusiasm is so great, why don't we go the whole hog?" In fact, Hitler had by now decided to do just that. Half-measures were no longer enough, and only complete annexation would now suffice. As Göring later recorded, "the decision to wipe out Austria was taken after the reception in Linz."[22]

The State Secretary at the Ministry of the Interior, Dr. Wilhelm Stuckart, was hurriedly summoned from Berlin to Linz, where, "to his surprise," Hitler bluntly told him to "draft a law providing for the direct, total Anschluss, that is, providing for Austria's status as a province of the German Reich."[23] He spent Sunday morning in the hotel drafting the necessary legislation, the "Law for the Re-Unification of Austria with the German Reich." At midday he flew to Vienna to submit it for approval to the newly created Austrian Ministerial Council, which unanimously accepted the draft at 5 P.M., after a meeting lasting just five minutes. President Miklas, however, refused to sign the new law, and resigned his post there and then. Seyss-Inquart took on the President's powers in addition to those of Chancellor and with Keppler traveled to Linz to present the new Anschluss Law to the Führer for signature. At the moment of signing, Seyss later recorded, Hitler "was deeply moved and wept."[24] At 8 P.M. foreign journalists in Vienna were called to the Chancellery, where they were informed of Miklas's resignation, as well as the provisions of the new law. Article 1 stated blandly that "Austria is a province of the German Reich." Article 2 promised retrospective sanction for the Anschluss. "On Sunday, April 10, 1938, a free and secret plebiscite of the German men and women over 20 years of age shall be held on reunion with the German Reich."[25]

Hitler left Linz for Vienna at 11 A.M. the following morning, escorted by a cavalcade of thirteen police cars. The British military attaché in Berlin, who had spent the previous day in Vienna, witnessed the passing convoy from a garage forecourt outside Linz. The Mercedes were "filled with S.S. bristling with tommy guns and other lethal weapons," he recalled. Hitler sat "impassively" in his car, "with the black cowlick and the toothbrush moustache, gazing fixedly ahead and taking no account whatever of his surroundings."[26] Once again, the crowds and the abandoned tanks slowed his journey, which took six hours. In one village a woman was brought to a microphone to tell "a touching little story about how she and Adolf had been to school together in Braunau."[27] When they finally reached Vienna soon after 5 P.M., in glorious spring sunshine, the church bells were pealing, and swastikas were flying from the steeples. Hitler was still standing, tense and unsmiling in his brown overcoat, his right arm extended in what seemed like a perpetual salute, his left hand nervously gripping the top of the windshield. The houses were decked out in both German and Austrian flags, and every spare inch of space on the rooftops and in windows was taken. The cheers were deafening. As the Vienna correspondent of the *Daily Telegraph* reluctantly observed: "To say that the crowds which greeted him along the Ringstrasse were delirious with joy is an understatement."[28]

"It is impossible to deny enthusiasm," confirmed Palairet to Halifax, "with which both the new régime and last night's announcement of incorporation in the Reich have been received here."[29] Hitler's car made its way through the crowds to the Hotel Imperial—as an impoverished young man he had been turned away from its doors on numerous occasions. Now its facade was decked out in bright red swastika banners, hanging from the roof. He acknowledged the vast crowds from the balcony of the presidential suite, and was forced to reappear, again and again, by the continuous chanting: "We want to see our Führer! We want to see our Führer!" That evening he sat up late, reminiscing with his officers about the cold, youthful nights he had spent peering jealously through the hotel's windows. Keitel, meanwhile, whose room overlooked the front of the hotel, was unable to get a hoped-for early night, so long as the huge, noisy crowd remained outside.[30] From Linz, Hitler had telephoned Eva Braun and summoned her to be by his side, and to share his triumph in Vienna. She arrived, chaperoned by her mother, and stayed so discreetly in the room directly across the corridor from Hitler's, that no one was even aware of her presence. But she too was swept away by the emotion of the occasion. "*Ich bin verrückt* [I'm crazy]," she scribbled on a postcard to her sister Ilse.[31]

There was more spring weather the following day, as Hitler addressed a vast, delirious crowd in the Heldenplatz (Heroes' Square), estimated at a quarter of a million people. Throughout Vienna, factories, offices and schools closed for the day, while crowds were bused in from all parts of Austria. Hitler spoke from the balcony of the Hofburg, the imperial palace of the Habsburgs, and a potent symbol of the Holy Roman Empire. The once independent country of Austria was, he told the crowd, to be renamed as the German province of Ostmark, while Seyss-Inquart, who was standing alongside him, was to be stripped of the title of Chancellor, and to be known henceforth as Reichsstadthalter, little more than a provincial governor.

> I now proclaim for this land its new mission. The oldest eastern province of the German people shall be from now on the youngest bulwark of the German nation. I can in this hour report before history the conclusion of the greatest aim in my life: the entry of my homeland into the German Reich.[32]

Once the prolonged cheering had died down, Hitler made his way down to a saluting base in front of the Hofburg, where he stood, right arm extended, acknowledging the march-past that followed. He was, according to Papen, "in a state of ecstasy."[33]

On the morning of Monday, March 14, while Hitler was basking in the adulation of the Viennese masses in the Heldenplatz, the British Cabinet sat down to prepare its response to the Anschluss, to be made public that afternoon by the Prime Minister in the House of Commons. Chamberlain proposed that "condemnation should be applied to the methods used by Herr Hitler and the shock that had been given to world confidence by those methods." It was, however, the case "that so far there had not been much bloodshed." Only the Secretary of State for War, Leslie Hore-Belisha, spoke out at length against this laissez-faire attitude, quoting from *Mein Kampf,* and warning that the British were now "up against new methods and a man who had gone a long way in the development of German armament." There would be "a grave risk if our only reply to Germany's real effort was a dilatory expansion." Having predicted that Germany would be prepared to talk, "Sir Nevile Henderson had been proved wrong just as Mr. Palairet had been proved right." Hore-Belisha's warning was barely even acknowledged by Chamberlain, who had a more pressing engagement. The Prime Minister "pointed out that it was now 12.30 P.M. He was due to lunch with his Majesty the King at 1 o'clock."[34]

Chamberlain's speech in the Commons that afternoon was, according to one onlooker, "a very restrained matter of fact affair."[35] He recounted the sequence of events of the previous few days, and read out the British note of protest and Neurath's reply in full. He then reiterated Göring's assurance to the Czech Minister in Berlin that Czechoslovakia had nothing to fear, and a further one, given that morning to Henderson, that German troops would be withdrawn from Austria as soon as possible. Neither assurance was to have any value. His strong words of condemnation of the methods employed by the Nazis to achieve Anschluss won the quiet support of the House. Privately, however, he believed that events in Austria had proved him right over Eden's resignation. "Well it is all very disheartening and discouraging," he wrote to his sister. "It is tragic to think that very possibly this might have been prevented if I had had Halifax at the F.O. instead of Anthony at the time I wrote my letter to Mussolini."[36]

Political opinion was deeply divided over the Anschluss, although the majority view was one of relief that the issue of Austria was now out of the way. Even those who knew the country well, and would have liked to see more decisive action in support of Austrian independence, had mixed feelings. "It is a real Black Letter day," recorded the pro-Austrian Conservative backbencher Victor Cazalet. "Overwhelmed by news. Furious, raging impotent. Everyone is indignant. But one can't fight if the Austrians won't."[37] The oleaginous Chips Channon wrote of "an unbelievable day, in which two things occurred. Hitler took Vienna and I fell in love with the Prime Minister. Will my adorable Austria become Nazi-fied?"[38] The previous month the veteran Conservative MP Leo Amery had written to Eden offering to organize a speaking visit to London by Schuschnigg, to help shore up the Chancellor's position. Eden had dismissed the idea on the grounds that such a visit "would inevitably give rise to wild speculation and suspicion," and would be "embarrassing and should therefore be discouraged."[39] Now Amery admitted that news of the Anschluss "came to me as a terrible blow," and that "the best hope of peace now lies in telling Germany that if she touches Czechoslovakia we are in it too."[40]

Such sentiments, however, represented the minority view. On March 14 *The Times* told its readers that "our correspondent leaves no room for doubt about the public jubilation with which [Hitler] and his army were greeted everywhere." The Labour Party, recalling the brutality of Dollfuss a few years earlier against Austrian socialists, had little inclination to speak up now for Schuschnigg, although 10,000 protesters congregated in Trafalgar Square on March 13 and, led by the left-wing publisher Victor Gollancz, processed to the nearby German embassy shouting "Hands off Austria."[41] Even the Archbishop of Canterbury appealed to the House of Lords for "calmness and balance of judgement." The union of Germany and Austria "sooner or later was inevitable" he told his fellow peers, and "finally, may bring some measure of stability to Europe."[42] At the Foreign Office too, the general feeling was one of relief. "Thank Goodness, Austria's out of the way," Cadogan wrote to Henderson, from Nancy Astor's seaside home in Kent.

> I can't help thinking that we were very badly informed about feeling in that country. I've no doubt there's a section of the population hiding in cellars, and a number of them waving Swastika flags may come to rue the day later, but we should evidently have been very wrong to try to prevent the Anschluss against the wishes of a very considerable proportion of the population. After all, it wasn't our business.[43]

Even allowing for the comparatively limited knowledge Cadogan may have had of events in Vienna at the time, his remarks appear surprisingly callous. With the benefit of hindsight, they seem spectacularly ill-judged. As early as March 12 Halifax warned Palairet that "considerable anxiety is evinced here regarding position of Jews and Socialists in Austria," and requested that the ambassador "take any opportunity that offers of impressing . . . that maltreatment of Jews and Socialists in Austria can only deepen the painful impression produced in this country."[44] In reality, it was already too late. The flight from Austria had begun as soon as Schuschnigg announced his resignation. Some senior officials, mindful of the way in which political events were unfolding, had chosen not to wait for the inevitable, but had already fled across the Czech border, and were among the few who made it safely to Bratislava and on into exile. By 8 P.M. on March 11 the roads out of Vienna toward the border were clogged with every conceivable make of vehicle. Some routes soon became impassable, as refugees abandoned their cars, and made their escape on foot, hoping to escape unnoticed through the woods and mountain border passes. There were lengthy queues at the airport and railway stations. At Aspern, the Baron Louis de Rothschild attempted to board a plane to Rome, only to have his passport torn up and thrown back in his face by a German officer. "You Jews will never have passports again," he was told.[45]

At the East Station, the last train out of Vienna, the night express, was due to leave for Prague at 11:15 P.M. Hours beforehand the vast crowd on the platform could have filled the train several times over. Those who succeeded in getting on board thought themselves the lucky ones, but just as the train was due to pull out of the station, Nazi storm troopers arrived. Running through the carriages, armed with dog whips, they dragged off to certain imprisonment and probable death all those they deemed, quite arbitrarily, to be "undesirable." Even those left on the train had their possessions confiscated. Twenty minutes after its departure, the train was stopped again, and forced to return to Vienna, where the searches, looting and forced removals were repeated. When the remaining passengers finally reached what they thought was the safety of Czechoslovakia, the local authorities in the border town of Breclav refused them permission to enter the country, and sent them back on the next train. Most of those arrested that night "went practically straight to Dachau."[46]

At first the beatings, torture and looting were randomly perpetrated by Austrian Nazi thugs. Anarchy reigned and a full-blown pogrom appeared imminent. Jewish shops were ransacked, while Jews were stripped of their possessions in the street, and forced to hand over cars, jewelry and money, before being beaten up. But it was not long before Himmler and Heydrich assumed control, setting up Gestapo headquarters at the Hotel Metropole. The tyranny became more organized. The borders were sealed for good, and a reign of terror began. For a few weeks, one American journalist witnessed "an orgy of sadism" worse than anything he had seen even in Germany.[47] Jewish men and women, of all ages, were systematically dragged from their homes and offices, or press-ganged off the streets. Herded together by truncheon-wielding storm troopers, and surrounded by jeering crowds, they were put to work in so-called cleaning squads, forced to scrub Schuschnigg propaganda slogans off the pavements on their hands and knees, using an acid solution which burned their hands. "Work for the Jews at last, work for the Jews!" chanted the gloating mob, as Nazi supervisors kicked and soaked the Jewish workers. "We thank our Führer for finding work for the Jews."

The National Labour MP Harold Nicolson described to his wife how on Sundays the Nazis would round up at random everyone who was out for an afternoon walk in the Prater park. Having separated out the Jews, they forced the men, of whatever age, to strip naked and "walk on all fours on the grass." Meanwhile they made "the old Jewish ladies get up into the trees by ladders and sit there. They then told them to chirp like birds. . . . The suicides have been appalling. A great cloud of misery hangs over the town."[48] Another form of entertainment in the Prater involved the most elderly Jews being put through a series of so-called physical exercises for which they were hopelessly ill-prepared, while being kicked and tormented by the storm troopers for hours upon end; the crowd's favorite was the compulsory goose step. Nor did the professional classes escape. Doctors and university professors were put to work cleaning out the toilets in the SS and SA barracks, using only their bare hands and the leather straps of a Tefillin, the sacred prayer band, from a nearby synagogue.

While such apparently random brutality was being perpetrated on the streets, Himmler quietly set up the "Office for Jewish Emigration," the sole agency authorized to allow Jews to leave the country. It was administered by

Adolf Eichmann, "the rising star of the S.D.'s Jewish Department."[49] Given immediate access to Austrian police records, he quickly identified all likely "undesirables," and assumed responsibility for a lucrative trade in human freedom, as almost 100,000 Jews were allowed to leave the city in exchange for their worldly possessions. From the richer Jews, the Nazi haul was substantial. The Baron Louis de Rothschild, having failed to make good his escape on March 11, first had to watch while his palace was looted of all its paintings, silver and tapestries, before eventually buying his own freedom by turning over his steel mills to the Nazis. But Himmler was not to be satisfied with the mere expulsion of Jews, and within a few weeks of arriving in Austria he had begun work on a new concentration camp at Mauthausen, on the north bank of the Danube, near Linz. The *Daily Telegraph* correspondent in Vienna, who was himself expelled soon after, described how women would receive a small parcel with the message: "To pay, 150 marks, for the cremation of your husband—ashes enclosed from Dachau." For many there was only one way out: "the acceptance of suicide as a perfectly normal and natural incident by every Jewish household" became commonplace.[50]

▪ ▪ ▪

In the aftermath of the Anschluss it was obvious to everyone that Czechoslovakia had been left hopelessly vulnerable, both economically and defensively. There was now a continuous Fascist block running from the Baltic to the Adriatic. Czechoslovakia's great natural and artificial mountain fortifications in Bohemia had been rendered worthless. The frontier with the former Austria was flat, and largely unfortified, and her borders were now exposed on all sides, in particular to a German advance from the southwest. With three-quarters of Czechoslovakia's trade passing through Germany, Hitler had also acquired an effective economic stranglehold over her communications with the outside world. Chamberlain summed up the situation succinctly in a letter to his sister.

> You have only to look at the map to see that nothing that France or we could do could possibly save Czecho-Slovakia from being over-run by the Germans if they wanted to do it. The Austrian frontier is practically open; the great Skoda munition works are within easy bombing distance of the

German aerodromes, the railways all pass through German territory, Russia is 100 miles away.[51]

The Republic of Czechoslovakia was a creation of the 1919 postwar peace treaties, when seven and a half million Czechs were put in a position of authority over three and a quarter million Germans, two and a half million Slovaks, half a million Hungarians, another half a million Ruthenes, and 80,000 Poles. Carved out of the remains of the Austro-Hungarian Empire, its creators had "reproduced the racial jigsaw" of that empire "in miniature."[52] Built on those same unstable foundations, from its very creation Czechoslovakia was prone to the same fissile tendencies as had plagued the Habsburgs for centuries. Democracy had somehow been maintained, although only the ruling Czech majority were truly happy with the existing order, and there was widespread discontent within the minority communities, and a natural propensity to seek support from their "mother" countries. Hungarians and Ruthenes looked to an increasingly bellicose Hungary. The predominantly Catholic Slovak People's Party, which had enjoyed electoral success in 1935, also now demanded greater autonomy. And even the small Polish minority in Teschen, or more specifically their profitable coalfields, was eyed covetously by Warsaw.

However, by far the largest ethnic minority was German. Although never actually part of Germany, they had historically always enjoyed political influence in Bohemia and Moravia. Indeed, the Czechs had often felt themselves to be victims of pro-German discrimination under Habsburg rule. Now the situation had been reversed. The *Sudetendeutsch* lived mostly in the industrial area known as the Sudetenland, along the north- and southwestern borders of the country, and had always enjoyed relative prosperity in a region that was vital both to Czechoslovakia's economy and to her defenses. The industrial decline of 1931 to 1933, however, had been particularly harsh in the Sudeten region, with unemployment rising to over 25 percent. Germans were traditionally laid off before Czechs, and nationalist feelings ran deep. The Sudeten German regarded the Czech as "a half-educated . . . creature, to some extent saved by German influence, politically intolerable and unreliable, socially never satisfied and always pushing for his nation." The Czech, on the other hand, considered the Sudeten German to be "the invader, the remorseless conqueror, the apostle of German world hegemony, the economic tyrant who only lives in the land in order to subject the Czech people socially, politically, and in every other way."[53]

It is generally acknowledged by historians that, in spite of the centralized nature of Czechoslovakia, the minorities there were treated with greater tolerance than many others in Europe. Eric Gedye, the central European correspondent of the *Daily Telegraph*, who moved to Prague following the Anschluss after twelve years in Vienna, described the Sudeten German minority as "easily the most privileged in the whole of Europe. . . . At no time politically persecuted, always arrogantly conscious of the backing of Germany's sixty-six millions."[54] They enjoyed full democratic and civil rights, including the right to vote, while the minority party leaders often served as ministers in central government. However, the Czech majority, having themselves been oppressed for centuries by the Austrians, were their own worst enemies. They could frequently be tactless and intolerant, and made no attempt to end the localized bureaucratic and economic discrimination that occurred within the minority communities. The result was a growing catalogue of minor grievances, generally brought on by petty local officialdom, including a disproportionate allocation of official posts, the building of Czech schools in non-Czech areas, and the sole use of the Czech language. As Hitler's power increased, the German minority grew increasingly restless, while the Nazi propaganda machine successfully exaggerated minor grievances to the point where the Sudeten Germans were able to portray themselves as "a cruelly repressed minority."[55]

In 1933 the Sudetendeutsche Partei (Sudeten German Party), or SdP, was created under the leadership of Konrad Henlein, an earnest, mild-mannered, and shortsighted gymnastics instructor from northern Bohemia. Born in 1898 near Liberec, he was the son of a German bookkeeper and a Czech mother, a fact he always did his best to conceal. During the First World War he served as a volunteer in the Austrian army, and was wounded and taken prisoner by the Italians in 1918. After the war he spent some time working as a bank clerk, before taking up teaching gymnastics as a profession, a move which enabled him to gather together a supportive political following from the gymnastics clubs, "which always had a strong political tinge of German nationalism."[56] Although he only formally joined the Nazi Party in 1933, as organizer for many years of the "German Gymnastics

League" he was always considered "from top to toe the perfect Nazi official."[57]

By 1935 the SdP was being secretly subsidized by the Foreign Ministry in Berlin to the tune of 15,000 marks a month, and for the parliamentary elections, held in May of that year, Henlein was awarded a subsidy of some 330,000 reichmarks, an astronomical amount by the standards of the time.[58] In a stunning success, the SdP emerged victorious in the Sudeten districts, coming top of the poll with one and a quarter million votes and forty-four seats, principally at the expense of the more moderate Social Democrats. Mimicking Hitler's disdain for parliamentary democracy, Henlein refused to stand as a candidate himself, believing such a move to be beneath his dignity as party leader. The sudden arrival of such a large, and obviously hostile, force into the Czech Parliament should have set alarm bells ringing. In an echo of Hitler's orders to his Nazi Reichstag deputies in the summer of 1932, Henlein summoned all the newly elected SdP deputies to appear before him at Eger (Cheb), to swear allegiance to him personally before they had a chance to take the formal constitutional oath in Parliament. Many of them routinely appeared in Parliament wearing jackboots.

In spite of his obvious contempt for democracy, Henlein was warmly welcomed to London in August 1935, and again in December, when he shamelessly told the *Daily Telegraph* that he had "never at any time had any relations with the present German government. I have never seen Herr Hitler," he continued, "I have never spoken with him, corresponded with him or negotiated with him in any way."[59] During a speech to the influential Royal Institute of International Affairs, at Chatham House in London, he pursued a similar theme, claiming that he was a man of "honest goodwill," whose sole desire was to act as a mediator for the Sudeten Germans "between their German mother country and the Czech people," and that he would "work loyally with the State." He was "not the local representative of Hitler," and "his party was not a covert Nazi party."[60] In spite of critical questioning from the politically well-informed audience, the Foreign Office official at the meeting was impressed by Henlein's "moderation and freedom from the fanaticism" he had expected.[61] During his visit, he managed to impress even such anti-appeasers as Churchill and Vansittart, while the Czech Minister in London, Jan Masaryk, regarded him as "an amiable and possibly useful person."[62]

Hitler's "antagonism towards the Czechs was profound and long-standing,"[63] in part as a result of his Austrian upbringing, when a deep-seated hatred of all things Czech would have been endemic. While it now suited him to represent the alleged persecution of the Sudeten Germans as a pretext for action, with himself cast as their protector, he had never previously expressed any affection for them, or shown any interest in their plight. In reality, Czechoslovakia's greatest crime was her threatening geographical position: the figurative dagger, thrust menacingly from the east into the heart of the newly created *Grossdeutschland*. Czechoslovakia blocked Hitler's path to the conquest of Poland and, further afield, to the commodity-rich lands of the Ukraine and Russia. Worse still, she was an ally of his archenemy, Soviet Russia. The preparation of Case Green in June 1937, and Hitler's comments at the Hossbach conference in November, had left no room for doubt. Greater autonomy for the Sudetenland, or even its incorporation into the Reich, was no longer enough. Only the complete destruction of Czechoslovakia itself would now suffice.

Hitler's Austrian triumph was of enormous political and psychological significance. He spent ten days personally campaigning throughout the extended Reich, and in the plebiscite held on April 10 both the Anschluss, and his list of candidates for the Reichstag, were overwhelmingly approved; by 99.08 percent in Greater Germany, and 99.75 percent in Austria. His popularity at home soared to ever-greater levels, as the euphoria of the German public peaked. In the hour of his greatest triumph, an ecstatic populace forgot army scandals, and ignored the methods used to conquer Austria. Once again, expansion abroad served to avert any lingering discontent at home. By his bold leadership he had tightened his hold on the army, and boosted still further his own sense of infallibility. Now he was impatient for more. Within days he was busy studying maps with his Propaganda Minister. "First comes now Czechia [*Tschechei*]," recorded Goebbels, "and drastically, at the next opportunity. . . . The Führer is wonderful. . . . A true genius. Now he sits for hours over the map and broods."[64]

News of the Anschluss fired nationalist aspirations in the Sudetenland to fresh heights. The British consul in Liberec reported that it had "set in motion an avalanche of national feeling amongst the Sudeten Germans which will soon lead to a united front of all Germans and will be hard to control unless the Government is prepared to make concessions."[65] The British military attaché went further still. "Nazism has gone to their heads like wine," he warned.[66] "Nothing short of incorporation in the German Reich will satisfy the majority of the people."[67] On March 28 Henlein was summoned to Berlin, where he spent three hours closeted with Hitler, Ribbentrop and Hess. Hitler announced that he could "no longer tolerate Germans being oppressed or fired upon," and that he "intended to settle the Sudeten German problem in the not-too distant future." Henlein was to be his "Viceroy [*Statthalter*]," and was instructed that "demands should be made by the Sudeten German Party which are unacceptable to the Czech Government." Henlein understood the Führer's orders perfectly. "We must always demand so much," he summarized, "that we can never be satisfied."[68]

■ ■ ■

On November 20, 1936, in a speech to his constituents in Leamington Spa, the then Foreign Secretary Anthony Eden attempted to clarify where Britain's national interests lay in central Europe. "Nations cannot be expected," he warned, "to incur automatic obligations save for areas where their vital interests are concerned." In Britain's case, those interests most certainly did not extend eastwards beyond the Rhine.[69] On March 3, 1937, Halifax reiterated the warning in a speech to the House of Lords. "We are unable to define beforehand," he confirmed, "what might be our attitude to a hypothetical complication in Central or Eastern Europe."[70] Chamberlain's personal view was more outspoken still. He explained Czechoslovakia's defensive vulnerability to his sister.

> Therefore we could not help Czecho-Slovakia—she would simply be a pretext for going to war with Germany. That we could not think of unless we had a reasonable prospect of being able to beat her to her knees in a reasonable time and of that I see no sign. I have therefore abandoned any idea of giving guarantees to Czecho-Slovakia or to France in connection with her obligations to that country.[71]

France had indeed signed a treaty of mutual assistance, guaranteeing Czechoslovakia's borders, in December 1925, but could only fullfil its terms by launching an attack against Germany across the Rhine. The Soviet Union had concluded a similar pact in 1935, but was obliged to intervene on Czechoslovakia's behalf only if France did so first. On March 17 the Russian Foreign Commissar, Maxim Litvinov, announced Soviet willingness to participate in mutual action, possibly within the remit of the League of Nations, to deter further German aggression. The British ambassador in Moscow, Viscount Chilston, recorded that Litvinov had assured foreign journalists "that U.S.S.R. would intervene in defence of Czechoslovakia if France did." When pressed to describe how this would be achieved in the absence of a common frontier, Litvinov had replied that "means would be found."[72] But Chilston thought this was bluff, and had little confidence in Soviet military capacity. Stalin's purges of the Red Army had recently reached their peak. The British military attaché's assessment was that 65 percent of the higher ranks had been wiped out, which "cannot but have had a disastrous effect on the morale and also on the efficiency of the Red army." He concluded that, while the Russians might be able to defend their own borders, they were "not capable of carrying the war into the enemy's territory with any hope of ultimate success."[73]

The Soviet Union shared a common border with neither Czechoslovakia nor Germany. It was therefore difficult enough logistically to deploy forces in support of Czechoslovakia, while both Poland and Romania would almost certainly have forbidden Russian troops the necessary right of passage through their territory, thus rendering military action politically unpalatable also. Chamberlain was concerned that an alliance involving Britain, France and the Soviet Union (the so-called Grand Alliance strongly favored by Churchill) might "aggravate the tendency towards the establishment of exclusive groups of nations which must . . . be inimical to the prospects of European peace."[74] He apparently thought that neither the Rome-Berlin Axis, nor the Comintern Pact, were remotely relevant to this argument. He would have been more honest had he admitted publicly what he confided to his sister in confidence, that he believed the Russians were "stealthily and cunningly pulling all the strings behind the scenes to get us involved in war with Germany (our Secret Service doesn't spend all its time looking out of the window)."[75] The Soviet ambassador in London, Ivan Maisky, probably came closest to the truth. Chamberlain, he claimed, frequently referred to Russia as "our enemies," and was "bitterly anti-Russian."[76]

The Prime Minister was not alone in believing that it would require a full-blown European war to protect Czechoslovakia. At the Foreign Office Cadogan held similar views. "We are helpless as regards Austria," he recorded, "that is finished. We *may* be helpless as regards Czechoslovakia, etc." He argued strongly against giving a guarantee to Czechoslovakia. "I shall be called 'cowardly,' " he conceded, but "I have come to the conclusion that is the least bad. We *must* not precipitate a conflict now—we shall be smashed. It *may* not be better later, but anything may happen (I recognise the Micawber strain)."[77] Not everyone at the Foreign Office agreed. An internal memorandum concluded that Chamberlain was working on the premise that "some general and lasting arrangement with both dictators . . . was not only desirable but possible." According to Cadogan's own Private Secretary, Gladwyn Jebb, "there was hardly a Foreign Office official who could swallow this preposterous theory."[78]

The Foreign Policy Committee of the Cabinet met on March 18 to consider a paper prepared by Halifax and Cadogan which set out three clear options. The first was Churchill's so-called Grand Alliance; the second was to give a guarantee to Czechoslovakia, either directly, or indirectly by guaranteeing France; and the third, made attractive by the obvious disadvantages of the other two, was for Britain and France to persuade Czechoslovakia "to make the best terms she can with Germany." This ran directly contrary to the plea made by the French Foreign Minister, and former Prime Minister Joseph Paul-Boncour, just three days earlier to the British ambassador in Paris, Sir Eric Phipps. In the course of the interview Paul-Boncour had "urged that His Majesty's Government should declare publicly that, if Germany attacked Czechoslovakia and France went to the latter's assistance, Great Britain would stand by France."[79] However, Sir Thomas Inskip, the Minister for Coordination of Defence, spelled out the reality of the military position.

It seemed certain that Germany could overrun the whole of Czechoslovakia in less than a week . . . it was difficult to see how we could effectively exercise any military pressure against Germany in time to save Czechoslovakia.[80]

Although one or two ministers supported giving a guarantee to France, Halifax persuaded the committee to choose the third option. Cadogan expressed relief that the committee had been "unanimous that Czechoslovakia is not worth the bones of a single British Grenadier. And they're quite right too!"[81]

When the full Cabinet met on March 22, they too were presented with a thoroughly pessimistic report from the chiefs of staff, entitled "Military Implications of German Aggression against Czechoslovakia." Its conclusion was that "no pressure which this country and its possible allies could exercise would suffice to prevent the defeat of Czechoslovakia." Chamberlain told his colleagues that "he was not in a position to recommend a policy involving the risk of war," and would instead be sending a note to the French warning that Britain would not necessarily support them in a war over Czechoslovakia.[82] Only Duff Cooper demurred, pointing out that "when France fought Germany, we should have to fight too, whether we liked it or not, so that we might as well say so."[83] It was, however, agreed that France should be asked to put as much pressure as possible on the Czech government to appease the Sudeten Germans, "a disagreeable business," acknowledged Halifax, "which had to be done as pleasantly as possible."[84] A few days later the Dominions Secretary, Malcolm MacDonald, summed up the effect of the military chiefs' report on his colleagues.

> We are really not strong enough to risk a war. It would mean the massacre of women and children in the streets of London. No Government could possibly risk a war when our anti-aircraft defences are in so farcical a condition. No Cabinet, knowing as they do how pitiable our defences are, could take any risk. All we can do is by wise retreat and good diplomacy to diminish the dangers being arrayed against us. The Cabinet knows full well that we are shirking great responsibility. But they cannot undertake such responsibility.[85]

When Chamberlain addressed the Commons on March 24 he caught the mood of the House. The government would not fetter its discretion over declaring war by a commitment, either to the Czechs or to France; nor would they take up the Soviet offer of a mutual pledge against aggression. Chamberlain did, however, sound a note of caution.

> But while plainly stating this decision I would add this. Where peace and war are concerned, legal obligations are not alone involved, and, if war

broke out, it would be unlikely to be confined to those who have assumed such obligations. It would be quite impossible to say where it would end and what Governments might become involved. The inexorable pressure of facts might well prove more powerful than formal pronouncements, and . . . other countries, besides those which were parties to the original dispute, would almost certainly become involved.[86]

In the aftermath of the Anschluss, Blum and Paul-Boncour had attempted to reassure Prague, warn Berlin and rally London. But on April 10 their "Popular Front" government fell, much to Phipps's delight. The following day Halifax made clear his irritation that French policy had hitherto been one of encouraging the Czechs to live in a thoroughly unreal world, based on the illusion of Anglo-French power and prestige.

> Unless the French and Czechoslovak Governments can be brought to face the realities of the present position, it is to be feared that the Czechoslovak Government will not realise the necessity of making drastic concessions to the German minority, but will content themselves with superficial measures which, though they might have been adequate in the past, will no longer meet the case.[87]

And when it appeared that the new Prime Minister, Edouard Daladier, might invite Paul-Boncour to stay on as Foreign Minister, Phipps took the extraordinary step, with Halifax's approval, of intervening to have "Daladier informed indirectly that it would be most unfortunate if Paul-Boncour were to remain."[88] Instead, Daladier chose Georges Bonnet, a noted appeaser, to fill the post.

At the end of April the new French ministers came to London for two days of talks. They made a show of trying to convince Chamberlain that Hitler was determined to destroy Czechoslovakia, that the Czechs were ready and able to fight, and that the French would support them. But Daladier's moving pleas were largely for the record, and to safeguard his own reputation. It was made clear to an agent of the German embassy that Daladier hoped "Chamberlain and Halifax would themselves suggest that pressure should be put on Prague," so that he could "acquiesce without seeming to have taken the initiative in the matter."[89] Chamberlain played his part to perfection, arguing that Czechoslovakia was militarily weak, that Soviet Russia would be of no help, and that preventing a German takeover of Czechoslovakia was therefore nigh on impossible. To threaten Germany would be to indulge in a game of bluff which would do nothing to deter Hitler. Although Chamberlain told his sister that the talks "came out all right in the end but they were pretty difficult,"[90] in truth the French were only too happy to fall in behind Chamberlain, and to follow his lead.

▪ ▪ ▪

On the evening of April 21, Palm Sunday, Hitler summoned Keitel to the Reich Chancellery to discuss Case Green, and to order him to institute preliminary studies for an invasion of Czechoslovakia. Hitler wanted the problem sorted out quickly, fearing that Czechoslovakia's strategic geographical importance would be "the greatest danger to the Reich" when the time came "for the big reckoning with the east and . . . particularly the Bolsheviks." Czechoslovakia, he warned Keitel, could not be allowed to become "a springboard for the Red Army and Air Force. In no time at all the enemy could be at the gates of Dresden and in the heart of the Reich."[91] The following day, Hitler's new army adjutant, Major Rudolf Schmundt, prepared a summary of the discussion, which outlined three possible scenarios.

(1) Idea of strategic attack out of the blue without cause or possibility of justification is rejected. Reason: hostile world opinion which might lead to serious situation.

(2) Action after a period of diplomatic discussions which gradually lead to a crisis and war.

(3) Lightning action based on an incident (for example the murder of the German Minister in the course of an anti-German demonstration).

The Führer, who evidently considered certain members of his diplomatic corps to be wholly expendable, preferred the third option; such an "incident" had of course been planned to foment discord in Austria, when Papen was to have been assassinated. Above all, Hitler emphasized to Keitel, speed would be of the essence.

The first four days of military action are, politically speaking, decisive. In the absence of outstanding military successes, a European crisis is certain to arise.[92]

In spite of the apparent caution of such remarks, Hitler was in reality confident that neither Britain nor France possessed the will or the strength to go to war. But at the back of his mind there still lurked sufficient uncertainty for him to feel the need for additional insurance. On April 18 Britain and Italy had finally signed their long-awaited, but largely meaningless, agreement (described by Churchill as "a complete triumph for Mussolini")[93] and on May 2 Hitler therefore set off for Rome with the express intention of winning the blessing and support of his sole ally. The visit was notable for the sheer scale of the German delegation, all of whom were kitted out in specially tailored ornate uniforms, approved by Frau Ribbentrop. The Foreign Ministry delegates were more used to the standard diplomatic dress of morning tails, but the *chef de protocole*, Count von Bülow-Schwante, drew up an intricate timetable, carefully detailing which uniform should be worn on which occasion. Three special trains were provided to transport the vast retinue of 500 diplomats, generals, party officials and security officers, and once the journey had begun it was not long before the "compartments looked like actors' dressing rooms."[94]

From the Italian perspective, the visit was memorable for lavish hospitality, as well as for the surly behavior of King Victor Emmanuel toward Hitler, whom he and the Queen treated with utter disdain. Hitler was already intensely irritated that they, rather than Mussolini, were to be his official hosts and, to the intense amusement of his staff, clearly felt ill at ease surrounded by the pomp and pageantry of the royal court. The accommodation at the royal place, the Quirinal, was not at all to his taste, and a rumor soon spread through both delegations that on his first night he had demanded the services of a woman. "This caused a great commotion," chuckled Ciano. "Then it was explained—apparently he can't get to sleep unless with his own eyes he sees a woman remake his bed. It was difficult to find one, but at last a hotel chambermaid arrived and the problem was solved." The King also complained to Ciano that Hitler "injects himself with stimulants and narcotics," while Mussolini was intrigued that the Führer appeared to put rouge on his cheeks.[95]

At the glittering banquet held to welcome him, Hitler's discomfort was painfully clear for all to see when he was called on to escort the Queen, a statuesque lady who towered over him, into dinner on his arm. He was even more horrified when the Italian ladies lining the corridor curtsied low, knelt down, or even kissed the hem of the Queen's dress; the two failed to exchange a single word for the rest of the evening. State Secretary Ernst von Weizsäcker, however, had a more enjoyable evening. When Ribbentrop pompously ticked him off for having agreed to sit in a place unbefitting of his rank, Weizsäcker reminded him of the timeless truth that "the lower down I was at the table the prettier my neighbours were likely to be."[96]

The final straw for Hitler came after a gala performance of *Aida* at the Opera House in Naples, when without warning he was invited to inspect a guard of honor alongside the King, who was dressed in full uniform and decorations. Hitler, on the other hand, was bareheaded and still in his evening tails, but was forced to suffer the ignominy of walking down the line, right arm outstretched in salute, left thumb (which he normally hooked into his belt) left limply across his chest, and the tails of his coat fluttering in the breeze behind him. "The German Führer and Reich Chancellor," wrote his amused adjutant Wiedemann, "looked like a head waiter at the peak of business in a restaurant, and he himself must have realised what a ridiculous figure he made."[97] In fact he realized it only too well, and the hapless Bülow-Schwante, whose sartorial fastidiousness had come to nothing, paid for the Führer's humiliation with his job.

For once, however, Hitler was prepared to tolerate such insults, both real and imagined, if it meant winning Mussolini's blessing for his proposed Czech adventure. The problem was that Ciano had planned the social program meticulously, precisely to avoid any serious political discussion. Ribbentrop had come to Rome hopefully clutching the draft text of a proposed German-Italian treaty, which he hoped would formalize the existing Axis agreement, and allow both countries jointly to direct their diplomatic fire against Britain and France. As usual, he clumsily chose the wrong moment to present the document to Ciano, who duly returned it a day or two later with so many amendments that it had lost virtually all meaning. Mussolini was contemptuous of Ribbentrop, telling his son-in-law that he "belongs to the category of Germans who are a disaster to their country. He talks about making war right and left, without naming an enemy or defining an objective."[98] Hitler, however, fulfilled his principal ambition, which was "to return with Czechoslovakia in his pocket."[99] At a dinner at the Palazzo Venezia on May 7, he calmed any lingering Italian fears by ruling out any German claim to the South Tyrol, and "succeeded pretty well in melting the ice around him."[100] On returning to Berlin, Ribbentrop was able to report to German missions abroad that "as far as the Sudeten German question is concerned, the conversations clearly brought out the fact that the Italians understood our concern for the fate of Sudeten Germans."[101]

At the same time Weizsäcker was briefing his colleagues that "France and Britain would probably not be prepared to intervene by armed force in favour of Czechoslovakia."[102] Indeed, it was becoming increasingly clear that the British government was prepared to go out of its way to do Hitler's work for him. Having taken the decision to avoid war at any cost, the logical consequence was inexorably to increase the pressure on Czechoslovakia to concede to Sudeten German demands. That pressure, recalled Lord Birkenhead, Halifax's Parliamentary Private Secretary and later biographer, was "to increase in force and meaning with every apparent Czech hesitation, until it almost seemed as though Czechoslovakia was herself a predatory state rather than a passive victim."[103] On May 2 Halifax summoned the Czech Minister, Jan Masaryk, the son of the country's founder, and bluntly warned him that if the problem was to be resolved, the "Czechoslovak Government would have to be prepared to go a very long way." Militarily, he continued, it was "a physical impossibility for any of Czechoslovakia's friends to prevent the country being overrun by Germany," and even if a war was fought and won against the Reich, it was "doubtful whether, in fact, the Czechoslovak State would be re-created in its present form."[104]

Ribbentrop's successor as ambassador in London, Herbert von Dirksen, quoted Halifax as saying that "Britain wished to make her contribution," and would shortly issue a démarche in Prague "which would aim at inducing [Czechoslovak President Edvard] Beneš to show the utmost measure of accommodation to the Sudeten Germans."[105] In Berlin, the message was the same. On May 7 Henderson called at the Foreign Ministry to give Ribbentrop and Weizsäcker his own view of the situation. "France," he said, "was acting for the Czechs and Germany for the Sudeten Germans. Britain was supporting Germany in this case."[106] Kirkpatrick, meanwhile, proposed that if the German government "would advise the British Government confidentially what solution of the Sudeten German problem they were striving after," then they would "bring such pressure to bear in Prague that the Czechoslovak Government would be compelled to the German wishes."[107]

On April 24, at the annual congress of the SdP at Karlsbad, Henlein had famously set out eight demands of the Czech government. All had been approved in advance by the German Foreign Ministry. The most important of these were recognition for the Sudeten areas as a distinct legal entity; full equality for Czechs and Germans within the state, including proportional appointment to government posts; and, most crucially, the right to hold and disseminate Nazi beliefs. Effectively they amounted to complete autonomy for the Sudeten Germans. En route for London on May 12, Henlein paid a secret visit to the Wilhelmstrasse to be briefed by Ribbentrop. "Herr Henlein will deny in London that he is acting on instructions from Berlin," recorded Weizsäcker. "His Karlsbad speech was not known in Berlin prior to its publication." In London, he was continually to emphasize "the progressive disintegration of the Czech political structure actually taking place, in order to discourage those circles which consider that their intervention on behalf of this political structure may still be of use."[108] On the same day the German Minister in Prague telegraphed Berlin urging greater caution in concealing from the Czech government that "almost every week Legation officials transmit secret consignments of money and documents to members of Sudeten German party."[109]

The tactic worked to perfection. Vansittart, who had been on "very friendly terms with Herr Henlein for some years past," thought that it would be a "pity to rebuff Herr Henlein's initiative." In the course of a four-hour meeting Henlein complained "how lamentably slow the Czech Government had been in making any advance," and that "he had always been the apostle of conciliation." Vansittart found him "far more reasonable and amenable than I had dared to hope."[110] Churchill agreed to meet Henlein at his Westminster flat and, when he later described the conversation to Masaryk, was relieved to find the Czech representative "contented with a settlement along these lines."[111] He also told Chamberlain that Henlein had "insisted, and offered to give his word of honour, that he had never received orders or even recommendations from Berlin."[112] Harold

Nicolson hosted a tea party for Hitler's *Statthalter*, to enable him to meet some of the younger generation of MPs, at which Henlein stressed that he himself "would not wish to join Germany, although many of his followers desire it."[113] This was the same man who, only the previous November, had proudly written to his "Führer and Reich Chancellor" that "an understanding between Germans and Czechs in Czechoslovakia is practically impossible and that a settlement of the Sudeten German question is only conceivable on a German basis."[114]

Hitler, meanwhile, was resting at Obersalzberg, and was becoming impatient to know what progress had been made with Case Green. Keitel and Jodl had deliberately dragged their feet in preparing the battle plans for Czechoslovakia, and had "prudently concealed the matter from the Army General Staff . . . to avoid unnecessary alarm."[115] However, Beck had gotten wind of the plans and on May 5 prepared his own memorandum, analyzing both the political and military lack of merit in fighting a war over Czechoslovakia. He was convinced that an attack on Czechoslovakia would unleash a European war in which Britain, France and Russia would unite in opposition to Germany, while the United States would become the arsenal of the West. He emphasized Germany's military inability to win such a war, largely on account of her lack of raw materials, and concluded that Germany's "military economic situation is worse than it was in 1917–18," when the Kaiser's armies had begun to collapse.[116] It is a measure of how terrified the army high command had by now become of Hitler that Brauchitsch and Keitel agreed not to show him the more damaging conclusions of the memorandum.

On May 16 Schmundt sent an urgent and "most secret" telegram from Berchtesgaden to OKW headquarters, demanding to know how many divisions on the Czech border were "ready to march within twelve hours, in the case of mobilisation." The reply, which came by return, indicated that twelve divisions were ready and waiting. This, however, failed to satisfy Hitler. "Please send the numbers of the divisions," retorted Schmundt, to which he received a more detailed breakdown. The "7th, 17th, 10th, 24th, 4th, 14th, 3rd, 18th, 8th PZ [Panzer] and Geb. [mountain troops]" were the divisions in question.[117] On May 20 Keitel forwarded to the Berghof the final draft directive for Case Green, promising that it would not be discussed with the military commanders until it "has been approved by you, my Führer."[118] The opening sentence of the new directive made Hitler's wishes clear.

> It is not my intention to smash Czechoslovakia by military action in the immediate future without provocation, unless an unavoidable development of the political conditions *within* Czechoslovakia forces the issue, or political events in Europe create a particularly favourable opportunity which may perhaps never recur.[119]

In the immediate aftermath of the Anschluss Jodl had recorded in his diary that "the Führer mentions that there is no hurry in solving the Czech question, because Austria has to be digested first."[120] Curiously, Chamberlain had used similar imagery himself, likening "Germany to a boa constrictor that had eaten a good meal and was trying to digest the meal before taking anything else."[121] Now, as Hitler again grew restless, the digestive process was all but complete, and his thoughts were turning to his next meal.

6

■

Crisis in May

The seizure of the whole of Czechoslovakia would not be in accordance with Herr Hitler's policy. . . . If Germany could obtain her desiderata by peaceful methods there was no reason she would reject such a procedure in favour of one based on violence.

Neville Chamberlain, March 18, 1938

It is my unalterable decision to smash Czechoslovakia by military action in the near future.

Adolf Hitler, May 30, 1938

I bear the burden of German proximity, but I bear it for all.

President Edvard Beneš to Anthony Eden, April 4, 1935

By the spring of 1938 Chamberlain felt confident that his political position was unassailable. He exercised a firm authority over the Cabinet, while his powerful Chief Whip, Captain David Margesson, used strong-arm tactics to deliver dominance over the parliamentary party also. Typically gratifying was the view of Lord Beaverbrook, as recounted to Chamberlain by the former Canadian Prime Minister R. B. Bennett, that he was "the best P.M. we've had in half a century . . . dominating Parliament but the country has not yet taken to him." If he so wished, claimed Beaverbrook, he could "be Prime Minister for the rest of his life."[1] With characteristic self-regard,

Chamberlain described his speech to the House of Commons on March 24 as "an éclatant success. In fact I never remember a speech by a British Minister at a critical time which has won such universal approval in Europe." Writing to his sister from the comfort of a weekend at Cliveden, the home of Nancy Astor, he continued that "as for the House of Commons there can be no question that I have got the confidence of our people as S[tanley] B[aldwin] never had it."[2]

Even the potentially damaging loss of a by-election to Labour in West Fulham on April 6, which caused consternation at the Conservative Central Office and led to a motion of censure in the Commons, failed to dampen his enthusiasm. "It was so long since our people had heard a real fighting speech that they went delirious with joy," he boasted to his sister,[3] while Harvey recorded that the "Conservatives in H. of C. were hysterically behind the P.M. . . . as the man who had preserved peace in face of the dictators."[4] At Westminster Chamberlain's Conservative critics found the going difficult. Since Eden's resignation a number of the younger dissidents had begun to meet discreetly, and to plot possible changes in the government. "The H. of C. is humming with intrigue," noted Chips Channon in his diary. "The so-called 'Insurgents' are rushing about, very over-excited. They want to bring back Anthony Eden and their Shadow Cabinet is alleged to include Lloyd George, Winston and Eden."[5] Harold Nicolson, for instance, was forced to resign as vice-chairman of the influential backbench Foreign Affairs Committee for failing to make it clear whether he was "pro-Eden or pro-Chamberlain."[6] But to the despair of his supporters, Eden showed not the slightest inclination to put himself forward as a stalking horse.

The Prime Minister, however, did not have it all his own way. Lord Swinton, the Secretary of State for Air, was one of his oldest political friends, but in May 1938 was unceremoniously sacked as the consequence of a parliamentary row about the slow progress of air rearmament. While his view was obviously colored by bitterness at his sacking, which was typically poorly handled, Swinton still spoke for many when he criticized Chamberlain as overly "autocratic and intolerant of criticism," and for assuming "the pretensions of the Presidential system of one-man government." Chamberlain had, claimed Swinton, become "intolerably self-assertive," and interpreted any expression opposed to his own as "disloyal and personally hostile."[7] Worse still, he had become suspicious to the point of paranoia, employing the shadowy Sir Joseph Ball, with the support of MI5, to gather information on the contacts and financial arrangements of his political opponents, and even to intercept their telephone calls. He was openly contemptuous of those who disagreed with him, "one of his least attractive attributes" being the "freedom with which he showed this contempt."[8] Indeed, he was positively proud of this combative style of debate, and made no attempt to tone down his abrasive manner, causing his predecessor, Lord Baldwin, to complain that all his own work "in keeping politics national instead of party" had been rendered worthless.[9] Eden expressed concern at "a return to class warfare in its bitterest form,"[10] while even Halifax was "aware of the harm which the P.M. is doing by hitting up the opposition."[11]

While Chamberlain was self-confident, decisive and autocratic in public, in private by contrast he could be painfully shy, difficult to befriend, and apparently aloof. He "did not mix easily with people," and attempts to humanize him were doomed to failure. Although it is hardly unusual for a Prime Minister to arouse dislike on the Opposition benches, Chamberlain managed to raise the art to an altogether higher form than usual. His Deputy Chief Whip later recalled "the chilling scorn he used when dealing with Opposition attackers," and noticed that he "got under the skin of some of the Members opposite to a quite remarkable degree." That said, it is generally considered customary to attempt to build a rapport of sorts with one's own backbenchers, but even this proved an ordeal too far for Chamberlain. Typical was one occasion when his Parliamentary Private Secretary, Lord Dunglass (later, as Sir Alec Douglas-Home, to become Prime Minister himself), escorted him to the Smoking Room in a bid to encourage dialogue with some of his fellow Tories. A painful silence ensued, broken only by a noisy interjection from the outspoken socialist Clydesider James Maxton. "Ach Jimmy, ye'll have to do better than that," he teased. "Anybody could see how unhappy ye all were."[12] And while Dunglass remained loyal to Chamberlain long after his death, he did later concede that his chief had been "economic in humour and select to the point of fastidiousness in his choice of friends."[13]

One distinguished historian, in critically analyzing Chamberlain's voluminous collection of letters to his two spinster sisters, Hilda and Ida, writes that the correspondence offers an "extraordinary insight into his mind and emotions," and reveals a "personality with marked traits of inferiority [and a] hunger for flattery that nourished a growing vanity and self-righteousness." His letters are "almost completely devoid of self-criticism or self-doubt [and] portray a man with an obsessive sense of mission, making predictions which were invariably optimistic and invariably wrong." His demeanor at all times is described as "self-satisfied" and "intolerably smug."[14] Another historian, Donald Cameron Watt, is blunter still: "It is extremely difficult to like Neville Chamberlain," he asserts. In Watt's view, the Prime Minister's worst attribute "was his distrust and dislike of public opinion." He regarded the British public "as too easily swayed by emotion to be trusted with the full facts," and accordingly set out deliberately to conceal as much of the truth from them as possible.[15]

To facilitate this deception, Chamberlain created and supervised the most sophisticated press management system until then seen at Downing Street, purposely setting out to court a select group of favored lobby journalists. "His aim had nothing remotely to do with open Government, access to information and the strengthening of the democratic process," wrote one contemporary journalist. "It had everything to do with the exploitation of the Press to espouse and defend Government thinking."[16] Indeed, some of his briefings were "so patently contrary to all other existing evidence that many civil servants were at a loss to understand why the lobby journalists were prepared to transcribe what he had to say without any independent evaluation or critique of the veracity of his comments."[17] The technique employed by Chamberlain, with his head of press, George Steward, was a combination of carrot and stick.

In an interesting pre-echo of modern-day spin doctoring, Chamberlain managed to convince certain journalists that they were "part of the Establishment, partners sharing power, authority and special knowledge."[18] The healthy adversarial relationship which a journalist should enjoy with any politician was replaced by one that was cozy and comfortable. Their job was made easier by two briefings a day, and the ultimate flattery was to be welcomed by Chamberlain into the small group of blue-chip journalists who were acknowledged as enthusiastic supporters, and were briefed in private at the St. Stephen's Club in Westminster. Meanwhile the distinction between government and party was distorted by the presence at such meetings of Sir Robert Topping, the director-general of the Conservative Central Office. One or two select correspondents even enjoyed unfettered personal access to the Prime Minister, for example W. W. Hadley, the editor of the *Sunday Times*, who was perhaps the most extravagant of all in his praise. Every Friday at 3:30 P.M. he visited Downing Street, and "every Sunday morning the paper's leading articles and reports faithfully reflected the Prime Minister's appeasement projects."[19]

Those journalists, however, who were not prepared to toe the party line found themselves marginalized, even bullied. Chamberlain refused to accept off-the-cuff questions, instead demanding four hours' notice from certain journalists. According to one of them, his intention was "to manipulate the Press into supporting his policy of appeasing the dictators," and increasingly he "abandoned persuasion, turning instead to the use of threats and suppression to coerce the Press into co-operation." As his obsession with the media grew, so the "old cosy relaxed atmosphere [was] replaced by a cold arrogance and intolerance." He resented critical, even probing, questions, to which he would reply with a "haughty sneer." After a pause, he would ask the journalist in question which publication he represented, before implying that the proprietor would be unhappy at his employee's "lack of patriotism." He made no attempt to conceal his anger, and "would attempt to snub a correspondent with frozen silence," before snapping, "Next question please!" His extraordinary chosen put-down to any question about such legitimate issues as the "persecution of the Jews, Hitler's broken pledges or Mussolini's ambitions," was to express surprise "that such an experienced journalist was susceptible to Jewish-Communist propaganda."[20]

Ignorance about central Europe, even among politicians and journalists, was still widespread; Members of Parliament would frequently refer during their speeches to Czechoslavia and Czechoslovenia, without provoking correction, or even mild amusement among their colleagues. As he walked past 10 Downing Street one day, Jan Masaryk, the Czech Minister in London, ruefully remarked that he spent most of his "official time in there explaining to the gentleman inside that Czechoslovakia is a country and not a contagious disease."[21] Certainly Chamberlain did not feel particularly sensitive toward Czech concerns, believing that he had more important issues with which to deal. In November 1937, after Halifax's visit to Germany, Chamberlain had privately speculated to his sister that Hitler only wanted "much the same things for the Sudetendeutsche as we did for the Uitlanders in the Transvaal,"[22] a reference to the expatriate British workers whose cause his father had famously espoused as Colonial Secretary in the late 1890s, leading in part to the outbreak of the Boer War.

In the aftermath of the Anschluss, Chamberlain soon recovered his equilibrium, and turned his thoughts back to how best to improve Anglo-German relations. The answer, he believed, was to approach Hitler, "and say something like this":

> It is no use crying over spilt milk. . . . Everyone is thinking that you are going to repeat the Austrian coup in Czecho-Slovakia. The best thing you can do is to tell us exactly what you want for your Sudeten Deutsch. If it is reasonable we will urge the Czechs to accept it.[23]

At a meeting of the Cabinet's Foreign Policy Committee, Sir Thomas Inskip described Czechoslovakia as "an unstable unit in Central Europe," and stated that he could "see no reason why we should take any steps to maintain such a unit in being." When he asked the Prime Minister whether he believed that Germany would be satisfied with the Sudetenland, or in fact wished to absorb the whole country, Chamberlain displayed an appalling lack of understanding of Hitler's intentions.

> The seizure of the whole of Czechoslovakia would not be in accordance with Herr Hitler's policy, which was to include all Germans in the Reich but not to include other nationalities. If Germany could obtain her *desiderata* by peaceful methods there was no reason she would reject such a procedure in favour of one based on violence.[24]

On April 11 Halifax wrote to Phipps in Paris, stressing that it was of the "greatest importance that every effort should be made by the Czechoslovak Government to reach a settlement of the German minority problem," and that it should be done "by direct negotiation with Herr Henlein."[25] This was the same Herr Henlein who just six days earlier had told the Hungarian Foreign Minister that "whatever the Czech government might offer, he would always raise still higher demands . . . he wanted to sabotage an understanding by all means because this was the only method to blow up Czechoslovakia quickly."[26] The government's faith in Henlein was hardly surprising, given that he had successfully pulled the wool over the eyes of even Churchill and Vansittart. According to the latter's intelligence sources, the Sudeten leader urgently needed to "have his hand strengthened and it would be profitable to anybody if we did the strengthening."[27] On May 4 Halifax told the Cabinet that "it would be very useful if the Germans would tell us at some time what would satisfy them." Chamberlain was delighted with this form of words. He "wanted, if possible," he confirmed "to get the Germans to say what kind of settlement would be acceptable."[28]

On May 12 Chamberlain attended a lunch given by Nancy Astor at her London mansion in St. James's Square. Organized with the help of Joseph Driscoll, a prominent Canadian journalist who contributed to the *New York Herald Tribune*, the purpose of the select gathering of American and Canadian journalists was that "a dozen hard boiled toughs" should meet Chamberlain, and listen to his views in an informal, off-the-record environment. For once, however, his sure touch with the press deserted him. "I addressed them on the situation in Europe and then answered questions," he told his sister. In fact he made it clear that, in his opinion, neither France, Russia, nor indeed Britain, would fight for Czechoslovakia, a state that was wholly unsustainable in its present form. He personally would favor ceding the Sudeten German districts to the Reich. As usual, both his modesty and his instinct subsequently deserted him. "So far as I can tell from what the Astors heard afterwards the experiment was a success," he told his sister. "They concluded that I was sincere, reasonable and moreover had a sense of humour."[29] In fact, Nancy Astor was only too happy to tell him exactly what he wanted to hear.

Two days later the *New York Times*, under an anonymous byline, printed a detailed account of the lunch which concluded that "Mr. Chamberlain . . . certainly favours a more drastic measure—namely separation of the German districts from the body of the Czechoslovak Republic and the annexation of them to Germany."[30] Similar articles by Joseph Driscoll appeared in both the *New York Herald Tribune* and the *Montreal Daily Star*. Driscoll disclosed what had until then been largely unknown to the public, and indeed to most MPs: that Eden's resignation had been caused by serious differences with Chamberlain, not only over Italy, but also over Roosevelt's offer. Driscoll added conspiratorially that he was also "now privileged to shed what can truly be called official light on the real British attitude towards Czechoslovakia," the accuracy of which could "not be disputed."[31]

> Perhaps the most dangerous spot in the world is Czechoslovakia. What do the British in authority think about it? Nothing seems clearer than that the British do not expect to fight for Czechoslovakia and do not anticipate that France or Russia will either. That being so, then the Czechs must accede to the German demands, if reasonable.[32]

Although the articles were not published in Britain, word soon leaked out and questions were asked in Parliament. Since appointing Halifax, a peer, as Foreign Secretary, Chamberlain himself had replied for the government on foreign affairs in the Commons, and in a highly unusual development for a Prime Minister he was forced to attend a late night debate on the reports initiated by a Liberal MP, Geoffrey Mander. Chamberlain began his reply by lying to the House, claiming that there had been no difference between him and Eden over Roosevelt's offer. He then tried to brush the issue aside by joking that Mander was well known as the "*enfant terrible*" of the Commons and dismissing the debate as "restless and mischievous curiosity . . . a fishing inquiry."[33]

The following day, the Liberal leader, Sir Archibald Sinclair, returned to the subject. In a masterful display of parliamentary obfuscation, Chamberlain protested that just because he refused to deny having given an interview, it did not mean that he was therefore admitting it. Unfortunately, he then succumbed to a fate dreaded by all party leaders, the unhelpful intervention from a backbench colleague, mistakenly assumed to be helpful. When Sinclair challenged him as to whether the lunch had taken place at all, Nancy Astor leapt to her feet "to say that there is not a word of truth in it."[34] A few days later, amid widespread hilarity, she was forced to retract her remark by making a personal statement to the House.

> I never had any intention of denying that the Prime Minister had had luncheon at my house. The Prime Minister did so attend, the object being to enable some American journalists who had not previously met him to do so privately and informally—(Opposition laughter). What I did deny, and still deny, is the suggestion that what took place on this particular occasion

was an interview. An interview is a meeting arranged with a view to the communication of information intended specifically to be made the subject of articles in the Press—(More Opposition laughter).[35]

Chamberlain was furious. "Heaven save me from my friends," he complained to his sister.[36]

A very public demonstration of the lengths to which some would go to appease Hitler occurred on May 14, when the England football team, including the legendary Stanley Matthews, played Germany at the Olympic Stadium in Berlin. Although Hitler himself was not present, a crowd of over 100,000 included Goebbels, Göring, Hess and Ribbentrop. As the two teams lined up before kick-off, the England captain, Eddie Hapgood, led his team in giving the Nazi salute during the playing of the German national anthem. There was immediate and widespread condemnation in the British press. It later transpired that there had been a good deal of soul searching among the players as to whether or not to acquiesce in the order to give the salute, which had emanated from the Foreign Office, and had been enforced by the Secretary of the Football Association, Stanley Rous. England won the game 6–3, with goals from Matthews and Arsenal striker Cliff Bastin, but Hitler already had his propaganda coup. Henderson, who watched the game from the Führer's private box alongside the Nazi dignitaries, without a trace of irony remarked that the spirit in which the match had been played gave the "promise of cordial relations in future insofar as sporting fixtures are concerned."[37]

▪ ▪ ▪

By the middle of May, a number of SIS intelligence reports had reached the Foreign Office which suggested that a German attack on Czechoslovakia was imminent; they included the intercept of Reichenau's telephone call from Cairo and also, most probably, details of the exchanges between Hitler and the Bendlerstrasse concerning the battle-readiness of certain frontier divisions and Keitel's latest draft directive for Case Green. The speed with which Germany had acted during the Anschluss had in itself created a sense of anxiety throughout Europe, and the prospect of the Czech local elections scheduled for the weekend of May 21 and 22 heightened the tension still further, as did the increasingly belligerent tone of the German press. On

May 19 Henlein broke off negotiations between the SdP and the Czech government.

In February 1937, a disaffected officer of the Abwehr, Paul Thümmel, had written to the head of Czech military intelligence, General František Moravec, volunteering his services. He quickly established his credentials by revealing a set of secret Czech plans that had fallen into German hands, and by betraying a senior Czech officer who was spying for the Abwehr. The officer was arrested and hanged, whereupon Thümmel was formally recruited by Moravec and given the code name A-54. By the spring of 1938 Thümmel was regularly passing over high-grade intelligence to Moravec, claiming that, although he was paid a considerable sum of money for his treachery, it was not his sole motivation; he had a Serb fiancée, a member of an oppressed Slav minority in East Prussia, and accordingly hated Nazis. Moravec was delighted with the quality of Thümmel's intelligence, but far from convinced by his explanation. "Spies, being human," he noted, "often invent a better-sounding motive if their sole reason for betraying their country is money."[38] It soon became apparent that Thümmel enjoyed access to high-grade intelligence, in particular concerning the structure of both the Abwehr and the Sicherheitsdienst, the SD, or Nazi security service. He also produced documents on Wehrmacht battle orders, mobilization plans, and German frontier defenses; indeed Moravec learned the details of Case Green barely a month after Blomberg had first commissioned it in June 1937, intelligence he undoubtedly shared with the SIS.

During the night of May 12, 1938, agent A-54 met Czech intelligence officers in secret at a police station in the Sudetenland. The picture he painted for them was alarming.

The Germans are preparing a campaign of provocation and sabotage which will erupt on the eve of the Czech local elections on 22 May. In the last few days, arms, explosives and munitions have been smuggled into Czechoslovakia. Shock troops, mainly led by high-ranking officers of the SS and SA, are waiting to invade Czech territory. Officials of the Henlein Sudeten Party are to listen regularly to German broadcasts. As soon as they hear the password they are to declare a state of alert. This will be a signal for sabotage: destruction of railway lines, main roads and bridges, and armed attacks on frontier posts and Czech sentries. This action is expected

to come to a head on 22 May. . . . Sudeten German Freikorps, supported
by SS troops, will then invade Czechoslovakia.[39]

Reports of unusual German troop concentrations near the Czech border
had been reaching Prague at an alarming rate since the beginning of May.
Czech military intelligence passed details of Thümmel's claims on to Major
Harold "Gibby" Gibson, the veteran passport control officer and SIS station
chief in Prague, who in turn passed the information to London. During the
evening of May 19, Henderson sent a dispatch to the Foreign Office reporting that the British consul in Dresden believed German troops were forming
up along the Czech frontier in Saxony, Silesia and northern Austria; his
French colleague in Berlin was receiving similar reports. The following
morning the British military attaché in Prague, Lieutenant Colonel H. C. T.
Stronge, was summoned to a meeting at the Czech Ministry of Defense.
Moravec, using a pointer and wall map, indicated "the reported movements
of certain Wehrmacht formations." They were considered, he said, "to be a
threat to Czech national security."[40]

On the afternoon of Friday, May 20, Henderson called on State Secretary
Weizsäcker at the Foreign Ministry to challenge him over the reports.
Weizsäcker assured him that he knew nothing of any troop movements, and
dismissed the rumors out of hand. However, in an effort to reassure the
ambassador, he promised to telephone Keitel at the Bendlerstrasse to obtain
military confirmation of this. Henderson expressed himself satisfied, but
before returning to his embassy, tactfully reminded Weizsäcker that similar
assurances had been given to his military attaché by the OKW on March 11,
shortly before the Anschluss, assurances that had turned out to be wholly
false. He asked that Keitel bear this in mind when replying. At 6:50 P.M.
Henderson telephoned London to say that he had heard back from
Weizsäcker who reported Keitel as having also described the "rumours of
troop concentration as absolutely nonsense." He gave his word of honor.
"No troops have been assembled in Saxony."[41] Henderson also released
details of Keitel's denial to Reuters for dissemination to the British press.
Similar assurances were given by the Foreign Ministry to the Czech Minister
in Berlin, and to the government in Prague.

However, memories of the Anschluss were still fresh, and the belligerent
attitude of the German press did nothing to calm the wild rumors. Late that

evening the British Minister in Prague, Basil Newton, drafted a series of telegrams for dispatch to London in the early hours. They arrived at 9:30 the following morning.

> Latest reports received by the Czechoslovak General Staff are to the effect that German 7th and 17th infantry divisions are advancing in the direction of Bavarian-Czechoslovak frontier. Czechoslovak General Staff believes movement of German troops in the direction of Czechoslovak frontier to be general.[42]

The significance of the message lies in the fact that the two divisions mentioned are also the first two named in the list of twelve divisions, described as being ready to march, which had been sent to Hitler just a few days earlier. This has led at least one historian to conclude that Czech fears "seem to have derived from detailed and at least superficially plausible reports of German troop movements."[43] A further telegram from Newton claimed that the troop movements were part of "a general plan of provocation and intimidation," including Luftwaffe flights over Czechoslovak territory. The Czech General Staff had recommended immediate mobilization.[44]

The Czech government was also concerned by a typically violent interview that its minister in Berlin had endured with Ribbentrop that afternoon. It was no surprise, therefore, when Beneš called an emergency meeting of the Cabinet and the Supreme Defense Council, which lasted all afternoon and well into the evening. At 9 P.M. an immediate partial mobilization was ordered, principally of reservists, some 180,000 men. Throughout the night troop trains rolled out of Prague and by dawn on Saturday, May 21, Czech troops occupied the border fortifications and all Sudeten territory. Henderson decided to dispatch his military attaché, Colonel Mason-MacFarlane, together with the assistant military attaché, on a reconnaissance mission through Saxony and Silesia, similar to the one that he had undertaken at the time of the Anschluss. Having done so, Henderson returned to the Wilhelmstrasse to see Ribbentrop, whom he found in "a highly excitable and pugnacious frame of mind."[45] Unfortunately a British newspaper had quoted Keitel by name as having been the source of the denial issued to Henderson, and the Foreign Minister was furious.

Ribbentrop's long-standing personal antagonism toward Keitel was well known, and he was no fan of the languid British ambassador, whom he found typical of the old-school, gentlemanly style of British diplomacy that he had so despised during his time in London. Now he was infuriated that the two men appeared to be colluding. "You have gone behind my back, ambassador," he shouted, "and asked General Keitel about alleged German troop movements on the Czechoslovakian border. I shall see to it that in future you are given no information on military matters." Henderson remained unperturbed. "I shall have to report that to my Government," he replied calmly. "I can only conclude from your remarks that Keitel's statement to me was incorrect."[46] Ribbentrop attempted to change the subject, complaining bitterly about the reported deaths of two SdP couriers early that morning near Eger. When challenged by a Czech policeman at a checkpoint, they had apparently refused to stop their motorbikes, and had been shot dead.[47] Ribbentrop launched into a torrent of abuse about the "mad" Czechs, who would, he assured Henderson, "all be exterminated, women and children and all." When Henderson dryly observed that while the death of two Germans was greatly to be deplored, it was surely better than that hundreds of thousands should die in war, Ribbentrop replied that "every German was ready to die for his country."[48]

In London, the mood at the Foreign Office was one of increasing concern. Further telegrams from Newton emphasized that the Czech government believed the news of German troop concentrations to be genuine, and that an attack was considered likely. Halifax was summoned back from his weekend in Oxford by Cadogan, while Chamberlain was given the news while fishing on the River Test in Hampshire with Sir Joseph Ball. His first reaction was that "those d—d Germans have spoiled another week end for me," but he still managed to carry on with his sport, in spite of "a general uneasiness on my part that deepened into anxiety after I got the message, and made it difficult to concentrate properly on the fishing."[49] Henderson was instructed to call on Ribbentrop a second time, and to hand him a still stronger warning. He was to stress that there was no letup in the "persistent stories of troop movements in the direction of Czechoslovakia," and that the British were "doing their utmost to promote a peaceful solution" to the problem.[50] Henderson warned that if the French honored their obligations, by intervening on behalf of Czechoslovakia, then "His Majesty's Government could not guarantee that they would not be forced by circumstances to do so also." Ribbentrop's mood had changed since their morning meeting, and he listened in sullen silence, becoming hysterical again when Henderson had finished. "If France were really to be so crazy as to attack us," he warned, "it would lead to perhaps the greatest French defeat in world history and, if Britain were to join her, then once again we should have to fight to the death."[51]

By now, the nerves of all those involved had become distinctly frayed. The British naval attaché in Berlin was due to return home on leave with his family, and another member of the embassy staff asked if he might send his own children home also, in the attaché's care. Unfortunately there was no remaining space on the train, but the railway company offered to add an extra carriage if it could be filled. Two further members of the staff were persuaded to enroll their families as well, and once the requisite number had been reached, the additional carriage was ordered. The rumor that the British embassy was being evacuated spread like wildfire through the diplomatic community. François-Poncet turned up in person to inquire what was happening, while Weizsäcker telephoned Henderson, and implored him not to be the cause of panic. When the news reached London, even Cadogan appeared at first to believe that the rumor was genuine, while Halifax was "horrified at such alarmist action and telephoned to stop them."[52] That evening, Henderson was dining with Frau von Dirksen, the stepmother of the German ambassador in London, when builders began to dynamite a nearby building which was being demolished. Henderson commented sarcastically to François-Poncet "that the war seemed to have begun," while Göring, who also heard the explosion, joked that his immediate reaction had been that "those cursed Czechs have begun it."[53] In Prague, the German ambassador was burning sensitive papers.

Mason-MacFarlane and his deputy returned to Berlin from their reconnaissance mission early on the morning of Sunday, May 22. In just twenty-four hours they had covered over a thousand miles between them, and had discovered no evidence whatsoever of any unusual or significant military activity. Later that morning Henderson called again at the Wilhelmstrasse to see Weizsäcker, Ribbentrop having left for Berchtesgaden. A further warning for Hitler from Halifax stressed the gravity of the situation.

If resort is had to forcible measures, it is quite impossible for me or for him to foretell results that may follow, and I would beg him not to count on this country being able to stand aside if from any precipitate action there should start European conflagration.[54]

At 5 P.M. the British Cabinet met for an hour, in a rare emergency session on a Sunday. "The general feeling," complained Duff Cooper, "seemed to be that great, brutal Czecho-Slovakia was bullying poor, peaceful little Germany. Such at least was the opinion of the Lord Chancellor [Lord Maugham], whom I find a most undesirable addition to the Cabinet."[55]

In truth, by Sunday afternoon the crisis was already over. Germany did not, after all, intend to invade Czechoslovakia. The immediate threat had passed. But the recriminations over who should bear responsibility for bringing the crisis about in the first place continued for some time, dividing opinion. The British military attachés in Berlin and Prague later laid the blame for the crisis squarely at the door of the Czechs. "I have always been inclined," wrote Stronge from Prague, "to suspect the Czechs, as they were the only party to benefit from the scare at that time. Britain and France were embarrassed as they were forced to come into the open, the very last thing they wanted to do, and administer a warning to Hitler."[56] Similarly Mason-MacFarlane concluded that the Czech General Staff "appear to have drawn many false deductions and they have been guilty of much exaggeration and of invention as well. They have possibly done this deliberately."[57]

In London, however, the mood was one of self-congratulation. Vansittart, through his private intelligence channels, remained convinced that a coup against Czechoslovakia had been under preparation, and had been thwarted. He dismissed Mason-MacFarlane's contradictory evidence as being "typical of those who served under the 'appeasement'-minded Henderson."[58] In reality, Mason-MacFarlane had little sympathy for his ambassador's views. Major General Henry Pownall, the Director of Military Intelligence, also believed that "Germany *were* [sic] up to some monkey tricks." The chief of the SIS had informed him that "someone in Germany called it off on Monday, influenced no doubt partly by the firm front shown by the C[zech]-S and French assurances. In fact their hand was called and they climbed down."[59]

Chamberlain too dramatized the weekend's events for his sister.

The more I hear about last week end the more I feel what a "d—d close run thing" it was. It is all very well for the German Press to make light of it now, but why did Ribbentrop abuse Henderson? I cannot doubt in my own mind (1) that the German Government made all preparations for a coup (2) that in the end they decided after getting our warnings that the risks were too great (3) that the general view that this was just what had happened made them conscious that they had lost prestige and (4) that they are venting their spite on us because they feel that we have got the credit for having given them a check.

He was suffering from a bad attack of gout, and had been feeling depressed. The "Czecho crisis was a plateful," he complained, "but I am recovering my spirits."[60]

In London, Paris, Prague, and even Moscow, world leaders breathed a sigh of relief. The crisis had been successfully negotiated, and Hitler had been taught a lesson; the diplomatic firmness with which he had been confronted had forced him to back down. The Western press had a field day at the Führer's expense. Pownall summed up the feeling in London. "The Germans are mighty sore," he reported, "the more so that French newspapers proclaim it as a victory for England, giving all the credit to British (and French) diplomacy and none to Germany's (alleged) moderation."[61] Intelligence reaching the Foreign Office led to a similar conclusion. "Our sources tend to show that Hitler had really intended to go for Czechoslovakia," recorded Harvey, "but that he has shied off in face of our warnings."[62] Vansittart wrote that "the best way to deal with Germany is firmness. The last days have shown that it pays and that no other method does."[63] And for once, Henderson's analysis too was accurate. "What Hitler could not stomach," he told Halifax, "was the triumphant outcry of the foreign Press, and particularly the British, to which above all he is susceptible."[64]

▪ ▪ ▪

In one respect at least, Chamberlain was quite correct. Hitler most certainly did intend to vent his spite upon his enemies. Whether or not he had indeed been on the point of invading Czechoslovakia was now largely immaterial. He felt deeply humiliated by the successful Czech mobilization, and shocked by the widespread support they had received. Britain and France

1. Field Marshal Werner von Blomberg is congratulated by Adolf Hitler on forty years of service in the German army, in March 1937. Standing apart (left to right) are General Werner von Fritsch, Hermann Göring, and Admiral Erich Raeder.

"Great Britain and every country owe a debt of gratitude... for the encouragement given to sport by this exhibition"—
LORD HALIFAX

NAZI HUNTING EXHIBITION.

2. "Nazi Hunting Exhibition" by the contemporary cartoonist David Low, from the *Evening Standard* of November 19, 1937. Lord Halifax, who was visiting Berlin under the pretext of attending the hunting exhibition, is shown Hitler's trophies—the empty plaques await the heads of Austria, Czechoslovakia and Poland.

3. "The high-water mark of Halifax's appeasement." Lord Halifax is welcomed to the Berghof by Hitler on November 19, 1937. The Führer's ever-present interpreter, Paul Schmidt, stands beside Halifax, while the German Foreign Minister, Constantin von Neurath, is partially hidden by Hitler. In the background are Ivone Kirkpatrick and Sir Nevile Henderson from the British embassy in Berlin.

4. Anthony Eden leaves the Foreign Office on February 20, 1938, after resigning as Foreign Secretary. Close behind him is his (and later Halifax's) Private Secretary, Oliver Harvey.

5. Hitler enjoys the welcome of the Austrian crowds during a stop for lunch in the town of St. Pölten, on the road from Linz to Vienna, on March 14, 1938.

6. Arthur Seyss-Inquart, the newly appointed *Reichsstadthalter* (Reich Governor) of the German province of Ostmark, welcomes Hitler to Vienna on March 14, 1938. Behind Seyss-Inquart are Heinrich Himmler (left) and Reinhard Heydrich.

7. Hitler addresses the vast, delirious crowd, estimated at a quarter of a million people, in Vienna's Heldenplatz on March 15, 1938.

8. Hitler reviews a march-past of troops in Rome on May 6, 1938, flanked by Benito Mussolini (left) and King Victor Emmanuel III and Queen Elena (right). In the second row (left to right) are Joachim von Ribbentrop, Joseph Goebbels, Rudolf Hess and Himmler. The Italian King treated Hitler with disdain throughout the state visit, and complained to Count Galeazzo Ciano that Hitler "injects himself with stimulants and narcotics."

9. Lord Runciman (left) meets President Edvard Beneš for the first time at Hradčany Castle in Prague, on August 4, 1938.

10. Sir Nevile Henderson (left), who had been recalled from Berlin, and Lord Halifax arrive at 10 Downing Street for the emergency meeting of ministers on August 30, 1938.

11. "Hitler's Spy Princess." Stephanie von Hohenlohe (with arms crossed) sitting next to Magda Goebbels. Standing (left to right) are Hohenlohe's "mentor," Lord Rothermere—"a strong supporter of the Führer" according to Joseph Goebbels; the interpreter Paul Schmidt; Hitler; his adjutant, and Hohenlohe's lover, Fritz Wiedemann; and Joseph Goebbels. The photograph was taken at the Berghof in January 1937.

12. Sir Robert Vansittart and Sir Alexander Cadogan leave Downing Street on Sunday September 11, 1938, after the meeting at which it was decided that Henderson should not issue a formal warning to Hitler at Nuremberg. "Van furious," recorded Cadogan.

13. Sir Nevile Henderson and the Reich Propaganda Minister, Joseph Goebbels, at a supper given by Himmler in the SS camp at Nuremberg on September 12, 1938.

14. Arthur Seyss-Inquart (left) and the Sudeten German leader, Konrad Henlein, at Nuremberg, September 1938.

15. Hitler reviews 100,000 troops on Army Day at the Zeppelinwiese, Nuremberg—September 12, 1938, the last day of the party congress.

16. Neville Chamberlain and Hitler enjoy a "macabre tea party" at the Berghof, during the Prime Minister's visit to Berchtesgaden on September 15, 1938. Schmidt and Henderson take a contrasting interest in the proceedings.

17. Chamberlain welcomes the French Prime Minister, Edouard Daladier (right), to Croydon Aerodrome on Sunday, September 18, 1938. The French Foreign Minister, Georges Bonnet, a staunch appeaser, stands between them.

18. Chamberlain leaves Heston in a Lockheed 14 Super Electra, on September 22, 1938, bound for Cologne and his second meeting with Hitler at Bad Godesberg. The M4 motorway now runs through the center of the photograph, and the landing ground is the site of the Heston service station.

had called his bluff, his word had been doubted, and he had suffered a major diplomatic defeat in full view of the whole world. "Because of Germany's self-restraint," noted Jodl, the Führer had "suffered a loss of prestige which he is not willing to suffer again."[65] Hitler was all the more enraged that he had been prematurely accused of being on the point of committing a crime that he did indeed intend to commit, but had not yet had the opportunity to carry out. The events of the weekend of the so-called May Crisis reinforced his determination, and accelerated his preparations. "After 21 May it was quite clear that this problem had to be solved one way or the other," he later recalled. "Every further postponement could only make the question more difficult and the solution thereby bloodier."[66]

For a week Hitler sat alone at the Berghof, high above Berchtesgaden, silently brooding, and plotting his revenge. On May 28, however, he suddenly reappeared in Berlin, and immediately summoned his ranking military leaders, including Göring, Beck, Keitel and Raeder, together with Ribbentrop and Neurath, to a meeting at the Reich Chancellery. The previous day he had ordered Admiral Raeder to speed up the construction program for battleships and submarines, with the express intention of creating a bargaining tool over any future conflict with Britain. But he did not believe that the British would go to war over Czechoslovakia. As the Reich's finest assembled outside the Wintergarten, the general assumption was that the Führer would announce further military measures. An agitated Göring took Wiedemann to one side. "Doesn't the Führer realise what he is doing?" he asked plaintively. "This will mean war with France!" He promised to speak when the moment was right.[67]

Hitler spoke calmly, but purposefully, for two hours. The speech was similar in many ways to what he had delivered the previous November, the crucial difference being that he now considered the invasion of Czechoslovakia to be imminent. The incomplete state of Czech fortifications and the slow pace of rearmament in Britain made early action essential. Construction work on the great West Wall, the formidable fortification on Germany's western front, otherwise known as the Siegfried Line, was to be greatly speeded up, to allow for a "lightning march into Czechoslovakia."[68] Britain and France would be unable to intervene, so long as the war was won quickly. All preparations for military action were to be completed by 2 October. "It is my unshakeable will," he concluded to his shocked audience, "to wipe Czechoslovakia from the map. We shall have to use methods which, perhaps, will not find the immediate approval of you older officers." As soon as Hitler had finished, Göring pushed forward excitedly, his eyes gleaming. "Mein Führer," he exclaimed, grasping Hitler by the hand and forgetting his earlier promise to Wiedemann. "Let me congratulate you wholeheartedly on your unique concept!" There were no protests, nor even further discussion.[69]

Two days later, on May 30, Hitler signed the new directive for Case Green, which differed from earlier drafts in only two respects. The first paragraph now read:

> It is my unalterable decision to smash [*zerschlagen*] Czechoslovakia by military action in the near future. It is the business of the political leadership to await or bring about the suitable moment from a political and military point of view.
>
> An unavoidable development of events within Czechoslovakia, or other political events in Europe providing a suddenly favourable opportunity which may never recur, may cause me to take early action.

The propaganda war, meanwhile, was to begin in earnest, "to intimidate the Czechs by means of threats and wear down their power of resistance." In a covering letter Keitel explained the meaning of "near future." The directive's "execution," he ordered, "must be assured by October 1, 1938, at the latest."[70]

Meanwhile over half a million men were put to work, day and night, under the command of Fritz Todt, the architect of the autobahn system, as construction of the West Wall was greatly accelerated; fortifications that were designed to halt any French incursion into Germany, with a minimum of troops, while Czechoslovakia was seized in the east with a lightning strike. On June 18, more detailed guidance was issued for senior officers. From October 1, confirmed Hitler, he intended to "make full use of every favourable political opportunity for the realization of this aim." As he had done in the Rhineland in 1936 and in Austria a few months earlier, however, he would only take action against Czechoslovakia once he was "firmly convinced that France will not march and therefore Britain will not intervene either."[71] The date was fixed and, in spite of a growing rift between Hitler and his army leadership, he was to adhere to it unflinchingly throughout the coming months.

Opposition to Hitler's military plans was led by General Ludwig Beck, the Chief of the Army General Staff. A "sensitive, intelligent, decent but indecisive man," according to one contemporary journalist,[72] the British embassy in Berlin recognized that he was not "in sympathy with the present régime."[73] Beck had initially welcomed Hitler's rise to power, and although he was later to oppose the Nazi regime on broader, more idealistic grounds, during the spring of 1938 his defiance of the Führer was based solely on professional differences of opinion. He had not questioned the proposed use of force against Austria, and agreed that the destruction of Czechoslovakia was a necessary prerequisite for achieving *Lebensraum*. However, Beck's "cardinal point" of disagreement with Hitler was that Germany was not yet mighty enough to take on the world powers and that any conflict would inevitably spread throughout Europe.[74] After hearing Hitler's speech on May 28, Beck responded with two written memoranda on May 29 and June 3, both highly critical of Hitler's assumptions in relation to Britain and France, and of the operational viability of Case Green. Having criticized Hitler's plans point by point, he concluded that the new directive was "militarily unsound," and suggested to the commander-in-chief of the army, General Walther von Brauchitsch, that the army high command should reject it.

Brauchitsch had, of course, been the principal beneficiary of the Blomberg scandal, having been appointed by Hitler to succeed Blomberg at the newly created OKW. He came from a distinguished Prussian family, as a child had served as pageboy to the Empress Augusta Victoria, and had been married to his heiress wife for twenty-eight years. A highly strung, albeit cultured, man, he was "quiet, dignified, rather reserved, perhaps even somewhat introverted,"[75] but in February 1938 he shocked Berlin society by suddenly leaving his wife. That he then became personally indebted to Hitler seems certain. For once the Führer put aside his prejudice against divorce, and offered Brauchitsch a substantial sum of money to facilitate his divorce and almost immediate remarriage to a much younger wife, herself an ardent Nazi. However, the importance of this bribery should not be overstressed, Hitler's biographer arguing that "Brauchitsch's subservience to Hitler was not purchased; it came naturally."[76] Other historians have observed that "the man without a backbone could not be provided with one by his associates,"[77] and that the shallow Brauchitsch became tongue-tied and "practically paralyzed" when in Hitler's presence. "When I confront this man," Brauchitsch once admitted, "I feel as if someone were choking me and I cannot find another word."[78]

On June 13 Hitler summoned forty senior army commanders to a gathering at Barth in Pomerania. Following Fritsch's complete exoneration at the military court chaired by Göring, there were growing murmurs of dissent within the officer corps. Fritsch had been widely revered, and talk of collective resignations in protest at his treatment had reached Hitler's ears. He now gambled that news of his proposed Czech adventure would provide the perfect distraction to head off any discontent among his officers. Before Hitler arrived, Brauchitsch spent the morning session preparing the ground, informing the assembled officers, most of whom knew nothing of Case Green, of the Führer's decision to take Czechoslovakia by force. There was widespread surprise, but in the course of a tense meeting Brauchitsch successfully appealed for loyalty. When Hitler arrived at lunchtime, he followed up Brauchitsch's introduction with his own carefully rehearsed analysis of the Fritsch case, which, remarkably, seems to have satisfied his critics. He concluded by echoing Brauchitsch's appeal for loyalty, demonstrating, in the words of one historian, his "exceptional insight into the tendency of men torn between conscience and self-interest to welcome what made it easier to opt for the latter."[79]

With Brauchitsch now identifying himself so closely with Hitler's policy, and the majority of senior officers having meekly fallen into line, Beck's hopes of winning support for a united front quickly faded. In mid-June his position was further weakened when army war games appeared to demonstrate that, despite his gloomy predictions, Czechoslovakia could quite easily be overrun within just eleven days. On July 16 he wrote a third, final memorandum for Brauchitsch, in which he effectively advocated industrial action, even mass resignation by the military leadership, to "avoid a general catastrophe for Germany."[80]

The soldierly duty has a limit at the point where their knowledge, conscience, and responsibility prohibits the execution of an order. If their advice and warnings in such a situation are not listened to, they have the right and duty to the people and to history to resign from their posts. They will thereby have saved their Fatherland from the worst, from destruction. . . . Extraordinary times demand extraordinary action.[81]

Beck delivered his paper to Brauchitsch in person. If the Wehrmacht's senior commanders could not persuade Hitler to abandon his proposals for war, he told him, then they must all tender their resignations. "But that is a collective act of insubordination that you are demanding of them," Brauchitsch exclaimed. "It fringes on rebellion."[82]

▪ ▪ ▪

Throughout the spring and summer of 1938 Chamberlain received strong, indeed near-unanimous, support from the press, in particular from those titles owned by the two great media barons of the day, the lords Beaverbrook and Rothermere. Although Beaverbrook exercised greater caution in his dealings with the Nazi leadership than did Rothermere, by 1935 he was already on good terms with Ribbentrop, entertaining him at his country home in Surrey, and ensuring that any critical articles in his newspapers were quickly corrected. In August 1936 he attended the Berlin Olympic Games as Ribbentrop's guest, and when Ribbentrop was appointed ambassador to London in October of that year, both the *Daily Express* and *Evening Standard* "bathed him in flattery."[83] In February 1938, when Ribbentrop was promoted to become Foreign Minister, Beaverbrook wrote to him in gushing terms.

It is with great pleasure that I hear today of your appointment to the highest office in the gift of your leader. I know full well that you will take full advantage of your great authority and immense power to develope [sic] still further the policies of peace and tranquillity. And you will have the loyal support of my newspapers in this pursuit.[84]

As one biographer comments, his conclusion "could be regarded as the single most ill-advised and damaging line Beaverbrook ever wrote."[85]

On March 10, the *Daily Express* was the first of his titles to use the celebrated strapline which was to feature regularly throughout the coming months, "There will be no European war." It was generally accompanied by the slogan "Britain will not be involved in a European war this year, or next year either." Under his own byline, Beaverbrook asked, "What concern is it of ours whether the Germans in Czecho-Slovakia are governed from Prague or have their home rule?" His biographer, the distinguished historian A. J. P. Taylor, insists that his motives were not as simplistic as has been alleged. "His dislike of dictators," maintains Taylor, "was second only to his dislike of war [and] his insistence on the need for armaments was as strong as his insistence on isolation."[86] Less commendable were the views expressed in some of his personal correspondence:

> The Jews have got a big position in the press here. I estimate that one third of the circulation of the *Daily Telegraph* is Jewish. The *Daily Mirror* may be owned by Jews. The *Daily Herald* is owned by Jews. And the *News Chronicle* should really be the *Jews Chronicle*. Not because of ownership but because of sympathy. The Jews may drive us into war. They do not mean to do it. But unconsciously they are drawing us into war. Their political influence is drawing us in that direction.[87]

Although his views on foreign affairs were at odds with those of Beaverbrook, since 1936 Churchill had contributed a fortnightly column to the *Evening Standard*. But as the situation in Europe deteriorated, even that became a source of controversy. In February, the *Standard*'s stable-mate, the *Daily Express*, attacked Churchill for his "violent, foolish and dangerous campaign,"[88] and Churchill's efforts to rally *Evening Standard* readers to support the Czech cause finally led to him being sacked. "It has been evident," wrote the editor, R. J. Thompson, "that your views on foreign affairs and the part which this country should play are entirely opposed to those held by us." In response, Churchill angrily referred to the views of David Low, the brilliant New Zealander, whose notorious cartoons in the *Standard* were considerably more outrageous than his own articles. "I rather thought," he concluded "that Lord Beaverbrook prided himself upon forming a platform in the *Evening Standard* for various opinions including of course his own." He took his column instead to the more sympathetic *Daily Telegraph*.[89]

Although Churchill would not have known it at the time, even Low had not been immune from Beaverbrook's intervention. During his visit to Germany the previous year, Halifax had been lectured at length by Goebbels about the British press. The Nazi leadership, he had been told, were out-raged at the vituperative personal attacks made on them; the worst offender was Low, and Goebbels had even gone to the trouble of compiling a collec-tion of the offending cartoons. On his return to London, Halifax contacted Beaverbrook, who in turn ordered the managing director of the *Evening Standard*, Michael Wardell, to resolve the situation. During an awkward lunch on the roof terrace of Wardell's London flat overlooking Hyde Park, Halifax warned Low of the "intense bitterness among the Nazi bosses over attacks on them. . . . Every Low cartoon attacking Hitler was taken to the Führer at once—and he blew up." Halifax was clearly embarrassed by his task. "Do I understand you to say," inquired Low, "that you would find it easier to pro-mote peace if my cartoons did not irritate the Nazi leaders personally?" Halifax agreed that he would. For a while Low ceased to draw cartoons of individuals, and instead created his famous character "Muzzler" by merging the best-known features of Hitler and Mussolini. But he bitterly regretted being forced to back down at all.[90]

Lord Rothermere enjoyed a far closer relationship with the foremost Nazi leaders, and had been visiting Germany regularly since 1930, when he had first written about Hitler under the headline "A NATION REBORN." In July 1933 he wrote one of the *Daily Mail*'s most infamous leaders, from "Somewhere in Naziland," under the headline "Youth Triumphant." Any "minor misdeeds of individual Nazis," he assured his readers, "would be submerged by the immense benefits the new regime is already bestowing upon Germany."[91] From 1933 onward Rothermere entered into a regular exchange of correspondence and gifts with Hitler, and met him for the first time in Berlin in December 1934. Having first been received at the Reich Chancellery, Rothermere returned the favor by hosting a dinner for Hitler at the Hotel Adlon, attended by guests including Neurath, Goebbels, Ribbentrop and Göring, together with their wives. He was to visit Hitler on a number of further occasions, including three trips to the Berghof between September 1936 and May 1937.

The result of this curious friendship was that, while other newspapers con-demned the Nazis' worst excesses, those owned by Rothermere carefully promoted the notion that the Führer's intentions were entirely peaceful, and that he was the savior of a defeated Germany. In George Ward Price, the central European correspondent of the *Daily Mail*, Rothermere employed the most enthusiastic supporter of the Nazi regime on Fleet Street. Ward Price always accompanied his chief to see Hitler, and soon became well acquainted with all the Nazi leaders himself, from whom he received preferential treatment. He entered Vienna with the German troops, and stood close by Hitler as he addressed the crowds from the balcony of the Hofburg. From there he traveled to Prague, where he urged anyone who would listen that Czechoslovakia should succumb to Germany's demands, leading another correspondent who met him to describe him as "a Nazi heart and soul."[92] On the way home he visited Göring at Karinhall, after which he submitted a lengthy memorandum to the Foreign Office. He described an idyllic day spent with Göring, walking about the estate and "working the Marshal's elaborate miniature toy railway system." Göring, he reported, had words of caution for the British government. "Why have you driven us into the ranks of your enemies?" he had exclaimed. "The sands of a possible reconciliation between Britain and Germany are fast running out."[93]

Of all the newspapers of the day, perhaps the one which followed the government's line most slavishly was *The Times*. Widely regarded as "the semi-official conduit of the British Government's thinking abroad," in the words of one historian, "every nuance of its long and elegant leaders was scrupulously scrutinized in the chancelleries and embassies of the world."[94] It was edited by Geoffrey Dawson, one of Halifax's oldest and most intimate friends; both were Old Etonians and Fellows of All Souls, both lived and hunted regularly in North Yorkshire, and both were high Anglicans and long-standing members of a close-knit circle of imperialist Conservatives. In April 1937, the Berlin correspondents of *The Times* had temporarily been expelled by the German Propaganda Ministry, after the paper had correctly identified German airplanes as having been responsible for the appalling carnage caused by the bombing of the north Spanish town of Guernica, an action which had caused worldwide outrage. Dawson professed himself perplexed. He could not understand, he wrote to his Geneva correspondent, what had "produced this antagonism in Germany. I did my utmost," he continued, "night after night, to keep out of the paper anything that might have hurt their susceptibilities."

Dawson was convinced that "the peace of the world depends more than anything else on our getting into reasonable relations with Germany,"[95] and he made sure that the paper's leaders reflected this view. But a rift soon opened up between the editor and some of his correspondents on the ground in Europe. The latter increasingly "felt bothered by the practice of excluding anything that the Germans might choose to regard as 'unfair,' " and thought that their dispatches "were being 'trimmed' to fit a policy."[96] The Vienna correspondent wrote privately to Dawson, describing the Anschluss. "In my wildest nightmares I had not foreseen anything so perfectly organised, so brutal, so ruthless, so strong. When this machine goes into action, it will blight everything it encounters like a swarm of locusts." The Nazis' ultimate object, he warned, was "precisely the destruction of England. . . . Their real hatred is for England." From Prague, *The Times* correspondent wrote that he was "convinced that Nazi Germany has a long-term programme which she is determined to carry out." He had no doubt that Hitler intended "both to break up this country and to challenge the British Empire," and therefore needed to be confronted.[97]

On June 3 *The Times*'s first editorial offered the opinion that "the Germans of Czechoslovakia ought to be allowed, by plebiscite or otherwise, to decide their own future—even if it should mean their secession from Czechoslovakia to the Reich."

> It is easily intelligible that the Czech Government might not willingly agree to a plebiscite likely to result in a demand for the transfer of the Sudetens and the loss of their territory for the Republic. Nevertheless, if they could see their way to it . . . they might in the long run be the gainers in having a homogeneous and contented people.[98]

The article caused an immediate outcry and the Foreign Office was forced to issue a formal denial that it had been government-inspired. Halifax telegraphed Newton, fearing that it might have been "misinterpreted by the Czechoslovak Government as representing a change of policy on the part of His Majesty's Government." Newton was to let it be known in Prague "that this is not the case and that the article in no way represents the view of His Majesty's Government."[99] Even the manager of *The Times*, John Walter, remonstrated with Dawson.

> I feel that our leader on Czechoslovakia yesterday must have come as a shock to many readers of *The Times*, advocating as it did the cause of the

Wolf against the Lamb, on the grounds of Justice. No wonder there is rejoicing in Berlin.[100]

Not only was there rejoicing in Berlin, the German government knew better than to believe the Foreign Office's denial. Fritz Hesse, the head of press at the German embassy, and a close friend of Chamberlain's own press officer, informed his ambassador that the article was "based on Chamberlain's interview with representatives of the British Press on Wednesday evening," and that "no part of the article has been disavowed" by the Prime Minister.[101] Not for the first time a Foreign Office denial had been undermined by a briefing from Downing Street. *The Times* persisted, declaring on June 14 that "it would really be the bankruptcy of European statesmanship if this question of the future of something over three million German Czech subjects were allowed to plunge a continent into devastating war."[102]

This at last prompted Halifax to complain officially to Dawson. He was, he told his old friend, "rather disturbed" by the paper's support for a plebiscite, since the government was doing its "utmost to bring Dr. Beneš and Herr Henlein together on a basis of negotiations for meeting the Sudeten claim within the framework of the Czechoslovak state." He then managed to undermine his own complaint by conceding that "it may be ultimately necessary to fall back on a plebiscite in order to forestall a worse catastrophe."[103] Dawson, who anyway saw Halifax privately on a daily basis, thought his disapproval was halfhearted. He had supposed that he was doing Halifax a favor, and "that this was one of the cases in which *The Times* could do something that the Foreign Office could not do so well."[104]

▪ ▪ ▪

On July 6 Halifax received an early morning visitor at his house in Eaton Square. Lady Snowden was the widow of Philip Snowden, the Chancellor of the Exchequer in the Labour governments of 1924 and 1929. Although an active socialist, suffragist and peace campaigner, Ethel Snowden had for the past three years attended the Nuremberg party rallies, and had written enthusiastically about them for the *Daily Mail*. In September 1937, Goebbels confided to his diary that "Lady Snowden writes an enthusiastic article on Nuremberg. A woman with guts. In London they don't understand that."[105] Now Halifax recounted to Cadogan that she had received a message "through a personage who was in a very intimate relationship with Hitler and whom I understand from her to be Princess Hohenlohe." The Führer "wished to ascertain whether it would be agreeable . . . that he should send over to England for the purpose of unofficial conversations, one of his intimate friends." The implication was that this referred to Göring, although Hitler was concerned whether he could safely visit England "without being too greatly and openly insulted."[106]

Princess Stephanie von Hohenlohe had been born Stephanie Richter, in Vienna in 1891, the illegitimate daughter of a Jewish mother from Prague, and her lover, a Jewish money-lender. Throughout her colorful life, however, Stephanie always claimed to be of the purest Aryan descent. Her mother's husband, whom she always regarded as her true father, was a Viennese lawyer who at the time of her conception was serving a prison sentence for embezzlement of his clients' funds. In her early twenties she became pregnant by the son-in-law of the Emperor Franz Joseph I, a scandal that was quickly hushed up by her marriage in London to another Austro-Hungarian prince, Friedrich Franz von Hohenlohe. Her son was born in Vienna in 1914, but at the end of the First World War she took Hungarian, rather than Austrian, citizenship, and after her divorce in 1920 she moved to Paris. In 1932, however, she was forced to leave France also, almost certainly because the authorities discovered that she had become involved in espionage. She began a new life in London.

In 1925 Hohenlohe met Lord Rothermere for the first time in Monte Carlo. He was immediately taken by this "*femme fatale*," who had risen, "by virtue of pulchritude and flair, opportunism and cunning, from the ranks of the dull bourgeoisie of Vienna to the heady stratosphere of the super-rich."[107] He immediately began to lavish money and jewelry on her, before setting her up at the Dorchester Hotel on Park Lane, and contracting her to act as his roving ambassador throughout Europe. She would use her society contacts to interview the rich and famous for an occasional column in the *Daily Mail*. She was soon given her most important task, that of establishing personal contact between Rothermere and Hitler. Between 1933 and 1938 she acted as a courier of letters and gifts between the Führer and the press baron, also organizing Rothermere's visits to Berlin and Berchtesgaden. In January 1937, Goebbels recalled how Rothermere, Hohenlohe and Ward Price visited the Berghof as Hitler's guests.

Very small party for lunch. Rothermere pays me great compliments. Enquires in detail about German press policy. Strongly anti-Jewish. The princess is very pushy. Rothermere writes good and useful articles in favour of an Anglo-German alliance. He is a strong supporter of the Führer.[108]

In early 1938 Hohenlohe received the Nazi Party's Gold Medal of Honor from Hitler in person, an extraordinary honor for him to bestow on a woman, let alone one who was generally known to be Jewish.

In the course of her frequent visits to the Reich Chancellery and the Berghof, Hohenlohe became friendly with Hitler's senior adjutant. Fritz Wiedemann had known Hitler since they had served together in the same regiment during the First World War; he had, in fact, been the Führer's immediate superior. In Berlin he was well known as a womanizer, and it came as no surprise when the handsome, but married, adjutant began a passionate affair with the Hungarian princess. The daughter of the American ambassador in Berlin, Martha Dodd, later recalled the "strong-man" of Hitler's inner circle, "with the shrewdness and cunning of an animal." "Tall, dark, muscular," she wrote, "he certainly had great physical brawn and the appearance of bravery."[109] On June 27 Hohenlohe received a cable from her lover, summoning her from London to Berlin. On her arrival she was driven out to Karinhall to meet Göring, who told her that he wished to visit Britain, and that she was to arrange the meeting. He believed that war could yet be avoided, if only he could spend some time alone with Halifax. In the meantime, Wiedemann would travel in secret to London to take initial soundings. Ribbentrop must know nothing of the proposed meeting.

The idea of Göring visiting England was nothing new. In May Halifax had admitted to Harold Nicolson that Göring "would be pleased by an invitation to Sandringham."[110] As Halifax had correctly suspected, Hohenlohe had enticed her best friend in London, Ethel Snowden, to sound him out. He was concerned, however, at the bizarre nature of the approach, and recognized that they were not "exactly the go-betweens one would choose," given that Hohenlohe was "a well-known adventuress, not to say a blackmailer."[111] Only the previous year, the British ambassador in Vienna, Sir Walford Selby, had warned that Hohenlohe was an "international adventuress," who was known "to be Hitler's agent."[112] Halifax nevertheless agreed to meet Wiedemann, insisting only "that the sole purpose of W.'s call was to discuss the actual visit [of Göring] itself." A visit to London by Göring could not possibly be kept secret, he warned, and "would not be without result."[113]

At 10 A.M. on Monday, July 18, the British Foreign Secretary received Hitler's envoy at his home at 88 Eaton Square. The only other person present was Cadogan, acting as interpreter. Wiedemann confirmed that he had come to London "with Hitler's knowledge, to explore the possibility of some important German personage coming over here in the near future, with the idea of full discussion of Anglo-German relations." Halifax expressed a cautious welcome in principle for any idea that might improve relations, but warned that the moment for such a visit would need to be chosen carefully, since it "would inevitably attract public attention," and might very well "do more harm than good." Wiedemann went on to assure Halifax that the Führer's view of England "had always been one of admiration and friendship, but Herr Hitler felt that he had on various occasions been rebuffed." He referred in particular to a lack of progress after Halifax's own visit to Germany, and resentment at the gleeful reaction of the British press following the May Crisis. He did, however, admit that "Ribbentrop had not managed that business well."

Halifax warned his guest that "the present moment might not be altogether favourable," unless there was to be a peaceful resolution in Czechoslovakia. Could Wiedemann give him any assurances in that respect? Wiedemann replied, wholly disingenuously, that he had not been charged with a political mission, and was therefore "hardly in a position to discuss such a question." He then immediately contradicted himself by giving "the most binding assurance—in fact, he was authorised to do so—that the German Government were planning no kind of forcible action," unless forced to do so by some unforeseen incident; this from a man who, on May 28, had heard in person Hitler's promise to "smash the Czechs." The conversation ended cordially, with Wiedemann reminiscing about his time in the trenches with Hitler. He had not then noticed "the great qualities that Herr Hitler possessed," although he had been a "brave, reliable and cool soldier, the sort on whom one could rely." He had not, however, had any "idea of the capabilities of which Herr Hitler had subsequently given proof."[114]

The Foreign Office was cautiously encouraged by the meeting. Wiedemann had "made a good impression," recorded Harvey, "and appeared serious and straightforward."[115] However, the presence of Hitler's adjutant in the Foreign Secretary's home caused considerable disquiet elsewhere in Europe. On his arrival at Croydon, Wiedemann had been recognized and followed by a British journalist. The following morning the left-leaning *Daily Herald* led with a banner headline revealing the secret meeting. Diplomatic messages flashed around Europe. François-Poncet informed the Quai d'Orsay that the "idea that Captain Wiedemann should be received by Lord Halifax was cooked up by Princess Hohenlohe, who is extremely well known to the secret services of all the Great Powers." While pretending to "serve the interests of Britain," she in fact felt "herself chiefly committed to the interests of Germany." Masaryk wrote indignantly to his masters in Prague:

> If there is any decency left in this world, then there will be a big scandal when it is revealed what part was played in Wiedemann's visit by Steffi Hohenlohe, *née* Richter. This world-renowned secret agent, spy and confidence trickster, who is wholly Jewish, today provides the focus of Hitler's propaganda in London.[116]

A visibly embarrassed Ribbentrop reacted furiously when news of the visit reached Berlin. As a result, when Wiedemann returned to Berchtesgaden, he was kept waiting at the Berghof for several hours while Hitler was out walking with Unity Mitford, the infamous British aristocrat who was such an ardent admirer of the Führer. That evening Hitler allowed him just five minutes to make his report, then angrily ruled out a visit to London by Göring, and refused to discuss the subject again. Wiedemann was left to prepare a heavily embellished written report for Ribbentrop, in which he famously made the extraordinary allegation that Halifax had asked him "to remember him to the Führer, and to tell him that he (Halifax), before his death, would like to see, as the culmination of his work, the Führer entering London, at the side of the English King, amid the acclamations of the English people."[117] A few months later, Wiedemann was packed off into exile as consul-general in San Francisco, taking Stephanie von Hohenlohe with him. The meeting with Halifax had achieved nothing at all. In the words of one historian, the episode "must belong to one of the most picaresque chapters in Anglo-German diplomatic relations. It inevitably left neither side the wiser."[118]

7

■

A Faraway Country

But what a cockpit Bohemia has always been. For 800 years they have quarrelled and fought. Only one king kept them at peace, Charles V, and he was a Frenchman! How then can we succeed?

Lord Runciman to Neville Chamberlain, August 1, 1938

Was brauchen wir'nen Weihnachtsmann,
Wir haben unser'n Runciman!
[What do we need Father Christmas for,
We have our Runciman evermore!]

Popular Sudeten German song, August 1938

Punctual to the minute, at 11:15 A.M. on August 3, 1938, in the hazy sunshine of a central European summer morning, the Paris–Prague express crossed the German frontier, and pulled into the station in the Czech border town of Eger. From the first-class compartment, a small, distinguished-looking man, with thinning gray hair, peered inquisitively out of the window, carefully taking in his surroundings. He was wearing a pale gray suit and, somewhat conspicuously on such a hot summer's day, a high wing collar. Customs and passport officers were on the platform to meet the train, but there was no official welcoming committee for the eminent visitor; no Czech government ministers, or Sudeten German officials. Yet just outside Eger station stood the Victoria Hotel, the headquarters of the Sudeten German leader, Konrad Henlein, while his home was only a few miles north, in the border town of Asch.

The border formalities did not take long, and the elderly man in first-class was soon once again immersed in the book he was reading, as the train pulled out of Eger, and continued its journey through the rolling Sudeten countryside; the hills swathed with pine trees, through which flowed streams teeming with trout; the gold cornfields already half-harvested; the small lakes in which children were having a noisy morning swim; and the white-walled, red-roofed cottages shining in the midday sun. The train's next stop was the spa town of Marienbad, once a favorite summer resort of King Edward VII, while further north was another famous spa town, Karlsbad (Karlovy Vary), once visited before the Great War by a young Neville Chamberlain seeking a cure for his gout—it was the only visit he was ever to make to the faraway country of Czechoslovakia. From Marienbad the train steamed on, through Pilsen, and past the towering chimneys of the Skoda munitions works, eyed so covetously by those planning war in Berlin. Once the train had crossed another, unseen border, the one that separated the Sudetenland from the rest of Czechoslovakia, the station names appeared only in Czech. An hour later, the train pulled into the Wilson Station in Prague, "named in that flush of post-war hopefulness after the American President" who had helped to create the state of Czechoslovakia.[1]

First off the train, noted a critical British observer, were "a number of gentlemen and one lady with the consciously superior air of Britons on foreign soil," accompanied by "a mountain of luggage." Finally, the distinguished visitor himself disembarked, "a stooping, bald-headed man with a clean-shaven, beak-nosed face, carrying a brief-case."[2] This was Walter Runciman, the first Viscount Runciman of Doxford, accompanied by his wife, who, to the consternation of the waiting Czechs, was heard loudly to complain about "Bolshevik influence" in Czechoslovakia.[3] Runciman had come to Prague as the officially appointed mediator of the British government, a fact reflected by the welcoming committee assembled on the platform to meet him: the Lord Mayor of Prague, the President's *chef de Cabinet*, and the British Minister, Basil Newton, who was wearing a black homburg of the kind made fashionable by Anthony Eden.[4] Ostentatiously keeping their distance a few paces away, and eyeing the Czech representatives with obvious suspicion, was another, smaller delegation. Ernst Kundt and Wilhelm Sebekovsky were two of the most senior members of Henlein's

SdP, and in an indication of the emphasis that the mission was to assume, Newton made a great show of introducing them to Runciman on the platform. As his entourage left the station, bound for the smartest lodgings in Prague, the Hotel Alcron off Wenceslas Square, Runciman nodded curtly to the waiting journalists. "The hangman with his little bag came creeping through the gloom," muttered Eric Gedye of the *Daily Telegraph* to a Czech friend.[5]

Throughout his journey from London, Runciman had been regularly accosted by journalists, anxious to secure a first interview with the British mediator. At 6 P.M. that evening he therefore held a press conference in the hotel's dining room, where some 300 journalists from around the world crammed in to hear his words of wisdom. By now wearing a black suit, but still with the ever-present wing collar, Runciman more than ever resembled the Liberal Victorian politician that in spirit he was. He made his way through the throng, and up on to a slightly raised dais, which at the last moment had been moved from one end of the room to the other. It had been realized that the sabbatarian and teetotal peer would otherwise have had to be photographed standing in front of a fetching bronze of a nude girl, her hands invitingly stretched out in welcome. It was also discreetly pointed out that with the dais now positioned next to the door, it would be easier for him to make a quick getaway, should the Czech journalists present take exception to the uninvited mediator. The newsreel arc lights accentuated the oppressive heat and atmosphere in the room, but Runciman addressed his audience calmly, in a measured, low voice.

"I am the friend of all and the enemy of none," he began. "I have learned that permanent peace and tranquillity can be secured only on a basis of mutual consent. There is much to be said for the exercise of patience."[6] In fact, Runciman had no need to fear for his safety. His reception was a sympathetic one, although one or two of the Czech journalists were unhappy that he appeared to go out of his way to thank the Sudeten German leaders for their welcome at the station. The following morning the local newspapers, beneath the headline "THE LORD ARRIVES," gave a generally warm welcome to the Runciman Mission, as it had now become known. The enthusiasm, however, was far from universal. The American journalist, and later historian, William Shirer, was in Prague reporting for CBS Radio. That night he recorded in his diary his belief that Runciman had arrived "to gum up the works and sell the Czechs short if he can." A journalist from the *Herald Tribune* had already distributed copies of the paper's earlier article reporting Chamberlain's remarks at Nancy Astor's now infamous lunch. Shirer's view was typical of the American press corps. "Runciman's whole mission smells," he wrote, before retiring to bed.[7]

▪ ▪ ▪

The Runciman Mission had been a considerable time in gestation. In all fairness to Runciman, it was not a job he had either coveted, or even accepted gracefully. As long ago as early June, Halifax had first considered the idea of sending a mediator to Prague if, as seemed likely, negotiations between the Czech government and Henlein's SdP reached an impasse. On June 16 he told the Cabinet's Foreign Policy Committee that he was considering the appointment of a distinguished person to act as an intermediary and, two days later, confirmed to Newton that he intended to approach the Czech government to ascertain whether they would be "ready to accept the services of an independent British expert who would try and reconcile the two parties."[8] As a former Viceroy of India, Halifax initially regarded an ex-governor of an Indian province as the best man for the job, but Newton was unhappy at the implication of such an appointment, which he thought "might be considered derogatory by both sides." He replied that he would far prefer "an outstanding figure whose impartiality and judgement could more readily be accepted by both parties."[9]

As summer progressed it became obvious that the prospect of the two sides reaching agreement was fast diminishing. The so-called First Plan, put forward by the Czech government, would have conferred full autonomy on three new Diets, in the historic provinces of Bohemia, Moravia and Silesia. This was rejected by Henlein's negotiators on the somewhat obvious grounds that the Sudeten Germans would not hold a majority in any of them. At the same time, the British government was becoming ever more desperate in its attempts to force Beneš to make concessions. "I earnestly hope that the French Government," wrote Halifax to the British ambassador in Paris, "will feel not less urgently than do His Majesty's Government the importance of putting the greatest possible pressure upon Dr. Beneš in person without delay." He referred to an earlier warning of the new French Foreign Minister that if the Czechs "were really unreasonable," the time might soon come when the French would consider releasing themselves from their promises to Czechoslovakia. "My feeling is that the moment has now come," continued Halifax, "for a warning to be given to the Czechoslovak Government on these lines."[10]

Of course, neither Britain nor France could know that the private understanding reached by Hitler and Henlein ensured that there was no prospect whatsoever of agreement being reached, however substantial the Czech concessions. The Czechs themselves reacted with increasing indignation to the British attitude. A senior Foreign Ministry official complained to a British journalist that Chamberlain was "treating the head of our State as though he were a nigger chieftain ruling some troublesome Colonial tribe." British diplomatic pressure was "becoming more and more intolerable."[11] On the ground in Prague, only Newton demonstrated a true understanding of the dilemma facing the Czechs. He made it clear that he could see no likelihood of Beneš being able to persuade the Czech public, army and all shades of non-German political opinion to accept concessions that would satisfy Henlein. He urged his Foreign Office masters to "show sympathetic appreciation of the fact that the Czechoslovak Government have hitherto accepted very far-reaching and doubtless unpalatable advice and appear to have been doing their utmost of late."[12]

Meanwhile, an increasingly confident Henlein had only to ratchet up the pressure, by persistently declaring that it was the Czechs who were being deliberately dilatory, and were taking neither the negotiations, nor the pressure from London, seriously enough. In an interview with the ever-pliant Ward Price, he gave warning that the government now had three simple choices. First, to give the Sudeten Germans everything that they demanded; second, to allow a plebiscite on possible secession to Germany; or, ultimately, to go to war. The third choice, he believed, "would be simpler still."[13] On June 8 his negotiators presented a memorandum to the government elaborating on the Karlsbad demands. Czechoslovakia would be divided into racial areas, each with full independence, as well as a continuing say in the affairs of central government. In effect, the Sudetenland would become an independent Nazi state. Under pressure from London, the government accepted this as a basis for discussion, but balked at two specific measures: that legislative powers should be conferred on the SdP's Volkstag, or party congress, and that Henlein should assume control of the local police, effectively putting Nazi storm troopers in charge of law and order throughout the Sudetenland. In reply the government proposed further schemes of their own, but the gulf between the two sides remained unbridgeable, as Henlein's chief negotiator, Ernst Kundt, refused compromise after compromise.

It was against this inauspicious backdrop that Halifax drew up a list of suitable candidates for the job of mediator. By June 29, he was in a position to interview Runciman for the first time, having been advised that his fellow peer's "wide and varied experience" gave him a "record that would impress." He was warned, however, somewhat worryingly, that "someone would have to accompany him and do most of the work."[14] A shipbuilding magnate from the northeast of England, Runciman had served in the Campbell-Bannerman and Asquith Liberal governments before the First World War, earning forever the enmity of Lloyd George—the former Prime Minister once said of Runciman "that he would make a thermometer drop, even at a distance."[15] He fought the 1931 election as a National Liberal, and joined the resulting National Government as President of the Board of Trade. But when Chamberlain became Prime Minister in May 1937, Runciman was offered no more than a junior Cabinet post and, deeply affronted, he left the Cabinet, albeit with a viscountcy to his name.

Runciman's first reaction was one of severe doubt, both as to his own suitability for the mission, and indeed of its very viability. On June 30 he wrote to Halifax refusing the offer, perceptively commenting that "an ambassador at large seldom succeeds."[16] Halifax, however, was not to be rebuffed, and pursued Runciman with a series of telegrams to his Scottish holiday retreat. Finally, on July 16, after an hour of persuasive argument at the Foreign Office with Cadogan, Sargent and Strang, Halifax was able to report to Newton that Runciman had accepted the position, subject only to the condition that he would not be asked to proceed unless "both sides agree to receive him and to explain to him fully their respective points of view."[17] Runciman still remained deeply skeptical about the entire project. "I quite understand," he told Halifax, "you are setting me adrift in a small boat mid-Atlantic." The Foreign Secretary thought for a moment. "That is exactly the position," he replied.[18]

If Runciman still had doubts of his own, then it is fair to say that anyone else who was likely to be involved was equally underwhelmed. When

Newton called on Beneš on July 20 to give him the news, he reported that the President "seemed greatly taken aback and much upset, flushing slightly and hardly recovering his full equanimity by the end of a conversation which lasted over two hours." The proposal, Beneš warned with some justification, gravely "affected the country's sovereignty," and would "provoke a most serious crisis in the country and might entail resignation of the Government."[19] In the end, Czech objections were overcome by a blunt threat to Beneš that the British government would publicize the offer, and its subsequent rejection by the Czechs. The SdP leadership offered no public opinion, although Kundt did assure Newton that his party would "welcome any objective study of conditions which might in any way help to achieve a positive result."[20] In Berlin, Ribbentrop complained bitterly "that public announcement had preceded communication to German Government,"[21] and later wrote a vitriolic letter to Halifax asserting that "the Government of the Reich must refuse to take any responsibility for the efforts of Lord Runciman, whether they are crowned with success or not."[22] Also in Berlin, Henderson could not resist the opportunity once again to make clear his own prejudices. "I do not envy Lord Runciman the difficult and thankless task he is undertaking," he wrote to Halifax. "The Czechs are a pig-headed race and Beneš not the least pig-headed among them."[23]

On July 26, after the story had leaked out in the *News Chronicle*, Chamberlain was rushed into announcing to the House of Commons that Runciman was indeed going to Prague, even though Runciman's stipulation that he should be accepted by both parties had still not been met. Chamberlain was first forced to deny "the rumour" that Britain was "hustling the Czech Government," in fact an accurate, if colloquial, description of British involvement since the May Crisis.[24] The Prime Minister then told a flagrant lie to the House, claiming that Runciman would be traveling to Prague "in response to a request from the Government of Czechoslovakia." He praised Runciman's personal qualifications for the job, his "fearlessness, freedom from prejudice, integrity and impartiality." He would be "independent of His Majesty's Government," and would "act only in his personal capacity." Finally he stressed that Runciman would not be "in any sense an arbitrator," but rather "an investigator and mediator," fulfilling a role well known to him, that "of a man who goes down to assist in settling a strike."[25]

In his business life, Runciman was indeed an acknowledged expert in settling industrial disputes, although it is impossible to tell quite what the Czech government made of their country's very existence being described in the dry language of industrial relations. Possibly mindful of any lingering resentment, Chamberlain wrote to Runciman the following day, "to say how much I admire your courage and public spirit in undertaking such a difficult and delicate task."[26] In spite of such warm words, the Czechs would no doubt have been interested to know that before becoming Prime Minister, and sacking the friend of whom he claimed to be "very fond," Chamberlain believed that Runciman was "not a very valuable colleague in Cabinet as he seldom opened his mouth," and considered him to be "lazy."[27] Runciman was now sixty-eight years old and, although a year younger than Chamberlain (and a "fellow devotee of the winged collar"[28]), his political career appeared to be well and truly over. He was also in noticeably declining health, his physical appearance giving alternately cause for concern and humor—"a taciturn, thin-lipped little man with a bald head so round it looks like a misshapen egg" was how Shirer described him on his arrival in Prague.[29]

Chamberlain's announcement met with a distinctly lukewarm reception. The *News Chronicle*, which had first broken the story, complained that "no-one—certainly no Czech and no German—is going to accept Mr. Chamberlain's bland assurance that the British Government has really nothing to do with his success or failure."[30] Even the pro-appeasement, Beaverbrook-owned *Evening Standard* questioned "whether the British Government should ever have persuaded the Czech Government to assent to the appointment—on terms so capable of being misunderstood, and for a purpose so fraught with complications."[31] Old political foes of Runciman such as Leo Amery were equally unimpressed. "I am not sure yet whether the appointment of Runciman as adviser and mediator is comic or a stroke of genius," he mused sarcastically. "It may well be that his bland, invincible ignorance and incapacity even to realise the emotions and aspirations on both sides may help to bring down the temperature."[32]

"RELIEF" shouted the unusually large headline in the *Observer* on July 31, above a signed article by its celebrated editor, the noted appeaser J. L. Garvin.

If the nation is justified in packing up for its holidays with a free heart, it is not only because of Lord Runciman's devoted pilgrimage of peace to a cockpit of discords, but on broader and more guarded grounds. The pilgrimage is the original and hardy idea of the Prime Minister himself.[33]

There was indeed a holiday air in Whitehall, as Chamberlain packed his fishing rod and headed off to what was to be the first of a number of large Scottish estates to which he had been invited to stay. His holiday could not come soon enough. "I am astonished myself at the way I stand the strain," he complained to his sister, "for I don't get much let up."[34] Unfortunately, after just one day on the river with the Duke of Westminster at Lochmore, north of Inverness, he suffered an acute attack of sinusitis. So bad was the pain that he was forced to cut short his holiday and return to London for specialist treatment. "I was so very sorry to hear that you had to return to London for treatment of your nose," commiserated the King, "which sounds both very painful & unpleasant." He trusted that it would not preclude Chamberlain from visiting Balmoral later in the month. "The German attitude," he concluded, with masterful royal understatement, "certainly gives cause for anxiety."[35]

▪ ▪ ▪

On August 4, twenty-four years to the day since Britain had entered the First World War, and the morning after his arrival in Prague, Lord Runciman went to work with a vengeance. In spite of the searing heat of a beautiful summer's day—it was in the high eighties in the shade—he donned full morning dress and top hat, and set off to pay a series of courtesy calls on members of the Czech government. He made his way first to Hradčany Castle, for 300 years the epicenter of Germanic Habsburg rule over the Czechs, the tall spires of St. Vitus's Cathedral dominating the Prague skyline. As his car, escorted by a cavalcade of police motorcycle outriders, swept into the courtyard, he would have noticed an obvious reminder of Czechoslovakia's hard-won independence at Versailles. Instead of the regular khaki-green uniforms of the Czech army, the sentries who saluted Runciman wore the First World War uniforms of the French, Italian and czarist Russian armies, into whose foreign legions the Czechs had been organized to fight their former German rulers.

Runciman was received first by the President, Edvard Beneš, in his high-ceilinged office, its floor-to-ceiling windows overlooking the River Moldau, winding through the valley below. An academic who had studied and taught in both Prague and in Paris, Beneš was a quiet, scholarly man who largely eschewed all outward signs of ostentation. He had spent most of the First World War in exile in Paris, one of the leading organizers of the Czech independence movement then seeking recognition from Britain and France for an independent Czechoslovakia. Together with the new state's first President and founding father, Tomáš Masaryk, he represented Czechoslovakia at Versailles, and became Foreign Minister. In December 1935 he succeeded his old friend Masaryk, who was to die in 1937, and remained President of Czechoslovakia until 1948, albeit spending seven of those years in exile.

After visiting Beneš, Runciman called next on his Prime Minister, Dr. Milan Hodža, a Slovakian who before the war had represented the Slovak minority in the Hungarian parliament, and accordingly lacked the natural Czech antagonism toward the Germans. He was known to favor a compromise with Henlein. "Stocky, well dressed, precise, with a pince-nez and a stubborn chin," he could easily have passed for "a successful bank manager."[36] Runciman's third call of the morning was on the Foreign Minister, Dr. Kamil Krofta, a close ally of Beneš, who at the age of sixty-five had given up the chair of history at Prague University to join the government after Masaryk's death. Like Beneš, Krofta led a discreet, unostentatious life, going quietly about his work from his office at the Czernin Palace, formerly the home of Count Czernin, the Austrian Foreign Minister during the First World War. In spite of their earlier reservations, it was clear that all these ministers were desperately keen to cooperate with Runciman in any way they could. However, that in itself caused him embarrassment. "The doors have been opened to me freely," he wrote to Halifax that evening, "and I am very uncomfortable, for they are all apt to expect too much."[37]

That evening Runciman returned to the Hotel Alcron, where he commandeered the main sitting room of the hotel for his interviews, and held a lengthy meeting with the two Sudeten German leaders, Kundt and Sebekovsky. Henlein himself did not attend, having refused to travel to Prague, insisting instead that he would only meet Runciman when the British mediator came to see him in the Sudetenland. The very length of this first meeting, compared to the brief courtesy calls he had paid on the Czech ministers, set the tone for the coming weeks, and was enough to arouse the unsympathetic attention of many of the waiting journalists. The criticism that "the contacts with the Henleinists were long and deep, those with the Government brief and distinctly cool,"[38] was to plague him throughout his stay,

Runciman had been accompanied to Prague by a team of advisers whose composition gave the lie to Chamberlain's insistence that the mission was independent of government; it was led by Frank Ashton-Gwatkin, the head of the Economic Section at the Foreign Office, and an acknowledged expert on trade negotiations, who knew Runciman from his time as President of the Board of Trade.[39] The problem was that they had no formal terms of reference, and only the tersest brief from Halifax, who had warned Runciman before he left that he must not "take any action that would have the effect of committing this country further than it is already committed, to take action in the event of Germany taking military action."[40] Even if Runciman had wished to appear more sympathetic to the Czech cause, this formula would almost certainly have prevented him from doing so. As it was, after his first, brief meeting with Beneš he was quick to come to his own judgment that the President did "not show much sign of an understanding or respect for the Germans in Czechoslovakia."[41] Geoffrey Peto, a former Conservative MP who was accompanying the mission with his wife, was blunter still. Just three days after arriving, he horrified the Czechs by telling a German diplomat that "he understood why the Sudeten German Party disliked Jews."[42]

Runciman's evenhandedness was further called into question by his apparent inability to comprehend that Henlein and the SdP were not the sole representatives of German opinion in Czechoslovakia. The moderate Social Democrat Party, although it had been badly squeezed in the elections of 1935, did still exist, headed by its young and engaging leader, Wenzl Jaksch. On his first day in Prague Runciman was asked by a British journalist who lived there whether he intended to hold talks with the Social Democrats. In reply, the British mediator "looked blank," as if "he did not have the faintest idea until that moment" that they existed. "They have not so far communicated with me," he explained.[43] When he did finally get around to meeting them, according to Jaksch the meeting did not go well.

Lord Runciman emphasised that we Social Democrats were only a small party compared to Henlein's. I agreed. I told him our problem is that we are a party of peace and freedom, ideals which are not very popular these days, so we don't compete very well with parties which don't believe in such things.[44]

Prague in August was hot and stifling, and Lord and Lady Runciman were understandably keen to escape the city at weekends to enjoy the fresh air of the Czech countryside. However, their choice of hosts was far from ideal. "Like many rich Liberals of middle-class origins and dissenting connections," recalled Harold Macmillan many years later, Runciman "had a curious penchant towards the aristocracy. He therefore spent his weekends at the castles of the great Austrian nobility, survivors of the old Austrian Empire, who had never in their hearts accepted Czechoslovakia as their country."[45] The great country estates of Czechoslovakia did tend to be in the Sudetenland, and were owned by the Germanic nobility, many of whom harked back to the days of Viennese rule, and resented their loss of power and prestige under the Czech government. Runciman spent his second weekend in Czechoslovakia staying with Prince Ulrich Kinsky, a member of the SdP, at his castle near Brünn. The German chargé d'affaires in Prague proudly reported back to Berlin that not only did the SdP have a "political staff" in place to negotiate with Runciman, there was also a "social staff under [the] leadership of Prince Ulrich Kinsky, the big landowner."[46] Yet it never seems to have occurred to Runciman that hobnobbing at the weekends with the German aristocracy, as well as the Sudeten leaders who were usually his fellow guests, might have appeared at best tactless, and at worst a public relations disaster in the eyes of the Czechs.

▪ ▪ ▪

Although he was too busy to meet Runciman in Prague, on August 5 Henlein traveled to Zurich, to participate in a bizarre secret meeting with a former British air force officer and diplomat, Group Captain Malcolm Christie, a figure of whom it has been said that he might well "have stepped straight from the pages of John Buchan." Christie had been educated at Aachen University, where he had first met Göring, before going on to win the Military Cross as a pilot with the Royal Flying Corps during the First

World War. He then served as air attaché, first in Washington, and from 1927 to 1930 in Berlin, before embarking on a business career. He was subsequently recruited by Sir Robert Vansittart to become a leading member of his private intelligence network and, working discreetly from his home on the German-Dutch border, Christie used his business as cover to move easily among the higher echelons of the Nazi Party in Berlin. He delighted in the cloak-and-dagger nature of his work, counting Göring, and his deputy at the Reich Air Ministry, General Erhard Milch, among his closest acquaintances. From 1936 onward he provided Vansittart with a steady flow of intelligence material, in particular that gleaned from Milch concerning the Luftwaffe's rearmament program.[47]

Christie knew both Henlein and the Sudetenland well, having "smoothed the path for Henlein" when he visited London in 1935, organizing his itinerary, and securing the prestigious invitation for him to speak at Chatham House.[48] He also introduced him to Vansittart, then still Permanent Under-Secretary at the Foreign Office. "He makes a most favourable impression," recorded Vansittart of the Sudeten German leader. "I should say that he was moderate, honest and clear-sighted. He speaks with a frankness and decision that inspire confidence." When Henlein assured him that the Sudeten Germans had no wish to be part of the Reich, Vansittart concluded: "I think he is speaking the truth."[49] The endorsement of so ardent an anti-appeaser was to be of considerable value to Henlein, while Vansittart was also taken in by another intermediary, the German-Bohemian Prince Max Hohenlohe-Langenburg, "an owner of large estates whose English education and impeccable manners obviously made a big impression on the diplomats he met." In May 1938 Vansittart tried to persuade Chamberlain to meet Hohenlohe, on the grounds that the aristocrat "might influence Henlein,"[50] yet no one ever seems to have discovered that Hohenlohe, like his princess namesake (but not relative), was in fact "one of the most skilful Nazi agents."[51]

Hohenlohe also attended the meeting in Zurich on August 5, when Henlein at last abandoned all pretense, launching an astonishing tirade against Czechoslovakia, a "state of crooks and criminals . . . an abortion of a state." All pretence disappeared. It was, he warned, time "to rob the British of the illusion that stability could be achieved in a combined State under Czech sovereignty." It was no longer merely a matter of the rights of

Sudeten Germans, but rather of the ultimate battle, "Germany versus Czechoslovakia." In the long run, he declared, "Germany cannot tolerate such an abscess on its body. . . . If England thinks that she must protect this State come what may, then England will bear the blame for an extension of the conflict."[52] In his written report of the meeting for Vansittart, Christie uses more moderate language, but warned that Runciman, "however distinguished and experienced he might be, remained an Englishman with an English attitude of mind that . . . would be quite unable to penetrate the fog of misleading statements."[53] Henlein still refused to meet Runciman, and had given explicit instructions to his negotiators that such an encounter was to be avoided for as long as possible.

The SdP's negotiating tactics were simple. They involved "cramming the British with information and with very copious documentary evidence," while simultaneously exploiting every possible incident which might put the Czechs in a bad light.[54] They paid frequent visits to the Hotel Alcron, bringing with them thick bundles of documents, usually in both English and German, which they then insisted on explaining well into the small hours. Runciman also received numerous telegrams from the Sudeten areas, all carefully coordinated by the SdP, and all protesting at the suffering being endured under the Czech yoke; he was always invited to visit to view the persecution for himself. A typical incident occurred on the night of August 7, in Gasterwald, a remote forest village in the Sudetenland. A young German woodcutter, a supporter of Henlein, was stabbed to death in a drunken brawl outside the local inn by a fellow German, a Social Democrat. The German press fell upon the story with glee. In spite of the fact that both men were German, here was yet another example of Czech brutality. The dead man's funeral was turned into a major propaganda coup, complete with Nazi parade, weeping mother, and an oration over the coffin by Henlein's hard-line deputy, Karl Hermann Frank.

"Curiously enough," Runciman reported to the Foreign Office on August 10, with a rare trace of humor, "Henlein has not been seen, although he must be somewhere in Czechoslovakia." But he knew that he was no closer to brokering an agreement between the parties, and the burden of responsibility was beginning to weigh heavy. "Success," he recognized, "depends on whether or not the Führer wants to go to war."

It is a pathetic side of the present crisis that the common people here, and, I am told, elsewhere are looking to me and my mission as the only hope for an established peace. Alas, they do not realise how weak are our sanctions, and I dread the moment when they find that nothing can save them. It will be a terrible disillusionment.

After only one week in Prague he already felt the need to enquire of Halifax "how long in your opinion I ought to hold the fort?" If hostilities were to break out, he hoped that he would at least "get some warning."[55] After two weeks of fruitless discussions with the SdP and the Czech government, the negotiations had reached deadlock and, on August 17, Kundt warned that "the patience of our people, which has seen no sign of good will on your part, is less than our patience."[56]

At last Runciman decided that if further progress was to be made he must tackle Henlein in person. A meeting was hurriedly arranged for the following day at Schloss Rothenhaus, Prince Hohenlohe's castle near Komotau, just fifteen miles from the German border. Runciman was driven up into the Sudeten mountains, a "fortress built by God in the heart of Europe" as Bismarck had described them, and just before midday his convoy swept into the castle's broad drive, to be greeted by a guard of honor composed of Prince Hohenlohe's gamekeepers, all of whom wore swastika badges in their lapels, and greeted Runciman with the Nazi salute. Ten minutes later two open-top cars, traveling at high speed and containing Frank, Kundt, and Henlein himself, were greeted even more enthusiastically. Geoffrey Cox of the *Daily Express* recalled that Henlein's brown sports jacket and gray flannel trousers reminded him of "an English bank clerk on holiday."

In spite of Runciman's best efforts to keep the meeting secret, the press had followed from Prague in a cavalcade of their own, and were now left to their own devices outside the front gate. Unfortunately, in typically British fashion, neither Runciman nor any member of his delegation had made the slightest effort to endear themselves to the large contingent of the world's press that had been dispatched to Prague. Their daily communiqués were brief and factual, and Ashton-Gwatkin in particular could not conceal his "tight-lipped disdain" for journalists, reserving special contempt for the American correspondents. After lunch, the waiting journalists could just glimpse Prince Hohenlohe and his guests sipping coffee in the summer sunshine on the castle's terrace, while, somewhat incongruously, children and dogs played on the manicured lawns. Hohenlohe's gamekeepers, meanwhile, reinforced by gray-uniformed Sudeten German storm troopers, ensured that the press was kept at bay, although German and Sudeten German journalists were allowed into the castle's inner courtyard. The scene reminded Cox of "the Cliveden touch, the art of country house diplomacy, being applied with skill in Central Europe."[57]

Runciman and Henlein talked for five hours, Hohenlohe and Ashton-Gwatkin acting as interpreters. According to Ashton-Gwatkin, Henlein offered nothing new, insisting that the eight demands he had made at Karlsbad must be met in full.

> The German people in Czechoslovakia, he said, must defend their homes and livelihood and the future of their children against a formidable Czech invasion which is promoted and assisted by the Government.

He repeated his now familiar, but wholly disingenuous, assurances that he would prefer a negotiated settlement to a plebiscite, that he wished to preserve the frontiers of Czechoslovakia, and that he would continue to urge moderation on his supporters. "But," he warned, "he was afraid that time was running out," and that with the additional hardship of a severe winter in prospect, his position might soon be under threat from his own people.[58] Henlein's own notes of the meeting record that Runciman did at least refuse to take everything he was told at face value. When Henlein claimed that the Czech government advocated "the extermination of the Sudeten Germans and the destruction of their homes," and that its "highest political and military circles wanted war," Runciman looked at him "in astonishment," and demanded to know what possible evidence he had for such an assertion. And when Henlein described the alleged hardship of the Sudeten Germans, Runciman replied dryly that "there was temporary economic trouble everywhere, even in England."[59]

At 6 P.M. Runciman was driven away at high speed, followed soon after by Henlein. It was left to Ashton-Gwatkin to brief the non-German press, but he chose instead to issue a bland two-line communiqué, confirming that the meeting had taken place and that Henlein had put his views to

Runciman. Having waited for six hours, tempers were frayed among the waiting journalists, and Walter Kerr of the *New York Herald Tribune* asked on behalf of them all how they were supposed to compile their reports without further information. "You can use your imagination," snapped back Ashton-Gwatkin. When confronted with the additional complaint that German correspondents and photographers had been given the free run of the castle courtyard, he again angrily dismissed their protest. "You ought to consider yourself lucky to be allowed within the grounds at all," he replied.[60] It is not surprising that history should have judged the Runciman Mission harshly, when much of it has been written by the British and American journalists whose job it was to report on it at the time.

A few days later, on August 22, Ashton-Gwatkin followed up the meeting at Schloss Rothenhaus by again motoring to the Sudetenland to visit Henlein at Marienbad, where the political committee of the SdP had gathered. In the course of their discussion, Ashton-Gwatkin was utterly deceived by Henlein, accepting at face value his "emphatic" denial:

(1) that he was a dictator; (2) that he had any sympathy whatever with the "terror" of the German Nazis; (3) that he would ever permit any "Judenhetze" [Jew baiting]; (4) that he aimed at political totalitarianism or anything other than the honourable treatment of opponents and opposition.[61]

Once again, Henlein's notes of the meeting are considerably more revealing than the official British record. So far removed was he from the reality of the situation that Ashton-Gwatkin made the apparently serious suggestion that the "moderate" Henlein should be sent to Hitler as a peacemaker. Would Henlein, he asked, be "prepared to sound out the Führer as to the desirability of a meeting between British representatives and the Führer"?[62] "I like him," concluded Ashton-Gwatkin in a note to his seniors at the Foreign Office. "He is, I am sure, an absolutely honest fellow."[63]

On August 24 Ashton-Gwatkin returned to London for few days, to brief Halifax and to receive further instructions. Halifax gave short shrift to the idea that Henlein should be employed as some sort of surrogate British peace envoy. "I am surprised," he scolded Runciman, "at the suggestion that Henlein should in any way speak on behalf of His Majesty's

Government either as regards your mission or as regards the conditions for an Anglo-German settlement." To allow Henlein such a role, he warned, "would be quite unsuitable and might lead to all sorts of complications."[64] However, the general principle of a visit to Hitler was more warmly received, and Halifax suggested that Runciman himself should make the trip to Berlin. Not surprising, Runciman politely but firmly declined, on the grounds that he would be extending his remit beyond that of neutral mediator.

▪ ▪ ▪

By mid-July, the military planning for Case Green was well advanced and becoming increasingly frenzied. Mussolini now knew of the strategy, and its approximate timing; autumn maneuvers had been brought forward to the summer, at the climax of which troop units would be deployed in the correct positions for an invasion of Czechoslovakia; the German air attaché in Prague was busy reconnoitering suitable landing strips for German planes in the Sudetenland; and plans had been drawn up for the establishment of ten army headquarters, with their corresponding commanders and staffs—five to carry out the invasion and five to protect Germany's other borders in the west and with Poland.[65] Hitler, meanwhile, remained in his mountain hideaway, bombarding his military commanders with demands and orders: construction of the West Wall was to be speeded up still further, special exercises were to be held to perfect the art of capturing heavily armed fortifications by surprise, and foreign military attachés were to be forbidden from visiting Germany's frontier regions. What, he wanted to know, was the current state of Czech armaments? Would Russia intervene?

General Beck, who had so far failed in his attempts to persuade Brauchitsch to warn Hitler of the dangers of military action, now made one last effort, as he believed, to avert war. It had finally dawned on him that Brauchitsch, while expressing private sympathy with his analysis, was simply not passing his concerns on to Hitler. Instead, Beck persuaded him to convene a meeting of all commanding generals for August 4 and, distrustful of Brauchitsch's own oratorical abilities, Beck prepared a robust speech for him to deliver. Unfortunately, when the generals met, Brauchitsch's courage again failed him, and it was left to Beck to read aloud his own memorandum of July 16. Only the army, he warned, could now halt Hitler's preparations for war.

> In full consciousness of the magnitude of such a step but also of my responsibilities I feel it my duty to urgently ask that the Supreme Commander of the Armed Forces call off his preparations for war, and abandon the intention of solving the Czech question by force until the military situation is fundamentally changed. For the present I consider it hopeless, and this view is shared by all the higher officers of the General Staff.[66]

Beck achieved widespread support among the twenty assembled generals. General Wilhelm Adam immediately endorsed his views and, as the general who would be in command of the western front, concurred that the fortifications there were wholly inadequate. With the bulk of the army concentrated against Czechoslovakia, he would have only five active divisions at his disposal, and would quickly be overrun by the French. "I paint a black picture," he conceded, but added that he was more than happy to repeat his views to Hitler in person.[67] There was a consensus that while Germany might possess the military capability to overrun Czechoslovakia, a war involving the Western powers was an altogether different proposition, and that no one believed the Sudetenland to be a cause for which it was worth risking the security of the nation.

Yet the apparent unanimity of the meeting soon began to unravel. Too many of those present had been dazzled by Hitler's successes to date, or were beholden to him in some way, or let their ambition and fear of disloyalty overcome their concerns. General von Reichenau, the most pro-Nazi general present, boasted of his "personal knowledge of the Führer," and warned his colleagues against confronting him individually.[68] "The question of knowing whether it is proper or not to make war does not concern us," he declared. "That is the Führer's business. We must rely on him to choose the best solution." He was supported by the outspokenly pro-Hitler General Ernst Busch, who assumed the moral high ground, and spoke earnestly of obedience and loyalty, falling back on the time-honored cliché that it was not the duty of soldiers to question political decisions. "Nothing can release us from our oath of loyalty to the Führer," he lectured his colleagues. "I know the weaknesses of our army, but nevertheless I would carry out his orders because any other course would be an act of indiscipline."[69] Finally Colonel General Gerd von Rundstedt, one of the most senior and respected officers, spoke for many when he declared himself unwilling to provoke a new crisis between Hitler and the army.

The meeting broke up without agreement, although Brauchitsch did pluck up the courage to send Beck's latest memorandum to Hitler. His reaction was predictable. Demanding to know who else had seen the document, he exploded with rage, and summoned Brauchitsch to the Berghof, where he dished out a "ferocious high-decibel verbal assault,"[70] which lasted several hours and forced those sitting on the terrace below to move inside out of sheer embarrassment. Hitler was, however, sufficiently concerned that Beck's memorandum had been read aloud to the generals to take a highly unorthodox step. On August 10, in an attempt to bypass the top military leadership, he summoned to the Berghof the next tier of officers below the ranking generals, many of whom were expecting to be given staff jobs with the commanding generals. They were a younger, and he therefore thought more unquestioning group, whose expectation of rapid promotion in time of war he believed would yield greater loyalty.

Such an obvious snub to his senior generals was a serious breach of military protocol, and his audience was clearly uneasy. After lunch he embarked on a three-hour *tour d'horizon* of his military ambitions, which unfortunately for him failed to impress those present any more than it had their commanding officers. When he had concluded his harangue, the ranking officer in the room, General Gustav Anton von Wietersheim, bravely rose to challenge Hitler's assumptions about Anglo-French nonintervention. As the designated chief of staff to General Adam on the western front, he also quoted Adam's warning of the previous week that, with the bulk of the army committed to Czechoslovakia, the West Wall defenses could probably not be held against the French for more than three weeks at most. At this, unsurprising, Hitler lost his temper. If that were indeed to be the case, he responded furiously, "the whole Army would not be good for anything. I say to you, Herr General, the position will be held not only for three weeks but for three years."

The meeting at the Berghof on August 10, 1938, was, according to one of those present, General Erich von Manstein, a historic one. It was the last at which Hitler was ever to permit questions from, or even discussion with, his military commanders. Although Jodl confided to his diary that Adam's and Wietersheim's "despondent opinion" was "held very widely within the Army General Staff," largely because they did "not believe in the genius of the Führer," it was no longer to find public expression.[71] Five days later, after watching a military review at the artillery range at Jüterborg, south of Berlin, Hitler again attempted to counter the effect of Beck's memorandum. Having gathered his generals together in the mess hall, he reiterated that he intended to solve the question of Czechoslovakia by force, and in a thinly veiled threat, he referred directly to Stalin's recent purge of his military top brass. "I too, would not recoil from destroying ten thousand officers if they opposed themselves to my will," he warned. "What is that in a nation of eighty millions? I do not want men of intelligence. I want men of brutality."[72]

On August 18 Beck finally tendered the letter of resignation which he had prepared a month earlier, and tried in vain to persuade Brauchitsch to join him. "You thought they would follow you?" asked Canaris, who had taken note of Hitler's disparaging reference to men of intelligence. "I know them well, they are serfs."[73] Yet even at the moment of his resignation, Beck missed one final trick. Ordinarily the departure of the chief of the army staff, especially at a time of international tension, would have caused uproar among military circles at home, and probably led to repercussions abroad. But Hitler, although he accepted his resignation with alacrity, cunningly persuaded Beck that the news should be suppressed. Out of a misplaced sense of patriotism Beck agreed, and Hitler thus cleverly avoided publicizing the fact that there existed a significant body of opposition to him. One of the last opportunities to create a coalition that might have stood up to him was squandered, and Hitler had now acquired the acquiescence, albeit reluctantly, of the military leadership to his plans. "I warned," Beck complained several months later, "and in the end I was alone."[74]

By August 19, Ribbentrop felt sufficiently confident to be able to confide in Weizsäcker that "the Führer was firmly resolved to settle the Czech affair by force of arms. He designated the middle of October as the latest possible date because of technical reasons governing air operations." Weizsäcker, who favored a diplomatic solution to hasten the so-called chemical dissolution process [*chemischer Auflösungsprozess*] in Czechoslovakia, argued against such a move. But Ribbentrop responded angrily that "the Führer had never yet made a mistake," and that Weizsäcker should "believe in his genius, just as he did from long years of experience." Ribbentrop also made the bizarre claim that Hitler intended "to move into Czechoslovakia himself at the head of the leading armoured division."[75] On August 24, Jodl prepared an urgent memorandum for Hitler, entitled "Timing of the X-Order and the Question of Advance Measures." He began by describing the conflicting wishes of the army and Luftwaffe as to the period of notice needed for a successful invasion. The Luftwaffe wanted the order to be given as late as possible, so as to "take the enemy air force by surprise on their peacetime airfields." The army, on the other hand, mindful of the chaotic mobilization prior to the Anschluss, were requesting as long a lead time as possible to prepare.

The document also described in detail plans to fabricate an incident, as had been intended in Austria also, which would serve as a casus belli.

Operation Grün will be set in motion by means of an "incident" in Czechoslovakia which will give Germany provocation for military intervention. The fixing of the *exact time* for this incident is of the utmost importance. It must come at a time when weather conditions are favourable for our superior *Luftwaffe* to go into action and at an hour which will enable authentic news of it to reach us by midday of X-day minus 1. No advance measures may be taken before X-day minus 1 for which there is not an innocent explanation as we shall otherwise appear to have manufactured the incident.

So crucial was it that there should be no hint of mobilization until the very last moment, that Jodl acknowledged it would even be impossible to warn their own diplomatic staff in Prague of the first air raid, "although the consequences could be very grave in the event of their becoming victims of such an attack."[76]

On August 22 Hitler interrupted his day-to-day preparations for invasion to spend two days watching naval maneuvers at Kiel. He invited the Hungarian regent, Admiral Miklós Horthy, accompanied by his Prime Minister, Béla Imrédy, as his guests. While the ostensible purpose of the visit was to attend the launch of the heavy cruiser *Prinz Eugen,* more important for Hitler was the opportunity to sound out the Hungarians as to the likelihood of their signing up with Germany in a joint military action against Czechoslovakia. Horthy and Imrédy found themselves confronted by a dilemma. On the one hand, so long as negotiations between the Czech government and the Sudeten Germans were ongoing, they hoped that the significant Magyar minority in Czechoslovakia could benefit from any concessions made to other minorities. On the other hand, it was becoming increasingly obvious that a German attack on Czechoslovakia was imminent, which would almost certainly result in that country's dismemberment. In that case, actual territorial revision, to the benefit of Hungary, was a distinct possibility, and they were naturally eager to acquire their share of the spoils.

Throughout the spring and summer the Hungarian leadership had been flattered by suggestions, from Göring in particular, that "in the event of a German-Czech conflict Hungary could presumably take part herself and receive her share." However, Göring had also stressed that Hungary "ought not to rely on Germany's pulling the chestnuts out of the fire alone."[77] The dangers for Hungary if war broke out were considerable. In 1921 Czechoslovakia, Yugoslavia and Romania had signed the so-called Little Entente, an alliance designed to provide a common defense against Hungarian territorial ambitions. Now, if Hungarian troops moved northward in a campaign against Czechoslovakia, Hungary's southern border would immediately become exposed to attack from Yugoslavia, an eventuality for which Hungary was militarily hopelessly unprepared. Horthy was also fearful that in a general European war Germany would be defeated and Hungary crushed. His concerns had been heightened just a few days earlier when a secret emissary of Canaris, whom Horthy had known as a fellow naval officer during the First World War, suddenly appeared in Budapest to warn that Hitler had arrived at an "irrevocable" decision to "settle accounts with Czechoslovakia by the end of September or beginning of October."

On the second day of the visit, Hitler and Horthy held talks on board the German warship *Patria,* in the course of a cruise to the island of Heligoland, while Imrédy and the Hungarian Foreign Minister were closeted with Ribbentrop. To the intense irritation of the Germans, not only did Horthy refuse to commit to military support for an invasion of Czechoslovakia, but he then presumed to lecture the Führer as to why it should not take place at all, principally because Britain would undoubtedly join in and would "inevitably win!" Although this was like "waving a red flag to a bull,"[78] Hitler persevered in trying to persuade Horthy to change his mind, offering Slovakia and the Carpatho-Ukraine as the prize if Hungary would join in.[79] Eventually, however, he was reluctantly forced to accept that he could expect no help from the Hungarians, but warned that "anyone who wanted to sit down to the meal would have first to help in the cooking of it."[80] Once his guests had left for Budapest, Hitler was privately scathing over their attitude and their inability to pluck up the courage for action. They preferred instead, he grumbled, to sit around "listening to gypsy music."[81]

Hitler quickly got over his disappointment, and once again took to the road. On August 26, accompanied by Himmler, Jodl and Fritz Todt, the engineer in charge of building works, he set off on a tour of inspection of the West Wall. The following day General Adam joined the Führer's special train at Aachen, and remained with his entourage as far as the Swiss border. At one point, at the French border near Strasbourg, Hitler made a great show of walking halfway across the bridge over the Rhine that marked the frontier, while the French troops looked on in amazement from the far river bank. The tour, noted Adam, "took on the air of a triumphal procession," as SS and Hitler Youth bands came out in force to cheer the Führer, who quickly became "intoxicated by such display." Adam, however, was far from impressed. Now over sixty, and affectionately known as the "father" of the Reich's mountain troops, he was one of the two most senior, and highly regarded, members of the Bavarian officer corps, and was the obvious choice to take command of the German forces on the western front. However, he was also notoriously stubborn, and had already shown that he was not afraid to speak his mind when the need arose.

Adam now demanded to speak to Hitler alone, insisting that the accompanying Nazi Party cronies, including Himmler, should leave the car so that he could discuss purely military matters with the Führer. Once Himmler had reluctantly agreed to go, Adam did not mince his words. The West Wall, he told Hitler, in spite of all the boasts made about it, was still entirely unfit for purpose and he could not possibly hold it with the troop strength he had at his disposal. There would be no improvement unless the shipping of raw materials was greatly speeded up, and he repeated his belief that the

British and French "would be at war as soon as the first German shot was fired against the Czechs, and the French would soon break through."[82] Hitler became hysterical. "We have no time to listen any longer to this stuff," he interrupted. "You don't understand that. We produce in Germany 23 million tons of steel a year, the French only 6 millions and the English only 16 millions. The English have no reserves and the French have the greatest internal difficulties. They'll beware of declaring war on us."[83] Adam replied sarcastically that in that case there was little need for him at all on the western front. "The man who does not hold these fortifications," screamed Hitler, "is a scoundrel. I only regret that I am the Führer and Reichschancellor, and that therefore I cannot be Supreme Commander of the Western Front."[84]

▪ ▪ ▪

The first SIS reports on the details of Case Green had reached Whitehall in early July. While they indicated that increased German military preparation was being undertaken "not necessarily with the immediate object of attacking Czechoslovakia," the clear implication was that "trouble may be in store for us in the autumn." German company commanders were being ordered to barracks due to a "continual state of alarm," increased numbers of reservists were being called up, and all leave outside Germany had been forbidden since August 1. The construction of the western fortifications had been greatly accelerated, and substantial fuel stocks were being laid up by both the army and Luftwaffe. Although "no serious trouble" was expected before the party rally at Nuremberg in early September, some sources suggested that there was "a definite plan for a German attack on Czechoslovakia after the harvest is in."[85] From Berlin, the normally imperturbable Henderson reported that all Luftwaffe leave had been canceled, while "all the best pilots were being quickly recalled from Spain." However, unable as usual to resist the temptation to blame the Czechs, he qualified his warning by pointing out that "these calculated indiscretions" all emanated from sources close to Göring, and were probably "a policy of deliberate bluff conceived in response to delays at Prague and in distrust of M. Beneš."[86]

By mid-August these warnings were reinforced by further information from Vansittart's private intelligence network. In a memorandum prepared for Halifax on August 18, based on a conversation with a "well-informed German acquaintance," he wrote that he had been told emphatically that "war was now a certainty unless we stopped it." There was "only one real extremist and that is Hitler himself. He is the great danger and he is doing this entirely on his own."[87] That afternoon Vansittart met an emissary of the moderate opposition movement in Germany, Ewald von Kleist-Schmenzin, who assured him that he could speak for "all the Generals in the German Army who are friends of mine. They are all dead against war," he continued, "but they will not have the power to stop it unless they get encouragement and help from outside. As I have already told you, they know the date and will be obliged to march at that date." Vansittart inquired what the date was, as which Kleist laughed. "Why of course you know it. Well anyhow, your Prime Minister knows it. After the 27th September," he concluded quietly, "it will be too late."[88]

The proposal that Kleist should be sent to London to sound out establishment opinion there was the brainchild of Colonel Hans Oster, the head of Section Z at the Abwehr (responsible for administration and organization), and effectively second-in-command to Admiral Canaris. However, it was clearly made at the behest of his chief. A young British journalist in Berlin, Ian Colvin of the *News Chronicle*, had already had his "first glimpses" of Canaris's "separate diplomacy," and Kleist confided to Colvin that Canaris wished to know for certain whether Britain would fight if Germany invaded Czechoslovakia. "The Admiral wants someone to go to London and find out," he whispered conspiratorially. "We have an offer to make to the British and a warning to give them."[89] Kleist, the owner of a large estate in Pomerania, was the ideal choice to undertake such a mission. A devout Christian, he was "pre-eminently a gentleman, an unwavering opponent of Hitler [and] had charm of manner, honesty of bearing and deep sincerity."[90] He was a member of the Old Conservative Party, a staunchly pro-monarchist group which had somehow managed to retain a voice behind the scenes in Nazi Germany on behalf of the old Junker landowners of Prussia.

When Nevile Henderson found out about Kleist's visit, he was far from happy, fearing giving offense to the German government. "It would be unwise for him to be received in official quarters," he urged, but Halifax insisted that Kleist "should not be rebuffed,"[91] and preparations were duly made in Berlin. "If you can bring me from London positive proof that the British will make war if we invade Czechoslovakia," Kleist was told by a conspiratorial Beck, "then I will make an end of this regime." All that he needed was "an open pledge to assist Czechoslovakia in the event of war."[92] Canaris, meanwhile, demonstrating the "spy-chief's usual cavalier attitude towards the passport system,"[93] procured for Kleist a fresh identity, new passport and sufficient sterling, and arranged for a Mercedes from the OKW car pool to deliver him to the foot of the aircraft steps, thus bypassing customs and passport control. At Croydon his arrival was noted and, after taking the coach to London, he made his way to the Park Lane Hotel. He had, he told Vansittart, "come out of the country with a rope around his neck," and "had no illusions as to the fate that awaited him if he failed."[94]

The following morning Kleist was driven down to Chartwell to see Churchill, whose son, Randolph, recorded the meeting. Kleist repeated what he had told Vansittart the previous day, insisting that Hitler was determined upon war, and that "an attack upon Czechoslovakia was imminent," probably after the Nuremberg party rally, and certainly before the end of September. There would be no ultimatum, just a lighting invasion, although "there was nobody in Germany who wanted war except H. who regarded the events of May 21 as a personal rebuff." His generals were "all for peace [and] if only they could receive a little encouragement they might refuse to march," in spite of their fear of Hitler's fury. "Some gesture was needed," concluded Kleist, "to crystallise the widespread and indeed, universal anti-war sentiment in Germany." If a senior British politician could only send a positive signal, the generals would "insist on peace and there would be a new system of government within forty-eight hours."[95]

Churchill was clearly impressed, and telephoned Halifax in the course of the meeting to seek authority from him to state formally to Kleist that Chamberlain's declaration in the House of Commons on March 24 still held good as government policy. Having done so, he gave Kleist an open letter with which to return to Berlin.

> I have welcomed you here as one who is ready to run risks to preserve the peace of Europe and to achieve a lasting friendship between the British, French and German peoples for their mutual advantage. . . . I am sure that the crossing of the frontier of Czecho-Slovakia by German armies or

aviation in force will bring about a renewal of the world war. I am as certain as I was at the end of July 1914 that England will march with France and that . . . the spectacle of an armed attack by Germany upon a small neighbour and the bloody fighting that will follow will rouse the whole British Empire and compel the gravest decisions. Do not, I pray you, be misled upon this point. Such a war, once started, would be fought out like the last to the bitter end, and one must consider not what might happen in the first few months, but where we should all be at the end of the third or fourth year.[96]

Kleist returned to Berlin, where the letter was delivered to him a few days later by a secret courier, Fabian von Schlabrendorff, an Abwehr lawyer. Copies were made for Beck and Canaris, on whom Kleist called at Abwehr headquarters on Tirpitzufer. Reluctantly, however, he was forced to concede that he had returned empty-handed, and had "found nobody in London who wishes to take this opportunity to wage a preventive war."[97] His inference was correct. After reading Vansittart's minute of his meeting with Kleist, Chamberlain wrote to Halifax from Chequers.

I take it that Von Kleist is violently anti-Hitler and is extremely anxious to stir up his friends in Germany to make an attempt at his overthrow. He reminds me of the Jacobites at the Court of France in King William's time and I think we must discount a good deal of what he says.[98]

Canaris ordered one of his Abwehr agents to approach Mason-MacFarlane, the British military attaché, in an effort to reinforce the message: clandestine mobilization was continuing, the invasion was scheduled for the end of the September, and the General Staff was "staggered by the fact that it was being taken so lightly abroad." As always, however, Henderson watered down the message by including his own health warning. The informant's anti-Nazi views were well known, he wrote, and "his pronouncements," said the ambassador, "are clearly biased and largely propaganda."[99]

Meanwhile, fears within the British intelligence community that German military action was imminent were strengthened by the first direct Nazi action against the "passport control officer" system. On the morning of August 17, Captain Thomas Kendrick, the PCO and SIS station chief at the consulate in Vienna, was arrested near Freilassing, a town to the west of Salzburg, while being driven to Munich with his wife. He was returned to Vienna and detained in the Hotel Metropole, the Gestapo headquarters, where a number of high-profile detainees, including Schuschnigg and Baron Rothschild, were then being held. Although the official British line was that "no details whatever of the alleged evidence against Captain Kendrick were produced,"[100] and it was suggested that his arrest was the result of a minor passport irregularity, *The Times* soon disclosed that he had been driving "partly through or near territory where German manoeuvres were understood to be in progress."[101]

Kendrick's arrest and his subsequent grueling interrogation at the hands of the Gestapo caused consternation at SIS headquarters at Broadway Buildings in Victoria. Admiral Sir Hugh Sinclair was forced to ask Henderson to intervene personally in Berlin and, after a meeting with Weizsäcker, the ambassador succeeded in having Kendrick released on Sunday, August 21. However, in a pre-echo of modern-day spy scandals, the Germans were determined to cause maximum embarrassment to the British government. "EXPELLED FROM GERMANY AS A SPY" proclaimed *The Times*, confirming that the charge against Kendrick was indeed "one of espionage," while the Germans claimed that he had made a full confession. On his release, he barely had time to clear out his Vienna apartment, before being expelled to Hungary, and then flying on to London. The "restraint with which the German Government have acted," crowed the German press, "in merely requiring Captain Kendrick to leave the country, is proof of a desire to maintain good relations with Britain."[102]

The significance of Kendrick's arrest was that, having worked in Vienna for more than twelve years, his dual role as PCO and SIS officer must have long been known to the German authorities. Why had they waited until now to arrest and deport him, when they could have done so at any time since the Anschluss? Either their action signaled a newfound "determination to expose SIS activities," or, more ominous, a need to "prevent [Kendrick] collecting intelligence on Operation 'Green.' "[103] In either scenario, according to one historian of MI6, the arrest was "an unfortunate one for all concerned," and was to have serious "repercussions all over Europe." The remaining SIS staff in Vienna were recalled to London, as were their counterparts in Berlin and Prague, along with the station chiefs there, Major Frank Foley and Major "Gibby" Gibson. This had a serious short-term effect on British intelligence gathering at a crucial moment, in what were then the most important capital cities in Europe. For Sinclair it was a "sobering experience" and "a warning of events to come."[104]

On August 27 Sir John Simon, the Chancellor of the Exchequer, and a former captain of the Royal and Ancient Golf Club, interrupted his golfing holiday at North Berwick. What was to have been the low-key constituency summer fete of Lord Dunglass's Lanark Unionist Association was seized upon by Chamberlain as a suitable vehicle for a restatement of government foreign policy. Simon had been invited to speak by Dunglass some months earlier, but now Lanark racecourse was hurriedly booked and, although persistent rain forced the abandonment of a cricket match between Dunglass's XI and a Lanark XI, 2,000 people still braved the Scottish weather to hear Simon's speech.

> I repudiate altogether the outlook which is tempted to say that war is inevitable, as though certain countries were bound to be our enemies. The beginning of a conflict is like the beginning of a fire in a high wind. It may be limited at the start, but who can say how far it would spread, or how much destruction it would do, or how many may be called upon to beat it out?[105]

Although the previous day a senior Foreign Office official had warned the King's Private Secretary that Simon was "not really going to say anything very epoch-making,"[106] the speech was a subtle reiteration of Chamberlain's declaration to the House of Commons on March 24: that "if Hitler used force against Czechoslovakia, it might well be impossible to localise the resulting war, and we might ourselves be involved."[107] Although it satisfied neither the advocates of appeasement nor those who favored taking a firmer stand against Hitler, it did receive a relatively warm welcome from the British press, on the grounds that it had "been received with satisfaction almost everywhere but in Berlin."[108] Unfortunately that was the one place where it mattered. "It would be impossible," Weizsäcker told Henderson, "to convince Ribbentrop that England would ever move under any circumstances."[109] The German press greeted Simon's speech "with disappointment and anger," and interpreted it as "encouragement to

Prague to continue the policy of 'procrastination' and 'obstinacy.' "[110] With a number of self-corroborating reports from the SIS, Vansittart, Kleist and Mason-MacFarlane now landing thick and fast on the Prime Minister's desk, Chamberlain finally grasped the seriousness of the situation, and declared himself "sufficiently impressed to be inclined to make some warning gesture" to Hitler before his Nuremberg speech on September 12.[111]

Chamberlain's "gesture" was to recall Henderson from Berlin for emergency talks in Whitehall, and to "take care that everyone knew it." Indeed Henderson was to let it be known in Berlin that "he was sent for to consult about the serious position in connection with Czecho."[112] However, Chamberlain had a further, ulterior motive, and on his arrival in London on Monday, August 29, Henderson was summoned directly to Downing Street, where he was ushered into the presence of the Prime Minister and Sir Horace Wilson, Chamberlain's most senior adviser. As he confided to his sister, Chamberlain had for some time been "racking his brains to try & devise some means of averting a catastrophe if it should seem to be upon us." Now he believed that he had come up with an answer "so unconventional and daring that it rather took Halifax's breath away,"[113] and he wanted to try it out on Henderson. Wilson later recalled that "it was quite a surprise to Sir Nevile who did not know why he had been sent for,"[114] but he soon recovered his composure and agreed with Chamberlain that his "idea might save the situation at the 11th hour."[115] It was, however, to be another two weeks before the Prime Minister's scheme was revealed to the rest of the world.

8

Czechoslovakia Stands Alone

THERE WILL BE NO WAR. . . . There will be no European war. Why? Because the decision of peace and war depends on one man, the German Führer. And he will not be responsible for making war at present.
Lord Beaverbrook, Daily Express, September 1, 1938

Long live the war, even if it lasts two to eight years.
Adolf Hitler to Konrad Henlein, Berchtesgaden, September 2, 1938

It might be worth while for the Czechoslovak Government to consider whether they should exclude altogether the project, which has found favour in some quarters, of making Czechoslovakia a more homogeneous State by the secession of that fringe of alien populations who are contiguous to the nation with which they are united by race.
The Times, September 7, 1938

On August 27 the newly appointed Cabinet Secretary, Edward Bridges, wrote to the King's Private Secretary, Sir Alec Hardinge, who was at Balmoral with the King.

The Prime Minister has decided that a Meeting of such Ministers as are readily available should be held . . . to discuss recent developments in the international situation, with particular reference to Czechoslovakia. The Prime Minister attaches importance to this meeting not being described—at any rate publicly—as a Cabinet Meeting, and steps have been taken to avoid the fact that this meeting is to be held getting known in advance.[1]

The previous day, every member of the Cabinet had received a similarly conspiratorial letter, summoning them to a meeting on Tuesday, August 30, and warning them that, in order "to avoid alarmist speculation in the Press," they should "be good enough to avoid publicity as to [their] movements."[2] Unfortunately, the Prime Minister's precautions had little effect. By August 29 even *The Times* felt able to report that Henderson's emergency recall from Berlin was an illustration of the "wider misgivings aroused by the manner in which the Sudeten demands have been supported from Germany."[3]

The majority of ministers managed to alter their holiday plans to attend the meeting. Duff Cooper, who had been enjoying a Baltic cruise on the Admiralty yacht, *Enchantress,* arrived back at Tilbury early that morning. Lord Hailsham was on a cruise to South America, and Lord Stanley was in Canada on official business.[4] Only Leslie Burgin, the Minister of Transport, refused to alter his arrangements and had traveled to Switzerland as planned. The eighteen ministers who were able to attend duly assembled at Downing Street at 11 A.M., the headlines in the morning newspapers demonstrating that Chamberlain's attempts to avoid alarmism, let alone to ensure secrecy, had failed hopelessly. "Ministers Meet To-Day," confirmed the *Daily Mail.*[5] Chamberlain began by apologizing for interrupting his colleagues' holidays, but stressed that "the situation was so grave that members of the Cabinet should know how matters stood." Halifax then spoke for an hour, giving a *tour d'horizon* of the situation, first explaining that Runciman's mission had enjoyed a "chilly reception from the German Ministry of Foreign Affairs."[6] He then warned that reports suggested that "Germany's military preparations were in full swing." Military maneuvers "were on a large scale, commodities were being bought heavily, labour was being impressed, and all service leave stopped."[7] Furthermore, the chief of the French air force, General Joseph Vuillemin, had recently visited Berlin and had been "a good deal impressed, in an unfavourable sense, by Field Marshal Göring."

There were, continued Halifax, two possible scenarios. The first was that

Hitler, "against the advice of the Army and the moderate party," was determined on war, possibly because he genuinely believed that to be the best solution, or because "he wished to wipe out the flavour left by the events of 21st May," or even because "he wanted a spectacular success for internal reasons." If that were the case, Halifax warned, "the only deterrent which would be likely to be effective would be an announcement that if Germany invaded Czechoslovakia we should declare war on her." His personal view was that such a threat would divide public opinion, and he could not guarantee the support of the country in carrying it out. Furthermore, if the "deterrent intimidation failed," there was still nothing to prevent Czechoslovakia being overrun, and it was unlikely that the country could ever be re-created in its present state. There was not, he thought, "much point in fighting a war for an object which one could not secure." Was it therefore "justifiable," he asked his colleagues, "to fight a certain war now in order to forestall a possible war later"? In conclusion, he could see no alternative but to maintain the existing policy of "keeping Hitler guessing," while giving all possible support to Lord Runciman.

Chamberlain praised Halifax's statement as "full and masterly," and endorsed his Foreign Secretary's conclusion. "No State, certainly no democratic State," he told the Cabinet, "ought to make a threat of war unless it was both ready to carry it out and prepared to do so. This was a sound maxim."[8] This view was in turn supported by Nevile Henderson, who, in an unusual but not unique break with tradition, was attending the meeting. Based on his experiences in Berlin, he insisted that there was no evidence whatsoever that Hitler had already decided on the use of force. The Home Secretary, Sir Samuel Hoare, was unimpressed by Henderson's performance. While the ambassador was evidently "as profoundly intent upon preventing war as Chamberlain," in contrast to the Prime Minister he was "governed by his nerves," and appeared "overwrought." Indeed, "so anxious was he that war should be averted that, no doubt unconsciously, he quite obviously took sides against anyone who seemed to be obstructing the way of peace." If international peace was to be maintained, Henderson told the meeting, then countries such as Austria and Czechoslovakia "must accept virtual absorption in the Reich."[9]

Only Duff Cooper spoke out against the consensus.

The great danger was that Hitler might think he could get away with a lightning attack which would give him the Sudeten territories before France or England had had time to move. He would then stop—declare for peace, and give good terms to the Czechs. If such a policy were to come off it would be disastrous from the point of view of the future of Europe. All the smaller Powers would give up hope and would immediately make the best terms they could with Germany. England would be humiliated and the Government would be very hard hit.[10]

When, as First Lord of the Admiralty, Cooper then suggested a partial mobilization of the fleet, Chamberlain dismissed the suggestion as being "in the nature of pin pricks," and warned that "it was very important not to exacerbate feeling in Berlin against us."[11] After two and three-quarter hours, the meeting had achieved almost nothing. There was to be no change in policy, no new diplomatic initiative, and no warning sent to Berlin. No decision had even been taken as to what Britain's response should be if Germany did indeed attack Czechoslovakia. Chamberlain, however, had got exactly what he wanted: collective Cabinet support for his leadership, and backing for his policy to avert war at any cost.

That afternoon the American ambassador, Joseph Kennedy, called on Chamberlain at Downing Street. If Hitler went ahead and invaded Czechoslovakia, "it would be hell," Kennedy told the Prime Minister, but he assured him that Roosevelt had resolved to "go in with Chamberlain" whatever course he decided upon.[12] Later that afternoon, having been checked over by his doctors, Chamberlain set off for Balmoral where he was to stay as minister in attendance on the King. He left a short, handwritten note for Halifax, again stressing the importance of underplaying any press statement about the morning's meeting. "There is already deep depression and anxiety on the Stock Exchange," he wrote, "and Kennedy, who has just been to see me, expressed the fear that U.S.A. should get into an 'economic tailspin' as a result of the construction [the press] put upon the meeting of Ministers." He was particularly anxious that "the atmosphere should not be unduly thickened or encouragement given to the idea put forward in the 'Mail' and 'Express' this morning that Henderson is taking a message (threat or warning) to Hitler from the Cabinet."[13]

Unsurprising, the blandest of communiqués was issued.

The Foreign Secretary made a full report of the international situation, and at the conclusion of the meeting Ministers expressed their entire agreement with the action already taken and the policy to be pursued in the future.[14]

There were to be no further meetings, although ministers were encouraged to stay as near as possible to London. Chamberlain, however, left for Scotland, while Henderson boarded a plane to take him back to Berlin. The following morning the *Daily Express* ignored the Foreign Office's attempts to minimize the significance of the meeting. Below the banner headline "THERE WILL BE NO WAR" Beaverbrook attached his own signature to the front-page leader.

There will be no European war. Why? Because the decision of peace and war depends on one man, the German Führer. And he will not be responsible for making war at present. Hitler has shown himself throughout his career to be a man of exceptional astuteness.

This view was endorsed by Joseph Kennedy who, after his meeting with Chamberlain, confidently informed the readers of the *New York Herald Tribune* that "1938 WILL PASS OUT WITHOUT WAR."[15]

The Prime Minister's stay at Balmoral, without even the support of his wife, Annie, who had remained in London, was a gloomy affair. The depression he felt at the state of events in Europe was compounded by the atrocious weather, and even his favorite pastimes of shooting and fishing could not lift his sense of despair. "The crisis atmosphere was unmistakably present," he complained to his sister of the meeting at Downing Street. "Is it not positively horrible," he continued, "to think that the fate of hundreds of millions depends on one man and he is half mad?"[16] In the King's presence he maintained an outward show of confidence, but to his wife he confided that "the thing hangs over me like a nightmare all the time and I often wish I was in Downing Street." He "didn't feel like fishing," and when the house party finally braved the weather on the moor, they were greeted by a hailstorm. "I shot badly," he told Annie, "and was also unlucky as fewer grouse came to my butt than to anyone's."[17] Yet even in the midst of such despondency, he could not resist a self-reassuring claim about his fitness. "I created rather a sensation at Balmoral," he boasted to his sister, "by showing myself to be neither tired nor stiff after a long walk which wore out some of the others."[18]

Halifax had stayed in London to hold the fort in Chamberlain's absence, and he began work on a speech which he proposed to deliver in advance of the Nazi Party rally at Nuremberg. Its conclusion, he confided hopefully to Henderson, would be a warning that "Europe is not prepared to have its peace disturbed either by unreasonable Czechs or by acquisitive Germans."[19] Henderson, however, refused to support any statement that might antagonize Hitler. On the night of his return to Berlin he had dined with Weizsäcker at the British embassy, and the conversation over dinner had involved a curious reversal of roles. It was the moderate Weizsäcker who issued a subtle word of caution, expressing his regret that "war in 1914 might possibly have been avoided if Great Britain had spoken in time." It was left to the British ambassador to argue that it would be "undesirable" to use a form of language which might have the effect of "damaging Herr Hitler's prestige and provoking his resentment."[20]

Debate within the Foreign Office, meanwhile, focused on the wisdom of issuing a formal warning to Hitler. Intelligence reports predicting that war was imminent continued to arrive from Germany. The latest came from Professor Philip Conwell-Evans, a friend of Malcolm Christie, who held a chair at the University of Königsberg. He was a key figure in the Anglo-German Society, a body dedicated to improving relations between the two countries, had long been impressed by the Nazi regime, and was known as a strong advocate for making concessions to Germany. Conwell-Evans had recently returned from a visit to Berlin, where he had held meetings with Ribbentrop and other senior figures. Back in London he briefed Halifax, Vansittart and Wilson. In spite of his pro-German sympathies, he was now firmly convinced that Hitler had indeed made up his mind to invade Czechoslovakia, and to "incorporate Bohemia and parts of Moravia"—that is to say Czech, as well as Sudeten German areas. Hitler had overruled the objections of his generals, assuring them "that France and Great Britain will remain neutral," and military action would commence "at any time between the end of September and October 15." Only a formal warning, "a firm declaration," would now restrain him.[21]

On Friday, September 2, Cadogan was finally recalled from a golfing holiday in Le Touquet, and spent the weekend catching up on his reading. There was "enough in the Secret Reports," he discovered, "to make one's hair stand on end." On balance, he too was in favor of sending a private warning to Hitler.[22] By the Sunday, all of the top officials at the Foreign Office had reassembled from their holidays. Even Halifax, whose habit it had been only "to visit the Foreign Office in the middle of each week," had been forced by "events in Central Europe . . . to return earlier and stay longer."[23] Only Chamberlain lingered, having begun his holiday later than everyone else after his illness in August. While he was at Balmoral, the situation was considered so serious that the King arranged for him to be flown back to London, if necessary at a moment's notice, in an aircraft of the royal flight. Chamberlain declined the offer "on the grounds that he had not been in a plane before and did not intend to break the habit of a lifetime at this stage."[24] On September 5 the "Londoner's Diary" column of the *Evening Standard* reported on the Prime Minister's whereabouts, alongside the paper's latest literary serialization, of Graham Greene's *Brighton Rock.*

The Prime Minister is shooting to-day with the man who ranks among the six best shots in England, Captain Ivan Cobbold, at Millden in Angus. Captain Cobbold belongs to the wealthy Ipswich brewing family. He enjoys sufficient leisure from city activities to enable him to fire as many as 40,000 cartridges in a season, at grouse in Scotland, and at partridges and pheasants on his estate in East Anglia.

Readers were also furnished with the fascinating society titbit that Cobbold's wife, Lady Blanche, the sister of the Duke of Devonshire, was "one of the few English Moslems and a noted traveller in the Near East."[25]

In Chamberlain's absence, Sir Horace Wilson, his most trusted ally and confidant, had assumed many of his responsibilities at Downing Street. A career civil servant, Wilson had made his name as an accomplished arbitrator of industrial disputes, first as Permanent Under-Secretary at the Ministry of Labour (he played a significant role in the settlement of the General Strike in 1926) and, since 1930, as Chief Industrial Adviser to the government, a post specifically created for him. In 1935 the then Prime Minister Stanley Baldwin had moved him to the Treasury (he also played a key role in the abdication crisis), where he soon became a close friend of Chamberlain, then the Chancellor of the Exchequer; both men "set the highest store upon hard work, efficiency and plain-speaking." When Chamberlain became Prime Minister, he unexpectedly took Wilson with him to 10 Downing Street. A self-made man, Wilson had no public school or Oxbridge connections, and held his position "solely because his abilities . . . were outstanding."[26] Hoare described him as "in every respect the orthodox, conscientious and efficient Civil Servant . . . as an administrator, he was of outstanding reputation in Whitehall."[27]

By 1938, according to Lord Woolton with whom he enjoyed a close friendship, Wilson found himself "enjoying tremendous power—in fact a power unequalled by any member of the Cabinet."[28] As a result, he was the "most widely photographed and most frequently written about civil servant of his day." He worked from an office immediately adjacent to the Cabinet Room, and answered only to Chamberlain, whom he provided with "an alternative source of opinions and information."[29] Chamberlain trusted Wilson absolutely and there was a "high degree of intellectual and personal sympathy, even affinity, between the two men."[30] Both resented the air of authority and finality with which the Foreign Office spoke (there were "too many dilettantes" there according to Wilson), a feeling of mistrust which was entirely mutual. Within the rarefied atmosphere of the Foreign Office, Wilson was regarded as an éminence grise; his lowly background was a source of contempt (Sir Orme Sargent nicknamed him "creeping Jesus"), and his lack of expert knowledge in the field of foreign affairs considered disastrous. Even Clement Attlee described his abilities as "Not National, only Midland Regional."[31] Yet as a fellow enthusiast for Chamberlain's obsession with improving Anglo-German relations and appeasing the dictators, Wilson had made himself indispensable.[32]

On the evening of September 5 Wilson was visited at Downing Street by Theodor Kordt, the Counselor at the German embassy. Kordt was acting on instructions from his brother, Erich Kordt, who had served with Ribbentrop during his London ambassadorship, and had then returned with him to Berlin to run his private office at the Foreign Ministry. A close friend of Weizsäcker, it was Erich Kordt who had persuaded Ribbentrop to promote Weizsäcker to become State Secretary. When Ribbentrop inquired about Weizsäcker's qualities, Kordt replied that as a former naval officer and a skilled diplomat he "would know how to obey," a quality that greatly endeared him to Ribbentrop. By 1938, "a core Opposition group was already in process of formation around Erich Kordt," while, after his appointment as State Secretary, Weizsäcker "became the sponsor and, ultimately, the head of this circle."[33]

Theo Kordt told Wilson that he had "put conscience before loyalty," and had come to warn the British government that Hitler had decided to "march in" on September 19 or 20. Although we now know this information to be inaccurate, it was considered sufficiently serious for Wilson to set about recalling Chamberlain from his Scottish holiday, and for Halifax to cancel a planned trip to the League of Nations.[34] The following morning Kordt returned to Downing Street, surreptitiously sneaking into No. 10 by the garden gate. On this occasion, Halifax was waiting for him with Wilson. Kordt repeated what he had said the previous day, and refined the details of the timing for invasion. Mobilization, he told the Foreign Secretary, would commence on September 16, with a view to attacking Czechoslovakia no later than the first day of October. He suggested a warning broadcast to the German nation, an idea that found little favor with Halifax. There was, he assured them, sufficient opposition to Hitler's plans within the German Foreign Ministry and among senior generals, that "all that was required of Britain and France was to remain firm and not to give ground before the fury of Hitler's forthcoming diatribes" at Nuremberg.[35]

Kordt's warning was entirely consistent with others received by the Foreign Office, as was his Shakespearean suggestion that the political and military opposition to Hitler was prepared to "take arms against a sea of troubles and by opposing end them."[36] Unlike Kleist, however, Kordt was not some little-known emissary from within Germany, but was the officially accredited second-in-command at the German embassy, and was a respected figure in diplomatic circles. It seems extraordinary in hindsight that, because his suggested course of action was so out of step with British policy at the time, no further action was taken or advice sought. When it was reported from Prague that evening that negotiations had broken down there, and that German troops might already be on the move, Cadogan was again put to work to draft a suitable warning to Hitler. But the BBC assured Wilson that the reports were false, and by the following morning the danger appeared to have passed.

Chamberlain arrived back in London early on September 8, and at 11 A.M. called together a small gathering at Downing Street, involving Wilson, Halifax, Cadogan and Simon. "P.M. doesn't think warning message much good," recorded Cadogan. "Thinks he should go himself. I agree."[37] Halifax, who had not been present when Chamberlain had first discussed the idea of his visiting Hitler with Wilson and Henderson, appears to have been surprised by the suggestion, and insisted that Vansittart should join the meeting. With the exception of Sir Samuel Hoare, who had taken Chamberlain's place at Balmoral, the group assembled in the Cabinet Room that morning constituted the first meeting of the so-called Inner Circle that was to meet regularly over the next few weeks. Vansittart quickly provoked a row, arguing forcefully against the proposal that Chamberlain should visit Hitler. "He mentioned the word Canossa," recalled Cadogan, while the Prime Minister sat with "his elbows on the Cabinet table and his head between his hands and never said a word."[38]

▪ ▪ ▪

During the last few days of August the diplomatic activity in Czechoslovakia became increasingly frenetic, as Runciman exerted ever-greater pressure on the Czech government to accede to the Sudeten German demands. Slowly, but surely, Beneš began to bow to the British pressure, offering further concessions to the SdP, which in turn led their negotiating team to seek advice from Berlin. On one such occasion the German chargé d'affaires in Prague chose the unlikely time of 1 A.M. to wake Ribbentrop, seeking guidance on a particular dilemma. The Foreign Minister was, unsurprisingly, furious. Henlein "had already received clear instructions . . . and he and his people must learn to stand on their own feet." Their orders were clear—"always to negotiate and not to let the link be broken [and] always to demand more than could be granted by the other side."[39]

On August 24 Beneš submitted further proposals to Kundt and Sebekovsky. The so-called Third Plan represented a considerable advance on those put forward previously, and contained significant new concessions relating to language issues, quotas of German officials and subsidies for distressed areas. Most far-reaching was the proposal that Bohemia and Moravia should be divided into autonomous cantons (*Gaue*), three of which would enjoy a German majority, thus giving the Nazis control over at least part of

Czechoslovakia. On Saturday, August 27, Runciman was due to spend the weekend at the Teplitz castle of Prince Clary-Aldringen, another Bohemian aristocrat sympathetic to the Sudeten German cause. Before leaving Prague, Runciman called on Beneš to "transmit a warning about . . . the necessity of going to the limit and beyond in meeting the wishes of the Sudetens."[40] That evening, Ashton-Gwatkin, who had arrived back from London that afternoon and had traveled to Teplitz with Runciman, left for the nearby castle of Prince Hohenlohe at Rothenhaus. There, the following day, he again held talks with Henlein and his deputy, Karl Hermann Frank.

The conversation began with an entirely fictitious account by Frank of a visit he had recently made to see Hitler in Berlin. He assured Ashton-Gwatkin that the Führer "would welcome a peaceful solution of Sudeten question if it comes quickly," and also a visit by Henlein, provided that he brought with him "a definite statement" of what the British government proposed. In particular, Hitler insisted that Runciman make a formal recommendation to the Czech government that they should "adopt the eight point programme of Herr Henlein's Karlsbad speech as general basis for solution of Sudeten question."[41] In fact, Frank's story was a total fabrication. He had confided the true nature of his conversation with Hitler to a senior Abwehr officer, Helmuth Groscurth, shortly before leaving Berlin. "The Führer," recorded Groscurth, "is determined to wage war. He gives orders to arrange incidents in Czechoslovakia. Insulted Beneš. He wants to catch him alive and to hang him personally on the rope."[42]

Hitler's order to Frank, that he should initiate a campaign of provocative incidents, represented the next step toward invasion and the ultimate implementation of Case Green. All acts of provocation were to lead inexorably to one, final incident, which would provide the necessary pretext for military intervention. Handpicked SA officers, with a proven track record in organizing such incidents, slipped discreetly across the border, while hard-line Sudeten Germans traveled in the opposite direction and were formed into a special legion close to the Czech frontier. Within the Sudetenland, scuffles broke out more frequently between Germans and Czechs, while spurious reports of Czech attacks on German villages increasingly filled the pages of the German press. The Czech police discovered mounting evidence of explosives being freely moved around the area, and there was an accompanying rise in the number of arrests for arms smuggling across the border.

On 30 August Beneš met Kundt and Sebekovsky, and handed them a written memorandum containing his "Third Plan" proposals. He assured them that he was, in effect, accepting Henlein's eight Karlsbad terms. Frank conceded this, and was forced to admit that the proposals were "comparatively far-reaching" and "could not be rejected out of hand."[43] The following day, however, Kundt resiled from this position, complaining to Runciman that the proposals still did not go far enough. Remarkably he was supported in this view by the British so-called mediator, who was now increasingly playing the role of arbitrator, exactly what Chamberlain had assured the world would not occur. In a particularly intemperate letter to Halifax, Runciman described Beneš's latest plan as a bitter disappointment, "covered with bolt holes and qualifications—no use for publication." Czechoslovakia, he moaned, was an "accursed country," where the "signs of bad government accumulate day by day and at any moment H. may find an excuse for crossing the frontier in order to maintain order." Mindful that Chamberlain was touring the estates of Scotland with his guns and rods, Runciman particularly resented that he had not even "been able to take a day off for their wonderful partridge shooting."[44]

On the same day Ashton-Gwatkin traveled to Marienbad, where he urged Henlein to report the latest Czech offer to Hitler in person. In one of the more curious episodes in the annals of twentieth-century diplomacy, the British Foreign Office official supplied Henlein, the irredentist leader in a country allied to Britain, with two messages to transmit to Hitler on behalf of the British government. Furthermore, in a break with established diplomatic practice, both were first translated into German. One sought Hitler's endorsement of Runciman's continuing efforts as mediator, while the second dealt with the wider issue of Anglo-German relations. Runciman justified this approach on the grounds that Henlein's "attitude may influence Hitler,"[45] while Henlein agreed to make the journey on the strict condition that it was made clear that he was traveling solely at the request of the British government. He did not want, he told Ashton-Gwatkin without a trace of irony, "to be accused of taking orders from Hitler."[46]

On September 1, in spite of a streaming cold, Henlein left for Berchtesgaden, promising Runciman that he was "anxious to dissociate his movement from identification with the Reich Nazis."[47] Henlein spent two days locked away at the Berghof with Hitler, Göring and Goebbels. Hitler divulged none of the details of Case Green, but left Henlein in no doubt that they were now firmly set on the path to war, although the SdP must continue to negotiate, in order to give the impression that no imminent crisis was at hand. As for timing, he would only promise that the "finishing off [*Erledigung*]" would come in September. "Long live the war," Hitler declared as Henlein took his leave—"even if it lasts two to eight years."[48] Henlein returned to Czechoslovakia on Friday, September 2, convinced that Hitler had now decided on a military solution. "Everywhere there's talk of war," recorded Goebbels. "The hot topic: war and Prague."[49] *The Times* reported that antiaircraft guns had appeared on public buildings throughout Berlin, including the Reichstag.

In Prague, meanwhile, the pressure on Beneš was ratcheted up still further. After the emergency meeting of ministers on August 30, Halifax wrote to Newton emphasizing that all available intelligence indicated Hitler "committing himself to extreme action" at Nuremberg the following week, or soon after; he hoped to "win a diplomatic success" by solving the Sudeten problem "this autumn—by force if necessary." It was therefore critical that "these unpleasant but unavoidable facts" should be strongly impressed upon Beneš, who needed to dispel the widely held suspicion that he was "merely manoeuvring for position and spinning out the negotiations without any sincere intention of facing the immediate and vital issue." The only way to do this was to offer the necessary concessions "immediately, publicly, and without reservation."[50] Faced with a choice between "acceptance of Karlsbad programme or war," Runciman warned Beneš, "he should be under no illusion as to what British choice would be."[51] Newton was blunter still. If war came, Czechoslovakia would become a "theatre of war and would be likely, whatever the ultimate issue, to be overrun and occupied for a long period . . . it was vital for Czechoslovakia to accept great sacrifices and even if necessary considerable risks."[52]

In Ashton-Gwatkin's assessment, Beneš was "a clever man, an adroit political balancer and an optimist always hoping for salvation just round the corner."[53] With the British warnings ringing in his ears, he decided to pull his very last chestnut out of the fire and, on the morning of September 5, he invited Kundt and Sebekovsky to Hradčany Castle. With scarcely a greeting, and no preamble, he pushed a blank sheet of paper across the table. "Please write your party's full demands," he suggested. "I promise you in advance to grant them immediately." The two men were temporarily "thunderstruck." Kundt stared incredulously across the table, while Sebekovsky sat in angry and suspicious silence. "Go on; I mean it," said Beneš. "Write!" Fearful of being lured into a cunning Czech trap, the sullen Sudeten Germans shifted uncomfortably in their chairs, but refused to commit themselves to paper in their own hand. Hitler's orders had not prepared them for this unforeseen eventuality—apparently total surrender to their demands. "Very well," continued Beneš. "If you won't write it down, I will. You tell me what to say." Taking back the blank sheet of paper, he slowly unscrewed the top of his fountain pen and sat at his desk, poised to write.[54]

By the time that Kundt and Sebekovsky had finished dictating, the completed document, which was to become known as the "Fourth Plan," embodied almost every demand Henlein had ever made. Beneš signed the paper, and handed it back to the Sudetens, before enduring a difficult four-hour meeting with his Cabinet at which he eventually secured their reluctant agreement to the plan. Privately, however, he thought it unlikely that even these proposals would be accepted.

> I was aware that I succumbed in this struggle against Nazi totalitarianism and for the rescue of Czech democracy, to the exaggerated and improper pressure which . . . forced us to concessions clothed in the mantle of ethnic justice and having as their real aim the destruction of our State and national existence. I wanted to convince the French and British Governments that not even the biggest concessions . . . could satisfy either Berlin or the Sudeten Pan-Germans. I saw in it the only and last way . . . to bring the Western Powers onto our side should an armed conflict break out between us and Germany.[55]

An accompanying press communiqué emphasized that the concessions had only been made "because of extraordinary pressure from foreign friends," which had created "considerable dissatisfaction and surprise."[56]

The surprise felt by Czech patriots, and even German democrats, at the capitulation to Henlein's demands was ironically shared by the SdP hierarchy—such sweeping concessions caused immediate confusion, and a meeting was hurriedly arranged in Eger to discuss the latest developments. "My God, they have given us everything!" was the anguished reaction of the hard-line Frank, while Henlein too reacted furiously, and immediately left for Nuremberg where he was to be Hitler's personal guest. Frank too flew to Germany to receive further orders and, although there had been some initial surprise and confusion in Berlin also, his Nazi puppet masters soon regained their composure. It was made clear to him that the time for talking was at an end, and that the hitherto low-key campaign of civil disobedience was to be fomented throughout the Sudetenland with still greater enthusiasm. It was a task to which the Sudeten leaders quickly applied themselves with alacrity.

On September 7 a group of Sudeten German deputies, headed by the radical Fritz Köllner, visited the industrial town of Mährisch-Ostrau in northeastern Moravia. Although predominantly Czech, some 20,000 Germans lived in the town, and the authorities had recently stepped up a campaign of arrests for arms smuggling across the nearby German border. By the day of the visit there were eighty-two SdP members in custody, and Köllner and his colleagues made an ostentatious display of visiting the local police station to inquire after the well-being of their incarcerated comrades. While they were in the cells, a crowd of 200 young Germans, most of whom had been hastily recruited from the local German high school, gathered outside and began to chant and jeer. This in turn attracted a counter-demonstration by Czechs, and mounted police were soon called in to restore order. When the deputies heard the commotion outside, some of them came out to investigate and, in the ensuing melee, one of them, Franz May, was struck by a policeman.

The Germans claimed that May had loudly affirmed his parliamentary immunity, at which the policeman had shouted, "I do not care," and had hit him with a riding whip.[57] The Czech version was that the SdP deputy had himself become involved in a fight, and was accidentally struck as the police tried to separate the combatants. The policeman told the *Daily Express* that he had no means of knowing that May was a deputy. "I did not recognise him. I felt it my duty to intervene because he was holding a Czech civil servant by the throat."[58] Although no one was hurt, there were only six temporary arrests, and the entire scuffle was over in half an hour, the SdP quickly realized the public relations potential of the incident. *The Times* reported that Köllner and May had dispatched an urgent telegram to the Czech Prime Minister.

Mounted police are taking brutal action with riding-whips against peaceful men and women who are gathered at Mährisch-Ostrau to welcome members of Parliament. We members of Parliament, in spite of showing our passes, are being threatened with riding-whips, thrashed, and pushed against walls by the horses of the police. We protest passionately against this brutal and offensive action of the State police and we demand the punishment of those responsible.[59]

The SdP leadership was quick to use the incident as an excuse to suspend their consideration of the "Fourth Plan," on the grounds that "the proceedings of the State police at Mährisch-Ostrau are in direct contradiction to the proposals of the Government."[60] In the course of the same day, an observer from the British legation hurried to the scene of the alleged crime to investigate. He soon concluded:

(i) that the so-called "riot" had been deliberately staged by the Sudeten representatives, (ii) that the Deputy had not been "beaten" and probably had not been struck at all, (iii) that he was actually assaulting a Czech at the moment when the "beating" was said to have taken place, and (iv) that, if he had been "beaten," he "would have got no more than he deserved" for his own conduct.[61]

Ashton-Gwatkin complemented this rather outspoken report by confirming that May was a "well-known bruiser," who was generally referred to by his colleagues as "Siegfried."[62] Although he gloomily told Runciman that he "thought it meant the end of the Runciman Mission," Ashton-Gwatkin went anyway to see Prime Minister Hodža, and persuaded him that the government should agree to Sudeten demands for redress, including punishment of the policeman.[63] That evening, Kundt also visited Hodža to tell him that no further negotiations could take place "until the Mährisch-Ostrau incidents had been liquidated,"[64] while Ashton-Gwatkin spent the evening at the Hotel Alcron trying to persuade Frank to agree to a resumption of negotiations.

The unfortunate policeman was dismissed, the local chief of police allowed to resign, and four of his officials were suspended pending trial for the alleged ill-treatment of prisoners. Yet again the SdP had run out of demands and, on September 10, they reluctantly agreed that talks should resume three days later, after Hitler's speech at Nuremberg. However, although he did not realize it at the time, Runciman's work in Czechoslovakia was now effectively at an end. Whether the incident at Mährisch-Ostrau had been deliberately staged as part of Hitler's planned provocation, or whether it was a happy coincidence, the Sudeten Germans showed themselves more than up to the task as they "seized upon it as a drowning man seizes a life raft."[65] Runciman acknowledged that it had been "used in order to provide an excuse for the suspension, if not the breaking off, of negotiations."[66] In fact, the resumption of talks planned for September 13, never took place. The situation in Czechoslovakia was to alter radically in the aftermath of Hitler's speech at Nuremberg a few days later. The drawn-out negotiations had now fully served Hitler's purpose, and the Sudeten German leadership thereafter steadfastly refused to reengage in any further debate.

■ ■ ■

On September 7 a further event took place which all but destroyed any last slim chance that agreement could be reached between Czechs and Sudeten Germans. At breakfast tables all over Britain, and in the chancelleries of Europe, readers of *The Times* turned to the middle of their morning newspaper to read that day's leading article, since described by one press historian as "probably the most famous, and certainly the most controversial leader ever to appear in a British newspaper."[67] In a lengthy article, blandly entitled "NUREMBERG AND AUSSIG,"[68] the anonymous editorial writer considered the prospects for Hitler's opening speech at the party rally, and examined the merits of Beneš's "Fourth Plan," welcoming the new proposals as a genuine attempt to remove local grievances and to give Sudeten Germans greater local self-determination. He also acknowledged that the Czech government was within its rights to retain central government control over issues such as defense, foreign policy and finance.

As is so often the case, however, the sting was in the tail, hidden away at the end of the article in dry, almost academic language.

If the Sudetens now ask for more than the Czech Government are apparently ready to give in their latest set of proposals, it can only be inferred that the Germans are going beyond the mere removal of disabilities and do not find themselves at ease within the Czechoslovak Republic. In that case it might be worth while for the Czechoslovak Government to consider whether they should exclude altogether the project, which has found favour in some quarters, of making Czechoslovakia a more homogeneous State by the secession of that fringe of alien populations who are contiguous to the nation with which they are united by race . . . the advantages to Czechoslovakia of becoming a homogeneous State might conceivably outweigh the obvious disadvantages of losing the Sudeten German districts of the borderland.[69]

On August 25 the deputy editor of *The Times*, Robin Barrington-Ward, a noted appeaser who had long since accepted the thesis that the Treaty of Versailles had been unjust and the Anschluss inevitable, had visited Halifax at the Foreign Office. He found him overly concerned by the reports of the German military buildup and Hitler's apparent determination to settle the Czech question by force, but Barrington-Ward refused to believe them. That day he wrote to his editor, Geoffrey Dawson, that he continued "to doubt, as I think you will, whether Hitler will really be ready to take all the risks implicit in forcible action."[70] On August 31, the day after the meeting of ministers at Downing Street, it was reported under the byline of the paper's "Diplomatic Correspondent" that official sources in London had "no reason to doubt Herr Hitler's own declarations of peaceful aims,"[71] prompting a telephone call of complaint from Halifax to Barrington-Ward that afternoon.

In early September Dawson was spending what remained of the summer holidays at his country home in Yorkshire. Barrington-Ward, meanwhile, was due to leave for his own holiday in Scotland on September 3, but was hesitating as to whether he should leave London at such a critical time. Dawson, however, persuaded him to do so, and the newspaper was left in the hands of the third-in-command in the editorial chain. On Sunday, September 4, the duty editorial writer, the paper's diplomatic correspondent Leo Kennedy, whose earlier anti-Czech dispatches from Prague had already influenced editorial policy, prepared his article for the Monday morning. Having done so, he drafted a further editorial dealing in general terms with the Czech problem, to lie on file for editing and use at a later date. Late on the afternoon of Tuesday, September 6, Dawson returned to the office from

Yorkshire, to find this incomplete second editorial on his desk. "It ventilated rather crudely," he recorded that night, "the idea which we had often raised before, of a secession of the Sudeten fringe to Germany."[72]

Dawson deleted one passage he disliked, ordered another to be rewritten, and sent the remainder of the article down to the composing room to be made ready for the morning paper. He then "departed to dine." When he returned much later he decided that he was still dissatisfied with the corrected draft, and set to work to make further amendments himself. It was by now 11:45 P.M., and he sought advice from the sole senior member of the editorial staff still in the office. William Casey, who was to become editor himself ten years later, traditionally played little or no part in editorial policy concerning foreign affairs and, having asked his advice about the redrafted leader, Dawson then ignored his forcefully expressed doubts. The crucial changes to the draft were the addition of the words "which has found favour in some quarters," and the final sentence suggesting that the disadvantages to Czechoslovakia of losing the Sudetenland might "conceivably" be outweighed by the advantages of becoming a "homogeneous State." At 12:05 A.M., just a few minutes before the presses were due to roll, Dawson sent the final version down to be printed.[73]

The following morning Kennedy "to his horror woke to find that the last paragraph of his leader had been entirely rewritten so as to suggest the immediate cession of the Sudeten lands to Germany."[74] Dawson was unrepentant. "There was a hubbub, as I fully expected, over this morning's leader," he recorded, and the following day almost every other newspaper "broke out in a volley of abuse."[75] Indeed, the article caused an outcry almost everywhere that *The Times* was read. The expression "which has found favour in some quarters" led to the near-universal assumption that the proposal that the Sudetenland should be ceded to Germany was an accurate reflection of current government policy. Most people drew the obvious conclusion that the article had been inspired by an official source at the very highest level. Jan Masaryk called at the Foreign Office early that morning to lodge a strong complaint with Halifax. Although he had reassured his government that *The Times* was "quite independent in its political opinions," he was perfectly well aware that "the knowledge of the above mentioned newspaper's independence is not shared by a very large section of the population abroad."[76]

19. The Dreesen Hotel in Godesberg, one of Hitler's favorite hotels and the scene of his second meeting with Chamberlain, on September 22 and 23, 1938.

20. Hitler welcomes Chamberlain back to the Dreesen for their resumed discussion on September 23, 1938.

21. While the world waits nervously, Hitler addresses a crowd of 20,000 Nazi supporters at the vast Sportspalast in Berlin, on the evening of September 26, 1938.

22. Sir Horace Wilson arrives back at Heston from Berlin on September 27, 1938, after his last, failed attempt to negotiate with Hitler—"a very violent hour."

24

"How horrible, fantastic, incredible it is that we should be digging trenches and trying on gas masks here because of a quarrel in a far-away country between people of whom we know nothing." Neville Chamberlain's radio broadcast on September 27, 1938, as the country prepared for war during the week preceding Munich.

26. Hitler explains to Mussolini and the Duce's son-in-law and Foreign Minister, Count Galeazzo Ciano (right), how he intends "to liquidate Czechoslovakia," during the journey from Kufstein to Munich in Hitler's private train, on September 29, 1938.

27. Joachim von Ribbentrop (right) welcomes Chamberlain to Munich on September 29, 1938. Between them is Chamberlain's Parliamentary Private Secretary, Lord Dunglass, later to become Prime Minister himself as Sir Alec Douglas-Home.

28. Chamberlain, Daladier, Hitler, Mussolini and Ciano at the Führerbau in Munich, on September 29, 1938.

29. Chamberlain and Hitler meet in the Führer's Munich apartment on the morning of September 30, 1938, for "a very friendly and pleasant talk," during which they sign the piece of paper agreeing "never to go to war with one another again." As usual, Schmidt interprets. On the table in the foreground is Richard Wagner's death mask.

30. After leaving Hitler's apartment on September 30, 1938, Chamberlain was taken on a short sightseeing tour of Munich. Here he is pictured paying a controversial visit to the Sterneckerbräu, the former beer hall that was the spiritual birthplace of the Nazi Party.

31. "This morning I had another talk with the German Chancellor, Herr Hitler, and here is a paper which bears his name upon it as well as mine." Chamberlain returns to Heston from Munich on September 30, 1938.

32. The police hold back the crowds that had flocked to Heston throughout the afternoon, as Chamberlain makes his way to his car for the journey to London.

33. King George VI (right) and Queen Elizabeth, later the Queen Mother (left), welcome Neville and Annie Chamberlain to Buckingham Palace on September 30, 1938. They later appeared together on the palace balcony.

34. "My good friends, this is the second time in our history that there has come back from Germany to Downing Street peace with honour. I believe it is peace for our time." Chamberlain addresses the crowds from an upstairs window at Downing Street on September 30, 1938.

35. By order of the Lord Mayor the swastika flies over Cardiff City Hall on October 2, 1938, in celebration of the Munich agreement. After two councillors had torn the flag down in protest, the Mayor insisted on it being hoisted again.

36. Hitler is welcomed to the town of Eger by thousands of Sudeten Germans as he crosses the border into Czechoslovakia on October 4, 1938.

With unfortunate timing, Halifax and Dawson were due to meet for lunch at the latter's club, the Travellers in Pall Mall. Yet Halifax seemed curiously unconcerned about the furor. "I have just had Edward Halifax lunching with me," Dawson wrote to Barrington-Ward that afternoon. "He reported, as I expected, that the last paragraph of Kennedy's leader this morning had disturbed his office, though he did not seem to dissent from it himself."[77] A salvo of diplomatic complaints rained down on the Foreign Office. Vansittart described the article as "calamitous," fearing that it would lead "to a most dangerous misconception of the British attitude," and would only encourage the Sudeten Germans to turn down any future concessions. One of his intelligence contacts confirmed that in Berlin the consequences were likely to be "disastrous, since it gives the impression that His Majesty's Government is on the run."[78] Theodor Kordt told Ribbentrop that the article had "caused [a] great sensation in London." While he believed that it had not been inspired by the Foreign Office, it was likely that it "derived from a suggestion which reached *The Times* editorial staff from the Prime Minister's entourage."[79] Phipps reported that the French wished to know whether the article "expressed the views of His Majesty's Government," while Runciman cabled from Prague that *The Times* "has added to our difficulties," noting that the "last paragraph of article is a recommendation of an Anschluss."

That evening the Foreign Office finally issued a formal statement that "a suggestion appearing in 'The Times' this morning to the effect that the Czechoslovak Government might consider as an alternative to their present proposals the secession of the fringe of alien populations in their territory in no way represents the views of His Majesty's Government."[80] But it was too little too late. Harvey recorded that the article had produced a "calamitous effect in spite of *démenti* from Foreign Office." It had been broadcast throughout Germany and had been "interpreted everywhere as a *ballon d'essai* and as foreshadowing a fresh surrender by H.M.G., especially in the U.S.A." He was furious with "that little defeatist Dawson."[81] The Russian ambassador, Ivan Maisky, also called at the Foreign Office to complain that the article's publication "had had the worst possible effect." Halifax could only reply, somewhat lamely, that he "did not in any way disagree with his judgement in this matter," but when Maisky invited him to reinforce the *démenti* of the previous day, the Foreign Secretary told him that it was not his "habit to repeat contradictions."[82]

London, meanwhile, was awash with conspiracy theories. Harold Nicolson was assured by a source at *The Times* that the article had been "written by Leo Kennedy and was merely glanced at by Geoffrey Dawson."[83] Chips Channon's Foreign Office informant assured him "that Lord Halifax dined with Geoffrey Dawson on Monday night, the 5th." The article "was definitely inspired, a *ballon d'essai,* to see how the public would react."[84] Claud Cockburn, the left-wing editor of the *Week,* who had first coined the phrase the "Cliveden Set" to describe the group of appeasers loosely collected around Nancy Astor, claimed that not only had the article been written at the instigation of the government, but it had actually been first referred to the German embassy for approval. Dawson told Barrington-Ward that Halifax did "not dissent privately from the suggestion that any solution, even the secession of the German minorities, should be brought into free negotiation at Prague."[85]

However, while the article may have had Halifax's tacit approval, in reality its genesis lay in Dawson's rushed return from holiday, leaving him, in the words of the official history of *The Times,* "insufficient time, before or after dinner, in which to bestow upon such an article the consideration and correction it needed in the actual circumstances."[86] The consequences for the Czechs were catastrophic. For the first time, it had been formally proposed that Czechoslovakia should be partitioned, voluntarily offering Hitler what he wanted before the suggestion had even passed his own lips. With the work of the Runciman Mission drawing to a close, and all eyes turning to Nuremberg, the suggestion that the British government was happy for the Sudetenland to become part of the Reich, even if erroneous, brought to an end any further negotiations. The Sudeten German negotiators had only to delay reaching agreement for long enough and they knew that Hitler and his invading army would do their work for them.

∎

9

In Full War Cry

I didn't raise my son to be a soldier,
  I brought him up to be my pride and joy,
Who dares to put a rifle on his shoulder,
  To kill some other mother's darling boy?

Sir Nevile Henderson, June 1, 1937[1]

What king, going to war against another king, sitteth not down first, and consulteth whether he be able with ten thousand to meet him that cometh against him with twenty thousand?
  Or else, while the other is yet a great way off, he sendeth an ambassage and desireth conditions of peace.

Luke 14: 31–32

Is it not positively horrible to think that the fate of hundreds of millions depends on one man and he is half mad?

Neville Chamberlain, September 3, 1938

"HITLER RETIRES TO MOUNTAINS TO DECIDE," screamed the *Daily Express* headline on September 1. "Brooding . . . in the loneliness of the Bavarian Alps, he will decide within the next four days his policy towards Czecho-Slovakia and the Sudeten German problems."[2] In fact, notwithstanding the occasional excursion to inspect fortifications or watch troop maneuvers, Hitler had spent most of the summer hidden away at the Berghof. It was his favorite time of year to be in the mountains, and he was dismissive of the supposed joys of winter Alpine life, and in particular of the attraction of skiing—"what pleasure can there be in prolonging the horrible winter artificially by staying in the mountains? If I had my way I'd forbid these sports, with all the accidents people have doing them."[3] Even during a time of international crisis, his relaxed daily routine varied little. He would begin the day with a leisurely breakfast in bed, from where he could enjoy the spectacular view across to the sheer wall of mountains that made up the Untersberg massif. It was here, according to legend, that the Emperor Charlemagne still slept, sword in hand, awaiting the clarion call to restore the great German empire to its former glory. "It is no accident," Hitler would tell his visitors, "that I have my residence opposite it."[4]

His formal day began later, when he would appear downstairs, often wearing traditional Bavarian costume or a country suit. He would spend some time studying the latest press summaries, brought to him by his head of press, Otto Dietrich, or diplomatic telegrams and military reports. As he insisted on being surrounded only by his closest friends and advisers at the Berghof, the late lunch would be an intimate affair, for up to twenty guests, but with all the trappings of formality. The guests would enter the first-floor dining room in pairs and, if there were no outside visitors, Eva Braun would sit on his left. According to his architect Albert Speer, who had helped completely to remodel the house, the room was a "mixture of artistic rusticity and urban elegance." The walls and ceiling were paneled with larch wood, while the guests sat in ornate, heavy chairs, covered with red morocco leather; they were served by towering SS waiters, immaculately turned out in white mess jackets and black trousers, and ate off plain white china, which was engraved with Hitler's personal monogram. Even the knick-knacks on the table bore a swastika emblem.

After postprandial chocolate and cakes in the large drawing room downstairs, with its huge picture window,[5] the party would set off for a daily walk, no more than half an hour long, in single file, to the so-called tea house, a small cabin built precariously on a rocky outcrop for its panoramic views. Here Hitler would chat to Eva Braun, be served tea, and doze for a while in an armchair, before, at the end of the afternoon, being driven back to the Berghof in a waiting black Mercedes. Occasionally he would venture further afield with a few chosen friends, to the nearby mountain woods, or the banks of a local lake, and enjoy a specially prepared picnic—while his every action was recorded for posterity by his personal photographer, Heinrich Hoffmann, for use in a new book on the Führer. Some evenings Hitler would summon Speer, and spend hours having "fun with compass and protractor," perusing architectural plans for new building projects. More usually after dinner a film would be shown, often one featuring Hitler's favorite star, Greta Garbo—"she is so Nordic"—or records played on a gramophone. "For days and even weeks this idyllic existence goes on," wrote Ivone Kirkpatrick, who twice had an opportunity to witness the Führer's lifestyle at the Berghof. "Hitler may claim that it is no holiday," he continued, "but every German soldier and every German workman would gladly give up his leave for a few days' rest in the enchanting atmosphere of Berchtesgaden."[6]

Having given Henlein his orders at the Berghof on September 2, the following day Hitler summoned Brauchitsch and Keitel to discuss the latest version of Case Green; the two generals were forced to listen to a lengthy monologue from the Führer, who expressed his dissatisfaction with almost every aspect of the planning for the invasion of Czechoslovakia. Brauchitsch drew attention to the poor condition of the motorized divisions, the likely shortage of reinforcements for the front line, and the obvious lack of training of some military leaders. But Hitler brushed aside all his objections. The 2nd Army under Rundstedt, he asserted, which was scheduled to bear the brunt of the action in isolating Bohemia and Moravia from the rest of Czechoslovakia, was neither the right force, nor in the right place, to lead the invasion. It would be faced with the greatest concentration of Czech troops, and the most heavily fortified stretch of border. He feared a "possible repetition of Verdun," and refused to see his troops "bleeding to death for a task which cannot be accomplished." The troops, he ordered, were to be assembled and ready to march at just two days' notice, while the commanders, he warned ominously, "must know when X-day is by 12 noon on September 27."[7] The final date for invasion had been set.

Monday, September 5, was the official "Day of Welcome" at the tenth annual congress of the National Socialist Party at Nuremberg. Hitler arrived by train from Munich, to be greeted at the historic city's brightly decorated railway station by his deputy Rudolf Hess; as church bells pealed, he was driven through the afternoon sunshine to the town hall. The congress, he told the assembled crowd, was to be known as the "First Parteitag of Greater Germany," in honor of the homecoming of Austria to the Reich— 35,000 Austrians had made the trip to Nuremberg. Train after train arrived at the station, bringing Nazis from all over the Reich and guests from other countries, swelling the town's population by over half a million people. Two hundred and fifty journalists attended from all over the world; the colors of Nationalist Spain were everywhere, in honor of the delegation from the "new Spain," led by General Milan Astray, the legendary founder of the Spanish Foreign Legion; and, for the first time, even the ambassador of the United States had agreed to attend. Only the Papal Nuncio and the Soviet ambassador had remained in Berlin. The minds of all those present, wrote the correspondent of *The Times*, were "dominated by a single thought— whether the Führer will be able to make a statement on Czechoslovakia."[8]

The following morning saw the formal opening of the congress, in front of 14,000 supporters in the great Congress Hall. Hitler's opening proclamation was read, in a rasping voice reminiscent of his own, by Adolf Wagner, the Gauleiter of Bavaria. The speech dwelt at length on the undying faith of the German people in the Führer's divine mission, and on Hitler's joy at welcoming Austria into the Reich.

> It is Great Germany which in these days makes its appearance at Nuremberg for the first time. If the insignia of the old Reich have returned for the future to this old German city, they have been brought hither and accompanied by 6½ million Germans, united in spirit to-day with all other men and women of our people. For us and for all those who come after us the Reich of the Germans will now always be only Great Germany [*Großdeutschland*].[9]

The reference to the insignia of the old Reich was explained during a ceremony later that morning at the ancient St. Katharine's Church, famous as the setting for Act I of *Die Meistersinger*. Seyss-Inquart, at the head of a blue-uniformed Austrian delegation, presented the ancient regalia of the Holy Roman Empire to the Burgomaster of Nuremberg. The jeweled crown, the imperial sword, the golden orb and the scepter had all been removed to the Hofburg in Vienna in 1809, to place them out of Napoleon's reach. Now, vowed Hitler, they would be restored to the German nation for all time, and he invited the town of Nuremberg to act as their custodian.

That evening Hitler attended the Culture Congress in the Opera House. Goebbels supervised the presentation of the National Prizes for Art and Science to Fritz Todt, the builder of Germany's autobahns and the West Wall; Professors Willy Messerschmitt and Ernst Heinkel for their aircraft designs; and Ferdinand Porsche, the designer of the so-called people's car, the Volkswagen Beetle.[10] On the fringe of the congress was the political exhibition "*Kampf im Osten*" (The Struggle in the East). Hitler himself had written a prominently displayed explanatory statement, stressing the interdependent ties which bound together the west European nations—their cultures, histories and futures—and emphasizing their supposed mutual struggle for living space and racial purity. Germany was depicted as the "bulwark against the penetration of Europe and the destruction of Western culture by invading hordes from the East, Huns, Turks, [and] the modern equivalent, Communists inspired by Russia." Czechoslovakia was identified on a huge map as giving access to Russian bombers into the heart of Europe. Other exhibits attacked the Jews, and the iniquities of "political freemasonry," illustrated by a photograph of King Edward VII, when Prince of Wales, in full masonic regalia.[11]

Although the first few days of the congress were marred for Hitler by the persistent heavy rain, nothing could dampen the spirits of the 40,000 members of the Reich Labour Service, who gathered in the vast Zeppelinwiese (Zeppelin Meadow) on National Labour Service Day. "Sunbrowned and steeled," in six broad gray-brown columns, the cream of Nazi youth paraded before the Führer, their 40,000 spades glinting in the sunlight which broke through the clouds from time to time. "This is a parade which repetition cannot stale," gushed *The Times* correspondent. "It never fails to raise the pride of every German and the envy of most foreign visitors." Meanwhile the massed ranks sang to Hitler:

> Austria suffers no longer. The Führer came as the orderly of God and made it free. . . . Blood is stronger than enemy power, and what is German must belong to Germany.

At these words, Göring turned to Henderson, who was standing next to him and "smilingly directed" the British ambassador to their implicit message.[12] Henderson was easily impressed. "In my opinion," he wrote privately to Halifax, the march-past was "the finest thing in the whole of the Nazi régime."[13]

Henderson was attending his second annual party congress. His predecessor, Sir Eric Phipps, had always refused to go to Nuremberg, but one of Henderson's first acts on his arrival in Berlin had been to announce his intention of attending, without any prior consultation with the Foreign Office, thus infuriating Vansittart. In 1938 he left Berlin on the evening of September 6 and arrived in Nuremberg early the next morning. The possibility of his issuing a strongly worded warning to Hitler remained very much under discussion in London, and that same day Halifax wrote to Chamberlain suggesting a line to take should the opportunity arise of a conversation with Hitler. His own suggestion was that Henderson should make it clear that if Hitler attacked Czechoslovakia, "this country would inevitably have to come to her assistance."[14] But Henderson refused to do anything of the kind. "An official démarche," he warned Halifax, "will drive [Hitler] to greater violence or greater menace . . . another warning will not help." Incredibly, he was still confident that Hitler would come down on the side of peace. "I do wish it might be possible," he continued, "to get at any rate 'The Times,' Camrose, Beaverbrook Press &c. to write up Hitler as the apostle of peace. It will be terribly shortsighted if this is not done. Cannot the News Dept. help?"[15]

Since returning to Berlin from London on August 31, with the discussion at the meeting of ministers still ringing in his ears, Henderson's sole concern had been to do all he could to deter his political masters from issuing a formal warning to Hitler. The practice of issuing pointless threats as a diplomatic tactic was one he had argued against throughout his career and, in the aftermath of the May Crisis, his fear of further antagonizing Hitler had become close to an obsession. In the first place, it was his strongly held opinion that Hitler's increasingly irrational behavior would render such a warning counterproductive. From Nuremberg he reported that Hitler was "in a state of extreme nervous tension," and that "his abnormality seemed greater than ever."[16] It was quite possible that "driven by megalomania inspired by military force . . . he may have crossed the border-line of insanity."[17] A further explanation for Henderson's reluctance was that he fundamentally believed the Sudeten German claim for autonomy, even secession, to be a just one. In a typical telegram to Halifax earlier that year, he had argued that the Sudeten Germans had "a moral right at least to self-administration and eventually to self-determination. It is morally unjust," he continued, "to compel this solid Teuton minority to remain subjected to a Slav central Government at Prague."[18] Nor had he made any secret of his views in Berlin, frequently emphasizing in the company of senior Germans that "Great Britain would not think of risking even one sailor or airman for Czechoslovakia."[19]

Few postwar historians have been prepared to speak up for Nevile Henderson, and the week he spent at Nuremberg represents for many the low-water mark of his career. The most generous interpretation of his behavior is that he demonstrated "the not unusual ambassadorial propensity towards sympathy with the country with which he was accredited."[20] Those who served with him, however, have been less charitable. Cadogan's Private Secretary, Gladwyn Jebb (later Lord Gladwyn), described his term in Berlin as a "disaster . . . from the first he tended to side absolutely with the Nazi point of view." Henderson allegedly believed "that the expansion of Nazi Germany into central Europe was a good thing," and that Britain "ought to give the Germans their head," and allow them "to absorb Czechoslovakia."[21] A still more extreme criticism was that of Con (later Sir Con) O'Neill, who served under Henderson as Third Secretary in Berlin. He described the Central Department at the Foreign Office as "a hotbed of hatred against Henderson [who] inspired nothing but horror and detestation in the bosoms of all those dealing with what he did," and whose "attitudes and principles in relation to Germany were really horrifying."[22]

Even Henderson's sole sympathetic biographer concedes that his "behaviour at Nuremberg was certainly odd," and has "opened him up to both criticism and ridicule."[23] It was not, however, his fault that the foreign diplomatic corps were all forced to live, sleep and work in exceedingly cramped conditions in the sleeping car of a train parked in a railway siding. The hotels had all been reserved for Hitler's guests. He found it impossible to sleep, and complained bitterly about the conditions, which were undoubtedly made worse by the fact that he was already badly afflicted by the throat cancer that was to force him to return home for medical treatment a month later, and of which he was to die in 1942. He took no cipher machine with him, fearing a lack of security, and had no means of communicating directly with either Berlin or London. Worse still, he had inexplicably forgotten to take any writing materials with him, and was forced instead "to use for the purpose the blank pages torn from some detective stories which I happened to have taken with me."[24]

On the afternoon of September 7 Henderson attended Hitler's reception for the diplomatic corps. The atmosphere was cozy to say the least. Hitler was "in quite good form and made himself generally agreeable, except to the Czech Minister." But the Führer still steadfastly refused to discuss politics and talked to Henderson only of the weather and the Labour Corps march-past that morning, boasting that he could "keep his arm stretched out for hours at a time by pure will-power."[25] François-Poncet, the senior diplomat present, did at least try to broach a more serious subject, taking the trouble to speak German so that Hitler would understand.

> One sentiment moves us all if I may be permitted to express it. It is the hope that peace will be preserved for humanity, which has suffered for so many years. For the fairest laurel that a statesman can receive is that which does not cause the tears of mothers to flow. May that laurel be yours! That is what we all wish you.

In spite of this impassioned plea, Hitler's "face remained impenetrable," recalled François-Poncet.[26] "I trust that no mother will ever have cause to weep in consequence of any action of mine," replied Hitler, before shaking the ambassador by the hand, and sweeping from the room.[27]

On September 9, to Hitler's delight, the sun finally shone on Nuremberg. At the Zeppelinwiese, a hundred thousand spectators applauded as thousands of athletes, mostly members of the SS, the SA and the Hitler Youth, took part in the "community games" on the "Day of Fellowship." That evening a huge torchlit procession passed through the city. In London the Inner Circle of ministers met almost continuously throughout the day. The only break came at lunchtime, when Eden, who had returned especially from a trip to Ireland, called at the Foreign Office to see his successor. He "strongly advocated a further and more definite warning being sent to Hitler," and confided to Harvey that he had found

Halifax "very depressed," and that he was "very much afraid H.M.G. may yet run away and let the Czechs down."[28] Henderson was sent further instructions by way of Kirkpatrick in Berlin, who forwarded them on to Nuremberg by the night train. He was to request an immediate interview with Ribbentrop, and to emphasize that the British were "greatly disturbed by the signs of deterioration in the atmosphere surrounding the negotiations at Prague." If war ensued and the French fulfilled their treaty obligations to Czechoslovakia, it seemed "inevitable that the sequence of events must result in a general conflict from which Great Britain could not stand aside."[29]

That night Hitler addressed a gathering of 180,000 supporters in the Zeppelinwiese—dressed in brown shirts, they were drawn up in ten broad columns, each 200 yards long, separated by wide, open passages. Hitler made his appearance at the far end of the stadium from the platform, and marched on foot up the central passage, surrounded by his senior officers. His arrival was greeted by the sudden illumination of 300 searchlights, creating a "great stadium crowned by a dome of blue light."[30] The lights had been placed forty feet apart, and the beams shone 25,000 feet into the night sky, colliding at the top, according to Speer, who had designed the effect, like the roof of "a vast room, with the beams serving as mighty pillars of infinitely high outer walls."[31] Behind Hitler came the standard-bearers, their huge swastikas lit up, giving the "indescribably picturesque" impression of "rivers of red and gold rippling" through the assembled masses. "The effect," wrote Henderson, "which was both solemn and beautiful, was like being inside a cathedral of ice."[32]

The exhilarating atmosphere at Nuremberg always produced an intoxicating effect on Hitler and, after this display of homage, he returned to his hotel, the Deutscher Hof, feeling even more assertive than usual. The presence of the crawling Keitel only served to enhance his sense of self-confidence,[33] and he summoned Brauchitsch, Keitel and General Franz Halder, Beck's successor as chief of staff, to a meeting which began shortly before midnight. Halder opened with a strong defense of the latest plans for Case Green, which, in spite of Hitler's criticisms at the Berghof the previous week, still entrusted the main thrust of the invasion to Rundstedt's 2nd Army. Hitler remained unconvinced and highly critical. Military plans, he insisted, should be based not on "wishful thinking, but on the probable course of action pursued by the enemy." The fortifications facing Rundstedt were the most formidable in Czechoslovakia, yet his commanders had failed to provide the necessary force to drive through them, into the heart of Czechoslovakia, dividing the country in a pincer movement. Above all, he insisted on a "rapid success. . . . The first week is politically decisive, within which a far-reaching territorial gain must be achieved."[34]

While the pliant Keitel was only too happy to concur with every word spoken by the Führer, to his dismay Brauchitsch and Halder continued to argue, causing Hitler to lecture them with ever-greater ferocity. Finally, at almost four o'clock in the morning, Hitler lost his patience; he suddenly called the meeting to a close, peremptorily ordered his generals to do his bidding, and angrily dismissed them from his presence. On the way out of the hotel, the three generals stopped off in the hotel bar for a late nightcap. "What is he really after?" demanded Halder, his voice shaking with indignation. "If you haven't found out," replied Keitel, sounding irritated, "then you have my sympathy." Brauchitsch smoothed over the argument, and new orders were drawn up to Hitler's satisfaction. "Why do you fight with him," asked Keitel, "when you know that the battle is lost before it's begun? Nobody thinks there is going to be any war over this, so the whole thing wasn't worth all that bitter rearguard action."[35] Keitel's chief of staff, Jodl, spoke for both them in his diary.

> There is only one undisciplined element in the army—the generals, and in the last analysis this comes from the fact that they are arrogant. They have neither confidence nor discipline because they cannot recognise the Führer's genius.[36]

On Saturday, September 10, the world awoke to banner headlines in the British press. "MINISTERS' MIDNIGHT DECISION" announced the *Daily Mail* in huge bold type. "BRITAIN WARNS GERMANY TODAY—WILL NOT STAND ASIDE IF CZECHS ARE ATTACKED—INSTRUCTIONS SENT TO AMBASSADOR."

> The British Government decided just before midnight last night to inform the German Government in precise and formal terms that Britain will not stand aside if Czecho-Slovakia is the subject of military aggression.

A diplomatic note to this effect will be delivered by Sir Nevile Henderson, the British Ambassador, probably to Herr Hitler himself in Nuremberg within the next few hours.[37]

The *Daily Express* concurred: "BRITAIN WILL SEND 'STRONGLY WORDED' NOTE TO HITLER—AMBASSADOR'S TALK WITH VON RIBBENTROP WAS 'UNSATISFACTORY.' " Yet in spite of the apocalyptic nature of the headlines, on the leader page Beaverbrook did his best to allay his readers' fears.

The *Daily Express* repeats over and over again that this nation will not be involved in a struggle this year nor next year either. The mother trembling for her son, the girl dreading the parting from her sweetheart—they can be calm.[38]

Henderson, however, was appalled and somehow got through to the Foreign Office by telephone at 8:30 A.M. He was "sending reply by air," recorded Cadogan, "but couldn't get further than Cologne. I got an aeroplane off the ground here at 9:30 to pick up Messenger at Cologne. We announce some naval moves (which impress German Naval Attaché)."[39] Henderson's reply was blunt and to the point. A formal warning "would be ill-timed and disastrous in its effect."[40] He had, he assured Halifax, already spoken at length with Göring, Goebbels, Neurath and Ribbentrop, and had "*made British position as clear as daylight to people who count.* . . . It is essential to keep cool as the atmosphere is electric. As it is, the tale of a London aeroplane with a message for me is enough to start stories of another May 21 and must be avoided at all costs. It will drive Hitler straight off the deep end."[41]

Later that morning, as part of Hitler Youth Day, the party congress was treated to what was the highlight of the week to date—an inordinately long speech by Göring.

We know what is going on down there. We know how intolerable it is that that little fragment of a nation down there—goodness knows where it hails from—should persistently oppress and interfere with a highly civilized people. But we know that it is not these absurd pygmies who are responsible. Moscow and the eternal grimacing Jewish-Bolshevist rabble are behind it.[42]

Only the correspondent from *The Times* appears to have failed to identify the venomous nature of the speech. Göring was, he wrote, "in excellent form. Vigorous, often humorous, and sometimes vulgar, he was able at will to rock his audience with laughter or raise it to a pitch of patriotic fervour."[43]

Although a Saturday, it was a hectic day for politicians and diplomats alike in the capitals of Europe. In London, news of the partial mobilization of the British fleet caused consternation at the German embassy. The naval attaché hurried round to the Admiralty to complain to the Director of Naval Intelligence at the Admiralty, who retorted that the measures had been taken in response to the European situation. The attaché told the admiral that "no one in Germany believed that Great Britain would, in any circumstances, come in against Germany," although he now realized, for the first time, that this was a very real possibility, and was "deeply moved at the prospect."[44] That afternoon the counselor at the German embassy warned the Wilhelmstrasse that press and public opinion in Britain had undergone a sea change in the past few days. The general view was that Hitler was being "incorrectly informed about the attitude of British Government and public opinion," that the "Czech proposals to Sudeten Germans are extremely far-reaching," and that there was therefore "no justification whatsoever for German action by force." The whole of Britain, he concluded, was "accordingly reckoning with the possibility of a war."[45]

Henderson's report reached London at 4 P.M., and was immediately considered by the Inner Circle of ministers at Downing Street; Hoare's return had brought the group up to full complement, after he had stayed on at Balmoral for a further day's shooting at the King's request.[46] Henderson's protest was accepted. "N.H. violently against a warning and Ministers decided to hold their hand," recorded Cadogan. "I think right. Van furious."[47] Halifax replied to Henderson that evening. "In view of strong expression of opinion in your communications received today," he wrote, "and on understanding that you have in fact already conveyed to Herr von Ribbentrop and others substance of what you were instructed . . . I agree you need make no further communication."[48] As the four ministers and their advisers left the Cabinet Room, they found the menacing presence of Winston Churchill waiting for them in the anteroom. He had come to "demand an immediate ultimatum to Hitler," which he was "convinced was our last chance of stopping a landslide."[49] But his views were ignored. Instead, a telegram was dispatched to the British embassies in Paris, Berlin and Prague, contradicting the morning's press reports. "It can be stated authoritatively that no such statements should be regarded as authentic."[50] Henderson had, for the time being at least, won the day.

The following morning, Sunday, September 11, Chamberlain briefed a select group of journalists at Downing Street that Britain "could not stand aside if a general conflict were to take place in which the security of France might be menaced."

> Undoubtedly it is of the first importance that the German Government should be under no illusions in this matter and that they should not, as it has been suggested they might, count upon it that a brief and successful campaign against Czechoslovakia could be safely embarked upon.[51]

In Nuremberg that afternoon, Ribbentrop held his annual tea party for 300 foreign dignitaries. Britain was well represented, and Lord Brocket, a fanatical appeaser and favorite of the Nazis, was given the honor of sitting next to the Führer. He had been "deliberately picked," lamented Horace Wilson, because he was "weak." Brocket embarked on a paean of praise for all things Nazi, during which even Hitler, who was "really very amusing [and] laughed a good deal," seemed embarrassed by his sycophancy. "Foreign Affairs and the weather," Hitler joked to his guests, "were both rather depressing." But when the conversation turned to Czechoslovakia he agreed with Brocket when he described Beneš as "a danger to the world." "I shall have to speak some stern words on Monday about all this," Hitler concluded.[52]

In Prague, "you could cut the tension with a knife" according to the American journalist William Shirer. On the evening of Göring's speech, Beneš addressed the nation on the radio. Speaking in both Czech and German he appealed for calm, but his speech was too "reasonable" for Shirer's liking, who assumed that he was "obviously trying to please the British."[53] Rumors abounded that 200,000 German troops were massed on the Austro-Czech border, and Newton reported that the Czech General Staff "were becoming increasingly anxious regarding their own lack of any precautionary measures in view of present great strength and state of preparedness of German army."[54] The airport and railway station in Prague were besieged by Jews desperately trying to flee the country, while gas masks were distributed, in expectation of a lightning attack by German bombers.[55] Runciman, meanwhile, spent the weekend with Count Czernin at his castle near Karlsbad, and found himself subjected to a new form of pressure. On the Sunday, several hundred Sudeten Germans, led by the local SdP deputy, marched up to the castle gates, and proceeded to give a lusty rendition of "Deutschland über Alles" and the "Horst Wessel Song." So enthusiastic was the crowd that Runciman was forced to appear on the castle's balcony; he saluted the throng, and spoke a few conciliatory words in English. He was answered with cries of "Sieg Heil!" and "Heil Hitler!," and a new song in his honor: *"Lieber Runziman mach uns frei, Von der Tschechoslowakei."*[56]

As Monday, September 12, dawned, the day of Hitler's closing speech at Nuremberg, *The Times* reported that "the Parteitag is drawing to a close in an atmosphere of indescribable tension."[57] The *Daily Express* ran a photograph on its front page of Hitler and a nervous Henderson together at Nuremberg. The Cabinet met at 11 A.M., Chamberlain expressing the hope that the mere act of calling the meeting "would assist in keeping public opinion steady." Halifax gave his colleagues a *tour d'horizon* of events since they had last met. The French had "called up reservists and manned the Maginot Line." He described Beneš's latest proposals as a "satisfactory basis for negotiation," and complained about his friend Geoffrey Dawson's "unhappy leading article" in *The Times*. The French Prime Minister had advised Phipps that "if Germany entered Czechoslovakia France would mobilise and declare war," while Henderson had repeated previous warnings to Ribbentrop at Nuremberg. He, Halifax, had held meetings with both Churchill and Eden. He concluded that "if Herr Hitler had made up his mind to attack, it was probable that there was nothing which we could do would stop him." His own opinion was that he "was possibly or even probably mad."

As had been the case on August 30, the principal source of dissent during the ensuing discussion was Duff Cooper, who expressed concern at the failure to issue a warning to Hitler on Henderson's advice alone. "It seemed that the solution which Sir Nevile contemplated," he told the meeting, "would result in a complete surrender on the part of the Czechs."[58] Privately he was more scathing still. The Cabinet had been presented with "a series of messages from Henderson which seemed to me almost hysterical, imploring the Government not to insist upon his carrying out these instructions. . . . And the Government had given way."[59] But Chamberlain would tolerate no criticism. "If Herr Hitler had made up his mind to use force," he declared, "the proposed message would not stop him, and if he had not made up his mind, the proposed message would be likely to drive him to adopt the course which we were anxious to avoid." Cooper's concerns were dismissed by Chamberlain emphasizing that Henderson was "on the spot and familiar with the local atmosphere."[60]

The air of expectancy as the world awaited the climax at Nuremberg was overwhelming, the tension unbearable. Hitler spent the last day of the congress, traditionally known as "Army Day," admiring the displays of Nazi military might paraded in front of a crowd of over 100,000 in the Zeppelinwiese. Among the attractions was the first modern-day helicopter, which made a dramatic vertical landing and takeoff in the middle of a mock battle.[61] That night 30,000 handpicked followers thronged to the Congress Hall, where Hitler arrived just before 7 P.M. He made his way slowly to the stage; the orchestra, in spite of its size and the predominance of brass, was drowned out by the cries of *"Sieg Heil!"* A sudden hush fell as Hess introduced him to the crowd, and Hitler began with his usual lengthy discourse on the Nazi Party, from its earliest struggles to its present-day triumphs. Then, just as some foreign observers were beginning to hope that he was not even going to raise the very subject for which everyone was waiting, the mood suddenly changed as the crowd realized that he was indeed moving on.

It was "intolerable," he roared, that a country existed "where a great part of our people is delivered up to shameless ill-treatment without any apparent means of self-defence."

> This State is a democracy, that is to say it was founded on democratic principles. . . . As a genuine democracy this State forthwith began to oppress, to ill-treat, and to deprive of its vital rights the majority of its inhabitants. Amongst the majority of the nationalities which are suffering oppression

in this State there are to be found three and a half million Germans. . . .
The conditions in this State, as is generally known, are intolerable. In economic life seven and a half millions are being systematically ruined and
thus devoted to a slow process of extermination. This misery of the
Sudeten Germans is indescribable. It is sought to annihilate them. As
human beings they are oppressed and scandalously treated in an intolerable fashion. . . . The depriving of these people of their rights must
come to an end. . . . I have stated that the Reich would not tolerate any
further oppression of these three and a half million Germans, and I
would ask the statesmen of foreign countries to be convinced that this is
no mere form of words.[62]

The written word fails to do justice to the violence of Hitler's delivery, or the
wild enthusiasm with which it was received by his adoring followers. "At
every pause," recorded one historian, "the deep baying of the huge crowd
gathered . . . and the roar of '*Sieg Heil! Sieg Heil! Sieg Heil!*' supplied a sinister background."[63] Experienced observers agreed that "the frenzy reached
heights never before seen at a party rally," while the *New York Times* correspondent eulogized that it had been "more beautiful, if not more impressive
than ever."[64] The speech was carried in full by over a hundred radio stations
across the United States, and in New York Wall Street came to a standstill
shortly before closing time.

In London, the British press compared "Hitler Night" to the night of
King Edward VIII's abdication; throughout the country families gathered
around their wireless sets. At 5:30 P.M. there were 300 people gathered in
Downing Street, cheering each appearance by a minister as he came and
went; but by 9 P.M. the crowd had risen to 10,000 people, and theatergoers
at the Whitehall Theatre, dressed in their evening finery, were booed for
being out on the town on such an important night. The *Evening Standard*
printed 150,000 copies of a special "Hitler Speech Edition,"[65] while the BBC
interrupted their scheduled programs three times between 8 and 11 P.M. to
carry live reports from Nuremberg.[66] In Prague, meanwhile, it had been a
dull, dismal day, and the cold, driving rain had forced most people off the
streets; the city was almost deserted by the time Hitler got to his feet.
Huddled around a radio with a group of fellow journalists in a smoke-filled
room, Shirer, who had heard Hitler speak many times before, recorded that

he had never "heard the Adolf quite so full of hate," his words "dripping with venom."[67]

Oliver Harvey listened at the home of a colleague, and pictured Hitler as a "madman or rather an African chieftain haranguing his tribe."[68] Leo Amery thought "the raving tone and the fierce cheers of the crowd were terrifying."[69] Harold Macmillan tuned in at his Sussex home, his wife doing her best to translate thanks to "a string of German governesses." They were joined by their near neighbor, Lord Cecil, who had no radio of his own, and listened to the broadcast "lying at full length" on Macmillan's sofa, "with his long, emaciated body, his splendid head, and the great beak nose—like a modern Savonarola." Macmillan later recalled that, however inadequate their German, "no listener could fail to grasp the import of the venomous insulting sentences hissed out by the orator—raucous, maniacal, almost inhuman—and of the roars of '*Sieg Heil!*' from the frenzied audience, bawled out like the battle-cry of a horde of savages." At the end of the speech Cecil "slowly uncoiled himself from his recumbent position," and gravely declared, "This means war."[70]

But the speech did not bring war. However brutal its delivery, Hitler had deliberately shied away from an outright declaration of war. He abused the Czechs in violent tones, describing the President as "Beneš the Liar." But having supplied a wealth of detail about the "intolerable oppression" under which the Sudeten Germans were allegedly laboring, he merely demanded "justice" for them, which was to be achieved by self-determination. Cleverly, he reserved the right to deal with the problem in his own way and in his own time. Cadogan was relieved that the speech "pulled no triggers."[71] In Rome, Mussolini switched off his radio with the words, "I had expected a more threatening speech . . . Nothing is lost."[72] The following day almost a million of the Führer's followers began the long journey home from Nuremberg. "Good-bye Until 1939" declared the huge banner hanging across the main road out of the city. In fact, although none of them knew it, they had attended the last ever Nuremberg rally. By September the following year, the world would be at war.[73]

▪ ▪ ▪

At 9:30 P.M., almost as soon as Hitler had finished speaking at Nuremberg, the Inner Circle of ministers convened in the Cabinet Room at Downing

Street, translated copies of the speech laid out on the table before them. Although this was in effect the fifth such meeting, it was the first to be formally minuted by the new Cabinet Secretary, Edward Bridges.[74] The four ministers present were Chamberlain, Halifax, Simon and Hoare, supported by Vansittart, Cadogan and Wilson. There was relief that the "first impressions of the speech . . . were that Herr Hitler had not committed himself to any violent action." There was also a short discussion about the wisdom of sending two bodyguards to Prague to protect Runciman; French intelligence sources had warned that there was "a grave and very real danger of some murderous attack . . . on Lord Runciman from a supposedly Czech quarter, engineered by the Germans, with a view to alienating the British."[75] Newton, however, argued that "the Germans would hail the arrival of two English detectives to guard Lord Runciman as a proof of the incapacity of the Czech Government to preserve order."[76]

Two weeks later, Chamberlain was to tell the House of Commons that the general effect of Hitler's speech had been "to leave the situation unchanged, with a slight diminution of the tension."[77] If that was indeed true, then it was only for a matter of hours at most. While stopping short of a declaration of war, Hitler's words provided the signal for a rising in the Sudetenland. Within minutes of the speech ending at 8:40 P.M., Henlein's supporters were out on the streets chanting *"Ein Volk, Ein Reich, Ein Führer,"* and indulging in sporadic acts of violence against the Czech police.[78] Within two hours the fighting had escalated, and there was widespread rioting throughout the night. SdP storm troopers had been under instructions to gather in town centers to listen to the speech and, around Eger and Karlsbad in particular, they took it as their cue to bring rifles, grenades and machine guns out onto the streets; the hope was that German tanks would soon be rolling into Czechoslovakia to support them. In Prague, meanwhile, the SdP quietly closed their offices, burning all records, while married and older members of staff were sent away on indefinite leave.

By the following morning, the streets of a number of Sudeten towns and villages were strewn with broken glass and the looted wreckage of Czech and Jewish shops. Overnight police stations had been attacked, and attempts made to seize railway stations, post offices and customs houses. Nearly all public buildings were now flying huge swastika banners. The streets were manned by Nazi storm troopers, and even the majority of civilians were going about their business wearing swastika armbands. During the day the revolt spread further afield. Four Czech gendarmes were killed trying to halt an attack on a local school, and several others died during rioting in the frontier districts. A larger group of twenty-six gendarmes, sent to provide assistance for their colleagues, was kidnapped and spirited away over the border into Germany, never to be heard of again. By the end of the day the death toll was in the region of twenty-three, of whom thirteen were Czechs, mostly gendarmes, and ten were Sudeten Germans; there were dozens of walking wounded.[79]

The government in Prague refused to panic and, in an attempt to restore order, declared a state of emergency and proclaimed martial law in a number of Sudeten areas. Civil courts were granted the power to try and condemn the accused, and if necessary to carry out the death penalty, with no right of appeal, within three days. Meetings and processions were banned, and large numbers of police and troops were bused into the affected areas. The Sudeten German gangs, who for twenty-four hours had been so conspicuous on the streets, simply melted away and the towns were quietly reoccupied. In some, force was needed and a number of bloody battles ensued. By late afternoon on September 13 order had been restored to the majority of the affected Sudeten areas, only the small border town of Schwaderbach holding out, as it was impossible for the Czechs to fire into it without the bullets falling on German soil.[80] The rebellion was over almost before it had begun. It had failed to provoke civil war and, from Hitler's point of view, as a provocation designed to prompt the accusation that the government had lost control and thus justify armed intervention, it had come to nothing.

Runciman had been scheduled to meet Henlein in Prague that afternoon, to resume the postponed negotiations. But the SdP leader had fled the city during the night, and the SdP executive committee met instead at Eger later that day. At 4 P.M. Frank transmitted an ultimatum to Hodža by telephone. Henlein deprecated the "large number of Sudeten Germans killed and injured by State authorities," and made a number of demands which were to be met within six hours. Failure to do so would result in Henlein being forced to "disclaim any responsibility for further developments."[81] The demands included: "1) Withdrawal of the State police, 2) Repeal of martial law, 3) Confinement of the military to barracks and their withdrawal from the streets, and 4) Transfer of control of the police and Security Service to local authorities."[82] In a remarkable display of self-control, the Czech government agreed to the demands, but insisted that the Sudetenland should not be left without a formal mechanism for guaranteeing law and order. They asked that the SdP should send a representative to Prague to discuss security arrangements, but the request was refused.

In a last, desperate attempt to save the Runciman Mission, Ashton-Gwatkin traveled that evening to Asch in the Sudetenland, arriving at 1:30 A.M. Unfortunately, Henlein was not at home, and instead they were presented with a pre-signed letter from him, formally breaking off negotiations and disbanding his SdP delegation. At 2 A.M. Ashton-Gwatkin returned to Eger, to Frank's party headquarters, the "Arbeitstelle der S.d.P. . . . quite a fortress with steel doors." There he was "received by a chorus of toughs with 'Heil Hitler,' " and Frank in his upstairs office brandishing a revolver. Together they walked the streets of Eger until 3:30 A.M., observing the Czech soldiers enforcing the peace, but Frank had become "so inflated with the eloquence of Nuremberg and his own importance, that no common-sense or sense of responsibility were to be got out of him."[83] At 11 A.M. Ashton-Gwatkin returned to Asch for one last meeting with Henlein. Although it was friendly, and the Sudeten leader did not say so in as many words, it was obvious that the British mission was at an end.

In Prague that night there was war fever; the widely shared expectation was that the expiry of Henlein's ultimatum would mark the beginning of the conflict. Shirer and a group of fellow foreign journalists sat up through the night, ears pricked for the sound of the German bombers which were assumed already to be in the air, en route for the Czechoslovak capital. In the lobby of the Ambassador Hotel, a traditional haunt for diplomats and correspondents, "the tension and confusion [was] indescribable," as rumors abounded that a German invasion was imminent. The sole telephone operator was besieged by journalists trying to file their stories, and the tension was broken only briefly when the correspondent of the *Chicago Tribune* received a cable from his editor. "Wars always start at dawn," he was told. "Be there at dawn." A grave-faced official from the Foreign Ministry arrived with the news that Henlein's ultimatum had been turned down. "The correspondents fly again to the telephone," recorded Shirer. "Several

Jews scurry out." From the Sudetenland a *Daily Express* correspondent telephoned with his report: he was standing in a police station, the bodies of four Czech gendarmes, covered with sheets, laid out beside him.[84]

Ashton-Gwatkin returned exhausted to Prague, only to learn that the Runciman Mission was indeed over. Their party had already "moved from the troubled atmosphere of the hotel for the calmer regions of H.M. Legation."[85] During the night, Frank's fortress at Eger had been stormed by the Czech army, while Henlein and several other senior members of the SdP had fled across the border into Bavaria, setting up a new headquarters there. He had left behind him a proclamation, addressed to the Sudeten Germans. It was one last act of defiance and treason.

> *We wish to live as free Germans! We want peace and work again in our homeland! We want to return to the Reich! [Wir wollen heim ins Reich] God be with us and our righteous struggle.*[86]

By now, all that was irrelevant to Runciman. As a mediator, he was shortly to be superseded by the Prime Minister himself, who, it was announced, would be flying to see Hitler at Berchtesgaden the following morning. In Prague, the newsboys were selling the evening paper. "Extra! Extra! Read all about how the mighty head of the British Empire goes begging to Hitler!"[87] Two days later, on September 16, Runciman and his team returned to London for the last time.

10

■

On the Razor's Edge

As Priam to Achilles for his son,
So you, into the night, divinely led,
To ask that young men's bodies, not yet dead,
Be given from the battle not begun.

> Sir John Masefield, poet laureate, *The Times*, September 16, 1938

I had established a certain confidence which was my aim and . . . I got the
impression that here was a man who could be relied upon when he had given
his word.

> Neville Chamberlain to Ida Chamberlain on his return from
> Berchtesgaden, September 19, 1938

Chamberlain and his adviser, Sir Horace Wilson, stepped into diplomacy
with the bright faithfulness of two curates entering a pub for the first time;
they did not observe the difference between a social gathering and a rough-
house; nor did they realise that the tough guys assembled did not speak or
understand their language.

> Harold Nicolson, *Why Britain Is at War*, 1939

The genesis of the idea that the Prime Minister should visit Hitler was a late night conversation on Sunday, August 28, between Chamberlain and Wilson, and again later following the meeting of ministers, when Chamberlain chose to confide in Halifax, Simon and Henderson, who had been summoned to London for the meeting. The idea was "so unconventional and daring," Chamberlain told his sister, "that it rather took Halifax's breath away." Henderson, however, gave it a cautious welcome, accepting that it could conceivably be used to "save the situation at the 11th hour."[1] After discussing it further with Henderson, Wilson drafted an initial outline for the visit.

> There is in existence a plan, to be called Plan Z, which is known and must be known only to the Prime Minister, the Chancellor of the Exchequer, the Foreign Secretary, Sir Nevile Henderson and myself. It is to come into operation only in certain circumstances. . . . The success of the plan, if it is to be put into operation, depends upon its being a complete surprise, and it is vital that nothing should be said about it.[2]

"Plan Z" was to stand for zero hour, and Chamberlain was to be referred to in any correspondence as "X." If suitable circumstances arose for the plan to be put into action, Henderson was to be given as much warning as possible, so that the necessary arrangements could be made.

There was no discussion of Plan Z for a further week, until the Inner Circle met for the first time on September 8; discussion revolved around the twin proposals of sending a warning to Hitler, and Chamberlain visiting Germany. "P.M. doesn't think warning message much good," recorded Cadogan. "Thinks he should go himself. I agree."[3] Vansittart, on the other hand, became "thoroughly worked up and fought the idea tooth and nail," comparing the suggestion to "Henry IV going to Canossa over again."[4] On September 9 the Inner Circle met in almost continuous session—"We sat most of the day in our usual huddle," recalled Cadogan.[5] Chamberlain was becoming increasingly enthusiastic about his visit, and was now contemplating a dramatic gesture: he would descend unannounced on Hitler at Nuremberg or, the following week, in Berlin. That afternoon Wilson sent a confidential letter to Henderson by special air courier. The Inner Circle had taken "another look at Z, and at the moment are inclining to the view that the moment is approaching when it might have to be decided to adopt it."

There was, however, one major cause of concern for everyone. What if the Prime Minister was to arrive unannounced, and the Führer caught a diplomatic cold and refused to see him? "This would be very awkward," mused Wilson with masterly understatement, "and would not look very well over here. Would the kudos to him of a visit so appeal to him as to deter him from administering such a rebuff?"[6] Henderson replied from his sleeping car at Nuremberg. "The moment for X is not come in my opinion. Here at Nuremberg it would be out of the question." He was anyway "against it without previous arrangement with Hitler."[7] Having received a further inquiry from London that evening, he replied again at midnight, leaving Wilson in no doubt as to his views. "While I greatly doubt H. being ill and refusing to see X," he wrote, "he might if things had gone so far that he regarded German honour would not allow him to stop. I do not feel that such a risk should be run as such a rebuff to X could scarcely be tolerated." He concluded by emphasizing yet again his earlier advice. "*I don't really like the idea of proceeding without previous arrangement.*"[8]

When Hoare returned to London from Balmoral on the morning of Saturday, September 10, he went directly to Downing Street, where he found Chamberlain alone in the Cabinet Room. The Prime Minister gloomily informed his Home Secretary that "the situation had become exceedingly critical," and that "some dramatic intervention was needed to stop an appalling calamity." Hoare warned that he was "taking a great political risk by personally intervening in a way that was quite likely to fail." But Chamberlain, in a variation of a theme that was to become familiar over the coming weeks, replied that he "would never forgive himself if war broke out and he had not tried every expedient for averting it." That afternoon Hoare joined the Inner Circle for the first time and, after a lengthy discussion about Henderson's increasingly frantic messages from Nuremberg, the conversation returned to Chamberlain's visit. "The Ministers were all agreed that it should be made," recorded Hoare, "and that the Cabinet should be asked to approve of it."[9]

In spite of this agreement, there was no mention of Plan Z when the full Cabinet met on September 12, the morning of Hitler's speech. Indeed, Inskip, who had been let in on the secret, was specifically warned by Wilson beforehand "to be careful not to mention it either in, or out, of the Cabinet."[10] Chamberlain did, however, sound out Runciman in Prague. "I must express my whole-hearted admiration of the patience, tact and skill with which you are pursuing your thankless task," he began. "If you could be left to finish your task alone, I should feel confident of a settlement." However, as that now appeared unlikely, Chamberlain revealed his intention instead to implement Plan Z immediately, although he did "not propose to reveal it to the Cabinet until the last minute," as there would be "less likelihood of leakage." He also requested that Runciman might play a leading role himself in the unfolding drama; he intended to suggest to Hitler that Runciman should abandon his attempts at mediation, and assume the role of final arbitrator in the Sudeten dispute.[11] Runciman was far from impressed, but agreed that "with great reluctance & as the last resort I would do as you suggest. It would of course mean an end to my mediation here."[12]

By now, an important further consideration for British ministers was the attitude of their French counterparts. If Hitler's Nuremberg speech had caused uncertainty in London, in Paris it had created chaos and confusion. Although Hitler had made no definitive declaration of war, he had described himself as the protector of the Sudeten Germans, and made it clear that he intended to honor that obligation. For France the dilemma was now critical. As Czechoslovakia's closest ally, the French government would have to decide whether or not to come to the aid of the Czechs if Hitler mobilized his troops in support of the Sudeten Germans. The weight of that responsibility was bearing down heavily on the shoulders of the leading French politicians. The Prime Minister, Edouard Daladier, had consistently asserted that his country would stand by Czechoslovakia. On September 8 he "declared most positively" to Phipps that "if German troops cross the Czechoslovak frontier, the French will march to a man . . . not for *les beaux yeux* of the Czechs but for their own skins, as, after a given time, Germany would . . . turn against France."[13] Two days later Halifax found the French ambassador in London, Charles Corbin, "full of fight," claiming that France "would have to mobilise and declare war if a German attack was made on Czechoslovakia."[14] General Maurice Gamelin, the French chief of staff, had recently declared "that the French army were in a position not only to hold the Maginot line but to carry out successfully a series of offensives into German territory."[15]

Yet on September 10 the French Foreign Minister, Georges Bonnet, summoned Phipps to the Quai d'Orsay and anxiously inquired whether he could pose a question to him as a friend, rather than as the British ambassador. "Supposing the Germans attacked Czechoslovakia and France mobilised, as she at once would," Bonnet asked. "Supposing France then turned to Great Britain and said 'We are going to march; will you march with us?' What would your answer be?" Phipps was puzzled, but Bonnet repeated the question, emphasizing that it was "tremendously important," but should be treated as "very private" and was not to be recorded officially. At last, Phipps replied that, "speaking personally," not only could he "not give an answer to this hypothetical question, but that [he] really did not believe that His Majesty's Government could either."[16] Two days later Halifax sent Phipps a cautious reply.

> So far as I am in a position to give any answer at this stage to Monsieur Bonnet's question, it would have to be that while His Majesty's Government would never allow the security of France to be threatened, they are unable to make precise statements of the character of their future action, or the time at which it would be taken, in circumstances that they cannot at present foresee.[17]

This telegram provoked an almost hysterical reaction from Bonnet, who called Phipps back to see him again. The ambassador found him "in a complete state of collapse."[18]

> M. Bonnet was very upset and said that peace must be preserved at any price as neither France nor Great Britain were ready for war. Colonel [Charles] Lindbergh had returned from his tour [of Germany] horrified at the overwhelming strength of Germany in the air. . . . He declares Germany has 8000 aeroplanes and can turn out 1500 a month. M. Bonnet said that French and British towns would be wiped out and little or no retaliation would be possible.

Phipps thought Bonnet's "collapse so sudden and so extraordinary,"[19] that he requested an immediate interview with Daladier, who had spent the day chairing a hopelessly divided Cabinet meeting. It soon became clear that Bonnet's attitude was part of a trend, and that Daladier too now showed an "evident lack of enthusiasm" for fulfilling French commitments to Czechoslovakia. "M. Daladier of today was quite a different one to the M. Daladier of September 8," Phipps reported to Halifax, "and tone and language were very different indeed." He feared that the French had been bluffing—"although I have constantly pointed out that one cannot bluff Hitler."[20]

On the morning of September 13 the British government learned "from secret service sources . . . that all German embassies and legations had been informed that Hitler intended to invade Czechoslovakia on September 25th."[21] Vansittart's private sources quoted Wiedemann as having described Hitler as "fanatically determined to destroy Czechoslovakia this autumn." Mobilization would take place on September 15, and the invasion ten days later; it would be carried out with such speed that German troops would be in Prague on the fifth day.[22] From Berlin, even Henderson reported that "only *immediate* action by Czechoslovak Government can avert recourse to force by Germany. If Czechoslovak Government cannot or will not give satisfaction, war will ensue whatever the consequences."[23] It had become obvious to Chamberlain that he must act immediately. He sat down and wrote to the King.

> I have been considering the possibility of a sudden and dramatic step which might change the whole situation. The plan is that I should inform Herr Hitler that I propose at once to go over to Germany to see him. If he assents, and it would be difficult for him to refuse, I should hope to persuade him that he had an unequalled opportunity of raising his own prestige and fulfilling what he has so often declared to be his aim, namely the establishment of an Anglo-German understanding, preceded by a settlement of the Czech-Slovakian question.[24]

The Inner Circle met at 3 P.M., and a last-minute proposal from France that a four-power conference should be held was briefly discussed. It was agreed, however, that "the proposal would not be in any way attractive to Germany, except in so far as it involved the exclusion of Russia." The last two items on the agenda were:

(9) The "Z" Plan. (Prime Minister's visit to Herr Hitler)
(10) Publicity for "Z" Plan.

No minutes were taken of the discussion.[25] At 6 P.M. the service ministers and chiefs of staff were called to a meeting at Downing Street. Duff Cooper tried to get approval for mobilizing the fleet, but was palmed off by Chamberlain with a promise to raise the matter at Cabinet next day.[26] In fact, the Prime Minister's thoughts were elsewhere. Inskip, who was also at the meeting, vividly described the sense of crisis.

> About 3 o'clock things began rattling down to war. German troop movements, fighting in Czechoslovakia, fierce German and Sudeten propaganda. Phipps reported that Bonnet was in a state of collapse. Daladier tried to telephone to P.M. who would not speak to him. Phipps saw Daladier. . . . He declared that "at all costs" Germany must be stopped from moving. Some way out must be found. If Czechoslovakia was invaded, France would be "faced with her obligations." This seemed to appal Daladier. Everything showed that the French didn't want to fight, were not fit to fight, and wouldn't fight.[27]

Chamberlain later explained to the House of Commons that by that evening "a highly critical situation had developed in which there was immediate danger of the German troops now concentrated upon the frontier entering Czechoslovakia to prevent further incidents occurring in the Sudetenland." He therefore decided "to put into operation a plan which I had had in my mind for a considerable period as a last resort."[28] It was "essential," he told his sister, "first that the plan should be tried just when things looked blackest, and second that it should be a complete surprise." He had intended to seek Cabinet approval on the Wednesday morning, "but on Tuesday night I saw that the moment had come & must be taken if it was not to be too late."[29] Simon had already advised Wilson that he did not believe that the Cabinet needed to be summoned. "I do *not* think it is necessary. Cab will trust/thank P.M. S[am] H[oare] agrees."[30] At 10 P.M. Chamberlain, Halifax, Cadogan and Wilson met in the Cabinet Room; Plan Z was the only item on the agenda. It was recorded that "contact had been established on the telephone with Sir Nevile Henderson, who had made some quiet soundings as to Herr von Ribbentrop's whereabouts."

After some discussion, it was further agreed that "the proposed message should be dispatched, but that, in view of the late hour, Sir Nevile Henderson should not attempt to get into touch with Herr von Ribbentrop until early on the morning of 14th September."[31] A telegram was therefore hastily drafted, approved and, late that night, telephoned through to Henderson. He was instructed to see Ribbentrop at the earliest opportunity, with the object of delivering the "following message to Herr Hitler, as personal message to him from Prime Minister."

> In view of increasingly critical situation I propose to come over at once to see you with a view to trying to find peaceful solution. I propose to come across by air and am ready to start tomorrow. Please indicate earliest time at which you can see me and suggest place of meeting. Should be grateful for very early reply.[32]

Chamberlain also wrote again to the King, who was still at Balmoral.

> Events on the Continent of Europe have moved so rapidly and the situation appears to have become so critical that I have sent a personal message to Herr Hitler that I propose to travel to Germany by air and I am ready to start tomorrow.[33]

The King decided to travel south immediately, "in order to have further time for discussion of the international situation with his Ministers."[34]

At 9 A.M. the following morning Henderson called on Weizsäcker at the Wilhelmstrasse to deliver Chamberlain's telegram. It proved, he told the State Secretary, "to what extent the PM of England was prepared to go to avoid another war between Britain and Germany, which would be quite inevitable if Germany intervened in Czechoslovakia."[35] Ribbentrop was in Munich, where he had gone for a few days so as to be closer to Hitler, who had returned to Berchtesgaden after leaving Nuremberg. At 9:30 A.M. Weizsäcker dictated Chamberlain's message to him over the telephone, adding that the plan was "not new," but that the fact that a man of Chamberlain's age should be prepared to "intervene personally on behalf of peace . . . showed his intention to make a last step at the cost of great sacrifice." At 12:15 P.M. an anxious Henderson called Weizsäcker to inquire what progress was being made, and was assured that Ribbentrop had by now arrived at Berchtesgaden and that a reply from Hitler himself would be forthcoming shortly. It was not until 2:40 P.M. that Ribbentrop called both

Weizsäcker and Henderson to tell them that Hitler would be pleased to receive the Prime Minister.[36]

At 11 A.M. in London, Chamberlain began the morning Cabinet meeting by stating that Hitler had vindicated British policy during his speech at Nuremberg, since he had "not done anything irrevocable." He conceded, however, that the "speech gave no encouragement and contained some ominous phrases." For fifty minutes he then unveiled the key elements of Plan Z, which he hoped "would have some chance at the eleventh hour of preserving peace." He had been encouraged by Henderson's view that "if Herr Hitler had decided to invade Czechoslovakia, this new idea might cause him to cancel that intention." He apologized for not having informed his colleagues of the plan earlier, but its vital element was surprise, and he had "thought it better to postpone mentioning it until the last moment." He had abandoned his original idea of arriving in Germany unannounced, and had brought the visit forward in the light of increasingly serious incidents in the Sudetenland, and a "remarkable communication" from Phipps, indicating that Bonnet was "in a state of collapse" and "thoroughly cowed." The telegram to Hitler, he now admitted, had already been sent. "He hoped that the Cabinet would feel that he had not gone beyond his proper duty in taking this action . . . without consulting the full Cabinet." He hoped that his initiative would "appeal to the Hitlerian mentality . . . it might be agreeable to his vanity that the British Prime Minister should take so unprecedented a step."[37]

The Prime Minister's announcement "came as a bombshell" to his colleagues. The Secretary of State for War, Leslie Hore-Belisha, thought it "not without risk," and warned that Hitler's actions were clearly "all part of a relentless plan on the lines of *Mein Kampf*." The government should immediately "intensify the rearmament programme."[38] Several ministers expressed concern at the concept of a plebiscite, Oliver Stanley arguing that such a concession would "give Herr Hitler everything which he was now demanding by force and would be a complete surrender." Chamberlain conceded that he did not like the idea of a plebiscite, which would almost certainly result in the secession of Sudeten territory to the Reich, but argued that it was "impossible for a democracy like ourselves to say that we would go to war to prevent the holding of a plebiscite." He doubted whether Czechoslovakia "could ever have peace so long as the

Sudeten Germans were part of the country."[39] It was all but inevitable that "the Sudetens would be incorporated in the Reich either by force of arms, or by an expression of their own desire by means of a plebiscite," and there was "no question which of these two alternatives was the lesser evil."[40]

Duff Cooper argued that the "choice was not between war and a plebiscite, but between war now and war later," but although he had earlier proposed the full mobilization of the fleet, he was now content to give Chamberlain's proposal a chance.[41] Privately, however, he was furious that the Cabinet was "being told, not consulted, for the telegrams had already gone off."[42] Lord Hailsham asked what would happen if other minorities also demanded a plebiscite, to which Chamberlain replied that he "did not expect any such demand to be made." This provoked a mild rebuke from Halifax, who warned that the idea of a plebiscite could well be "infectious." Sir John Simon asked what would become of the rest of Czechoslovakia, once the Sudeten areas had been ceded to the Reich. For Chamberlain, this was the most difficult question of all; since the Anschluss he had steadfastly refused to contemplate the offer of a formal guarantee to Czechoslovakia. Now, however, he reluctantly agreed that perhaps "this country should join in guaranteeing the integrity of the rest of Czechoslovakia. . . . The value of the guarantee would lie in its deterrent effect. Czechoslovakia should be guaranteed by France, Russia, Germany and Great Britain and would become a neutral state."

Only the Minister of Health, Walter Elliot, expressed hostility to Chamberlain's proposal, complaining at the lack of consultation, and warning that the government was "being led by pressure to do something which we should not have done of our own free will."[43] Otherwise, recorded Inskip, "almost everyone spoke with admiration of the P.M.'s bold stroke," while Simon "finished by his usual shower of compliments to P.M."[44] Never one to miss an opportunity to ingratiate himself, Simon had indeed saved his own observations until last. He "felt sure the Prime Minister must feel deeply moved" by his colleagues" endorsement of his "brilliant proposal." He invited the Cabinet to "record their unanimous approval of the action taken [and] to express their confidence and trust in the Prime Minister."

> His absence from this country, if only for a short time, was a grievous matter, but if he came back with the seeds of peace with honour he would

be universally acclaimed as having carried out the greatest achievement of the last twenty years.

Chamberlain thanked his colleagues, and repeated that "he would not have done his duty to his conscience if he did not make this effort to avert the threatened catastrophe." He was "much touched by the confidence placed in him."[45]

As soon as the two-and-a-half-hour meeting ended, Phipps telephoned from Paris to confirm the complete volte-face of the French ministers, who still knew nothing of Plan Z. Bonnet had told him that France would "accept any solution of Czechoslovak question to avoid war," and that the French people would not allow the "sacrifice of ten million men in order to prevent three and a half million Sudetens joining the Reich." In order to "avoid German aggression," and as a last resort, "they would consent to a plebiscite on [the] general question whether Sudetens shall remain inside or shall be allowed to join Reich." In support of this stance, Bonnet had "given a broad hint to M. Beneš that France may have to reconsider her obligations towards Czechoslovakia."[46] Phipps told the Conservative MP Leo Amery, who was passing through Paris that day, that the French were "so frightened of war that they may be looking for any sort of excuse in the manner of breaking out of trouble in order to get out of their obligations to Czechoslovakia."[47] "What was abundantly clear," recorded the Secretary of State for India, Lord Zetland, was "that in the face of an imminent probability of German aggression the French Government were behaving like a pricked balloon."[48]

At 3:30 P.M. Henderson telephoned Cadogan to say that Hitler would be "entirely at the disposal" of the Prime Minister.[49] The Labour leader, Clement Attlee, and other Opposition leaders were told of the visit, while telegrams were drafted to Phipps and Runciman informing them that Chamberlain would be leaving for Germany the following morning. Runciman was put on standby to travel there at short notice if required, while Daladier, reported Phipps, "did not look very pleased" when given the message.[50] All afternoon, a "large and anxious but undemonstrative crowd" gathered outside Downing Street, as rumors circulated that an important announcement was imminent, and by the time a formal communiqué was issued at 9 P.M., there were several thousand people in Whitehall. As soon as the news was released, dozens of waiting journalists raced from Downing

Street in an attempt to be the first to reach the telephone kiosks at the end of the road, while the public thronged around them trying to listen in as reports were filed with news desks across the world.[51]

That evening the chiefs of staff issued a report, as requested by Inskip a few days earlier, analyzing Britain's military preparedness in the event of a German invasion of Czechoslovakia. As Inskip himself described, it made salutary reading.

> It re-affirmed their view that no pressure we and France could bring to bear, by sea, land or air, could stop Germany overrunning Bohemia, and inflicting a decisive defeat on Czechoslovakia. The war would be an unlimited war, in which while we should initiate no air bombardment, sooner or later we must experience to the tune of possibly 500 or 600 tons of bombs a day for 2 months.[52]

Nothing, however, could dampen Chamberlain's enthusiasm. "Hitler was entirely at my disposal," he boasted to his sister, "and would not Mrs. Chamberlain come too!" What was more, he had heard that Hitler, on hearing of his proposal, "was struck all of a heap and exclaimed 'I can't possibly let a man of his age come all this way; I must go to London.' "[53] Hitler's actual reaction appears to have been that he could scarcely believe his luck. "*Ich bin vom Himmel gefallen* [I fell from Heaven]," he supposedly commented "with a chuckle," when he first heard the news.[54]

▪ ▪ ▪

"A gasp of amazement rang round the world," reported the *Daily Express* the following morning, "followed by a new sense of relief in the worried capitals." Both at home and abroad there was near-unanimous praise for Chamberlain's bold stroke, and admiration at his determination to undertake his maiden flight at the age of sixty-nine. "The issues at stake are too big for him to consider his own comfort or convenience," the paper told its readers.[55] Even those papers usually critical of his foreign policy joined in the praise. Under the headline "GOOD LUCK CHAMBERLAIN!" the Labour-supporting *Daily Herald* welcomed the Prime Minister's "bold course, which will receive general support. It is an effort to stave off war which has seemed to be growing dreadfully near," the article continued, "and, as such, it must win the sympathy of opinion everywhere, irrespective of party."[56] The Liberal-leaning *News Chronicle* applauded "one of the boldest and most dramatic strokes in modern diplomatic history."[57] *The Times*, below the headline "A CORDIAL WELCOME FROM THE FÜHRER," reported that Chamberlain's initiative "throws all other news of the European crisis into the shade." The announcement of his visit had brought "a sense of relief and profound satisfaction to all," and provided "proof of his courage and common sense." The financial pages, however, reported a falling stock market, strong demand for U.S. dollars, and rising premiums for war-risk insurance.

Political and public opinion was almost universally supportive. The polling organization Mass-Observation recorded an immediate swing in Chamberlain's favor, with 70 percent of those polled believing that the trip was "a good thing for peace."[58] In Geneva, news of the visit was announced at a banquet given by the British delegation at the League of Nations. Diana Cooper was sitting next to the Irish Taoiseach, Eamon de Valera, who declared that it was "the greatest thing that has ever been done."[59] At the same dinner, Chips Channon described Chamberlain's initiative as "one of the finest, most inspiring acts of all history . . . the company rose to their feet electrified, as all the world must be, and drank his health." He was only disappointed that "of course some Jews and many of the more shady pressmen who hang about Geneva are furious."[60] The Archbishop of Canterbury, meanwhile, announced that Westminster Abbey would remain open, day and night, "for a period of unbroken intercession in connection with the present crisis." A makeshift prayer area was created with seats and kneelers around the Tomb of the Unknown Soldier, and when the abbey opened its doors at 8 A.M. there was already a lengthy queue.

The Labour leadership felt reassured. The previous week, at a Labour rally in County Durham, the Shadow Foreign Secretary Hugh Dalton had told his supporters that war could be "averted now only in one way. Hitler must be warned in the clearest and most unmistakable language that if he commits this crime Britain will join with France and Soviet Russia in armed resistance to his aggression."[61] Now Dalton confided in Douglas Jay of the *Daily Herald* that "Chamberlain had assured him he was going to Germany to inform Hitler that if he made any further aggressive moves, we should be ready to fight."[62] The Canadian High Commissioner, Vincent Massey, spoke for the usually skeptical Dominion governments, praising Chamberlain's initiative as "a very brave thing to do," which he felt could not "make matters worse, and might make them better."[63] Even the staunch anti-appeaser Leo Amery considered it "a bold stroke and one which might just conceivably save the situation, though one cannot help thinking of Schuschnigg." When he met Annie Chamberlain in Whitehall, he congratulated her "on Neville's courageous action."[64]

Churchill, on the other hand, described the visit as "the stupidest thing that has ever been done,"[65] while Eden was "infuriated" when he first heard the news.[66] In Prague too reaction was muted, as the Czechs came to terms with Henlein's flight to Germany; the government declared him a traitor and ordered that he be arrested on sight if he set foot back on Czech soil. Shirer reported that the Czechs were "dumbfounded . . . they suspect a sell-out."[67] There were spontaneous demonstrations, as crowds massed in the streets urging Beneš to resist what was being done in their name. "Good for peace, bad for Czechoslovakia" was the general view.[68] In Rome, Mussolini too was astonished. "There will not be war," he exclaimed to Ciano, "but this is the liquidation of English prestige."[69] In Berlin, the news "came as a bomb-shell and was greeted by the public with enormous relief and satisfaction."[70] Details of the visit were splashed across the front pages of the newspapers: "A WEIGHT OFF THE HEART" was how the local *Times* correspondent described the news. He had been lunching in a packed Berlin gentlemen's club, when the news had been announced; all the diners had gotten to their feet and drunk Chamberlain's health. Berliners thought that Chamberlain's visit was a "manly action," and offered the "best hope for peace that has appeared for many a day, and a great compliment to Germany."[71]

A beaming Chamberlain left Downing Street at 7:45 A.M., waving cheerfully to the large crowd that had assembled, even at such an early hour. At Heston Aerodrome, a half-hour drive west of London, a small crowd of dignitaries had gathered to see him off, including Lord and Lady Halifax, who had been driven to the airport by Cadogan; Theodor Kordt, the Counselor from the German embassy, in full morning dress; the chairman and managing director of British Airways; and Lord Brocket, fresh from his trip to Nuremberg. As Chamberlain was making his way across the tarmac to the plane, another of Hitler's British friends, Lord Londonderry, "arrived out of the sky" in his private airplane, and joined the group waiting to send the Prime Minister off on his way.[72] A solitary protester was held back behind a barrier, but was still close enough to shout "Stand by Czechoslovakia. No concessions to Hitler" as Chamberlain passed by.[73] At 8:30 A.M. he spoke to the BBC.

> I am going to meet the German Chancellor because the present situation seems to me to be one in which discussions between him and me may have useful consequences. My policy has always been to try to ensure peace, and the Führer's ready acceptance of my suggestion encourages me to hope that my visit to him will not be without results.[74]

With that he boarded the gleaming silver, twin-engined Lockheed Electra, with his traveling companions, Sir Horace Wilson and William Strang, the head of the Central Department at the Foreign Office. *The Times* reassured its readers that it was the most modern aircraft in the British Airways fleet, equipped with "every navigational and safety device known to modern science"; Chamberlain would be able to relax in its "deep-seated adjustable armchairs in a sound-proof cabin," while cruising at 175 mph.[75] In fact his first flight proved to be a bumpy one, and it took him a while to get over his initial nervousness, later admitting to "some slight sinkings" as the plane climbed over the London suburbs.[76] He soon relaxed enough, however, to enjoy the ham sandwiches and whisky which had been provided for the journey.[77] Wilson did his best to distract Chamberlain's attention by reading a selection of the laudatory letters and telegrams which had already arrived at Downing Street, ensuring, in the words of one critical historian, that Chamberlain was "thus wafted to Berchtesgaden in a cloud of commendation."[78] Strang, on the other hand, found the Prime Minister curiously unaffected by the excitement of his first flight, even when the plane flew into a violent storm as they neared Munich; he was "as always, aloof, reserved, imperturbable, unshakably self-reliant."[79]

They touched down half an hour early at 12:35 P.M. and, as an eyewitness later recalled, "a very nice old man with an umbrella appeared" off the plane.[80] He was met at the foot of the aircraft steps by Henderson, who had come from Berlin by train, Dirksen, from the London embassy, and Ribbentrop, who inquired how the flight had been. "I stood the passage very well," Chamberlain replied, "although we had bad weather part of the way, and I had never been in an aeroplane before."[81] The Prime Minister was smiling, reported the *Daily Mail*, and "looked fresh and ruddy, and his eyes were sparkling." As he shook hands with the German dignitaries, his "stiff wing-collar and his tie of heavy grey silk struck an unmistakable and rather old-fashioned English note among the black uniforms of the Schütz-Staffel Corps."[82] "I'm tough and wiry," he reassured Henderson.[83]

A crowd of between 3,000 and 4,000 had turned up in the rain to catch a glimpse of the visiting Prime Minister, who was invited to inspect a guard of honor, to the accompaniment of beating drums. A fleet of fourteen soft-topped Mercedes, with the hoods up to keep out the rain, were waiting on the tarmac, and as he and Ribbentrop were driven the five miles to the railway station, it quickly became apparent that the people of Munich had turned out in force to line the streets and loudly cheer him along the route. According to Paul Schmidt, Hitler's interpreter, who rode with them, the warmth of the welcome was considerably greater than that which had greeted Mussolini the previous year. This seems to have had a restorative effect on Chamberlain after the long flight, who expressed himself "delighted with the enthusiastic welcome of the crowds who were waiting in the rain and who gave me the Nazi salute and shouted 'Heil' at the tops of their voices all the way to the station."[84] Ribbentrop, on the other hand, sulked, and was clearly "livid."[85]

Hitler had sent his own train, made up of six gray-green coaches, for Chamberlain to make the three-hour journey to Berchtesgaden. The ubiquitous Ward Price of the *Daily Mail* was also on board, and thought that the Prime Minister was clearly enjoying himself. Lunch was taken in the Führer's maple-lined dining car at a table laid for fifteen, Chamberlain sitting next to Ribbentrop—"turtle soup, a special German fish called Renken (found in the Alpine lakes), roast beef and Yorkshire pudding, cheesed fritters and fruit." As the coffee, liqueurs and cigars were served, Chamberlain became increasingly "animated."[86] Outside, the picturesque Bavarian scenery rushed past, as the train climbed into the mountains, but Schmidt observed that Chamberlain was more interested in the other trains, as "troop transports rolled past, making a dramatic background, with soldiers in new uniforms and gun barrels pointing skywards."[87] Crowds lined the route, gathering at stations and level crossings to cheer the passing envoy of peace, and at Berchtesgaden the station was a hive of bustling activity. Hitler had sent his head of Chancellery, Otto Meissner, and all three of his service adjutants to greet his guest, while the town was swarming with journalists from around the world. The Prime Minister's entourage made a brief stop to check into the Grand Hotel, where an SS guard of honor had formed up in welcome, before making their way up the mountain with the Führer's chauffeur at the wheel. It had started to rain and the sky had darkened, so that the view of the mountains was obscured by the cloud and mist.

Having been on the road since dawn, the sixty-nine-year-old Chamberlain pulled up at the foot of the Berghof steps just before 5 P.M. To the accompaniment of yet another drum roll, a black-uniformed guard of honor, composed of members of the SS-Leibstandarte Adolf Hitler, snapped smartly to attention. Hitler, with Keitel at his side, came down the steps to shake the Prime Minister's hand. Chamberlain "waved his hat in a friendly way" and, after inspecting the guard of honor, "waved his hat again, an umbrella hanging from his left arm."[88] Chamberlain observed his host closely. "On first view," he later told the Cabinet, "Herr Hitler was unimpressive."[89]

> He was bareheaded and dressed in a khaki coloured coat with a red armlet and a swastika on it and the military cross on his breast. He wore black trousers such as we wear in the evening and black patent leather lace-up shoes. His hair is brown, not black, his eyes blue, his expression rather disagreeable, especially in repose and altogether he looks entirely undistinguished. You would never notice him in a crowd and would take him for the house painter he once was.[90]

Hitler led the way along a sparsely furnished corridor to the great hall, with its famous picture window looking out over the Untersberg, where a "macabre" tea party ensued, at a low, round table.[91] Chamberlain seemed absorbed by the quantity and scale of the paintings of nudes which were hung throughout the house, but tactfully refrained from introducing them into the conversation. The tension was palpable. Hitler was tense, and the talk over tea was stilted. He expressed regret at the length of Chamberlain's journey, while the Prime Minister in turn admired the scenery, and spoke of his disappointment that it was partially hidden from view because of the weather. "I have often heard of this room," he continued, "but it is much larger than I expected."

"It is you who have the big rooms in England," replied Hitler.

"You must come and see them sometime."

"I should be received with demonstrations of disapproval," said Hitler, at last allowing himself a shadow of a smile.

"Well perhaps it would be wise to choose the moment."[92]

After half an hour of such platitudes, Hitler brought the conversation to an abrupt halt by inquiring how Chamberlain wished to proceed. It was agreed that the two heads of state would carry on the formal part of the conversation alone, with only Schmidt in attendance to translate. This was a scheme that had been devised in advance by Henderson and Weizsäcker, with Hitler's acquiescence, so as to exclude Ribbentrop from the conversation. It worked, but consequently left Ribbentrop brooding furiously at the snub, and he exacted revenge in a particularly petty fashion the following day. Hitler took Chamberlain upstairs to his private study, a bare wood-paneled room, furnished only with a stove, a sofa, and a small table with three chairs. It was the room where both Halifax and Schuschnigg had held their respective, and contrasting, meetings with the Führer in recent months. Hitler made no effort to offer his guest a glass of water from the bottles which had been left for them on the table.

It must by now have become all but obvious to Hitler that Chamberlain had arrived in Germany with a compromise in mind. On first receiving the Prime Minister's telegram, his initial reaction had been quite the opposite. He later told the Polish ambassador in Berlin that he had been "taken aback by Chamberlain's proposition to come to Berchtesgaden . . . but it was of course impossible for him not to receive the British Prime Minister. He thought Chamberlain was coming to make a solemn declaration that Great Britain was ready to march."[93] Any such concern soon evaporated. In the wake of Hitler's Nuremberg speech, and the day before the visit to Berchtesgaden was made public, the Prime Minister's press secretary briefed German correspondents in London that Chamberlain had been "disappointed and hurt by [the] Führer's speech." He considered "war to be unavoidable if matters were allowed to run the same course," but he was "still prepared to examine far-reaching German proposals, including [a] plebiscite, to take part in carrying them into effect, and to advocate them in public."[94] Hitler already knew Chamberlain's negotiating position.

By the time Chamberlain arrived at the Berghof, the situation had altered again. As he traveled by train from Munich, German radio stations broadcast details of Henlein's proclamation, under the slogan *"Wir wollen heim ins Reich!,"* demanding the annexation of the Sudeten areas to the Reich. Henlein had sent a copy of the proclamation to Hitler, with a personal covering letter.

> In the event of its being approved by you, my Führer, as a short-term solution by stages, permit me to submit two proposals:
> 1) No plebiscite, but immediate cession of regions with more than 50% German population.
> 2) Occupation of this region within 24 hours (48) by German troops (reason: to put an end to further murders resulting from Czech fanaticism).
> Heil my Führer![95]

If Chamberlain had come to Berchtesgaden intending to discuss the possibility of a plebiscite in the Sudeten areas, or even a partial cession of territory, then these two negotiating options were suddenly no longer available to him. Hitler had set himself up as the champion of the oppressed Sudeten Germans, and if their leader now demanded their incorporation in the Reich, such a condition had de facto become the minimum requirement.

Hitler warmly welcomed Henlein's proclamation. On the one hand, he was well aware that to satisfy world opinion it had been necessary to agree to the meeting with Chamberlain. In spite of that, he remained determined to invade Czechoslovakia, for which he had been preparing for many months, even if it led to a European war. Agreeing to see Chamberlain was one aspect of a twin-track approach, which also required Henlein to generate the provocations which Hitler believed would provide an excuse for war, and might even deter Britain and France from intervening. "I have arranged for these provocations," he told those around him at the Berghof.[96] At the same time, Henlein's reference in his letter to a "short-term solution by stages," gives the game away. The annexation of the Sudetenland was to be no more than a stepping-stone toward the ultimate occupation of the whole of Czechoslovakia.

Chamberlain began the meeting by welcoming the "opportunity for bringing about a new understanding between England and Germany," which had long been his ambition. Until now it had proved impossible, but he wanted to put that right. Hitler, however, intervened almost immediately to reply that while that, and other issues, were undoubtedly important, the plight of the Sudeten Germans was "of the utmost urgency and could not wait."[97] Reports received that very day indicated that 300 Sudeten Germans had been killed during clashes with the Czech authorities. It was essential to discuss this matter first of all. Schmidt quickly realized that Hitler was still in party rally mode. Having insisted that Czechoslovakia should be the first topic for discussion, he in fact began as if making a set-piece speech, reciting a lengthy tirade extolling his achievements on behalf of the German people, and listing Germany's numerous grievances. Chamberlain listened patiently as he was offered Hitler's views on the Treaty of Versailles, the League of Nations, disarmament, unemployment and a host of issues to do with National Socialism. "Nothing in his clear-cut, typically English features," remarked Schmidt, "with their bushy eyebrows, pointed nose and strong mouth, betrayed what went on behind his high forehead."[98]

When Hitler's monologue finally moved on to the subject of Anglo-German relations, he first complained of perceived British threats, and then surprised Chamberlain by questioning the validity and purpose of the Anglo-German Naval Agreement. For the first time, Chamberlain reacted, gently pointing out the difference between a threat and a warning. Hitler, however, brushed aside such linguistic niceties and, as he became increasingly agitated, began to develop in detail his theory of racial unity, which was the basis of his demand that all Germans should "return to the Reich, to which they had belonged for a thousand years." He had already answered the call of seven million Germans in Austria, and now it was the turn of the three million Sudeten Germans, "whose earnest desire it was to return to Germany." This he would make possible at any cost.[99] "I am ready to face a world war," he shouted at Chamberlain. "I am forty-nine years old, and I want still to be young enough to lead my people to victory."[100]

At this point, Chamberlain again intervened.

Hold on a minute; there is one point on which I want to be clear and I will explain why: you say that the three million Sudeten Germans must be included in the Reich; would you be satisfied with that and is there nothing more you want? I ask because there are many people who think that is not all; that you wish to dismember Czechoslovakia.

Hitler launched into another rambling speech. It was "impossible that Czechoslovakia should remain like a spearhead in Germany's side [but] he did not want a lot of Czechs, all he wanted was Sudeten Germans." Nor would he feel safe so long as there was a mutual treaty between Czechoslovakia and Russia. Although he had no mandate to do so, Chamberlain suggested possible modifications to the treaty, but Hitler brushed him aside and declared that once the Sudeten Germans were part of the Reich, the Hungarian, Polish and Slovak minorities would secede also, "and what was left would be so small that he would not bother his head about it."[101]

Chamberlain then embarked on a detailed analysis of the practical difficulties in resolving which communities should be ceded to Germany, and what percentage of population should be the benchmark. Even if those areas containing 80 percent Germans became part of the Reich, there would still be a considerable number of Germans left in Czech areas, and vice versa; it would require not only a change of boundaries, but a transfer of population also. Chamberlain promised to do his utmost to ensure that German grievances were settled, so long as the use of force was ruled out. But Hitler was utterly disinterested in such minutiae. Percentages were not the problem; where the Germans were in a majority, the territory should pass to the Reich. The discussion, he complained, was becoming far too academic. Three hundred Sudeten Germans had been killed. "Force!" he exclaimed. "Who speaks of force? Herr Beneš applies force against my countrymen in the Sudetenland, Herr Beneš mobilised in May, not I." As the rain lashed against the windows, and the wind howled outside, Hitler finally exploded. "I shall not put up with this any longer. I shall settle this question one way or another. I shall take matters into my own hands."[102]

For the first time Chamberlain reacted angrily. "If I've understood you correctly," he replied, "then you're determined in any event to proceed against Czechoslovakia. If that is your intention why have you had me coming to Berchtesgaden at all? Under these circumstances it's best if I leave straight away. Apparently it's all pointless."[103] It proved an effective retort. Until then, Schmidt had feared the worst—either Chamberlain gave in, or it would be war. "At that moment," he later recalled, "the question of peace or war was really poised on a razor's edge."[104] Yet now, to Schmidt's astonishment, Hitler backed down; his manner changed, and he spoke more quietly. "If you recognize the principle of self-determination for the treatment of the Sudeten question," he told Chamberlain, "then we can discuss how to put the principle into practice."[105] It was true that the principle of self-determination for the Sudeten Germans had already been all but accepted by Chamberlain, and it would have been simple enough for him to give the assurance that Hitler was seeking there and then. Indeed, he wrote to his sister later that evening, admitting that he personally "didn't care two hoots whether the Sudetens were in the Reich or out of it."[106] But perhaps sensing that for the first time he had Hitler's full and undivided attention, he insisted that he would have to return home to consult his Cabinet colleagues first. Hitler initially looked concerned, but then appeared relieved when Schmidt made it clear that Chamberlain intended to return for a further meeting subsequently.

At the end of the meeting Hitler escorted Chamberlain downstairs, and out to a waiting car. His mood was friendlier, and he even invited his guest to return the following day to admire the scenery. The guard of honor once again stood to attention, the drums rolled, and Chamberlain was driven back down the mountain to his hotel, where he told the waiting press that it had been "a very friendly talk."[107] A joint press communiqué described the meeting as a "comprehensive and frank exchange of views," and added that after Chamberlain had consulted his Cabinet, "in the course of a few days a further conversation will take place."[108] At the Berghof, life began to return to normal; Hitler talked about Chamberlain, and "Eva Braun's friends emerged from the shadows." At dinner that night he was joined by the Speers and the Bormanns, while the women "made fun of the old-fashioned Englishman who was so attached to his umbrella." Hitler could not resist a boast. "The old man took an aeroplane for the first time in his life in order to come and see me," he told his admirers, adding sarcastically that Chamberlain would "have to be prepared to pay if he becomes a target for your mockery once more."[109]

Hitler was well satisfied with his day's work. He gave a "lively and joyful description of the conversation" to Ribbentrop and Weizsäcker, and "clapped his hands as after a highly successful entertainment. He felt that he had managed to manoeuvre the dry civilian into a corner." He was confident, he told them, that "by his brutally announced intention to solve the Czech question now, even at the risk of a European war, as well as by the promise that he would be satisfied in Europe, Chamberlain had been induced to work for the cession of the Sudetenland." He, Hitler, would not refuse a plebiscite, but, if the Czechs refused one, "the road would be clear for the German invasion." If Czechoslovakia yielded on the Sudetenland, the rest of the country would anyway be annexed the following spring. In either scenario, he could not lose; he would have his longed-for war during his own lifetime.[110]

At the conclusion of the meeting, Chamberlain had requested that no military action should be taken against Czechoslovakia before they met again. "The German military machine is a mighty instrument," Hitler replied. "Once set in motion it cannot be stopped. But, provided there is no further grave provocation by the Czechs, I will not set it in motion until our talks are resumed."[111] Back at his hotel, Chamberlain drafted a statement which he had sent back up to the Berghof.

> In order that we may pursue our conversations undisturbed and to avoid further loss of life and injury to persons we hope that the Czechs and Sudetendeutsche alike will abstain from all provocative action and remain quiet.[112]

Unfortunately, this request too played into Hitler's hands. He willingly made what appeared to be a concession, when his strategy for Case Green did not envisage an invasion of Czechoslovakia for another fortnight anyway. He had even had the gall to suggest that Chamberlain should appeal to the Czechs "to recall their State Police from the Sudeten German districts, confine their soldiers to barracks and withdraw mobilisation," thus leaving the frontier open for his invading tanks.[113]

Hitler remained determined to invade Czechoslovakia, even at the risk of a wider war. He felt confident that Chamberlain would fail to obtain Cabinet approval for his demands, but needed insurance against the "danger" that, by some miracle, those demands might indeed be met. He therefore began a program of action designed to "minimize the chances of being cheated out of at least a little war."[114] That evening Schmidt, who was staying in the same hotel as the British delegation, dictated his notes from the meeting. Henderson looked in several times, impatiently asking when a copy of the transcript would be available for the Prime Minister. It was common diplomatic etiquette that such a transcript should be made available, not least since Chamberlain had deliberately refrained from having an interpreter of his own present. But when Ribbentrop found out, he reacted furiously. "You think you're still in Geneva," he shouted at Schmidt, "where all secret papers were freely handed about to everybody. We don't have that sort of thing in National Socialist Germany. This report is intended for the Führer alone."[115] Schmidt then had the unpleasant task of explaining to Henderson that he was not after all to be given a record of the meeting. It was assumed that Ribbentrop's instruction was the result of pique at being excluded from the meeting. In fact, the order came from Hitler, who spotted an opportunity to preserve the flexibility of his bargaining position; he could avoid too proscriptive a form of words, and even later deny much of what had actually been said.

As Chamberlain left his hotel the following morning, he was asked by a British journalist if he had a message for the public at home. He was returning to London, he replied, and was therefore "now in a position to take the message to England himself."[116] He was driven to Munich with Ribbentrop by Hitler's personal chauffeur, along seventy-five miles of newly constructed autobahn, while Wilson and Strang traveled in the car behind with Dirksen. Everyone at the Berghof, Dirksen told Wilson, had "obviously been impressed by the Prime Minister," and Hitler had particularly appreciated the "directness with which he talked and the rapidity with which he had grasped the essentials of the situation." Chamberlain's "master-stroke in diplomacy" had appealed to the Führer "as something after his own heart." Weizsäcker too told Wilson that Chamberlain had "made just the right impression on Hitler," while Walther Hewel, the head of Ribbentrop's personal staff, said that Hitler had "felt he was speaking to a *man*." Even Schmidt joined in the charm offensive, claiming that "what impressed Hitler most was Mr. Chamberlain's directness and clarity of thought and speech."

Characteristically, only Ribbentrop could not bring himself to join in the general approval of Chamberlain, sulking throughout the car journey and during lunch in Munich. Wilson took the opportunity to chide him about the persistent reports that had reached the Berghof the previous day, during the meeting, that 300 Sudeten Germans had been massacred at Eger. In an attempt to verify or deny these reports, Wilson had put through several telephone calls the previous evening to London, to Berlin and to Runciman in Prague. "Nonsense," had been the reply. There had been no such massacre, indeed there had been no casualties at all that day. The total death toll currently stood at twenty-eight, including both Germans and Czechs. "It would be well if everyone concerned," commented Wilson rather primly, "would remember that it is a good rule to have the facts before deciding action."[117]

On the tarmac at Munich, with Ribbentrop at his side, Chamberlain expressed his thanks in English for the "warmth and friendliness of his reception, not only by the Government, but by the people of Germany"; he looked forward to his return. "Good-bye, Henderson," he concluded. "I shall be seeing you soon."[118] It was still raining and the SS guard of honor presented arms, to the accompanying roll of drums, one last time. The ham sandwiches and whisky that had provided sustenance on the outbound trip had been replaced by chicken sandwiches and claret for the flight home, and the pilot, Commander Pelly, told *The Times* that Chamberlain had cheerfully admitted that flying "was not as bad as he had been led to believe . . . he had travelled very comfortably." There was a strong headwind, and the plane was forced to refuel at Cologne, but the time was made up and soon after 5 P.M. they landed at Heston; a large crowd was waiting to greet the Prime Minister. "I hope you feel that you were successful," inquired Theodor Kordt. "At any rate you have conquered the hearts of my countrymen."[119]

A BBC television camera crew was also waiting to record Chamberlain's arrival. At 5:15 P.M. his words were broadcast live on the radio, the cheers of the crowd clearly audible in the background.

> I have come back again rather quicker than I expected, after a journey which, had I not been so preoccupied, I should have found thoroughly enjoyable. Yesterday afternoon I had a long talk with Herr Hitler. It was a frank talk, but it was a friendly one, and I feel satisfied now that each of us fully understands what is in the mind of the other. You will not, of course, expect me to discuss now what may be the results of these talks. What I have got to do now is discuss them with my colleagues. Later—perhaps in a few days—I am going to have another talk with Herr Hitler; only this time he has told me that it is his intention to come half-way to meet me. That is to spare an old man such another long journey.

The Prime Minister's words, according to a BBC written report, were greeted with "laughter and cheers."[120]

■

11

A New and Sharper Sword

The callous and irresponsible betrayal
Of the Czech Republic has brought not peace
But a new and sharper sword . . .

>Hugh MacDiarmid, "When the Gangs Came to London,"
>October 1938[1]

Veracity is not, I regret to say, the strongest point of the average French politician.

>Sir Eric Phipps to Lord Halifax, September 17, 1938

We had no other choice, because we were left alone.

>Czechoslovak government statement, September 21, 1938

As Chamberlain drove back into London from Heston, with Halifax at his side, he was entitled to feel quietly satisfied that reaction to his visit had been almost universally positive. *The Times* had that morning published a specially commissioned poem by the poet laureate, Sir John Masefield, paying a glowing tribute to Chamberlain's courage, and the same paper subsequently reported that the warmth of his welcome home "indicated a deep feeling of gratitude for his personal effort to preserve peace."[2] His short speech at Heston had been enthusiastically received by the press, and he returned to Downing Street to be met by a crowd of almost 3,000 people. When newsreels featuring scenes from the Berghof were shown that evening in London cinemas, Chamberlain was cheered while Hitler was booed and hissed.[3] On his arrival at Heston, Chamberlain had been given a handwritten letter from the King, asking that he be given firsthand news of the visit at the earliest opportunity.

> I am sending this letter to meet you on your return, as I had no opportunity of telling you before you left how much I admired your courage and wisdom in going to see Hitler in person. You must have been pleased by the universal approval with which your action was received.[4]

The King was taking a keen interest in the developing crisis. He had been forced to travel south from Balmoral anyway for the funeral of his cousin, Prince Arthur of Connaught, and he arrived back in London on the morning that Chamberlain left for Berchtesgaden. While the Prime Minister was away in Germany, the King conferred at Buckingham Palace with several Cabinet ministers, including Halifax, Hoare, Simon and Inskip. He was contemplating making a diplomatic approach of his own, encouraged by his Private Secretary, Sir Alexander Hardinge, that it would "represent the only real contribution that Your Majesty could make to a peaceful solution by approaching the question from an entirely non-political angle."[5] The King duly drafted a handwritten letter to Hitler, "not as one Head of State to another, but rather as one ex-serviceman to another." He recalled the slaughter of the First World War, convinced that Hitler too would be "appalled at the possibility of such a calamity recurring." There were, he continued, too many "hot-heads of a younger generation who do not know the horror that war means, as you and I do."[6] However, when he asked Halifax whether such an initiative might be helpful, the Foreign Secretary's reaction was distinctly lukewarm.

Chamberlain returned to Downing Street at 6:30 P.M., and immediately convened a meeting of the Inner Circle. Runciman, whose flight from Prague had touched down at Heston just a few minutes after the Prime Minister's, joined the usual group of four ministers and three officials. It soon became clear that Chamberlain's private assessment of his meeting with Hitler was not as optimistic as his public statements had implied. Almost as soon as he had arrived at the Berghof, "he had appreciated that the position was well-nigh desperate. Everything was ready for an immediate blow." He was not sure whether Hitler had definitely made up his mind to invade Czechoslovakia, but the air had been "full of fantastic stories," and he thought that Hitler "definitely contemplated that he might strike at any moment." Wilson referred to the unsubstantiated rumors of 300 dead Sudeten Germans, and confirmed that "the atmosphere on arrival in Berchtesgaden had been so excited that they feared that the conversations would not take place."

Chamberlain described his conversation with Hitler in detail, before drawing his own conclusion. "Speaking personally," he told his colleagues, he "did not object to the principle of self-determination, or, indeed, attach very much importance to it." He believed that it was "impossible that the Sudeten Germans and the Czechs would settle down together," and equally inconceivable that Britain should go to war to prevent self-determination for the Sudeten Germans.[7] The Prime Minister looked exhausted, thought Cadogan, but at least he had "held Hitler for the moment"; it was "quite clear that nothing but 'self-determination' will work."[8] When the meeting broke up, Chamberlain answered the royal summons and, at 9:30 P.M., made his way to Buckingham Palace, where he found the King "as excited as a boy."[9] He again described his meeting with Hitler, and told the King of his fear that the Führer was "not bluffing but was fully determined to settle the matter" by force. He believed that his arrival in Germany had delayed the invasion of Czechoslovakia, and that he had "won a breathing-space of a week." King George was not impressed, confessing afterward to his assistant Private Secretary, Alan Lascelles, that he felt "both distressed and perplexed at this news."[10]

In the course of his broadcast at Heston, Chamberlain had accurately, but perhaps foolishly, drawn attention to the fact that he had returned from Germany earlier than expected. The brevity of his talks with Hitler had not gone unnoticed. A junior minister, Harry Crookshank, claimed that everyone was "astounded at Neville's return. No sign of what it means, but one assumes Peace at the expense of the Czechs (morally with dishonour)."[11] Inskip too recorded that it was "a complete surprise to read in the morning press that he was on his way back"; even Mrs. Chamberlain had not known he was returning until she opened her morning copy of *The Times*.[12] Chamberlain had gone to Germany expecting to negotiate with a fellow world leader; he had assumed that he would be able to develop an argument, make concessions where necessary, and finally reach an amicable agreement. In fact, he had been presented with a single, peremptory demand, backed up by the threat of immediate war if it were not met. While his bold stroke in flying to see Hitler had captured the imagination of even his critics, few of them realized that he had gone to Germany hoping not only to solve the Czech crisis, but also to establish a personal relationship with Hitler, and to build a lasting Anglo-German settlement.

Incredibly he returned to London convinced that he had "established a certain confidence" with Hitler, and that "in spite of the hardness and ruthlessness I thought I saw in his face, I got the impression that here was a man who could be relied upon when he had given his word." He regularly repeated the bogus praise that Wilson had been fed by Hitler's closest associates, and boasted that he had heard from a reliable source that he was "the most popular man in Germany."[13] Even Chamberlain's most sympathetic biographer concedes that this reliance on his much vaunted "personal touch" was a "tragic misapprehension,"[14] while Hitler's biographer contends that such claims demonstrate the extent to which he "allowed himself to be deluded by the personality and assurances of Germany's dictator."[15] Halifax's biographer, meanwhile, states that Chamberlain had become "unbearably pleased with himself [and] had suspended all critical judgement of the Führer."[16] A year later, in 1939, Harold Nicolson compared Chamberlain and Wilson's attempt at diplomacy to "the bright faithfulness of two curates entering a pub for the first time; they did not observe the difference between a social gathering and a rough-house; nor did they realise that the tough guys assembled did not speak or understand their language. They imagined that they were as decent and honourable as themselves."[17]

Chamberlain had set out his stall in support of self-determination for the Sudeten Germans and, once that principle had been conceded, it only remained to agree on the mechanics for achieving it; the means chosen, either a plebiscite or a direct transfer, would have a considerable bearing on the amount of territory to be handed over. While Chamberlain was in Germany, the Inner Circle met to discuss the concept of a plebiscite and how it would work. On the morning of September 16 Halifax was visited at the Foreign Office by his old friend, Leo Amery, an acknowledged expert on Czech affairs. Amery had been working for Lloyd George, and therefore present in Paris, during the peace conference of 1919, and knew both Thomas Masaryk and Beneš well; he was also a close friend of Masaryk's son, Jan, now the Czech Minister in London. Amery's advice to Halifax was blunt: "Czechoslovakia should declare itself neutral and be guaranteed," and while a plebiscite was "quite unworkable, it might be possible to make a definite cession of the north west corner which Masaryk had wanted to give up in 1919." Halifax "rather boggled" at the suggestion,[18] but just two days earlier Newton had had a similar conversation with Beneš. The Czech President had "mentioned that some Sudeten Germans lived in areas such as Egerland which in his opinion could have been excluded from Czechoslovakia without endangering the existence of the State." Indeed in 1919 he had himself "suggested their exclusion but the suggestion had never been seriously discussed nor had it been agreed to by other members of his Delegation."[19]

By the time the Cabinet met in emergency weekend session on Saturday, September 17, the rumblings of discontent were growing louder. Several Cabinet ministers had privately expressed doubts of their own. Chips Channon heard "from a private source that Duff [Cooper], Walter Elliot, [Lord] Winterton and, of course, that gloomy Oliver Stanley—'Snow White' as we call him—are likely to be troublesome."[20] Harold Nicolson encountered Vincent Massey, the Canadian High Commissioner, at his club, and asked if Massey thought that the government was likely to agree to Hitler's demands. "It is better to have smallpox three years from now than at once," replied Massey. "Yes, but if we have it now, we shall recover," countered Nicolson. "If in three years, we shall die."[21] Oliver Harvey felt "disgust . . . that we should be reduced to treating with Hitler under a threat."[22] The meeting opened with a pessimistic report from Runciman. He was forced to admit that Henlein "had been in much closer touch with Hitler throughout the period of negotiation than he had previously imagined." Beneš, in his opinion, was "extremely clever . . . on the whole he was inclined to think that he was less dishonest than he appeared to be."[23] Unfortunately the Czech government remained "blind to what was going on around them," and he had therefore "reached the conclusion that Czechoslovakia could not continue to exist as she was today. Something would have to be done, even if it amounted to no more than cutting off certain fringes."[24]

Chamberlain then took up the story. He began with a lengthy description of his journey, the scene at the Berghof, and Hitler's appearance—"the commonest little dog he had ever seen."[25] But even this outspoken criticism of his host failed to impress Duff Cooper. The "curious thing," Cooper recorded, was that Chamberlain "recounted his experiences with some satisfaction." He was clearly delighted by reports of the good impression he had made, and repeated "with obvious satisfaction how Hitler had said to someone that he had felt that he—Chamberlain—was 'a man.' "[26] He had seen "no signs of insanity but many of excitement. Occasionally Herr Hitler would lose the thread of what he was saying and would go off into a tirade. It was impossible not to be impressed with the power of the man. He was extremely determined; he had thought out what he wanted and he meant to get it and he would not brook opposition beyond a certain point." Unbelievably, Chamberlain "had formed the opinion that Herr Hitler's objectives were strictly limited." It all came down, concluded the Prime Minister, to whether or not Hitler meant what he said. "The Prime Minister's view," recorded the official minutes, "was that Herr Hitler was telling the truth."[27]

At this point Chamberlain must have "noted consternation on the faces of some of his colleagues,"[28] as he quickly sought to reassure the Cabinet. When he had arrived in Germany, the situation "had been one of desperate urgency. If he had not gone, hostilities would have started by now. The atmosphere had been electric." Yet again he repeated that all the "information from other sources had been to the effect that the Führer had been most favourably impressed,"[29] but he conspicuously failed to achieve the same effect around the Cabinet table. Cooper recorded that:

> The bare facts of the interview were frightful. None of the elaborate schemes that we had discussed in Cabinet . . . had even been mentioned. He had felt that the atmosphere did not allow of it. After ranting and raving at him, Hitler had talked about self-determination and asked the P.M. whether he accepted the principle. The P.M. had replied that he must consult his colleagues. The P.M. seemed to expect us all to accept that principle without further discussion because the time was getting on.[30]

Even the ultra-loyal Inskip felt uneasy. "The impression made by the P.M.'s story was a little painful," he thought. "It was plain that H. had made all the running: he had in fact blackmailed the P.M."[31]

When the meeting reconvened after lunch the discussion was thrown open to the wider Cabinet. The Lord Chancellor, Lord Maugham, began with a rather tedious exposition of the foreign policy principles of Canning and Disraeli. "Two conditions had to be satisfied before we intervened," he intoned solemnly. "First, that British interests were seriously affected; secondly, that we should only intervene with overwhelming force."[32] British interests, he concluded, were not involved. Cooper thought the intervention "deplorable"; if that argument was taken to its logical extreme, he reasoned, then Britain was unlikely ever again to possess sufficient force to intervene in Europe. Privately, he concluded, "we were in fact finished."[33] He warned that the Cabinet was "in danger of being accused of truckling to Dictators, and offending our best friends." Britain should "make it plain that we would fight rather than agree to an abject surrender."

Cooper was supported, with varying degrees of enthusiasm, by a number of his colleagues. Oliver Stanley objected vigorously to Hitler's "ultimatum," and declared that "if the choice for the Government in the next four days is between surrender and fighting, we ought to fight." Lord Hailsham attempted to rally the Cabinet to Chamberlain's cause with a spectacularly defeatist assertion. While it was not in Britain's interests to see any single power dominate Europe, in effect "that had now come to pass and he thought we had no alternative but to submit to humiliation." This in turn provoked Lord Winterton to make a tangential comparison between the cession of the Sudetenland and British acquiescence "in the invasion of Kent or the surrender of the Isle of Wight." Winterton had already written to Chamberlain, threatening at least three Cabinet resignations if a plebiscite was forced upon the Czechs. Finally, the leader of the National Labour Party, Lord De La Warr, was the sole member of the Cabinet to state categorically that he was "prepared to face war in order to free the world from the continual threat of ultimatums."

Chamberlain, however, would brook no dissent. In what was patently a deeply divided Cabinet, he found himself taking the middle way, supporting neither the pacifist views of the lawyers, nor the more belligerent stance of Cooper and Stanley. Gradually, he reasserted his position, pointing out that the Cabinet had "accepted the principle of self-determination and given him the support he had asked for." In conclusion, he fell back on that well-worn refuge of politicians, the apocryphal postbag. He wished that he could show his colleagues "some of the many letters which he had received in the last few days, which showed the intense feeling of relief throughout the country, and of thankfulness and gratitude for the load which had been lifted, at least temporarily."[34] The meeting ended at 5:40 P.M. with no formal decision having been taken, Chamberlain bragging to his sister that he had "finally overcome all critics, some of whom had been concerting opposition beforehand."[35]

That evening Chamberlain, Halifax and Wilson received a delegation at Downing Street from the National Council of Labour: Hugh Dalton and Herbert Morrison represented the leadership of the Labour Party, and Sir Walter Citrine the Trades Union Congress. The two groups sat three abreast opposite each other across the Cabinet table and, in the course of the hour-and-a-half meeting, the Labour representatives gave the Prime Minister a "rough time."[36] Citrine stated that "British prestige had been gravely lowered by Chamberlain going to see Hitler,"[37] while Dalton emphasized that these were unlikely to be the last of Hitler's demands. "I believe that he intends to go on and on," he told the Prime Minister, "until he dominates first all Central and South Eastern Europe, then all Europe, then the world."[38] Chamberlain responded with platitudes and boasts: "while not wishing to appear egotistical," he believed that he "made a considerable impression on Hitler." That night Dalton wrote a scathing assessment of the Prime Minister.

> The best that can be said of the P.M. is that, within the limits of his ignorance, he is rational, but I am appalled how narrow these limits are, and it is clear that Hitler produced an enormous impression on him, partly by hustling intimidation and partly by a few compliments and words of courtesy. If Hitler had been a British nobleman and Chamberlain a British working man with an inferiority complex, the thing could not have been done better.[39]

The following morning, Sunday, September 18, a French delegation arrived in London. Bonnet had already made clear his irritation at not having been consulted immediately upon Chamberlain's return from Berchtesgaden, a conscious decision by the Foreign Office, for fear that any important information given to the French would inevitably leak.[40] At 11 A.M. Daladier,

Bonnet and various officials from the Quai d'Orsay sat down across the Cabinet table from the usual members of the Inner Circle: Chamberlain, Halifax, Simon and Hoare, who were in turn supported by Cadogan, Vansittart, Wilson and Strang. Chamberlain began with a lengthy, typically matter-of-fact analysis of Runciman's report, and a similarly exhaustive description of his own meeting with Hitler, which, according to Hoare, conveniently provided "the sedative of a long narrative."[41] He brought this dreary monologue to a conclusion by bluntly warning that unless the Sudetenland was transferred to Germany forthwith, "we must expect that Herr Hitler's reply would be to give the order to march."[42]

The ensuing discussion was arduous in the extreme. "We had to listen to Daladier," complained Cadogan, "with voice trembling with carefully modulated emotion, talking of French honour and obligations."[43] It was clear that Daladier and Bonnet were overwhelmed by the emotional strain of attempting both to fulfill their treaty obligations to Czechoslovakia, while at the same time averting war at any cost. Desperate to preserve French diplomatic dignity, they were clearly "at their wits end."[44] Daladier, recorded Hoare, sat "square and squat, his face flushed redder than ever," while Bonnet was "as white as Daladier was red, sensitive, and apparently on the verge of a *crise de nerfs*, made especially sensitive as he had discovered that there were no gas-masks in France."[45] Eventually Daladier was forced to concede that the dilemma he faced was "to discover some means of preventing France from being forced into war as a result of her obligations and at the same time to preserve Czechoslovakia and save as much of that country as was humanly possible."[46]

"As so often in international discussions," recalled Chamberlain the following day, "he had found that the darkest hour was before lunch." However, at lunch the mood lightened. During the morning Daladier had expressed strong opposition to the idea of self-determination by plebiscite, fearing that it would lead to a rush of similar demands from other minorities, but he now told Chamberlain that "he thought he could get M. Beneš to agree to a cession of territory in the particular case of the Sudeten Germans." Bonnet informed Halifax that the major difficulty was "whether Britain was prepared to join us in some form of international guarantee in Czechoslovakia."[47] In all other respects Daladier appeared to be "altogether under the influence" of his Foreign Minister, and for the remainder of the conversation, he sat "glum and silent, acquiescing in Bonnet's sardonic acceptance of the transfer to Germany of the territory of France's ally."[48]

Immediately after lunch, Chamberlain called the Inner Circle together at Downing Street. It was agreed to "offer to join France in a guarantee to Czechoslovakia," conditional on the Czech government agreeing both "to accept a position of neutrality [and] agreeing to act on our advice on issues of peace and war." There followed a perfunctory discussion as to the relative merits of a plebiscite or a direct transfer of territory; no one challenged Hitler's insistence that a German population of over 50 percent would suffice as a condition for transfer. Halifax posed the crucial question: would the Czechs, or would they not, accept such a proposal? "It should be stated pretty bluntly," he continued, "that if Dr. Beneš did not leave himself in our hands we should wash our hands of him." It was concluded that "it should be made quite clear to Dr. Beneš that unless he gave a prompt acceptance of the present proposals the French and British Governments would not hold themselves responsible for the consequences. There was no time to be lost."[49]

The two delegations met again in the Cabinet Room at 3:30 P.M. and within an hour there was sufficient common ground for work to begin across the road at the Foreign Office, drafting a joint Anglo-French telegram to Beneš. When the discussion resumed, Chamberlain agreed to Daladier's proposal that the cession of Sudeten territory should be made by direct transfer rather than plebiscite, but warned that a British guarantee of the remainder of Czechoslovakia would be a "very serious additional liability for this country," one to which he nevertheless agreed.[50] After a further adjournment for dinner, during which the French returned to their embassy to consider the Foreign Office draft, Daladier announced that while he found the proposals deeply "distressing," in "the interests of European peace . . . he felt it was his duty in these painful circumstances to agree."[51] Shortly after midnight, showing signs of considerable strain, Daladier accepted the draft of the telegram to be sent to Beneš, with what Simon described as "the greatest show of gratitude I have ever seen in a spokesman of France."[52] He knew that he was both sacrificing an ally and weakening a strategic border outpost of France, but it was the only choice left available to him.

Chamberlain wanted to dispatch the telegram to Prague immediately, but Daladier insisted on first returning to Paris early the following morning to obtain the approval of his Cabinet. Chamberlain agreed reluctantly, emphasizing that he had no wish to postpone his next meeting with Hitler beyond September 21. Finally, he put one last question to Daladier: what if Beneš said no? Daladier brushed aside such a notion as inconceivable; it could lead only to war and there was no question of the Czechs being left to take a decision of such momentous importance on their own. "The strongest pressure would have to be brought to bear on Dr. Beneš," concluded the French Prime Minister, "to see that the Czechoslovak Government accepted the proposed solution."[53] The meeting finally ended at 12:15 A.M., and Harvey saw the French ministers off from Croydon Aerodrome, noting that "they looked wretched."[54]

At a stormy Cabinet meeting Daladier was vigorously opposed by some of his Cabinet colleagues, most notably the Minister of Colonies, Georges Mandel, and Paul Reynaud. Daladier was forced to concede that the Anglo-French proposals should only be disclosed to Hitler once Prague had agreed to them, and that, in spite of what he had said to Chamberlain just a few hours earlier, no pressure would be put on the Czech government. If the offer was not accepted in its entirety, then existing French obligations to Czechoslovakia would hold good. This assurance was broken almost immediately. When the genial Czech Minister, Stefan Osuský, called on Bonnet at the Quai d'Orsay an hour later, his pleas that France resist Hitler's demands were "met with a terse and sardonic '*Acceptez.*' "[55] "My country has been tried and condemned by a court which did not even summon us to appear," he complained bitterly to the waiting journalists outside. "One of the judges previously went to see Herr Hitler and heard his evidence, but nobody heard ours. Yet one of the judges is a pledged ally and we had hoped that the other was a powerful friend."[56]

The British Cabinet also met that morning, and was once again invited by Chamberlain to ratify a major foreign policy initiative about which he had failed to seek their approval in advance; indeed, unknown to the Cabinet, the Anglo-French proposals had already been dispatched to Prague overnight, and were only awaiting French Cabinet approval before being handed to Beneš. The Cabinet was deeply divided, and a lengthy debate ensued about the proposed guarantee to Czechoslovakia. What other countries would be involved? What precise obligations did it entail? Was it to be a "joint" guarantee, to be implemented only when each and every guarantor wished to enforce it, or was it to be a "several" guarantee, meaning that in theory Britain could be called on to defend Czechoslovakia alone? In response to widespread alarm, Halifax conceded that he too "felt considerable misgivings about the guarantee, but . . . it would have been disastrous if there had been any delay in reaching agreement with the French."[57]

Hore-Belisha was most vociferous in voicing his concerns, principally on the strategic grounds that Czechoslovakia could not be defended. Once the Sudeten German areas had been transferred, it would become "an unstable State economically, would be strategically unsound, and there was no means by which we could implement the guarantee. It was difficult to see how it could survive." The proposals offered nothing more than "a postponement of the evil day."[58] He quickly got into an acrimonious discussion with a "tired and disspirited [sic]" Chamberlain,[59] who replied with disarming honesty that "it was not right to assume that the guarantee committed us to maintaining the existing boundaries of Czechoslovakia [but] merely related to unprovoked aggression. Its main value," he thought, "would be in its deterrent effect." As usual, it was Simon who came to Chamberlain's rescue, telling his colleagues that the French ministers had arrived looking "somewhat woebegone, but they had gone away with heart and courage restored to them by the Prime Minister."[60] The meeting once again endorsed Chamberlain's position.

▪ ▪ ▪

The growing sense of anxiety was not confined to the Cabinet alone. The consensus of approval for the Berchtesgaden "agreement" within the press was also beginning to fracture. On September 16 Lord Beaverbrook wrote to Chamberlain offering his assistance.

> I desire so much that a Minister be appointed to deal with the newspaper proprietors. They are all anxious to follow you. But we are in the dark. It is not information we need; it is guidance . . . to guide the newspapers in their policy, to strike out errors and to crush rumours.

Beaverbrook recommended his old friend Sam Hoare as a suitable go-between with the necessary "balance, judgement and prestige."[61] Hoare began to hold daily meetings with proprietors and editors, bypassing altogether the news departments at both Downing Street and the Foreign Office. His purpose was to calm the prevailing atmosphere of crisis by playing down the serious nature of the situation; his method was a naked appeal to the editors' patriotism. On September 17, the American ambassador Joseph Kennedy saw Hoare shortly after he had held meetings with the editor of the *Daily Herald* and Sir Walter Layton, the chairman of the *News Chronicle*. He had spent two and a half hours "trying to persuade them to have the papers strong on the side of peace. He felt that the *Herald* would play ball. He hoped that Layton would but was not quite sure yet."[62]

Layton did indeed "play ball," but his intervention caused widespread bitterness among his own staff at the *News Chronicle*; until now, the paper's editorial line had been resolutely anti-Hitler. He met Hoare on a regular basis during the latter half of September and, according to his biographer, "behaved more in his old role of Government adviser than as a newspaper man." When one of his young correspondents returned from Prague with a secret document of Henlein's, which purported to reveal the detailed timetable for the German invasion of Czechoslovakia, Layton had publication of the story suppressed; instead he sent the document to Chamberlain, for which he was privately thanked by Hoare.[63] The staunchly anti-appeasing Vernon Bartlett also had his reports from Prague suppressed, and when the paper's editor, Gerald Barry, wrote an anti-Chamberlain editorial, Layton promptly had him replaced as editor.[64]

Nor was it solely the written press that fell under the spell of Downing Street. Although they later denied it, the hierarchy at the BBC also allowed themselves to submit to censorship, in their case under the influence of Sir Horace Wilson. A subsequent internal BBC report on the crisis of September 1938 revealed that "towards the end of August, when the international situation was daily growing more critical," Wilson made a number of veiled threats, for instance that the BBC should "pay particular attention to opinions expressed in talks such as Harold Nicolson's 'The Past Week.' " The same BBC report later confirmed that "news bulletins as a whole inevitably fell into line with Government policy at this critical juncture."[65] On September 22 Paramount News released a newsreel featuring interviews with two senior British journalists who were critical of Chamberlain. British cinema audiences greeted "with considerable applause" the warning that "Germany is marching to a diplomatic triumph. . . . Our people have not been told the truth." The Conservative Central Office complained, Halifax approached Kennedy, and while "there was no question of censorship," Hoare demanded that the offending interviews be removed. Kennedy brought his influence to bear on Paramount's American holding company, and the offending newsreel was quickly withdrawn.[66]

Clearly, however, the mood on Fleet Street was shifting. In spite of Layton's best efforts, on September 19 the *News Chronicle* typified the sense of deep concern. "Would it be considered indelicate," it inquired, "if at this point in this crisis one put in a word for the Czechs?" Two days later it protested that "bewilderment is giving place to a feeling of indignation that Great Britain should be one of the instruments used to compel a small democratic country to agree to self-mutilation under the threat of force."[67] The *Daily Herald* commented angrily that the Czechs had been "betrayed and deserted by those who had given every assurance that there should be no dismemberment of their country,"[68] while the *Daily Telegraph* warned that "a policy which does not command general approval is worse than useless."[69] Even the solidly appeasing *Times*, in its editorial on September 20, conceded that "the general character of the terms submitted to the Czechoslovak Government could not, in the nature of things, be expected to make a strong *prima facie* appeal to them."[70]

Across the political divide too, individual politicians took a stand against the Prime Minister. On September 19 the National Council of Labour, meeting at Southport, heard from Clement Attlee about his meeting with Chamberlain earlier that day. The council subsequently issued a manifesto, stating that it viewed

> with dismay the reported proposals of the British and French Governments for the dismemberment of Czechoslovakia under the brutal threat of armed force by Nazi Germany and without prior consultation with the Czechoslovak Government. It declares that this is a shameful betrayal of a peaceful and democratic people and constitutes a dangerous precedent for the future.[71]

Chamberlain ignored Attlee's accompanying letter demanding the recall of Parliament to discuss the crisis. Sir Archibald Sinclair told the Liberal Party

Council that "we have merely submitted to Herr Hitler's demands and our submission has been extracted, not by a sudden conversion to the justice of his case, but by the threat of war."[72] An unhappy Anthony Eden told a constituency meeting that the "British people know that a stand must be made. They pray that it will not be made too late."[73] Leo Amery had initially written to Chamberlain welcoming his flight to Germany as "a great thing. . . . If the peace of the world is going to be saved, yours will have been the outstanding contribution."[74] Now, however, he was appalled to discover that the terms to which Chamberlain had signed up "amounted to nothing less than [Czechoslovakia's] destruction as an independent state."[75]

Winston Churchill, "in absolute despair at H.M.G.'s policy,"[76] paid a flying visit to Paris, and held a series of meetings with MPs such as Mandel and Reynaud in an attempt to whip up political opposition to the Anglo-French proposals. He only succeeded, however, in offending Bonnet, who was furious at his meddling in French affairs, while Phipps complained bitterly to the Foreign Office that he was "busy giving bad advice to M. Osuský [the Czech Minister] and to certain French politicians."[77] On his return to London Churchill issued an unequivocal statement.

> It is necessary that the nation should realise the magnitude of the disaster into which we are being led. The partition of Czechoslovakia under Anglo-French pressure amounts to a complete surrender by the Western Democracies to the Nazi threat of force . . . the prostration of Europe before the Nazi power.[78]

The Prime Minister did receive staunch support from one quarter, albeit one that was not particularly welcome. During his stay at Balmoral, Chamberlain had discussed with the King the increasingly persistent demands from the Duke of Windsor that he should be permitted to visit Britain. A lengthy exchange of correspondence ensued, as Chamberlain tried to smooth the exiled Duke's ruffled feathers. On September 18, the Duke wrote again from his bolt-hole in the south of France.

> Let me first of all say how much I regret that circumstances should have made my raising of the question of the Duchess' and my return to England coincide with the major European crisis which has descended

upon us. . . . I would wish to express on behalf of the Duchess and myself, our very sincere admiration for the courageous manner in which you threw convention and precedent to the winds by seeking a personal meeting with Herr Hitler and flying to Germany. It was a bold step to take, but if I may so, one after my own heart, as I have always believed in personal contact as the best policy in "a tight corner."[79]

In fact, Chamberlain came closer than he probably realized to a potentially nightmarish diplomatic incident. Having visited Hitler at Berchtesgaden the previous year, the Duke now seriously considered making a "bold step" of his own. His plan was to offer himself as a mediator, and to make a second impromptu visit to Germany, where he would "expostulate with Hitler."[80] Fortunately he was talked out of it by friends who feared that such a visit would have been "disastrous in its effect on public opinion both in England, which was on the brink of war with Germany, and in the United States, where it would revive the legend of his Nazi sympathies."[81]

Although the Czech reply to the Anglo-French proposals had still not been received, the Cabinet met during the afternoon of September 21 to agree on the guidelines that Chamberlain should adopt in his next conversation with Hitler. A Foreign Office discussion paper warned that "if Hitler is true to form, we must be prepared . . . for him to make further demands under the threat of war." At Berchtesgaden he had fabricated the massacre of 300 Sudeten Germans, and on the next occasion he would "no doubt be able to invent a state of affairs which will enable him to maintain that the situation has deteriorated . . . in such a way that he is no longer able to accept as a settlement what he had then demanded."[82] Cadogan agreed that such a scenario was likely, but even so stressed that "it was quite clear that we have gone to our limit," and that if Hitler was again to up his demands, "he will have gone beyond our limit, and there will be nothing more to be done but to oppose them. . . . Our moral position will be all the stronger for having strained to the utmost to give him satisfaction, and his position before the world will be all the worse."[83]

The Cabinet was consequently warned that there was increasing evidence that Hitler might add the territorial claims of Hungary and Poland to those of the Sudeten Germans. Chamberlain "did not think that Herr Hitler was likely to take up this attitude," but agreed that if the matter were raised he would refuse to discuss it and would "say that he must return home to consult his colleagues."[84] Regarding the proposed guarantee to Czechoslovakia, it was agreed that he should negotiate on the basis that France, Great Britain and Russia would act as joint guarantors, and that Germany should sign a nonaggression pact of her own with Czechoslovakia. Finally the meeting discussed at length the proposed modus operandi for effecting the transfer of the Sudeten areas. Chamberlain thought that there was a "good deal to be said on practical grounds for allowing the occupation at an early date by regular German troops of those areas in which the German inhabitants constituted a very large majority." He also suggested that British troops might be utilized as peacekeepers in areas with a mixed population. Both suggestions drew immediate criticism from his colleagues. Stanley was unhappy at the idea that a single German soldier should cross the border, while Cooper assumed that German troops would simply find an excuse to overrun the rest of Czechoslovakia. The Prime Minister, he suggested, "should indicate to Herr Hitler that if he made any further demands we should go to war with him, not to prevent the Sudeten Germans from exercising self-determination, but to stop Herr Hitler from dominating Europe."[85]

■ ■ ■

Chamberlain was convinced that he had single-handedly prevented the outbreak of war and, if he could only persuade his own, the French and the Czechoslovak governments to agree to the annexation of the Sudetenland to the Reich, that war could be averted in the long run also. In fact, while British and French ministers met in London to debate how best to carve up Czechoslovakia, Hitler had carried on regardless with his preparations for invasion. Before leaving Berlin to join the gathering at Berchtesgaden, Keitel[86] had called in the chiefs of staff of the army and Luftwaffe to consider "what could be done if the Führer insists on advancing the date [for invasion], owing to the rapid development of the situation." All three men agreed that this would be logistically impossible, principally because the railway schedules for the transportation of troops could not be altered. Jodl noted that "the new railway schedule is effective only as of September 28th. Thus we are bound to the date which the Führer has chosen."[87] Furthermore, every available day was needed to complete the construction of the West Wall. On September 16, as Chamberlain was traveling home to London, the order was given that the Reinforced Frontier Guard should be arranged along the Czech border; and all spare railway rolling stock was to be secretly made ready for the strategic movement of the army, to commence on September 28.[88]

"Führer told Chamberlain yesterday," began the confidential telegram sent by the German Foreign Ministry to its overseas delegations, "that he was finally resolved to put an end in one way or another to the intolerable conditions in Sudetenland within a very short time. Autonomy for Sudeten Germans is no longer being considered, but only cession of the region to Germany." Ominously, the telegram concluded that "methods of doing this are still being arranged."[89] Jodl, meanwhile, collaborated with the Propaganda Ministry over "joint preparations for refutation of our own violations of international law."[90] It was Goebbels's job to justify Nazi excesses, and his propaganda machine was already in full swing. "WOMEN AND CHILDREN MOWED DOWN BY CZECH ARMOURED CARS," announced one headline, while the *Börsen Zeitung* alleged "POISON GAS ATTACK ON AUSSIG."[91] On September 17 the Foreign Ministry ordered the Prague legation to instruct all "Reich-Germans in regions with Czechoslovak population, without attracting attention and only verbally, to send women and children out of the country."[92] On September 18 the jumping-off schedule for five armies, comprising thirty-six divisions, was dispatched to commanders.

Meanwhile Hitler played host at the Berghof to a second English guest, George Ward Price of the *Daily Mail*, who had succeeded in securing an exclusive interview with the Führer. Hitler's remarks should have left readers of the *Daily Mail* in no doubt as to his intentions. The interview opened peacefully enough, with Hitler maintaining that he was "convinced of Mr. Chamberlain's sincerity and good will." But his language quickly became more menacing, as he began to address Ward Price "in a low tone of grim determination."

This Czech trouble has got to be ended once and for all, and ended now. It is a tumour which is poisoning the whole European organism. . . . Herr Gott, what couldn't I do in Germany and for Germany if it were not for this infernal Czech tyranny over a few million Germans. But it must stop. It *shall* stop. To set an intellectually inferior handful of Czechs to rule over minorities belonging to races like the Germans, Poles, Hungarians, with a thousand years of culture behind them, was a work of folly and ignorance.[93]

By referring to Poles and Hungarians in the same breath as Germans, Hitler was giving notice that they formed an important part of his planning for the dismemberment of Czechoslovakia. On September 20 he received the Hungarian Prime Minister and Foreign Minister at Berchtesgaden and "reproached the Hungarian gentlemen for the undecided attitude of Hungary." He was "determined to settle the Czech question even at the risk of a world war," and this was "Hungary's last opportunity to join in." He suggested that they should immediately demand a plebiscite in the territory over which Hungary had staked a claim, and should refuse to join any international guarantee of Czechoslovakia's proposed new borders. "The Führer declared," read the official minute of the meeting, "that he would present the German demands to Chamberlain with brutal frankness. In his opinion, action by the Army would provide the only satisfactory solution," although he was worried by the prospect of the "danger of the Czechs submitting to every demand."[94]

The Polish ambassador, Józef Lipski, arrived at the Berghof almost as soon as the Hungarian delegation had left. Göring had recently suggested to Lipski that "Poland should categorically insist on a plebiscite in the region inhabited by Polish population, using all possible means of pressure agitation." Now, with Ribbentrop also present, Hitler railed against the Czechs, although Lipski found him distracted and "very much absorbed by his approaching talk with Chamberlain." However, he again told the ambassador that he intended to "use armed force to annex the Sudetenland to the Reich," and promised unconditional support if Poland joined in the conflict.[95] On September 21 Poland formally demanded a plebiscite in the contested Teschen region of Czechoslovakia, and moved troops up to the border. This led the Soviet Vice-Commissar for Foreign Affairs, Vladimir Potemkin, to present a strongly worded note to the Polish chargé d'affaires in Moscow, warning that any incursion into Czechoslovakia by Polish troops would lead to Russia denouncing the Polish-Soviet nonaggression pact.

Hitler recognized the need to take additional steps to ensure that war would indeed break out once his elaborate military preparations were complete. Having assured Chamberlain that no military action would be undertaken before they met again, he now set about doing exactly the opposite. He had repeatedly insisted on the proviso, in his conversations with both Chamberlain and with foreign diplomats, that he could only guarantee that he would take no action against Czechoslovakia in the continuing absence of any unforeseen acts of aggression against the German population there. Unfortunately for Hitler, in the aftermath of Henlein and his hard-line associates fleeing the country, a relative calm had settled on the Sudeten areas, which now threatened to undermine the political pretext of disorder that was needed to justify invasion. Hitler therefore set about doing what he had promised Chamberlain he would not do, namely arranging for acts of provocation to take place throughout the Sudeten areas that would provide him with his pretext for war.

Henlein's parting proclamation had failed to induce a spontaneous uprising among his people, and Hitler therefore needed to find an alternative means of fomenting revolt. His chosen method was the establishment of the Sudeten German Freikorps, a terrorist organization which brought together and armed all those Sudeten Germans who had fled Czechoslovakia for Germany. They were given the job of protecting the Sudeten German population in the border areas, arranging clashes and disturbances in the Sudetenland, and mounting attacks on Czechoslovak frontier installations along the length of the German-Czechoslovak border. Although Henlein was placed nominally in command, he was provided with a high-level Wehrmacht adviser, Lieutenant Colonel Köchling, who received his orders direct from the Führer.[96] By September 19, membership of the Freikorps was reported to have reached 40,000 and on the same day the legation in Prague reported that it had commenced "small-scale actions."[97] In fact, the Freikorps was to prove excessively successful, and became if anything too zealous for the tastes of the Wehrmacht high command. When its operations led to sizable units of the Czech army being brought up to the border, Hitler was forced to instruct Köchling that the Freikorps should show some restraint.

■ ■ ■

While British and French ministers met in London, and Hitler prepared for war at the Berghof, the people of Prague spent the weekend bathed in glorious late-summer sunshine, "waiting in a mood of stunned stoicism to learn their fate."[98] The respective Czech ministers in London and Paris, Masaryk and Osuský, had tried to some extent to prepare their political masters in Prague for what was about to happen. On September 18, while the British and French Prime Ministers were still in conference, Masaryk had anticipated the likely outcome by presenting an official démarche to Halifax. He warned that the Czechs took it "for granted that no decision will be taken without their previously being consulted," but that in the absence of such consultation, they "could not take any responsibility for decisions made without them."[99] When, on September 19, the British and French Cabinets approved the text of their joint message to Beneš, they realized that their very worst fears had indeed been confirmed.

At 2 P.M. that afternoon, Newton and his French counterpart, Victor de Lacroix, made their way to Hradčany Castle to present the so-called Anglo-French plan to Beneš. It was to be made clear to him that both governments now agreed that it was impossible for "the districts mainly inhabited by the Sudeten-Deutsch" to remain within Czechoslovakia "without imperilling the interests of Czechoslovakia herself and of European peace." The territory in question should be "transferred to the Reich" forthwith, to ensure "the maintenance of peace and the safety of Czechoslovakia's vital interests." This could be effected either by plebiscite or direct transfer—the British and French favored the latter—and "would probably have to include areas with over 50 per cent of German inhabitants." Where necessary, frontier revision would be negotiated by "some international body including a Czech representative," and the same body would be responsible for "questions of possible exchange of population." Finally, the British government was willing to join in "an international guarantee of the new boundaries of the Czechoslovak State against unprovoked aggression," but only on the strict condition that Czechoslovakia agreed to revoke all existing military treaties.

After dealing with Runciman all summer, Beneš had long since appreciated that he could not rely on British support when standing up to Hitler. Now, however, he was also confronted by the defection of his closest ally, France, the likely loss of Czechoslovakia's militarily strategic frontier, and a demand to sever his vital military treaty with Russia. This presented him with a cruel dilemma. To accept was inconceivable: it would entail surrendering all Czechoslovakia's frontier fortifications to the Reich, and would create a minority of as many as 800,000 Czechs living under Nazi rule. Yet to reject the proposals would lead to war, certainly between Czechoslovakia and Germany, and probably a general European conflict, for which the blame would be laid squarely at his door. With appalling insincerity, the French and British governments claimed to "recognise how great is the sacrifice thus required of the Czechoslovak Government in the cause of peace." They nevertheless insisted on a reply "at earliest possible moment" since Chamberlain "must resume conversation with Herr Hitler not later than Wednesday [September 21]."[100]

After Newton had finished speaking, Beneš was initially so "greatly moved and agitated" that he refused to discuss the matter at all; he was "a constitutional President and would need to consult both his Government and Parliament." A visibly embarrassed Newton explained that speed was of the essence. The Prime Minister's return visit to Hitler could be delayed by no more than a further forty-eight hours, and it was imperative that he was in possession of Prague's reply before he traveled. When Beneš finally collected his thoughts sufficiently to respond, he spoke "with self-control but with bitterness." He understood, he told the two diplomats, that "after all the efforts which he and his Government had made, they were being abandoned." The guarantees he already possessed had been proved worthless. Furthermore, far from providing closure, the proposed solution would ultimately prove to be no more than "a stage towards eventual domination by Germany." As justification, he referred Newton to Ward Price's interview with Hitler in that morning's *Daily Mail.*

Newton nevertheless reported to London that Beneš was "more likely to accept than to refuse," and was "very receptive to any reason which will help him to justify acceptance to his people."[101] By the time that Newton and de Lacroix left Hradčany Castle, the contents of the Anglo-French proposals were widely known throughout Prague. While British newspapers had maintained an attitude of coy discretion, their French counterparts, "owing to a leakage from French sources" according to Phipps,[102] had carried lengthy and accurate details of the terms that were to be forced upon the Czechs. The Prague press faithfully reproduced the proposals and, throughout the day, small groups of bewildered people gathered together around the city's newspaper vendors, as the bare facts of their betrayal slowly dawned on them. Initial disbelief soon gave way to anger and defiance, and a "grim and bitter mood,"[103] especially toward France, settled on Prague and the Czech people. The leading local newspaper, the *Lidové noviny*, tersely summed up the mood with a banner headline over its leading article: "UNACCEPT-ABLE."[104]

On the afternoon of September 19 Beneš summoned his ministers, the leaders of the six coalition parties, and his military chiefs of staff to an emergency Cabinet meeting; they sat for a day and a half, throughout the night, in almost continuous session. Even the pessimists among them had not expected to be presented with such peremptory demands; but still no one spoke up in favor of accepting the proposals. At 11 A.M. the following morning a message reached Newton that a reply was expected by early afternoon. But the hours ticked by, and at 2:15 P.M. Phipps reported a conversation with Bonnet, who had been told that the Czechs were wavering between two possible solutions: "(1) appeal to arbitration or (2) accept basis of Franco-British plan." Bonnet had subsequently ordered de Lacroix to intervene urgently, and to warn Beneš "that (1) would be folly and would mean war and that (2) is the only possible course for M. Beneš to take." He suggested that Newton should make similar representations.[105] At 3:30 P.M. an enciphered telephone message reached the Quai d'Orsay from de Lacroix. He had carried out Bonnet's instructions and, during a meeting with the Czech Foreign Minister, Dr. Kamil Krofta, had "urged the impossibility for Czechoslovakia in the present circumstances of retaining within her frontiers . . . a population which was now animated by a positive hatred for the state and which furthermore, had the backing of that huge country Germany."[106]

When the Czech reply had still not been received by 6:30 P.M., it was reluctantly decided in London that Chamberlain's second visit to Hitler would have to be postponed, at least for a further day. Finally, at 7:45 P.M. the reply was handed to Newton and de Lacroix by Krofta, although the full text did not reach London until the early hours of the following morning. In a dignified response, the Czech government rejected the Anglo-French plan. They did not believe that the proposals would bring about peace; they had not been consulted; and such substantial frontier revision could not take place without the approval of Parliament. Acceptance of the proposals would be unconstitutional, and would lead to the "complete mutilation of [the Czechoslovak] State in every respect." Instead, the entire Sudeten question should be submitted to international arbitration under the terms of the German-Czech Treaty of Arbitration, signed at Locarno in 1925. The French in particular were reminded of their own treaty obligations toward Czechoslovakia.

> Czechoslovakia has always been bound by the most devoted esteem and friendship as well as by an alliance in respect of which no Government and no single Czechoslovak will ever fail.[107]

Newton beseeched a clearly distressed Krofta to reconsider, and warned that rejection of the Anglo-French plan "meant the destruction of his beautiful country." He reminded Krofta that Chamberlain was flying back to see Hitler again the following day, and "how disastrous it would be for Czechoslovakia if he came without any satisfactory reply from Prague." The suggestion of arbitration could only lead to war.[108] De Lacroix had the even more unenviable task, as the representative of Czechoslovakia's principal ally, of endorsing Newton's warning. Soon after the meeting had ended, de Lacroix was summoned to see the Czech Prime Minister, Mílan Hodža. "Could Czechoslovakia count on French help or could she not?" he was asked. De Lacroix was initially too overcome to respond, and burst into tears. Although he had no definite instructions, he replied, his personal belief was that French military support would not be forthcoming. At this, Hodža insisted that de Lacroix obtain written confirmation from Paris, emphatically stating that France would back out of their treaty if it came to war. "It was the only way of saving the peace," Hodža asserted.[109]

In London the Czech reply was received with ill-disguised petulance. Chamberlain had waited anxiously all day and, after persistent requests from Berlin and Berchtesgaden for clarification of his travel plans, had eventually been forced to agree to a suggestion from Ribbentrop that his visit should be postponed by a day. Therefore, when news of the Czech refusal eventually came through that evening, the Prime Minister was furious. However, in an attempt to soften the blow, Newton claimed to have information from "an even better source" that the official Czech refusal was not necessarily the last word in the matter. It is possible that he too had been privately told by the apparently duplicitous Hodža that the Czech government would capitulate if sufficient pressure was applied. He suggested that he should deliver an "ultimatum" to Beneš that the proposals be accepted "without reserve and without further delay failing which His Majesty's Government will take no further interest in the fate of the country."[110] At 11 P.M. Halifax was hurriedly summoned back to Downing Street from his home, where he, Chamberlain and Wilson, in the words of Cadogan, "drafted [a] reply driving the screw home on [the] poor Czechs."[111]

At 1:20 A.M. on Wednesday, September 21, Newton received further instructions.

> You should at once join with your French colleague in pointing out to Czech Government that their reply in no way meets the critical situation which Anglo-French proposals were designed to avert, and if adhered to would, when made public, in our opinion lead to an immediate German invasion. You should urge the Czech Government to withdraw this reply and urgently consider an alternative that takes account of realities.

If the Czech refusal became publicly known, Halifax warned Newton, there would be no point in Chamberlain returning to Germany.

> We therefore beg Czech Government to consider urgently and seriously before producing a situation for which we could take no responsibility. If on reconsideration the Czech Government feel bound to reject our advice, they must of course be free to take any action they think appropriate. Please act immediately on receipt at whatever hour.[112]

Newton took the Foreign Secretary at his word and, soon after 2 A.M., an exhausted Beneš was hauled out of bed at Hradčany Castle to meet the British and French ministers. It was barely an hour since he had gotten to sleep for the first time in three days, and he was clearly not thinking straight. Both diplomats read out the identical instructions they had received from their respective political masters. De Lacroix made it clear that if Czechoslovakia refused to accept the Anglo-French plan and war were to break out, then the Czech government would be held solely responsible and France would take no part. "*La France ne s'y associera pas,*" he concluded unequivocally.[113] Beneš noticed that the Frenchman had "tears in his eyes," while Newton behaved coldly, shuffling uneasily and constantly looking down at the floor. The meaning of the double démarche was clear. Britain would not fight to protect Czechoslovakia, while France was repudiating treaty obligations which, until now, had been considered sacrosanct. "I had the impression," wrote Beneš, "that both of them were ashamed to the bottom of their hearts of the mission they had to discharge."[114]

Beneš, still exhausted, tried to argue. He produced a map, and raised all sorts of technical difficulties about the proposed transfer of population, the problems of refugees, and the offer of a guarantee. Again and again Newton and de Lacroix repeated that they were unable to discuss the minutiae of the proposals, which had to be accepted without reservations. But still Beneš could not bring himself to acknowledge the inevitable. The proposals, he claimed, were an ultimatum, and he was constitutionally obliged once again to consult his government; they would have a reply by midday. Dawn was breaking over Prague when Newton and de Lacroix finally left the Hradčany at 4 A.M. A few Western correspondents, tipped off that something important was afoot, made their way to the castle, and found that Beneš had already summoned his senior ministers to a meeting. It took just an hour for them to agree that they had no option but to accept the Anglo-French proposals, and at 6:30 A.M. the full Cabinet began a three-hour meeting. Meanwhile Hodža's Private Secretary telephoned Newton to convey the "personal and preliminary information" that the reply was to be "affirmative," and that the "official reply will be sent as soon as possible." This news reached London at 7:30 A.M.[115]

Although the full Cabinet ratified the decision, the army chiefs of staff and the leaders of the other political parties urged Beneš to reject the proposals. But persistent pressure was applied on the Czechs throughout the day, both in Prague and in London, where Masaryk had "taken to his bed with grief," and was either "unable or unwilling" to visit Halifax to receive a further demand.[116] Beneš asked Newton for written confirmation of the verbal assurances he had been given during their meeting in the early hours, in particular that "if Czechoslovakia accepts the Anglo-French proposals and if none the less German Government attacks Czechoslovakia the two Governments will come to her assistance." Newton bluntly warned him that "it was extremely dangerous to make new conditions for acceptance at this last minute."[117] By late afternoon, there was still no reply from the Hradčany.

As the news spread that surrender was imminent, everyday life in Prague came to a standstill, as offices, factories and even apartments emptied. All day the city's streets swarmed with people, the great Wenceslas Square serving as a vast amphitheater where loudspeakers were fitted to the lampposts along its length. Armed troops were posted outside the British legation for its protection. At 5 P.M. the Czech government finally and "sadly" capitulated—"*forcé par les circonstances et les insistences des gouvernements français et britannique.*" Krofta summoned Newton and de Lacroix to the Foreign Ministry and reluctantly handed them Czechoslovakia's acceptance of the Anglo-French proposals.[118] "We have been disgracefully betrayed," protested Beneš. At 7 P.M. the news that all Prague had been dreading was broadcast over the loudspeakers in Wenceslas Square. "We had no other choice," declared the Government, "because we were left alone." History, continued the Propaganda Minister, would "pronounce its judgement on the events of these days. Let us have confidence in ourselves. Let us believe in the genius of our nation. We shall not surrender, we shall hold the land of our fathers."[119]

Almost at once, in the gathering darkness, a huge crowd began to make its way toward the Hradčany, a vast dark silhouette against the sky. At the head of the procession was the red, white and blue tricolor, the national flag of Czechoslovakia; the crowd sang the national anthem. Crossing the river by the Baroque-styled Charles Bridge, they marched up the hill to the square below the castle's gates. The *Daily Express* correspondent, Geoffrey Cox, recorded the scene:

> There was little fanaticism, only a mixed air of confusion and determination. Here was a man carrying a briefcase, on his way home from work. There a group of students. Behind them factory workers in black leather jackets, their hands still black from the work bench. Women led children by the hand. Well-dressed people came out of cafés to join the march. They all pressed on up the hill, under the blue-shaded street lights.

At the entrance to the street that wound up to the castle, their way was blocked by fifty mounted police; but after a halfhearted attempt to break through the cordon, the crowd stayed where it was, and the police mingled with the demonstrators.

Violence was not their aim. Instead they stood in the darkness, singing and chanting their slogans until after a couple of hours they began to drift away.[120]

The following morning there was a general strike in Prague, and an even larger mass demonstration; thousands congregated in factories, in the suburbs and in the surrounding villages, before marching to Wenceslas Square. There, over 100,000 people demanded a military government, and a program of national resistance. At 10 A.M. it was announced from the balcony of Parliament that Hodža's government, by now a symbol of capitulation, had resigned. In its place Beneš appointed a new, nonpolitical Government of National Defense, to be headed by General Jan Syrový, the Inspector General of the army. Syrový's appointment was greeted ecstatically. He was a heroic military figure, untainted by politics, who had commanded the legendary Czechoslovak Legion in Russia during the First World War. Having first battled against the Germans, the legion had subsequently fought its way back to freedom from Siberia, this time against the Bolsheviks. His status as a national hero was personified by the black patch he wore over his right eye, disguising an old war wound. Syrový addressed the crowds from the same balcony.

> I guarantee that the Army stands and will stand on our frontiers to defend our liberty to the last. I may soon call upon you here to take an active part in the defence of our country in which we all long to join.[121]

At these words the population of Prague began to drift away and return to work, relieved that the policy of surrender was apparently to be consigned to the past.

■

12

On the Banks of the Rhine

I labour for peace, but when I speak unto them thereof, they make them ready to battle.

Psalm 120: 7

In his view Herr Hitler had certain standards; he would not deliberately deceive a man whom he respected, and he was sure that Herr Hitler now felt some respect for him. . . . He thought that he had now established an influence over Herr Hitler, and that the latter trusted him. The Prime Minister believed that Herr Hitler was speaking the truth.

Neville Chamberlain, Cabinet minutes, September 24, 1938

Chamberlain left Heston at 10:45 A.M. on the morning of September 22, bound for the spa town of Bad Godesberg near Cologne. He again addressed the assembled press on the tarmac.

A peaceful solution of the Czechoslovakia problem is an essential preliminary to a better understanding between the British and German peoples; and that, in turn, is the indispensable foundation of European peace. European peace is what I am aiming at, and I hope this journey may open the way to get it.[1]

He was relieved to read the weather report issued by the Air Ministry at 8:30 A.M. "Conditions generally good. Wind 20–30 m.p.h. Not likely to be 'bumpy.' "[2] *The Times* reported that the plane in which he was to fly, a Lockheed 14 Super Electra, had the previous Sunday "established a civil aviation record by flying from London to Stockholm and back in a single day," and was soon to be put into service on a new route to West Africa. The same two pilots were to be in charge of the Prime Minister's flight.[3]

For this journey Chamberlain took with him not only Wilson, but also a small Foreign Office team, comprising William Strang, the head of the Central Department, Sir William Malkin, the head of the Legal Department, and two secretaries. Malkin's presence was a sure sign that Chamberlain hoped to use this meeting to deal with the practical intricacies of implementing the understanding he had already reached with Hitler at Berchtesgaden. The party landed at Cologne soon after 12:30 P.M., where they were met by Henderson and Kirkpatrick, as well as by a still more impressive welcoming committee than had greeted Chamberlain the previous week. Waiting on the tarmac was a "galaxy of dignitaries," including Ribbentrop, Weizsäcker and Ambassador Dirksen from the London embassy.[4] Chamberlain was invited to inspect an SS "guard of honour of youthful giants, with black steel helmets, black uniforms, white collars and white gloves." Meanwhile the band of the SS-Leibstandarte Adolf Hitler struck up with gusto their own rendition of "God Save the King."[5]

From the airfield Chamberlain was driven to his hotel in a large black Mercedes, the Union Jack and swastika flying side by side on the hood; the roads were lined with cheering crowds, and decked out with alternately hung swastikas and Union Jacks. The sumptuous Hotel Petersberg sat on a hilltop across the Rhine from Godesberg, and enjoyed spectacular views from its terraces and windows over the river, the town, and the local countryside. "Hitler is Germany's greatest travel agent," the *Daily Express* breathlessly told its readers. "The season has been bad this year, but he has sold a trip to the Rhine to Britain's Prime Minister."

The hotel enjoys the finest view in Germany, on the top of the first of the Seven Hills of the Rhine. The Prime Minister undoubtedly has the better view. His balcony looks straight out on the furry-backed mountains, and fields spreading like lawns under his window. The harvest is stacked in the valley, and the swastika flags wave like poppies in the village below.

However, 1,000 feet below the river looks placid and smooth. The hotel looks out on the Drachenfels, those shadowy mountain crags, where the Lorelei and Goth legends were bred.

Two floors had been reserved for the exclusive use of Chamberlain and his entourage. After an inspection of the rooms, the German Foreign Ministry had

ordered a complete change in the furnishing and telephoned for a suite of Louis Quinze furniture from Munich. Hydrangeas were imported, and the marble dining hall, which looks like a tiled bathroom, has been flooded with flowers. A double guard of Scotland-Yard men and Stormtroopers will watch the corridors.[6]

The hotel was owned by Peter Mülhens, the heir to the Eau de Cologne empire, which had been founded by an ancestor 150 years earlier. According to the "Londoner's Diary" column of the *Evening Standard*, Mülhens was now "one of the richest industrialists and largest landowners in Germany"; he owned farms and vineyards, and more than a hundred racehorses, all of which ran in the blue and gold livery which also graced his cologne bottles. He was "the only man alive to know the secret formula for manufacturing Eau de Cologne. He mixes the necessary essences himself, behind locked double-doors, and at his death will pass the secret on to his son."[7] To the delight of the British delegation, their rooms were well stocked with fruit, cigars and no fewer than fifteen samples of Mülhens's products: hair lotion, shaving cream, soap and bath salts. Kirkpatrick, like many hotel guests before and since, "appropriated a discreet number . . . as compensation" for his wife.[8]

Hitler knew the Petersberg well; he was a frequent visitor for coffee on the terrace, from where he enjoyed the panoramic views. On the opposite bank of the Rhine, in the town of Godesberg itself, he set up his own headquarters at the Hotel Dreesen, which was also to be the venue for the talks. Once again, the *Daily Express* emphasized the positive. "The Dreesen family—father Fritz, his wife and their very blond sons and daughters—entertain the Führer in a simple, easy way. Here he is happiest, and usually on holiday." It was true that Hitler did have permanent access to his own suite overlooking the river, with double soundproofed doors. He had stayed every autumn for the past ten years, although the room was held reserved for him throughout the year, and in his absence the hotel sold off his towels, pillowcases and water bottles as souvenirs; large photographs of him adorned the common parts.[9] However, what the correspondent failed to tell his readers was that Herr Dreesen was widely known as the "Führer of the German hotel industry," that his Nazi Party card bore one of the earliest membership numbers, and that it was at the Dreesen that Hitler had plotted the so-called Night of the Long Knives, resulting in the murder of Ernst Röhm and his SA cronies in Munich on June 30, 1934.[10]

For the talks with Chamberlain the Dreesen had been emptied of guests; like the Petersberg it had been given a spring-cleaning, and decked out with dozens of swastikas and the occasional Union Jack. Hitler had arrived by train from Berlin that morning and the whole town had turned out to see him driven from the station; a lorry with a film camera drove in front of his car to record his every move. William Shirer had traveled from Prague to Godesberg to cover the meeting for CBS radio, and was having breakfast on the terrace of the Dreesen that morning. As Hitler strode past on his way to the riverbank to inspect his yacht, Shirer observed that he "was in a highly nervous state." He also noticed that the Führer had a "very curious walk indeed, very ladylike," and a "peculiar tic" which caused him nervously to cock his right shoulder. That, and the "ugly, black patches under his eyes," led Shirer to presume that Hitler "seemed to be on the edge of a nervous breakdown." A popular rumor within the German press corps was that when in a rage Hitler would lose control, and "fling himself to the floor and chew the edge of the carpet." Hence he had acquired the sobriquet "*Teppichfresser*," or "carpet-eater."[11]

After a light lunch at the Petersberg, Chamberlain was driven down the hill and on to a waiting ferry to make the short trip across the river, escorted by two police launches. Thousands of onlookers lined both banks, as far as the eye could see, in a scene that reminded Henderson of the Thames on the day of the University Boat Race. It was a short drive from the ferry to the Dreesen, and the streets were again packed with silent crowds. Kirkpatrick noted that the hotel lobby was "filled with a mob of Third Reich nabobs in variegated uniforms";[12] Chamberlain, however, "looking the image of an owl" according to Shirer, "was smiling and apparently highly pleased in his vain way with some manufactured applause by a company of S.S. guards." An air of expectancy filled the lobby as the word went round: *"Der Führer kommt."*[13] As bodies were pressed flat against the walls, Hitler swept in, looking neither to the left nor to the right. With ostentatious affability he shook Chamberlain warmly by the hand, and inquired politely about the quality of the accommodation at the Petersberg. The two leaders then made their way upstairs, preceded by an SS guard, to the first-floor room where the talks were to take place.

The most striking thing about the small, unimpressive conference room was the magnificent view over the Rhine and the Siebengebirge mountains. There were twenty chairs around a long table, covered with a green baize tablecloth. A writing pad and propelling pencil was neatly laid out, one at each place setting; a bunch of scarlet and purple dahlias had been arranged as a centerpiece; and a framed photograph of the Führer, draped in a garland of bay leaves, dominated the wall at one end of the room.[14] Hitler took his place at the head of the table, and motioned to the Prime Minister to take the chair to his right. Not wishing to repeat the mistakes of Berchtesgaden, Chamberlain was this time accompanied by Kirkpatrick, to act as his interpreter, who took his place to Hitler's left alongside the ubiquitous Paul Schmidt. Beyond the four men lay "a long vista of green baize and empty chairs." There was silence, until Hitler motioned toward Chamberlain, as if to say "your move."[15]

The Prime Minister had arrived in Godesberg in confident mood. Having accepted the principle of self-determination for the Sudeten Germans at Berchtesgaden, he had subsequently succeeded in persuading first his own Cabinet, then the French ministers, and finally the Czech government that they too should all abide by the agreement he had reached with Hitler. In doing so, he had scored a success which most people, including Hitler, had thought impossible. Now he was returning to Germany as the peacemaker; the warmth of the welcome he received from the crowds at the airport, and in the towns and villages through which he had passed, only confirmed his belief that the German and British people were at one in their burning desire for peace. He had chosen to ignore the recent warning signs emanating from Germany—the violent attacks on the Czechs in the Berlin press, and the rumors of Hitler's meetings with Hungarian and Polish ministers. He now looked forward to an amicable discussion with the Führer, one that would deal solely with the practical implementation of the Anglo-French plan. "I had only to discuss with him the proposals I had brought with me," he later told the House of Commons.[16]

Chamberlain had prepared a lengthy opening statement, which he was determined to deliver in full. He recalled the agreement reached at Berchtesgaden, and gave a protracted explanation of how he had secured the acquiescence of the British Cabinet, the French government, and finally the Czechs themselves. It now remained only to discuss the ways and means of transferring the territory in an orderly manner from Czechoslovakia to Germany. He outlined the comprehensive plan he had drawn up for this, suggesting that an international commission, composed of one Czech, one German, and a neutral chairman, should be appointed to demarcate the new frontier. He spoke of safeguards for those who found themselves on the wrong side of the new border, the question of the ownership of state property, and concluded by describing the international guarantee which was to be given to Czechoslovakia, and the proposed nonaggression pact with Germany. At last he finished speaking, and leaned back in his chair with a self-satisfied look on his face, one that Schmidt construed as implying: "Haven't I worked splendidly during these five days?"[17]

Hitler thanked Chamberlain "for his great efforts to reach a peaceful solution," and cautiously inquired whether the proposals that he had just outlined "were those he had submitted to the Czechoslovak Government."

"Yes," replied Chamberlain, without hesitation.[18]

To Schmidt's surprise, and Kirkpatrick's horror, Hitler gazed down at the table and in a dry, rasping voice, replied almost regretfully: *"Es tut mir furchtbar leid, aber das geht nicht mehr."*[19] With that he pushed his chair back from the table, crossed his legs and folded his arms, and turned to scowl at the Prime Minister while Schmidt interpreted. "I'm awfully sorry, Mr. Chamberlain, but this is not possible any more. I can no longer discuss these matters. This solution, after the developments of the last few days, is no longer practicable."[20] Chamberlain sat bolt upright, his face flushed with anger, and for a few moments was too astonished to speak. After what seemed like an interminably painful silence, he at last composed himself sufficiently to ask Hitler the reason for his sudden change of mind.

As the Foreign Office had warned was likely, Hitler calmly introduced two entirely new demands into the discussion. First, he insisted that he was now unable to contemplate any agreement until the territorial demands of Hungary and Poland, "which had his full sympathy," were also met. Second, he now demanded that the timetable be greatly speeded up.

> He must emphasise that the problem was now in a most critical stage. In his view no delay was possible. . . . There were, as the whole world knew, military preparations on both sides, but this situation could not be held for very long and a solution must be found one way or another, either by agreement or by force. He desired to say, categorically, that the problem must be settled definitely and completely by the 1st October at the latest.

Warming to his theme, he worked himself up into a fury, painting a lurid picture of Sudeten Germans being terrorized by the Czech authorities. The "people of the streets were being mobilised, and the Bolsheviks were threatening to take the rudder." In the Sudetenland entire villages had been deserted after "the men had been arrested or conscripted [and] there were only the children left wandering uncared for in the streets or the fields." From time to time messages were brought into the room reporting fresh atrocities against the Sudeten Germans.

With masterful understatement, Chamberlain could only manage to reply that he was "both disappointed and puzzled" by what he had heard, and repeated his earlier assurance that Hitler had achieved everything he had demanded at Berchtesgaden "without the expenditure of a drop of German blood." Plaintively, he remarked that in persuading his critics to accept Hitler's demands, "he had been obliged to take his political life into his hands"; as an illustration of his difficulties, "he had actually been booed on his departure today." Hitler, however, was utterly unimpressed by this display of self-indulgence. Producing a map, he declared that "a frontier line must be drawn at once . . . from which the Czechs must withdraw the army, police and all State organs; this area would at once be occupied by Germany." The border would be demarcated on the basis of language, and he would accept a plebiscite in the occupied territory using the 1918 census; any German who had emigrated since 1918 would still be allowed to vote, while all those Czechs "who had since been planted there" would not. He would not consider the issue of indemnification of any Czechs for their property, nor join in any international guarantee to the rump of Czechoslovakia.

After three hours the meeting broke up in disarray. Ribbentrop, Wilson and Henderson joined in briefly toward the end to consider the new map, and a "desultory discussion" took place about plebiscite numbers. Even this was interrupted when a message was brought in stating that twelve Sudeten German hostages had been executed, prompting a further outburst from Hitler. His sole concession was to assure Chamberlain that, pending a further meeting, "he would give instructions at once to General Keitel that no military action was to be taken."[21] This was, of course, no concession whatsoever, since the invasion was still scheduled to begin on October 1. In fact Keitel did telephone OKW headquarters in Berlin. "Date cannot yet be ascertained," he reported. "Continue preparations according to plan. If Case Green occurs, it will not be before September 30. If it occurs sooner, it will probably be improvised."[22] The two leaders agreed to meet again the following morning and, as they left the hotel, Hitler underwent a sudden change of temperament. "Oh, Mr. Prime Minister," he murmured. "I am so sorry. I had looked forward to showing you this beautiful view of the Rhine, but now it is hidden by the mist."[23] A despondent Chamberlain was ferried back across the Rhine to the safety of the Petersberg.

▪ ▪ ▪

While Chamberlain argued with Hitler in Godesberg, war fever had gripped London. On the night of September 22 the Ministry of Health issued a statement on the BBC.

> 34 hospitals in the London area have been allotted as clearing stations for air raid casualties, and detailed plans have been prepared for removing between three and four thousand patients by ambulance trains to towns over 50 miles from London. Casualties would be taken to the railway stations in motor coaches converted to carry stretchers.[24]

At the same time, the Prime Minister's stock was falling. A Mass-Observation poll found that 44 percent of those questioned expressed themselves to be "indignant" at Chamberlain's policy, while only 18 percent were supportive.

Noticeably, men who were questioned expressed their readiness to fight, 67 percent responding positively to the "indignant" question. The *Daily Star* ran a cartoon of Chamberlain flying to see Hitler above the caption "Coming Sir."[25] And that evening a crowd of over 10,000 people massed in Whitehall, shouting "Stand by the Czechs!" and "Chamberlain must go!"[26]

Political opinion too was shifting. Chamberlain was rapidly losing the confidence of some of his senior ministers, most notably his Foreign Secretary. On the morning of September 22 Duff Cooper arrived at the Admiralty to discover copies of Foreign Office telegrams suggesting that the Cabinet's agreed line had been overturned, and which instead "seemed to envisage our agreeing to the early occupation of Czechoslovakia by German troops." He immediately wrote to Halifax to complain, and received a reply to the effect that the Foreign Secretary "entirely agreed [and] that he had no intention of allowing German troops to enter Czechoslovakia except with the consent of the Czechoslovak Government."[27] At 3 P.M., just as Chamberlain was sitting down with Hitler at the Dreesen, the Inner Circle convened in his absence in Halifax's room at the Foreign Office. The usual group was joined by the Dominions Secretary, Malcolm MacDonald, and Sir Thomas Inskip; the meeting began with a discussion about the wisdom of drafting a statement for the BBC, given the "possibility of a break with Germany if things went badly" in Godesberg. "There was all the difference in the world," it was agreed, "between an immediate but orderly settlement of the German-Sudeten question, and forcible annexation to be followed by the activities of the Gestapo."[28]

The sense of unease was heightened by disturbing telegrams from both Prague and Berlin, with the news that the Sudeten towns of Asch and Eger had been occupied overnight by Freikorps troops, who had crossed the border into Czechoslovakia from Germany. In Berlin, François-Poncet and the British Counselor, Sir George Ogilvie-Forbes (acting in Henderson's absence in Godesberg), called at the Wilhelmstrasse to present notes of protest; both men were given a "laconic" answer, to the effect that the stories were a "complete fabrication." However, the official German news agency, Deutsches Nachrichten Büro, was not so modest. "Swastika flags are flying over the town hall at Eger and over the church," it reported. By late afternoon the Berlin evening press was openly boasting that the "German flag is flying over Asch."[29] Meanwhile, the official Nazi Party newspaper, the *Völkischer Beobachter,* made its views clear: "Away with the Beneš State!"[30]

The previous week, on September 18, while the French ministers were in London, the British and French governments had jointly persuaded the Czech government to postpone any mobilization of its armed forces pending the further negotiations at Godesberg. Since then, the more militant Syrový had assumed control, and was demanding that the advice be lifted. The assembled members of the Inner Circle now conceded that "it would be very difficult for us to defend the action taken in urging the Czechoslovak Army not to mobilise if an immediate German attack was launched against the country."[31] The French agreed, and at 8 P.M. the instruction was dispatched to Newton that the "Czechoslovak Government be informed that French and British Governments cannot continue to take responsibility of advising them not to mobilise." The message was not, however, to be delivered until 9 P.M. that night.[32]

Open disagreement now broke out between London and the British delegation in Godesberg. On their return to the Hotel Petersberg after the initial meeting with Hitler, Wilson telephoned the Foreign Office to report that the "conversations today had been 'pretty difficult' and they were all rather exhausted." Both he and the Prime Minister strongly opposed any move to allow the Czechs to mobilize, and hoped that they "may just hold the fort for tonight."[33] They were both adamant that "nothing should be done which would result in a rupture of the Prime Minister's conversation. It was feared that the effect of an announcement that night in Prague of mobilisation, coupled with a statement that this was taken on our advice, might have disastrous consequences on the Bad Godesberg conversations." Therefore when the Inner Circle met again at 9:30 P.M., for the second time that day, it was reluctantly agreed to tell Newton to delay delivery of the proposed message to the Czech government.

After the disastrous first round of talks, the British delegation in Godesberg spent the rest of the evening pondering their next move. While Kirkpatrick was up until 4 A.M. writing up the minutes of the meeting, Chamberlain spoke to Halifax at 10:30 P.M. to inform him, with splendid understatement, that the "interview with Herr Hitler had been most unsatisfactory," and that he "might have to return tomorrow."[34] At 2 A.M. a telegram further informed the Foreign Secretary that Chamberlain had decided to write to Hitler "giving cogent reasons why his proposal is unacceptable."[35] Wilson worked virtually throughout the night and, the following morning soon after breakfast, a letter was dispatched across the Rhine. In spite of the cordial nature of Chamberlain's greeting—"My dear Reich Chancellor"—the Prime Minister made clear his objections to Hitler's proposals; according to Schmidt, "its impact was explosive."[36]

Chamberlain made no reference to the territorial claims of the Hungarian and Polish minorities, but instead focused on Hitler's unreasonable demand that military occupation should be immediate. While he was happy to submit the Führer's proposed new frontiers to the Czech government, he insisted that occupation of those areas by German troops "would be condemned as an unnecessary display of force."

> I do not think you have realised the impossibility of my agreeing to put forward any plan unless I have reason to suppose that it will be considered by public opinion in my country, France and indeed in the world generally as carrying out the principles agreed upon in an orderly fashion and freedom [*sic*] from threat of force.

In the event that German troops entered the Sudetenland, he was sure that "the Czechoslovak government would have no option but to order their forces to resist." As an alternative, he proposed suggesting to the Czech government that "there could be an agreement whereby law and order in certain agreed Sudeten German areas would be entrusted to Sudeten Germans themselves by creation of a suitable force."[37] Hitler reacted by canceling the meeting that was to have taken place that morning, and instead spent several hours closeted with Ribbentrop at the Dreesen.

Across the river at the Petersberg, Chamberlain and Henderson spent the morning pacing nervously up and down the terrace of the hotel, awaiting Hitler's reply, and with nothing more than the magnificent view to console them. It was, according to *The Times*, "a day of the most acute suspense."[38] Lunchtime came and went, and there was still no word from the Führer, while dozens of journalists representing the world's press waited impatiently for news on both sides of the river. Meanwhile a fleet of black cars was kept on permanent standby, with their engines running. At 1:30 P.M. a telegram arrived from Halifax, warning that the French were now extremely concerned that the advice against mobilization, previously given to the Czech government, had not been withdrawn. At 2 P.M. Wilson telephoned the Foreign Office, pointing out that they were still waiting for Hitler's reply, and that they "thought the Foreign Secretary should wait a little longer before making the communication [to the Czechs]. It was added that the communication should point out that such action by them may very well precipitate action by others."[39]

Wilson spent much of the morning on the telephone to Downing Street, planning the next stage in this remarkable early example of shuttle diplomacy; he was clearly enjoying the cloak-and-dagger atmosphere. At 10 A.M. he asked the duty officer at Downing Street to ensure that "the two aeroplanes which took the Prime Minister's party to Godesberg were standing by and were ready for all emergencies." He emphasized particularly "that they could be used if necessary for a journey to some other destination than London." All communication with the pilots at Cologne was to be done through Downing Street and British Airways, so that the delegation at Godesberg "should not have to send any message to the pilots which might arouse excitement in Germany." Early that afternoon Wilson ordered the pilots to be placed on standby, and to "be ready to proceed anywhere at short notice—even Egypt." From this remark the duty officer deduced "that it might be necessary for the party to go to Prague; the direct route from Cologne to Egypt would pass over Prague." Although the Prime Minister's plane had a range of a thousand miles, the pilots did not have the relevant maps with them; ironically, they would have "to borrow them from Luft Hansa," who had "a very complete library in Cologne."[40]

Just how seriously Chamberlain considered making a flying visit to Prague, presumably to promote Hitler's terms to Beneš in person, will never be known. At 3 P.M. there was finally some sign of life at the Dreesen, as Schmidt emerged from the hotel carrying a large brown envelope; he was chauffeured across the river in a black Mercedes, keenly watched by hundreds of pairs of eyes. As he climbed out of the car at the entrance to the Petersberg, he was surrounded by a crowd of journalists. "Do you bring peace or war?" shouted out one American correspondent, but Schmidt gave no clue as to the contents of the envelope, pushing his way through the throng and into the hotel.[41] Upstairs he found Chamberlain on his balcony, who greeted Hitler's emissary with a remarkable display of sangfroid;

"undismayed, with the calmness of a summer visitor enjoying his holiday," Schmidt noted admiringly.[42] There had been no time to provide a written translation of the five-page letter, so Chamberlain invited Schmidt into the room he was using as a study, where the interpreter translated it in person, with Henderson, Wilson and Kirkpatrick also present.

Hitler's reply, wrote a contemporary historian, was "written in the spirit of a military commander, who, in the middle of a war, demands the surrender of some town or district that lies at his mercy."[43] With considerable understatement, Chamberlain later told the Cabinet that "the tone was not as courteous or as considerate as one would wish, but it was worth remembering that the Germans were apt to express themselves curtly."[44] The letter contained a largely predictable reiteration of the previous day's demands, as well as age-old Nazi grievances: the brutal repression of the Sudeten Germans, the alleged iniquities of the Treaty of Versailles, and the Reich's lack of faith in promises from whatever quarter. Hitler was not interested "in the recognition of the principle" that the Sudetenland should be annexed to Germany, but "solely the realization of this principle . . . which both puts an end in the shortest time to the suffering of the unhappy victims of Czech tyranny, and at the same time corresponds to the dignity of a Great Power." He concluded with yet another threat of force. If, as now appeared to be the case, Germany found it impossible "to have the clear rights of Germans in Czechoslovakia accepted by way of negotiation," then she would be "determined to exhaust the other possibilities which then alone remain open to her."[45]

When Schmidt returned to the Dreesen, having had once again to battle his way through the waiting horde of journalists, Hitler appeared visibly anxious. "What did he say? How did he take my letter?" he asked nervously. An hour later, at 6 P.M., Wilson and Henderson crossed the river, and handed Chamberlain's conciliatory reply to Ribbentrop: the Prime Minister offered to act as an intermediary with the Czechs, and invited Hitler to set out his proposals in a memorandum, with an accompanying map, which he could forward on to them. In the meantime, he again sought reassurance that there would be no recourse to military force while this process continued and announced that, once he had received the required document, he would be returning to London. This threat of departure appears to have had the desired effect. After leaving Wilson and Henderson alone while he conferred with Hitler, Ribbentrop returned to propose that a further meeting should take place between the two leaders later that evening, at which Hitler would explain the memorandum to Chamberlain in person.

Unfortunately for the Prime Minister, he was no longer negotiating in a vacuum. Although Godesberg must have seemed a long way from London, he still could not fail to have realized from the exchange of telegrams that sympathy for his stance in the face of Hitler's demands was on the wane, even among some of his most loyal supporters. At 3 P.M., just as Schmidt was reading Hitler's letter to Chamberlain at the Petersberg, Halifax convened a further meeting of the Inner Circle in his room at the Foreign Office; the usual group was again joined by MacDonald and Inskip. Halifax informed his colleagues that he had decided to ignore the strong opinions expressed by Chamberlain and Wilson in Godesberg, and that it had "accordingly been agreed to dispatch [the] telegram to Prague authorising our Minister to withdraw the advice" against Czech mobilization. The only proviso, with one eye on events in Germany, was that Vansittart should urge upon Masaryk "the importance of avoiding needless publicity, in Czechoslovakia's own interests."

Ominously for Chamberlain, the Foreign Secretary also reported that there were "rumblings from unnamed Cabinet Ministers that they didn't know what was going on." He failed to admit that by now he counted himself among their number, indeed that the messages emanating from Godesberg were considered increasingly opaque by everyone who had read them.[46] "I think we are in the soup over this," he complained to Harvey as the mobilization telegram was dispatched to Prague.[47] At 4 P.M. Duff Cooper was summoned to a meeting with Sir John Simon, along with several other skeptical ministers. To Cooper's great surprise he found Chamberlain's most ardent cheerleader "in a robust mood—quite prepared for the fray," and quite happy that the ban on Czech mobilization had been lifted, "in spite of a rather feeble protest from the Prime Minister." When he returned to the Admiralty, Cooper took it upon himself to authorize the recalling of men from leave, the increase of all crews to full complement, and the dispatch of almost 2,000 men to the Mediterranean to support the fleet there and to man the defenses in the Suez Canal.[48]

According to the Foreign Secretary's biographer, Hitler's demands on September 23 "marked the turning-point in Halifax's attitude towards

Hitler and Nazism. The positive, Christian side of appeasement, that of balming wounds and righting legitimate grievances, was wholly absent from this crisis."[49] At 9:30 P.M. the Inner Circle met again, and considerable disquiet was expressed at the substance of yet more messages from Wilson in Godesberg. The Prime Minister was to cross the river to see Hitler one last time and "if there is any loophole we shall stay," reported Wilson. "If not we shall come home. We are telling Prague that we are expecting a Memorandum later this evening and that they may like to defer their decision until they see it when they get it tonight." This further attempt to delay Czech mobilization was too much for Halifax, who was particularly anxious that "the Godesberg conversations should end on some simpler and stronger statement than, on the available information, the Prime Minister seemed to contemplate."[50]

At 10 P.M. Halifax sent a strongly worded message to Chamberlain in his own name.

> It may help you if we give you some indication of what seems predominant public opinion as expressed in press and elsewhere. While mistrustful of our plan but prepared perhaps to accept it with reluctance as alternative to war, great mass of public opinion seems to be hardening in sense of feeling that we have gone to limit of concession and that it is up to Chancellor to make some contribution. . . . From point of view of your own position, that of Government, and of the country, it seems to your colleagues of vital importance that you should not leave without making it plain to Chancellor if possible by special interview that, after great concessions made by Czechoslovak Government, for him to reject opportunity of peaceful solution in favour of one that must involve war would be an unpardonable crime against humanity.[51]

At 10:30 P.M. Chamberlain again crossed the Rhine, and was greeted by Hitler in the lobby of the Dreesen; the two leaders posed for photographs that were to be flashed around the world. The presence of Henderson, Kirkpatrick, Ribbentrop and Weizsäcker, and the need for space to spread out the maps that had been prepared for the meeting, necessitated that it took place in the hotel's ground-floor dining room. "All the best people are invited," joked one of Schmidt's colleagues sarcastically, after hearing that

Ribbentrop had finally managed to inveigle his way into the talks. The three-hour meeting, "one of the most dramatic in the whole Sudeten crisis," according to Schmidt, began shortly before 11 P.M.[52] Hitler surprised Chamberlain with the warmth of his welcome, thanking him effusively for his efforts to preserve peace and his political courage; he hoped that it would still be possible to reach a peaceful solution. However, the illusion did not last long. Schmidt was asked to translate the memorandum that had been prepared for the Prime Minister and it soon became clear that Hitler's demands were even more extreme than previously feared.

According to Hitler's memorandum, the latest reports from the Sudetenland proved "that the situation has become completely intolerable for the Sudeten people and, in consequence, a danger to the peace of Europe." It was essential that the transfer of territory "should be effected without any further delay." Hitler now demanded the complete withdrawal of all Czech forces from an area depicted on an accompanying map; the evacuation was to begin on September 26, and to be completed two days later. The territory to be ceded immediately was shaded red on the map, while other areas, where plebiscites would be held, were shaded green. Only voters who had been resident in the area in 1918 would be eligible to vote. Furthermore, the territory was to be handed over "in its present condition," and no attempt was to be made to destroy or "render unusable in any way military, economic or traffic establishments"; the same restriction applied to all utility services. The precise wording of the appendix to the memorandum made clear the severity of this stipulation: "Finally no food-stuffs, goods, cattle, raw materials etc. are to be removed."[53] The Czechs of the Sudetenland were to begin the evacuation of their homes in just over two days' time, and were to be gone within four, without taking so much as a single cow with them.

Chamberlain was appalled. "But that's an ultimatum," he exclaimed, throwing his copy on the table in disgust, and getting up from his chair as if to leave. "*Ein Diktat,*" interjected Henderson, who always enjoyed an opportunity to show off his German, and knew it to be an emotive word for Hitler, who had for years used it to describe the Treaty of Versailles. "With the most profound regret and disappointment, Chancellor," continued Chamberlain, "I have to state that you have made no effort to assist my attempts to secure peace."[54] Hitler, who was wholly unaccustomed to being addressed in such language, in turn "looked pained" at the vehemence of the Prime Minister's reaction. Chamberlain was, Hitler assured him, "grievously mistaken."[55] It was "nothing of the sort," he continued. "It is not a *diktat* at all: look, the document is headed by the word 'memorandum.' "[56] But Chamberlain remained unimpressed by such semantics and now spoke "very frankly." It was not, he later recalled, the contents of the memorandum that caused him such offense, but rather the "language and the manner of the document, which . . . would profoundly shock public opinion in neutral countries, and I bitterly reproached the Chancellor for his failure to respond."[57]

At this crucial moment a message was brought into the room and handed to Hitler. After reading it slowly, he gave it to Schmidt. "Read this to Mr. Chamberlain," he asked. The interpreter cautiously read it out aloud: "Beneš has just announced over the wireless general mobilisation of the Czechoslovak forces." There was a stunned silence in the room, everyone sharing the same thought, that war was now inevitable.[58] Eventually Hitler himself broke the silence. "In spite of this provocation, this unheard-of provocation," he murmured, in a scarcely audible voice, "I shall keep to my undertaking not to proceed against Czechoslovakia, not to use force while these negotiations are on—at any rate while you, Mr. Chamberlain, remain on German soil."[59] The tension relaxed noticeably. "After the big-drum beat of Czech mobilisation," recorded Schmidt, "there was silence for a few bars." Chamberlain removed his spectacles and a pencil from his pocket, and began to go through the memorandum line by line. By the time he had finished, he had secured a few minor textual alterations and one modest concession from Hitler. "To please you Mr. Chamberlain," he said, "I will make a concession over the matter of the time-table. You are one of the few men for whom I have ever done such a thing." Chamberlain appeared delighted by this bogus flattery. The new deadline for the transfer of the Sudetenland was to be October 1; conveniently, of course, long since Hitler's projected date for the invasion of Czechoslovakia.

It was by now 2 A.M., and the meeting concluded, according to Schmidt, "in a thoroughly amiable atmosphere."[60] The two leaders shared a few words in private, before Chamberlain bid Hitler a "hearty farewell." The Prime Minister "had the feeling that a relationship of confidence had grown up between himself and the Führer as a result of the conversations of the last few days," and that once the current crisis had been resolved, "then he would be glad to discuss other problems still outstanding with the Führer in the same spirit."[61] Crucially, Hitler then repeated "with great earnestness" the assurance he had given at Berchtesgaden, that "this was the last of his territorial ambitions in Europe and that he had no wish to include in the Reich people of other races than Germans."[62] William Shirer, who had stayed up to report on the conclusion of the conference and was in a makeshift broadcasting studio in the hotel lobby, watched at close quarters as the two leaders said their farewells; he was "struck by their cordiality to each other."[63] In the small hours of Saturday, September 24, the British delegation were once again ferried back across the Rhine. "Oh I am tired," complained Chamberlain, as he arrived back at the Petersberg. "Is the position hopeless, sir?" he was asked by a waiting journalist. "I would not like to say that," he answered. "It is up to the Czechs now."[64]

▪ ▪ ▪

Shortly after 10 P.M. on the evening of Friday, September 23, the Prague correspondent of the *Daily Express*, Geoffrey Cox, had just finished dictating his copy for that night's edition over the telephone to his London office. Although Chamberlain and Hitler were still negotiating in Godesberg, word had got out that Hitler's demands were severe, and Prague was a city preparing for war. As Cox was about to hang up, his Czech assistant motioned to him that he should stay on the line. An army reservist, he had just been called by a friend in the War Ministry to advise him to leave work immediately and go home to say goodbye to his wife— a general mobilization was to be announced in a few minutes' time. Sure enough, acting on the advice of the British and French governments that had finally been communicated by Newton and de Lacroix that evening, Beneš had ordered an immediate mobilization. At 10:30 P.M. the announcement was broadcast on the radio, in the six languages of the Republic: Czech, Slovak, German, Hungarian, Ruthenian and Polish. Cox was able to dictate a further story, confirming the mobilization, moments before all telephone lines out of Czechoslovakia were cut off. He had secured himself a scoop.[65]

Hardly had the proclamation been broadcast than army reservists began to obey the order to report at once to their muster station. Cox's report, which had to be smuggled out of the country, appeared in the following Monday's *Daily Express.*

> Men rushing wildly through the streets so as to get to their homes for their equipment, the crowds packing the Wenceslas Square, grim-faced, dreading the thought of war, but grateful that the chance of defending their country, rather than surrendering it without a fight, seemed near. The guards who were rushed to every public building, men and women taking farewells at street corners, in hotel lobbies, on the station platforms, here a man walking to the train with his ten-year-old son proudly carrying his suitcase, there a group of soldiers roaring off towards the frontier through cheering crowds. War seemed then right at hand. When the first black-out came at one A.M. there were few who did not expect to hear the roar of the bombers any minute. But there was no panic, little alarm.[66]

The willingness of the Czechs to fight was abundantly evident. They did not merely obey the call-up order, they "leapt to arms with an indescribable enthusiasm to face the onslaught." Theaters and cinemas cut short performances; cafés, restaurants and bars emptied within moments; all nonreservists were politely asked to vacate the trams to allow hordes of men to crowd in and be ferried across the city; civilian air raid wardens appeared, as if by magic, to replace the police on the streets who had answered the call-up; and those reservists who could not hitch a ride in a car, taxi or tram marched in groups to their gathering points, proudly led by one of their number carrying the national flag. Meanwhile, in spite of an appeal from Henlein on German-speaking radio that no German should obey the mobilization order, many German Social Democrats joined up with the same alacrity as their Czech neighbors.

Eric Gedye of the *Daily Telegraph* was in a restaurant at the time, sitting just a few feet away from two of Henlein's closest associates; one of them, Ernst Kundt, had led the negotiations with the Runciman Mission. Halfway through dinner, their waiter put down his tray, threw off his apron and ran out by the nearest door. Angrily they demanded to know where the waiter had gone, only to be told, to their dismay, that he had answered the call to mobilize. Both Kundt and his colleague were later arrested.[67] All street lamps in the city were extinguished, air raid wardens patrolled the streets, and everyone carried a gas mask; the management at the Hotel Alcron, formerly Runciman's headquarters, provided one for every guest. For all that anyone knew, the German bombers might arrive at any moment. The mobilization was complete within four hours, and by the end of the night Czechoslovakia's frontier fortifications were fully manned. "Calm in Prague," reported the German military attaché, almost approvingly, to Berlin. "Last mobilization measures taken. Total of men mobilized according to estimates, one million. Army in the field, eight hundred thousand."[68]

In fact there was to be no declaration of war that night, and the following day the Czech government received the gruesome details of Hitler's Godesberg demands. Chamberlain had promised that he would act as intermediary, and the German memorandum was communicated to Prague in two contrasting ways. Schmidt's translation was telegraphed direct to Newton overnight, who handed it to Foreign Minister Krofta that evening. However, it was also necessary somehow to present the Czechs with the original German text, and accompanying map. They were entrusted to the British military attaché in Berlin, Colonel Mason-MacFarlane. Known to everyone as "Mason-Mac," he was a larger-than-life figure who traveled around Germany inspecting military installations in his Rolls-Royce, and was hugely popular within the diplomatic community, where he was known as the "Austrian Scot" due to his strong Viennese accent. He is nowadays remembered for making the apparently serious proposition, to the Berlin correspondent of *The Times* in 1938, that he should assassinate Hitler to further the cause of world peace. His Berlin apartment overlooked the saluting platform where the Führer would review the army during his birthday parade. "Easy rifle shot," Mason-Mac remarked casually. "I could pick the bastard off from here easy as winking, and what's more I'm thinking of doing it."[69]

Mason-MacFarlane was a committed anti-appeaser who had little sympathy with either Chamberlain, or his own immediate chief, Henderson. He was far from happy at being asked to act as Hitler's courier, but recognized that after Czech mobilization there was no prospect of his making the journey to Prague by conventional means. Instead, he embarked on an expedition worthy of Richard Hannay. He returned to Berlin from Godesberg, before leaving by car with only the Czech assistant military attaché for company. They reached the frontier at Zinnwald at dusk, but were told by the border guards that the road ahead was impassable. As they pondered their next move, the Czech guardhouse at the frontier came under fire from a Freikorps patrol, and so they set off on foot through the forest. Two hours later, having cut their way through barbed wire fences, they reached the nearest town, Teplitz-Schönau—a "bedraggled spectacle, their hands and faces torn by brambles and bloody, clothes soaked and clinging to their bodies." There, a car was provided to take them to Prague, and the documents were finally handed over at the British legation after midnight. When Mason-MacFarlane crossed the border back into Germany the following morning, he was horrified to be welcomed by a group of local SS and Freikorps, and to be loudly thanked by their commanding officer "for having acted as the Führer's messenger."[70]

▪ ▪ ▪

After just a few hours' sleep at the Petersberg, Chamberlain left for London and arrived back at Heston at 1:15 P.M. He was reportedly given a "cordial reception by crowd," while "his attitude was cheerful and hopeful." He again addressed the press.

> My first duty, now that I have come back, is to report to the British and French Governments the result of my mission, and until I have done that it will be difficult for me to say anything about it. I will only say this: I trust that all concerned will continue their efforts to solve the Czechoslovakia problem peaceably, because on that turns the peace of Europe in our time.[71]

At 3:30 P.M. Chamberlain summoned the Inner Circle to Downing Street. He was, he assured his colleagues, entirely "satisfied that Herr Hitler was speaking the truth when he said that he regarded this question as a racial question," and that the Sudetenland represented the limit of his territorial ambitions. He was also sure that Hitler "regarded the terms offered as his last word, and that if they were rejected he would fight. If war broke out, in any case Czechoslovakia would be over-run . . . and there would be an end of the country." He concluded by boasting that he had won important concessions from the Führer, and of his certainty that "Herr Hitler would not go back on his word once he had given it him."

At this stage, only Hoare distanced himself from the mood of self-congratulation, although he chose his words carefully. The government, he warned, might well "find difficulty in carrying acceptance of the German proposals unless there was something to put on the other side."[72] Cadogan had already seen Hitler's memorandum, which he thought "awful," and had arrived at Downing Street privately thanking God that Chamberlain "hasn't yet recommended it for acceptance." In the course of the meeting, however, it gradually became clear that that was precisely what the Prime Minister intended to do. "I was completely horrified," recorded Cadogan. "He was quite calmly for total surrender. . . . Hitler has evidently hypnotised him to a point." Worse still, Chamberlain had in turn "hypnotised H[alifax] who capitulates totally." Simon, meanwhile, who had been surprisingly bellicose during Chamberlain's absence, now recognized "which way the cat was jumping" and once again fell into line behind the Prime Minister.[73]

After half an hour's rest, Chamberlain addressed the full Cabinet at 5:30 P.M., looking "none the worse for his experiences." He spoke for an hour, going over the detail of his talks with Hitler, and explaining the memorandum. Although he claimed that "he 'snorted' with indignation when he read the German terms," he still made it clear to his colleagues that "he considered we should accept those terms and that we should advise the Czechs to do so."[74] He believed that "Herr Hitler had certain standards . . . he would not deliberately deceive a man whom he respected and with whom he had been in negotiation, and he was sure that Herr Hitler now felt some respect for him." He was furthermore convinced that "Herr Hitler was speaking the truth," and it would be "a great tragedy" if the opportunity were lost of "reaching an understanding with Germany on all points of difference." With breathtaking conceit and naïveté, he concluded that "he thought that he had now established an influence over Herr Hitler, and that the latter trusted him and was willing to work with him."[75]

As soon as the discussion was thrown open to the floor, it became obvious that the Prime Minister had misjudged his audience. Hore-Belisha called for the army to be mobilized. It was, he contended, "the only argument Hitler would understand." To Chamberlain's intense annoyance, he then warned that the Cabinet "would never be forgiven if there were a sudden attack on us and we had failed to take the proper steps."[76] Hore-Belisha was supported by Duff Cooper, Walter Elliot, Oliver Stanley and the two peers, lords Winterton and De La Warr. Cooper, as at previous meetings, was the most vociferous. Hitherto he had anticipated only two possible outcomes to the crisis—"the unpleasant alternatives of peace with dishonour or war." Now he foresaw a third possibility, "namely war with dishonour," by which he meant "being kicked into war by the boot of public opinion, when those for who we were fighting had already been defeated." Chamberlain's supporters, Simon and Hoare in particular, remained unusually silent, as Cooper continued with his argument. The chiefs of staff, he pointed out, had already called for mobilization—"we might some day have to explain why we had disregarded their advice." This riled Chamberlain, who responded angrily that the advice had only been given on the assumption that war was imminent. Cooper commented dryly that it was "difficult to deny that any such danger existed." As it was agreed to adjourn the meeting until the following morning, Cooper reflected that "Hitler has cast a spell over Neville."[77]

This point of view was fast gaining currency. After the Cabinet meeting, Winterton hurried round to seek the advice of his friend and fellow Privy Counselor, Leo Amery. There were, he admitted, "at least four or five [Cabinet members] who were seriously contemplating resignation."[78] Amery was one of Chamberlain's oldest political friends, a protégé of his father, and a neighboring Birmingham MP for many years; until this moment he had offered the Prime Minister his qualified support. Now, however, as he wrote to the former Australian Prime Minister Billy Hughes, Chamberlain had "come back with Hitler's incredible ultimatum asking the Czechs to put their necks in his halter . . . and was inclined to think that we ought to tell the Czechs to accept!"[79] Over the next twenty-four hours Amery worked feverishly to try to change the government's mind. "Almost everyone I have met," he wrote to Halifax, "has been appalled by the so-called 'peace' we have forced upon the Czechs."[80] Early the next morning he composed an even stronger letter to Chamberlain, which he delivered to Downing Street himself. How, he asked, could Chamberlain expect the Czechs "to commit such an act of folly and cowardice"? If he failed to stand up to Hitler, he risked making Britain look "ridiculous as well as contemptible in the eyes of the world." Amery concluded with a prescient warning.

If the country and the House should once suppose that you were prepared to acquiesce in or even endorse this latest demand, there would be a tremendous feeling of revulsion against you.[81]

Although Amery was neither politically nor socially close to Eden, he chose this moment to seek the former Foreign Secretary's support. Eden was already busy canvassing opinion himself. When Jan Masaryk, the Czech Minister, heard the details of the Godesberg terms on the afternoon of September 24, he turned first to Eden. "He was in a state of great distress," Eden recorded, "and reiterated several times that his Government could not accept them. He thought it incredible that the Prime Minister of Great Britain could forward such a document to a friendly power."[82] Eden did not tell Masaryk what was in his own mind, that it was indeed "incredible that such terms could be recommended to H.M.G. and most unfortunate that they should be forwarded by Chamberlain to Prague." After speaking to a number of colleagues, the following morning Eden telephoned Halifax to urge that if Hitler's new proposals were indeed as they had been reported in the press, they should be rejected forthwith.[83]

It turned out to be an opportune moment. At the conclusion of the previous day's Cabinet, Halifax had returned to the Foreign Office to find an anxious Cadogan waiting for him. Cadogan was deeply upset to discover that the Foreign Secretary was "completely and quite happily défaitiste-pacifist," and when he drove Halifax home that night he "gave him a bit of [his] mind, but didn't shake him."[84] In fact, although Cadogan had not appreciated it, his effect on Halifax had been profound. He had already been deluged with letters and calls from friends urging a strong stand against Hitler. "Winston, A.E. and Amery," warned Harvey, "are horrified at the possibility of our urging Czechoslovakia to accept."[85] At 1 A.M. that night Halifax woke up, and was unable to go back to sleep. His conversation with Cadogan was preying heavily on his mind. "Alec, I'm very angry with you," he chided his Permanent Under-Secretary the next morning. "You gave me a sleepless night. . . . But I came to the conclusion you were right."[86] "It is not too melodramatic," writes Halifax's biographer, "to pinpoint that night as the time that Halifax underwent his almost Damascene conversion from appeaser to resister."[87]

Since his appointment as Foreign Secretary, Halifax had given

Chamberlain his absolute support in all foreign policy matters. But now he could do so no longer. When the Cabinet reconvened at 10:30 A.M. on Sunday, September 25, Halifax was invited by Chamberlain to lead off the discussion, and he pulled no punches. Speaking in a low voice, trembling with emotion, he confessed to his shocked colleagues that he had "found his opinion changing somewhat in the last day or so."

> Yesterday he had felt that the difference between acceptance of the prin-
> ciple of last Sunday's proposal and the scheme now put forward a week
> later for its application did not involve a new acceptance of principle. He
> was not quite sure, however, that he still held that view . . . he could not
> rid his mind of the fact that Herr Hitler had given us nothing and that he
> was dictating terms, just as though he had won a war but without having
> had to fight . . . he felt some uncertainty about the ultimate end which he
> wished to see accomplished, namely, the destruction of Nazi-ism. So long
> as Nazi-ism lasted, peace would be uncertain. For this reason he did not
> think it would be right to put pressure on Czechoslovakia to accept. We
> should lay the case before them.

If the Czechs were to reject Hitler's terms, Halifax continued, then France would come to their aid, and he imagined that Britain would follow suit. His reflections during the night had led him to this point of view and, as Chamberlain squirmed in his chair, he concluded that while "he had worked most closely with the Prime Minister throughout the long crisis . . . he was not quite sure that their minds were still altogether at one."[88] The Cabinet was stunned. Hore-Belisha thought that Halifax had given "a fine moral lead,"[89] while Cooper conceded that his intervention "came as a great surprise to those who think as I do."[90] There was further support from an unexpected source, Lord Hailsham; generally a staunch ally of Chamberlain, he had been influenced by the experience of his son Quintin Hogg, who was contesting the Oxford by-election against Sandy Lindsay, the Master of Balliol, who was fighting on an anti-appeasement platform. Hailsham theatrically produced a press cutting which listed in detail the many occasions on which Hitler had broken his word.

Only two ministers opposed Halifax and supported Chamberlain. Lord Stanhope, the President of the Board of Education, demonstrating just how far removed from reality he was, contradicted Hailsham and assured his colleagues that there was a big difference between Hitler's previous promises and his current ones, since "the Prime Minister had clearly exercised a considerable influence on him." Not to be outdone, Kingsley Wood, the Secretary of State for Air, exclaimed that Chamberlain's visits had "made a considerable impression in Germany and had probably done more to weaken Nazism than any other event in recent years."[91] Chamberlain, however, had only heard Halifax's contribution, and furiously scrawled a penciled note, which he passed to the Foreign Secretary across the Cabinet table.

Halifax's suggestion, that war might be an appropriate means for achieving the eradication of Nazism and the overthrow of the Führer, was completely at odds with Chamberlain's intention to agree to a long-term settlement with Hitler, after first disposing satisfactorily of the thorny problem of Czechoslovakia.

> Your complete change of view since I saw you last night is a horrible blow to me, but of course you must form your opinions for yourself. It remains to see what the French say. If they say they will go in, thereby dragging us in, I do not think I could accept responsibility for the decision. But I don't want to anticipate what has not yet arisen. N.C.

This thinly veiled threat of resignation elicited an apologetic reply from Halifax.

> I feel a brute—but I lay awake most of the night, tormenting myself, and did not feel I could reach any other conclusion at this moment, on the point of coercing Cz[echoslovakia]. E.

Chamberlain remained unimpressed. "Night conclusions are seldom taken in the right perspective," he jotted down in reply. "I should like the Czechs to agree on the facts," concluded Halifax, "but I do not feel entitled to coerce them into it."[92]

During a break for lunch it became obvious that Chamberlain was unable to carry the Cabinet with him. Harvey found Hore-Belisha "very stiff and bellicose," insisting that the Godesberg "proposals must be rejected and now was the time to fight Hitler."[93] By the time the meeting finished after five hours of discussion, Cooper, Hailsham, Stanley, De La Warr, Elliot and Hore-Belisha had all spoken in support of Halifax. Chamberlain was clearly flustered and summed up cautiously. He accepted that "there had been some difference of opinion, as was only to be expected," but nevertheless urged that the Cabinet should present a united front. Hitler's demands had been put to the Czechs, not to Britain, and it was therefore not necessary to come down on one side of the argument or the other, but merely to place the full facts before them.[94] Cooper was unimpressed—in his view "this was sophistical gerrymandering."[95] He then offered his resignation, on the grounds that his "continual presence in the Cabinet was only a source of delay and annoyance." Chamberlain claimed to have been expecting such a move, but rejected it, asking Cooper not to take "any precipitate action." It appears that Cooper hoped his offer would not be taken seriously anyway.[96]

The previous day Masaryk had warned Halifax that the "Czechs would sooner go down fighting than accept [Hitler's proposals)]."[97] Now, immediately after the Cabinet meeting, Masaryk called at Downing Street to deliver his government's formal reply. His letter contrasted "the unique discipline and self-restraint" of the Czechs, with the "unbelievably coarse and vulgar campaign of the controlled German press against Czechoslovakia." The original Anglo-French plan had been accepted by Czechoslovakia only "under extreme duress," but Hitler's new proposals represented a "*de facto* ultimatum of the sort usually presented to a vanquished nation," and were "absolutely and unconditionally unacceptable. The nation of St. Wenceslas, John Hus and Thomas Masaryk will not be a nation of slaves."[98] Chamberlain was clearly irritated. Did the Czechs not "realise the military facts"? Whatever happened, it was unlikely that Czechoslovakia could be protected or restored to her former frontiers after a war. But Masaryk was not prepared to be bullied. The British government's agreement to the withdrawal of the embargo on mobilization "must carry the implication that they could never be expected to accept Hitler's plan." Having now mobilized, it was inconceivable that the Czech army would stand down and hand over the country to Hitler without a fight.[99]

▪ ▪ ▪

In recent days, the signals emanating from Paris had become increasingly puzzling. On September 21 Bonnet had asked the British government's opinion on the merits of the French "placing seven divisions behind [the] Maginot line in battle positions," as a safeguard against possible German invasion.[100] Halifax refused to be drawn, replying only that the French "must of course be judges of requirements of their security," but that there would be no objection.[101] During the night of September 23 Daladier and Bonnet conferred in the light of the disconcerting news from Godesberg, the Czech mobilization, and reports of the quickening pace of German military preparations. With the support of the French chief of staff General Gamelin, a partial mobilization was ordered; the next morning two categories of reservists were called up, in all over half a million men, bringing the French mobilized force up to a million in total. The German military attaché in Paris reported with concern that this acceleration of French military measures made "it appear probable that, in the event of belligerent measures by Germany, general mobilisation and immediate attack will take place."[102]

On the same day the Foreign Office received what appeared to be a quite extraordinary telegram from Sir Eric Phipps in Paris, in which he submitted his "purely personal impressions."

> Unless German aggression were so brutal, bloody and prolonged as to infuriate French public opinion to the extent of making it lose its reason, war now would be most unpopular in France. I think therefore that His Majesty's Government should realise extreme danger of even appearing to encourage small, but noisy and corrupt, war group here. All that is best in France is against war, *almost* at any price.[103]

This communication caused consternation at the Foreign Office. "I have never seen anything like the defeatist stuff which Phipps is now sending us," recorded Harvey. "He is either not reporting honestly feeling in France or else is taking no trouble to find out opinions which may be unpalatable to H.M.G. It is tragic that at such a time we have three such wretched ambassadors [in Rome, Berlin and Paris]."[104] Cadogan sent a stiff reply, demanding to know exactly what Phipps meant by "small, but noisy and corrupt, war group," and insisting that he should cast his net further afield in ascertaining the views of a more representative sample of French political opinion.[105]

At 9:25 P.M. on Sunday, September 25, the Inner Circle again sat down around the Cabinet table with Daladier and Bonnet. William Strang, who had accompanied Chamberlain to both Berchtesgaden and Godesberg, later described the meeting as one of "the most painful which it has ever been my misfortune to attend." Clearly upset at the rough treatment he had received from Hitler and by his Cabinet's subsequent reaction, the Prime Minister "allowed his mortification to appear in his attitude to M. Daladier."[106] He began with a lengthy exposition of the Godesberg discussions, liberally peppered with self-congratulatory remarks as to how he had stood up to Hitler. Daladier retorted that a meeting of his Council of Ministers that afternoon had unanimously rejected the Godesberg demands. It was "no longer a question of reaching a fair arrangement," but was now apparent that Hitler's sole objective was "to destroy Czechoslovakia by force, enslaving her, and afterwards realising the domination of Europe."

Chamberlain brusquely inquired what the French therefore proposed to do next, at which Daladier suggested returning to the terms of the original Anglo-French plan. Chamberlain then asked what would happen if, as he thought inevitable, Hitler refused to agree to this. Daladier replied, somewhat cryptically, that each of them "would have to do his duty." This failed to satisfy Chamberlain's meticulous mind, and he subjected Daladier to a further cross-examination. They could no longer "fence about this question," he declared; it was time "to get down to the stern realities of the situation." The memorandum under discussion was undoubtedly Hitler's "last word," and if the Czechs refused its terms, then Hitler "would at once take military measures." What would be the attitude of the French if that happened? Daladier could only reply, rather lamely, that each of them "would do what was incumbent on him." Did that mean, persisted Chamberlain, that France would declare war on Germany? The matter was absolutely clear, replied Daladier—"in the event of unprovoked aggression against Czechoslovakia, France would fulfil her obligations." That was why a million Frenchmen had "gone calmly and with dignity" to the frontier.[107]

Sir John Simon, an eminent King's Counsel, then took up the "cold interrogation," addressing the Prime Minister of France with the faux courtesy of Counsel questioning a hostile witness.[108] Employing all his forensic skills, Simon directed a succession of brutally frank questions to Daladier and Bonnet. "He did not wish to appear to be playing the strategist," he began with labored diffidence, "for he was only an ordinary public man." But he needed answers to important questions. Would the French sit tight behind the Maginot Line, or would they invade Germany? Would they use ground troops alone, or would the French air force be put into the air over Germany? Indeed, was it the case that their air force was largely nonexistent? Was the French public mentally prepared for the aerial German bombardment that would undoubtedly ensue? What support did they expect from Russia? Unsurprisingly, Daladier grew increasingly resentful at this aggressive line of cross-examination, and his replies became more evasive. Adopting an even more patronizing tone, Simon repeated the questions, as they "seem to have been misunderstood." Daladier retorted that it would be "ridiculous to mobilise French land forces only to leave them under arms doing nothing in their fortifications." There would be a land offensive, while military and industrial targets would be attacked from the air.

A cursory reading of the official British minutes suffices to give an adequate flavor of the hectoring and patronizing attitude of the British delegation. Chamberlain repeatedly tried to "clear up any doubts or misunderstandings about Herr Hitler's proposals"; Simon repeated questions which he supposed had been misunderstood, and "wished to assure M. Daladier on behalf of all the British Ministers how deeply and truly sensible they were" of the French point of view. Even Hoare interrupted soothingly that he "fully understood M. Daladier's feelings and hoped he would not think that anyone present liked the German proposals." Eventually Daladier angrily asked three questions of his own. Did the British accept Hitler's memorandum? Were they prepared to bring the necessary pressure to bear on Czechoslovakia to accept it? And did they honestly "think that France should do nothing"?[109] Chamberlain evaded all three questions. It was not for the British to accept or refuse the proposals, but for the Czechs, nor was it for "the British Government to express an opinion as to what France should do. That is a matter for the Government of France."[110]

At 11:40 P.M. the meeting was adjourned for an hour while the Cabinet was summoned for a third time in twenty-four hours. Chamberlain complained that the French had been evasive, but Cooper thought it sounded as though "they hadn't been nearly so evasive as [Chamberlain] had," and made himself "pretty offensive."[111] The prospect of a damaging split loomed large when, to everyone's astonishment, Chamberlain announced yet another new initiative. He was sending Wilson to Berlin the following day with a letter addressed to Hitler, suggesting that the transfer of territory be settled by an international commission. "If the letter failed to secure any response from Herr Hitler," continued Chamberlain, "Sir Horace Wilson would be authorised to give a personal message from the Prime Minister to the effect that if this appeal was refused, France would go to war, and if that happened it seemed certain that we should be drawn in."[112] Chamberlain made the announcement "almost casually," and Cooper had to ask if he had heard correctly. "It was after all a complete reversal of what [Chamberlain] had advised us to do the day before. And it was a reversal of the policy which a majority of the Cabinet had supported. None of the 'yes men' who had supported his policy all day said a word in criticism of its reversal." Chamberlain "looked for the first time absolutely worn out."[113] That night Hugh Dalton called Jan Masaryk to inquire whether the British and French governments were now at last taking a firmer line. "Firm!" exploded Masaryk. "About as firm as the erection of an old man of 70!"[114]

■

13

Keep Calm and Dig

I think it is well also for the man in the street to realise that there is no power on earth that can protect him from being bombed. Whatever people may tell him, the bomber will always get through. . . . The only defence is in offence, which means that you have to kill more women and children more quickly than the enemy if you want to save yourselves.

Stanley Baldwin, House of Commons, November 10, 1932

The terror that seized London during the Munich crisis was that dumb, chattering terror of beasts in a forest fire.

Louis MacNeice, *The Strings Are False*, 1965

How horrible, fantastic, incredible it is that we should be digging trenches and trying on gas masks here because of a quarrel in a far-away country between people of whom we know nothing.

Neville Chamberlain, September 27, 1938

When Britain awoke on the morning of Monday, September 26, war seemed imminent. An unofficial but accurate version of the Godesberg demands appeared in *The Times*, apparently leaked by the Czechoslovak government, while the paper gave pride of place to a philippic from Leo Amery on the letters page.

Are we to surrender to ruthless brutality a free people whose cause we have espoused but are now to throw to the wolves to save our own skins, or are we still able to stand up to a bully.[1]

Throughout the weekend, the country had resolutely been preparing for war. For the majority of the population, their only knowledge of war had been the horror of the trenches and, even twenty years on, the memories were still fresh. Now they were warned to expect a conflict that would yield still greater carnage than ever witnessed before. It was an appalling prospect. The polling organization Mass-Observation revealed that some people would sooner contemplate suicide than face the consequences of war. "I'd rather see my two boys dead," remarked one woman, "than see them bombed like they are in some places. I'd poison them if I thought it was coming."[2]

After Godesberg, wrote Harold Macmillan, the British people were "grimly, but quietly and soberly, making up their minds to face war. They had been told that the devastation of air attack would be beyond all imagination. They had been led to expect civilian casualties on a colossal scale. They knew, in their hearts, that our military preparations were feeble and inadequate. Yet they faced their ordeal with calm and dignity." The threat of attack from the air, in particular with gas, was, for the first time, a very real one. Mussolini had used poison gas against the Abyssinians in 1935, and the terrible destruction wreaked on the northern Spanish town of Guernica by the Luftwaffe in 1937 had been widely reported and shown on cinema newsreels. "We thought of air warfare in 1938," wrote Macmillan at the height of the Cold War thirty years later, "rather as people think of nuclear warfare today."[3]

Sunday, September 25, had been nicknamed "gas mask Sunday" by the press. Throughout the country Air Raid Precautions stations opened to distribute gas masks, arousing conflicting emotions. The *Daily Express* reported that as the queues grew outside Chelsea Town Hall, "it might have been a church social. Everybody—titled girls and telephone girls—attended."[4] But the act of trying on one's mask was also for many the first tangible sign of the approaching slaughter, and gave rise to a sense of fear. The strong smell of rubber made people sick, the elderly sometimes fainted, and there were no masks available for children and babies. The

Home Office issued guidelines, urging everyone to "take great care of their masks," and not to allow children to play with them "as damaged masks become leaky, and therefore dangerous." However, they were also forced to admit that "the production of a satisfactory equivalent of a gas mask for babies has been very difficult." In the meantime, "a good measure of protection can be afforded in the event of a gas attack by wrapping the child up completely in a blanket, when it could with safety be carried through gas to the nearest gas-proof shelter."[5]

The distribution centers stayed open all weekend, often late into the night, and in London loudspeaker vans toured the streets: "Will every citizen of Westminster get his gas mask fitted as soon as possible? Please do not delay." Similar announcements were made "on the screens in cinemas, from the stage at theatres, from the pulpit in churches, and at sports and social gatherings." On the Saturday afternoon, at the football match between Brentford and Sunderland, a loudspeaker announcement urged 28,000 fans to have their masks fitted as soon as possible.[6] While her husband was busy at Downing Street making life difficult for the Prime Minister, Lady Diana Cooper volunteered for duty at her local ARP station; she spent the day "clamping snouts and schnozzles on to rubber masks, parcelling them and distributing them to queues of men and women. Mothers would ask me for small ones for children," she later recalled. "There was none as yet. . . . It was a grisly job for a neurotic but better than inaction."[7] Virginia Woolf wrote to her sister in Sussex.

> In London it was hectic and gloomy and at the same time despairing and yet cynical and calm. The streets were crowded. People were everywhere talking loudly about war. There were heaps of sandbags in the streets, also men digging trenches, lorries delivering planks. . . .[8]

The frantic digging of trenches in London's parks provided the other conspicuous evidence of the imminence of war. In Hammersmith, the borough council took on 2,000 unemployed men to dig trenches. Radio appeals were broadcast for able-bodied men to come forward. On Hampstead Heath and on Hackney Downs, in Hyde Park, St. James's Park, Green Park, Regent's Park and London Fields, men dug through the night, working by the light of flares and the headlamps of lorries. The

Home Office delivered an illustrated handbook to every home in the country, containing advice on "the choice and preparation of refuge rooms in houses, precautions against fire, and the operation of the Air Raid warden system." The booklet also showed how to construct "a quick refuge for six" in the back garden, using a "corrugated iron roof, sandbags or boxes filled with earth, and old boards." The occupants should nevertheless "have their gas masks with them, as the trench would not be gas-proof."

The Committee of Imperial Defence instructed that "the Precautionary Period was to be considered as being in force." Overnight, antiaircraft batteries appeared in Horse Guards Parade and on the Embankment, while a lone Hurricane patrolled the skies. "London this morning bristles with the long muzzles of high-velocity anti-aircraft guns," reported the *Daily Express.* "Vital buildings are padded with sandbags . . . hundreds of guns are now in place." The War Office announced the creation of a new organization, the Auxiliary Territorial Service, to enable women who wished to join up to do so, principally as drivers—"War Office Call for 25,000 women." The recruiting poster featured a photograph of a girl blowing a bugle. All police leave was canceled, doctors and nurses were urged to enroll on a central register, and the London County Council appealed for ARP workers, auxiliary firemen, women ambulance drivers, and air raid wardens.[9]

The government announced that food prices, including those of bacon, ham, butter, cheese, lard and cooking fats, would be frozen for fourteen days; and emergency measures for the wartime distribution of meat supplies were being actively discussed with the National Federation of Meat Traders' Associations.[10] The financial markets too were in turmoil, the pound slumping on the foreign exchanges. "Only vigorous action by the British Exchange Control authorities prevented a continental panic from overwhelming the City of London," reported the *Daily Express.* But in spite of Treasury intervention to the tune of £20 million, the pound lost 2¾ cents against the dollar when the market opened on September 27, and the New York Stock Exchange fell to its lowest since 1935.[11] The Postmaster General issued a warning that the telephone system was in danger of collapse due to the heavy demand being placed on it, and urged subscribers to limit their use to essential calls only.

The London Underground announced that many of its tube lines were to close for "urgent structural works"; the true purpose of this, to convert the stations into airraid shelters, was tactfully left unsaid. "The first ARP rule is to keep calm," the *Daily Express* told its readers. "Bombs cannot wipe out defended cities. It would take *train-loads*, not aeroplane-loads, of high explosive to wipe out London." Meanwhile the registry offices were all fully booked as "hundreds rush to get married," and advertisements appeared offering to have a "photograph taken of your bank account," which would then be stored away from London to prevent destruction by bombing. The sense of unreality was compounded by the continuing everyday nature of the rest of the news. Readers were encouraged to turn to the center pages to read the final installment of the serialization of Daphne du Maurier's *Rebecca*—"Surprise end to the story of Manderley and the de Winters."[12] The picture editor of the *Evening Standard* retained his sense of humor, featuring a photograph of a policeman, tactfully stationed in Lower Regent Street between the neighboring offices of the Czechoslovakian Travel Bureau ("Czechoslovakia—the hunter's paradise in Central Europe") and the German Railways Information Bureau ("a holiday of songs and smiles").[13]

Evacuation procedures were also getting into full swing. Three thousand blind children were the first to be evacuated from London, while plans were announced for further emergency evacuation procedures in time of war. "People who wish to leave London by the special arrangements should go to any of the main line stations," announced the BBC. "Refugees should take their respirators and should wear their warmest clothes. They may take only small hand luggage and they should have with them some food for the journey and a rug or a blanket. They will not be able to take domestic animals." Nor would it be possible "to allow anyone to choose his destination."[14] The roads to the coast were crammed with Bank Holiday quantities of traffic, while the American embassy issued advice to its citizens who were getting caught in the stampede to flee for home. Unfortunately, all berths on the transatlantic liners were fully booked, and the *Queen Mary* had a waiting list of over 200.

From her home at Sissinghurst in Sussex, the writer Vita Sackville-West wrote to her husband, Harold Nicolson, typifying the mood of anxiety. "I do not at all like the prospect of your staying Friday night in London," she wrote on September 27. "If Saturday is really to be the *giorno fatale*, the first raids on London will be launched directly after midnight on Saturday, I mean 1 A.M. on Sunday morning."[15] The crisis was considered too serious for the King to be allowed to leave London; so the Queen, accompanied only by the two young princesses, traveled to Clydebank for the launch of her namesake, the new liner *Queen Elizabeth*. For the first time she addressed the nation over the radio.

> I have a message for you from the King. He bids the people of this country to be of good cheer, in spite of the dark clouds hanging over them and, indeed, over the whole world. He knows well that, as ever before in critical times, they will keep cool heads and brave hearts.[16]

▪ ▪ ▪

Chamberlain's meeting with Daladier had concluded without agreement late on the evening of Sunday, September 25. The following morning the French chief of staff, General Maurice Gamelin, arrived in London to bolster the French delegation. During a meeting with Chamberlain, he was considerably more positive than his political masters had been the night before. He promised that the French would attack Germany within five days of an invasion of Czechoslovakia, both against known weak points in the still unfinished West Wall, and by air. The Czech army had thirty-four divisions available, along with 500 airplanes of their own, and half as many again from Russia. He thought that they would "give a good account of themselves." France had twenty-three divisions on the western front, opposite only eight German divisions, and the French army would be in a good position to "draw off German troops from Czechoslovakia."[17] However, Halifax also later reported to Phipps that, in the event of invasion, Gamelin had suggested that "Czech resistance is likely to be of extremely brief duration."[18]

Later that morning Chamberlain sat down again with Daladier and Bonnet. The French military attaché in London had earlier complained to Hore-Belisha that the French "were furious at their reception, that they had been browbeaten and cross-examined on technical military matters of which they knew nothing."[19] Now, however, there was a perceptible change of attitude on both sides. Chamberlain hoped that Hitler would make clear his intentions in the set-piece speech he was due to give in Berlin that night. Meanwhile, it was obvious that the Czechs would not accept the Godesberg terms and would resist invasion. If that was the case France would then go to the aid of her ally, and Britain would stand by France. Daladier was delighted, warmly welcomed Wilson's visit to Berlin, and admitted that he too had expressed himself badly the night before. Stiffened by Gamelin, Daladier now reassured Chamberlain that, "if Germany attacked Czechoslovakia and hostilities ensued, the French intended to go to war and to commence hostilities with Germany within five days."[20]

At noon the British Cabinet reconvened; Chamberlain read out a telegram that he had received during the night from President Roosevelt, which he had also addressed to Daladier, Beneš and Hitler.

> The fabric of peace on the continent of Europe is in immediate danger. The consequences of its rupture are incalculable. Should hostilities break out, the lives of millions of men, women and children in every country will most certainly be lost under circumstances of unspeakable horror . . . for the sake of humanity everywhere I most earnestly appeal to you not to break off negotiations.[21]

The Cabinet then dealt with a number of emergency defense measures. Officers and men of the antiaircraft and coastal defense units of the Territorial Army were to be called up that afternoon, while all Royal Air Force personnel had been recalled from leave. The Prime Minister would broadcast to the nation the following evening, and Parliament had been recalled and would meet in two days' time. Malcolm MacDonald had met the Dominion High Commissioners; they had "all said in the strongest possible terms that . . . if there was any possible chance of peace by negotiation the opportunity should not be lost. In their view acceptance of Hitler's proposals was better than war." He was certain that Australia and New Zealand would join in if it came to war, and equally thought it likely that South Africa and Eire would not.[22]

In conclusion, Chamberlain announced that Wilson was en route to see Hitler. He admitted that he "placed no particular hopes on this last appeal," but there was "just a chance that it might have some result." He hoped that Wilson would carry influence with Hitler as he would "speak personally on behalf of the Prime Minister as his Confidential Adviser." If Hitler did not agree to this last-minute appeal, Wilson was to hand him a letter from Chamberlain that had already been agreed with the French.

> The French Government have informed us that, if the Czechs reject the memorandum and Germany attacks Czechoslovakia, they will fulfil their obligations to Czechoslovakia. Should the forces of France in consequence become engaged in active hostilities against Germany, we shall feel obliged to support them.[23]

Cooper was so astonished at this complete volte-face, that he felt obliged to state that he was "in entire agreement with the policy now adopted." Somewhat shamefacedly, he added that "if in our recent meetings I had expressed my opinions too frequently and too forcibly and had thereby added to the Prime Minister's heavy burden, I was very sorry." He repeated that he was happy to surrender his portfolio if the Prime Minister wished to broaden the base of his government to include members of the Opposition.[24] Chamberlain had no intention of doing any such thing.

As the Cabinet dispersed, Wilson flew to Berlin, and the French ministers made their way to Croydon Aerodrome, Chamberlain had an audience with the King over lunch at Buckingham Palace. King George was deeply troubled by what he perceived as the relentless approach of war and during their talk he reverted to the idea, which he had already proposed to Halifax, of his making a personal appeal to Hitler. He believed that it would "reinforce the appeal to reason rather than force being made this afternoon by Sir Horace Wilson . . . before Hitler's speech to-night." However, to the King's disappointment, Chamberlain remained unconvinced that the moment was right, and the following day he finally vetoed the idea on the grounds that "Hitler might send an insulting reply, publish it, and thus add further to the ill feeling now rising to a head between the two countries."[25]

Not far from Buckingham Palace, another meeting was taking place, although not one at which Chamberlain would have enjoyed the conversation. It was not only within the Cabinet that opinion had hardened during his absence; there was growing evidence too of an organized revolt on the backbenches. Four days earlier, while Chamberlain was clashing with the Führer in Godesberg, a gathering of like-minded peers and MPs had crammed into Winston Churchill's small flat in Morpeth Mansions, near the House of Commons. Churchill had just returned from a private briefing at Downing Street, and he now stood "behind the fire-screen, waving a whisky-and-soda, rather blurry, rather bemused in a way." He was satisfied, he reassured his fellow parliamentarians, that Chamberlain would make a suitably strong stand, and that if Hitler refused the Anglo-French plan, "Chamberlain will return tonight and we shall have war." Among his colleagues, however, there was greater, and as it turned out, wholly justified skepticism. "It all boils down to this," Nicolson recorded in his diary. "Either Chamberlain comes back with peace with honour or he breaks it off. In either case we shall support him. But if he comes back with peace with dishonour, we shall go out against him."[26]

As news leaked out during the course of the evening, Churchill's mood darkened. An old friend called him at home, anxious to find out what was going on in Godesberg. "I don't know," Churchill replied, "but I suspect it is something shameful."[27] He took a number of further calls that evening, including one from a deeply concerned Masaryk, and another from Clement Attlee. The Labour Party's opposition to Chamberlain was understandable on party-political grounds alone, although with the vast parliamentary majority enjoyed by the National Government, it was one that the Prime Minister could afford largely to ignore. However, Attlee and many of his colleagues also believed that Chamberlain was morally in the wrong. "This Government is leading the country into war," he had written to his brother earlier in the year. "There is really no peace policy at all. Chamberlain is just an imperialist of the old school but without much knowledge of foreign affairs or appreciation of the forces at work. It is a pretty gloomy outlook."[28] On September 26 Attlee wrote to Chamberlain to complain that the Godesberg terms, "which you agreed to submit to the Czechoslovakian Government, have, I believe, profoundly shocked British public opinion."[29]

Churchill was back at Downing Street on the afternoon of September 26, and was present during a discussion between Chamberlain and Halifax which led to the issuing of a controversial Foreign Office communiqué later that evening.[30] He afterward gathered together a larger group of anti-appeasers in his flat, including some on the left of the party, such as Harold Macmillan, as well as those more traditionally to the right, such as Leo

Amery and Lord Lloyd. Nicolson was again present, as was the Liberal leader, Sir Archie Sinclair, but there was still no sign of Eden. It was, thought Amery, a "queer collection," but the cast list illustrated the growing cross-party opposition to the Prime Minister, and was to become known as the "Focus Group." Churchill described Chamberlain as "a very exhausted and broken man." He had "done his best valiantly, but he should never have attempted such a task with such slender qualifications."[31] Although the Cabinet had been "in a blue funk" the night before, he understood that a combination of Cabinet hard-liners and French ministers had "restored confidence"; Wilson's message was "not in the least a retreat . . . merely an attempt to save Hitler's face if he wants to climb down." After a long discussion, the group concluded that they should call for closer cooperation with the Soviet Union, a cross-party coalition government and the introduction of National Service. "If Chamberlain rats," wrote Nicolson, "we shall form a united block against him."[32]

■ ■ ■

In Berlin, Sunday, September 25, was a glorious, Indian summer's day. In contrast to the war fever that had gripped London, the crowds flocked to the lakes and woods that surrounded the city, as it seemed that the threat of war had actually receded. While Chamberlain spent the day in almost continuous meetings with his Cabinet and the French ministers, Hitler had at last returned to Berlin after an extended stay at Obersalzberg. He was furious to hear that attitudes in London and Paris were hardening. Worse still, in Prague news of the French mobilization and the Russian warning to Poland had raised hopes that Czechoslovakia might after all be able to count on French, Russian and even British support. "The Czech attitude towards Germany is stiffening increasingly," reported the German chargé d'affaires, who had the impression that Beneš was now "ready to let it come to war."[33]

Like his fellow Berliners, Hitler made the most of the glorious weather, in his case spending the afternoon strolling in the gardens of the Reich Chancellery, earnestly discussing his next moves with Goebbels, who recorded them in his diary.

He doesn't believe that Beneš will yield. But then a terrible judgement will strike him. On 27–28 September our military build-up will be ready. The

Führer then has five days' room for manoeuvre. He already established these dates on 28 May. And things have turned out just as he predicted. The Führer is a divinatory genius. But first comes our mobilization. This will proceed so lightning-fast that the world will experience a miracle. In 8–10 days all that will be ready. If we attack the Czechs from our borders, the Führer reckons it will take 2–3 weeks. But if we attack them after our entry, he thinks it will be finished in 8 days. The radical solution is the best. Otherwise, we'll never be rid of the thing.

Ever since the May Crisis, Hitler had been planning a single, lightning invasion of Czechoslovakia at the beginning of October. Now, however, he appears to have curbed his ambition, and to have been preparing instead for a two-tier invasion; first by establishing troops in the Sudetenland, before then overrunning the rest of the country.[34]

The following morning, Monday, September 26, Sir Horace Wilson left for Berlin. An intensely private man, he was horrified to find a pack of newspaper photographers camped outside his front door when he left for the airport. On arrival in Berlin, he went first to the British embassy and then, accompanied by Henderson and Kirkpatrick, made his way to the Reich Chancellery. At 5 P.M. they were ushered into the Führer's presence. Unfortunately Wilson had picked absolutely the wrong moment to confront Hitler, who was in a particularly ugly mood. As was his practice before making a big, set-piece appearance, he was focusing on the speech he was to deliver that evening in the Sportspalast; by the time Wilson arrived, Hitler had already worked himself up into the necessary fury. It was to be the first and only occasion on which Hitler "completely lost his nerve" in Schmidt's presence.[35]

Wilson handed Chamberlain's letter to Schmidt to translate, and asked that he might first say a few words by way of introduction. "The German memorandum has been published," he began, "and opinion in England has been profoundly shocked at its terms." But no sooner had he opened his mouth than Hitler turned pale, and grew increasingly agitated. "In that case," interrupted Hitler, "there is no use talking any more." Wilson, however, persevered, politely insisting that Hitler should listen to what he had to say. It was not the proposals themselves, but the speed at which they were to be carried out which had "shocked and roused public opinion." He then asked Schmidt to translate Chamberlain's message. But after just two sentences Schmidt reached a passage describing the Godesberg terms as "wholly unacceptable," according to Czech opinion.[36] At this Hitler let out a howl of rage, rose from his chair and made for the door, as if the meeting was already over. Wilson later described his own reaction.

> Schmidt got up. Ribbentrop got up. Henderson and Kirkpatrick got up. I stayed put. I thought Hitler was very rude to walk out. I was not accustomed to being treated like that. I was, after all, the representative of the British Government. I therefore clung to my armchair.[37]

Hitler was astonished at such an open display of defiance and, on reaching the door, he suddenly "seemed to realise how impossible his behaviour was," shrugged his shoulders, and "returned to his seat like a defiant boy."[38] Schmidt was allowed to continue, but was constantly interrupted by Hitler, who muttered and spluttered his way through the letter until, once Schmidt had finished, he exploded into another furious outburst. A shouting match ensued: Hitler raged against Beneš and the Czechs, Schmidt tried to interpret as everybody talked at once, and Wilson did his best to stay calm. Unfortunately Wilson's soothing, but cautionary, tone only served to enrage Hitler still further. "Germany was treated like niggers," he screamed. "One would not dare treat even the Turks like that." At one point Kirkpatrick became so transfixed by the extraordinary scene he was witnessing, that Wilson had to turn to him and remind him to keep taking notes. "On the 1st October," shrieked Hitler, "I shall have Czechoslovakia where I want her."[39] If France and England decided to strike, he concluded, let them strike. "I don't give a damn."[40]

Chamberlain's letter proposed that, since the Czechs had already agreed in principle to Hitler's demands, a meeting of Czech and German delegates should now take place "with a view to settling by agreement the way in which the territory is to be handed over." Chamberlain was quite happy to "arrange for the representation of the British Government at the discussions."[41] Hitler replied that he would negotiate with the Czechs only if they first accepted the Godesberg memorandum; they must agree to German troops occupying the Sudeten areas by October 1, and he must have their reply by 2 P.M. on September 28—that was to say within forty-eight hours. Meanwhile, he recommended that Wilson should come to the Sportspalast that evening to hear him speak. Wilson, who had still failed to deliver the most important part of Chamberlain's message, politely declined, but promised to listen on the radio. "That is not the same thing," replied Hitler. "You must be present to sense the atmosphere."[42] Wilson returned to the embassy and telephoned London; he had endured "fifty very hectic minutes," but would be staying the night in order to see Hitler again the following morning. When the Foreign Office official to whom he gave the message said "Good!" in reply to some minor observation, Wilson replied dryly: "That is not the word to use."[43] He later telegraphed Chamberlain to report that he had undergone a "very violent hour."[44]

At 8 P.M., with the world tuned in to listen to his every word, Hitler delivered his speech to 20,000 handpicked Nazi Party supporters, packed into the vast Sportspalast arena. William Shirer was watching from the gallery immediately above the platform, and described Hitler "shouting and shrieking in the worst state of excitement I've ever seen him in." During all the years he had been covering the Third Reich, for the first time Hitler "seemed tonight to have completely lost control of himself."[45] After a brief introduction, he quickly found his voice and launched into a furious, venomous tirade against the Czech nation in general, and its President in particular. "The question which in these last months and weeks has moved us so profoundly," he shouted, "has long been familiar to us. It is not so much a question of Czechoslovakia, it is a question of Herr Beneš."

> This Czech State began with a single lie and the father of this lie was named Beneš. . . . I have demanded that now after twenty years Mr. Beneš should at last be compelled to come to terms with the truth. On 1 October he will have to hand over to us this area. . . . Now two men stand arrayed one against the other: there is Mr. Beneš and here stand I.

Urged on by the approving crowd, a tumultuous roar greeted each and every argument, while for the benefit of world opinion there was an assurance that he had no territorial ambitions beyond Czechoslovakia. Cleverly, he praised Chamberlain for the efforts he had made to secure peace.

I am grateful to Mr. Chamberlain for all his efforts. I have assured him that the German people desires nothing else than peace. . . . I have further assured him, and I repeat it here, that when this problem is solved there is for Germany no further territorial problem in Europe. And I have further assured him that at the moment when Czechoslovakia solves her problems . . . then I have no further interest in the Czech State. And that is guaranteed to him! We want no Czechs!

His patience with Beneš, however, was at an end, and he concluded with a threat.

I have made Mr. Beneš an offer. . . . The decision now lies in his hands: Peace or War! He will either accept this offer and now at last give to the Germans their freedom or we will go and fetch this freedom for ourselves. We are determined! Now let Mr. Beneš make his choice.[46]

After seventy minutes on his feet, Hitler brought his speech to an end in a virtual paroxysm of violence. The massed ranks of Nazis, who had interrupted almost every sentence with cries of "*Sieg Heil*," cheered and chanted for several minutes: "Führer command, we will follow! [*Führer befiehl, wir folgen!*]"[47] At last, Goebbels sprang up and grabbed the microphone. "One thing is sure," he shouted to the crowd, "1918 will never be repeated!" At this, according to Shirer, Hitler "looked up to him, a wild, eager expression in his eyes," leaped back to his feet again, "and with a fanatical fire in his eyes . . . brought his right hand, after a grand sweep, pounding down on the table and yelled with all the power in his mighty lungs: '*Ja!*' Then he slumped into his chair exhausted."[48] The speech had been one of Hitler's most powerful. Goebbels described it as a "psychological masterpiece,"[49] and many of those who heard it over the radio commented on the sheer brutality of its delivery. Leo Amery, a fluent German-speaker, described it as "the most horrible thing . . . more like the snarling of a wild animal than the utterance of a human being, and the venom and vulgarity of his personal vilifications of 'Beneš the liar' almost made me feel sick. There was something terrifying and obscenely sinister in this outpouring of sheer hatred."[50]

Incredibly, when the Inner Circle met in London immediately after the speech was over, it was agreed that, although violent, it "did not justify a decision to issue immediate orders for general mobilisation."[51] Instead, two strongly contrasting statements were issued to the press. At 9:15 P.M. the Press Department of the Foreign Office issued an "authorised statement," attributed to "official circles," which was broadcast later that night, and was widely reported in the press the following morning.

> The German claim to the transfer of the Sudeten areas has already been conceded by the French, British and Czechoslovak Governments, but if in spite of all efforts made by the British Prime Minister a German attack is made upon Czechoslovakia the immediate result must be that France will be bound to come to her assistance, and Great Britain and Russia will certainly stand by France.[52]

To this day, the paternity of this statement, known as the "Leeper Telegram," remains the subject of conjecture. What seems certain is that it was drafted by Rex Leeper, the head of the Foreign Office Press Department, and that its release was authorized by Halifax that evening, in the erroneous belief that it was "completely in accord" with Chamberlain's view.[53] It caused widespread comment, both because of its claim to know the true position of the Soviet Union, and its vigorous insistence that Britain was ready to go to war alongside France.

The second statement was more conventional, and was issued on behalf of the Prime Minister at 1:50 A.M. that night, in response to Hitler's speech.

> I have read the speech of the German Chancellor and I appreciate his references to the efforts I have made to save the peace. I cannot abandon those efforts since it seems to me incredible that the peoples of Europe who do not want war with one another should be plunged into a bloody struggle over a question on which agreement has already been largely obtained.[54]

In the course of the night Wilson transmitted a lengthy telegram to Chamberlain, welcoming certain aspects of Hitler's speech. It had not been, he thought, "so violent as was expected"; Hitler had, after all, praised Chamberlain and given an assurance that Czechoslovakia was his last territorial claim in Europe. It was, however, now clear that the Godesberg memorandum represented his final word. Wilson also described a curious incident that had occurred during his meeting at the Chancellery. Both Hitler and Ribbentrop had told him, and Göring had later repeated it to Henderson, that the Germans had been tapping the telephone lines between Masaryk in London and Beneš in Prague. Masaryk had apparently told Beneš "to stand firm, that he need not bother to give up territory, that he, Masaryk, was in touch with Winston Churchill and others, and was convinced that the Chamberlain policy will fail." Wilson concluded by warning that he felt it was "very doubtful whether it is either necessary or wise to deliver that special message tomorrow morning."[55]

Shortly after noon the next day, Wilson returned to the Reich Chancellery. Kirkpatrick had found the previous day's experience so distasteful that he asked Wilson if he might be spared a second visit; there had been an "aura of such ruthless wickedness that it was oppressive and almost nightmarish to sit in the same room." But Wilson insisted that he accompany him. The Chancellery corridors and waiting rooms were heaving with hangers-on, all hoping to be allowed a moment of the Führer's precious time. Outside Hitler's office, the round antechamber was packed with SS guards and Nazi bigwigs. As the British were shown in, Colonel Bodenschatz, Göring's liaison officer at the Chancellery, whispered conspiratorially to Kirkpatrick "to be firm."[56]

Hitler's mood had improved only marginally, and Wilson opened the conversation with an outrageous bout of sycophancy. He had listened to Hitler on the radio, and "he desired to congratulate him on the reception he had received; it must be a wonderful experience for any man to receive such a reception." He then referred to the Prime Minister's overnight statement, drawing particular attention to the passage in which Chamberlain had declared himself "morally responsible" for ensuring that the Czechs carried out the transfer of territory "fairly and fully, and . . . with all reasonable promptitude." He was effectively offering to guarantee the handover of the areas in question. Did the Führer, asked Wilson, have a message that he could take back to London? Yes, replied Hitler, again growing increasingly agitated. The Czechs had but two, simple choices—"acceptance of the memorandum or rejection."[57] If they chose the latter, he shouted, there could only be one outcome. "*Ich werde die Tschechen zerschlagen*" he repeated, over and over again. This Schmidt faithfully translated as "I will smash-sh-sh the Czechs."

At last the moment had come for Wilson to deliver the crux of his message. Speaking quietly and deliberately, there was, he said, just one more thing. He would try to deliver Chamberlain's message in the tone he believed the Prime Minister himself would have employed, had he been present. "If, in pursuit of her Treaty obligations, France became actively involved in hostilities against Germany," he warned Hitler, then "the United Kingdom would feel obliged to support her."[58] Hitler was enraged. Since he had no intention of attacking France, "what it boiled down to was that if France elected to attack Germany, Great Britain was under an obligation to attack Germany also."[59] Wilson explained that he had misunderstood, but Hitler was past caring. Increasingly exasperated, he shifted uneasily in his chair, repeatedly slapped his knee, and drummed his heel on the parquet floor.

"If France and England strike," he shouted, "let them do so. It is a matter of complete indifference to me. I am prepared for every eventuality. I can only take note of the position. It is Tuesday today, and by next Monday we shall all be at war."[60] At one point there was an interruption when the young Third Secretary from the British embassy, Con O'Neill, arrived with a message for Henderson. "How's it going?" he inquired discreetly, as he passed it to Kirkpatrick, who stuffed the note in his pocket with barely a glance and replied in a stage whisper: "It's war!" This delighted the staunchly anti-appeasing O'Neill, who "went back to the embassy in high spirits."[61] Wilson, however, was not to be so easily outdone, and was still trying to engage Hitler in conversation when Henderson signaled that it was time to leave. As he left, Wilson took the Führer to one side. "A catastrophe," he told him, "must be avoided at all costs. I will still try to make those Czechos sensible."[62] Kirkpatrick remembered bidding Hitler farewell rather differently. "As I grasped his podgy hand," he recalled years later, "I felt an overwhelming sense of relief that I should never have to see him again."[63]

▪ ▪ ▪

Wilson returned to London on the afternoon of September 27, in time to attend an extended meeting of the Inner Circle at Downing Street. Inskip brought with him to the meeting the three chiefs of staff: the First Sea Lord, Admiral Sir Roger Backhouse, the Chief of the Imperial General Staff,

General the Viscount Gort, and the Chief of the Air Staff, Air Chief Marshal Sir Cyril Newall. To the assembled gathering their report appeared unremittingly bleak.

> It is our opinion that no pressure that Great Britain and France can bring to bear, either by sea, on land, or in the air, could prevent Germany from overrunning Bohemia and from inflicting a decisive defeat on Czechoslovakia. The restoration of Czechoslovakia's lost integrity could only be achieved by the defeat of Germany and as the outcome of a prolonged struggle, which from the outset must assume the character of an unlimited war.[64]

The outlook was made worse by Mason-MacFarlane, who had been invited to London to give his own views on the military situation in Germany, and to recount his brief experience while delivering the Godesberg terms to Prague. The morale of the Czechs "appeared to him to be poor, and much of the *matériel* preparations were not completed. The Customs Frontier Guards were definitely scared stiff. On the Southern frontier, opposite Vienna-Linz, the Czechs appeared to him to be very ill-prepared. He thought it would be very rash to base any policy on the assumption that the Czechs would fight like tigers."[65]

The meeting was joined by Malcolm MacDonald and the Australian High Commissioner, and former Prime Minister, Stanley Bruce. The Dominion governments, according to Bruce, were far from happy and were insistent that the Godesberg terms should be accepted. The High Commissioner of South Africa had spoken for them all, when he told MacDonald that "South Africa cannot be expected to take part in any war over Czechoslovakia."[66] After Wilson had reported on his experience in Berlin, the sense of gloom was compounded by a telegram from Henderson, who had spoken to Göring after Wilson's meeting with Hitler.

> It was quite evident from his attitude that every detail of the plan for occupying Sudeten districts was now finally prepared. He was neither nervous nor excited but absolutely confident that if the Czechs resisted, their opposition would be overcome by overwhelming force in the briefest possible time. It is quite obvious . . . that the die is cast, that British mediation is at

an end and that if delegates do not arrive at Berlin with full authority to make the best terms they can on their own with Germans before 2 P.M. tomorrow, general mobilization will be ordered at that hour and occupation of Sudeten areas will begin immediately.[67]

It was agreed that a preliminary telegram should be sent to Prague, from Chamberlain to Beneš, and this was done while the meeting continued.

I feel bound to tell you and Czechoslovak Government that the information His Majesty's Government now have from Berlin makes it clear that German forces will have orders to cross Czechoslovak frontier almost immediately, unless by 2 P.M. tomorrow Czechoslovak Government have accepted German terms. That must result in Bohemia being overrun and nothing that any other Power can do will prevent this fate for your own country and your people, and this remains true whatever may be the ultimate issue of a possible world war. His Majesty's Government cannot take responsibility of advising you what you should do but they consider this information should be in your hands at once.[68]

As the meeting drew to a close, Chamberlain asked Backhouse if he was satisfied that all necessary measures had been taken. The First Sea Lord replied that he would like to take one further step, that of mobilizing the fleet. Chamberlain hesitated for a few moments, before nodding. Backhouse gathered up his papers, and hurried back to set the process in motion. Later, when the various meetings had finished, Cadogan was still working alone in the Cabinet Room when Wilson looked round the door. "Do you realise that we have not told Duff the Fleet is to be mobilised?" he asked.[69]

Having told Beneš that they could offer no further advice, that was precisely what the British government then proceeded to do. Halifax and Cadogan had earlier prepared an alternative proposal for a phased German occupation of the Sudetenland. By early evening a draft document had been prepared, approved by the French, and dispatched to both Newton and Henderson. The new plan provided for the immediate occupation of the towns of Eger and Asch, on October 1; this was to be followed by the creation of an international boundary commission and a phased transfer of further Sudeten territories between October 3 and 10. The proposals were again accompanied by a veiled threat to the Czechs.

> The only alternative to this plan would be the invasion and dismemberment of their country by forcible means, and though that might result in general conflict entailing incalculable loss of life, there is no possibility that at the end of that conflict, whatever the result, Czechoslovakia could be restored to her frontiers of today.[70]

At 7:30 P.M., after a meeting lasting three hours, the remaining members of the Inner Circle were turned out of the Cabinet Room by BBC electricians rigging up the microphone for the Prime Minister's broadcast. Chamberlain, Halifax, Wilson and Cadogan adjourned to Wilson's room next door, where the meeting continued. Wilson then produced a draft of a further telegram that he proposed should be sent to Beneš; the Czechs were to be requested to accept immediate occupation of all those areas identified on the map accompanying Hitler's memorandum.

> In the light of the considerations set out in my earlier message, it seems to us that it would be wise for you to consider the withdrawal of your troops from the areas to be occupied, in this way leaving the German forces to effect a bloodless occupation. If you should decide that this is in all the circumstances a prudent course to adopt, it would be advisable for you to inform the German Government of your intention at the earliest possible moment and in any case before tomorrow afternoon.[71]

Cadogan was appalled by this message of "complete capitulation," and said so, while Halifax too distanced himself from the suggestion. Chamberlain, however, by now "quite exhausted," seemed ready to accept it. "I'm wobbling about all over the place," he admitted to Cadogan, and with that he returned to the Cabinet Room next door.[72]

At 8 P.M. Chamberlain broadcast to the nation over the radio. He was ill-prepared, and spoke slowly, his voice breaking with tiredness and emotion. He began, characteristically, by thanking all those who had "written to my wife or myself in these last weeks to tell us of their gratitude for my efforts and to assure us of their prayers for my success."

If I felt my responsibility heavy before, to read such letters has made it seem almost overwhelming. How horrible, fantastic, incredible it is that we should be digging trenches and trying on gas masks here because of a quarrel in a far-away country between people of whom we know nothing. It seems still more impossible that a quarrel that has already been settled in principle should be the subject of war.

He spoke of his visits to Germany, which had made him realize "vividly how Herr Hitler feels that he must champion other Germans," and reiterated his belief that the Sudetenland represented Hitler's last territorial claim in Europe. He would not, he promised his listeners, "give up the hope of a peaceful solution, or abandon my efforts for peace as long as any chance for peace remains"; indeed, he was only too happy to return to Germany for a third time if he thought it would do any good.

Chamberlain went on to describe the precautionary war measures that had been taken; they did not mean, he insisted, that war was imminent. He appealed for calm, and called for additional volunteers to play their part in the defense of the country. Then he signaled that there were likely to be further concessions to come.

However much we may sympathise with a small nation confronted by a big powerful neighbour, we cannot in all circumstances undertake to involve the whole British Empire in war simply on her account. If we have to fight it must be on larger issues than that. I am myself a man of peace to the depths of my soul. Armed conflict between nations is a nightmare to me; but if I were convinced that any nation had made up its mind to dominate the world by fear of its force, I should feel that it must be resisted . . . war is a fearful thing, and we must be very clear, before we embark on it, that it is really the great issues that are at stake, and that the call to risk everything in their defence, when all the consequences are weighed, is irresistible.[73]

Chamberlain has rightly been strongly criticized for these remarks, insular and naive as they now appear, and appeared to some at the time. British foreign policy had never hitherto been dependent on geographical proximity or public awareness. Cooper found the broadcast "a most depressing utterance," and was furious that Chamberlain had failed to mention the mobilization of the fleet as he had promised. He summed up the views of many: "There was no mention of France in it nor a word of sympathy for Czechoslovakia. The only sympathy expressed was for Hitler whose feelings about the Sudetens the Prime Minister said that he could well understand."[74] Churchill rang Cooper, "almost inarticulate with rage. The speech, he said, was a preparation to scuttle."[75] Amery was more scathing still. The broadcast was "the utterance of a very weary and heartbroken man . . . which will only encourage the Germans to go ahead. . . . If ever there was an essential citizen, a citizen accustomed to deal with fellow citizens on City Council or in Cabinet, and a man quite incapable of thinking in terms of force, or strategy or diplomacy, it is Neville."[76]

At 9:30 P.M. the Cabinet met in emergency session. The outlook, warned Chamberlain, was "gloomy." He repeated the defeatist reports that had been presented to the Inner Circle that afternoon: Henderson's telegram from Berlin, Mason-MacFarlane's pessimistic prognosis on the fighting ability of the Czech army, and the staunch opposition of the Dominion governments to any policy that might lead to war. He read a telegram from the Prime Minister of Australia warning that "the transfer of the Sudeten areas having been agreed upon in principle, the precise method of giving effect to that decision was not a matter of sufficient importance to warrant a dispute leading to war." Wilson then described his meetings with Hitler, concluding that Hitler thought Beneš "a twister, who would never implement his promises." He then reverted to his earlier suggestion that a telegram should be sent to Prague insisting that "the only plan which could prevent the country from being over-run would be for the Czechoslovak Government to withdraw their troops from the red areas and allow Germany to occupy them without loss of life." He was supported by Chamberlain; Wilson's proposal was the "last opportunity for avoiding war."[77]

Not for the first time, however, the Prime Minister had misread the mood of the meeting; Wilson's draft telegram proved too much for many Cabinet ministers. Cooper "thought it important to get my oar in first before the Big Four." He referred to Roosevelt's growing support, allied to a hardening of opinion in France; Mason-MacFarlane had clearly fallen under Henderson's pernicious spell, while Dominion backing was irrelevant anyway. He criticized Chamberlain for failing to praise the Czechs in his broadcast. "If we were now to desert the Czechs, or even advise them to surrender," he concluded, "we should be guilty of one of basest betrayals in history."[78] Crucially, Cooper was followed by Halifax, who agreed that he too could not support Wilson's telegram. The suggestion it contained "amounted to complete capitulation to Germany," and it would not be accepted by the House of Commons. Simon then eagerly jumped on the bandwagon, forcing Chamberlain reluctantly to concede that there were "powerful and convincing reasons against the adoption of his suggestion. . . . If that was the general view of his colleagues he was prepared to leave it at that."[79]

That night Chamberlain sat up late at Downing Street, preparing the speech he was to deliver in the House of Commons the following day. Those who had heard him on the radio that evening went to bed with a feeling of near certainty that they would wake up the following morning to find Britain at war. Even the King shared the anxiety of his subjects. At Buckingham Palace that night, he sat down to write to his mother, Queen Mary, describing the latest proposals that had been sent to Prague and Berlin.

> Beneš has been told, as he well knows, that his country will be overwhelmed anyhow, & that it would be wise for him to take this course. If Hitler refuses to do this then we shall know once and for all that he is a *madman*. It is all so worrying this awful waiting for the worst to happen.[80]

"I only know that as the hours went by," Chamberlain later wrote to his sister, "events seemed to be closing in and driving us to the edge of the abyss with a horrifying certainty and rapidity."[81]

▪ ▪ ▪

While London nervously held its breath, in Berlin preparations for the invasion of Czechoslovakia were nearing completion. Indeed, in the Sudeten border town of Asch, a salient jutting out into German territory, it could be said that it had already begun. The Czech army had retreated from the town, which was almost entirely populated by Germans, and had been replaced there first by the Freikorps, and then, on Hitler's orders, by two Death's Head battalions of the SS. The following day, shortly after

Wilson left the Chancellery, Hitler issued a "most secret" order that the seven divisions which comprised the invasion assault units should move forward from their exercise areas to the jumping-off points near the Czech border. They were to be ready "to begin action against 'Grün' on September 30, the decision having been made one day previously by 12:00 noon"[82]; ground troops would attack at 6:15 A.M., while the air force was left to decide on the most suitable time to commence operations, depending on the weather conditions.[83] The OKW warned the Nazi Party authorities that full mobilization was imminent; any demands made by the OKW of local party leaders should be "met immediately and without being referred to higher authorities."[84] Finally, that evening, the OKW issued an order "without warning," for the secret deployment of "the five regular west divisions" along the West Wall.[85]

At 6 P.M., as dusk fell on a dull autumn day in Berlin, a motorized division, fully equipped for war, made its way slowly through the streets, bound for the Czech frontier. The parade had been ordered by Hitler, partly to try to prepare the people of Berlin for war by appealing to their patriotism, and also to impress upon the foreign diplomats and correspondents in the city the full military might of the Reich. For three and a half hours the armored column, complete with heavy artillery, rumbled its way along the Wilhelmstrasse, while Hitler, in brown tunic and black trousers, stood motionless on the Chancellery balcony, flanked by his three military adjutants. The parade had been timed to catch Berliners as they hurried home from work, but if the aim had been to impress, it failed miserably. William Shirer arrived at the corner of the Linden, where the parade turned down the Wilhelmstrasse, expecting to see a public demonstration of noisy support, similar to that which had taken place at the outbreak of war in 1914. Instead, he noted, the people of Berlin "ducked into the subways, refused to look on, and the handful that did stood at the curb in utter silence." It was the "most striking demonstration against war I've ever seen."[86]

On the Wilhelmplatz, opposite the Chancellery balcony, a group of 200 civilians stood quietly and sullenly. They had come to see Hitler, but had not expected to see his guns. The *Daily Express* correspondent described how the "camouflaged trucks rumbled past with their loads of young stolid-faced German soldiers sitting bolt upright, rifles between their knees . . . looking grim and glum." No one smiled, no one cheered, no one waved.[87]

At the British embassy, a few doors down the Wilhelmstrasse from the Chancellery, Henderson too watched this defiant show of strength; it conjured up the image of a "hostile army passing through a conquered city."[88] Hitler was furious at such a brazen display of apathy, even displeasure. It was all in stark contrast to the adulation of the handpicked audience at the Sportspalast the previous night. Fritz Wiedemann was rebuked when he walked into the Chancellery observing loudly: "It looks like a funeral march out there!"[89] At last, clenching his fist, Hitler stepped back from the window and hid behind a curtain. "With such people," he complained, "I cannot wage war."[90]

Given this frenetic buildup of military activity, all of it geared toward an invasion on September 30, it is difficult to ascertain why, almost as soon as Wilson had left Berlin, Hitler instructed Weizsäcker to draft a reply to Chamberlain's letter; only the previous day he had refused even to listen to its being read. Some commentators have attributed his change of mind to the public reaction to the military parade; however, the time at which his reply was received in London demonstrates that the letter had been conceived earlier that afternoon.[91] Nor was he influenced by the mobilization of the British fleet, news of which was not made public until late that night. Ribbentrop's Private Secretary offers a more prosaic reason, giving the credit to Weizsäcker, who, "in his concern to keep at least a flicker of hope alive," persuaded Hitler that it was "only correct to send some sort of response."[92] When Schmidt was ordered to translate this "conciliatory" reply, he noticed that for the second time in a few days "Hitler shrank from the extreme step."[93] Henderson too thought the letter "constituted a perceptible attempt at conciliation and was indicative of a certain nervousness."[94] Weizsäcker was later told by Göring that Hitler had chosen peaceful methods at this late stage for two reasons: "first, doubt as to the war-like disposition of the German people; and second, the fear that Mussolini might definitely leave him in the lurch."[95]

Chamberlain received Hitler's reply at 10:30 P.M., and was immediately given renewed hope. While continuing to justify the unyielding attitude he had assumed at Godesberg, and with Wilson, Hitler's more moderate tone was cleverly designed to appeal to Chamberlain. He denied that he had any wish to "cripple Czechoslovakia in her national existence or in her political and economic independence." He neither contemplated occupying the entire country, nor would those Czechs left behind in the Sudeten areas suffer mistreatment. The Czechs were only holding out in the hope that they might "mobilise those forces in other countries, in particular in England and France, from which they hope to receive unreserved support for their aim and thus to achieve the possibility of a general warlike conflagration."

> I must leave it to your judgement whether, in view of these facts, you consider that you should continue your effort, for which I should like to take this opportunity of once more sincerely thanking you, to spoil such manoeuvres and bring the Government in Prague to reason at the very last hour.[96]

Chamberlain reflected that the differences between the two sides had now been "narrowed down still further to a point where really it was inconceivable that they could not be settled by negotiations." He decided that he must follow up his existing proposals with one final, "last last" letter to Hitler.[97]

▪ ▪ ▪

At 4 on the morning of September 28, the French ambassador in Berlin, André François-Poncet, was woken by the arrival of a telegram from the Quai d'Orsay. During the night, Phipps had informed Bonnet of the content of the British government's last-minute proposals to Hitler—the suggested phased occupation of the Sudetenland, beginning with the immediate occupation of Eger and Asch. Bonnet now instructed François-Poncet to present, in person to Hitler, similar proposals on behalf of the French government, "which would follow the methods of application contained in this latest British suggestion but would provide for the immediate occupation of a more considerable territory."[98] At 7 A.M., a few hundred yards away at the British embassy, Henderson was himself roused by a telephone call from François-Poncet, informing him of the receipt of these new instructions from Paris. The French ambassador had, he told Henderson, already requested an immediate audience with the Führer.

At 8:30 A.M. François-Poncet telephoned Weizsäcker to brief him on his instructions. Weizsäcker in turn tracked down Ribbentrop, who was staying at the Kaiserhof Hotel, and reported that the new French proposals were considerably more far-reaching than the more modest British proposals of the night before. The French government was now suggesting "the occupation of all four sides of the Bohemian quadrilateral by German troops; districts comprising Czech fortifications were also to be occupied. The smooth carrying-out of this occupation would, as far as possible, be guaranteed by the French Government." François-Poncet had stressed that Prague had not yet been informed of these plans, but that the Führer was to be consulted first. If Hitler agreed to them, the French "would demand acceptance from the Czech Government. If Czechoslovakia refused, conclusions could be drawn which he did not need to define more closely." As an afterthought, François-Poncet had helpfully added that, in his opinion, the British plan "was in any case useless."[99]

In Downing Street, Annie Chamberlain came downstairs for breakfast at 7:30 to find her husband busy drafting a reply to Hitler's latest letter, and an accompanying message to Mussolini in Rome. He had woken early, he told her, and "felt that to ask Mussolini to intervene with Hitler was the one hope left. The Germans were to march in that afternoon at 2 o'clock & war for us all would have started."[100] "I feel certain," wrote Chamberlain, "that you can get all essentials without war and without delay."

> I am ready to come to Berlin myself at once to discuss arrangements for transfer with you and representatives of Czech Government, together with representatives of France and Italy if you desire. I feel convinced we could reach agreement in a week. I cannot believe that you will take responsibility of starting a world war which may end civilisation for the sake of a few days' delay in settling this long standing problem.[101]

For Chamberlain, these two letters represented a "last desperate snatch at the last tuft of grass on the very verge of the precipice."[102] The young Lord Birkenhead, Halifax's Parliamentary Private Secretary and, later, his biographer, took a different view. "There was an ugly ring in this telegram," he wrote, "something almost effusive in the eagerness to continue the process of surrender." It was "the nadir of diplomacy."[103]

At 10 A.M. François-Poncet again called Henderson. He had still received no reply to his request for an audience with Hitler, and feared the worst.

Unknown to him, the delay was due entirely to the bellicose Ribbentrop, who had initially refused even to pass on the request, so annoyed was he "at the prospect of his game being upset, this time from Paris." He had spent much of the previous evening trying to strengthen Hitler's resolve to wage war; Weizsäcker now warned him that it was "a monstrous thing . . . to want to start a war when the real differences between the two sides are so small."[104] Henderson offered to come round to the French embassy immediately, but before leaving he first telephoned Göring. He told the field marshal that François-Poncet had requested an interview, that he had still not received a reply, and that he had fresh proposals to submit. It was, in short, a matter of peace or war, and he began to describe the proposals in greater detail. "You need not," interrupted Göring, "say a word more. I am going immediately to see the Führer."[105]

No sooner had Henderson arrived at the French embassy than a message came from Hitler that he would see François-Poncet at 11:15 A.M. At almost the same moment a telegram was brought from the British embassy, containing Chamberlain's "last last" message for the Führer, with instructions that Henderson should deliver it in person as soon as possible. The decisive intervention appears to have come from Göring, who had gone round to the Chancellery immediately upon hearing from Henderson. Somehow the former Foreign Minister, Neurath, had also inveigled his way into the Chancellery that day, and together the two men spent an hour with Hitler in the Wintergarten, doing their best to persuade him of the merits of a peaceful compromise. "Mein Führer," implored Neurath, "do you wish to start a war under any circumstances? Of course not!"[106]

As Göring left, he found Ribbentrop hanging around nervously outside. The Foreign Minister had been busily preparing for war, with what his biographer describes as "joyful excitement." Two days before, he had commandeered a special train for use as his personal mobile headquarters, and he had ordered in a supply of pistols, steel helmets and gas masks for himself and his staff. Now Göring rounded on him, calling him a "warmonger" and a "criminal fool."[107] Striding across the outer lobby of the Wintergarten, he shouted: "Herr von Ribbentrop, if war should break out, I will be the first one to tell the German people that you pushed things to this end!" While the assembled aides nervously pretended to ignore the row between "the two insulted 'primadonnas,' " Ribbentrop and Göring traded accusations. When Ribbentrop accused Göring of being afraid to go to war, the field marshal exploded. He knew precisely what war was, he told the Foreign Minister, and he did not want to go through it again. However, "as soon as the Führer said, 'March!' he would take off in the leading aeroplane—on condition that Ribbentrop sat in the seat beside him!"[108]

▪ ▪ ▪

In Rome, as in London and Berlin, a surreal atmosphere hung over the city as the prospect of war loomed ever closer. The staff at the British embassy was destroying archives and packing up to go home, trying hard not to give the impression of panic. There was a feeling among politicians and diplomats that Italy had so far been largely ignored during the crisis. There was currently no French ambassador in Rome, principally due to the strained relations between the two countries over events in Abyssinia and Spain, and even British diplomats felt that they had been sidelined. After Chamberlain's visit to Berchtesgaden, the embassy had dispatched a telegram to London, urging the Foreign Office to take advantage of the widespread feeling of relief in Italy, and to "associate Mussolini with any plans for a general settlement." The Duce, they believed, was "angling after an invitation to take part in the big central European game and longing to play a larger role."[109] They had received no reply.

On the evening of September 27, the British ambassador in Rome, the Earl of Perth, again contacted the Foreign Office requesting permission to "convey officially and immediately to Count Ciano the Prime Minister's declaration made after Herr Hitler's speech [at the Sportspalast]," and to ask if "Signor Mussolini would use his influence to induce Herr Hitler to accept proposals contained therein."[110] The following morning, the British chargé d'affaires, Pierson Dixon, arrived at work early to find a telegram from Halifax approving the approach, and immediately telephoned to request an interview for the ambassador with Ciano. Perth was "still enjoying a leisurely breakfast and not expecting war until 1 October," but at 10 A.M. Ciano's office called back and invited the ambassador to go round immediately to the Palazzo Chigi.[111] It was only two days since Ciano had learned from the Italian ambassador in Berlin, Bernardo Attolico, that Hitler had brought forward the expiry of his ultimatum to the Czechs to 2 P.M. on September 28. Mussolini, however, had no desire for a European war, into which an under-armed and under-prepared Italy would undoubtedly be drawn; it was therefore hardly surprising that, with less than four hours to go before a possible outbreak of hostilities, Perth found Ciano "looking very grave."

Ciano listened carefully to Chamberlain's letter, and Perth's accompanying statement that Mussolini was "perhaps the only man who could now induce Herr Hitler to accept a pacific solution." Ciano was impressed. "Then there is no time to be lost; it is a question of hours, not days."[112] He left Perth in his office and hurriedly made his way round to see Mussolini at the nearby Palazzo Venezia. Mussolini agreed at once to act on Perth's suggestion, and Ciano put through a personal call to Ribbentrop. The Foreign Minister, however, was not at the Wilhelmstrasse, but was busy arguing with Göring at the Chancellery, so Ciano instead asked the operator to connect him to the Italian embassy.

When Attolico came on the line, Mussolini seized the telephone. "The Duce here. Can you hear me?"

"Yes, I hear you."

"Ask for an audience with the Chancellor at once. Tell him that the British Government have asked me through Lord Perth to mediate in the Sudeten question. The point of difference is very small. Tell the Chancellor that we are behind him, I and fascist Italy. It is for him to decide. But tell him that in my opinion the proposal ought to be accepted. Do you hear me? Hurry!"[113]

Barely twenty minutes after leaving Perth, Ciano returned to the Palazzo Chigi. He was determined to milk the moment for as long as he could.

> I inform Perth that hostilities are to begin to-day and confirm that our place is beside Germany. His face quivers and his eyes are red. When I add that nevertheless the Duce has accepted Chamberlain's request and has proposed a delay of 24 hours, he bursts into a sobbing laugh and rushes off to his Embassy.[114]

Perth returned to the embassy soon after 11:15 A.M., only to find, as his Rolls-Royce pulled into the drive, Dixon waiting for him on the doorstep, brandishing a further telegram from London. This one contained the personal message for Mussolini that Chamberlain had drafted over breakfast that morning, together with a copy of his final appeal to Hitler. Perth duly turned his car round, and made his way back to see Ciano for the second time that morning.

▪ ▪ ▪

In Berlin, meanwhile, François-Poncet had arrived at the Chancellery for his interview with Hitler. The atmosphere was warlike and frenetic, the sense of crisis acute. The waiting rooms and corridors were crowded with an assortment of ministers, generals, high-ranking Nazi Party officials and aides-de-camp, all hurrying about frantically, and all eager to confer with the Führer. Hitler, recalled Schmidt, strolled around the Chancellery, holding impromptu conversations here and there with whomever he happened to find; from time to time he would retire to the privacy of the Wintergarten or his office, for further discussions with Göring, Ribbentrop or Keitel. As he passed through the rooms, politicians leaped to their feet, and generals snapped to attention; everyone, whatever their rank, would be forced to listen to a lengthy harangue on the current crisis, always reminiscent of his speech at the Sportspalast, albeit in a shortened form. The Reich Chancellery, thought Schmidt, resembled "more the camp of an army in the field than the centre of an organised government."[115]

François-Poncet's first impression was that the room next to Hitler's office was being laid up for lunch. On inquiring who were to be the guests, he was told that the Führer had invited the commanding officers of all the units that were shortly to invade Czechoslovakia. He found Hitler, tense and overwrought with excitement, sitting alone in his office with Ribbentrop; Schmidt sat quietly in a corner, a precautionary presence thanks to the ambassador's fluent German. François-Poncet laid out a map of Czechoslovakia, on which he had shaded in red the areas of the Sudetenland which were to be occupied immediately under the new French proposals. They were considerably larger than those in the latest British plan, which Hitler had not yet even seen. "You deceive yourself, Chancellor," he began, "if you believe that you can confine the conflict to Czechoslovakia. If you attack that country you will set all Europe ablaze." Hitler responded with a tirade against Beneš, but François-Poncet maintained his composure. "You are naturally confident of winning the war," he continued, "just as we believe that we can defeat you. But why should you take this risk when your essential demands can be met without war."[116]

At the Italian embassy, Attolico had reacted with alacrity to his instructions from Rome. Not realizing that Ciano had already tried unsuccessfully to contact Ribbentrop, he too telephoned the Wilhelmstrasse and was put through to Ribbentrop's outer office. The call was taken by Ribbentrop's Private Secretary, Reinhard Spitzy. Attolico's German was poor, and he pleaded in a mixture of Italian and broken English, his high-pitched voice causing great amusement among the listening officials. "Please, I must speak to the Führer immediately, please, quick, quick, it's a personal message from the Duce." Spitzy walked over to the Chancellery, where he found Hitler with Ribbentrop, who was clearly annoyed at the interruption. "So, what's new?" inquired Hitler. When Ribbentrop heard that Attolico was requesting a meeting, he did his best to discourage Hitler from agreeing; but Hitler quietly considered the news. "Tell Attolico," he said finally, "that I am to receive the French ambassador at eleven o"clock, but that he may come at 11:30!"[117]

As soon as this message was relayed to Attolico, he rushed from the embassy without his hat; unable to find his official chauffeur, he hailed a passing taxi, and arrived at the Chancellery at 11:40 A.M., breathless and sweating heavily. Hitler was still in his meeting with François-Poncet, but agreed to see Attolico in another room, leaving the French ambassador alone in his office. The "slightly stooping" Attolico, "his face flushed with excitement," was shown into Hitler's presence. "I have an urgent message to you from the Duce, Führer!" he shouted unceremoniously from the far side of the room. "The Duce informs you that, whatever you decide, Führer, Fascist Italy stands behind you," he continued, catching his breath. "The Duce is, however, of the opinion that it would be wise to accept the British proposal, and begs you to refrain from mobilisation." According to Schmidt, Hitler was "clearly impressed" by Mussolini's message and, after a moment of contemplation, turned back to Attolico. "Tell the Duce that I accept his proposals."[118]

▪ ▪ ▪

In Rome, Perth had hurried back to the Palazzo Chigi for his second meeting with Ciano in under an hour, arriving just as Attolico was being shown into Hitler's presence in Berlin. He told Ciano that he now had a further telegram from Chamberlain, a personal message for Mussolini, containing details of the Prime Minister's final appeal to Hitler; he had offered to visit Germany for a third time, and hoped that Mussolini would join him at an international conference there.

> I trust Your Excellency will inform German Chancellor that you are will-
> ing to be represented and urge him to agree to my proposal which will
> keep all our peoples out of war.[119]

Ciano was once again sufficiently impressed to take the message to Mussolini immediately, and the Duce again reacted promptly, instructing Attolico to return to the Chancellery. Twenty minutes later, Ciano returned to the waiting Perth. "Very good news; very, very good news," he reported. "Herr Hitler has agreed to Signor Mussolini's request to postpone the German mobilisation for twenty-four hours, and I am also authorised to tell you that Signor Mussolini will support with, and recommend to, Herr Hitler the acceptance of the proposals for a conference between the four Powers and ask to be represented at it." The two men shook hands. "We have done, I think, a very good morning's work," concluded Ciano.[120]

Henderson had by now replaced François-Poncet in Hitler's study, and was putting forward the new British plan, which had anyway already been trumped by France. When he arrived, Henderson had been encouraged by what he felt was a more cheerful atmosphere. Following the visits of the Italian and French ambassadors, there was a palpable sense of relief among the less bellicose Nazi officers who were still loitering outside Hitler's office. As he was shown in, Bodenschatz whispered to him: "*Das geht besser: halten Sie nur fest* [It is going better: only stick to it]." To Henderson's astonishment, Hitler began the interview with an announcement of his own. "At the request of my great friend and ally, Signor Mussolini, I have postponed mobilising my troops for twenty-four hours."[121] Henderson then spent an hour trying to persuade Hitler to accept the idea of a conference in Berlin, but Hitler would only reply that he was in the midst of negotiations with Mussolini, and would take no decision without first consulting his Axis ally.

For the second time that morning, Hitler's meeting with a foreign ambassador was interrupted by Attolico; this time he came bearing news of Mussolini's support for Chamberlain's proposed conference. Furthermore, he would be happy to attend himself. Having already agreed to postpone mobilization, Hitler was left with little choice but to accede to Mussolini's latest request. All that remained was to agree the venue and the precise terms under which the talks would be held. Early that afternoon Attolico was therefore summoned back to the Chancellery for a third time, to be told that Hitler would agree to the proposed conference on two conditions: that Mussolini's offer to participate still stood, and that it should be held immediately, either in Munich or Frankfurt. A telephone call between the two leaders subsequently confirmed that invitations would be sent to Chamberlain and Daladier to come to Munich the following morning. There was one last stipulation. In his message to Hitler, Chamberlain had originally suggested a five-power meeting, but there was absolutely no question whatsoever of Hitler inviting Czechoslovakia to attend.

With barely an hour to go before his ultimatum to Czechoslovakia was due to expire, and after months of preparing to unleash war, Hitler had changed his mind at the last moment. Did his change of heart represent a victory or a climb-down? That he was terrified of losing face is beyond dispute. After the May crisis he had promised that it was his "unalterable decision to smash Czechoslovakia," yet it could be said that by agreeing to a negotiated annexation of the Sudetenland, Hitler neither climbed down nor lost face. By postponing mobilization for a further twenty-four hours he conceded nothing; the threat of invasion would remain, like a "Damoclean sword," throughout any further discussions. The latest British and French proposals, while not going as far as those he had put forward at Godesberg, still guaranteed that his troops would cross the Czechoslovak border on his chosen date, to which he had publicly committed himself just two days earlier at the Sportspalast. In the words of one historian, he had in fact "had everything he wanted handed to him on a silver salver."[122]

Yet those closest to him were astounded. "One can't grasp this change," noted the Abwehr officer Helmuth Groscurth. "Führer has given in, and fundamentally."[123] As the hours had counted down to invasion, there had been growing pressure for him to pull back from the brink; only Ribbentrop had remained a steadfast advocate of war. During the night of September 27, President Roosevelt had sent a second message, begging Hitler to consider the lessons of the First World War, and suggesting "a conference of all the nations directly involved in the present controversy."

Although the United States would play no role in any negotiations, if Hitler would agree to a peaceful solution, "hundreds of millions throughout the world would recognize your action as an outstanding historic service to all humanity."[124] From London came news of Chamberlain's broadcast, his proposal for a conference, and the mobilization of the British fleet. At home Hitler had witnessed for himself the German people's apathy, even hostility, to war; and the faintheartedness, as he saw it, of his generals.

It was Henderson's view that "of the various factors which induced Hitler to abandon his idea of a Czech war," Göring's intervention had been far from the "least important."[125] Yet even on the morning of September 28 Göring was still predicting war. "A great war can hardly be avoided any longer," he told Jodl before Chamberlain's message and Mussolini's intervention. "It may last seven years and we will win it."[126] Hitler's biographer, on the other hand, identifies the "decisive intervention" as that of Mussolini.[127] Schmidt too believed that the moment when Hitler agreed to Attolico's request to postpone mobilization, just two hours before it was due to take place, was when "the decision in favour of peace was made," and Hitler "shrank back from the extreme brink."[128] In Rome, the telephonist who spent the day putting Mussolini's calls through to Berlin was rewarded by him with a gift of 2,000 lire. If the lines between Rome and Berlin had been cut that day, joked Attolico to Henderson, "there would have been war."[129] Yet Mussolini was not wholly satisfied with his day's work. "I am only moderately happy," he told Ciano that evening, "because, though perhaps at a heavy price, we could have liquidated France and Great Britain for ever. We now have overwhelming proof of this."[130]

14

■

The Flying Messenger of Peace

When I was a little boy I used to repeat: "If at first you don't succeed, try, try, try again."

Neville Chamberlain, Heston Aerodome, September 29, 1938

If at first you don't concede, fly, fly, fly again.

Foreign Office ditty, October 1938

People who carry an umbrella can never found an empire.

Benito Mussolini, October 1938

What one hates is the terrible, ghastly farce of that "victory drive"—that "triumphant" appearance on the balcony of Buckingham Palace when in the streets of Prague the people wept openly at being forsaken.

Ronald Cartland MP to his sister Barbara Cartland, October 1938[1]

Our enemies are small worms. I saw them at Munich.

Hitler addressing his generals, August 1939

Throughout the morning of September 28, the people of London, wholly ignorant of the diplomatic frenzy taking place in Berlin, continued to prepare for war. Men and women had woken with the overwhelming sensation that this was to be the last day of peace, and that by the following evening London could well be a scene of utter devastation, brought about by mass German bombing. The morning newspapers carried news of the mobilization of the fleet, and further details of the extensive ARP precautions that were now in place. The exodus from London continued;[2] Oxford and Cambridge universities announced that the start of the new term was to be postponed, and the Red Cross and St. John Ambulance were urgently appealing for new recruits. The BBC broadcast warnings that anyone hoarding food was "not playing the game towards the rest of the population," and to prevent panic buying everyone was assured that "petrol prices will remain unchanged during the next fourteen days."[3]

At 10:30 A.M. the King held a Privy Council at Buckingham Palace to ratify by royal proclamation the mobilization of the fleet, and the calling up of various auxiliary and territorial forces. A state of emergency was declared, giving the government emergency wartime powers. Duff Cooper stayed behind afterward for a private talk, and found the monarch cheerful, "envisaging the war with great equanimity."[4] Chips Channon flew back to London from France to attend the recall of Parliament, and found that at Heston Aerodrome "there was war atmosphere already, with young airmen lounging about, smoking; we heard the word 'Boche' again, and someone said 'mufti.' It was 1914 all over again."[5] At Churchill's flat near Westminster, feelings ran high at another meeting of anti-appeasers; Amery found "some of the young men, particularly Harold Macmillan, very wild, clamouring for an immediate pogrom to get rid of Neville and make Winston Prime Minister before the House met."[6]

That afternoon Members of Parliament made their way to the House of Commons to hear Chamberlain's speech. Nicolson encountered a large, "silent and anxious" crowd in Whitehall, some of whom were laying flowers on the Cenotaph—"They stare at us with dumb, inquisitive eyes."[7] Churchill walked to the Commons with his close ally Brendan Bracken and the Polish ambassador, Count Raczynski. He "would not allow Chamberlain to rat and to give in," he told Raczynski, and if necessary was "prepared to speak and to oppose any surrender."[8] The mood in the chamber was somber and apprehensive, the green benches and public galleries packed to overflowing; MPs sat huddled together on the steps between the benches. The Press Gallery was full. In the Peers' Gallery above the clock the Duke of Kent took his place, flanked by Halifax, the former Prime Minister Lord Baldwin, and the Archbishop of Canterbury. In the Speaker's Gallery sat Queen Mary, dressed in black, with the Duchess of Kent and Annie Chamberlain. The Diplomatic Gallery too was over-crowded, Jan Masaryk sitting just a few places away from the German ambassador, Dirksen, as well as those from France and the Soviet Union. The American ambassador, Joseph Kennedy, had brought along his twenty-one-year-old son, John F. Kennedy.

The business of the House began, as usual, with Prayers, followed by departmental questions. At 2:50 P.M., as the Speaker was announcing the death of a former Member, Chamberlain slipped into the chamber and took his place. He was greeted by a tremendous ovation, the government benches rising to their feet almost as one, cheering and waving their order papers. The Opposition, and one or two government backbenchers, remained in their places. On a pile of books on the dispatch box in front of him was an unfamiliar sight—a radio microphone, "a strange metal honeycomb . . . that filled us with mingled horror and pride in the occasion."[9] It had been planned to attempt the first-ever live broadcast from Parliament of the Prime Minister's speech, but at the last moment it was agreed that the microphone would serve only to relay proceedings as far as the library of the House of Lords, where peers had assembled to listen, and the gallery of the Commons for the benefit of Queen Mary. Chamberlain rose slowly, flanked on one side by Simon, and on the other by the Chief Whip, David Margesson; carefully, he spread his papers out on the dispatch box in front of him.

Chamberlain had stayed up late into the night working on his speech, and had then been up since dawn redrafting it, and sending telegrams to Hitler and Mussolini. Once they had been dispatched, there was little he could do but wait and hope. Walking in the garden at Downing Street that morning, he had told his wife that he "would gladly stand up against that wall and be shot if only I could prevent war."[10] Now he looked tired and haggard. Before entering the chamber he had at least received one piece of good news, one crumb of comfort. At 1 P.M. Perth had telephoned from Rome to report that Hitler had agreed to Mussolini's request to postpone mobilization by twenty-four hours; the Duce had also supported

Chamberlain's proposal for a conference, but a reply was still awaited from Berlin. He began to speak, calmly and deliberately, in measured tones. He had, he told the House, hoped to find a peaceful solution to the crisis, but "unhappily those hopes have not been fulfilled." "Today," he warned, "we are faced with a situation which has no parallel since 1914."[11]

He was listened to in almost deathly silence, the House in a more solemn mood than even the longest-serving members could recall. They fully expected to hear the worst, possibly even that war was to be declared in a few hours' time. The only noise was that of the tail-coated messengers, as they hurried about the chamber delivering the pink slips of paper that conveyed telephone messages and telegrams to members; Churchill, sitting in his usual aisle seat below the gangway, received so many that they were bundled together with an elastic band. Attlee listened motionless, his feet up on the table facing the Opposition front bench. Chamberlain continued with a lengthy and detailed chronological account of the crisis that had consumed the country since Parliament had adjourned for the summer recess. He explained the appointment of Lord Runciman back in July and, as members cheered at the mention of the Liberal peer's name, Chamberlain paused, "removed his pince-nez between his finger and thumb, and raised his face to the skylight."[12]

Gradually, as he recounted the events of the past few weeks, he brought the House up to date, describing his visits to Berchtesgaden and Godesberg; his audience realized that his remarks were gaining in importance. "This country," he intoned, "which does not readily resort to war, would not have followed us if we had tried to lead it into a war to prevent a minority from obtaining autonomy, or even from choosing to pass under some other Government." He concentrated on the rights of the Sudeten Germans, rather than those of the Czech population, and there were echoes of his radio broadcast the previous night. "However remote this territory may be, we knew, of course, that a spark once lighted there might give rise to a general conflagration, and we felt it our duty to do anything in our power to help the contending parties to find agreement."[13] His critics listened in silence, not daring to intervene on such a grave occasion to point out that the "contending parties" were in fact the sovereign Czech government and the Nazi dictatorship. Amery was typical; the speech, he thought, was "very polite to Hitler [and] on the whole lacking in sympathy to the Czechs."[14]

Nor had the influence exerted by Britain in trying to reach that agreement been entirely benign, as Chamberlain was implying. For the benefit of members, his oral account had been supplemented with a white paper, which had been published that morning, containing a number of relevant documents. However, it gave a far from honest picture of the situation. At their meeting the previous afternoon, the Inner Circle had discussed the wisdom of publishing a white paper at all, and Halifax in particular had been violently opposed. But Chamberlain had been pressed to do so by Attlee and, with great reluctance, it was agreed that it might be published "subject to the excision of the message sent by the Czechoslovak Government accepting the Franco-British proposals . . . since it referred to the strong and continuous pressure put upon the Czechoslovak Government by the French and British representatives." It was hoped that this remarkable act of deception would forestall demands for the publication of a number of further telegrams, which were also omitted for fear of revealing the full force, and at times brutally unpleasant language, used in applying pressure on the Czech government.[15]

At 3:15 P.M. Cadogan was in his room at the Foreign Office when the telephone rang; it was Nevile Henderson in Berlin. He had just been informed by the Wilhelmstrasse that "Herr Hitler invites the Prime Minister to meet him in Munich tomorrow morning. He has also invited Signor Mussolini, who will arrive at 10 A.M., and M. Daladier."[16] Cadogan hurriedly dictated a written message, and ran across Whitehall to Parliament, where he first "fished H[alifax] out of [the] Peers' Gallery," before they made their way downstairs together to the small lobby behind the Speaker's Chair.[17] There they knocked on the door to the small under-gallery beside the Speaker's Chair, used during a debate by a few government officials and advisers. Wilson took the note, and immediately motioned to Chamberlain's Parliamentary Private Secretary, Lord Dunglass, who was sitting on the bench behind the Prime Minister. With some difficulty Dunglass clambered over several colleagues, and reached the box to find a "bewildered" Wilson. "What on earth has happened," he asked, "has he marched in?" He could scarcely believe Wilson's reply, but took the note anyway and passed it to Simon, who was sitting in front of him alongside the

Prime Minister. Wilson, Dunglass told Simon, recommended that Chamberlain "should not announce it at once but keep it to follow on the passage dealing with the twenty-four hours reprieve."[18]

Simon was at first unsure how to communicate the news to Chamberlain, not wishing to "interrupt the current of his argument or throw him off his balance by suddenly interjecting this joyful piece of news." Chamberlain, who was in full flow, at first showed no sign of wishing to be distracted but, during a short pause to allow the House to cheer, Simon was able to tug at his coat and hand him the note.[19] Those sitting nearby realized immediately that something important was afoot—the Foreign Office crest was clearly visible at the head of the single, typed sheet of paper. Chamberlain again "adjusted his pince-nez and read the document . . . his whole face, his whole body seemed to change. He raised his face so that the light from the ceiling fell full upon it. All the lines of anxiety and weariness seemed suddenly to have been smoothed out; he appeared ten years younger and triumphant."[20] The peers listening on the radio relay in the Lords' library heard Chamberlain turn to Simon and ask, in a whispered aside, "Shall I tell them now?" Simon simply replied "Yes."[21]

It was now 4:15 P.M. and the Prime Minister had been on his feet for over an hour. He cleared his throat, and a faint hint of a smile crossed his face. He spoke of the telegrams he had sent to Hitler and Mussolini that morning—"a last last" effort for peace—and paid tribute to the Italian leader for intervening with Hitler. The Führer, he announced, had agreed to postpone German mobilization by twenty-four hours. "Whatever views honourable members may have had about Signor Mussolini in the past," he continued, "I believe that everyone will welcome his gesture of being willing to work with us for peace in Europe."[22] A rising murmur of relief reverberated around the Chamber. "How foolish the anti-Italians now looked," thought Chips Channon, "and Anthony Eden's face—I watched it—twitched, and he seemed discomforted."[23]

That is not all. I have something further to say to the House yet. I have now been informed by Herr Hitler that he invites me to meet him at Munich tomorrow morning. He has also invited Signor Mussolini and M. Daladier. Signor Mussolini has accepted and I have no doubt M. Daladier will also accept. I need not say what my answer will be.

After a split second of silence, as the significance of his words sank in, a roar of approval broke out in all corners of the House. "Thank God for the Prime Minister!" cried out one unidentified member.[24] "God has sent him a peroration," muttered Ernest Brown to Kingsley Wood on the front bench, "and it is in time."[25]

When the cheering finally died down, Chamberlain asked that the debate should be adjourned.

> Mr. Speaker, I cannot say any more. I am sure that the House will be ready to release me now to go and see what I can make of this last effort. Perhaps they may think it will be well, in view of this new development, that this Debate shall stand adjourned for a few days, when perhaps we may meet in happier circumstances.

Five brief speeches followed. Attlee for Labour, and Sinclair for the Liberals, readily agreed to the adjournment of the House, and wished the Prime Minister well. Only the Communist member, William Gallagher, objected, refusing to "be a party to what has been going on here. There are as many Fascists opposite as there are in Germany," he declared, "and I protest against the dismemberment of Czechoslovakia."[26] As the Chief Whip moved the formal motion to adjourn, the government benches began cheering again and rose to salute the Prime Minister. This time Opposition members, who had "sat glum and silent" at first, felt obliged to join in on a sign from Attlee, cheering Chamberlain as enthusiastically as their Conservative colleagues, "though looking a little foolish," thought Cooper.[27] As Dunglass was to write many years later, with only a hint of irony: "There were a lot of 'appeasers' in Parliament that day."[28]

The assistant editor of *The Times*, Barrington-Ward, was in the Press Gallery. "In a second the whole place was on its feet," he wrote. "A huge prolonged cheer and a tempest of waving order papers. I heard the unusual sound of loud clapping, looked round the partition and saw the public violently applauding in the Strangers' Gallery. It was electrifying."[29] Sir John Simon agreed. It was a demonstration unlike any he had experienced during thirty years in the House of Commons. "Ambassadors in the Diplomatic Gallery broke all the rules by rising and applauding," and on the floor of the House there was a "forest of waving hands and order papers." It was "incomparably the greatest piece of real drama that the House of Commons has ever witnessed."[30] For a full five minutes Chamberlain, his face "white and tightly set, as if he were making an effort to retain self-control," stood motionless as the uproar continued around him. "Tears came into the eyes of Queen Mary," reported the *News Chronicle*, while the Archbishop of Canterbury was "striking the rail in front with both hands and Earl Baldwin was banging the floor with his stick."[31] Channon was completely overcome; he stood on the green bench, waving his order paper, and cheering until he was hoarse. He felt "a gratitude, an admiration for the PM which will be eternal. I felt sick with enthusiasm, longed to clutch him."[32] As the Chamber emptied, Simon watched as many of Chamberlain's hardened enemies "crossed the floor in tears and with unrestrained emotion grasped him by the hand."[33]

Not every Member of Parliament, however, joined in the tumultuous acclamation. Harold Nicolson stayed firmly rooted to his seat, and recorded that "Liddall [the Conservative Member for Lincoln] behind me, hisses out, 'Stand up, you brute!'"[34] One seasoned commentator on Czech affairs enjoyed an uninterrupted view of the Conservative benches. He watched as members cheered and threw their order papers in the air, "some actually weeping with emotion and relief." Yet he would "never forget the grim, set faces of three men, who held aloof from the demonstration, realizing the dire consequences which the House was preparing for itself: they were Mr. Churchill, Mr. Eden and Mr. Amery."[35] All three initially stayed sitting in their places, before Eden "walked out of the Chamber pale with shame and anger."[36] Amery found it "a curious moment, immense relief tinged with the uncertainty whether it was more than a few hours respite." Churchill, he noticed, "looked very much upset."[37]

In fact Churchill had at first made as if to rise in his place, in an effort to catch the Speaker's eye and contribute to the debate. The Polish ambassador, with whom he had walked to the House earlier, observed that he "kind of half rose from his seat and then sat down, rather resigned." It was obvious that "contrary to what he had prepared before, he found that in the atmosphere then reigning in the House, no objections and no speech could kind of change the atmosphere."[38] Members sitting around him began to barrack, urging him to "Get up! Get up!" By then Chamberlain was enjoying his moment of glory, showing "great satisfaction and even greater self-satisfaction" as his supporters crowded around him. Churchill shook him by the hand, but his praise was barbed. "I congratulate you on your good fortune," he said, adding, to the Prime Minister's obvious annoyance, "You were very lucky."[39] However, having wished him "God Speed," Churchill later issued a statement to the press making it clear that he supported Chamberlain's initiative "from the bottom of my heart."[40]

Chamberlain returned home, the cheers of the crowds in Whitehall echoing those in the House of Commons. It had been, as he confessed himself, "a piece of drama that no work of fiction ever surpassed."[41] In Downing Street his car was surrounded by the throng; he smiled broadly and waved his hat. "It's all right this time," he told them, giving the *Daily Express* its banner headline for the following morning.[42] Dunglass joined Chamberlain and his wife for tea. "I want you to come back from Germany with peace with honour," Annie Chamberlain told her husband. "You must speak from the window like Dizzy did."[43] During the evening Chamberlain and Halifax met Masaryk in Halifax's room at the Foreign Office. It was a painful and distressing interview for the son of Czechoslovakia's founding father. Masaryk tried to insist that a Czech presence at Munich should be a precondition of the meeting, but was bluntly told that Hitler had only agreed to the conference on condition that Russia and Czechoslovakia were excluded. Masaryk struggled to control his emotions. "If you have sacrificed my nation to preserve the peace of the world," he told them, "I will be the first to applaud you. But if not, gentlemen, God help your souls."[44]

▪ ▪ ▪

Having agreed to the conference, the Axis powers lost little time in preparing for it. No sooner had the invitations to Chamberlain and Daladier been dispatched, than Weizsäcker went to work at the Chancellery, aided by Göring and Neurath, to prepare a draft agreement that would be acceptable to Germany during the negotiations. As soon as the document was ready, Göring secured Hitler's approval, Schmidt translated it into French, and it was presented to Attolico, who in turn telegraphed it to Mussolini before he left Rome. Ribbentrop was deliberately excluded from the drafting process. The Italian dictator was later able to produce this draft at Munich as his own work. Weizsäcker also issued a communiqué designed to ensure that a suitable propaganda message was sent out to the watching world; there was to be no suggestion of a climb-down by the Führer. The invitation to Munich had been issued only "after the British and French governments had stated themselves to be ready to make important concessions to the German demands. Because of this, the outlook in favour of peace is considerably improved."[45]

At 6 P.M. Mussolini and Ciano, accompanied by a vast entourage decked out in glittering uniforms, left Rome for Munich by special train; the cheers of the crowds were clearly audible at the nearby British embassy. "In the train," recorded Ciano, "the Duce is in good humour." Over dinner he gave vent to his views about the British.

> In a country where animals are adored to the point of making cemeteries and hospitals and houses for them, and legacies are bequeathed to parrots, you can be sure that decadence has set in . . . it is also a consequence of the composition of the English people. Four million surplus women. Four million sexually unsatisfied women, artificially creating a host of problems in order to excite or appease their senses. Not being able to embrace one man, they embrace humanity.[46]

In the early hours of September 29, the train was boarded at the Brenner Pass by a group of high-ranking Nazis, who informed Mussolini that the Führer would meet him at Kufstein, a small stop on the former Austro-German border. Their tone was far from reassuring. "The Führer is half-satisfied," Prince Philip of Hesse told Ciano.[47]

Hitler, meanwhile, had traveled overnight by train from Berlin, with Göring and Ribbentrop, and arrived early the following morning in Munich. He left again almost immediately and, shortly after 9 A.M., arrived at the deserted station at Kufstein, where Mussolini too alighted soon after, and joined Hitler in his dining car. As the two dictators sped toward Munich, Hitler was in a bellicose mood, spreading out several huge maps, which illustrated the Sudeten areas to be transferred, the layout of the fortifications at the West Wall and the precise deployment of his divisions on both the Czech and French borders. He intended "to liquidate Czechoslovakia as she now is," and reminded Mussolini that the delay in mobilization to which he had agreed expired at 2 P.M. that afternoon; after that, "either the Conference is successful in a short time or the solution will take place by force of arms." Mussolini listened carefully, with growing apprehension, but said little. "Besides," concluded Hitler, "the time will come when we shall have to fight side by side against France and England. All the better that it should happen while the Duce and I are at the head of our countries, and still young and full of vigour."[48]

▪ ▪ ▪

The British delegation that was to fly to Munich assembled at Downing Street early on the morning of Thursday, September 29; it was considerably larger than that which had traveled to Berchtesgaden or Godesberg. The ubiquitous Wilson, together with William Strang and Sir William Malkin of the Foreign Office, were all to fly again; they were joined this time by Frank Ashton-Gwatkin, fresh from his work with the Runciman Mission. Chamberlain's Downing Street staff was represented by Lord Dunglass, Cecil Syers of his Private Office, his personal doctor, and two secretaries and accompanying detectives. As he stepped into his car, the Prime Minister was cheered by a group of workmen, already hard at work stacking sandbags in front of the windows of the neighboring Foreign Office. Cheering crowds lined the route to Heston, where the party arrived shortly before 8:30 A.M. At Simon's suggestion, the entire Cabinet had risen early that morning, and had made their way to the airport in a surprise show of solidarity with the Prime Minister—all that is except "that absurd dissenting nanny-goat Eddie Winterton," according to Channon.[49] A steady drizzle was falling, as the large crowd of ministers, foreign diplomats and journalists prepared to wave Chamberlain off.

As he had done previously, the Prime Minister paused at the foot of the aircraft steps.

When I was a little boy I used to repeat: "If at first you don't succeed, try, try, try again." That is what I am doing. When I come back I hope I may be able to say, as Hotspur said in Henry IV, "Out of this nettle, danger, we pluck this flower, safety."[50]

The plane was once again well stocked for the journey. Luncheon hampers had been provided by the Savoy Hotel, containing grouse sandwiches, caviar, pâté and smoked salmon; for added sustenance there was a supply of beer, claret and cider. The mood during the three-hour flight was anxious. Wilson prepared his notes for the conference; it was hoped that the most recent British proposals would form the basis of any discussion. It was now Thursday, and it was expected that the conference would last until Sunday at the very earliest. Chamberlain said little, but confided in Dunglass that "this was his last throw, but that he could not see how it would pay Hitler to push things to the point of war."[51] The previous night he had sent a telegram to Beneš, promising that he would "have the interests of Czechoslovakia fully in mind," and was going to Munich "with the intention of trying to find accommodation between position of German and Czechoslovak Governments."[52] In fact, he had no such intention, nor would he have the strength of purpose to ensure that the request implicit in Beneš's reply would be agreed to either. "I beg that nothing may be done at Munich," pleaded the Czech President, "without Czechoslovakia being heard."[53]

The two British aircraft touched down at Oberwiesenfeld Aerodrome shortly before noon. Daladier had already arrived from Paris looking tired and worn out; even his own ambassador thought he looked "gloomy and preoccupied . . . his head buried deep between his shoulders, his brow deeply furrowed with wrinkles."[54] The French were escorted to their hotel, the Vier Jahreszeiten, by Ribbentrop, and had been astonished by the warmth of their reception from the people of Munich. According to *The Times* correspondent, however, the vast crowds at the airport and those thronging the streets had been "saving up their enthusiasm" for Chamberlain.[55] Ribbentrop returned to the airport in time to greet the British too, together with the inevitable military band, SS guard of honor, and much shouting of "Heil Hitler!" Henderson and Kirkpatrick had come from Berlin. Chamberlain stood briefly in an open-topped car acknowledging the cheers of the crowd, before the cavalcade set off through the streets of Munich; on the orders of the local Gauleiter, the city was decked out with flags and banners.

To their surprise, the British were not taken to their hotel, but direct to the Führerbau, the local Nazi Party headquarters, where the conference was to be held. The streets were lined with cheering crowds, "unbelievable in their enthusiasm," although it later turned out that Ribbentrop had deliberately chosen a route that would avoid those that were the most crowded.[56] The Führerbau, completed in 1937, was the latest addition to Nazi neoclassical design: "a characteristic specimen of Hitlerian architecture, it repudiated detail, ornament, curve, and roundness of form, seeking to impress by the Doric simplicity of its lines and the massive aspect of its proportions." The sole visible decoration on the cream and pink marble facade was a huge bronze eagle with outstretched wings.[57] It was one of two identical office blocks that had been built at one end of the wide-open Königsplatz on which stood the huge Glyptothek museum; one became Hitler's Munich headquarters, the other an administration building. They had been designed by Hitler's favorite architect, Paul Troost, before his death in 1934, and replaced the nearby former party headquarters, the so-called Braune Haus. Alongside the Führerbau were the two neoclassical open-air Temples of Honor, built in 1935 as a permanent resting place for the sixteen cast iron sarcophagi containing the bodies of the "martyrs" of the Nazi putsch of November 1923. The whole area was the heart of "Nazi ritual worship," the temples "the altars of the movement."[58]

Halifax had visited the building the previous autumn, after his visit to Berchtesgaden, and had been greatly impressed by the "modern German architecture." The buildings reminded the former Viceroy of India of the "two blocks of the Secretariat at Delhi." Inside it was "very spacious, with two good staircases, immense corridors, and a banqueting hall with quite good plaster bust reliefs of Hitler Youth, Agriculture, Industry, Storm Troops, etc." A huge central hall led to the stone double staircase that went up to the reception rooms and Hitler's own office. Everywhere there were marble columns and extravagant wood paneling, while the rooms were furnished with thick wool carpets, huge fireplaces, deep armchairs and expensive works of art. Hitler's office was "decorated with a death mask of Frederick the Great . . . who is evidently a hero,"[59] while *The Times* told its readers that the room was "dominated by a Lenbach painting of Emperor William I."[60] The "Londoner's Diary" column of the *Evening Standard* was not so impressed. The Führerbau, its readers were told, resembled "a second-rate barracks," while there was an air of absurdity about the "attendants in blue and gold uniform" standing outside the building.[61]

Chamberlain was met at the imposing entrance to the Führerbau by Keitel and, to an accompanying drum roll, they mounted the steps while the guard of honor saluted. Inside the building, Dunglass recalled the sensation of being "shepherded" to the room that had been assigned to them—"the feeling was as if one was under arrest."[62] The impact was deliberate, and was accentuated by the wide-open corridors, lined with "SS men with expressionless, rigid faces, who had been given orders to create the impression that they were ready to march." Chamberlain responded to their shouts of "Heil Hitler!" with "an amicable nod."[63] He was the first leader to arrive, and was shown into an upstairs drawing room where a buffet had been laid out. The British stood around nervously, outnumbered by the silent footmen, wearing breeches with white stockings, long black tailcoats with silver shoulder knots, and silver-buckled shoes. Fortunately they did not have long to wait. Daladier arrived soon after, accompanied by François-Poncet, and the State Secretary at the Quai d'Orsay, Alexis Léger; they had been collected from their hotel by Göring, "bedecked with braid and decorations, his face radiant." Chamberlain reminded François-Poncet of an elderly English lawyer—"grizzled, bowed, with bushy eyebrows and protruding teeth, his face blotchy, his hands reddened by rheumatism." He stood nervously between Wilson and Strang, all three of them dressed in drab, black suits.

Next to arrive was Mussolini, in a uniform that was slightly too tight for him, with "the features of a Caesar, patronizing, completely at ease as though in his own house." Behind him, at the head of a small army of Italian officers and diplomats, all wearing uniforms of varying degrees of gaudiness, accessorized with plenty of gold braid and decorations, came Ciano, "a tall healthy fellow, very solicitous of his master, more the orderly officer than the minister of foreign affairs."[64] Finally Hitler himself strode into the room, accompanied by his adjutants. Pale, tense and clearly agitated, he wasted no time on the niceties of polite introductions, and while he made a point of greeting Mussolini warmly, he exchanged cold handshakes with Daladier and Chamberlain. At first Mussolini remained in a corner of the room, surrounded by Nazis, with whom he chatted away happily like old acquaintances; the British and French, meanwhile, stood about awkwardly, trying to make conversation among themselves. At last, Chamberlain made his way over to introduce himself to Mussolini. "He thanks him for all that he has already done," recorded Ciano, "but the Duce, coldly, does not take advantage of the opening, and the conversation peters out."[65]

Hitler invited the principal participants into his private study. They took their places beside a large fireplace, sitting in a circle around a low coffee table that was too small to be of much use. Hitler sat with his back to the window so as to leave his face in the shadow, with Schmidt sitting between him and Chamberlain, and Wilson to the left of the Prime Minister next to the fireplace. Weizsäcker and Ribbentrop sat opposite, alongside Daladier and Léger, while Mussolini and Ciano made themselves comfortable on a deep sofa in the middle of the room, facing the fireplace. The ambassadors, other diplomats and soldiers were all left outside. The meeting began at 12:45 P.M. and it was immediately obvious that there had been little or no preparatory organization for the discussion. With everyone sitting in comfortable chairs, the atmosphere was far from businesslike; there was no agenda, no chairman, no one to take notes, and not even any paper or pencils for the leaders to take their own. The local telephone system had crashed. It was, wrote Strang, a "hugger-mugger affair."[66]

The informal atmosphere played into Hitler's hands. Henderson was told that "at no stage of the conversations did they become heated,"[67] while Schmidt detected from the start "an atmosphere of general goodwill."[68] Although Chamberlain had feared the worst, and later claimed that the day "was one prolonged nightmare," he found Hitler's opening remarks "so moderate and reasonable" that "he felt instant relief."[69] The record, however, shows that Hitler was in a hurry, and in no mood to argue.

> He had now declared in his speech at the Sportspalast that he would in any case march in on October 1. He had received the answer that this action would have the character of an act of violence. Hence the task arose to absolve this action from such a character. Action must, however, be taken at once.

Ciano noted that Hitler spoke "calmly, but from time to time he gets excited and then he raises his voice and beats his fist against the palm of his other hand."[70] The three guests thanked the Führer for his hospitality, and it was left to Mussolini to produce the written plan of action which he had brought with him, "in order to bring about a practical solution of the problem."

Mussolini's five-point memorandum was, of course, the same document as that which had been drawn up at the Reich Chancellery the previous day by Weizsäcker, and then transmitted to Rome. Yet in spite of its striking similarity to Hitler's Godesberg terms, neither Chamberlain nor Daladier seemed to grasp this obvious fact. To the relief of the British, Daladier "welcomed the Duce's proposal, which had been made in an objective and realistic spirit," and Chamberlain then "also welcomed the Duce's proposal and declared that he himself had conceived of a solution on the lines of this proposal."[71] The naïveté of the British and French leaders seems breathtaking. Henderson believed that Mussolini had "acted as a brake on Hitler," and had "tactfully put forward as his own a combination of Hitler's and the Anglo-French proposals,"[72] while François-Poncet somehow got the impression that the discussion was based on a British memorandum "drawn up by Sir Horace Wilson with Strang's assistance."[73]

The proposals were then debated clause by clause, and there was no argument over Clause 1, which allowed for the evacuation of the Sudeten areas to commence on October 1. However, the first sign of trouble arose over Clause 2, which stated that "the Guarantor Powers, England, France and Italy, will guarantee to Germany that the evacuation of the territory shall be completed by the 10th October, without any existing installations being destroyed."[74] In a halfhearted effort to honor his promise to Beneš, Chamberlain insisted that he could give no such guarantee without knowing whether the Czech government would consent to such a demand. For this purpose, he would need a formal assurance from an official Czech representative, who, he suggested, should be invited to join the conference forthwith. This proposal inspired a furious tirade from Hitler, the only one of any substance during the day, who launched into a familiar verbal onslaught against the Czechs in general and Beneš in particular.

Accounts of the meeting differ over the degree of support Chamberlain then received. According to François-Poncet, who was not in the room, it was at this stage that the taciturn Daladier made one of his rare contributions to the debate, "clearly and vigorously posing the crucial question"—did the conference wish Czechoslovakia to continue to exist, or did it not?

If the point was to prepare the dismemberment and disappearance of Czechoslovakia, then he, Daladier, had no business in this place. He refused to be associated with such a crime and would take his leave.[75]

Ciano grudgingly supports this version: "Daladier defends the cause of the Czechs without much conviction."[76] Schmidt, on the other hand, in the official German record, quoted Daladier as declaring that "the French Government would in no wise tolerate procrastination in this matter by the Czech Government. The Czech Government had given its word, and must honour it. There could be no talk of postponing the evacuation."[77] His views were, in any case, immaterial. Hitler refused to share the room with a Czech, and Chamberlain was forced to back down, although it was agreed that a Czech representative should be made available nearby in case he was needed.

Much to Hitler's annoyance, Chamberlain also attempted to demonstrate his credentials as a businessman, by stubbornly insisting on raising the question of compensation for the Czech government for the buildings and installations which would pass into German hands in the newly transferred territory of the Sudetenland. Hitler grew increasingly restive. Any such buildings had been constructed with money raised from taxes paid by the Sudeten Germans, and there could therefore be no question of any such indemnification. Chamberlain persisted, broadening his proposal to include indemnification for private individuals who, under the Godesberg terms, were forbidden from taking their possessions with them. "If the Czechoslovaks want to leave these regions and if they cannot take their cattle with them," asked Chamberlain, "who will indemnify them?"[78] At this Hitler finally exploded. "Our time is too valuable to be wasted on such trivialities," he shouted.[79]

At 3:15 P.M. the conference broke for lunch, under strict orders to be back at the Führerbau in little over an hour. Mussolini and Ciano were entertained by Hitler at his private apartment, while the French returned to their hotel, and the British made their way to theirs for the first time. According to Wilson, the British invited the French to join them at the Regina Palast Hotel to discuss the progress of the conference, but Daladier failed to appear. Instead the French took their lunch in the dining room at the Vier Jahreszeiten, with Göring, Ribbentrop and their wives at a nearby table. When proceedings resumed at 4:30 P.M. Hitler's mood had worsened. He returned to the Führerbau to find Chamberlain and Daladier deep in conversation on the first-floor gallery outside the conference room. Impatient to get started, he angrily sent Ribbentrop over to summon the two statesmen back to the meeting. The chaotic atmosphere of the morning's session became still more pronounced. François-Poncet took the lead by entering the conference room uninvited, whereupon a whole host of ambassadors, generals, adjutants, legal advisers and aides followed suit.

For two and a half hours, the discussion focused on Mussolini's paper, which had been translated into the various languages over lunch; a particular source of argument was the question of the guarantee to Czechoslovakia, and also the full extent of the territory to be occupied between October 1 and 10. The meeting became increasingly chaotic. Maps were unfolded and, as the participants broke up into smaller groups, the discussion became increasingly fragmented. The legal advisers assumed responsibility for drafting a final agreement. François-Poncet described the scene.

> No one was in the chair. There was no agenda. The discussion was uncontrolled, laborious, confused. It dragged along, handicapped by the burden of a double translation. It shifted from point to point; and came to a stop whenever there was a deadlock.[80]

Mussolini was "slightly annoyed by the vaguely parliamentary atmosphere" of the proceedings, and wandered "round the room with his hands in his pockets and a rather distracted air."[81] All the while Hitler "gazed intently upon him, subject to his charm and as though fascinated and hypnotized." When the Duce laughed, "the Führer laughed too; did Mussolini scowl, so scowled Hitler."[82]

Outside the formal proceedings of the conference, the hangers-on who had not been invited into Hitler's study did their best to keep themselves amused. Strang and Dunglass made themselves as comfortable as they could in the room set aside for the British delegation; through the open door they watched the hurried comings and goings of "flocks of spruce young SS subalterns in their black uniforms, haughty and punctilious." Of more interest was the makeshift beer hall in the cellar, to which they repaired at the most tedious moments.[83] They befriended Keitel and Neurath, and watched on in amazement as Göring, who remained in "boisterous good spirits throughout," changed his uniform several times during the day to impress everyone. Mussolini "strutted about with his chin in the air," exuding a confidence born of the fact that he was the only one of the four leaders who could understand and converse in all four languages. The Germans, noted Dunglass, "could not disguise their contempt for the Italians," which they were happy to share with their other guests.[84]

As day wore on into night, Hitler grew steadily more irritated. He had arranged an elaborate dinner at 9 P.M. to mark the conclusion of the conference, but it soon became obvious that proceedings would drag on long beyond then. The food was left to get cold, and the liveried footmen stood around with nothing to do. It was decided to call a further adjournment, but Chamberlain and Daladier declined Hitler's invitation to partake of the feast anyway, on the spurious grounds that they had to telephone home for advice. "They were obviously not in the mood to attend a banquet," observed Schmidt. "They had secured peace, but at the price of a serious loss of prestige."[85] Instead, they returned to their hotels to order room service, while in the grand hall of the Führerbau Hitler and Mussolini went ahead with the banquet anyway, at a table that was now much too long for the guests. Hitler talked incessantly and poured out a stream of venom against the Czechs, while Göring waxed lyrical about his favorite subject, the decadence of Western democracy.

Meanwhile, as Chamberlain had requested, two representatives of the Czech government had arrived in Munich. Dr. Voytech Mastný, the Czech Minister, arrived from Berlin, while Dr. Hubert Masařik, Private Secretary to the Foreign Minister, Krofta, flew in at short notice from Prague. Masařik, who traveled with his wife, was met at the airport by the Gestapo, and they were taken by police car directly to the Regina Palast Hotel, where the British were also staying. The atmosphere was oppressive. They knew no one, and the corridors were crowded with journalists and SS officers. Although they were shown into a comfortable room, it was soon apparent that they were effectively prisoners; they were not allowed to leave the hotel, and were denied use of the telephone. Finally, at 7 P.M., they were visited in their room by an evidently embarrassed Ashton-Gwatkin. He was "agitated and very silent" and, although he gave little away, it was obvious to Masařik that a plan was being hatched which "was already completed in its general lines and that this plan was much worse than the Anglo-French proposals."

Three hours later, at 10 P.M. during the break for dinner, Mastný and

Masařik were summoned to see Wilson in his room; he brusquely outlined the broad terms of the new agreement, and handed them a map on which the areas for immediate occupation were clearly marked. In response to a series of factual questions from the Czechs, dealing with particular towns and districts which they felt to be important, Wilson cut them short, and fell back on formality, declaring that he "had nothing to add to his communication." He then left them alone with Ashton-Gwatkin, who was more forthcoming, but no more sympathetic. It was difficult negotiating with Hitler, he explained. The British favored the new proposals and he gave them some blunt advice. "If you do not accept you will have to settle your affairs with the Germans absolutely alone," he warned. "Perhaps the French will say this to you more kindly, but believe me they share our views. They are disinterested."[86]

From 8:33 P.M., news of the proceedings had begun to filter out to the waiting world in a series of telegrams from the British United Press news agency. Based in the lobby of a local hotel, the agency had six reporters working on the story, and kept a series of telephone and telex lines permanently open between Munich and London. Their source of information was one of Hitler's closest aides, Fritz Wiedemann, and although the BBC later complained that the agency had consistently jumped the gun with its exclusives, the BUP left all other news organizations trailing in its wake. While "German sources" throughout the evening claimed that an agreement was imminent, at 9:26 P.M. it was reported that a British spokesman, presumably Wilson, on returning to the Regina Palast would only comment that the "discussions were of a friendly character. There are still a number of points to discuss." Four minutes later the agency reported that Italian journalists had been "officially informed that Mussolini hopes to be able to entrain for Rome about midnight."[87]

Shortly after 10 P.M. the conference resumed. By now the work was largely in the hands of a small drafting committee, on which Sir William Malkin was the British representative. Those who were not directly involved lounged around the fireplace, waiting for what seemed like an eternity for the definitive draft of the agreement. Daladier sat slumped in a deep armchair, while the ebullient Göring remained at the heart of all conversation. Hitler sat "moodily apart," shifting uncomfortably on his sofa, crossing and uncrossing his legs, folding his arms and glaring round the room. He made several unsuccessful attempts to join in the conversation.[88] At 1:30 A.M., the finished document, no more than a few typewritten sheets clipped together, was at last ceremoniously placed on the mahogany table in the center of the room, beside an enormous, ornate inkwell. Hitler was the first to sign, appearing almost reluctant to attach his signature, and even this moment did not pass off smoothly. "When the time had come to sign the final Agreements," Chamberlain told the Cabinet the following day, "it was found that the inkpot into which Herr Hitler dipped his pen was empty!"[89]

Under the terms of the Munich Agreement, the German army would, after all, begin its occupation of the "predominantly German territory" in Czechoslovakia on October 1, as Hitler had always insisted that it would. For the purposes of the "evacuation" the territory in question was to be divided into four distinct zones, clearly marked on a map that accompanied the agreement; the phased occupation would begin on October 1 and be completed by October 10. Britain, France and Italy would guarantee that the evacuation of the territory would take place on the dates agreed, "without any existing installations having been destroyed." The precise conditions for the evacuation would be set by a newly created international commission of the four powers, with a Czech representative in attendance, which would begin work in Berlin immediately; it would then be responsible for ascertaining the "remaining territory of preponderantly German character . . . to be occupied by German troops by 10 October." The commission was also charged with determining those further areas of the Sudetenland which would be subject to a plebiscite, and in fixing the conditions for those plebiscites, to be held before the end of November. Finally, it would propose a definitive new frontier, and was empowered to recommend to the four powers, "in certain exceptional cases, minor modifications in the strictly ethnographical determination of the zones which are to be transferred without plebiscite."[90]

At 1:57 A.M. British United Press put out its final telegram of the night.

The communiqué specifies that the agreement is between Germany, the United Kingdom, France and Italy and does not specify Czechoslovakia's agreement. It specifies that the evacuation shall be completed without any existing installations being destroyed. The Czech Government shall be held responsible for evacuation without damage.[91]

For the professional diplomats, the signing of the agreement was "a distressing event."[92] Kirkpatrick found it "a very sad affair . . . with no redeeming feature." Göring and Mussolini, he recorded, were "jubilant," while the image lingered long of the "watery smile of Himmler's fish-slab face."[93] Only François-Poncet, however, had the courage to speak out at the time. *"Voilà comme la France traite les seuls alliés qui lui étaient restés fidèles,"* he exclaimed bitterly.[94] Daladier too looked unhappy. "You will be cheered when you get back to France," a smiling Mussolini told him.[95]

At 2:30 A.M. the last cars finally left the Königsplatz. "It is terrible," Hitler said to Ribbentrop, on the steps of the Führerbau as they watched Chamberlain and Daladier drive away, "I always have to deal with nonentities."[96] William Shirer had stayed up until the bitter end, and was outside the Führerbau as the leaders left. He later recalled "the light of victory in Hitler's eyes as he strutted down the broad steps . . . the cockiness of Mussolini laced in his special militia uniform." Chamberlain too had "looked particularly pleased with himself" as he returned to the Regina Palast Hotel. Daladier, on the other hand, "looked a completely broken man." A journalist shouted out, asking if he was satisfied with the agreement. He "turned as if to say something, but he was too tired and defeated and the words did not come out and he stumbled out of the door in silence."[97]

Back at the Regina Palast Hotel, the British and French had one last, unpleasant duty to perform. The Czech representatives had been waiting throughout the night for news and they were now summoned to Chamberlain's private sitting room, to be confronted by the two prime ministers, as well as Wilson, Léger and Ashton-Gwatkin. They were all exhausted. "The atmosphere was oppressive," recalled Masařik, "judgement was about to be given. The French, visibly agitated, appeared to be expecting the blow to French prestige." Chamberlain made a long speech, defending the agreement, while Daladier handed a copy of the text and an accompanying map to Mastný, who read it quickly and began to ask questions. Chamberlain, meanwhile, "yawned continuously without the least embarrassment . . . and no longer concealed his fatigue." Masařik asked Daladier if a reply was expected from the Czech government, but the French Prime Minister was so "obviously embarrassed" that Léger answered for him, almost casually. Time was of the essence, so no reply would be required; "they regarded the plan as accepted." A Czech representative needed to be in Berlin that afternoon by 5 P.M. for the first meeting of the international commission.

"They were then finished with us," recorded Masařik, "and we were allowed to go. The Czechoslovak Republic as constituted within the frontiers of 1918 had ceased to exist."[98] Wilson gave Mastný "a pretty broad hint that—having regard to the seriousness of the alternative—the best course was for his Government to accept what was clearly a considerable improvement upon the German memorandum."[99] At this, Mastný burst into tears; François-Poncet did his best to console him. "Believe me," he said, "all this is not final. It is but one moment in a story which has just begun."[100] Unsurprisingly, Daladier rejected the suggestion that he should be responsible for taking the agreement to Prague, and it was agreed instead that Ashton-Gwatkin would accompany the Czechs back on their plane at 6 A.M. It was, recalled Ashton-Gwatkin, "one of the most cruel things I ever had to do," and the flight passed without a single word being said.[101] Just to make sure, Chamberlain dispatched a telegram to Newton in the early hours urging a "plain acceptance" of the terms. "You will appreciate," he concluded, "that there is no time for argument."[102] Daladier, on the other hand, did his best to soothe his Czech allies. He had, he assured Beneš, only signed the agreement with "deep emotion and . . . it was not by my choice that no representative of Czechoslovakia was present." He too, however, instructed the French Minister in Prague "to make sure of the President's agreement."[103]

In fact, the German Minister in Prague beat them all to it. He roused the Foreign Minister, Krofta, from his bed at 5 A.M., and peremptorily presented him with a copy of the agreement just a few hours after it had been signed. Beneš, his Cabinet and his military commanders spent the morning weighing up their options, while the British, French and Italian ministers all did their governments' bidding, and called to demand a decision by noon at the latest. At 12:30 P.M. Krofta informed the three ministers that Czechoslovakia accepted "the decisions taken at Munich without us and against us."

> The Government of the Czechoslovak Republic, in announcing this acceptance, declares also before the whole world its protest against the decisions which were taken unilaterally and without our participation.

At 5 P.M. General Syrový had the difficult task of announcing the country's capitulation over the radio.

> I am experiencing the gravest hour of my life. I would have been pre-pared to die rather than to go through this. We have had to choose between making a desperate and hopeless defence, which would have meant the sacrifice of an entire generation of our adult men, as well as of our women and children, and accepting, without a struggle and under pressure, terms which are without parallel in history for their ruthless-ness. We were deserted. We stood alone.[104]

▪ ▪ ▪

Before leaving the Führerbau the previous night, Chamberlain had asked Hitler if they might meet the following morning for a private talk; the Führer apparently "jumped at the idea."[105] Therefore on the morning of September 30 Chamberlain woke early after just a few hours' sleep, and summoned an exhausted William Strang to his room; he asked the official to draft a short statement on the future of Anglo-German relations. While he was dressing and having breakfast, Strang composed three short para-graphs for Chamberlain to approve; the resulting document remains one of the most famous documents of the twentieth century.

> We, the German Führer and Chancellor and the British Prime Minister, have had a further meeting today and are agreed in recognising that the question of Anglo-German relations is of the first importance for the two countries and for Europe.
>
> We regard the agreement signed last night and the Anglo-German Naval Agreement as symbolic of the desire of our two peoples never to go to war with one another again.
>
> We are resolved that the method of consultation shall be the method adopted to deal with any other questions that may concern our two coun-tries, and we are determined to continue our efforts to remove possible sources of difference and thus to contribute to assure the peace of Europe.

Chamberlain rewrote Strang's second paragraph and made one or two other minor changes, in spite of Strang complaining that the Anglo-German Naval

Agreement "was not a thing to be proud of." Chamberlain, however, replied that, on the contrary, it was exactly the kind of agreement he wished to reach with Germany. When Strang suggested that the Prime Minister should warn Daladier of his intention to reach a unilateral agreement with the Führer, Chamberlain brusquely replied that "he saw no reason whatever for saying anything to the French."[106] As he finished his breakfast, Chamberlain showed the draft to Dunglass and explained his thinking. "If he signs it and sticks to it that will be fine," he said, "but if he breaks it that will convince the Americans of the kind of man he is." On returning home, Chamberlain concluded, he would give the joint declaration "maximum publicity."[107]

As he was about to leave the hotel, Chamberlain asked why there was so much noise outside. It transpired that a huge crowd had gathered in the street, and they now refused to disperse until the Prime Minister saluted them. He duly picked up one of the many bunches of flowers that were stacked high in his room, and stepped out on to his balcony to acknowledge their cheers. Daladier too had a similar reception at his hotel. Chamberlain and Dunglass were driven to Hitler's private apartment at Prinzregentenplatz. He had lived there since 1929, "a modest apartment in a large building full of other residents," according to Ciano, who had accompanied Mussolini to lunch there the previous day. Ciano had, however, conceded that the Führer owned "many valuable pictures."[108] They found Hitler in a typically sullen and unresponsive mood. "Behind a dark table," recalled Dunglass many years later, "was this little, very grey, dull man . . . dressed in ordinary clothes, in a very, very dour mood."[109]

Hitler listened absentmindedly as Chamberlain opened the conversation with a lengthy list of topics he wished to discuss. He first urged the Führer to adopt a generous attitude in his implementation of the newly signed Munich Agreement. He was concerned lest "the Czech Government might be mad enough to refuse the terms and attempt resistance." If this was to happen, he hoped that Hitler would ensure that nothing was done "which would diminish the high opinion of him which would be held throughout the world in consequence of yesterday's proceedings." In particular, Chamberlain asked that there should be "no bombardment of Prague or killing of women and children by attacks from the air." Hitler replied nonchalantly that "he hated the thought of little babies being killed by gas bombs."[110]

The Prime Minister pressed on, his monologue becoming increasingly rambling. He also wished to discuss ways of bringing to an end the civil war in Spain, the generalities of Anglo-German relations, the world economy, and finally disarmament and the possible abolition of bombing. Although Chamberlain later described the meeting as "a very friendly and pleasant talk," in truth Hitler hardly contributed a word of his own, and Schmidt noticed that the Führer was becoming increasingly morose. Dunglass thought that Chamberlain would have to hold back the document in his pocket for fear of being rebuffed, but just as it appeared that the conversation had dragged on too long, he suddenly plucked the sheet of paper from his pocket and offered it to Hitler to read. Chamberlain later described to his sister the scene as Schmidt translated: "Hitler frequently ejaculated 'Ja! Ja!' and at the end he said 'Yes I will certainly sign it. When shall we do it?' I said 'Now,' and we went at once to the writing table and put our signatures to the two copies which I had brought with me."[111]

Although Chamberlain judged that Hitler had signed with enthusiasm, Schmidt thought quite the opposite, recording that the Führer had agreed to it "with a certain reluctance . . . only to please Chamberlain."[112] Nor was Dunglass, who was watching Hitler closely, fooled by the perfunctory manner in which he accepted. "He signed it with suspicious alacrity," he later claimed. "He was clearly disinterested by its content."[113] Chamberlain, on the other hand, was delighted, and "thanked the Führer warmly for his willingness and underlined the great psychological effect which he expected from this document."[114] He then tucked the piece of paper away in his breast pocket, signed the visitors' book and shook Hitler's hand enthusiastically. Before leaving, the two leaders posed for Hitler's photographer, Heinrich Hoffmann, on a red-velvet-covered sofa. When Eva Braun saw the photographs, she said conspiratorially to a friend: "If only Chamberlain knew the history of that sofa."[115] In the street, the Prime Minister doffed his hat genially in response to the SS guards' cries of "Heil Hitler."[116]

Back at the Regina Palast Hotel, the Foreign Office officials were concerned at Chamberlain's gullibility, and his obvious delight. When he saw Strang, he "complacently patted his breast-pocket and said 'I've got it!' "[117] Ashton-Gwatkin was told by a German friend that Hitler had said: "Well he was such a nice old gentleman I thought I'd give him my autograph as a souvenir!"[118] To his valet, Hitler boasted: "I gave him a noseful. He won't be visiting me again soon."[119] Later that day, when Ribbentrop expressed his concern at the wisdom of signing such a declaration, Hitler brushed him aside. "Oh, don't take it so seriously. That piece of paper is of no further significance whatsoever."[120] That was also the line taken by Germany with her allies. Fearing that the Italians might be upset by this apparently unilateral diplomacy, the Prince of Hesse was dispatched to Rome two days later with instructions to play down the significance of the document still further. "The Führer did not think he could refuse," he told Ciano. Mussolini was anyway philosophical. "Explanations are superfluous," he said. "You do not refuse a glass of lemonade to a thirsty man."[121]

On the way back to the hotel, Chamberlain was taken by his hosts on a short sightseeing tour of Munich. Among the sites he visited was the Sterneckerbräu, the former beer hall where Hitler had attended his first meeting of the DAP, the forerunner of the Nazi Party, in 1919. The party subsequently rented a room in the Sterneckerbräu as its first headquarters, and in 1920 it was also the venue for the founding of the notorious Sturm Abteilung (SA), the Storm Troop created to act as Hitler's bodyguard. By 1938, it had been converted into a shrinelike museum, full of Nazi memorabilia.[122] A month later, the diplomatic correspondent of the *Daily Herald*, William Ewer, wrote to Wilson inquiring about this "unexpected" visit to the birthplace of the Nazi Party, which he thought "seemed to indicate special interest." Wilson replied scornfully that "it would have been discourteous to decline" the offer of a "short drive . . . no political significance attaches to this visit, and it would of course be ridiculous to assume that there was any such significance."[123] Whatever the reason for the visit, Chamberlain appears either to have shown a remarkably poor grasp of Nazi history, or to have been deserted by his usually sure political touch.

▪ ▪ ▪

During the evening of September 29, while Chamberlain was in Munich, London waited for news with bated breath. The Other Club, a political dining club that had been founded by Churchill and F. E. Smith in 1911, was meeting for dinner at the Savoy Hotel. Since Smith's death in 1930, the club had been largely dominated by Churchill, and that night he was in a "towering rage and a deepening gloom." He had spent the afternoon trying to persuade various colleagues to sign an open telegram to Chamberlain, warning against making any further concessions at the expense of the Czechs; both Eden and Attlee had refused to sign. As news of the terms agreed at Munich filtered through in the course of the evening, a growing sense of despair descended on the company. Churchill directed his fury at the two ministers present, Duff Cooper and Walter Elliot. How, he asked, "could honourable men with wide experience and fine records in the Great War condone a policy so cowardly? It was sordid, squalid, sub-human, and suicidal."

As the tension grew, the atmosphere in the room became increasingly acrimonious. The editor of the *Observer*, J. L. Garvin, whose editorials throughout the crisis had been staunchly pro-Chamberlain, was forced to defend himself; he had, he pointed out, written a "stiff article" in the previous Sunday's paper. "What is the use of that," asked Bob Boothby, "after forty flabby ones?" Garvin stormed out of the room, and was not to renew his membership until 1945. Cooper, meanwhile, grew increasingly depressed as the evening went on. When someone went out into the Strand to buy an early edition of the morning newspaper, Cooper "seized it and read out the story with obvious anger and disgust. There was a silence as if all had been stricken dumb."[124] Cooper's face flushed, and he whispered to Boothby: "I shall resign tomorrow morning."[125] The evening finally concluded when "everybody insulted everybody else and Winston ended by saying that at the next General Election he would speak on every socialist platform in the country against the Government."[126] As Churchill was leaving, the sound of laughter alerted him to a party in the next-door restaurant. "Those poor people!" he exclaimed. "They little know what they will have to face."[127]

The following day Chamberlain returned from Munich in triumph. Halifax drove back into London with him from Heston, performing the role of the slave who, during the triumphs of ancient Rome, would accompany the victorious general in his chariot, and "whose duty it was constantly to whisper in his ear reminders of his mortality."[128] Halifax offered two pieces of advice. First, that there should be no snap general election to capitalize electorally on Chamberlain's success at Munich, in spite of the urgings of the Conservative Central Office; and second, that he should strengthen his parliamentary position by broadening the base of his

Cabinet, and creating a truly National Government. This would mean offering Cabinet posts to Churchill and Eden, as well as to members of both the Labour and Liberal parties. "All this will be over in three months," predicted Chamberlain, as their car struggled through the traffic to his appointment with the King at Buckingham Palace.[129]

That evening, ministers had to elbow their way through the cheering throngs, to reach Downing Street for the Cabinet meeting. Sir Orme Sargent, an Assistant Under-Secretary, watched the scene from a balcony at the Foreign Office across the road. "You might think that we'd won a major victory," he said distastefully, "instead of just betraying a minor country."[130] At 7:30 P.M. the Cabinet finally managed to assemble to hear Chamberlain's report. In a "departure from normal procedure," Simon spoke first, opening the proceedings with an effusive tribute. He wished to "express, on behalf of the whole Cabinet, their profound admiration for the unparalleled efforts the Prime Minister had made and for the success that he had achieved. He would also like to say how proud they were to be associated with the Prime Minister as his colleagues at this time." Even Chamberlain, who "felt that we could now safely regard the crisis as ended," appeared momentarily taken aback by such fulsome praise, and only mumbled that he was "deeply grateful."

He then described the proceedings at Munich, the protracted length of which had been "largely due to the inefficiency of the arrangements for the Conference made by the Germans." He assured his colleagues that he had only agreed with reluctance to the German refusal, on the grounds of lack of time, to allow a Czech representative to attend; Mussolini, he told them, "had already organised his own reception in Rome for Friday." He had nevertheless "done his best for Czechoslovakia in the absence of a Czech Government representative, and he thought that the arrangements secured could, taken as a whole, be regarded as satisfactory." He quoted at length from a document drawn up by Wilson on the return flight, which described the supposed differences between the Godesberg terms and the Munich Agreement. The latter, he claimed, was a "vast improvement," and it had been a "triumph for diplomacy that representatives of the Four Powers concerned should have met and reached a peaceful settlement of the matter."[131]

In the course of the half-hour meeting, only Duff Cooper voiced his dissatisfaction. On reading the Munich terms that morning, his first reaction had been that he must resign; he had spent the rest of the day "in high spirits at the prospect of my new liberty." When he arrived in Downing Street, the "scenes of indescribable enthusiasm" had made him feel "very lonely in the midst of so much happiness that I could not share."[132] He conceded that the difference between the Godesberg and Munich terms was indeed greater than he had initially realized, but he "nevertheless still felt considerable uneasiness in regard to the position." He had come to the meeting ready to resign, and "he still felt it was his duty to offer the Prime Minister his resignation."[133] Chamberlain smiled at him "in quite a friendly way," and said that it was a matter to be settled between the two of them. Hore-Belisha and Stanley both admitted to similar concerns, but urged Cooper not to resign, while Hoare grumbled that "it was most improper and quite without precedent to discuss personal matters of this sort in Cabinet, and he hoped the discussion would not be prolonged."[134]

The following morning, Cooper went to see Chamberlain to tender his resignation. The "interview was as friendly as it was brief." He then made his way to Buckingham Palace to hand in his seals of office; the King was polite but frank. "He said he could not agree with me, but he respected those who had the courage of their convictions."[135] In fact, the King was more preoccupied with the prospect of being able to resume his summer holiday. "We may be returning to Balmoral tomorrow night," he wrote to his mother the same day. The Prime Minister "could see no reason why we should not go." Before leaving London, King George VI issued a message to his people: "The time of anxiety is past. After the magnificent efforts of the Prime Minister in the cause of peace it is my fervent hope that a new era of friendship and prosperity may be dawning among the peoples of the world." Queen Mary herself was even more outspoken in her support for Chamberlain. "I am sure you feel as angry as I do at people croaking as they do at the P.M.'s action," she replied to her son a few days later. "He brought home Peace, why can't they be grateful?"[136]

For a brief period Chamberlain basked in the adulation of a largely uncritical press and a thankful people. "No conqueror returning from a victory on the battlefield," enthused *The Times*, "has come home adorned with nobler laurels than Mr. Chamberlain from Munich yesterday."[137] The often critical *Daily Telegraph* too had no reservations: "The news will be hailed with a profound and universal relief. . . . Never for a moment has Mr. Chamberlain spared himself in the pursuit of his mission." The *Daily Express* was typically effusive: "The Prime Minister's conquests are mighty and enduring—millions of happy homes and hearts relieved of their burden. To him the laurels!"[138] Even the Labour-supporting *Daily Herald* grudgingly admitted that "Herr Hitler has had to abandon the most brutal of his Godesberg terms," although the agreement remained "open to grave criticism on a number of points."[139] Lord Rothermere sent a brief telegram of his own, "You are wonderful,"[140] while President Roosevelt was more taciturn: "Good man."[141] The Duke of Windsor also wrote from the south of France: "The Duchess and I wish to join with millions who are acclaiming you throughout the world in expressing our deep gratitude and admiration for what you have done."[142]

In the days following Munich, Chamberlain received more than 20,000 letters and telegrams of thanks, while he was showered with an "embarrassing profusion" of gifts, including "countless fishing flies, salmon rods, Scottish tweed for suits, socks, innumerable umbrellas, pheasants and grouse, fine Rhine wines, lucky horseshoes, flowers from Hungary, 6000 assorted bulbs from grateful Dutch admirers and a cross from the Pope."[143] Lord Lee of Fareham, who had given Chequers to the nation in 1921, now presented the Chamberlains with a silver dinner service, "to express our admiration and gratitude in some tangible and lasting form."[144] *Paris Soir* opened a fund to present him with a property in France: "A corner of French soil. A simple house—for his tastes are simple—besides a river, since he likes to fish . . . the House of Peace." Charities sought to take advantage of the mood of relief by taking out advertisements in newspapers, asking readers to give generously: "Now that the great Tragedy of World War has been averted will you please send a thanksoffering [sic] for peace to The Royal Cancer Hospital and give invaluable help in another war that is being waged."[145] When the *Daily Sketch* offered readers a photograph of the Chamberlains, to be paid for with three-pence-worth of stamps, the paper received more than 90,000 applications, while a prominent businessman donated £10,000 to Birmingham University to fund a scholarship in Chamberlain's name.[146]

The overwhelming sensation for many people, as expressed by Sir Isaiah Berlin, was a combination of "shame and relief."[147] The anti-appeasing editor of the weekly magazine *Time and Tide* summed up the dilemma while trying to write a leading article on the agreement. Nine-tenths of her "mind and heart were stricken with not only shame but the certainty of ultimate disaster . . . one tenth was filled with a blessed feeling of relief: There will be no bombs tonight."[148] Harold Macmillan too shared in the general sense of relief. His son would "stay at school and go to Oxford in the autumn . . . my home and children, like all the other homes throughout the country, would be spared—at least for the time."[149] Even Halifax told Harvey that "he thought it was a horrid business and humiliating, no use blinking the fact, but yet better than a European war."[150]

On October 1 Chamberlain went to Chequers to prepare himself for the following week's parliamentary debate. While he was out walking on the estate that afternoon he had, he confessed to his sister, come "nearer there to a nervous breakdown than I have ever been in my life," as he contemplated the "fresh ordeal to go through in the House."[151] In his absence, the Inner Circle met at the Treasury, and agreed that "it would be a mistake to enter into a detailed discussion in the debate of the terms of the Munich Agreement, or to invite detailed comments on its provisions."[152] The full Cabinet then met on October 3, the morning of the debate. There had been a good deal of speculation in the press that there would be further ministerial resignations. Oliver Stanley, in particular, had written to complain that there was still "a considerable divergence of view" between himself and the Prime Minister, and that he remained "profoundly sceptical of Nazi promises"; he did not view "the present situation as 'peace in our time' but as an uneasy truce." However, he now agreed to accept Cabinet responsibility, and to acknowledge that the Munich terms were an improvement on those agreed at Godesberg.[153]

The four-day debate opened with Cooper's well-received resignation statement. He began by drawing on the lessons of 1914.

> I thought then, and I have always felt, that in any other international crisis that should occur our first duty was to make plain exactly where we stood and what we would do. I believe that the great defect in our foreign policy during recent months and weeks has been that we have failed to do so. During the last four weeks we have been drifting, day by day, nearer into war with Germany, and we have never said, until the last moment, and then in most uncertain terms, that we were prepared to fight.

He went on to criticize Chamberlain for his naïveté. The Prime Minister had "believed in addressing Herr Hitler through the language of sweet reasonableness. I have believed that he was more open to the language of the mailed fist." Cooper concluded with an emotional valediction.

> I have forfeited a great deal. I have given up an office that I loved, work in which I was deeply interested and a staff of which any man might be proud. . . . I have ruined, perhaps, my political career. But that is a little matter; I have retained something which is to me of great value—I can still walk about the world with my head erect.[154]

As he sat down, he received a note from Churchill: "Your speech was one of the finest parliamentary performances I have ever heard. It was admirable in form, massive in argument and shone with courage and public spirit."[155]

Chamberlain made no attempt to reply to Cooper's claims. Instead he argued that the agreement was justified because the principle that the Sudetenland should be ceded to "the German Reich . . . had been decided already. What we had to consider was the method, the conditions and the time of the transfer of the territory." This had to be done quickly to prevent "the outbreak of a conflict which might have precipitated the catastrophe." He particularly emphasized the positive differences between the terms agreed at Munich and those at Godesberg. The occupation was to be phased over ten days rather than immediate; the line of the German advance was to be fixed by the international commission, which would also define the plebiscite areas; and, finally, Britain would act as a guarantor of Czechoslovakia's new borders. "It is my hope, and my belief," he continued, "that under the new system of guarantees, the new Czechoslovakia will find a greater security than she has ever enjoyed in the past." As MPs interrupted his speech with cries of "Shame," Chamberlain even pleaded for a greater understanding of Hitler's role. "After everything that has said about the German Chancellor today and in the past, I do feel that the House ought to recognise the difficulty for a man in that position to take back such emphatic declarations as he had already made amidst the enthusiastic cheers of his supporters."[156]

That night Macmillan brought together the Conservative rebels and the Labour leadership, ostensibly to discuss the precise wording of the Opposition amendment, which was to be tabled the following day. Somewhat reluctantly,

Hugh Dalton accompanied Macmillan after midnight to the Westminster home of Brendan Bracken, where they found both Churchill and Eden. It was impressed upon Dalton that, in order to maximize the Tory abstention, the words used should be "neither too hostile nor too extravagant in their censure" of the government, for fear of frightening off wavering rebels on the Conservative backbenches.[157] One draft referred to "national unity and strength," but Dalton insisted: "That is not our jargon." When he then warned that some Labour MPs wished to see a strongly worded amendment to prove that they were "brave and uncompromising," Churchill in turn replied: "It is not enough to be brave. We must also be victorious." The meeting also considered the likelihood that Chamberlain planned to call an early general election, in which he, "as Saviour of Peace, would sweep the country." Any Conservative rebels at the end of the Munich debate would "be marked down for destruction and official Tory candidates run against them." Dalton, however, refused to commit immediately to an electoral pact whereby Labour would refuse to oppose those MPs, were they indeed to be challenged by a "loyalist" pro-Chamberlain candidate.[158]

The remaining days of the debate were, for Chamberlain, "a pretty trying ordeal," as the "ceaseless stream of vituperation being poured upon me had a somewhat depressing effect on my spirits."[159] It was certainly the case that those who opposed him were the most vociferous. When Harold Nicolson persistently tried to catch the Speaker's eye in the hope of voicing his own protest, the Speaker told him apologetically that he was "trying to spread things out; there are four days of bread and none too much butter."[160] Chamberlain was especially bitter that "Winston was carrying on a regular conspiracy against me with the aid of Masaryk," and it was hardly surprising therefore that when Churchill came to speak on the third day of the debate, he pulled no punches.

> I will begin by saying what everybody would like to ignore or forget but which must nevertheless be stated, namely, that we have suffered a total and unmitigated defeat.[161]

When Nancy Astor, sitting behind him, shouted out "Nonsense," Churchill retorted that "no doubt the Noble Lady has been receiving very recently a finishing course in manners."[162]

"All is over," continued Churchill. "Silent, mournful, abandoned, broken, Czechoslovakia recedes into the darkness." Hitler, "instead of snatching his victuals from the table, has been content to have them served to him course by course, while the differences between the Godesberg terms and the Munich Agreement could be "very simply epitomised."

> £1 was demanded at the pistol's point. When it was given, £2 were demanded at the pistol's point. Finally, the dictator consented to take £1 17s. 6d. And the rest in promises of good will for the future.

He did not "grudge," he went on, the British people their "natural, spontaneous outburst of joy and relief." But they should know that there had been "gross neglect and inefficiency in our defences; they should know that we have sustained a defeat without a war."

> And do not suppose that this is the end. This is only the beginning of the reckoning. This is only the first sip, the first foretaste of a bitter cup which will be proffered to us year by year unless . . . we arise again and take our stand for freedom as in the olden time.[163]

At 4 P.M. on October 6 the House of Commons divided at the end of the debate. Chamberlain had made a more confident speech winding up, and succeeded in persuading some of his wavering backbenchers to vote with him, especially when he ruled out the prospect of calling a snap election. Amery wrote to the Prime Minister that evening: "Your speech moved me very deeply, and very, very nearly persuaded both myself and Anthony Eden to vote. I only hope, most sincerely, that the misgivings which even you could not dispel today, will be disproved by the events of the near future."[164] In the end, between twenty and thirty Conservative dissidents decided to abstain rather than vote against the government; the majority made their point by ostentatiously remaining in their places in the chamber while the division took place. It was not the quantity of the rebels that mattered, but their "reputation"—Churchill, Eden, Amery, Macmillan, Cranborne and Cooper were all among their number. "That looks none too well in any list," recorded Nicolson, who also abstained. "The House knows that most of the above people know far more about the real issue than they do."[165]

In spite of the Conservative abstentions, the *Manchester Guardian* correctly predicted that "it would take a revolt of 200, not 20, Tories to disturb this Government." For the majority of Conservative MPs, Chamberlain had become "the deliverer, and they will vote for him to a man."[166] In the end, the government won the division comfortably, by 366 votes to 144, although Chamberlain remained incensed by the criticism he had endured. "I tried occasionally," he complained to his sister, "to take an antidote to the poison gas by reading a few of the countless letters and telegrams which continued to pour in expressing in most moving accents the writer's heartfelt relief and gratitude. All the world seemed to be full of my praises except the House of Commons."[167] Chamberlain left immediately after the vote for King's Cross, where he boarded the overnight sleeper to Scotland. Utterly exhausted by the events of the past fortnight, he had been advised by his doctor to take a complete rest, and now took advantage of an invitation from Dunglass's father, the Earl of Home, to take refuge for a few days at the Hirsel near Berwick. There, he was assured, he would find "good sport on one of the most famous beats of the Tweed," and excellent partridge shooting.[168]

Epilogue

■

Drawing the Sword

Chamberlain the Peacemaker: for one week only.

> London cinema billboard, October 1938

I shall not occupy Prague for six months or so. I can't bring myself to do such a thing to the old fellow at the moment.

> Adolf Hitler, October 1938

I am sure that some day the Czechs will see that what we did was to save them for a happier future.

> Neville Chamberlain, October 2, 1938

Our policy was never designed just to postpone war, or enable us to enter war more united. The aim of our appeasement was to avoid war altogether, for all time.

> Sir Horace Wilson, 1962

"The pact of Munich is signed," recorded Jodl in his diary. "Czechoslovakia as a power is out. The genius of the Führer and his determination not to shun even a World War have again won the victory without the use of force."[1] Yet in spite of returning to a hero's welcome in Berlin, Hitler did not share the general air of euphoria that peace had been preserved. "This has been my first international conference," he grumbled, "and I can assure you that it will be my last. If ever that silly old man comes interfering here again with his umbrella, I'll kick him downstairs and jump on his stomach in front of photographers."[2] Above all, he felt cheated out of the triumph which would assuredly have come from a war with Czechoslovakia for which he had been preparing all summer: "That fellow Chamberlain has spoiled my entry into Prague."[3] He had been deprived, in Henderson's words, of "the great satisfaction—to which he was ardently looking forward—of giving his army a little experience, of appearing himself in the role of conquering hero, and of wreaking vengeance on Beneš and the Czechs."[4] Goebbels recognized that the Führer was far from satisfied: "We have essentially achieved everything that we wanted according to the small plan. The big plan is for the moment, given the prevailing circumstances, not yet realizable."[5]

Hitler's senior commanders also understood the need for a show of military strength. "The present degree of mobilized preparedness is to be maintained completely," ordered Keitel on September 30. The peaceful entry into Czechoslovakia was to "be planned in such a way that it can easily be converted into operation 'Grün.' "

> Those units of the Armed Forces intended for the occupation of Sector I must cross the former Czech-German frontier by 1200 noon Oct 1st. Armed resistance in the area cleared for occupation must be broken. Czech soldiers and other armed personnel found within the sector are to be disarmed and taken prisoner. The conduct of the field units must be based on the realization that they are occupying a territory whose population, after being harassed for years, looks upon the German Armed Forces as Liberators.[6]

Sure enough, on October 1, the German forces which had been loitering on Czechoslovakia's borders for weeks finally began their push into the Sudetenland. As agreed at Munich, Zone I in southern Bohemia was occupied within two days. Zone II, in northern Bohemia, followed on October 2 and 3; and Zone III, which was much the largest and included Karlsbad, Eger and Asch, was occupied by forces under the command of Reichenau on October 3, 4 and 5. Zone IV, in northern Moravia, was taken by Rundstedt two days later.

On October 3 Hitler arrived before dawn at Asch, to be met by General

Guderian. Although he was unhappy with the field breakfast on offer—there was meat in the soup—his mood quickly improved as he began a tour of his newly won territory. At Eger he was greeted by Reichenau, Keitel, Himmler and Henlein.[7] "Mein Führer," began Reichenau, "the army today is making the greatest sacrifice that soldiers can make to their supreme commander, namely to march into enemy territory without firing a shot." Another general concurred: "I was with my old regiment this morning. The men were weeping for being forbidden to attack the Czech bunkers." Hitler was delighted. "And all along," he said, "those defeatists tried to tell me that my politics would lead to war!"[8] He rode on through the Sudetenland in a six-wheeled black Mercedes; in every village swastika flags were flying, and local people lined the roads. "*Endlich Heim ins Reich*"—"Back home in the Reich at last"—was on everyone's lips. As the Czech army moved out, the storm troopers moved in; some shops were already daubed with "*Jude.*" In Karlsbad, Hitler made a short, fiery speech from the theater balcony. "We were ready to draw the sword for you," he told the cheering crowd. "That I should one day stand here before you I never for a moment doubted."[9]

Immediately upon the proceedings at Munich coming to an end, Henderson, together with Weizsäcker, François-Poncet and Attolico, had returned to Berlin. The first meeting of the international commission, created under the terms of the Munich Agreement, took place on October 1, soon after the first German tanks had crossed the Czech border. For Henderson, the task was one that was "ungrateful in principle and distasteful in detail,"[10] while François-Poncet described it as a "surgical operation, the cutting up of the panting victim."[11] The ambassadors, including the Czech representative Mastný, soon found that they were dealing not with the amiable Weizsäcker, but with generals Keitel and Brauchitsch, who viewed the Munich Agreement as an entirely temporary settlement. When Hitler received the new Czech Foreign Minister, František Chvalkovský, he warned that at the first sign of Czech recalcitrance he would "make an end of Czechoslovakia in twenty-four, no, in eight hours."[12]

The commission's principal task was to agree on the boundary of the fifth zone, the "remaining territory of preponderantly German character," which was to be occupied after October 10. Mastný and François-Poncet both insisted that "preponderantly" should mean a majority of 75 or 80 percent.

Henderson, however, agreed with the German line, that a simple majority should suffice. A few days later it was agreed to dispense with the plebiscites in the remaining disputed areas. The Czechs duly lost considerably more territory than they had ever foreseen. Within a fortnight, virtually every major Czech border fortification was in German hands, and any defense of those that remained was impossible; Prague was less than forty miles from the new frontier. By the time the final settlement was agreed in November, Czechoslovakia had handed over to the Reich 11,000 square miles of territory, inhabited by 2,800,000 Sudeten Germans and 800,000 Czechs. The country's communications infrastructure had been disrupted beyond recognition, and it had lost up to three-quarters of its industrial production. "I never want to work with Germans again," Henderson wrote to Halifax.

> In my blackest pessimism I tried to console myself with two thoughts (a) that war would rid Germany of Hitler and (b) that it [would] remove me from Berlin. As it is by keeping the peace we have saved Hitler and his regime and I am still in Berlin.[13]

However, the bloodless coup by which he had won the Sudetenland was not nearly enough to satisfy the Führer. Not only had he been denied his military victory, but the vast industrial, arms-producing and mineral wealth of Czechoslovakia still remained beyond his grasp. On October 9 he made a speech at Saarbrücken, complaining bitterly that he had been deceived at Munich, and cautioning that Britain should "drop certain airs which they have inherited from the Versailles epoch. We cannot tolerate any longer the tutelage of governesses!" For those Germans who had doubted his Czechoslovak policy, he had a stern message. "A hard decision had to be made: even with us there were weaklings who perhaps had failed to understand that." The democratic British political system, he warned, allowed for uncertainty.

> It only needs that in England instead of Chamberlain Mr. Duff Cooper or Mr. Eden or Mr. Churchill should come to power, and then we know quite well that it would be the aim of these men immediately to begin a new World War. They make no secret of the fact. That obliges us to be watchful and to remember the protection of the Reich . . . at every hour ready to defend ourselves.[14]

There was, of course, a further militarily strategic reason for continuing the Wehrmacht's push beyond the Sudetenland, and on into the rump of Czechoslovakia. As Hitler had made clear to his military commanders at the Reich Chancellery on November 5, 1937, during the so-called Hossbach conference, the incorporation of Austria and Czechoslovakia into the Reich was not an end in itself, but was merely an opening gambit in the greater campaign for *Lebensraum* in eastern Europe, at the expense of Poland, the Ukraine and, ultimately, Russia herself. Czechoslovakia therefore provided a vital bridgehead for further military expansion eastward. On the same day he spoke at Saarbrücken, Hitler sent a message to Keitel, asking "what reinforcements are necessary in the present situation to break all Czech resistance in Bohemia and Moravia?" Keitel consulted his commanders in the field, and replied by return. There were now twenty-four German divisions in Czechoslovakia, and only limited reinforcements would be needed. "OKW believes," concluded Keitel, "that it would be possible to commence operations without these reinforcements, in view of the present signs of weakness in Czech resistance."[15]

On October 21 Hitler summoned Keitel to a conference at the Reich Chancellery, as a result of which a new directive was issued to the Wehrmacht to prepare for the "following eventualities":

1. Securing the frontiers of the German Reich and protection against surprise air attacks.
2. Liquidation of the remainder of the Czech State.
3. The occupation of Memelland.

The directive asserted that it must "be possible to smash at any time the remainder of the Czech State, should it pursue an anti-German policy." In the event of such a contingency, the objective would be "the speedy occupation of Bohemia and Moravia and the cutting off of Slovakia."[16] In the case of Slovakia, a twin approach, involving political, as well as military, pressure was to be used; Ribbentrop duly began work on a strategy designed to drive a diplomatic wedge between Slovakia in the east, and the rest of the country, so hastening the ultimate breakup of Czechoslovakia. A Foreign Ministry memorandum confirmed Hitler's intention to use Czechoslovakia as a springboard for further expansion:

"An independent Slovakia would be weak constitutionally and would therefore best further the German need for penetration and settlement in the East."[17]

On November 7 a junior diplomat at the German legation in Paris, Ernst vom Rath, was shot and mortally wounded by a seventeen-year-old Polish Jewish refugee, Herschel Grynspan, whose parents had been deported from Germany to Poland. Two nights later, after Rath had died of his wounds, Goebbels, with Hitler's undoubted approval, unleashed a night of coordinated terror in revenge against the Jews of Germany and Austria. In one of the most infamous episodes in the history of the Third Reich, synagogues were burned to the ground and thousands of Jewish homes were destroyed or set alight; the vast quantities of broken glass that littered the streets outside the ransacked Jewish shops gave the night its name, *Kristallnacht.* Almost a hundred Jews were killed, many more were beaten and injured, and tens of thousands arrested and sent to concentration camps. "The human misery of the victims," wrote Hitler's biographer, "was incalculable. Beatings and bestial maltreatment, even of women, children, and the elderly, was commonplace."[18] Not only were many Germans, including some senior Nazis, horrified by the scale and the savagery of this systematic anti-Semitic pogrom, but the shock to world opinion, in particular in the United States, did much to dissipate the post-Munich atmosphere of euphoria.

A wave of revulsion swept through the British press, reflecting public opinion. Yet an evidently mystified Chamberlain still harbored hopes that a long-term settlement with Hitler was possible. On October 31 he had summed up his policy to the Cabinet. "Our foreign policy is one of appeasement," he told them. "We must aim at establishing relations with the Dictator Powers which will lead to a settlement in Europe."[19] After *Kristallnacht* he wrote to his sister:

> I am horrified by the Germans' behaviour to the Jews. There does seem to be some fatality about Anglo-German relations which invariably blocks every effort to improve them. I suppose I shall have to say something on the subject. . . . It will be a problem how to avoid condonation on one side or on the other such criticisms as may bring even more things on the heads of these unhappy victims.[20]

At a meeting of the Cabinet's Foreign Policy Committee, he talked vaguely of the "disappointing way in which the situation had developed in Germany since the Munich settlement." Halifax was not so phlegmatic. It was time, he said, to correct "the false impression that we are decadent, spineless and could with impunity be kicked about."[21]

▪ ▪ ▪

"The Czechs will hardly appreciate Mr. Chamberlain's phrase that it is 'peace with honour,' " wrote the *Manchester Guardian*, in one of very few critical press comments in the immediate aftermath of Munich. "Politically, Czechoslovakia is rendered helpless with all that it means to the balance of forces in Eastern Europe, and Hitler will be able to advance again, when he chooses, with greatly increased force."[22] The diplomatic correspondent of the *Daily Herald* also accurately predicted the imminent plight of those who would be forced to flee Hitler's advancing tanks.

> Certainly, on the face of it, Adolf Hitler scores a personal triumph. He said he would march into the Sudetenland to-morrow. He marches into the Sudetenland to-morrow. Czechoslovakia, having made so many sacrifices, has had to make another one under peremptory pressure from the British and French Governments. Thousands of people (not so much Czechs as anti-Nazi Sudeten Germans) are going to suffer. They must run for their lives or face the rubber truncheons and the concentration camps.[23]

On October 3 the British Cabinet considered a request from Masaryk, on behalf of the Czech government, for an emergency loan of £30 million to assist with the flood of refugees that was expected from the Sudeten areas, and with rebuilding the country's shattered economy. Chamberlain first asserted that it was "impossible to accept every statement made by M. Masaryk," before Simon reminded the meeting that this was not "an occasion on which this country need adopt an apologetic attitude. It was not the case that Czechoslovakia had any legitimate grievance against us. . . . On the contrary the position was that a world war had been averted and thereby Czechoslovakia had been saved." While he supported a smaller, short-term combination of gift and loan, it was essential that any financial help should be given without any acceptance of guilt. The meeting was then informed that the Lord Mayor of London, Sir

Harry Twyford, had opened a Mansion House appeal fund to alleviate the suffering of Czech refugees. Chamberlain's incredible response was that he was "rather afraid that the opening of a Fund might have a bad effect on public opinion in Germany," and he hoped that Halifax would be able to persuade the Lord Mayor that he should do no such thing.[24]

In the end, the government granted 350 visas to Sudeten refugees, and Harold Macmillan was one of those who took in forty of them, at his Sussex estate, Birch Grove. Even that decision proved controversial. When Nancy Astor argued against the policy in the House of Commons, complaining that the Czechs were Communists and should have been sent to Russia, Macmillan wrote to her in fury. Among those to whom he had given shelter, he pointed out, was the former Mayor of Aussig and one of the leading advocates from the Sudetenland. They were "quiet and cultivated people, dazed . . . hard-working, courteous and grateful. With all that they have had to suffer," he continued, "I do not see why they should be insulted in our Parliament in addition."[25] On Bonfire Night, the Czechs joined in the usual celebrations, and the evening was given an added poignancy by the replacement of the usual straw effigy on the bonfire by a "splendid representation of Chamberlain." Macmillan had "sacrificed for the purpose a black Homburg hat in quite good repair, as well as a rolled umbrella."[26]

In Czechoslovakia itself, the republic founded by Masaryk in the aftermath of the Treaty of Versailles was in the process of unraveling. On October 5, at Hitler's insistence, Beneš resigned as President and flew to England and into exile. He was replaced for a few weeks by General Syrový, who in turn surrendered his office on November 30 to Dr. Emil Hácha, the Chief Justice of the Supreme Court; at sixty-six, Hácha was both weak-willed and physically ailing. After Munich, Prague was forced to grant Slovakia, as well as the region known as Ruthenia, a degree of autonomy; both now had a Cabinet and a parliament of their own. The parliamentary bill confirming Slovakia's autonomy also changed the country's name to Czecho-Slovakia; until then it had been an offense to spell the word with a hyphen. Poland's demands for territory in the Teschen district were conceded on October 10, to be followed by further forced annexations in November. Hungary's territorial claim, meanwhile, was partially granted by Ribbentrop and Ciano, on November 2, under the terms of the so-called Vienna Award. And all the while, the German Foreign Ministry continued actively to encourage the claims of the Slovak separatist movement. "A Czech State minus Slovakia is even more completely at our mercy," noted Göring. "Air base in Slovakia for air force for operation against the east very important."[27]

Of the supposed guarantee by the four powers to the "new" Czechoslovakia, Chamberlain had told the Cabinet on his return from Munich that for Britain and France it would "come into operation at once, while the guarantees of Germany and Italy come into operation after the Hungarian and Polish minorities question had been settled."[28] In fact, Germany ostentatiously failed to proceed with the guarantee in any form. "Czechoslovakia's future is in German hands," Weizsäcker told foreign diplomats, "and a guarantee from any other power would be worthless."[29] On January 12, 1939, the Czech Foreign Minister Chvalkovský reported to the German chargé d'affaires in Prague the rumor "that the incorporation of Czechoslovakia into the Reich was imminent." In a final effort to hold up the Wehrmacht, he emphasized that his government would "endeavour to prove its loyalty and good will by far-reaching fulfilment of Germany's wishes."[30] On January 21 Chvalkovský flew to Berlin, where he was harangued by Hitler, who bluntly warned him that it was "useless to cherish any hopes of assistance from Britain or France," and that Czechoslovakia was now "completely at the mercy of the German Reich."[31]

On the night of March 9, Hácha made one final attempt to hold the country together, by endeavoring to put a brake on the pace of Slovak separatism; it proved to be a disastrous blunder. The Slovakian Cabinet was dismissed, the government offices in Bratislava were occupied by Czech police, and the deposed Prime Minister, Father Jozef Tiso, a Catholic priest, was placed under house arrest; martial law was declared throughout Slovakia. Hitler immediately seized the opportunity. He canceled a trip to Vienna to celebrate the anniversary of the Anschluss, and eagerly told Goebbels, Ribbentrop and Keitel that this was his opportunity to "march in, smash the rump Czech state, and occupy Prague." The invasion would take place five days later on the Ides of March. "The Führer shouts for joy," recorded Goebbels. "This game is dead certain."[32] Göring, who was on holiday in the Mediterranean resort of San Remo, was told not to return suddenly for fear of raising suspicion abroad. The same day, a Friday, Henderson telegraphed Halifax to say that he doubted "whether Herr Hitler has yet taken any decision and I consider it therefore highly desirable that nothing be said or published abroad during the weekend which will excite him to precipitate action."[33] The following morning Keitel ordered the army and Luftwaffe to stand by to invade Czecho-Slovakia at 6 A.M. three days later.

That evening, Tiso, who had escaped from the monastery where he was supposedly under arrest, was summoned to Berlin. The following day, Hitler received him at the Chancellery, flanked by Keitel and Brauchitsch, whom he pointed out to the Slovak leader. "Tomorrow at midday," began the Führer, "I shall begin military action against the Czechs, which will be carried out by General Brauchitsch."[34] He had therefore sent for Tiso to "clear up this [Slovak] question *in a very short* time."

> It was a matter of complete indifference to him what happened there. The question was, did Slovakia want to lead an independent existence or not? It was a question not of days but of hours. If she hesitated or refused to be separated from Prague, he would leave the fate of Slovakia to events for which he was no longer responsible. Then he would look after German interests only.[35]

Tiso was in no mood to argue, and returned hastily to Bratislava where, the following day, the Slovak Diet declared independence, and Hungarian troops, as arranged with Germany, occupied Ruthenia in eastern Czechoslovakia.

That same afternoon the aging Hácha, accompanied by his daughter acting as his nurse, and Chvalkovský, traveled by train to Berlin; he was too frail to fly. Having arrived at 10:40 P.M. after a five-hour journey, they were kept waiting at their hotel until the small hours while Hitler watched one of his favorite films. At last, having first gone through the usual ritual of inspecting the SS guard of honor, a flushed and harassed Hácha was ushered into Hitler's vast study in Speer's brand-new Reich Chancellery. There, in front of a sizable audience of leading Nazis, the terrified Hácha was subjected to a ferocious browbeating. Hitler first launched into a familiar tirade against the spirit of Beneš, before warning that the Wehrmacht was poised to cross the border at 6 A.M., in just a few hours' time, and that the Luftwaffe would occupy all Czech airfields. When Hácha tried to argue, Hitler screamed that the invasion was irreversible; Hácha must immediately order the Czech army to remain in their barracks. If there was any resistance, it "would be broken by brute force with all available means."[36] With that, Hitler stormed out of the room.

Hácha and Chvalkovský were left alone with Göring and Ribbentrop, who produced a document that would give effect to the voluntary incorporation of Bohemia and Moravia into Germany, as a "protectorate" of the Third Reich. The two Germans quite literally pursued Hácha around the table, thrusting a fountain pen into his hand, and threatening dire consequences for Czecho-Slovakia if he refused to sign. Göring warned incessantly that hundreds of German bombers were awaiting his order to take to the skies, and that by dawn half of Prague would lie in ruins. "I should be sorry," he later confessed to telling Hácha, "if I had to bomb beautiful Prague."[37] Finally, at 3:55 A.M., Hácha agreed to sign. In the course of his browbeating, he had almost certainly suffered a heart attack, and he was by now so weak that he required several injections from Hitler's personal physician to sustain him through the night. After some time, a telephone line to Prague was secured, and Hácha ordered that Czech troops were not to fire on the invading Wehrmacht. Hitler was beside himself with excitement. "This is the happiest day of my life," he told two of his secretaries, as he demanded a kiss on each cheek from both of them. "I will go down as the greatest German in history."[38]

Two hours later the German army poured across the Czech frontier and marched on Prague. There was no resistance and, for the Wehrmacht, the occupation of the rump of Czechoslovakia represented little more than a routine training exercise. On December 17, 1938, Keitel had issued a further directive on behalf of Hitler. Preparations for the "liquidation of the Rump Czech State" were to be carried out "on the assumption that no appreciable resistance is to be expected. Outwardly it must be quite clear that it is only a peaceful action and not a warlike undertaking."[39] Although it was snowing heavily and the roads were icy, the first German tanks entered Prague at 9 A.M., and that evening Hitler arrived from Berlin by train, traveling the last few miles in an open-topped car, as always standing erect, his arm outstretched, in spite of the driving snow. As dusk fell he was driven through the gates of Hradčany Castle, where he was greeted by General Syrový,[40] before enjoying a makeshift picnic of ham, cheese and, surprisingly for Hitler, Pilsner beer, with his entourage. That night he sat at Beneš's desk, and drafted the formal proclamation incorporating Czechoslovakia into the Reich. "Czecho-Slovakia," it concluded, "has ceased to exist."[41]

Notes

PROLOGUE: HESTON

1. A. Christiansen, *Headlines All My Life*, Heinemann 1961, p. 143.
2. *The Times*, 1 October 1938, p. 13.
3. *Evening News*, 30 September 1938, p. 1.
4. T. Sherwood, *A Short History of Hounslow, Hanworth and Heston Aerodromes, 1911–1946*, Heritage Publications, Hounslow Cultural and Community Services 1999. Civilian air traffic stopped using Heston on the outbreak of war, and in 1946 the airport was closed when the decision was taken to expand nearby Heathrow. Nowadays there is little evidence that it was ever there. The tree-lined avenue which led to the airport terminal remains, but the fine airport buildings (including the first concrete control tower ever built) have all long since disappeared and the site now houses an industrial estate serving nearby Heathrow Airport. One or two of the old hangars, now used as warehouses, can still be identified. The huge landing ground and runway is now the site of the Heston Service Station, separated by both carriageways of the M4 motorway.
5. *The Times*, 1 October 1938, p. 12.
6. The National Archives, CAB 23/95/180, Cabinet 42 (38), 24 September 1938.
7. A large quantity of food had been provided for the flight by a Munich hotel. However, when Chamberlain discovered where it came from, he said that "it would give him great satisfaction if the food remained untouched." It was, recalled the flight engineer many years later, "digestive biscuits all the way home" (*Daily Telegraph*, 26 August 1992, p. 15).
8. J. Toland, *Adolf Hitler*, Doubleday, New York 1976, p. 493.
9. *Evening News*, 1 October 1938, p. 1.
10. BBC Written Archives, R34/325 Czechoslovak Crisis, General File 1938–1939, "Recorded Programmes Library," 30 September 1938.
11. *The Times*, 1 October 1938, p. 12.
12. The Royal Archives, RA PS/GVI/C 047/13, King George VI to Neville Chamberlain, 30 September 1938.
13. Neville Chamberlain Papers, NC 18/1/1070, Chamberlain to Hilda Chamberlain, 2 October 1938.
14. *The Times*, 1 October 1938, p. 12.
15. King George VI had originally intended to go to Heston in person to greet

his Prime Minister but was dissuaded from doing so. Some historians have since strongly condemned him for such an overt display of political approval. John Grigg, for example, described the invitation to Buckingham Palace as "the most unconstitutional act by a British Sovereign in the present century. Whatever the rights or wrongs of the Munich Agreement, the relevant point is that it was denounced by the official Opposition and was to be the subject of a vote in Parliament" (*The Times*, 11 November 1989).

16. J. Wheeler-Bennett, *King George VI: His Life and Reign*, Macmillan 1958, p. 354.
17. *Daily Herald*, 1 October 1938, p. 5.
18. BBC Written Archives, R19/2172, "I Was There" Series, Interview with Sir Alec Douglas-Home, 14 January 1968. Lord Dunglass (later Sir Alec Douglas-Home, later Lord Home) always believed that it had been Mrs. Chamberlain, who never left her husband's side during the return to Downing Street, who had persuaded him to change his mind.
19. *The Times*, 1 October 1938, p. 12.

1: HITLER SEES HIS CHANCE

1. J. Heineman, *Hitler's First Foreign Minister: Constantin Freiherr von Neurath, Diplomat and Statesman*, University of California Press, Los Angeles 1979, pp. 155–56.
2. I. Kershaw, *Hitler 1936–45: Nemesis*, Allen Lane 2000, p. 46 (original in Goebbels Diaries, 6 November 1937).
3. *Trial of the Major War Criminals Before The International Military Tribunal*, Volume IX, Nuremberg 1947, p. 307, Göring testimony, 14 March 1946 (hereafter cited as *TMWC*).
4. *Documents on German Foreign Policy 1918–1945*, Series D (1937–1945), Volume 1, "From Neurath to Ribbentrop," His Majesty's Stationery Office 1949 (hereafter cited as *DGFP* D/1), No. 19, p. 29, "Minutes of the Conference in the Reich Chancellery, Berlin, November 5, 1937." (The original German text of the minutes of the meeting, commonly known as the Hossbach Memorandum, is in *TMWC*, Volume XXV, pp. 402–13.)
5. A. Brissaud (trans. I Colvin), *Canaris: The Biography of Admiral Canaris*, Weidenfeld and Nicolson 1973, p. 60.
6. W. Shirer, *The Rise and Fall of the Third Reich: A History of Nazi Germany*, Secker and Warburg 1961, pp. 303–4.
7. *DGFP* D/1, No 19, pp. 29–34, "Minutes of the Conference in the Reich Chancellery, Berlin, November 5, 1937."
8. Kershaw, *Hitler*, p. 48.
9. *DGFP* D/1, No. 19, pp. 35–38, "Minutes of the Conference in the Reich Chancellery, Berlin, November 5, 1937."
10. J. Wright & P. Stafford, "Hitler, Britain, and the Hossbach Memorandum," *Militärgeschichtliche Mitteilungen*, Volume 42, No. 2, 1987, p. 86.
11. Brissaud, p. 62.

12. Heineman, p. 160.
13. *DGFP* D/1, No 19, pp. 35–38, "Minutes of the Conference in the Reich Chancellery, Berlin, November 5, 1937."
14. E. Raeder, *Struggle for the Sea*, William Kimber 1959, p. 122.
15. *TMWC*, Volume XVI, p. 640, Neurath testimony, 24 June 1946.
16. Shirer, *The Rise and Fall of the Third Reich*, p. 309.
17. *TMWC*, Volume XVI, pp. 640–41, Neurath testimony, 24 June 1946.
18. Brissaud, pp. 60–63.
19. Heineman, p. 163.
20. Hickleton Papers A4/410/3/2 (i), Parker to Halifax, 13 October 1937.
21. Hickleton Papers A4/410/3/3 (i).
22. W. Churchill, *The Second World War, Volume I: The Gathering Storm*, Cassell 1948, p. 194. In his memoirs Halifax made a point of describing this account by Churchill as "unwittingly inaccurate" (*Fulness of Days*, Collins 1957, p. 183). In 1946 he also took the trouble to write to Sir Orme Sargent, by then the Permanent Under-Secretary at the Foreign Office, to try to dispel the "legend that has been established that my going to Berlin was the decision of Chamberlain, bent on appeasement, against the wishes of a robust Anthony Eden." He in fact went, he claimed, because of the "joint exhortations" of Chamberlain and Eden (Hickleton Papers A4/410/3/3 (vi), Halifax to Sargent, 6 May 1946).
23. Lord Avon, *The Eden Memoirs: Facing the Dictators*, Cassell 1962, p. 509.
24. Hickleton Papers A4/410/3/3 (vi), Halifax to Sargent, 6 May 1946.
25. NC 18/1/1025, Chamberlain to Hilda Chamberlain, 24 October 1937.
26. P. Neville, "The Appointment of Sir Nevile Henderson, 1937—Design or Blunder?", in *Journal of Contemporary History*, Volume 33, No. 4, October 1998, p. 613 & p. 611, n20.
27. T. Jones, *A Diary with Letters, 1931–50*, Oxford University Press 1954, p. 208.
28. Neville, "The Appointment of Sir Nevile Henderson," p. 612.
29. I. Colvin, *Vansittart in Office*, Victor Gollancz 1965, p. 146.
30. N. Henderson, *Failure of a Mission, Berlin 1937–1939*, Hodder and Stoughton 1940, p. 13.
31. P. Neville, "Sir Nevile Henderson," in *Oxford Dictionary of National Biography*, H. Matthew & B. Harrison (eds.), Volume 26, Oxford University Press 2004, p. 330.
32. London School of Economics Archive, 1/3/7, "Munich 1938," interview with Sir Geoffrey Harrison, n/d. Harrison went on to enjoy a distinguished diplomatic career, culminating as British ambassador in Tehran, and then in Moscow. Unfortunately, his posting in Moscow was cut short in 1968 following an incident involving a Russian chambermaid and the KGB.
33. *Daily Telegraph*, 16 November 1937, p. 14.
34. I. Kirkpatrick, *The Inner Circle*, Macmillan 1959, pp. 90–91.
35. P. Neville, "Sir Noel Mason-MacFarlane," in *Oxford Dictionary of National Biography*, H. Matthew & B. Harrison (eds.), Volume 35, Oxford University Press 2004, p. 381.
36. LSE Archive, 1/3/7, "Munich 1938," interview with Sir Geoffrey Harrison, n/d.

37. In December 2007, Channel 4 broadcast a program about the life of the Duke, otherwise known as Prince Charles Edward, entitled "Hitler's Favourite Royal."

38. T. Conwell-Evans, *None So Blind: A Study of the Crisis Years 1930–1939, Based on the Private Papers of Group-Captain M. G. Christie*, Harrison & Sons 1947, p. 92.

39. N. Henderson, p. 20.

40. W. & M. Dodd (eds.), *Ambassador Dodd's Diary, 1933–1938*, Victor Gollancz 1941, p. 417.

41. N. Henderson, p. 96.

42. Hickleton Papers A4/410/3/2 (i).

43. Dalton Papers, I/18/29–34, Dalton Diary, 28 October 1937.

44. Avon, *Facing the Dictators*, pp. 503–4.

45. LSE Archive, 1/1/9, "Munich 1938," interview with Sir Frank Roberts, n/d. In 1938 Roberts was based in the Central Department of the Foreign Office in London, but he too was to go on to enjoy a glittering diplomatic career in a wide variety of posts, including as ambassador to Yugoslavia, NATO, the USSR and West Germany.

46. NC 18/1/1026, Chamberlain to Ida Chamberlain, 30 October 1937.

47. Hickleton Papers A4/410/3/2 (ii), Henderson to Halifax, 29 October 1937.

48. *Documents on British Foreign Policy 1919–1939*, Second Series, Volume XIX, Her Majesty's Stationery Office 1982 (hereafter cited as *DBFP* 2/XIX), No. 273, p. 447, "Minute by Mr. Eden," 27 October 1937.

49. *DBFP* 2/XIX, No. 264, p. 434, Eden to Ogilvie-Forbes (Berlin), 22 October 1937. Eden made a point of adding these words to the draft of the telegram from his Private Secretary informing the Berlin embassy of the invitation.

50. *DBFP* 2/XIX, No. 283, p. 459, Henderson to Foreign Office, 2 November 1937. (The comments of the two officials are attached to Henderson's telegram as note 4.)

51. *DBFP* 2/XIX, No. 294, p. 471, Henderson to Eden, 6 November 1937.

52. *DBFP* 2/XIX, No. 298, p. 476, Henderson to Eden, 7 November 1937. (Vansittart's written minute on the telegram is in note 2.)

53. Avon, *Facing the Dictators*, p. 510.

54. *DBFP* 2/XIX, No. 295, pp. 471–72, Eden to Henderson, 6 November 1937.

55. *DBFP* 2/XIX, No. 299, p. 476, Eden to Henderson, 8 November 1937.

56. A. Roberts, *"The Holy Fox:" The Life of Lord Halifax*, Weidenfeld and Nicolson 1991, p. 65.

57. J. Harvey (ed.), *The Diplomatic Diaries of Oliver Harvey, 1937–1940*, Collins 1970, 7 & 8 November 1937, pp. 57–58.

58. NC 18/1/1027, Chamberlain to Hilda Chamberlain, 6 November 1937.

59. NC 18/1/1025, Chamberlain to Hilda Chamberlain, 24 October 1937.

60. Harvey, 8 November 1937, p. 58.

61. Avon, *Facing the Dictators*, p. 510.

62. Harvey, 11 November 1937, p. 59.

63. *The Times*, 10 November 1937, p. 8.

64. *Evening Standard*, 10 November 1937, p. 1.

65. R. Rhodes James (ed.), *Chips: The Diaries of Sir Henry Channon*, Weidenfeld

and Nicolson 1967, 9 November 1937, pp. 140–41 (hereafter cited as *Channon Diaries*). Either Rhodes James, or possibly Channon himself, mistakenly included this entry for November 9. In fact, both the dinner at the Savoy, and Chamberlain's statement in the House of Commons earlier in the day following the death of Ramsay MacDonald, to which Channon also refers, took place on November 10. This is only important insofar as it rules out the possibility that Chamberlain's remarks at the dinner were the source for the leak in the *Evening Standard*, which had already appeared on the afternoon of November 10, before he spoke at the Guildhall.

66. NC 18/1/1028, Chamberlain to Ida Chamberlain, 14 November 1937.
67. Harvey, 11 November 1937, p. 59.
68. *Daily Express*, 12 November 1937, p. 2.
69. *Evening Standard*, 13 November 1937, p. 1.
70. *DBFP* 2/XIX, No. 321, pp. 525–26, Henderson to Eden, 14 November 1937 at 8:15 P.M.
71. *DBFP* 2/XIX, No. 322, p. 526, Henderson to Eden, 14 November 1937 at 9 P.M.
72. Hickleton Papers A4/410/3/3 (ii), Henderson to Eden, 14 November 1937 at 10:25 P.M.
73. *DBFP* 2/XIX, No. 324, pp. 527–28, Eden to Henderson, 15 November 1937.
74. C. Andrew, *Secret Service: The Making of the British Intelligence Community*, Heinemann 1985, p. 380.
75. R. Cockett, *Twilight of Truth: Chamberlain, Appeasement and the Manipulation of the Press*, Weidenfeld and Nicolson 1989, p. 37.
76. *Daily Telegraph*, 16 November 1937, p. 14.
77. *The Times*, 16 November 1937, p. 16.
78. Harvey, 16 November 1937, pp. 60–61.
79. *DGFP* D/1, No. 29, pp. 52–53, "Conversation with the Prime Minister's press chief," 18 November 1937.
80. Cockett, p. 15.
81. Lord Birkenhead, *Halifax: The Life of Lord Halifax*, Hamish Hamilton 1965, p. 367.
82. Hickleton Papers A4/410/3/3 (vi), Lord Halifax, "Diary of Visit," 17–21 November 1937.
83. Roberts, "*The Holy Fox*," p. 69.
84. Hickleton Papers A4/410/3/3 (vi), Lord Halifax, "Diary of Visit," 17–21 November 1937.
85. *Evening Standard*, 19 November 1937, p. 6 & p. 10.
86. A. Lane, "Sir Ivone Kirkpatrick," in *Oxford Dictionary of National Biography*, H. Matthew & B. Harrison (eds.), Volume 31, Oxford University Press 2004, pp. 807–8. Like so many of the other diplomats who played important roles during the Munich crisis, Kirkpatrick was to reach the pinnacle of his profession, serving as Britain's postwar High Commissioner in West Germany, and as Permanent Under-Secretary at the Foreign Office between 1953 and 1957, during which time he is best remembered for the part he played in the Suez crisis.

87. LSE Archive, 2/4/7, "Munich 1938," interview with Sir Con O'Neill. Although he was to resign in protest at the Munich Agreement, O'Neill resumed his Foreign Office career after the war, serving as ambassador to Finland, to the European Communities in Brussels, and finally becoming the Deputy Under-Secretary responsible for negotiating Britain's entry to the EEC.

88. Lord Halifax, *Fulness of Days*, Collins 1957, p. 185.

89. *Country Life*, 28 March 1936, pp. 322–23. In November 1938, *Homes and Gardens*, a sister title of *Country Life*, published a similarly gushing article about Hitler's lifestyle at the Berghof by the same correspondent. In 2003, IPC Media, the owner of both magazines, made a rather cack-handed attempt to gag a *Guardian* journalist who put the article up on his Web site, claiming "unauthorised reproduction" and "infringement of copyright." After an international media outcry, prompted in part by leading anti-Holocaust campaigners, IPC were forced to back down, and admitted to being "appalled" that the magazine had published what was essentially "Nazi propaganda" (*Guardian*, 3 November 2003).

90. H. Eberle & M. Uhl (eds.) (trans. G. MacDonagh), *The Hitler Book: The Secret Dossier Prepared for Stalin*, John Murray 2005, p. 24.

91. A. Lambert, *The Lost Life of Eva Braun*, Century 2006, p. 225.

92. Kirkpatrick, p. 95.

93. P. Schmidt (ed. R. Steed), *Hitler's Interpreter*, William Heinemann 1951, p. 76.

94. Roberts, "*The Holy Fox*," p. 67.

95. Hickleton Papers A4/410/3/3 (vi), Lord Halifax, "Diary of Visit," 17–21 November 1937.

96. *DGFP* D/1, No. 31, pp. 55–56, Memorandum, "Conversation between Lord Halifax and Herr Hitler," 19 November 1937.

97. Hickleton Papers A4/410/3/3 (vi), Lord Halifax, "Diary of Visit," 17–21 November 1937.

98. Ibid.

99. Avon, *Facing the Dictators*, p. 515.

100. Hickleton Papers A4/410/3/3 (vi), Lord Halifax, "Diary of Visit," 17–21 November 1937.

101. *DGFP* D/1, No. 31, p. 64, Memorandum, "Conversation between Lord Halifax and Herr Hitler," 19 November 1937.

102. Kirkpatrick, pp. 95–97.

103. Schmidt, p. 77.

104. Hickleton Papers A4/410/3/3 (vi), Lord Halifax, "Diary of Visit," 17–21 November 1937.

105. Schmidt, p. 77.

106. Eberle & Uhl, p. 25.

107. Halifax, p. 190.

108. Hickleton Papers A4/410/3/3 (vi), Lord Halifax, "Diary of Visit," 17–21 November 1937.

109. Duchess of Windsor, *The Heart Has Its Reasons*, Michael Joseph 1956, pp. 305–6.

110. Halifax, pp. 190–91.
111. Schmidt, p. 78.
112. Hickleton Papers A4/410/3/3 (vi), Lord Halifax, "Diary of Visit," 17–21 November 1937.
113. Birkenhead, *Halifax*, p. 372.
114. Halifax, p. 191.
115. Kirkpatrick, p. 101.
116. Hickleton Papers A4/410/3/3 (vi), Lord Halifax, "Diary of Visit," 17–21 November 1937.
117. *Evening Standard*, 22 November 1937, p. 1 & p. 12.
118. CAB 23/90A/165–67, Cabinet 43 (37), 24 November 1937.
119. NC 18/1/1030, Chamberlain to Ida Chamberlain, 26 November 1937.
120. Roberts, "*The Holy Fox*," p. 75.

2: SCANDAL IN BERLIN

1. Kershaw, *Hitler*, p. 51.
2. Vansittart Papers, VNST I/1/22, Kirkpatrick to Eden, "Record of Leading Personalities in Germany," 6 January 1938.
3. NC 18/1/1004, Chamberlain to Hilda Chamberlain, 15 May 1937.
4. *TMWC*, Volume XIV, p. 37, Raeder testimony, 16 May 1946.
5. *Documents on German Foreign Policy 1918–1945,* Series D (1937–1945), Volume VII, "The Last Days of Peace," Appendix III (K) (i), Her Majesty's Stationery Office 1956, pp. 635–36.
6. There is widespread confusion over Fräulein Gruhn's real name. She is variously referred to in contemporary newspaper reports and subsequent works of history as Erna Luise, Erna, Erika, Elli and Eva.
7. H. Gisevius (trans. R. & C. Winston), *To the Bitter End*, Greenwood Press, Connecticut 1975, p. 244.
8. H. Deutsch, *Hitler and His Generals: The Hidden Crisis, January–June 1938*, University of Minnesota Press, Minneapolis 1974, p. 87.
9. Shirer, *The Rise and Fall of the Third Reich*, p. 312 (original in *TMWC*, Volume XXVIII, p. 356, Jodl Diary).
10. W. Gorlitz (ed.) (trans. D. Irving), *The Memoirs of Field-Marshal Keitel*, William Kimber 1965, p. 42 (hereafter cited as Keitel).
11. Brissaud, pp. 66–67.
12. *Daily Mail*, 13 January 1938, p. 10.
13. *Daily Mail*, 18 January 1938, p. 13.
14. Gisevius, p. 220.
15. Deutsch, *Hitler and His Generals*, pp. 99–100.
16. Brissaud, pp. 68–69.
17. Gisevius, p. 220.
18. VNST I/1/22, Kirkpatrick to Eden, "Record of Leading Personalities in Germany," 6 January 1938.
19. Brissaud, p. 69.

20. Keitel, p. 44.
21. Brissaud, p. 70.
22. Gisevius, pp. 222–23.
23. Deutsch, *Hitler and His Generals*, pp. 105–6.
24. Kershaw, *Hitler*, p. 53.
25. T. Taylor, *Sword and Swastika: The Wehrmacht in the Third Reich*, Victor Gollancz 1953, p. 149.
26. Kershaw, *Hitler*, p. 53 (original in Goebbels Diaries, 27 January 1938).
27. Deutsch, *Hitler and His Generals*, p. 111.
28. Gisevius, p. 224.
29. Shirer, *The Rise and Fall of the Third Reich*, p. 315.
30. Deutsch, *Hitler and His Generals*, p. 116.
31. Shirer, *The Rise and Fall of the Third Reich*, p. 315.
32. Brissaud, p. 74.
33. W. Warlimont (trans. R. Barry), *Inside Hitler's Headquarters, 1939–1945*, Weidenfeld and Nicolson 1964, p. 13.
34. Deutsch, *Hitler and His Generals*, p. 120.
35. T. Taylor, pp. 150–51.
36. Keitel, pp. 45–46.
37. *Daily Express*, 7 February 1938, p. 10.
38. T. Taylor, p. 151.
39. Keitel, p. 49.
40. Deutsch, *Hitler and His Generals*, pp. 136–37.
41. Ibid., p. 140.
42. Ibid., p. 153.
43. Brissaud, p. 73.
44. Deutsch, *Hitler and His Generals*, p. 159.
45. Kershaw, *Hitler*, p. 55.
46. Shirer, *The Rise and Fall of the Third Reich*, p. 316.
47. Gisevius, p. 230.
48. Deutsch, *Hitler and His Generals*, p. 165.
49. Kershaw, *Hitler*, p. 862n (original in Goebbels Diaries, 30 January 1938).
50. Deutsch, *Hitler and His Generals*, p. 163.
51. T. Taylor, p. 149.
52. Deutsch, *Hitler and His Generals*, p. 205.
53. Brissaud, p. 77.
54. Deutsch, *Hitler and His Generals*, p. 181.
55. Ibid., p. 324.
56. Kershaw, *Hitler*, p. 57 (original in Goebbels Diaries, 28 January 1938).
57. Ibid., p. 58 (original in Goebbels Diaries, 1 February 1938).
58. Keitel, p. 51.
59. VNST I/1/22, Kirkpatrick to Eden, "Record of Leading Personalities in Germany," 6 January 1938.
60. W. Jędrzejewicz (ed.), *Diplomat in Berlin, 1933–1939: Papers and Memoirs of Józef Lipski, Ambassador of Poland*, Columbia University Press, New York 1968, p. 336 (hereafter cited as *Lipski Papers*).

61. *TMWC*, Volume XVI, p. 641, Neurath testimony, 24 June 1946.
62. Heineman, p. 168.
63. *TMWC*, Volume IX, p. 290, Göring testimony, 14 March 1946.
64. Heineman, p. 169.
65. *TMWC*, Volume IX, p. 290, Göring testimony, 14 March 1946.
66. Shirer, *The Rise and Fall of the Third Reich*, p. 318.
67. T. Taylor, p. 165.
68. *Daily Express*, 2 & 5 February 1938, p. 1.
69. H. Guderian (trans. C. Fitzgibbon), *Panzer Leader*, Michael Joseph 1952, p. 47.
70. T. Taylor, p. 173.
71. Kershaw, *Hitler*, p. 60.
72. Deutsch, *Hitler and His Generals*, p. 338.
73. Brissaud, p. 79.

3: THE LAST FRAIL CHANCE

1. Avon Papers, AP 20/1/18, Eden Diary, 5 January 1938.
2. RA EDW/3540, Duke of Windsor to Chamberlain, 22 December 1937.
3. D. R. Thorpe, *Eden: The Life and Times of Anthony Eden*, Chatto and Windus 2003, p. 201.
4. S. Welles, *Seven Major Decisions*, Hamish Hamilton 1951, p. 41.
5. PREM 1/259/84, Lindsay to Foreign Office, 11 February 1938.
6. PREM 1/259/81, Lindsay to Foreign Office, 12 February 1938.
7. PREM 1/259/82, Lindsay to Foreign Office, 12 February 1938.
8. NC 18/1/1031, Chamberlain to Ida Chamberlain, 12 December 1937.
9. G. Berridge, "Sir Alexander Cadogan," *Oxford Dictionary of National Biography*, H. Matthew & B. Harrison (eds.), Volume 9, Oxford University Press 2004, p. 413.
10. *DBFP* 2/XIX, No. 428, pp. 733–34, "Minute by Sir A. Cadogan for Mr. Chamberlain," 12 January 1938.
11. D. Dilks (ed.), *The Diaries of Sir Alexander Cadogan*, Cassell 1971, 12 January 1938, p. 36 (hereafter cited as *Cadogan Diaries*).
12. Welles, *Seven Major Decisions*, p. 41.
13. *DBFP* 2/XIX, No. 425, p. 732, Lindsay to Foreign Office, 12 January 1938.
14. NC 2/24A, Chamberlain Diary, 19 & 27 February 1938.
15. NC 18/1/1036, Chamberlain to Ida Chamberlain, 23 January 1938.
16. *Cadogan Diaries*, 13 January 1938, p. 36.
17. NC 2/24A, Chamberlain Diary, 19 & 27 February 1938.
18. R. Rhodes James, *Anthony Eden*, Weidenfeld and Nicolson 1986, p. 188.
19. Avon, *Facing the Dictators*, p. 548.
20. Ibid., p. 552.
21. Welles, *Seven Major Decisions*, p. 41.
22. *DBFP* 2/XIX, No. 443, p. 753, Eden to Lindsay, 16 January 1938.
23. Avon Papers, 20/1/18, Eden Diary, 16 January 1938.

24. *DBFP* 2/XIX, p. 758, Lindsay to Eden, 18 January 1938.

25. Harvey, 18 January 1938, p. 73.

26. AP 20/1/18, Eden Diary, 17 January 1938.

27. Thorpe, *Eden*, p. 204.

28. Harvey, 20 January 1938, p. 76.

29. *DBFP* 2/XIX, No. 455, p. 767, Eden to Lindsay, 21 January 1938.

30. *DBFP* 2/XIX, No. 462, p. 776, Lindsay to Eden, 22 January 1938.

31. Churchill, p. 199.

32. NC 18/1/1034, Chamberlain to Hilda Chamberlain, 9 January 1938.

33. Halifax, p. 376.

34. NC 1/17/5, Ivy Chamberlain to Chamberlain, 16 December 1937.

35. NC 1/17/6, Ivy Chamberlain to Chamberlain, 2 January 1938.

36. M. Muggeridge (ed.) (trans. A. Mayor), *Ciano's Diary 1937–1938*, Methuen 1952, 1 January 1938, p. 57 (hereafter cited as *Ciano's Diary*).

37. R. Rhodes James, *Memoirs of a Conservative, J. C. C. Davidson's Memoirs and Papers, 1910–37*, Weidenfeld and Nicolson 1969, p. 272. Lord Blake wrote of Sir Joseph Ball that he was the "quintessential *éminence grise* [whose] influence on affairs cannot be measured by the brevity of the printed references to him" (*Oxford Dictionary of National Biography*, Volume 3, 2004, p. 567).

38. W. C. Mills, "Sir Joseph Ball, Adrian Dingli, and Neville Chamberlain's 'Secret Channel' to Italy, 1937–1940," *The International History Review*, Volume XXIV (2), 2002, p. 284.

39. Ibid., p. 292.

40. Ibid., p. 293.

41. Ibid., pp. 294–95.

42. Avon, *Facing the Dictators*, p. 570.

43. NC 1/17/7, Ivy Chamberlain to Chamberlain, 2 February 1938.

44. PREM 1/276/105, Perth to Eden, 6 February 1938.

45. Andrew, p. 402.

46. *DBFP* 2/XV, p. 693n.

47. NC 1/17/7, Ivy Chamberlain to Chamberlain, 2 February 1938.

48. PREM 1/276/99 & 100, Eden to Chamberlain, 8 February 1938.

49. PREM 1/276/96, Chamberlain to Eden, 8 February 1938.

50. Mills, p. 295.

51. *Daily Mail*, 9 February 1938, p. 11.

52. Avon, *Facing the Dictators*, p. 574.

53. Harvey, 9 February 1938, p. 87.

54. Mills, p. 295.

55. Harvey, 14 February 1938, pp. 89–90.

56. *Ciano's Diary*, 7 February 1938, p. 71.

57. NC 18/1/1039, Chamberlain to Hilda Chamberlain, 13 February 1938.

58. *The Sunday Times*, 13 February 1938.

59. *Ciano's Diary*, 11 & 15 February 1938, pp. 73–75.

60. M. Muggeridge (ed.), *Ciano's Diplomatic Papers*, Odhams Press 1948, Ciano to Grandi, 16 February 1938, pp. 161–62.

61. PREM 1/276/87, Perth to Eden, 17 February 1938.

62. PREM 1/276/85, Perth to Eden, "Personal," 17 February 1938.
63. Mills, p. 297.
64. *Ciano's Diplomatic Papers*, Grandi to Ciano, 19 February 1938, p. 165.
65. PREM 1/276/83-84, Eden to Chamberlain, 17 February 1938.
66. NC 2/24A, Chamberlain Diary, 19 & 27 February 1938.
67. PREM 1/276/67–75, Halifax to Perth, 21 February 1938.
68. Avon, *Facing the Dictators*, pp. 581–82.
69. PREM 1/276/67–75, Halifax to Perth, 21 February 1938.
70. *Ciano's Diplomatic Papers*, Grandi to Ciano, 19 February 1938, p. 172.
71. Avon, *Facing the Dictators*, p. 581.
72. *Cadogan Diaries*, 18 February 1938, p. 50.
73. Avon, *Facing the Dictators*, p. 582.
74. *Cadogan Diaries*, 18 February 1938, p. 50.
75. S. Ball, *The Guardsmen: Harold Macmillan, Three Friends, and the World They Made*, HarperCollins 2004, p. 167.
76. Avon, *Facing the Dictators*, p. 584–85.
77. *Ciano's Diplomatic Papers*, Grandi to Ciano, 19 February 1938, p. 183.
78. Mills, p. 300.
79. Harvey, 18 February 1938, pp. 93–94.
80. NC 2/24A, Chamberlain Diary, 19 & 27 February 1938.
81. Hickleton Papers A4/410/4/11, "A Record of Events connected with Anthony Eden's resignation, February 19–20th 1938."
82. CAB 23/92/179–87, Cabinet 6 (38), 19 February 1938.
83. NC 2/24A, Chamberlain Diary, 19 & 27 February 1938.
84. CAB 23/92/191, Cabinet 6 (38), 19 February 1938.
85. Lord Norwich (ed.), *The Duff Cooper Diaries 1915–1951*, Weidenfeld and Nicolson 2005, 20 February 1938, p. 241.
86. CAB 23/92/212, Cabinet 6 (38), 19 February 1938.
87. NC 2/24A, Chamberlain Diary, 19 & 27 February 1938.
88. Avon, *Facing the Dictators*, p. 591.
89. Hickleton Papers A4/410/4/11, "A Record of Events connected with Anthony Eden's resignation February 19–20th 1938."
90. Mills, p. 301.
91. NC 2/24A, Chamberlain Diary, 19 & 27 February 1938.
92. Avon, *Facing the Dictators*, p. 592. In later life, having discovered the contributory role played by Sir Joseph Ball in his resignation, Eden was to comment ruefully in his memoirs that Ball had "certainly served Mussolini well" (Avon, *Facing the Dictators*, p. 578).
93. Mills, p. 301.
94. *Daily Express*, 21 February 1938, p. 1.
95. CAB 23/92/224–28, Cabinet 7 (38), 20 February 1938 at 3 p.m.
96. Thorpe, *Eden*, p. 207.
97. Harvey, 20 February 1938, p. 96.
98. *Daily Mail*, 21 February 1938, p. 13.
99. Mills, p. 302.
100. *Ciano's Diary*, 20 February 1938, p. 78.

101. CAB 23/92/254, Cabinet 8 (38), 20 February 1938 at 10 P.M.
102. *Channon Diaries*, 21 February 1938, p. 145.
103. Rhodes James, *Anthony Eden*, p. 197.
104. House of Commons, Official Report, Fifth Series, Volume 332, Col. 52, 21 February 1938.
105. Amery Papers, AMEL 7/32, Amery Diary, 21 February 1938.
106. Crookshank Papers, MS Eng. Hist.d.359/195, Crookshank Diary, 21, 23 & 24 February 1938.
107. Harvey, 27 February 1938, p. 103. "What says Lord Stanley? Will he bring his power?" asks Shakespeare's Richard III. "My Lord, he doth deny to come" (*King Richard III*, V, iii).
108. NC 7/11/31/10, Ball to Chamberlain, 21 February 1938.
109. *Daily Mail*, 21 February 1938, pp. 12–13.
110. Simon Papers, 84/180, Simon to Eden, 23 February 1938.
111. Harvey, 21 February 1938, p. 97.
112. NC 18/1/1040, Chamberlain to Hilda Chamberlain, 27 February 1938.
113. House of Commons, Official Report, Fifth Series, Volume 332, Cols. 257–58, 22 February 1938.
114. NC 1/17/8, Ivy Chamberlain to Chamberlain, 22 February 1938.
115. FO 800/313/1, Henderson to Halifax, 27 February 1938.
116. Churchill, p. 257.

4: THE LOADED PAUSE

1. Shirer, *The Rise and Fall of the Third Reich*, pp. 324–25.
2. B. Pauley, *Hitler and the Forgotten Nazis: A History of Austrian National Socialism*, Macmillan 1981, p. 157.
3. K. von Schuschnigg, *The Brutal Takeover*, Weidenfeld and Nicolson 1971, p. 5.
4. Pauley, p. 172.
5. Kershaw, *Hitler*, pp. 65–66.
6. G. Gedye, *Fallen Bastions*, Victor Gollancz 1939, p. 217.
7. *DGFP* D/1, No. 273, p. 486, Papen to Hitler, 21 December 1937.
8. G. Brook-Shepherd, *Anschluss: The Rape of Austria*, Macmillan 1963, p. 15.
9. F. von Papen (trans. B Connell), *Memoirs*, André Deutsch 1952, p. 406.
10. Kershaw, *Hitler*, p. 865, n27 (original in Goebbels Diaries, 15 December 1937).
11. G. Weinberg, *The Foreign Policy of Hitler's Germany: Starting World War II 1937–1939*, University of Chicago Press, Chicago 1980, p. 290.
12. Papen, pp. 407–8.
13. K. von Schuschnigg (trans. F. von Hildebrand), *Austrian Requiem*, Victor Gollancz 1947, pp. 18–19.
14. Kershaw, *Hitler*, p. 70.
15. Weinberg, p. 292.
16. Keitel, p. 57. Legend has it that Hitler chose his "most fearsome-looking gen-

erals to cow Schuschnigg with their scowls" (T. Taylor, p. 179). A quick glance at a photograph of Sperrle is enough to confirm that his selection was certainly well deserved on these grounds alone.

17. R. Spitzy (trans. G. Waddington), *How We Squandered the Reich*, Michael Russell 1997, p. 174.
18. Schuschnigg, *The Brutal Takeover*, pp. 191–92.
19. Schuschnigg, *Austrian Requiem*, p. 20.
20. Shirer, *The Rise and Fall of the Third Reich*, p. 326.
21. Schuschnigg, *Austrian Requiem*, pp. 21–25.
22. Gedye, p. 227.
23. Schuschnigg, *Austrian Requiem*, p. 26.
24. Papen, p. 415.
25. Spitzy, p. 175.
26. Schuschnigg, *Austrian Requiem*, p. 27.
27. *DGFP* D/1, No. 294, pp. 513–14, Draft "Protocol of the Conference of February 12, 1938."
28. Schuschnigg, *Austrian Requiem*, pp. 27–28.
29. Shirer, *The Rise and Fall of the Third Reich*, p. 329.
30. Schuschnigg, *Austrian Requiem*, p. 30.
31. Papen, p. 417.
32. Eberle & Uhl, p. 26.
33. Papen, p. 417.
34. Shirer, *The Rise and Fall of the Third Reich*, p. 329.
35. Schuschnigg, *Austrian Requiem*, p. 32.
36. Gedye, p. 226.
37. Shirer, *The Rise and Fall of the Third Reich*, p. 331.
38. *DGFP* D/1, No. 297, p. 518, Papen to German Foreign Ministry, 14 February 1938.
39. *Nazi Conspiracy and Aggression* (hereafter cited as *NCA*), Volume IV, Document 1780-PS, United States Government Printing Office, Washington 1946, p. 361, Jodl Diary, 13 February 1938.
40. Brissaud, p. 81.
41. *NCA*, Volume IV, Document 1780-PS, p. 361, Jodl Diary, 14 February 1938.
42. Pauley, p. 183.
43. Shirer, *The Rise and Fall of the Third Reich*, p. 332.
44. Brook-Shepherd, p. 27.
45. *DBFP* 2/XIX, No. 513, p. 892, Palairet to Eden, 13 February 1938.
46. *DBFP* 2/XIX, No. 516, p. 895, Palairet to Eden, 15 February 1938.
47. *Cadogan Diaries*, 15 February 1938, p. 47.
48. Harvey, 15 & 16 February 1938, pp. 90–91.
49. Kershaw, *Hitler*, p. 72.
50. *DBFP* 2/XIX, No. 516, p. 896, Palairet to Eden, 15 February 1938.
51. Brook-Shepherd, p. 80.
52. *Ciano's Diary*, 15 February 1938, p. 75.
53. *DBFP* 2/XIX, No. 522, p. 900, Palairet to Eden, 15 February 1938.

54. FO 800/313/3, Henderson to Halifax, 27 February 1938.
55. Kershaw, *Hitler*, p. 73.
56. *Daily Mail*, 21 February 1938, p. 14.
57. N. Baynes (ed.), *The Speeches of Adolf Hitler, Volume II, April 1922–August 1939*, Oxford University Press 1942, pp. 1404–6.
58. Gedye, p. 248.
59. Schuschnigg, *Austrian Requiem*, pp. 36–37 (the final line of the quotation rhymes in the German also).
60. CAB 27/623, Foreign Policy Committee 21 (38), 24 January 1938.
61. FO 800/313/1, Henderson to Halifax, 27 February 1938.
62. N. Henderson, pp. 115–16.
63. *DGFP* D/1, No. 138, p. 248, Ribbentrop to Henderson, 4 March 1938.
64. *DGFP* D/1, No. 139, p. 249, Henderson to Ribbentrop, 4 March 1938.
65. N. Henderson, p. 117.
66. Schuschnigg, *Austrian Requiem*, p. 39.
67. Pauley, p. 206.
68. Schuschnigg, *Austrian Requiem*, p. 41.
69. Brissaud, p. 83.
70. A. J. P. Taylor, *The Origins of the Second World War*, Hamish Hamilton 1961, p. 146.
71. Kershaw, *Hitler*, p. 74 (original in Goebbels Diaries, 10 March 1938).
72. *NCA*, Volume IV, Document 1780-PS, p. 362, Jodl Diary, 10 March 1938.
73. Spitzy, pp. 181–82.
74. CAB 23/92/325–27, Cabinet 11 (38), 9 March 1938.
75. Harvey, 10 & 11 March 1938, pp. 112–13.
76. *Documents on British Foreign Policy 1919–1939*, Third Series, Volume I, His Majesty's Stationery Office 1949 (hereafter cited as *DBFP* 3/I), No. 2, p. 2, Palairet to Halifax, 9 March 1938.
77. Harvey, 11 March 1938, p. 113.
78. *Cadogan Diaries*, p. 59, 10 March 1938.
79. Andrew, p. 391.
80. Brissaud, pp. 83–84.
81. Guderian, p. 50.
82. Brook-Shepherd, p. 133.
83. Kershaw, *Hitler*, p. 75–76.
84. Shirer, *The Rise and Fall of the Third Reich*, p. 336.
85. Schuschnigg, *Austrian Requiem*, pp. 45–46.
86. Papen, pp. 427–28.
87. *DGFP* D/1, No. 146, p. 263, Ribbentrop to Hitler, 10 March 1938.
88. Spitzy, p. 187.
89. E. Butler, *"Mason-Mac": The Life of Lieutenant-General Sir Noel Mason-MacFarlane*, Macmillan 1972, p. 66.
90. *DBFP* 3/I, No. 34, p. 17, Henderson to Halifax, 11 March 1938.
91. *DBFP* 3/I, No. 14, p. 8, Henderson to Halifax, 11 March 1938.
92. It is an intriguing, but infrequently commented upon, fact that during the lengthy period that the German embassy in the Mall was being refurbished,

the Ribbentrops rented Chamberlain's house in Eaton Square. Chamberlain was at the time Chancellor of the Exchequer, and was living at 11 Downing Street.

93. M. Bloch, *Ribbentrop*, Bantam 1992, p. 171.
94. *DGFP* D/1, No. 149, pp. 272–73, Ribbentrop memorandum, 11 March 1938.
95. Harvey, 7 March 1938, p. 111.
96. N. Smart (ed.), *The Diaries and Letters of Robert Bernays, 1932–1939*, Edwin Mellen Press, Lewiston 1996, p. 352.
97. Viscount Templewood, *Nine Troubled Years*, Collins 1954, p. 282.
98. Churchill, pp. 211–12.
99. NC 18/1/1041, Chamberlain to Hilda Chamberlain, 13 March 1938.
100. *DGFP* D/1, No. 150, pp. 274–75, Ribbentrop memorandum, 11 March 1938.
101. *Cadogan Diaries*, 11 March 1938, p. 60.
102. A. Bullock (ed.), *The Ribbentrop Memoirs*, Weidenfeld and Nicolson 1954, pp. 84–86.
103. *DBFP* 3/I, No. 44, p. 22, Halifax to Henderson, 11 March 1938.
104. Roberts, "*The Holy Fox*," p. 92.
105. NC 18/1/1041, Chamberlain to Hilda Chamberlain, 13 March 1938.
106. Duchess of Windsor, p. 306.
107. Papen, p. 410.
108. Deutsch, *Hitler and His Generals*, p. 343.
109. *TMWC*, Volume IX, p. 296, Göring testimony, 14 March 1946.
110. Schuschnigg, *Austrian Requiem*, p. 47.
111. Pauley, p. 208.
112. Schuschnigg, *Austrian Requiem*, p. 48–49.
113. Papen, p. 429.
114. Kershaw, p. 77.
115. Schuschnigg, *Austrian Requiem*, Appendix p. 253, Göring to Seyss-Inquart, 11 March 1938 at 5:26 P.M.
116. Schuschnigg, *Austrian Requiem*, Appendix p. 255, Göring to Keppler, 11 March 1938 at 6:28 P.M.
117. Shirer, p. 340.
118. Schuschnigg, *Austrian Requiem*, pp. 51–52.
119. Shirer, *The Rise and Fall of the Third Reich*, p. 341.
120. Brook-Shepherd, p. 173.
121. Brissaud, p. 84.
122. Shirer, *The Rise and Fall of the Third Reich*, p. 342.
123. Schuschnigg, *The Brutal Takeover*, p. 336, (original in *TMWC*, Volume XXXIV, Document 182-C, p. 774).
124. *DGFP* D/I, No. 352, pp. 575–76, Hitler to Mussolini, 11 March 1938.
125. Eberle & Uhl, p. 27.
126. Shirer, *The Rise and Fall of the Third Reich*, p. 343 (original in *TMWC*, Volume XXXI, p. 368).
127. J. Wheeler-Bennett, *Munich: Prologue to Tragedy*, Macmillan 1948, p. 22.
128. *Lipski Papers*, p. 351.
129. N. Henderson, p. 124.

130. H. Noguères (trans. P. O'Brian), *Munich, or the Phoney Peace*, Weidenfeld and Nicolson 1965, p. 19.
131. Wheeler-Bennett, *Prologue to Tragedy*, p. 25.
132. N. Henderson, pp. 124–25.
133. *TMWC*, Volume IX, Göring testimony, 14 March 1946, pp. 300–301.
134. *DGFP* D/I, No. 364, pp. 584–85, Foreign Ministry memorandum, 12 March 1938.
135. Keitel, p. 58.
136. Shirer, *The Rise and Fall of the Third Reich*, p. 346.

5: A SPRING STORM

1. Guderian, pp. 50–51.
2. Churchill, p. 210.
3. *DBFP* 3/I, No. 51, p. 27, Palairet to Halifax, 12 March 1938.
4. Keitel, p. 59.
5. Spitzy, p. 190.
6. Guderian, pp. 52–56.
7. Shirer, *The Rise and Fall of the Third Reich*, p. 347.
8. Spitzy, p. 191.
9. Shirer, *The Rise and Fall of the Third Reich*, p. 348.
10. *DGFP* D/I, No. 362, p. 583, Dieckhoff to German Foreign Ministry, 12 March 1938.
11. NC 18/1/1041, Chamberlain to Hilda Chamberlain, 13 March 1938.
12. CAB 23/92/345–55, Cabinet 12 (38), 12 March 1938. Contrary to the accepted version in a number of works on this period, Halifax's warning to Schuschnigg was in fact never delivered by Palairet, who knew that "it would not have done any good" (Weinberg, p. 297).
13. Heinemann, p. 174.
14. *DBFP* 3/I, No. 47, p. 25, Kirkpatrick to Neurath, 11 March 1938.
15. *DBFP* 3/I, No. 46, p. 24, Henderson to Halifax, 12 March 1938.
16. *DBFP* 3/I, No. 54, p. 29, Halifax to Henderson, 12 March 1938.
17. J. Gehl, *Austria, Germany and the Anschluss, 1931–45*, Oxford University Press 1963, p. 194.
18. E. Bukey, *Hitler's Austria, Popular Sentiment in the Nazi Era, 1938–1945*, University of North Carolina Press, Chapel Hill 2000, p. 25.
19. Toland, p. 452.
20. Kershaw, *Hitler*, p. 80.
21. B. Mussolini (trans. F. Lobb), *Memoirs 1942–1943*, Weidenfeld and Nicolson 1949, p. 190n.
22. Brook-Shepherd, p. 193.
23. *TMWC* Volume XV, p. 632, Stuckart affidavit, 10 June 1946.
24. *TMWC* Volume XV, p. 633, Seyss-Inquart testimony, 10 June 1946.
25. Brook-Shepherd, p. 195.
26. Butler, p. 70.

27. F. Jetzinger, *Hitler's Youth*, Hutchinson 1958, p. 55.
28. Gedye, p. 318.
29. *DBFP* 3/I, No. 76, p. 43, Palairet to Halifax, 14 March 1938.
30. Keitel, p. 60.
31. N. Gun, *Eva Braun, Hitler's Mistress*, Leslie Frewin 1969, p. 151.
32. Brook-Shepherd, p. 200.
33. Papen, p. 432.
34. CAB 23/92/365–77, Cabinet 13 (38), 14 March 1938.
35. Amery Papers, AMEL 7/32, Amery Diary, 14 March 1938.
36. NC 18/1/1041, Chamberlain to Hilda Chamberlain, 13 March 1938.
37. R. Rhodes James, *Victor Cazalet, A Portrait*, Hamish Hamilton 1976, p. 200.
38. *Channon Diaries*, 11 March 1938, pp. 150–51.
39. AMEL 2/2/10, Eden to Amery, 5 February 1938.
40. AMEL 7/32, Amery Diary, 12 March 1938.
41. *The Times*, 14 March 1938, p. 11 & p. 15.
42. House of Lords, Official Report, Fifth Series, Volume 111, Cols. 448–49, 29 March 1938.
43. FO 800/269/104, Cadogan to Henderson, 22 April 1938.
44. *DBFP* 3/I, No. 55, p. 30, Halifax to Palairet, 12 March 1938.
45. *The Times*, 14 March 1938, p. 14.
46. Gedye, p. 301.
47. Shirer, *The Rise and Fall of the Third Reich*, p. 351.
48. N. Nicolson (ed.), *Harold Nicolson, Diaries and Letters, 1930–1939*, Collins 1966, p. 347 (hereafter cited as *Nicolson Diaries*).
49. Kershaw, *Hitler*, p. 84.
50. Gedye, pp. 305–6.
51. NC 18/1/1042, Chamberlain to Ida Chamberlain, 20 March 1938.
52. Noguères, p. 28.
53. E. Wiskemann, *Czechs and Germans: A Study of the Struggles in the Historic Provinces of Bohemia and Moravia*, Oxford University Press 1938, p. 118.
54. Gedye, p. 396.
55. Toland, p. 459.
56. Gedye, p. 393.
57. J. Bruegel, *Czechoslovakia Before Munich: The German Minority Problem and British Appeasement Policy*, Cambridge University Press 1973, p. 110.
58. Bruegel, p. 120.
59. *Daily Telegraph*, 10 December 1935.
60. K. Henlein, "The German Minority in Czechoslovakia," *International Affairs*, Volume XV, No. 4, The Royal Institute of International Affairs 1936, pp. 568–69.
61. Bruegel, p. 135.
62. R. Shepherd, *A Class Divided: Appeasement and the Road to Munich 1938*, Macmillan 1988, p. 145.
63. Weinberg, p. 314.
64. Kershaw, *Hitler*, p. 83.
65. *DBFP* 3/I, No. 97, p. 68, Newton to Halifax, 22 March 1938.

66. *DBFP* 3/I, No. 120, p. 105, Newton to Halifax, 29 March 1938.
67. *DBFP* 3/I, No. 129, p. 121, Newton to Halifax, 6 April 1938.
68. *Documents on German Foreign Policy 1918–1945,* Series D (1937-1945), Volume II, "Germany and Czechoslovakia 1937–1938," His Majesty's Stationery Office 1950 (hereafter cited as *DGFP* D/II), No. 107, p. 198, unsigned report of German Foreign Ministry, 28 March 1938.
69. Wheeler-Bennett, *Munich,* p. 33.
70. House of Lords, Official Report, Fifth Series, Volume 104, Col. 498, 3 March 1937.
71. NC 18/1/1042, Chamberlain to Ida Chamberlain, 20 March 1938.
72. *DBFP* 3/I, No. 92, p. 65, Chilston to Halifax, 17 March 1938.
73. *DBFP* 3/I, No. 148, p. 161, Chilston to Halifax, 19 April 1938.
74. House of Commons, Official Report, Fifth Series, Volume 333, Col. 1406, 24 March 1938.
75. NC 18/1/1042, Chamberlain to Ida Chamberlain, 20 March 1938.
76. *Nicolson Diaries,* 7 March 1938, p. 329.
77. *Cadogan Diaries,* 12 & 16 March 1938, pp. 62–63.
78. Lord Gladwyn, *The Memoirs of Lord Gladwyn,* Weidenfeld and Nicolson 1972, pp. 74–75.
79. *DBFP* 3/I, No. 81, p. 50, Phipps to Halifax, 15 March 1938.
80. CAB 27/623, Foreign Policy Committee (36) 26th Meeting, 18 March 1938.
81. *Cadogan Diaries,* 18 March 1938, p. 63.
82. CAB 23/93/32–34, Cabinet 15 (38), 22 March 1938.
83. *Duff Cooper Diaries,* 27 March 1938, p. 245.
84. CAB 23/93/35, Cabinet 15 (38), 22 March 1938.
85. *Nicolson Diaries,* 29 March 1938, p. 333.
86. House of Commons, Official Report, Fifth Series, Volume 333, Cols. 1405–6, 24 March 1938.
87. *DBFP* 3/I, No. 135, p. 141, Halifax to Phipps, 11 April 1938.
88. FO 800/311/27, Phipps to Halifax, 11 April 1938.
89. *DGFP* D/II, No. 147, p. 257, Dirksen to German Foreign Ministry, 6 May 1938.
90. NC 18/1/1049, Chamberlain to Ida Chamberlain, 1 May 1938.
91. Keitel, p. 62.
92. *DGFP* D/II, No. 133, pp. 239–40, memorandum on Operation "Green" by Major Schmundt, 22 April 1938.
93. Churchill, p. 221.
94. Schmidt, pp. 81–83.
95. *Ciano's Diary,* 7 & 8 May 1938, p. 113.
96. E. von Weizsäcker (trans. J. Andrews), *Memoirs of Ernst von Weizsäcker,* Victor Gollancz 1951, p. 131.
97. Toland, p. 462.
98. *Ciano's Diary,* 6 May 1938, p. 112.
99. Weinberg, p. 307.
100. *Ciano's Diary,* 7 May 1938, p. 113.
101. *DGFP* D/I, No. 761, p. 1109, Ribbentrop to All German Embassies, 12 May 1938.

102. *DGFP* D/I, No. 762, p. 1110, Weizsäcker to Woermann, 12 May 1938.
103. Birkenhead, *Halifax*, p. 385.
104. *DBFP* 3/I, No. 166, p. 236-37, Halifax to Newton, 2 May 1938.
105. *DGFP* D/II, No. 145, p. 255, Dirksen to Foreign Ministry, 3 May 1938.
106. *DGFP* D/II, No. 149, p. 262, Woermann to Ribbentrop, 7 May 1938.
107. *DGFP* D/II, No. 151, p. 265, Bismarck Memorandum, 10 May 1938.
108. *DGFP* D/II, No. 155, p. 273, Weizsäcker memorandum, 12 May 1938.
109. *DGFP* D/II, No. 156, p. 274, Eisenlohr (Prague) to German Foreign Ministry, 12 May 1938.
110. Vansittart Papers, VNST II/2/17/, memorandum of meeting with Henlein, 16 May 1938.
111. Churchill, p. 223.
112. PREM 1/249/125, Churchill to Chamberlain, 15 May 1938.
113. *Nicolson Diaries*, 13 May 1938, p. 340.
114. *DGFP* D/II, No. 23, p. 50, Henlein to Hitler, 19 November 1937.
115. Keitel, p. 63.
116. Shirer, *The Rise and Fall of the Third Reich*, p. 367.
117. Bruegel, p. 189 n2 (original in *TMWC*, Volume XXV, p. 419).
118. *DGFP* D/I1, No. 175, p. 299, Keitel to Hitler, 20 May 1938.
119. *DGFP* D/I1, No. 175, p. 300, "Draft for the New Directive 'Green,' " 20 May 1938.
120. T. Taylor, p. 189.
121. Weinberg, p. 302.

6: CRISIS IN MAY

1. Beaverbrook Papers, BBK A/224, Beaverbrook to R. B. Bennett, 9 March 1938.
2. NC 18/1/1043, Chamberlain to Hilda Chamberlain, 27 March 1938.
3. NC 18/1/1046, Chamberlain to Hilda Chamberlain, 9 April 1938.
4. Harvey, 13 April 1938, p. 127.
5. *Channon Diaries*, 17 March 1938, pp. 151–52.
6. *Nicolson Diaries*, 7 April 1938, p. 333.
7. Lord Swinton, *Sixty Years of Power, Some Memories of the Men Who Wielded It*, Hutchinson 1966, pp. 111–14.
8. D. C. Watt, *How War Came: The Immediate Origins of the Second World War, 1938–1939*, Heinemann 1989, p. 78.
9. Harvey, 12 March 1938, p. 115.
10. Avon Papers, AP 8/2/13A, Eden to Baldwin, 11 May 1938.
11. Harvey, 19 May 1938, p. 140.
12. J. Stuart, *Within the Fringe: An Autobiography*, Bodley Head 1967, p. 83.
13. Lord Home, *Letters to a Grandson*, Collins 1983, p. 30.
14. S. Aster, " 'Guilty Men': The Case of Neville Chamberlain," in *Paths to War, New Essays on the Origins of the Second World War*, R. Boyce & E. Robertson (eds.), Macmillan 1989, pp. 240–41.

15. Watt, pp. 76–78.
16. J. Margach, *The Abuse of Power: The War Between Downing Street and the Media from Lloyd George to Callaghan*, W. H. Allen 1978, p. 50.
17. Cockett, p. 7.
18. J. Margach, *The Anatomy of Power: An Enquiry into the Personality of Leadership*, W. H. Allen 1979, p. 129.
19. Margach, *The Abuse of Power*, p. 53.
20. Ibid., pp. 50–53.
21. R. Bruce Lockhart, *Jan Masaryk: A Personal Memoir*, Dropmore Press 1951, p. 18.
22. NC 18/1/1030, Chamberlain to Ida Chamberlain, 26 November 1937.
23. NC 18/1/1042, Chamberlain to Ida Chamberlain, 20 March 1938.
24. CAB 27/623, Foreign Policy Committee (36) 26th Meeting, 18 March 1938.
25. *DBFP* 3/I, No. 135, p. 142, Halifax to Phipps, 11 April 1938.
26. Weinberg, pp. 334–35.
27. FO 371/21721/168, Vansittart memorandum for Halifax, 25 May 1938.
28. CAB 23/93/235, Cabinet 22 (38), 5 May 1938.
29. NC 18/1/1051, Chamberlain to Ida Chamberlain, 15 May 1938.
30. Gedye, p. 410.
31. Parliamentary Debates, House of Commons, Official Report, Fifth Series, Volume 337, Cols. 852–53, 20 June 1938.
32. Parliamentary Debates, House of Commons, Official Report, Fifth Series, Volume 337, Col. 955, 21 June 1938.
33. Parliamentary Debates, House of Commons, Official Report, Fifth Series, Volume 337, Col. 854–56, 20 June 1938.
34. Parliamentary Debates, House of Commons, Official Report, Fifth Series, Volume 337, Col. 958, 21 June 1938.
35. *The Times*, 28 June 1938, p. 9.
36. NC 18/1/1057, Chamberlain to Hilda Chamberlain, 25 June 1938.
37. Shepherd, p. 162.
38. F. Moravec, *Master of Spies: The Memoirs of General František Moravec*, Bodley Head 1975, p. 84. Thümmel continued to provide high-quality intelligence to the Czechs for another year, and correctly predicted German plans for the invasion of Czechoslovakia and Poland. When Prague fell, SIS transferred Moravec and his network to London, and Thümmel began work for SIS instead.
39. Andrew, pp. 392–93.
40. Stronge Papers, MS Eng. Hist. d. 150/154, "Personal Memorandum relating to the state of morale and general readiness for war of the army of the Czechoslovak Republic at the time of the Munich Crisis," 8 February 1974.
41. *DBFP* 3/I, No. 240, n4, p. 323, Henderson to Halifax, 20 May 1938.
42. *DBFP* 3/I, No. 244, p. 327, Newton to Halifax, 20 May 1938.
43. G. Weinberg, "The May Crisis 1938," *The Journal of Modern History*, Volume XXIX, University of Chicago Press 1957, p. 217.
44. *DBFP* 3/I, No. 245, p. 327, Newton to Halifax, 20 May 1938.
45. *DBFP* 3/I, No. 249, p. 329, Henderson to Halifax, 21 May 1938.

46. Schmidt, p. 84.
47. The funeral of the two Sudeten Germans was attended by the German military and air attachés from Prague, who laid wreaths decorated with swastikas and red ribbons bearing the name Adolf Hitler in gold letters (Bruegel, p. 190, n3).
48. N. Henderson, p. 136.
49. NC 18/1/1053, Chamberlain to Hilda Chamberlain, 22 May 1938.
50. *DBFP* 3/I, No. 250, p. 331, Halifax to Henderson, 21 May 1938.
51. *DGFP* D/II, No. 186, p. 317, Ribbentrop memorandum, 21 May 1938.
52. Harvey, 22 May 1938, p. 144.
53. N. Henderson, p. 139.
54. *DBFP* 3/I, No. 264, p. 341, Halifax to Henderson, 22 May 1938.
55. *Duff Cooper Diaries*, 29 May 1938, pp. 249–50. Lord Maugham, at seventy-one the oldest member of the Cabinet, had recently been appointed to the Woolsack by Chamberlain, "to the astonishment of the political and legal world." He was "entirely without political experience, either local or national. Indeed so divorced was he from the world of affairs that he had never even met the Prime Minister before their interview at No. 10 Downing Street on 9 March 1938." Even Maugham himself later confessed that "he had no idea how his name was placed before the Prime Minister" (R. Heuston, *Lives of the Lord Chancellors, 1885–1940*, Clarendon Press 1964, p. 553).
56. Stronge Papers, MS Eng. Hist. d.150/154–55.
57. *DBFP* 3/I, No. 316, p. 380, Henderson to Halifax, 25 May 1938.
58. D. C. Watt, "British Intelligence and the Coming of the Second World War in Europe," in E. May (ed.), *Knowing One's Enemies*, Princeton University Press 1984, p. 262.
59. B. Bond (ed.), *Chief of Staff: The Diaries of Lieutenant-General Sir Henry Pownall, Volume One 1933–1940*, Leo Cooper 1972, p. 147.
60. NC 18/1/1054, Chamberlain to Ida Chamberlain, 28 May 1938.
61. *Pownall Diaries*, p. 147.
62. Harvey, 24 May 1938, p. 144.
63. FO 371/21721/167, Vansittart memorandum for Halifax, 25 May 1938.
64. CAB 21/540/17, Henderson to Halifax, 10 March 1939.
65. *NCA*, Volume IV, Document 1780-PS, p. 363, Jodl Diary, n/d.
66. Kershaw, *Hitler*, p. 100.
67. Toland, p. 464.
68. Kershaw, *Hitler*, p. 101.
69. *NCA*, Volume V, Document 3037-PS, pp. 743–44, affidavit of Fritz Wiedemann, 21 November 1945.
70. *DGFP* D/II, No. 221, p. 358–59, "Directive for Operation Green," 30 May 1938.
71. *DGFP* D/II, No. 282, p. 473, "General Strategic Directive," 18 June 1938.
72. Shirer, *The Rise and Fall of the Third Reich*, p. 366.
73. Vansittart Papers, VNST I/1/22, Kirkpatrick to Eden, "Record of Leading Personalities in Germany," 6 January 1938.

74. Kershaw, *Hitler*, p. 101.
75. H. Deutsch, *The Conspiracy Against Hitler in the Twilight War*, University of Minnesota Press, Minneapolis 1968, p. 34.
76. Kershaw, *Hitler*, p. 874, n246.
77. Weinberg, p. 384.
78. Deutsch, *The Conspiracy Against Hitler*, p. 34.
79. Deutsch, *Hitler and His Generals*, p. 406.
80. Toland, p. 467.
81. Kershaw, *Hitler*, p. 102.
82. Brissaud, p. 110.
83. A. Chisholm & M. Davie, *Beaverbrook: A Life*, Hutchinson 1992, p. 333.
84. BBK C/275, Beaverbrook to Ribbentrop, 17 February 1938.
85. Chisholm & Davie, p. 348.
86. A. J. P. Taylor, *Beaverbrook*, Hamish Hamilton 1972, pp. 378–79.
87. BBK B/261, Beaverbrook to F. Gannett, 9 December 1938.
88. Chisholm & Davie, p. 349.
89. M. Gilbert, *Winston S. Churchill, Volume V, Companion Part 3, "The Coming of War 1936–1939,"* Heinemann 1982, pp. 958 & 987.
90. D. Low, *Low's Autobiography*, Michael Joseph 1956, p. 278–79.
91. S. Taylor, *The Great Outsiders: Northcliffe, Rothermere and the Daily Mail*, Weidenfeld and Nicolson 1996, pp. 290–92.
92. Cockett, p. 56.
93. FO 800/313/54–55, Ward Price memorandum, 30 March 1938.
94. Cockett, pp. 12–13.
95. *The History of The Times, Volume IV: The 150th Anniversary and Beyond, 1912–1948*, The Times 1952, p. 907.
96. Ibid., p. 908.
97. Ibid., p. 917.
98. *The Times*, 3 June 1938, p. 15.
99. *DBFP* 3/I, No. 374, p. 444, Halifax to Newton, 4 June 1938.
100. *The History of The Times*, p. 921.
101. *DGFP* D/II, No. 247, pp. 399–400, Dirksen to Foreign Ministry, 9 June 1938.
102. *The Times*, 14 June 1938, p. 17.
103. FO 800/309/183–84, Halifax to Dawson, 15 June 1938.
104. FO 800/309/186, Dawson to Halifax, 19 June 1938.
105. M. Schad (trans. A McGeoch), *Hitler's Spy Princess: The Extraordinary Life of Stephanie von Hohenlohe*, Sutton Publishing 2004, p. 78.
106. FO 800/313/166, Halifax to Cadogan, 8 July 1938.
107. S. Taylor, p. 257.
108. Schad, pp. 40–41.
109. M. Dodd, *My Years in Germany*, Victor Gollancz 1939, pp. 223–24.
110. *Nicolson Diaries*, 26 May 1938, p. 344.
111. Harvey, 11–16 July 1938, p. 161–62.
112. W. Selby, *Diplomatic Twilight*, John Murray 1953, p. 72.
113. Schad, p. 85.
114. FO 800/314/10–17, Halifax memorandum, 18 July 1938.

115. Harvey, 18 July 1938, p. 163.
116. Schad, pp. 86 & 89.
117. *DGFP* D/VII, Appendix III (H) (iii), p. 631, Wiedemann memorandum for Ribbentrop, n/d. Halifax's biographer writes that such a statement "completely fails to ring true," but does point out that when the editor of a Danish newspaper wrote to the *Manchester Guardian* about this incident in 1957, Halifax, then aged seventy-five, "decided to absent himself from Garrowby [his Yorkshire home] for the day and refused to take calls from the press about it" (Roberts, p. 103).
118. R. Bassett, *Hitler's Spy Chief: The Wilhelm Canaris Mystery*, Weidenfeld and Nicolson 2005, pp. 150–51.

7: A FARAWAY COUNTRY

1. G. Cox, *Countdown to War: A Personal Memoir of Europe 1938–1940*, William Kimber 1988, pp. 11–13.
2. Wheeler-Bennett, *Munich*, pp. 77–79.
3. P. Neville, *Hitler and Appeasement: The British Attempt to Prevent the Second World War*, Hambledon Continuum 2006, p. 92.
4. In June, Chips Channon had bumped into Chamberlain and his wife walking in St. James's Park, and had "doffed his bowler" to the Prime Minister. "Everyone wears bowlers now," he confided to his diary, "since the Eden debacle black homburgs are 'out.' " *Channon Diaries*, 14 June 1938, p. 159.
5. Gedye, p. 392. Eric Gedye had been expelled from Vienna by the Gestapo soon after the Anschluss, and spent the summer in Prague, covering events for the *Daily Telegraph*. He was sacked the following year when he published *Fallen Bastions*, from which this reference comes, and in which he fiercely criticized Chamberlain and his policies. Although the *Telegraph* was basically an anti-appeasing newspaper, the editor announced that Gedye had left "by mutual consent." "That is quite correct," commented Gedye. "It is equally correct that Herr Hitler invaded Czechoslovakia by 'mutual arrangement' with President Hácha" (*DNB*, Volume 21, p. 711). His quotation is not quite accurate. It should read "The hangman, with his little bag, Went shuffling through the gloom." Oscar Wilde, *The Ballad of Reading Gaol*, Part III.
6. Cox, p. 13.
7. W. Shirer, *Berlin Diary*, Hamish Hamilton 1941, p. 102.
8. *DBFP* 3/I, No. 425, p. 501, Halifax to Newton, 18 June 1938.
9. *DBFP* 3/I, No. 431, p. 505, Newton to Halifax, 21 June 1938.
10. *DBFP* 3/I, No. 354, p. 419, Halifax to Phipps, 31 May 1938.
11. Gedye, p. 410.
12. *DBFP* 3/I, No. 368, p. 439, Newton to Halifax, 2 June 1938.
13. *Daily Mail*, 26 May 1938.
14. PREM 1/265/232, Wilson to Halifax, 22 June 1938.
15. Noguères, p. 77.
16. FO 800/309/202, Runciman to Halifax, 30 June 1938.

17. *DBFP* 3/I, No. 493, p. 567, Halifax to Newton, 16 July 1938.
18. Parliamentary Debates, House of Lords, Official Report, Fifth Series, Volume 105, Col. 1282, 27 July 1938.
19. *DBFP* 3/I, No. 521, p. 600, Newton to Halifax, 20 July 1938.
20. *Documents on British Foreign Policy 1919–1939*, Third Series, Volume II, His Majesty's Stationery Office 1949 (hereafter cited as *DBFP* 3/II), No. 547, p. 8, Newton to Halifax, 26 July 1938.
21. *DBFP* 3/II, No. 552, p. 13, Henderson to Halifax, 27 July 1938.
22. PREM 1/265/206, Ribbentrop to Halifax, 21 August 1938.
23. FO 800/269/207, Henderson to Halifax, 26 July 1938.
24. On July 22 Chamberlain held a meeting at Downing Street with the German ambassador, Dirksen. So lengthy was their conversation that it attracted widespread comment in the press. Dirksen reported to Berlin that Chamberlain had "emphasised the earnest will of the British Government, by intensified and continued pressure on Prague, to bring about a settlement of the Czech crisis, and to secure the desired autonomy for the Sudeten Germans" (*DGFP* D/II, No. 266, p. 432, Dirksen to Foreign Ministry, 23 June 1938).
25. Parliamentary Debates, House of Commons, Official Report, Fifth Series, Volume 338, Cols. 2956–58, 26 July 1938.
26. PREM 1/265/221, Chamberlain to Runciman, 28 July 1938.
27. R. Self, *Neville Chamberlain: A Biography*, Ashgate 2006, p. 263.
28. Shepherd, p. 164.
29. Shirer, *Berlin Diary*, p. 102.
30. *News Chronicle*, 27 July 1938, p. 10.
31. *Evening Standard*, 26 July 1938, p. 6.
32. Amery Papers, AMEL 7/32, Amery Diary, 26 July 1938.
33. *The Observer*, 31 July 1938, p. 10.
34. NC 18/1/1060, Chamberlain to Ida Chamberlain, 16 July 1938.
35. RA PS/GVI/ C 047/09, King George VI to Chamberlain, 14 August 1938.
36. Cox, p. 38.
37. *DBFP* 3/II, No. 583, p. 51, Runciman to Halifax, 4 August 1938.
38. Gedye, p. 435.
39. The mission also included Robert Stopford, the former Secretary of the Simon Commission on Indian Constitutional Reform; Geoffrey Peto, a former Conservative MP and Parliamentary Private Secretary to Runciman from 1931 to 1935; Ian Henderson, the British consul in the Sudetenland; and Miss Miller, a Foreign Office secretary. They were later to co-opt a young Treasury clerk, David Stephens, who had made an extensive study of the issue of German minorities in Czechoslovakia, and who happened to be on a cycling holiday in the country at the time.
40. *DBFP* 3/II, No. 587, p. 55, Halifax to Henderson, 5 August 1938.
41. R. Douglas, *In the Year of Munich*, Macmillan 1977, p. 37.
42. Neville, *Hitler and Appeasement*, p. 92.
43. A. Henderson, *Eyewitness in Czecho-Slovakia*, George Harrap 1939, p. 145.
44. Cox, p. 39.
45. H. Macmillan, *Winds of Change, 1914–1939*, Macmillan 1966, p. 552.

46. *DGFP* D/II, No. 336, p. 535, Hencke to Foreign Ministry, 5 August 1938. In 2003, Kinsky's sixty-eight-year-old son, who has lived for most of his life in Argentina, initiated 150 lawsuits against the Czech government and private individuals to recover family properties which he claimed had been unlawfully confiscated from his family, under the so-called Beneš Decrees, at the end of the Second World War. They included the magnificent Kinsky Palace in the center of Prague and, presumably, the castle where Runciman stayed.

47. Andrew, p. 382.

48. Bruegel, p. 133.

49. FO 371/20374/25, Eden to Sir J. Addison (Prague), 27 July 1936.

50. *Cadogan Diaries*, 12 May 1938, p. 76.

51. Bruegel, p. 219.

52. Ibid., pp. 228–29.

53. VNST, II/2/19/6–12, report by Christie for Vansittart, 8 August 1938.

54. R. Laffan, "The Crisis over Czechoslovakia, January to September 1938," *Survey of International Affairs 1938*, Volume II, Oxford University Press 1951, p. 214.

55. *DBFP* 3/II, No. 602, pp. 74–75, Runciman to Halifax, 10 August 1938.

56. Cox, p. 55.

57. Ibid., pp. 55–56.

58. *DBFP* 3/II, Appendix II/I/1, p. 656, "Note of a Conversation between Viscount Runciman and Herr Henlein on August 18," 19 August 1938.

59. Bruegel, p. 233.

60. LSE Archive, "Munich 1938," 2/1/4, interview with Sir Geoffrey Cox. Cox, who was to enjoy a long and distinguished career in journalism, almost lost his job over a careless piece of reporting at the Schloss Rothenhaus. In an effort to make the waiting hours seem more worthwhile, he reported that he had seen Princess Stephanie Hohenlohe walking in the castle grounds during Runciman's visit. In fact, she was not there at all, and the *Daily Express* was forced to print a fulsome apology. Cox escaped sanction because Lord Beaverbrook enjoyed the discomfort of her "mentor," and his rival, Lord Rothermere.

61. *DBFP* 3/II, Appendix II/I/2, p. 658, "Note of a Conversation between Mr. Ashton-Gwatkin and Herr Henlein at Marienbad on August 22," 23 August 1938.

62. Bruegel, p. 236.

63. *DBFP* 3/II, Appendix II/III, p. 664, Ashton-Gwatkin to Strang, 23 August 1938.

64. *DBFP* 3/II, No. 710, p. 180, Halifax to Newton, 29 August 1938.

65. T. Taylor, p. 193.

66. Shirer, *The Rise and Fall of the Third Reich*, p. 368.

67. T. Taylor, p. 198.

68. Kershaw, *Hitler*, p. 103.

69. Brissaud, p. 111.

70. Kershaw, *Hitler*, p. 103.

71. *NCA*, Volume IV, Document 1780-PS, p. 364, Jodl Diary, 10 August 1938.

72. I. Colvin, *Chief of Intelligence*, Victor Gollancz 1951, p. 43.
73. Brissaud, p. 111.
74. Kershaw, *Hitler*, p. 104.
75. *DGFP* D/II, No. 374, pp. 593–94, unsigned minute by Weizsäcker, 19 August 1938.
76. *NCA*, Volume III, Document 388-PS, "Most Secret" memorandum submitted to Hitler by Jodl, 26 August 1938.
77. *DGFP* D/II, No. 284, p. 479, Weizsäcker to Ribbentrop, 7 July 1938.
78. T. Sakmyster, *Hungary's Admiral on Horseback, Miklós Horthy, 1918–1944*, Columbia University Press, New York 1994, pp. 214–16.
79. Weinberg, p. 408 & n132.
80. Weizsäcker, p. 139.
81. Sakmyster, p. 216. The leading historian of this period of Hungarian history, Thomas Sakmyster, elsewhere makes the point that Hitler's vigorous and repeated attempts to persuade the Hungarians to join with him in an invasion offer powerful support for the theory that Hitler had definitely, by the summer of 1938, determined to go to war that autumn (T. Sakmyster, "The Hungarian State Visit to Germany of August 1938: Some New Evidence on Hungary in Hitler's Pre-Munich Policy," *Canadian Slavic Studies*, Volume 3, No. 4, 1969, p. 684).
82. T. Taylor, p. 204. Although General Adam's memoirs had not then been published, Taylor based this account on an interview he conducted with Adam in early 1948, in preparation for one of the Nuremberg trials.
83. Kershaw, *Hitler*, p. 106.
84. T. Taylor, p. 205. This quotation is also in Jodl's Diary, where the word used by Hitler is *Hundsfott*, considerably stronger language than "scoundrel."
85. *DBFP* 3/I, No. 530, pp. 610–12, Strang to Henderson, 21 July 1938.
86. *DBFP* 3/I, No. 507, p. 580, Henderson to Halifax, 18 July 1938.
87. VNST, I/2/37/1, memorandum from Vansittart to Halifax, 18 August 1938.
88. VNST, I/2/37/2–3, memorandum from Vansittart to Halifax, 18 August 1938.
89. Colvin, *Chief of Intelligence*, pp. 46 & 60.
90. Bassett, pp. 151–52.
91. *DBFP* 3/II, Appendix IV, p. 683, Henderson to Halifax, 16 August 1938.
92. Colvin, *Chief of Intelligence*, p. 62.
93. Bassett, p. 152.
94. *DBFP* 3/II, Appendix IV (i), pp. 685–86, "Note of a Conversation between Sir R. Vansittart and Herr von Kleist," 18 August 1938.
95. FO 800/309/246–47, Churchill to Halifax, enclosing "Note of a Conversation between Mr. Winston Churchill and Herr von Kleist," 20 August 1938.
96. FO 800/309/243–45, Churchill to Kleist, 19 August 1938.
97. Colvin, *Chief of Intelligence*, p. 66. Kleist kept the original letter himself, in a desk at his country home. It was discovered there by the Gestapo during his arrest in the aftermath of the failed assassination attempt on Hitler of July 20, 1944, and was used as evidence against him in securing the death penalty,

which was carried out at Plötzensee prison in Berlin on April 16, 1945 (J. Wheeler-Bennett, *The Nemesis of Power*, 2nd ed., Palgrave Macmillan 2005, p. 413, n3). Beck was arrested on the day of the plot and was ordered to commit suicide the following day. When he failed, a sergeant was sent to his cell to shoot him in the back of the neck. Canaris and Oster were also among those arrested, and both were executed in Flossenburg concentration camp on April 12, 1945—Canaris was kept until last by the SS executioner, and then hanged "twice," the first time just enough "to give him a taste of death" (Bassett, p. 289). Schlabrendorff, although arrested and tortured by the Gestapo in a succession of concentration camps, miraculously survived the war.

98. FO 800/314/60, Chamberlain to Halifax, 19 August 1938.
99. *DBFP* 3/II, No. 658, p. 126, Henderson to Halifax, 21 August 1938.
100. Gedye, p. 353.
101. *The Times*, 19 August 1938, p. 12.
102. *The Times*, 22 August 1938, p. 12.
103. Andrew, p. 396.
104. N. West, *MI6, British Secret Intelligence Service Operations, 1909–1945*, Weidenfeld and Nicolson 1983, p. 58.
105. Simon Papers, 272/4, *Sunday Dispatch*, 28 August 1938.
106. FO 800/309/290, Hoyer-Millar to Hardinge, 26 August 1938.
107. Viscount Simon, *Retrospect*, Hutchinson 1952, p. 245.
108. *News Chronicle*, 29 August 1938, p. 10.
109. *DBFP* 3/II, No. 736, p. 204, Henderson to Halifax, 1 September 1938.
110. *The Times*, 29 August 1938, p. 12.
111. Self, p. 307.
112. *DBFP* 3/II, Appendix IV (ii), p. 686, Chamberlain to Halifax, 19 August 1938.
113. NC 18/1/1066, Chamberlain to Ida Chamberlain, 3 September 1938.
114. Colvin, *Vansittart in Office*, p. 232.
115. NC 18/1/1066, Chamberlain to Ida Chamberlain, 3 September 1938.

8: CZECHOSLOVAKIA STANDS ALONE

1. RA PS/GVI/PS 03348/001, Bridges to Hardinge, 27 August 1938.
2. PREM 1/265/193, Bridges to Cabinet ministers, 25 August 1938.
3. *The Times*, 29 August 1938, p. 12.
4. Stanley had only been appointed Dominions Secretary as recently as May, and the trip to Toronto was his first official tour abroad. He twisted his left ankle playing golf and, having fallen gravely ill in Canada, he returned to London in late September, and died at the age of forty-four on October 16, of lymphosarcoma—the crack in his foot had released cancerous bone marrow cells into his bloodstream. He accordingly played no role whatsoever in the Czech or Munich crisis (*DNB*, Volume 52, p. 202).
5. *Daily Mail*, 30 August 1938, p. 11.

6. CAB 23/94/286, "Meeting of Ministers," 30 August 1938.
7. Inskip Papers, INKP 1, Inskip Diary, 30 August 1938.
8. CAB 23/94/289–96, "Meeting of Ministers," 30 August 1938.
9. Templewood, p. 299.
10. *Duff Cooper Diaries*, 30 August 1938, p. 224.
11. CAB 23/94/315, "Meeting of Ministers," 30 August 1938.
12. PREM 1/265/184–85, Wilson memorandum, 30 August 1938.
13. PREM 1/265/180–81, Chamberlain to Halifax, 30 August 1938.
14. *The Times*, 31 August 1938, p. 10.
15. *Daily Express*, 1 September 1938, p. 1.
16. NC 18/1/1066, Chamberlain to Ida Chamberlain, 3 September 1938.
17. NC 1/26/530, Chamberlain to Annie Chamberlain, 2 September 1938.
18. NC 18/1/1067, Chamberlain to Hilda Chamberlain, 6 September 1938.
19. *DBFP* 3/II, No. 737, p. 205, Halifax to Henderson, 1 September 1938.
20. *DBFP* 3/II, No. 748, p. 216, Henderson to Halifax, 2 September 1938.
21. Conwell-Evans, p. 140.
22. *Cadogan Diaries*, 3 September 1938, p. 94.
23. *The Times*, 5 September 1938, p. 12.
24. D. R. Thorpe, *Alec Douglas-Home*, Sinclair-Stevenson 1996, p. 75.
25. *Evening Standard*, 5 September 1938, p. 6.
26. M. Gilbert, "Horace Wilson: Man of Munich?," *History Today*, Volume 32, No. 10, October 1982, p. 4.
27. Templewood, p. 260.
28. Lord Woolton, *Memoirs*, Cassell 1959, p. 140. In the immediate aftermath of the Anschluss, Lord Woolton (or Sir Frederick Marquis as he was still then known) decided to make a stand by initiating a boycott of German goods at all branches of John Lewis's department stores, where he was chairman; he then made a speech at Leicester urging other companies to follow his example. In spite of their close friendship, Wilson summoned Marquis to Downing Street and gave him a "high-powered rocket," protesting that Chamberlain "strongly disapproved" of his action, and that he had "no right to interfere in the foreign policy of the country" (Woolton, p. 132).
29. Gilbert, "Horace Wilson," pp. 3–5.
30. R. Lowe, "Sir Horace Wilson," in *Oxford Dictionary of National Biography*, H. Matthew & B. Harrison (eds.), Volume 59, Oxford University Press 2004, p. 574.
31. H. Dalton, *The Fateful Years, Memoirs 1931–1945*, Frederick Muller 1957, p. 176.
32. Gilbert, "Horace Wilson," p. 5.
33. Deutsch, *The Conspiracy Against Hitler*, pp. 17–18.
34. *Cadogan Diaries*, 6 September 1938, pp. 94–95.
35. Wheeler-Bennett, *The Nemesis of Power*, p. 418.
36. Colvin, *Vansittart in Office*, p. 236. The quotation is, of course, from Hamlet's most famous speech in Act III, Scene I.
37. *Cadogan Diaries*, 8 September 1938, p. 95.
38. Colvin, *Vansittart in Office*, p. 237. In 1076 the Holy Roman Emperor Henry

IV fell out with Pope Gregory VII in the so-called Investiture Contest, concerning papal jurisdiction over ecclesiastical appointments. In January 1077 the Emperor was forced to walk over the snow-covered Alps, and wait for three days outside the Pope's palace at Canossa to beg forgiveness. The term "to travel to Canossa" has been used ever since to describe a form of humiliation.

39. *DGFP* D/II, No. 369, p. 586, memorandum by Altenburg (Foreign Ministry), 18 August 1938.
40. *DBFP* 3/II, Appendix II, III, p. 666, Ashton-Gwatkin to Strang, 29 August 1938.
41. *DBFP* 3/II, No. 706, p. 177, Troutbeck (Prague) to Halifax, 29 August 1938.
42. Bruegel, p. 236.
43. *DGFP* D/II, No. 407, p. 661, Hencke (Prague) to German Foreign Ministry, 30 August 1938.
44. PREM 1/265/113–15, Runciman to Halifax, 30 August 1938.
45. *DBFP* 3/II, No. 731, p. 200, Newton to Halifax, 1 September 1938.
46. *DBFP* 3/II, Appendix II, III, p. 668, Ashton-Gwatkin to Strang, 6 September 1938.
47. *DBFP* 3/II, No. 734, p. 202, Newton to Halifax, 1 September 1938.
48. R. Smelser, *The Sudeten Problem, 1933–1938*, Dawson 1975, pp. 234–35.
49. Kershaw, *Hitler*, p. 107 (original in Goebbels Diaries, 1 September 1938).
50. *DBFP* 3/II, No. 727, pp. 195–96, Halifax to Newton, 31 August 1938.
51. *DBFP* 3/II, No. 753, p. 221, Newton to Halifax, 3 September 1938.
52. *DBFP* 3/II, No. 758, pp. 226–27, Newton to Halifax, 4 September 1938.
53. BBC Written Archives, T 56/177/1, *Ten Years After—A Munich Survey*, interview with Frank Ashton-Gwatkin, 11 October 1948.
54. Wheeler-Bennett, *Munich*, p. 91.
55. Bruegel, p. 248.
56. Laffan, p. 239.
57. Ibid., p. 253.
58. *Daily Express*, 8 September 1938, p. 1.
59. *The Times*, 8 September 1938, p. 12.
60. Laffan, p. 254.
61. *DBFP* 3/II, No. 801, p. 265, n1, report of Major Sutton-Pratt, 8 September 1938.
62. *DBFP* 3/II, Appendix II, III, p. 671, Ashton-Gwatkin to Strang, 17 September 1938.
63. BBC Written Archives, T56/177/1, *Ten Years After—A Munich Survey*, interview with Ashton-Gwatkin, 11 October 1948.
64. *DBFP* 3/II, No. 801, p. 265, Newton to Halifax, 8 September 1938.
65. Smelser, p. 237.
66. Laffan, p. 255.
67. Cockett, p. 72.
68. The SdP leadership had announced plans to hold their own Nuremberg-style rally on October 15 and 16. It was to be held at Aussig in Bohemia.
69. *The Times*, 7 September 1938, p. 13.

70. *The History of The Times*, p. 927, n1, Barrington-Ward to Dawson, 25 August 1938.

71. *The Times*, 31 August 1938, p. 10.

72. Dawson Papers, 42/132, Dawson Diary, 6 September 1938.

73. *The History of The Times*, pp. 929–30. In this official history of *The Times*, published in 1952, Dawson was strongly criticized for taking the responsibility for publishing such a contentious article on the night "without recourse to the opinion of a [foreign affairs] specialist inside or outside" the building. However, it was also acknowledged that this was the consequence of a "defect in the organization of Printing House Square," following a decision taken ten years earlier not to employ a specialist Foreign Editor in the mold of such celebrated occupants of that post as Chirol or Wickham Steed. This had resulted in the deputy editor, Barrington-Ward, a "general journalist," assuming de facto the role of "virtual Foreign Editor" (*The History of The Times*, pp. 930–31).

74. C. Coote, *Editorial: The Memoirs of Colin R. Coote*, Eyre & Spottiswoode 1965, p. 170.

75. Dawson Papers 42/133, Dawson Diary, 7 & 8 September 1938.

76. *DBFP* 3/II, p. 271, n1.

77. Dawson Papers, 80/24, Dawson to Barrington-Ward, 7 September 1938.

78. FO 371/21735/186 & 189, Vansittart to Halifax, 7 September 1938.

79. *DGFP* D/II, No. 443, pp. 722–23, Kordt to German Foreign Ministry, 8 September 1938.

80. *DBFP* 3/II, p. 271, n1.

81. Harvey, 8 September 1938, p. 171.

82. *DBFP* 3/II, No. 808, p. 271, Halifax to Chilston (Moscow), 8 September 1938.

83. *Nicolson Diaries*, 9 September 1938, p. 358.

84. *Channon Diaries*, 10 September 1938, pp. 164–65.

85. *The History of The Times*, p. 934.

86. Ibid., p. 932. Over thirty years later, in an apparent attempt to make amends, *The Times* acknowledged its mistake in 1938 in a front-page article and accompanying leader. *Der Spiegel* had recently revealed the suggestion made by General (formerly Colonel) Mason-MacFarlane that he had had an opportunity to assassinate Hitler when military attaché in Berlin. Britain should not have taken up that idea said *The Times*, "but should have done something more substantial in 1938. It should, against the advice of this newspaper at the time, have stood firm at Munich. That would really have affected history" (*The Times*, 6 August 1969, p. 9).

9: IN FULL WAR CRY

1. See Chapter 1, notes 37, 38 & 39, for details of Henderson's speech and the audience. The "American pacifist doggerel" is the refrain of a popular American antiwar ballad of 1914 (Conwell-Evans, p. 93). The speech quickly

earned Henderson the sobriquet in certain British newspapers of "our Nazi British Ambassador at Berlin" (N. Henderson, p. 20).

2. *Daily Express*, 1 September 1938, p. 2.
3. A. Speer (trans. R. & C. Winston), *Inside the Third Reich*, Weidenfeld and Nicolson 1970, p. 47.
4. Ibid., p. 86.
5. In his memoirs, Speer points out that a major design fault of the house, one he blames on Hitler rather than himself, was that the garage was situated directly below this famous window. As a result, when it was left open on warm days and there was a light breeze, a "strong smell of gasoline" blew into the room (Speer, p. 86).
6. Kirkpatrick, pp. 98–99.
7. *NCA*, Volume III, Document 388-PS, pp. 334–35, "Notes by Major Schmundt of Conference at the Berghof," 4 September 1938.
8. *The Times*, 6 September 1938, p. 12.
9. Baynes, pp. 1470–72, Hitler's opening proclamation at Nuremberg, 6 September 1938.
10. H. Burden, *The Nuremberg Party Rallies: 1923–39*, Pall Mall Press 1967, p. 151.
11. *The Times*, 6 September 1938, p. 12.
12. *The Times*, 8 September 1938, p. 12.
13. FO 800/314/141, Henderson to Halifax, 13 September 1938.
14. FO 800/314/108, Halifax to Chamberlain, 5 September 1938.
15. FO 371/21737/112, Henderson to Halifax, 6 September 1938.
16. *DBFP* 3/II, No. 837, p. 296, Henderson to Halifax, 12 September 1938.
17. *DBFP* 3/II, No. 839, p. 299, Henderson to Halifax, 12 September 1938.
18. FO 800/313/75, Henderson to Halifax, 7 April 1938.
19. *DGFP* D/II, No. 337, p. 536, Foreign Ministry memorandum for Ribbentrop, 6 August 1938.
20. Douglas, *In the Year of Munich*, p. 19.
21. LSE Archive, "Munich 1938," 1/1/7, interview with Lord Gladwyn.
22. LSE Archive, "Munich 1938," 2/4/7, interview with Sir Con O'Neill.
23. P. Neville, *Appeasing Hitler: The Diplomacy of Sir Nevile Henderson 1937–39*, Macmillan 2000, pp. 97–98.
24. N. Henderson, p. 145.
25. FO 800/314/141–42, Henderson to Halifax, 13 September 1938.
26. Laffan, p. 300.
27. Burden, p. 152 (original in *New York Times*, 8 September 1938).
28. Harvey, 9 September 1938, p. 172.
29. FO 371/21737/19–20, Halifax to Kirkpatrick, 9 September 1938.
30. *The Times*, 10 September 1938, p. 10.
31. Speer, p. 59.
32. N. Henderson, p. 71.
33. Keitel was widely derided among his military colleagues as Hitler's lapdog, and he acquired the nickname "Lakaitel," a play on his own name and the German word for lackey, "Lakai."

34. *DGFP* D/II, No. 448, p. 729, "Manuscript Notes by Hitler's Adjutant (Schmundt) on Conference at Nuremberg," 10 September 1938.
35. Keitel, pp. 69–70.
36. Toland, p. 472.
37. *Daily Mail*, 10 September 1938, p. 1.
38. *Daily Express*, 10 September 1938, p. 1.
39. *Cadogan Diaries*, 10 September 1938, p. 96.
40. *DBFP* 3/II, No. 818, p. 279, Ogilvie-Forbes (Berlin) to Halifax, 10 September 1938.
41. *DBFP* 3/II, No. 819, p. 280, Ogilvie-Forbes (Berlin) to Halifax, 10 September 1938 (italics Henderson's own).
42. Laffan, p. 302.
43. *The Times*, 11 September 1938, p. 14.
44. *DBFP* 3/II, No. 827, pp. 286–87, Halifax to Henderson, 10 September 1938.
45. *DGFP* D/II, No. 452, pp. 734–35, Selzam (London) to German Foreign Ministry, 10 September 1938.
46. The Hoares were close friends of the King and Queen. A plan had been devised that if the royal couple were forced to leave London to escape the bombing, they were to stay at Lady Maud Hoare's family home, Madresfield Court in Worcestershire (A. Roberts, *Eminent Churchillians*, Weidenfeld and Nicolson 1994).
47. *Cadogan Diaries*, 10 September 1938, p. 96.
48. FO 371/21737/24, Halifax to Henderson, 10 September 1938.
49. Templewood, p. 302.
50. PREM 1/265/14, Downing Street memorandum, 10 September 1938.
51. *DBFP* 3/II, Appendix III, p. 681, "Text of the Prime Minister's Statement to the Press," 11 September 1938.
52. PREM 1/249/65–70, Wilson memorandum for Chamberlain, enclosing memorandum of Lord Brocket, written in Nuremberg, 12 September 1938.
53. Shirer, *Berlin Diary*, p. 105.
54. *DBFP* 3/II, No. 820, pp. 280–81, Newton to Halifax, 10 September 1938.
55. Shirer, *The Rise and Fall of the Third Reich*, p. 383.
56. *DBFP* 3/II, Appendix II, III, p. 672, Ashton-Gwatkin to Strang, 17 September 1938.
57. *The Times*, 12 September 1938, p. 12.
58. CAB 23/95/3–14, Cabinet 37 (38), 12 September 1938.
59. *Duff Cooper Diaries*, 12 September 1938, pp. 257–58.
60. CAB 23/95/15, Cabinet 37 (38), 12 September 1938.
61. Burden, p. 157.
62. Baynes, pp. 1489–91.
63. A. Bullock, *Hitler: A Study in Tyranny* (revised edition), Odhams 1965, p. 453.
64. Burden, p. 159 (original in *New York Times*, 13 September 1938).
65. C. Madge & T. Harrison, *Britain by Mass-Observation*, Penguin 1939, p. 58.
66. BBC Written Archives, R34/325 Czechoslovak Crisis, General File 1938–1939.
67. Shirer, *Berlin Diary*, p. 106.

68. Harvey, 12 September 1938, p. 176.
69. Amery Papers, AMEL, 7/32, Amery Diary, 11 September 1938.
70. Macmillan, p. 554.
71. *Cadogan Diaries*, 12 September 1938, p. 97.
72. Noguères, p. 116.
73. Burden, p. 160.
74. The meeting on September 12 is variously referred to by historians as the second or third meeting of the Inner Circle, albeit the first at which formal minutes were taken. In fact, the same group of ministers and officials met together on September 8, 9, 10 & 11, Hoare joining for the first time on the 10th. These four meetings are identified in the diaries of both Harvey and Cadogan.
75. *DBFP* 3/II, No. 833, p. 292, Phipps to Halifax, 11 September 1938.
76. CAB 27/646/7–9, "The Czechoslovakian Crisis 1938, Notes of Informal Meetings of Ministers," 1st Meeting, 12 September 1938. The minutes of the seventeen meetings of the Inner Circle (sometimes referred to as the "Big Four"), between September 12 and October 2, 1938, are neatly filed in a black, leather-bound foolscap volume, marked "SECRET." Critics of Chamberlain have pointed out that the correct forum for these discussions should have been the Cabinet's Foreign Policy Committee, which did not meet between June 16 and November 1938. However, the smaller group of loyal supporters (there were never more than the four ministers present) undoubtedly suited Chamberlain's purpose in achieving a consensus (I. Colvin, *The Chamberlain Cabinet*, Victor Gollancz 1971, p. 146).
77. Parliamentary Debates, House of Commons, Official Report, Fifth Series, Volume 339, Col. 12, 28 September 1938.
78. Cox, p. 67.
79. Laffan, pp. 312–13.
80. Gedye, p. 449.
81. Noguères, p. 117.
82. *DGFP* D/II, No. 466, p. 751, German Foreign Ministry memorandum, 13 September 1938.
83. Karl Hermann Frank was the most hard-line of the Sudeten German leaders and, during the war, became the most ruthless. As police leader for the former Czechoslovakia he enjoyed the patronage of Himmler, and rose steadily through the ranks of the SS. He frequently indulged in the harsh suppression of dissident Czechs and after the war he was arrested by the Americans and handed over to the Czech government. On May 22, 1946, he was hanged in Prague for war crimes, in front of a crowd of 5,000 people.
84. Shirer, *Berlin Diary*, pp. 108–9.
85. "Wilson Papers" T 273/404, Ashton-Gwatkin to Wilson, 13 September 1938.
86. *DGFP* D/II, No. 490, p. 802, "Proclamation by Konrad Henlein to the Sudeten Germans," 15 September 1938 (emphasis in original).
87. Shirer, *Berlin Diary*, p. 110.

10: ON THE RAZOR'S EDGE

1. NC 18/1/1066, Chamberlain to Ida Chamberlain, 3 September 1938.
2. PREM 1/266A/363, Wilson memorandum, 30 August 1938.
3. *Cadogan Diaries*, 8 September 1938, p. 95.
4. Inskip Papers, INKP 1, Inskip Diary, 7 September 1938 (see Chapter 8, note 38).
5. *Cadogan Diaries*, 9 September 1938, p. 96.
6. PREM 1/266A/359–60, Wilson to Henderson, 9 September 1938.
7. FO 800/314/117–18, Henderson to Wilson, 9 September 1938.
8. FO 800/314/124, Henderson to Wilson, 9 September 1938 at midnight (Henderson's emphasis).
9. Templewood, pp. 300–1.
10. INKP 1, Inskip Diary, 9 September 1938.
11. PREM 1/266A/320–23, Chamberlain to Runciman, 12 September 1938.
12. PREM 1/266A/319, Runciman to Chamberlain, 13 September 1938.
13. *DBFP* 3/II, No. 807, p. 269, Phipps to Halifax, 8 September 1938.
14. INKP 1, Inskip Diary, 12 September 1938.
15. Zetland Papers, Mss Eur D609/10/57, Zetland to Brabourne, 16 September 1938.
16. Phipps Papers, PHPP III/1/20/67, Phipps to Halifax, 10 September 1938.
17. PHPP III/1/20/76, Halifax to Phipps, 12 September 1938.
18. Mss Eur D609/10/57, Zetland to Brabourne, 16 September 1938.
19. PHPP III/1/20/70, Phipps to Halifax, 13 September 1938.
20. *DBFP* 3/II, No. 857, p. 312, Phipps to Halifax, 13 September 1938.
21. *Duff Cooper Diaries*, 13 September 1938, p. 259.
22. Conwell-Evans, pp. 144–45.
23. *DBFP* 3/II, No. 849, p. 306, Henderson to Halifax, 13 September 1938.
24. RA PS/GVI/C 235/02, Chamberlain to King George VI, 13 September 1938.
25. CAB 27/646/15, "The Czechoslovakian Crisis 1938, Notes of Informal Meetings of Ministers," 2nd Meeting, 13 September 1938 at 3 P.M.
26. D. Cooper, *Old Men Forget*, Rupert Hart-Davis 1953, p. 228.
27. INKP 1, Inskip Diary, 13 September 1938.
28. Parliamentary Debates, House of Commons, Official Report, Fifth Series, Volume 339, Col. 13, 28 September 1938.
29. NC 18/1/1069, Chamberlain to Ida Chamberlain, 19 September 1938.
30. PREM 1/266A/316, Wilson memorandum, 13 September 1938.
31. CAB 27/646/18, "The Czechoslovakian Crisis 1938, Notes of Informal Meetings of Ministers," 3rd Meeting, 13 September 1938.
32. *DBFP* 3/II, No. 862, p. 314, Halifax to Henderson, 13 September 1938.
33. RA PS/GVI/C 235/03, Chamberlain to King George VI, 13 September 1938.
34. RA PS/GVI/PS 03348/004, Press announcement, 14 September 1938.
35. FO 800/309/305, Henderson to Halifax, 14 September 1938.
36. *DGFP* D/II, No. 480, p. 763, Weizsäcker minute, 14 September 1938.
37. CAB 23/95/34-41, Cabinet 38 (38), 14 September 1938.

38. R. Minney, *The Private Papers of Hore-Belisha*, Collins 1960, pp. 139–40.
39. CAB 23/95/41 & 49, Cabinet 38 (38), 14 September 1938.
40. Mss Eur D609/10/57, Zetland to Brabourne, 16 September 1938.
41. CAB 23/95/55, Cabinet 38 (38), 14 September 1938.
42. *Duff Cooper Diaries*, 14 September 1938, p. 259.
43. CAB 23/95/46, Cabinet 38 (38), 14 September 1938.
44. INKP 1, Inskip Diary, 14 September 1938.
45. CAB 23/95/56–58, Cabinet 38 (38), 14 September 1938.
46. *DBFP* 3/II, No. 874, p. 323, Phipps to Halifax, 14 September 1938 at 2:20 P.M.
47. AMEL 7/32, Amery Diary, 14 September 1938.
48. Mss Eur D609/10/57, Zetland to Brabourne, 16 September 1938.
49. *Cadogan Diaries*, 14 September 1938, p. 98.
50. *DBFP* 3/II, No. 883, p. 329, Phipps to Halifax, 14 September 1938 at 10 P.M.
51. *The Times*, 15 September 1938, p. 10.
52. INKP 1, Inskip Diary, 14 September 1938.
53. NC 18/1/1069, Chamberlain to Ida Chamberlain, 19 September 1938. Although Chamberlain is sometimes mocked for using this kind of language, on this occasion his claim was accurate. Weizsäcker's handwritten minute, describing his conversations with Ribbentrop that day, confirms that an invitation was indeed issued to Mrs. Chamberlain, and that the idea that Hitler should fly to see Chamberlain was briefly considered. So too was a plan to meet in neutral waters on board Hitler's yacht, the *Grille*. Both were dropped, in favor of Chamberlain traveling to Berchtesgaden.
54. L. Namier, *Diplomatic Prelude 1938–1939*, Macmillan 1948, p. 35, n1.
55. *Daily Express*, 15 September 1938, pp. 1–2.
56. *Daily Herald*, 15 September 1938, p. 8.
57. *News Chronicle*, 16 September 1938, p. 10.
58. Madge & Harrison, p. 65.
59. *Duff Cooper Diaries*, 14 September 1938, p. 260.
60. *Channon Diaries*, 14 & 15 September 1938, p. 166.
61. B. Pimlott, *Hugh Dalton*, Macmillan 1985, p. 256.
62. D. Jay, *Change and Fortune: A Political Record*, Hutchinson 1980, p. 75.
63. V. Massey, *What's Past Is Prologue: The Memoirs of the Right Honourable Vincent Massey CH*, Macmillan 1963, p. 258.
64. AMEL 7/32, Amery Diary, 14 & 16 September 1938.
65. Harvey, 15 September 1938, p. 180.
66. Colvin, *Vansittart in Office*, p. 250.
67. Shirer, *Berlin Diary*, p. 110.
68. *The Times*, 16 September 1938, p. 12.
69. *Ciano's Diary*, 14 September 1938, p. 156.
70. *DBFP* 3/II, No. 890, p. 334, Henderson to Halifax, 15 September 1938.
71. *The Times*, 15 September 1938, pp. 10 & 11.
72. Cadogan Papers, ACAD 1/7, Cadogan Diary, 15 September 1938.
73. *The Times*, 16 September 1938, pp. 11 & 14.

74. BBC Written Archives, R34/325 Czechoslovak Crisis, General File 1938–1939.
75. *The Times*, 15 September 1938, p. 10.
76. NC 18/1/1069, Chamberlain to Ida Chamberlain, 19 September 1938.
77. Madge & Harrison, p. 58.
78. Wheeler-Bennett, *Munich*, p. 108, n2.
79. Lord Strang, *Home and Abroad*, André Deutsch 1956, p. 137.
80. LSE Archive, "Munich 1938," 1/2/3, Reinhard Spitzy interview.
81. Schmidt, p. 90.
82. *Daily Mail*, 16 September 1938, p. 12.
83. N. Henderson, p. 149.
84. NC 18/1/1069, Chamberlain to Ida Chamberlain, 19 September 1938.
85. Spitzy, p. 239.
86. *Daily Mail*, 16 September 1938, p. 12.
87. Schmidt, p. 91.
88. Eberle & Uhl, p. 29.
89. CAB 23/95/71, Cabinet 39 (38), 17 September 1938.
90. NC 18/1/1069, Chamberlain to Ida Chamberlain, 19 September 1938. The "military cross" which Chamberlain noticed specifically was the Iron Cross, First Class.
91. Strang, p. 137.
92. NC 18/1/1069, Chamberlain to Ida Chamberlain, 19 September 1938.
93. *Lipski Papers*, p. 408.
94. *DGFP* D/II, No. 470, p. 754, Kordt to German Foreign Ministry, 13 September 1938.
95. *DGFP* D/II, No. 489, p. 801, Henlein to Hitler, 15 September 1938.
96. Conwell-Evans, p. 145.
97. CAB 23/95/72, Cabinet 39 (38), 17 September 1938.
98. Schmidt, p. 92.
99. *DBFP* 3/II, No. 896, p. 345, "Translation of notes made by Herr Schmidt of Mr. Chamberlain's conversation with Herr Hitler at Berchtesgaden," 15 September 1938.
100. Dalton, p. 178.
101. *DBFP* 3/II, No. 895, pp. 339–40, "Notes by Mr. Chamberlain of his conversation with Herr Hitler at Berchtesgaden," 15 September 1938.
102. Schmidt, p. 92.
103. Kershaw, *Hitler*, p. 111.
104. Schmidt, p. 93.
105. Kershaw, *Hitler*, p. 111.
106. NC 18/1/1069, Chamberlain to Ida Chamberlain, 19 September 1938.
107. *Daily Express*, 16 September 1938, p. 1.
108. *DBFP* 3/II, No. 896, p. 351, "Translation of notes made by Herr Schmidt of Mr. Chamberlain's conversation with Herr Hitler at Berchtesgaden," 15 September 1938.
109. Eberle & Uhl, pp. 29–30.
110. Weizsäcker, pp. 150–51.

111. Dalton, p. 179.
112. NC 8/26/1, handwritten note, Chamberlain to Hitler, n/d (16 September 1938).
113. *DBFP* 3/II, No. 895, p. 341, "Notes by Mr. Chamberlain of his conversation with Herr Hitler at Berchtesgaden," 15 September 1938.
114. Weinberg, p. 433.
115. Schmidt, p. 94.
116. *The Times*, 17 September 1938, p. 10.
117. NC 8/26/2, "Notes by Sir Horace Wilson on conversations during Mr. Chamberlain's visit to Berchtesgaden," 16 September 1938.
118. *Evening Standard*, 16 September 1938, p. 1.
119. *The Times*, 17 September 1938, p. 10.
120. BBC Written Archives, R34/325 Czechoslovak Crisis, General File 1938–1939.

11: A NEW AND SHARPER SWORD

1. I am grateful to D. R. Thorpe for this reference; the poem lay undiscovered for over sixty years. Another verse describes Chamberlain as "The meanest man who ever sneaked into high political place . . . Even littler, than Hitler" (M. McCulloch, "Littler than Hitler," *Times Literary Supplement*, 17 March 2000).
2. *The Times*, 17 September 1938, p. 10.
3. Madge & Harrison, p. 69.
4. RA PS/GVI/C 235/08–9, King George VI to Chamberlain, 16 September 1938.
5. RA PS/GVI/C 235/04, memorandum, Hardinge to King George VI, 15 September 1938.
6. RA PS/GVI/C 235/05, draft handwritten letter, King George VI to Hitler, 14 September 1938.
7. CAB 27/646/25–29, "The Czechoslovakian Crisis 1938, Notes of Informal Meetings of Ministers," 5th Meeting, 16 September 1938.
8. *Cadogan Diaries*, 16 September 1938, p. 99.
9. NC 18/1/1069, Chamberlain to Ida Chamberlain, 19 September 1938.
10. J. Wheeler-Bennett, *King George VI*, pp. 349–50.
11. Ms. Eng. Hist. d.359/215, Crookshank Diary, 16 September 1938.
12. INKP 1, Inskip Diary, 16 September 1938.
13. NC 18/1/1069, Chamberlain to Ida Chamberlain, 19 September 1938.
14. Self, p. 314.
15. Kershaw, *Hitler*, p. 112.
16. Roberts, *The Holy Fox*, p. 110.
17. H. Nicolson, *Why Britain Is at War*, Penguin 1939, p. 106.
18. AMEL 7/32, Amery Diary, 16 September 1938.
19. *DBFP* 3/II, No. 888, p. 333, Newton to Halifax, 15 September 1938.
20. *Channon Diaries*, 16 September 1938, p. 166.

21. *Nicolson Diaries*, 16 September 1938, p. 360.
22. Harvey, 16 September 1938, p. 182.
23. Mss Eur D609/10/58, Zetland to Brabourne, 16–20 September 1938.
24. CAB 23/95/65–69, Cabinet 39 (38), 17 September 1938.
25. INKP 1, Inskip Diary, 17 September 1938.
26. *Duff Cooper Diaries*, 17 September 1938, p. 260.
27. CAB 23/95/72–76, Cabinet 39 (38), 17 September 1938.
28. Colvin, *The Chamberlain Cabinet*, p. 156.
29. CAB 23/95/79–80, Cabinet 39 (38), 17 September 1938.
30. *Duff Cooper Diaries*, 17 September 1938, p. 260.
31. INKP 1, Inskip Diary, 17 September 1938.
32. CAB 23/95/86, Cabinet 39 (38), 17 September 1938.
33. *Duff Cooper Diaries*, 17 September 1938, pp. 260–61.
34. CAB 23/95/107, Cabinet 39 (38), 17 September 1938.
35. NC 18/1/1069, Chamberlain to Ida Chamberlain, 19 September 1938.
36. Harvey, 17 September 1938, p. 184.
37. Dalton, p. 176.
38. Pimlott, p. 256.
39. Dalton Diary, I/18, 17 September 1938.
40. Harvey, 16 September 1938, p. 182.
41. Templewood, p. 305.
42. *DBFP* 3/II, No. 928, p. 379, "Record of Anglo-French Conversations held at No. 10 Downing Street," 18 September 1938.
43. *Cadogan Diaries*, 18 September 1938, p. 100.
44. Simon Papers 10/2, Diary, 29 September 1938.
45. Templewood, p. 305.
46. *DBFP* 3/II, No. 928, p. 387, "Record of Anglo-French Conversations held at No. 10 Downing Street," 18 September 1938.
47. CAB 23/95/116–17, Cabinet 40 (38), 19 September 1938.
48. Wheeler-Bennett, *Munich*, p. 114.
49. CAB 27/646/41–44, "The Czechoslovakian Crisis 1938, Notes of Informal Meetings of Ministers," 6th Meeting, 18 September 1938.
50. CAB 23/95/119, Cabinet 40 (38), 19 September 1938.
51. *DBFP* 3/II, No. 928, p. 397, "Record of Anglo-French Conversations Held at No. 10 Downing Street," 18 September 1938.
52. Simon Papers 10/3, Diary, 29 September 1938.
53. *DBFP* 3/II, No. 928, p. 399, "Record of Anglo-French Conversations Held at No. 10 Downing Street," 18 September 1938.
54. Harvey, 19 September 1938, p. 186.
55. Wheeler-Bennett, *Munich*, p. 116.
56. *The Times*, 20 September 1938, p. 12.
57. CAB 23/95/121, Cabinet 40 (38), 19 September 1938.
58. Minney, p. 142.
59. INKP 1, Inskip Diary, 19 September 1938.
60. CAB 23/95/125–26 & 131, Cabinet 40 (38), 19 September 1938.
61. BBK C/80, Beaverbrook to Chamberlain, 16 September 1938.

62. A. Adamthwaite, "The British Government and the Media, 1937–1938," *Journal of Contemporary History*, Volume 18, No. 2, April 1983, p. 288.

63. D. Hubback, *No Ordinary Press Baron: A Life of Walter Layton*, Weidenfeld and Nicolson 1985, pp. 157–58.

64. Cockett, p. 79.

65. BBC Written Archives C41, "Compilations, 'September Crisis 1938.' " Nicolson had begun a series of thirteen weekly talks in July, which became increasingly contentious and outspoken as the Czech crisis developed. By September his scripts were being vetted by the Foreign Office and, following Wilson's intervention, the BBC themselves censored the talks.

66. Adamthwaite, pp. 288–89.

67. *News Chronicle*, 19 September 1938, pp. 11 and 21 September 1938, p. 10.

68. *Daily Herald*, 21 September 1938, p. 8.

69. *Daily Telegraph*, 20 September 1938.

70. *The Times*, 20 September 1938, p. 13.

71. Ibid., p. 14.

72. *News Chronicle*, 22 September 1938, p. 13.

73. Ibid., p. 1.

74. AMEL 2/1/28, Amery to Chamberlain, 17 September 1938.

75. L Amery, *My Political Life, Volume III: The Unforgiving Years, 1929–1940*, Hutchinson 1955, p. 268.

76. Harvey, 20 September 1938, p. 189.

77. *DBFP* 3/II, No. 1001, p. 444, Phipps to Halifax, 21 September 1938.

78. Gilbert, *Winston S. Churchill*, pp. 1171–72.

79. RA EDW/3745, Duke of Windsor to Chamberlain, 18 September 1938.

80. N. Rose (ed.), *Baffy: The Diaries of Blanche Dugdale 1936–1947*, Vallentine Mitchell 1973, p. 127.

81. Monckton Papers, Dep Monckton Trustees 16/150, Philip Guedalla to Monckton, 21 September 1938.

82. Weinberg, pp. 445–46.

83. PREM 1/266A/267–68, Cadogan memorandum, 20 September 1938.

84. CAB 23/95/145–46, Cabinet 41 (38), 21 September 1938.

85. CAB 23/95/154–60, Cabinet 41 (38), 21 September 1938.

86. In his letter to his sister describing his visit to Berchtesgaden, Chamberlain described Keitel as a "youngish pleasant-faced smart-looking soldier" (NC 18/1/1069, Chamberlain to Ida Chamberlain, 19 September 1938).

87. T. Taylor, p. 215.

88. *NCA*, Volume IV, Document 1780-PS, Jodl Diary, 16 September 1938.

89. *DGFP* D/II, No. 500, p. 810, German Foreign Ministry to German Missions Abroad, 16 September 1938.

90. Shirer, *The Rise and Fall of the Third Reich*, p. 387.

91. Shirer, *Berlin Diary*, p. 113.

92. *DGFP* D/II, No. 517, p. 825, German Foreign Ministry to Prague Legation, 17 September 1938.

93. *Daily Mail*, 19 September 1938, p. 13.

94. *DGFP* D/II, No. 554, pp. 863–64, Kordt minute for Weizsäcker, 21 September 1938.
95. *Lipski Papers*, pp. 403 & 408–11.
96. *NCA*, Volume III, Document 388-PS, p. 344.
97. *DGFP* D/II, No. 528, p. 836, Hencke to German Foreign Ministry, 19 September 1938.
98. Cox, p. 68.
99. *DBFP* 3/II, No. 929, p. 400, Masaryk to Halifax, 18 September 1938.
100. *DBFP* 3/II, No. 937, pp. 404–5, Halifax to Newton, 19 September 1938.
101. *DBFP* 3/II, No. 961, pp. 416–17, Newton to Halifax, 19 September 1938.
102. *DBFP* 3/II, No. 959, p. 414, n2, Phipps to Halifax, 19 September 1938.
103. *The Times,* 20 September 1938, p. 12.
104. Bruegel, p. 279.
105. *DBFP* 3/II, No. 967, p. 419, Phipps to Halifax, 20 September 1938.
106. Noguères, p. 145.
107. *DBFP* 3/II, No. 986, pp. 432–34, Newton to Halifax, 21 September 1938 at 12:20 A.M.
108. *DBFP* 3/II, No. 981, p. 426, Newton to Halifax, 20 September 1938.
109. Toland, p. 477.
110. *DBFP* 3/II, No. 979, p. 425, Newton to Halifax, 20 September 1938. Some historians have accused Hodža, a Slovak, of having separatist designs of his own, and of persistent treachery toward Beneš throughout the crisis, until his removal on September 22. It certainly appears that he told both de Lacroix and Newton that if Britain and France refused to support Czechoslovakia, then his government would be forced to concede.
111. *Cadogan Diaries,* 20 September 1938, p. 102.
112. *DBFP* 3/II, No. 991, pp. 437–38, Halifax to Newton, 21 September 1938 at 1:20 A.M.
113. Wheeler-Bennett, *Munich,* p. 123.
114. Bruegel, p. 280.
115. *DBFP* 3/II, No. 993, pp. 438–39, Newton to Halifax, 21 September 1938 at 7:30 A.M.
116. Harvey, 19 September 1938, p. 187.
117. *DBFP* 3/II, No. 998, p. 442, Newton to Halifax, 21 September 1938 at 3:45 P.M.
118. *DBFP* 3/II, No. 1005, p. 447, "Note from the Czechoslovak Government to the British Legation, Prague," 21 September 1938.
119. H. Ripka, *Munich: Before and After,* Victor Gollancz 1939, pp. 106–8.
120. Cox, p. 70.
121. Gedye, p. 467.

12: ON THE BANKS OF THE RHINE

1. BBC Written Archives, R34/325 Czechoslovak Crisis, General File 1938–1939.

2. NC 8/26/5, "Memorandum for the Prime Minister," 22 September 1938.
3. *The Times*, 23 September 1938, p. 12.
4. I. Macleod, *Neville Chamberlain*, Frederick Muller 1961, p. 242.
5. *The Times*, 23 September 1938, p. 12.
6. *Daily Express*, 21 September 1938, p. 10.
7. *Evening Standard*, 21 September 1938, p. 6.
8. Kirkpatrick, p. 113.
9. *Daily Express*, 21 September 1938, p. 10.
10. Noguères, p. 160.
11. Shirer, *Berlin Diary*, p. 115. Two of Hitler's leading biographers emphasize that Hitler's sobriquet, the "carpet-eater," was in fact an urban myth, resulting from a misinterpretation by American journalists of the German slang expression; it should have been colloquially translated as "climbing the wall" rather than "eating the carpet" (Toland, p. 480 and 481. Kershaw, *The Hitler Myth: Image and Reality in the Third Reich*, Clarendon Press 1987, p. 187).
12. Kirkpatrick, p. 114.
13. Shirer, *Berlin Diary*, p. 115.
14. *Daily Express*, 21 September 1938, p. 10.
15. Kirkpatrick, p. 114.
16. House of Commons, Official Report, Fifth Series, Volume 339, Col. 20, 28 September 1938.
17. Schmidt, p. 96.
18. *DBFP* 3/II, No. 1033, p. 465, "Notes of a conversation between Mr. Chamberlain and Herr Hitler at Godesberg," 22 September 1938.
19. N. Henderson, p. 155.
20. Schmidt, p. 96.
21. *DBFP* 3/II, No. 1033, pp. 466–73, "Notes of a conversation between Mr. Chamberlain and Herr Hitler at Godesberg," 22 September 1938.
22. *NCA*, Volume IV, Document 1780-PS, p. 367, Jodl Diary, 21 September 1938.
23. A. Maurois (trans. D. Lindley), *Tragedy in France*, Harper & Brothers, New York 1940, p. 13.
24. BBC Written Archives, R34/325 Czechoslovak Crisis, General File 1938–1939.
25. Madge & Harrison, p. 75.
26. *Daily Herald*, 23 September 1938.
27. *Duff Cooper Diaries*, 22 September 1938, p. 263.
28. CAB 27/646/65, "The Czechoslovakian Crisis 1938, Notes of Informal Meetings of Ministers," 9th Meeting, 22 September 1938 at 3 P.M.
29. Noguères, p. 164.
30. Harvey, 22 September 1938, p. 192.
31. CAB 27/646/65, "The Czechoslovakian Crisis 1938, Notes of Informal Meetings of Ministers," 9th Meeting, 22 September 1938 at 3 P.M.
32. *DBFP* 3/II, No. 1027, p. 461, Halifax to Newton, 22 September 1938.
33. PREM 1/266A/183, Gladwyn Jebb memorandum of telephone conversation with Sir Horace Wilson, 22 September 1938 at 8:14 P.M.

34. CAB 27/646/70 & 76, "The Czechoslovakian Crisis 1938, Notes of Informal Meetings of Ministers," 10th Meeting, 22 September 1938 at 9:30 P.M.

35. *DBFP* 3/II, No. 1035, p. 474, British Delegation (Godesberg) to Halifax, 23 September 1938 at 2 A.M.

36. Schmidt, p. 98.

37. *DBFP* 3/II, No. 1048, p. 482, British Delegation (Godesberg) to Halifax, 23 September 1938, enclosing text of Chamberlain to Hitler.

38. *The Times*, 24 September 1938, p. 10.

39. CAB 27/646/78, "The Czechoslovakian Crisis 1938, Notes of Informal Meetings of Ministers," 11th Meeting, 23 September 1938 at 3 P.M.

40. PREM 1/266A/173–77, Downing Street memorandum of telephone conversations with Sir Horace Wilson, 23 September 1938.

41. Schmidt, p. 99.

42. Noguères, p. 167.

43. Laffan, p. 382.

44. CAB 23/95/173, Cabinet 42 (38), 24 September 1938.

45. *DGFP* D/II, No. 573, pp. 890–91, Hitler to Chamberlain, 23 September 1938.

46. CAB 27/646/78–79, "The Czechoslovakian Crisis 1938, Notes of Informal Meetings of Ministers," 11th Meeting, 23 September 1938 at 3 P.M.

47. Harvey, 23 September 1938, p. 194.

48. *Duff Cooper Diaries*, 23 September 1938, pp. 263–64.

49. Roberts, "*The Holy Fox*," p. 113.

50. CAB 27/646/86–89, "The Czechoslovakian Crisis 1938, Notes of Informal Meetings of Ministers," 12th Meeting, 23 September 1938 at 9:30 P.M.

51. *DBFP* 3/II, No. 1058, p. 490, Halifax to British Delegation (Godesberg), 23 September 1938.

52. Schmidt, p. 100.

53. *DBFP* 3/II, No. 1068, pp. 495–96, British Delegation (Godesberg) to Newton, 24 September 1938, enclosing text of memorandum.

54. Schmidt, pp. 100–1.

55. Kirkpatrick, p. 121.

56. N. Henderson, p. 157.

57. House of Commons, Official Report, Fifth Series, Volume 339, Col. 21, 28 September 1938.

58. Schmidt, p. 101.

59. BBC Written Archives, T 56/177/1, *Ten Years After—A Munich Survey*, interview with Paul Schmidt, 11 October 1948.

60. Schmidt, pp. 101–2.

61. *DGFP* D/II, No. 583, p. 907, "Memorandum on the Conversation Between the Führer and the British Prime Minister," 23 September 1938.

62. House of Commons, Official Report, Fifth Series, Volume 339, Col. 22, 28 September 1938.

63. Shirer, *Rise and Fall of the Third Reich*, p. 395.

64. *The Times*, 24 September 1938, p. 10.

65. Cox, p. 71.

66. *Daily Express*, 26 September 1938, p. 2.

67. Gedye, pp. 471–72.
68. Noguères, p. 176.
69. Butler, p. 75. Mason-MacFarlane's extraordinary suggestion was first revealed by *Der Spiegel* in August 1969, and the story was followed up on the front page of *The Times*, below the headline "Should He Have Shot Hitler?" This in turn led to a correspondence on the letters page which lasted several days, as the ethical and practical merits of the proposal were debated at length. One contributor was Brigadier Stronge, who had been military attaché in Prague in 1938, and who was strongly critical of Mason-MacFarlane (*The Times*, 6 and 8 August 1969).
70. Butler, pp. 81–83.
71. BBC Written Archives, R34/325 Czechoslovak Crisis, General File 1938–1939.
72. CAB 27/646/91–92, "The Czechoslovakian Crisis 1938, Notes of Informal Meetings of Ministers," 13th Meeting, 24 September 1938.
73. *Cadogan Diaries*, 24 September 1938, p. 103.
74. *Duff Cooper Diaries*, 24 September 1938, p. 264.
75. CAB 23/95/179–80, Cabinet 42 (38), 24 September 1938.
76. Minney, p. 145.
77. *Duff Cooper Diaries*, 24 September 1938, p. 264–65.
78. AMEL 7/32, Amery Diary, 24 September 1938.
79. AMEL 2/1/28, Amery to Billy Hughes, 25 September 1938.
80. J. Barnes & D. Nicholson (eds.), *The Empire at Bay: The Leo Amery Diaries 1929–1945*, Hutchinson 1988, p. 483.
81. NC 7/2/81, Amery to Chamberlain, 25 September 1938.
82. Eden Diary, AP 20/118, 24 September 1938 (Thorpe, p. 225).
83. Lord Avon, *The Eden Memoirs: The Reckoning*, Cassell 1965, p. 27.
84. *Cadogan Diaries*, 24 September 1938, p. 103.
85. Harvey, 25 September 1938, p. 196.
86. *Cadogan Diaries*, 25 September 1938, p. 105.
87. Roberts, "*The Holy Fox*," p. 114.
88. CAB 23/95/198–200, Cabinet 43 (38), 25 September 1938 at 10:30 A.M.
89. Minney, p. 146.
90. *Duff Cooper Diaries*, 25 September 1938, p. 265.
91. CAB 23/95/202 & 207, Cabinet 43 (38), 25 September 1938 at 10:30 A.M.
92. Hickleton Papers, A4/410/3/7/2–4, exchange of penciled notes between Chamberlain and Halifax, n/d (25 September 1938).
93. Harvey, 25 September 1938, p. 197.
94. CAB 23/95/224, Cabinet 43 (38), 25 September 1938 at 3 P.M.
95. J. Charmley, *Duff Cooper: The Authorized Biography*, Weidenfeld and Nicolson 1986, p. 120.
96. *Duff Cooper Diaries*, 25 September 1938, p. 266. Interestingly, the official Cabinet minutes make no reference to this, Duff Cooper's first offer to resign.
97. CAB 23/95/189, Cabinet 42 (38), 24 September 1938.
98. *DBFP* 3/II, No. 1092, pp. 518–19, "Note from the Czechoslovak Minister to Viscount Halifax," 25 September 1938.

99. Wilson Papers, T 273/406, note of meeting between Chamberlain, Halifax and Masaryk, 25 September 1938.
100. *DBFP* 3/II, No. 1009, p. 451, Phipps to Halifax, 21 September 1938.
101. *DBFP* 3/II, No. 1015, p. 456, Halifax to Phipps, 22 September 1938.
102. *DGFP* D/II, No. 647, p. 977, German military attaché (Paris) to German Foreign Ministry, 27 September 1938.
103. Phipps Papers, PHPP III/1/20/90, Phipps to Halifax, 24 September 1938.
104. Harvey, 24 September 1938, p. 195.
105. PHPP III/1/20/91, Halifax to Phipps, 25 September 1938.
106. Strang, p. 140. William Strang (later Lord Strang) served as Permanent Under-Secretary at the Foreign Office from 1949 to 1953. In the course of a long and distinguished career he was involved in many important negotiations, for instance with Stalin—the meeting with the French ministers must, therefore, have been pretty bad.
107. *DBFP* 3/II, No. 1093, pp. 523–27, "Record of an Anglo-French Conversation held at No. 10 Downing Street," 25 September 1938.
108. Strang, p. 141.
109. *DBFP* 3/II, No. 1093, pp. 527–34, "Record of an Anglo-French Conversation held at No. 10 Downing Street," 25 September 1938.
110. Wheeler-Bennett, *Munich*, p. 143.
111. *Duff Cooper Diaries*, 25 September 1938, pp. 266–67.
112. CAB 23/95/241, Cabinet 44 (38), 25 September 1938 at 11:30 P.M.
113. *Duff Cooper Diaries*, 25 September 1938, p. 267.
114. Dalton Papers I/18, Diary, 26 September 1938.

13: KEEP CALM AND DIG

1. *The Times*, 26 September 1938, p. 13.
2. Madge & Harrison, pp. 49–50.
3. Macmillan, p. 560 & p. 575.
4. *Daily Express*, 26 September 1938, p. 6.
5. BBC Written Archives, R34/325 Czechoslovak Crisis, General File 1938–1939, "Special Announcements and Bulletins," 26 & 27 September 1938.
6. *The Times*, 26 September 1938, p. 14.
7. Diana Cooper, *The Light of the Common Day*, Rupert Hart-Davis 1959, p. 243.
8. N. Nicolson (ed.), *Leave the Letters Till We're Dead: The Letters of Virginia Woolf, Volume VI: 1938–1941*, Hogarth Press 1980, p. 275.
9. *Daily Express*, 26 September 1938, pp. 5–6.
10. BBC Written Archives, R34/325 Czechoslovak Crisis, General File 1938–1939, "Special Announcements and Bulletins," 26 September 1938.
11. *Daily Express*, 27 September 1938, p. 2, and Madge & Harrison, p. 91.
12. *Daily Express*, 28 September 1938, pp. 5–12.
13. *Evening Standard*, 29 September 1938, p. 6.
14. BBC Written Archives, R34/325 Czechoslovak Crisis, General File 1938–1939, "Special Announcements and Bulletins," 27 September 1938.

15. *Nicolson Diaries*, Vita Sackville-West to Nicolson, 27 September 1938, p. 368.
16. Wheeler-Bennett, *King George VI*, p. 352.
17. CAB 23/95/258, Cabinet 45 (38), 26 September 1938.
18. *DBFP* 3/II, No. 1143, p. 575, Halifax to Phipps, 27 September 1938.
19. Duff Cooper, p. 237.
20. CAB 23/95/249, Cabinet 45 (38), 26 September 1938.
21. S. Welles, *The Time for Decision*, Hamish Hamilton 1944, p. 58.
22. CAB 23/95/256, Cabinet 45 (38), 26 September 1938.
23. CAB 23/95/247–48, Cabinet 45 (38), 26 September 1938.
24. *Duff Cooper Diaries*, 26 September 1938, p. 267.
25. RA PS/GVI/C 235/10, Hardinge memorandum, 26 & 29 September 1938.
26. *Nicolson Diaries*, 22 September 1938, p. 364.
27. Jay, p. 75.
28. Attlee Papers, MS Eng. c.4792/85, Clement Attlee to Tom Attlee, 29 April 1938.
29. PREM 1/266A/96, Attlee to Chamberlain, 26 September 1938.
30. See Note 53 below.
31. AMEL 7/32, Amery Diary, 26 September 1938.
32. *Nicolson Diaries*, 26 September 1938, p. 367.
33. *DGFP* D/II, No. 603, p. 930, Hencke to German Foreign Ministry, 25 September 1938.
34. Kershaw, *Hitler*, p. 115–16 (original in Goebbels Diaries, 26 September 1938).
35. Schmidt, p. 103.
36. *DBFP* 3/II, No. 1118, p. 555, "Notes of a Conversation between Sir Horace Wilson and Herr Hitler at Berlin," 26 September 1938.
37. Gilbert, "Horace Wilson: Man of Munich?," p. 7.
38. Schmidt, p. 103.
39. *DBFP* 3/II, No. 1118, p. 555, "Notes of a Conversation between Sir Horace Wilson and Herr Hitler at Berlin," 26 September 1938.
40. Kershaw, *Hitler*, p. 116.
41. *DBFP* 3/II, No. 1097, p. 542, Chamberlain to Hitler, 26 September 1938.
42. Kirkpatrick, p. 124.
43. PREM 1/266A/79, Gladwyn Jebb memorandum, 26 September 1938.
44. *DBFP* 3/II, No. 1115, p. 552, Henderson to Halifax, 26 September 1938.
45. Shirer, *Berlin Diary*, p. 118.
46. Baynes, p. 1509, p. 1517 & pp. 1525–27.
47. Kershaw, *Hitler*, p. 117.
48. Shirer, *Berlin Diary*, pp. 118–19.
49. Kershaw, *Hitler*, p. 117 (original in Goebbels Diaries, 27 September 1938).
50. Amery, p. 278.
51. CAB 27/646/95, "The Czechoslovakian Crisis 1938, Notes of Informal Meetings of Ministers," 14th Meeting, 26 September 1938 at 10 P.M.
52. *DBFP* 3/II, No. 1111, n1, p. 550.
53. Gilbert, *Winston S. Churchill*, p. 1182, Halifax to Churchill, 24 July 1947. In *The Gathering Storm* (pp. 277–78), Winston Churchill claimed that he had

been present with Halifax and Chamberlain in the Cabinet Room on the afternoon of September 26 when the communiqué was drafted (see Note 30 above). However, when in 1947 he sought confirmation of this, Halifax replied that he believed Churchill's "recollection was at fault." While there might have been a general discussion that afternoon, the actual draft communiqué was only brought to him for approval that evening by Rex (later Sir Reginald) Leeper. Halifax alone authorized its release, in the belief that it was "completely in accord" with Chamberlain's view. However, to his surprise, "Neville was much put out when the Communiqué appeared, and reproached me with not having submitted it to him before publication" (Gilbert, *Winston S. Churchill*, p. 1182, Halifax to Churchill, 24 July 1947). The statement acquired its sobriquet from the fact that it was Leeper who issued it to the press, while in French diplomatic circles it was assumed to be a fake, or the work of Sir Robert Vansittart.

54. *The Times*, 27 September 1938, p. 12.
55. PREM 1/266A/76–77, Wilson to Foreign Office, 26 September 1938.
56. Kirkpatrick, p. 124.
57. *DBFP* 3/II, No. 1129, p. 565, "Notes of a Conversation between Herr Hitler and Sir Horace Wilson at Berlin," 27 September 1938.
58. N. Henderson, p. 160.
59. *DBFP* 3/II, No. 1129, p. 566, "Notes of a Conversation between Herr Hitler and Sir Horace Wilson at Berlin," 27 September 1938.
60. N. Henderson, p. 160.
61. LSE Archive, "Munich 1938," 1/1/8, interview with Sir Con O'Neill, n/d. The twenty-six-year-old O'Neill was a Fellow of All Souls and the son of Sir Hugh (later Lord) O'Neill, a Privy Counselor and senior Conservative MP. In the immediate aftermath of Munich, the young Con O'Neill resigned his Foreign Office position in disgust at the terms of the agreement. Fearing for his son's future career, Sir Hugh appealed directly to Sir Horace Wilson, asking that he might seek to persuade his son to withdraw his resignation, and help to have him reinstated. Wilson not only refused to do so, he insisted that O'Neill should go. He was, he said, a "hot-headed young man. . . . As a civil servant you are not justified in criticising the Government. What had it to do with him? He was addressing envelopes or something. He didn't matter a row of beans" (Gilbert, "Horace Wilson: Man of Munich?," p. 8).
62. *DGFP* D/II, No. 634, p. 965, "Memorandum on the Conversation between the Führer and Sir Horace Wilson," 27 September 1938 (the phrase is in English in Schmidt's original German notes).
63. Kirkpatrick, p. 126.
64. *Cadogan Diaries*, p. 108.
65. CAB 27/646/101, "The Czechoslovakian Crisis 1938, Notes of Informal Meetings of Ministers," 15th Meeting, 27 September 1938.
66. PREM 1/242/27, Te Water memorandum, 27 September 1938.
67. *DBFP* 3/II, No. 1126, pp. 561–62, Henderson to Halifax, 27 September 1938.
68. *DBFP* 3/II, No. 1136, p. 570, Halifax to Newton, 27 September 1938 at 5:45 P.M.

69. *Cadogan Diaries,* p. 108.
70. *DBFP* 3/II, No. 1138, p. 571, Halifax to Newton, 27 September 1938 at 6 P.M.
71. PREM 1/266A/115, draft telegram, Chamberlain to Beneš, 27 September 1938.
72. *Cadogan Diaries,* 27 September 1938, p. 107.
73. N. Chamberlain, *The Struggle for Peace,* Hutchinson 1939, pp. 274–76.
74. *Duff Cooper Diaries,* 27 September 1938, p. 268.
75. Diana Cooper, p. 245.
76. AMEL, 7/32, Amery Diary, 27 September 1938.
77. CAB 23/95/261–70, Cabinet 46 (38), 27 September 1938.
78. *Duff Cooper Diaries,* 27 September 1938, pp. 268–69.
79. CAB 23/95/272-4, Cabinet 46 (38), 27 September 1938.
80. Wheeler-Bennett, *King George VI,* p. 352.
81. NC 18/1/1070, Chamberlain to Hilda Chamberlain, 2 October 1938.
82. *NCA,* Volume III, Document 388-PS, p. 352, memorandum, 28 September 1938.
83. *NCA,* Volume III, Document 388-PS, p. 379, "Coordinated Time of Attack by Army and Air Forces on X Day," 27 September 1938.
84. *NCA,* Volume III, Document 388-PS, p. 351, Keitel memorandum, "Mobilization Measures," 27 September 1938.
85. *NCA,* Volume III, Document 388-PS, p. 350, "Most Secret" Keitel memorandum, 27 September 1938.
86. Shirer, *Berlin Diary,* p. 119.
87. *Daily Express,* 28 September 1938, p. 2.
88. N. Henderson, p. 161.
89. Toland, p. 45.
90. *TMWC,* Volume XII, p. 219, Gisevius testimony, 25 April 1946.
91. Hitler's reply to Chamberlain's letter was received at the Foreign Office at 8:40 P.M. that evening (see note 96 below). Given that by then it had been drafted, translated by Schmidt, handed to Henderson and transmitted to London, it must have been written before the parade in Berlin that evening.
92. Spitzy, p. 246.
93. Schmidt, p. 105.
94. N. Henderson, p. 161.
95. Weizsäcker, p. 154.
96. *DBFP* 3/II, No. 1144, pp. 576–79, Henderson to Halifax, 27 September 1938.
97. House of Commons, Official Report, Fifth Series, Volume 339, Col. 25, 28 September 1938.
98. Laffan, p. 423.
99. *DGFP* D/II, No. 656, pp. 988–89, Weizsäcker minute for Ribbentrop, 28 September 1938.
100. NC 8/26/13, Munich File, note by Annie Chamberlain, n/d.
101. *DBFP* 3/II, No. 1158, p. 587, Halifax to Henderson, enclosing message from Chamberlain to Hitler, 28 September 1938.
102. NC 18/1/1070, Chamberlain to Hilda Chamberlain, 2 October 1938.
103. Birkenhead, *Halifax,* p. 405.

104. Weizsäcker, p. 153.
105. N. Henderson, p. 163.
106. Toland, p. 487.
107. Bloch, pp. 195–96.
108. Toland, p. 487.
109. P. Dixon, *Double Diploma: The Life of Sir Pierson Dixon, Don and Diplomat*, Hutchinson 1968, p. 48.
110. *DBFP* 3/II, No. 1125, p. 561, Perth to Halifax, 27 September 1938.
111. Dixon, p. 50.
112. *DBFP* 3/II, No. 1231, pp. 642–43, Perth to Halifax, 30 September 1938.
113. Noguères, p. 222.
114. *Ciano's Diary*, 28 September 1938, p. 165.
115. Schmidt, p. 106.
116. Schmidt, p. 106 (translated from the original in A. François-Poncet, *Souvenirs d'une Ambassade à Berlin*, Flammarion, Paris 1947, p. 328).
117. Spitzy, pp. 248–49.
118. Schmidt, p. 107.
119. *DBFP* 3/II, No. 1159, p. 587, Halifax to Perth, 28 September 1938.
120. *DBFP* 3/II, No. 1231, p. 644, Perth to Halifax, 30 September 1938.
121. N. Henderson, p. 164.
122. Wheeler-Bennett, *Munich*, p. 167.
123. Kershaw, *Hitler*, p. 119 (original in Groscurth Diary, 28 September 1938).
124. Laffan, p. 407.
125. N. Henderson, p. 164.
126. Wheeler-Bennett, *Munich*, p. 167 n4.
127. Kershaw, *Hitler*, p. 119.
128. Schmidt, pp. 107–8.
129. N. Henderson, p. 166.
130. *Ciano's Diary*, 28 September 1938, p. 166.

14: THE FLYING MESSENGER OF PEACE

1. One of the youngest MPs in the House, Cartland was to argue bravely against Chamberlain's policy throughout 1939. He died during the retreat to Dunkirk in May 1940 (B. Cartland, *The Isthmus Years*, Hutchinson 1943, p. 177).
2. Wheeler-Bennett compares the orderly, and relatively low-key, exodus from London that day with that taking place in Paris where "they were fighting for seats on trains, and the roads out of the city were choked with traffic" (*Munich*, p. 167).
3. BBC Written Archives, R34/325 Czechoslovak Crisis, General File 1938–1939, "Special Announcements and Bulletins," 28 September 1938.
4. *Duff Cooper Diaries*, 28 September 1938, p. 269.
5. *Channon Diaries*, 28 September 1938, p. 170.
6. AMEL, 7/32, Amery Diary, 27 September 1938.

7. *Nicolson Diaries,* 28 September 1938, p. 369.
8. LSE Archive, "Munich 1938," 1/1/3, Interview with Count Raczynski.
9. *Nicolson Diaries,* 28 September 1938, p. 369.
10. Self, *Neville Chamberlain,* p. 322.
11. House of Commons, Official Report, Fifth Series, Volume 339, Col. 5, 28 September 1938.
12. *Nicolson Diaries,* 28 September 1938, p. 369.
13. House of Commons, Official Report, Fifth Series, Volume 339, Col. 6, 28 September 1938.
14. AMEL, 7/32, Amery Diary, 28 September 1938.
15. CAB 27/646/105, "The Czechoslovakian Crisis 1938, Notes of Informal Meetings of Ministers," 15th Meeting, 27 September 1938. Among other vital telegrams that were deliberately omitted from the white paper were the Anglo-French ultimatum of September 21; the most recent British proposals to Hitler; and Chamberlain's telegram to Beneš of September 27 warning that if war ensued and the Allies were successful, it was still unlikely that Czechoslovakia would be reconstituted in her present form. It is highly likely that the threatening language of some of these dispatches would have given some MPs pause for thought.
16. *DBFP* 3/II, No. 1174, pp. 593–94, "Note by Sir A. Cadogan," 28 September 1938.
17. *Cadogan Diaries,* 28 September 1938, p. 109.
18. Hirsel Archive, ADH, "Notes on Munich" by Lord Dunglass, later Sir Alec Douglas-Home, later Lord Home (the handwritten notes are not dated, but are described as having been "written immediately after Munich").
19. Simon Papers 10/11, Simon Diary, 29 September 1938.
20. *Nicolson Diaries,* 28 September 1938, p. 370.
21. *The Times,* 28 September 1938, p. 12.
22. House of Commons, Official Report, Fifth Series, Volume 339, Cols. 25–26, 28 September 1938.
23. *Channon Diaries,* 28 September 1938, p. 171.
24. House of Commons, Official Report, Fifth Series, Volume 339, Col. 26, 28 September 1938.
25. Hirsel Archive, SB/7.
26. House of Commons, Official Report, Fifth Series, Volume 339, Cols. 26–28, 28 September 1938.
27. *Duff Cooper Diaries,* 28 September 1938, p. 269.
28. Lord Home, *The Way the Wind Blows,* Collins 1976, p. 65.
29. *The History of The Times,* p. 943.
30. Simon Papers 10/12, Simon Diary, 29 September 1938. Simon had been on the Front Bench in 1914 when Sir Edward Grey had announced the beginning of the First World War.
31. *News Chronicle,* 29 September 1938, p. 1.
32. *Channon Diaries,* 28 September 1938, p. 171.
33. Simon, p. 247.
34. *Nicolson Diaries,* 28 September 1938, p. 371, n1.

35. R. Seton-Watson, *A History of the Czechs and Slovaks*, Hutchinson 1943, p. 367n.
36. Wheeler-Bennett, *Munich*, p. 170.
37. AMEL, 7/32, Amery Diary, 28 September 1938.
38. LSE Archive, "Munich 1938," 1/1/3, interview with Count Raczynski.
39. *Nicolson Diaries*, 28 September 1938, p. 371.
40. G. Stewart, *Burying Caesar: Churchill, Chamberlain and the Battle for the Tory Party*, Weidenfeld and Nicolson 1999, p. 324.
41. NC 18/1/1070, Chamberlain to Hilda Chamberlain, 2 October 1938.
42. *Daily Express*, 29 September 1938, p. 1.
43. Hirsel Archive, ADH, "Notes on Munich" by Lord Dunglass. This quotation has never been published before, and is perhaps the earliest available reference to Chamberlain's subsequent remark from the window at Downing Street; it gives a strong indication that it was Annie Chamberlain who encouraged him to say it. Lord Hailsham also saw Annie Chamberlain that evening, and reported that she said to him: "I think Neville will bring back Peace from Munich and I hope that it will be Peace with Honour" (Heuston, p. 490).
44. Wheeler-Bennett, *Munich*, p. 171.
45. *DGFP* D/II, No. 662, p. 994, German Foreign Ministry to German Missions Abroad, 28 September 1938.
46. *Ciano's Diary*, 29 September 1938, p. 166.
47. Laffan, p. 437.
48. *Ciano's Diary*, 29 September 1938, p. 166.
49. *Channon Diaries*, 29 September 1938, p. 172.
50. BBC Written Archives, R34/325 Czechoslovak Crisis, General File 1938–1939, "Recorded Programmes Library," 29 September 1938.
51. Thorpe, *Alec Douglas-Home*, pp. 80–81.
52. *DBFP* 3/II, No. 1184, p. 599, Halifax to Newton, 28 September 1938.
53. *DBFP* 3/II, No. 1194, p. 604, Newton to Halifax, 28 September 1938.
54. A. François-Poncet (trans. J. LeClercq), *The Fateful Years*, Victor Gollancz 1949, p. 269.
55. *The Times*, 30 September 1938, p. 12.
56. Hirsel Archive, ADH, "Notes on Munich."
57. François-Poncet, *The Fateful Years*, p. 269.
58. J. von Halasz, *Hitler's Munich*, Foxley Books 2007, pp. 72–73. The Führerbau is one of the few buildings of the Nazi era in Munich still standing intact. Its facade is now a dirty brown, although the outline of the massive bronze eagle with swastika that hung above the main entrance is still clearly visible. Today the building houses the Munich Academy of Music, and Room 105, on the first floor directly above the entrance, where the agreement was signed, is now used for piano rehearsals. There is a small, A4-sized framed plaque on the wall which briefly describes the room's history.
59. Hickleton Papers, A4/410/3/3/vi, "Diary of Visit," 19 November 1937.
60. *The Times*, 30 September 1938, p. 12.
61. *Evening Standard*, 29 September 1938, p. 7.
62. Hirsel Archive, ADH, "Notes on Munich."
63. Eberle & Uhl, p. 33.

64. François-Poncet, *The Fateful Years*, p. 269–70.
65. *Ciano's Diary*, 30 September 1938, p. 167.
66. Strang, p. 144.
67. N. Henderson, p. 166.
68. Schmidt, p. 109.
69. NC 18/1/1070, Chamberlain to Hilda Chamberlain, 2 October 1938.
70. *Ciano's Diary*, 30 September 1938, p. 167.
71. *DGFP* D/II, No. 670, pp. 1005–6. "Memorandum on the First Meeting Between the British and French Prime Ministers, the Duce, and the Führer at Munich," 29 September 1938.
72. N. Henderson, p. 167.
73. François-Poncet, *The Fateful Years*, p. 271. The fact that Mussolini's proposals had their origin in the Wilhelmstrasse was not discovered until the relevant German documents were seized after the war. It has to be assumed, therefore, that both Chamberlain and Henderson went to their graves believing that they had been drafted by Mussolini.
74. *DBFP* 3/II, No. 1227, p. 634, "Note by Sir H. Wilson on the Munich Conference," Appendix A, 1 October 1938.
75. Noguères, p. 265.
76. *Ciano's Diary*, 30 September 1938, p. 167.
77. *DGFP* D/II, No. 670, p. 1006, "Memorandum on the First Meeting Between the British and French Prime Ministers, the Duce, and the Führer at Munich," 29 September 1938.
78. Noguères, p. 268.
79. Schmidt, p. 110.
80. Laffan, p. 441, n3.
81. *Ciano's Diary*, 30 September 1938, p. 167.
82. François-Poncet, *The Fateful Years*, p. 271.
83. Strang, p. 145.
84. BBC Written Archives, T56/177/1, "Ten Years After—A Munich Survey," 11 October 1948, interview with Lord Dunglass.
85. Schmidt, p. 111.
86. Wilson Papers, T 273/408, memorandum of Dr. Hubert Masařik, 30 September 1938.
87. BBC Written Archives, R28/297325, Czechoslovak Crisis, "News Agencies 1938".
88. Kirkpatrick, p. 129.
89. CAB 23/95/280, Cabinet 47 (38), 30 September 1938.
90. *DBFP* 3/II, No. 1224, pp. 627–28, United Kingdom Delegation (Munich) to Halifax, enclosing text of Munich Agreement, 30 September 1938.
91. BBC Written Archives, R28/297325, Czechoslovak Crisis, "News Agencies 1938."
92. Strang, p. 146.
93. Kirkpatrick, p. 127.
94. *Ciano's Diary*, 30 September 1938, p. 168.
95. Noguères, p. 284.

96. Wheeler-Bennett, *Munich*, p. 172, n2.

97. Shirer, *Berlin Diary*, p. 121.

98. T 273/408, Memorandum of Dr. Hubert Masařik, 30 September 1938. Kirkpatrick, who it is by no means certain was in the room, contradicts Masařik's account of Chamberlain's attitude. The Prime Minister, he contends, showed the "greatest sympathy and understanding," in contrast to the "peremptory attitude of Daladier who did not mince his words" (Kirkpatrick, pp. 129–30).

99. *DBFP* 3/II, No. 1227, p. 633, "Note by Sir H. Wilson on the Munich Conference," 1 October 1938.

100. François-Poncet, *The Fateful Years*, p. 273.

101. BBC Written Archives, T56/177/1, "Ten Years After—A Munich Survey," 11 October 1948, interview with Frank Ashton-Gwatkin.

102. *DBFP* 3/II, No. 1225, p. 630, British Delegation (Munich) to Newton, 30 September 1938.

103. Wheeler-Bennett, *Munich*, p. 175.

104. Ripka, pp. 231–32.

105. NC 18/1/1070, Chamberlain to Hilda Chamberlain, 2 October 1938.

106. Strang, p. 147.

107. Thorpe, *Alec Douglas-Home*, p. 83.

108. *Ciano's Diary*, 30 September 1938, p. 167. When the American war correspondent Lee Miller arrived at the flat in May 1945, she observed: "Superficially, almost anyone with a medium income and no heirlooms could have been the proprietor of this flat. It lacked grace and charm, it lacked intimacy, but it was not grand" (L. Miller, *Lee Miller's War*, Condé Nast Books 1992, p. 191). Today the block of flats is a police station.

109. Hirsel Archive, SB/104, interview with Lord Home, 28 August 1989.

110. *DBFP* 3/II, No. 1228, p. 636, "Note of a Conversation between the Prime Minister and Herr Hitler at the Latter's Flat in Munich," 30 September 1938.

111. NC 18/1/1070, Chamberlain to Hilda Chamberlain, 2 October 1938. Chamberlain's notes of the meeting, fourteen pages of penciled handwritten jottings in a small notebook, are in his papers at Birmingham University. His original of the signed piece of paper, complete with fold marks, is on display at the Imperial War Museum.

112. Schmidt, pp. 112–13.

113. BBC Written Archives, R19/2172, "I Was There" series, interview with Sir Alec Douglas-Home, 14 January 1968.

114. *Documents on German Foreign Policy 1918–1945*, Series D (1937–1945), Volume IV, "The Aftermath of Munich," HMSO 1951, No. 247, p. 292, "Conversation between the Führer and the British Prime Minister," 30 September 1938.

115. Lambert, p. 276.

116. Eberle & Uhl, p. 35.

117. Strang, p. 148.

118. BBC Written Archives, T56/177/1, "Ten Years After—A Munich Survey," 11 October 1948, interview with Frank Ashton-Gwatkin.

119. Toland, p. 493.
120. Spitzy, p. 254.
121. *Ciano's Diary*, 2 October 1938, p. 172.
122. von Halasz, pp. 36–37, 40. The Sterneckerbräu is now a computer shop.
123. T 273/407, Ewer to Wilson, 20 October 1938, & Wilson to Ewer, 21 October 1938.
124. C. Coote, *The Other Club*, Sidgwick & Jackson 1971, pp. 88–91.
125. Charmley, *Duff Cooper*, p. 124.
126. *Duff Cooper Diaries*, 29 September 1938, p. 270.
127. Coote, *The Other Club*, p. 91.
128. Roberts, "*The Holy Fox*," p. 123.
129. Avon, *The Reckoning*, p. 36.
130. LSE Archive, 1/1/5, "Munich 1938," interview with Sir John Colville.
131. CAB 23/95/280–85, Cabinet 47 (38), 30 September 1938.
132. *Duff Cooper Diaries*, 30 September 1938, pp. 270–71.
133. CAB 23/95/287, Cabinet 47 (38), 30 September 1938.
134. *Duff Cooper Diaries*, 30 September 1938, p. 271.
135. Duff Cooper, p. 243.
136. Wheeler-Bennett, *King George VI*, pp. 354–56.
137. *The Times*, 1 October 1938, p. 13.
138. W. Hadley, *Munich: Before and After*, Cassell 1944, pp. 94–95.
139. *Daily Herald*, 1 October 1938.
140. NC 7/11/31/228, Rothermere to Chamberlain, 1 October 1938.
141. Self, *Neville Chamberlain*, p. 328.
142. RA EDW/3760, Duke of Windsor to Chamberlain, n/d.
143. Self, *Neville Chamberlain*, p. 329.
144. NC 7/11/31/168, Lee to Chamberlain, 12 November 1938.
145. *The Times*, 1 October 1938, p. 1.
146. D. Dutton, *Neville Chamberlain*, Arnold 200, p. 55.
147. Shepherd, p. 223.
148. B. Morris, *The Roots of Appeasement: The British Weekly Press and Nazi Germany During the 1930s*, Frank Cass 1991.
149. Macmillan, p. 562.
150. Harvey, 1 October 1938, p. 208.
151. NC 18/1/1070, Chamberlain to Hilda Chamberlain, 2 October 1938.
152. CAB 27/646/108, "The Czechoslovakian Crisis 1938, Notes of Informal Meetings of Ministers," 16th Meeting, 1 October 1938.
153. PREM 1/266A/23–24, Stanley to Chamberlain, 3 October 1938.
154. House of Commons, Official Report, Fifth Series, Volume 339, Cols. 31–34 & 40, 3 October 1938.
155. Charmley, *Duff Cooper*, p. 130.
156. House of Commons, Official Report, Fifth Series, Volume 339, Cols. 42–47, 3 October 1938.
157. Macmillan, p. 568.
158. Dalton, pp. 198–99.
159. NC 18/1/1071, Chamberlain to Ida Chamberlain, 9 October 1938.

160. *Nicolson Diaries*, 4 October 1938, p. 375.
161. House of Commons, Official Report, Fifth Series, Volume 339, Col. 360, 5 October 1938.
162. Nancy Astor Papers, 1416/1/7/78, *News Review*, 13 October 1938.
163. House of Commons, Official Report, Fifth Series, Volume 339, Cols. 361 & 373, 5 October 1938.
164. AMEL 2/1/28, Amery to Chamberlain, 6 October 1938.
165. *Nicolson Diaries*, 6 October 1938, pp. 375–76.
166. N. Thompson, *The Anti-Appeasers: Conservative Opposition to Appeasement in the 1930s*, Clarendon Press 1971, pp. 182–83.
167. NC 18/1/1071, Chamberlain to Ida Chamberlain, 9 October 1938.
168. Hirsel Archive, SB/8, 1938–40.

EPILOGUE: DRAWING THE SWORD

1. *NCA*, Volume IV, Document 1780-PS, p. 368, Jodl Diary, 29 September 1938.
2. Kirkpatrick, p. 135.
3. Shirer, *The Rise and Fall of the Third Reich*, p. 427.
4. N. Henderson, pp. 174–75.
5. Kershaw, *Hitler*, p. 122 (original in Goebbels Diaries, 30 September 1938).
6. *NCA*, Volume III, Document 388-PS, pp. 357–58, "Green" File, Keitel to Hitler, 30 September 1938.
7. T. Taylor, pp. 224–25.
8. Toland, p. 494.
9. Cox, pp. 76–77.
10. N. Henderson, p. 168.
11. François-Poncet, *The Fateful Years*, p. 273.
12. Kirkpatrick, p. 131.
13. Weinberg, p. 459.
14. Baynes, pp. 1533–35.
15. *NCA*, Volume III, Document 388-PS, pp. 372–74, "Green" File, 9 and 11 October 1938.
16. *DGFP* D/IV, No. 81, p. 99–100, "Directive by the Führer for the Wehrmacht," 21 October 1938. The third point referred to the town of Memel, a Baltic seaport of some 40,000 inhabitants, the majority of whom were German. The area had been ceded by Germany to Lithuania under the terms of the Treaty of Versailles.
17. *DGFP* D/IV, No. 45, p. 46, "Memorandum for the Führer," 7 October 1938.
18. Kershaw, *Hitler*, p. 141.
19. CAB 23/96/92, Cabinet 51 (38), 31 October 1938.
20. NC 18/1/1076, Chamberlain to Ida Chamberlain, 13 November 1938.
21. Self, *Neville Chamberlain*, p. 345.
22. Hadley, p. 103.
23. T 273/407, *Daily Herald*, 1 October 1938.
24. CAB 23/95/292–94 & 301, Cabinet 48 (38), 3 October 1938.

25. Nancy Astor Papers, MS 1416/1/2/188, Macmillan to Astor, October 1938.
26. Macmillan, p. 573.
27. *DGFP* D/IV, No. 68, p. 83, note of Göring conversation, n/d (17 October 1938).
28. CAB 23/95/284, Cabinet 47 (38), 30 September 1938.
29. T. Taylor, p. 230.
30. *DGFP* D/IV, No. 156, pp. 188–89, Hencke (Prague) to German Foreign Ministry, 12 January 1939.
31. Wheeler-Bennett, *Munich*, p. 316.
32. Kershaw, *Hitler*, p. 169 (original in Goebbels Diaries, 11 March 1939).
33. *Documents on British Foreign Policy 1919–1939*, Third Series, Volume IV, "1939," HMSO 1951, No. 203, p. 223, Henderson to Halifax, 11 March 1939.
34. *DBFP* 3/IV, No. 473, p. 439, Newton to Halifax, 21 March 1939.
35. *DGFP* VI, No. 202, pp. 243–44, "Conversation between the Führer and Tiso," 13 March 1939. After the war, Tiso was arrested by the Americans and handed over to the Czech government for trial, as a result of which he was hanged on April 18, 1947.
36. *DGFP* D/IV, No. 228, p. 267, "Conversation between the Führer and President Hácha," 15 March 1939.
37. Toland, p. 517n.
38. Kershaw, *Hitler*, p. 171.
39. *DGFP* D/IV, No. 152, pp. 185–86, Keitel directive, 17 December 1938.
40. Syrový was arrested after the liberation of Czechoslovakia, and tried on a charge of collaboration. On April 21, 1947, he was sentenced to twenty years' imprisonment, ten with hard labor.
41. Baynes, p. 1585.

Bibliography

MANUSCRIPT COLLECTIONS

King George VI	The Royal Archives (RA)
The Duke of Windsor	The Royal Archives
(By gracious permission of Her Majesty the Queen)	

Leo Amery	Churchill Archives Centre
Lady Astor	Reading University
Lord Attlee	Bodleian Library, Oxford
Lord Avon	Birmingham University Library
	National Archives (FO 800)
Lord Baldwin	Cambridge University Library
Lord Beaverbrook	Parliamentary Archive
Sir Alexander Cadogan	Churchill Archives Centre
	National Archives (FO 800)
Lord Caldecote	Churchill Archives Centre
Neville Chamberlain	Birmingham University Library
Lord Cranborne	National Archives (FO 800)
Lord Crookshank	Bodleian Library, Oxford
Lord Dalton	British Library of Political and Economic Science
Geoffrey Dawson	Bodleian Library, Oxford
Paul Emrys-Evans	British Library
Lord Gladwyn	Churchill Archives Centre
Lord Halifax	Borthwick Institute, University of York (The Hickleton Papers)
	National Archives (FO 800)
Lord Hankey	Churchill Archives Centre
Sir Nevile Henderson	National Archives (FO 800)
Lord Home	The Hirsel Archive
Lord Margesson	Churchill Archives Centre
Lord Monckton	Bodleian Library, Oxford
Lord Norwich	Churchill Archives Centre
Sir Eric Phipps	Churchill Archives Centre
Lord Runciman	National Archives (FO 800)

Sir Orme Sargent   National Archives (FO 800)
Lord Simon   Bodleian Library, Oxford
Lord Strang   Churchill Archives Centre
Brigadier H. C. T. Stronge   Bodleian Library, Oxford
Lord Templewood   Cambridge University Library
Lord Vansittart   Churchill Archives Centre
Sir Horace Wilson   National Archives (T273)
Lord Zetland   British Library

Cabinet Papers   National Archives (CAB)
Foreign Office Papers   National Archives (FO)
Prime Minister's Papers   National Archives (PREM)
Treasury Papers   National Archives (T)

BBC Written Archives   Caversham Park, Reading
British Library of Political   London School of Economics
 and Economic Science
Newspapers   British Library, Colindale

PUBLISHED OFFICIAL DOCUMENTS

Documents on British Foreign Policy 1919–1939, Second Series, Volume XIX, "European Affairs, July 1, 1937–August 4, 1938," W. Medlicott & D. Dakin (eds.), Her Majesty's Stationery Office 1982.

Documents on British Foreign Policy 1919–1939, Third Series, Volume I, "1938," E. Woodward & R. Butler (eds.), His Majesty's Stationery Office 1949.

Documents on British Foreign Policy 1919–1939, Third Series, Volume II, "1938," E. Woodward & R. Butler (eds.), His Majesty's Stationery Office 1949.

Documents on British Foreign Policy 1919–1939, Third Series, Volume IV, "1939," E. Woodward & R. Butler (eds.), His Majesty's Stationery Office 1951.

Documents on German Foreign Policy 1918–1945, Series D (1937–1945), Volume I, "From Neurath to Ribbentrop, September 1937–September 1938," His Majesty's Stationery Office 1949.

Documents on German Foreign Policy 1918–1945, Series D (1937–1945), Volume II, "Germany and Czechoslovakia, 1937–1938," His Majesty's Stationery Office 1950.

Documents on German Foreign Policy 1918–1945, Series D (1937–1945), Volume IV, "The Aftermath of Munich, October 1938–March 1939," His Majesty's Stationery Office 1951.

Documents on German Foreign Policy 1918–1945, Series D (1937–1945), Volume VII, "The Last Days of Peace," Her Majesty's Stationery Office 1956.

The History of The Times, Volume IV, The 150th Anniversary and Beyond, 1912–1948, The Times 1952.

Nazi Conspiracy and Aggression, Volumes I–VIII, United States Government Printing Office, Washington 1946.

Parliamentary Debates, House of Commons, Official Report, Fifth Series.
Oxford Dictionary of National Biography, H. Matthew & B. Harrison (eds.), Oxford University Press 2004.
Trial of the Major War Criminals Before the International Military Tribunal, Nuremberg 1946.

PUBLISHED BOOKS

L. Amery, *My Political Life, Volume III: The Unforgiving Years, 1929–1940,* Hutchinson 1955.
C. Andrew, *Secret Service: The Making of the British Intelligence Community,* Heinemann 1985.
Lord Avon, *The Eden Memoirs: Facing the Dictators,* Cassell 1962.
———, *The Eden Memoirs: The Reckoning,* Cassell 1965.
S. Ball, *The Guardsmen: Harold Macmillan, Three Friends, and the World They Made,* HarperCollins 2004.
J. Barnes and D. Nicholson (eds.), *The Empire at Bay: The Leo Amery Diaries 1929–1945,* Hutchinson 1988.
V. Bartlett, *I Know What I Liked,* Chatto and Windus 1974.
R. Bassett, *Hitler's Spy Chief: The Wilhelm Canaris Mystery,* Weidenfeld and Nicolson 2005.
N. Baynes (ed.), *The Speeches of Adolf Hitler, Volume II, April 1922–August 1939,* Oxford University Press 1942.
N. von Below (trans. G. Brooks), *At Hitler's Side: The Memoirs of Hitler's Luftwaffe Adjutant, 1937–1945,* Greenhill Books 2001.
Lord Birkenhead, *Halifax: The Life of Lord Halifax,* Hamish Hamilton 1965.
———, *Walter Monckton: The Life of Viscount Monckton of Brenchley,* Weidenfeld and Nicolson 1969.
M. Bloch, *Ribbentrop,* Bantam 1992.
B. Bond (ed.), *Chief of Staff: The Diaries of Lieutenant-General Sir Henry Pownall, Volume One 1933–1940,* Leo Cooper 1972.
P. Brendon, *The Dark Valley: A Panorama of the 1930s,* Jonathan Cape 2000.
A. Brissaud (trans. I. Colvin), *Canaris: The Biography of Admiral Canaris,* Weidenfeld and Nicolson 1973.
G. Brook-Shepherd, *Anschluss: The Rape of Austria,* Macmillan 1963.
R. Bruce Lockhart, *Jan Masaryk: A Personal Memoir,* Dropmore Press 1951.
J. Bruegel, *Czechoslovakia Before Munich: The German Minority Problem and British Appeasement Policy,* Cambridge University Press 1973.
E. Bukey, *Hitler's Austria: Popular Sentiment in the Nazi Era, 1938–1945,* University of North Carolina Press, Chapel Hill 2000.
A. Bullock, *Hitler: A Study in Tyranny* (revised edition), Odhams 1965.
A. Bullock (ed.), *The Ribbentrop Memoirs,* Weidenfeld and Nicolson 1954.
H. Burden, *The Nuremberg Party Rallies: 1923–39,* Pall Mall Press 1967.
E. Butler, *"Mason-Mac": The Life of Lieutenant-General Sir Noel Mason-MacFarlane,* Macmillan 1972.

B. Cartland, *The Isthmus Years*, Hutchinson 1943.

N. Chamberlain, *The Struggle for Peace*, Hutchinson 1939.

J. Charmley, *Chamberlain and the Lost Peace*, Hodder & Stoughton 1989.

————, *Duff Cooper: The Authorized Biography*, Weidenfeld and Nicolson 1986.

A. Chisholm & M Davie, *Beaverbrook: A Life*, Hutchinson 1992.

A. Christiansen, *Headlines All My Life*, Heinemann 1961.

W. Churchill, *The Second World War, Volume I: The Gathering Storm*, Cassell 1948.

R. Cockett, *Twilight of Truth: Chamberlain, Appeasement and the Manipulation of the Press*, Weidenfeld and Nicolson 1989.

I. Colvin, *The Chamberlain Cabinet*, Victor Gollancz 1971.

————, *Chief of Intelligence*, Victor Gollancz 1951.

————, *Vansittart in Office*, Victor Gollancz 1965.

T. Conwell-Evans, *None So Blind: A Study of the Crisis Years 1930–1939, Based on the Private Papers of Group-Captain M. G. Christie*, Harrison & Sons 1947.

Diana Cooper, *The Light of the Common Day*, Rupert Hart-Davis 1959.

D. Cooper, *Old Men Forget*, Rupert Hart-Davis 1953.

C. Coote, *Editorial: The Memoirs of Colin R. Coote*, Eyre & Spottiswoode 1965.

————, *The Other Club*, Sidgwick & Jackson 1971.

R. Coulondre, *De Staline à Hitler: Souvenirs de deux ambassades 1936–1939*, Hachette, Paris 1950.

M. Cowling, *The Impact of Hitler: British Politics and British Policy 1933–1940*, Cambridge University Press 1975.

G. Cox, *Countdown to War: A Personal Memoir of Europe 1938–1940*, William Kimber 1988.

H. Dalton, *The Fateful Years: Memoirs 1931–1945*, Frederick Muller 1957.

R. de Felice (ed.), *The Complete, Unabridged Diaries of Count Galeazzo Ciano*, Phoenix Press 2002.

H. Deutsch, *The Conspiracy Against Hitler in the Twilight War*, University of Minnesota Press, Minneapolis 1968.

————, *Hitler and His Generals: The Hidden Crisis, January–June 1938*, University of Minnesota Press, Minneapolis 1974.

D. Dilks (ed.), *The Diaries of Sir Alexander Cadogan*, Cassell 1971.

H. von Dirksen, *Moscow, Tokyo, London—Twenty Years of German Foreign Policy*, Hutchinson 1951.

P. Dixon, *Double Diploma: The Life of Sir Pierson Dixon, Don and Diplomat*, Hutchinson 1968.

M. Dodd, *My Years in Germany*, Victor Gollancz 1939.

W. & M. Dodd (eds.), *Ambassador Dodd's Diary, 1933–1938*, Victor Gollancz 1941.

R. Douglas, *Between the Wars 1919–1939: The Cartoonists' Vision*, Routledge 1992.

————, *In the Year of Munich*, Macmillan 1977.

O. Dutch, *The Errant Diplomat: The Life of Franz von Papen*, Edward Arnold 1940.

D. Dutton, *Neville Chamberlain*, Arnold 2001.

H. Eberle & M. Uhl (eds.) (trans. G. MacDonagh), *The Hitler Book: The Secret Dossier Prepared for Stalin*, John Murray 2005.

R. Evans, *The Third Reich in Power 1933–1939*, Allen Lane 2005.

N. Farrell, *Mussolini: A New Life*, Weidenfeld and Nicolson 2003.

K. Feiling, *The Life of Neville Chamberlain*, Macmillan 1946.

A. François-Poncet, *Souvenirs d'une Ambassade à Berlin*, Flammarion, Paris 1947.

A. François-Poncet (trans. J. LeClercq), *The Fateful Years*, Victor Gollancz 1949.

L. Fuchser, *Neville Chamberlain and Appeasement: A Study in the Politics of History*, W. W. Norton, New York 1982.

G. Gedye, *Fallen Bastions*, Victor Gollancz 1939.

J. Gehl, *Austria, Germany and the Anschluss, 1931–1938*, Oxford University Press 1963.

M. Gilbert, *Winston S. Churchill, Volume V, Companion Part 3, "The Coming of War 1936–1939,"* Heinemann 1982.

H. Gisevius (trans. R. & C. Winston), *To the Bitter End*, Greenwood Press, Connecticut 1975.

Lord Gladwyn, *The Memoirs of Lord Gladwyn*, Weidenfeld and Nicolson 1972.

W. Gorlitz (ed.) (trans. D. Irving), *The Memoirs of Field-Marshal Keitel*, William Kimber 1965.

H. Guderian (trans. C. Fitzgibbon), *Panzer Leader*, Michael Joseph 1952.

N. Gun, *Eva Braun, Hitler's Mistress*, Leslie Frewin 1969.

W. Hadley, *Munich: Before and After*, Cassell 1944.

J. von Halasz, *Hitler's Munich*, Foxley Books 2007.

Lord Halifax, *Fulness of Days*, Collins 1957.

J. Harvey (ed.), *The Diplomatic Diaries of Oliver Harvey, 1937–1940*, Collins 1970.

J. Heineman, *Hitler's First Foreign Minister, Constantin Freiherr von Neurath, Diplomat and Statesman*, University of California Press, Los Angeles 1979.

A. Henderson, *Eyewitness in Czecho-Slovakia*, George Harrap 1939.

N. Henderson, *Failure of a Mission, Berlin 1937–1939*, Hodder & Stoughton 1940.

F. Hesse (trans. F. A. Voight), *Hitler and the English*, Allan Wingate 1954.

R. Heuston, *Lives of the Lord Chancellors, 1885–1940*, Clarendon Press 1964.

F. Hinsley, *British Intelligence in the Second World War, Volume One*, HMSO 1979.

H. Höhne (trans. J. Brownjohn), *Canaris*, Secker & Warburg 1979.

Lord Home, *Letters to a Grandson*, Collins 1983.

———, *The Way the Wind Blows*, Collins 1976.

A. Horne, *Macmillan 1894–1956*, Macmillan 1988.

D. Hubback, *No Ordinary Press Baron: A Life of Walter Layton*, Weidenfeld and Nicolson 1985.

I. Hunter (ed.), *Winston and Archie: The Letters of Sir Archibald Sinclair and Winston S. Churchill, 1915–1960*, Politico's 2005.

D. Jay, *Change and Fortune: A Political Record*, Hutchinson 1980.

W. Jędrzejewicz (ed.), *Diplomat in Berlin, 1933–1939: The Papers and Memoirs of Józef Lipski, Ambassador of Poland*, Columbia University Press, New York 1968.

F. Jetzinger, *Hitler's Youth*, Hutchinson 1958.

T. Jones, *A Diary with Letters, 1931–50*, Oxford University Press 1954.

J. F. Kennedy, *Why England Slept*, Greenwood Press, Connecticut 1961.

I. Kershaw, *Hitler 1936-45: Nemesis*, Allen Lane 2000.

———, *The "Hitler Myth": Image and Reality in the Third Reich*, Clarendon Press 1987.

I. Kirkpatrick, *The Inner Circle*, Macmillan 1959.

A. Lambert, *The Lost Life of Eva Braun*, Century 2006.

D. Low, *Low's Autobiography*, Michael Joseph 1956.

I. Macleod, *Neville Chamberlain*, Frederick Muller 1961.

R. Macleod & D. Kelly (eds.), *The Ironside Diary, 1937–1940*, Constable 1962.

H. Macmillan, *Winds of Change, 1914–1939*, Macmillan 1966.

C. Madge & T. Harrison, *Britain by Mass-Observation*, Penguin 1939.

J. Margach, *The Abuse of Power: The War Between Downing Street and the Media from Lloyd George to Callaghan*, W. H. Allen 1978.

———, *The Anatomy of Power: An Enquiry into the Personality of Leadership*, W. H. Allen 1979.

V. Massey, *What's Past Is Prologue: The Memoirs of the Right Honourable Vincent Massey CH*, Macmillan 1963.

Viscount Maugham, *At the End of the Day*, William Heinemann 1954.

A. Maurois (trans. D. Lindley), *Tragedy in France*, Harper & Brothers, New York 1940.

L. Miller, *Lee Miller's War*, Condé Nast Books 1992.

R. Minney, *The Private Papers of Hore-Belisha*, Collins 1960.

F. Moravec, *Master of Spies: The Memoirs of General František Moravec*, Bodley Head 1975.

B. Morris, *The Roots of Appeasement: The British Weekly Press and Nazi Germany During the 1930s*, Frank Cass 1991.

R. Moseley, *Mussolini's Shadow: The Double Life of Count Galeazzo Ciano*, Yale University Press 1999.

M. Muggeridge (ed.), *Ciano's Diplomatic Papers*, Odhams Press 1948.

M. Muggeridge (ed.) (trans. A. Mayor), *Ciano's Diary 1937–1938*, Methuen 1952.

B. Mussolini (trans. F. Lobb), *Memoirs 1942–1943*, Weidenfeld and Nicolson 1949.

L. Namier, *Diplomatic Prelude 1938–1939*, Macmillan 1948.

P. Neville, *Appeasing Hitler: The Diplomacy of Sir Nevile Henderson 1937–1939*, Macmillan 2000.

———, *Hitler and Appeasement: The British Attempt to Prevent the Second World War*, Hambledon Continuum 2006.

H. Nicolson, *Why Britain Is at War*, Penguin 1939.

N. Nicolson (ed.), *Harold Nicolson: Diaries and Letters, 1930–1939*, Collins 1966.

N. Nicolson (ed.), *Leave the Letters Till We're Dead: The Letters of Virginia Woolf, Volume VI: 1938–1941*, Hogarth Press 1980.

H. Noguères (trans. P. O'Brian), *Munich, or the Phoney Peace*, Weidenfeld and Nicolson 1965.

Lord Norwich (ed.), *The Duff Cooper Diaries 1915–1951*, Weidenfeld and Nicolson 2005.

R. Ovendale, *"Appeasement" and the English Speaking World*, University of Wales Press, Cardiff 1965.

F. von Papen (trans. B. Connell), *Memoirs*, André Deutsch 1952.

R. Parker, *Chamberlain and Appeasement: British Policy and the Coming of the Second World War*, Macmillan 1993.

B. Pauley, *Hitler and the Forgotten Nazis: A History of Austrian National Socialism*, Macmillan 1981.

B. Pimlott, *Hugh Dalton*, Macmillan 1985.

B. Pimlott (ed.), *The Political Diary of Hugh Dalton, 1918–40, 1945–60*, Jonathan Cape 1986.

E. Raeder, *Struggle for the Sea*, William Kimber 1959.

N. Reynolds, *Treason Was No Crime: Ludwig Beck, Chief of the German General Staff*, William Kimber 1976.

R. Rhodes James, *Anthony Eden*, Weidenfeld and Nicolson 1986.

———, *Memoirs of a Conservative: J. C. C. Davidson's Memoirs and Papers, 1910–37*, Weidenfeld and Nicolson 1969.

———, *Victor Cazalet, A Portrait*, Hamish Hamilton 1976.

R. Rhodes James (ed.), *Chips: The Diaries of Sir Henry Channon*, Weidenfeld and Nicolson 1967.

H. Ripka, *Munich: Before and After*, Victor Gollancz 1939.

K. Robbins, *Munich 1938*, Cassell 1968.

A. Roberts, *Eminent Churchillians*, Weidenfeld and Nicolson 1994.

———, *"The Holy Fox": The Life of Lord Halifax*, Weidenfeld and Nicolson 1991.

F. Roberts, *Dealing with Dictators: The Destruction and Revival of Europe 1930–70*, Weidenfeld and Nicolson 1991.

N. Rose, *Vansittart: Study of a Diplomat*, Heinemann 1978.

N. Rose (ed.), *Baffy: The Diaries of Blanche Dugdale 1936–1947*, Vallentine Mitchell 1973.

T. Sakmyster, *Hungary's Admiral on Horseback: Miklós Horthy, 1918–1944*, Columbia University Press, New York 1994.

H. Schacht (trans. E. Fitzgerald), *Account Settled*, Weidenfeld and Nicolson 1949.

M. Schad (trans. A. McGeoch), *Hitler's Spy Princess: The Extraordinary Life of Stephanie von Hohenlohe*, Sutton Publishing 2004.

P. Schmidt (ed. R. Steed), *Hitler's Interpreter*, William Heinemann 1951.

K. von Schuschnigg (trans. F. von Hildebrand), *Austrian Requiem*, Victor Gollancz 1947.

K. von Schuschnigg, *The Brutal Takeover*, Weidenfeld and Nicolson 1971.

P. Schwarz, *This Man Ribbentrop: His Life and Times*, Julian Messner, New York 1943.

W. Selby, *Diplomatic Twilight*, John Murray 1953.

R. Self, *Neville Chamberlain: A Biography*, Ashgate 2006.

R. Self (ed.), *The Neville Chamberlain Diary Letters, Volume 4: The Downing Street Years, 1934–40*, Ashgate 2005.

R. Seton-Watson, *A History of the Czechs and Slovaks*, Hutchinson 1943.

R. Shepherd, *A Class Divided: Appeasement and the Road to Munich 1938*, Macmillan 1988.

T. Sherwood, *A Short History of Hounslow, Hanworth and Heston Aerodromes, 1911–1946*, Heritage Publications, Hounslow Cultural and Community Services 1999.

W. Shirer, *Berlin Diary*, Hamish Hamilton 1941.

———, *The Rise and Fall of the Third Reich: A History of Nazi Germany*, Secker and Warburg 1961.

Viscount Simon, *Retrospect*, Hutchinson 1952.

N. Smart (ed.), *The Diaries and Letters of Robert Bernays, 1932–1939*, Edwin Mellen Press, Lewiston 1996.

R. Smelser, *The Sudeten Problem, 1933–1938*, Dawson 1975.

A. Speer (trans. R. & C. Winston), *Inside the Third Reich*, Weidenfeld and Nicolson 1970.

R. Spitzy (trans. G. Waddington), *How We Squandered the Reich*, Michael Russell 1997.

G. Stewart, *Burying Caesar: Churchill, Chamberlain and the Battle for the Tory Party*, Weidenfeld and Nicolson 1999.

Lord Strang, *Home and Abroad*, André Deutsch 1956.

K. Strong, *Intelligence at the Top: The Recollections of an Intelligence Officer*, Cassell 1968.

J. Stuart, *Within the Fringe: An Autobiography*, Bodley Head 1967.

Lord Swinton, *Sixty Years of Power: Some Memories of the Men Who Wielded It*, Hutchinson 1966.

A. J. P. Taylor, *Beaverbrook*, Hamish Hamilton 1972.

———, *The Origins of the Second World War*, Hamish Hamilton 1961.

S. Taylor, *The Great Outsiders: Northcliffe, Rothermere and the Daily Mail*, Weidenfeld and Nicolson 1996.

T. Taylor, *Sword and Swastika: The Wehrmacht in the Third Reich*, Victor Gollancz 1953.

Viscount Templewood, *Nine Troubled Years*, Collins 1954.

N. Thompson, *The Anti-Appeasers: Conservative Opposition to Appeasement in the 1930s*, Clarendon Press 1971.

C. Thorne, *The Approach of War, 1938–1939*, Macmillan 1967.

D. R. Thorpe, *Alec Douglas-Home*, Sinclair-Stevenson 1996.

———, *Eden: The Life and Times of Anthony Eden*, Chatto and Windus 2003.

J. Toland, *Adolf Hitler*, Doubleday, New York 1976.

Lord Vansittart, *Lessons of my Life*, Hutchinson 1943.

———, *The Mist Procession*, Hutchinson 1958.

W. Wark, *The Ultimate Enemy: British Intelligence and Nazi Germany, 1933–1939*, I. B. Tauris 1985.

W. Warlimont (trans. R. Barry), *Inside Hitler's Headquarters, 1939–1945*, Weidenfeld and Nicolson 1964.

D. C. Watt, *How War Came: The Immediate Origins of the Second World War, 1938–1939*, Heinemann 1989.

G. Weinberg, *The Foreign Policy of Hitler's Germany: Starting World War II 1937–1939*, University of Chicago Press, Chicago 1980.

E. von Weizsäcker (trans. J. Andrews), *Memoirs of Ernst von Weizsäcker*, Victor Gollancz 1951.

S. Welles, *Seven Major Decisions*, Hamish Hamilton 1951.

———, *The Time for Decision*, Hamish Hamilton 1944.

N. West, *MI6, British Secret Intelligence Service Operations, 1909–1945*, Weidenfeld and Nicolson 1983.

J. Wheeler-Bennett, *King George VI: His Life and Reign*, Macmillan 1958.

———, *Munich: Prologue to Tragedy*, Macmillan 1963.

———, *The Nemesis of Power: The German Army in Politics 1918–1945*, 2nd ed., Palgrave Macmillan 2005.

Duchess of Windsor, *The Heart Has Its Reasons,* Michael Joseph 1956.

E. Wiskemann, *Czechs and Germans: A Study of the Struggles in the Historic Provinces of Bohemia and Moravia,* Oxford University Press 1938.

Lord Woolton, *Memoirs,* Cassell 1959.

K. Young (ed.), *The Diaries of Sir Robert Bruce Lockhart: Volume One 1915–1938,* Macmillan 1973.

PUBLISHED ARTICLES

A. Adamthwaite, "The British Government and the Media, 1937–1938," *Journal of Contemporary History,* Volume 18, No. 2, April 1983.

S. Aster, " 'Guilty Men': The Case of Neville Chamberlain," in *Paths to War: New Essays on the Origins of the Second World War,* R. Boyce & E. Robertson (eds.), Macmillan 1989.

D. Dilks, " 'We Must Hope for the Best and Prepare for the Worst': The Prime Minister, the Cabinet and Hitler's Germany, 1937–1939," *Proceedings of the British Academy,* Volume 73, Oxford University Press 1988.

R. Douglas, "Chamberlain and Eden, 1937–38," *Journal of Contemporary History,* Volume 13, No. 1, 1978.

M. Gilbert, "Horace Wilson: Man of Munich?," *History Today,* Volume 32, No. 10, October 1982.

K. Henlein, "The German Minority in Czechoslovakia," *International Affairs,* Volume 15, No. 4, The Royal Institute of International Affairs 1936.

R. Laffan, "The Crisis over Czechoslovakia, January to September 1938," in *Survey of International Affairs 1938,* Volume II, Oxford University Press 1951.

M. McCulloch, "Littler than Hitler," *Times Literary Supplement,* 17 March 2000.

W. C. Mills, "Sir Joseph Ball, Adrian Dingli, and Neville Chamberlain's 'Secret Channel' to Italy, 1937–1940," *The International History Review,* Volume 24, No. 2, 2002.

P. Neville, "The Appointment of Sir Nevile Henderson, 1937—Design or Blunder?," *Journal of Contemporary History,* Volume 33, No. 4, October 1998.

——, "Nevile Henderson and Basil Newton, Two British Envoys in the Czech Crisis 1938," in *Diplomacy and Statecraft,* Volume 10, No. 2, "The Munich Crisis 1938," I. Lukes & E. Goldstein (eds.), Frank Cass 1999.

——, "Sir Alexander Cadogan and Lord Halifax's 'Damascus Road' Conversion over the Godesberg Terms 1938," in *Diplomacy and Statecraft,* Volume 11, No. 3, Frank Cass 2000.

T. Sakmyster, "The Hungarian State Visit to Germany of August 1938: Some New Evidence on Hungary in Hitler's Pre-Munich Policy," *Canadian Slavic Studies,* Volume 3, No. 4, 1969.

P. Schroeder, "Munich and the British Tradition," *The Historical Journal,* Volume 19, Cambridge University Press, 1976.

B. Strang, "Two Unequal Tempers: Sir George Ogilvie-Forbes, Sir Nevile Henderson and British Foreign Policy, 1938–39," in *Diplomacy and Statecraft,* Volume 5, No. 1, Frank Cass 1994.

H. Stronge, "The Czechoslovak Army and the Munich Crisis: A Personal Memorandum," in *War and Society*, B. Bond & I. Roy (eds.), Croom Helm 1975.

W. Wallace, "The Foreign Policy of President Beneš in the Approach to Munich," *The Slavonic and East European Review*, Volume 39, University of London 1961.

———, "The Making of the May Crisis of 1938," *The Slavonic and East European Review*, Volume 41, University of London 1963.

D. C. Watt, "Appeasement: The Rise of a Revisionist School?," *Political Quarterly*, Volume 36, Thomas Nelson & Sons 1965.

———, "British Intelligence and the Coming of the Second World War in Europe," in *Knowing One's Enemies*, E. May (ed.), Princeton University Press 1984.

———, "Chamberlain's Ambassadors," in *Diplomacy and World Power*, M. Dockrill & B. McKercher (eds.), Cambridge University Press 1996.

G. Weinberg, "The May Crisis 1938," *The Journal of Modern History*, Volume 29, University of Chicago Press 1957.

J. Wright & P. Stafford, "Hitler, Britain, and the Hossbach Memorandum," *Militärgeschichtliche Mitteilungen*, Volume 42, No. 2, 1987.

Acknowledgments

I am most grateful to the copyright owners and archivists at the various libraries and archive centers where I have undertaken the research for this book. These include the Royal Archives at Windsor Castle, the National Archives, the British Library (including the Newspaper Collection at Colindale), the Bodleian Library, the University of Birmingham Library, the Churchill Archives Centre, the Parliamentary Archive, the University of Reading Library, the British Library of Political and Economic Science at the London School of Economics, the Borthwick Institute at the University of York, the BBC Written Archives at Caversham, and Getty Images. I am especially grateful to Lord and Lady Home for their hospitality at the Hirsel during my research into the papers of the late Lord Home.

I owe a very great debt of gratitude to all the staff at the London Library, where this book was written, for whom nothing is ever too much trouble; also, to many of my fellow readers there for their encouragement. In particular, Joachim von Halasz, who has had the bad luck to sit only a tap on the shoulder away, has been an ever-present source of advice and assistance in relation to all things to do with the topography of the Third Reich. He has acted as interpreter and overseer of German spelling, as well as name checker and a source of photographs. He even generously organized a trip to Munich, where he gained access for us to the room where the Munich Agreement was signed, much to the amusement of the young pianist whose rehearsal we interrupted.

Colin Lee has again given generously of his time, reading the manuscript not once but twice, and has been a source of advice on many topics, especially relating to political and parliamentary matters. I am also very grateful to Niall Murphy at Radley College for reading the book with the keen eye of an expert historian on the period. D. R. Thorpe has again taken a close interest throughout, and has steered me toward suitable references that he has come across in the course of his own research.

At Simon & Schuster, Andrew Gordon bravely set the ball rolling, while my editor, Mike Jones, has since encouraged and advised me with the voice of experience and a sure touch. Rory Scarfe has worked tirelessly on the manuscript and put up with my often fastidious approach to the editing process. I am extremely grateful to them all for the confidence they have demonstrated in me, as I am to three others who have shown spectacular patience in helping to deliver the finished article: my copy editor, Hugo de Klee, proofreader Martin Bryant, and indexer Andy Armitage. My thanks go also to my agent, Michael Sissons at PFD, and to Fiona Petheram.

In the United States I am also very grateful to everyone at Simon & Schuster, especially Dedi Felman and Michele Bové; to my agent, Peter Matson; and to my painstaking copy editor, Fred Chase.

Lastly, but by no means least, I thank my family from the bottom of my heart. My wife has once again tolerated my near-obsessive behavior, in this case with some pretty unsavory characters; without her at my side this book would quite simply never have been written. My daughters, in spite of their years, have been a constant source of encouragement, while it has been a joy to be able to discuss the progress of the book, and the story contained within it, with my son; I only hope I may have been of some use to him in preparing for his history GCSE! Finally, I thank my mother, who lived through these times and met many of the characters involved. She has never once failed to encourage me, without question, in absolutely everything I have done, even when she disapproved. I could never have contemplated reaching this moment without her unwavering support, and that of my late father. I dedicate this book to her.

Index